THE EPIC OF GESAR OF LING

THE EPIC OF

Gesar of Ling

GESAR'S MAGICAL BIRTH,
EARLY YEARS, AND
CORONATION AS KING

TRANSLATED BY

Robin Kornman, PhD
Sangye Khandro &
Lama Chönam

Forewords by
His Holiness the Fourteenth Dalai Lama
Alak Zenkar Rinpoche
Sakyong Mipham Rinpoche

SHAMBHALA
Boston & London
2012

Shambhala Publications, Inc.
Horticultural Hall
300 Massachusetts Avenue
Boston, Massachusetts 02115
www.shambhala.com

9 8 7 6 5 4 3 2 1

First Edition
Printed in Thailand

∞ This edition is printed on acid-free paper that meets the
American National Standards Institute z39.48 Standard.
♻ Shambhala Publications makes every effort to print on recycled paper.
For more information, please visit www.shambhala.com.

Distributed in the United States by Random House, Inc.,
and in Canada by Random House of Canada Ltd

Designed by Lora Zorian

LIBRARY OF CONGRESS CATALOGING-IN-PUBLICATION DATA

Gesar. Volume 1–3. English.
The epic of Gesar of Ling: Gesar's magical birth, early years, and coronation
as king / translated by Robin Kornman, Sangye Khandro, and Lama Chönam;
forewords by Alak Zenkar Rinpoche and Sakyong Mipham Rinpoche.
p. cm.
Includes bibliographical references and index.
ISBN 978-1-59030-842-4 (hardcover: alk. paper)
1. Epic literature, Tibetan—Translations into English.
I. Kornman, Robin, 1947–2007 II. Khandro, Sangye. III. Chonam, Lama. IV. Title.
PL3748.G4E5 2012
895'.41—dc22
2011014496

CONTENTS

THE DALAI LAMA

THE EPIC, GESAR OF LING, IS A GREAT WORK drawn from centuries of oral tradition that combines cultural, literary, musical, and historical elements with Tibetan Buddhist values. The Gesar story is one of the Tibetan people's most popular epics, its stories being enacted and sung at festivals and on important ceremonial occasions.

Many ancient peoples have recited epics as a source of inspiration, the renowned Mahabharata and Ramayana in India, the Hamzanama in Persia, the Iliad and Odyssey in Greece, for example. Tales of the heroic feats of Gesar of Ling enjoy a similar status among the people of Tibet.

By making the epic of Gesar available in English, the translators are offering the modern reader a chance to experience the particular character of this Tibetan tradition that has brought hope and fortitude to many generations across the Tibetan-speaking world; we have sound reasons to be grateful to them.

AUGUST 14, 2012

Foreword by

ALAK ZENKAR RINPOCHE

IT HAS COME TO MY ATTENTION that Lama Chönam and Lotsawa Sangye Khandro have been able to successfully complete the English translation of *The Events Leading to Gesar's Incarnation in the Land of Ling,*[*] *Gesar's Birth and Childhood in the Land of Ling,*[†] and *Gesar Wins the Horse Race and Becomes the King of Ling*[‡] which are the first three volumes of the great epic of King Gesar of Ling. For those of us who are dedicated to the preservation of the Gesar epic, this great news, like the melodious beating of the drums in the heavenly realms, brings the epic one step closer to worldwide awareness and appreciation.

These three initial volumes, like a fountainhead, are the source for the entire body of the many hundreds of episodes that comprise the great body of this epic. The first volume, *The Events Leading to Gesar's Incarnation in the Land of Ling,* describes the wisdom intent of all one thousand buddhas of this fortunate *kalpa,* and accords with the spiritual mandate of the great Vajra Master Padmasambhava. It chronicles the way the young godling who was known by the name Thöpa Gawa, or Joyful to Hear, lived in the higher god realm of Gaden[§] [Tuṣita] and how he formed the enlightened intent to take rebirth in the lower realm of human beings (Jambudvīpa), where the purpose and goal for this rebirth is then established. This sets the stage for the account of how this great hero Gesar is able to uplift and maintain the continuity of the lineage of Ling through the profound and secret deeds that he performs, like opening a precious jeweled receptacle.

The second volume, *Gesar's Birth and Childhood in the Land of Ling,* describes the astonishing arrangement of the *rūpakāya* (enlightened body of form), which he

---

[*] Tib. *lha gling.*

[†] Tib. *'khrungs gling.*

[‡] Tib. *rta rgyug.*

[§] Tib. *dga' ldan.*

ix

emanates to actually appear in the world of human beings. By displaying an array of magical manifestations that virtually transcend thought, speech, and expression, he then enacts enlightened deeds that pacify, enrich, magnetize, and wrathfully subdue all beings. In order to establish the basis for the battleground to defeat the border-land negative forces of Hor and Düd, he seizes the land of Ma and spends the early years of his life preparing this domain for the future deeds to occur.

The third volume, *Gesar Wins the Horse Race and Becomes the King of Ling,* is based on the wager that is won by the winner of the race. Gesar is the victor and becomes the sovereign ruler of the six districts of Ling. As the proverb tells us:

> *The hammer that pounds the previously untamed enemies;*
> *The parent who cares for those who are helpless.*

And in his own words, "Except for the enemies of the Buddha's doctrine and those who bring harm to sentient beings, I, Gesar, have no enemies."

Hence, according to this authentic quote, to that end Gesar spent his entire life enacting great waves of enlightened activity. Among the great epics that exist in this world, this epic life story of King Gesar of Ling is a beacon of light that will once again shine forth through these efforts. To that end I offer my heartfelt gratitude to the translators for their kindness in making this possible.

THUBTEN NYIMA
[ALAK ZENKAR RINPOCHE]
Fall 2010

Foreword by
SAKYONG MIPHAM RINPOCHE

AS A DESCENDANT OF GESAR OF LING, I am delighted that this new translation of the Gesar epic has come to the Western readership. The timing could not be better. As our modern world experiences a loss of heart and humanity, and climactic changes and disasters occur, we need the compassionate, wise, and potent energy of Gesar more than ever. He was an incredibly brave and heroic being who believed in the goodness of humanity and was able to raise the spirits and energy of the people of Ling at a time when they were experiencing confusion and chaos.

The epic of Ling has all the aspects of a great story—love, hope, despair, and finally victory. I'm extremely pleased that the late Dr. Robin Kornman and my friends Lama Chönam and Sangye Khandro—in the spirit of Gesar—all persevered to produce this wonderful translation. I have no doubt that it will be of great benefit to the world.

SAKYONG MIPHAM RINPOCHE
Halifax, Nova Scotia
Summer 2011

PREFACE

WE HAVE TAKEN GREAT CARE to ensure that this translation is faithful in form and meaning to the original Tibetan. The version that we worked from is a typewritten copy based on the original of a woodblock carved at Derge Lingtsang. Derge (Tib. *sde dge*) is a district in Kham (eastern Tibet) in the watershed of the Dri and Ma Rivers, which are the headwaters of the Yangtze River. Derge itself is about 13 kilometers east of the Dri Chu (Yangtze River), now the westernmost area of Sichuan Province of China. The Derge printing house was built between 1729 and 1750 C.E. and was never destroyed during the Cultural Revolution. The press has returned to printing original woodblocks since that time. It houses tens of thousands of engraved blocks of religious classics of Tibetan Buddhism, as well as histories, literature, art, and science materials, all in the Tibetan script.

This particular text was compiled by Gyurmed Thubten Jamyang Dragpa, who was a close disciple of Ju Mipham Jampel Gyepai Dorje (1846–1912). It was later edited and arranged under the direction of Thubten Nyima (Alak Zenkar Rinpoche) and others. As is clarified in the postscript to volume 3, they made additions, particularly to *Gesar Wins the Horse Race and Becomes the King of Ling* (volume 3), which included the addition of a table of contents, the likes of which is not found in the first two volumes. In addition, four-line verses have been added at the beginning of each chapter to foreshadow the events of that chapter. We have gone on to change the titles of the volumes to make the English more descriptive of the narrative; the original titles are given in endnotes.

The work in Tibetan is divided into sections that are written in prose and poetry. This is mirrored in the text of the translation. The verse sections are primarily songs that are sung by various characters in the epic, and the melodies referred to are specific tunes that correspond to that character and the mood that is being portrayed.* Italicized sections within the verse are lines that have been identified as traditional

---

* Much as we might say, for example, that a song is sung to the tune of "Row, Row, Row Your Boat."

Tibetan proverbs. Proverbs in colloquial life were the style of the day in the time of Gesar of Ling and have continued to be prevalent in the Golog culture up through this present generation. They are used in abundance throughout the epic. The appearance of words in boldface type in volume 3 indicates the root verses of the Horse Race Supplication written by Ju Mipham Rinpoche himself, the source for the epic and commentary.

The names of people and places have been written in phonetic transliteration in the text itself, and at the first appearance, the English translation is given in brackets. The Wylie spelling also appears in many of the glossary entries. In some instances the English translation of a name seemed awkward to use in the text, so the original Tibetan was maintained; however some of the place names appear only in English when that was judged to be expressive and elegant. The glossary is not exhaustive, but it contains names and important places that recur throughout these first three volumes of the epic. In the glossary of terms we have opted not to include too many of the Buddhist terms that appear, since so many of these terms have permeated Western culture over the past decades and are familiar to readers.

Here are a few comments about pronunciation. We have tried to be phonetically descriptive, but at the same time we distinguish sounds that are close but not exactly the same in Tibetan. This is most problematic with aspirated sounds: for example, the sounds "p" and "ph" differ in that the first is like the "p" in "pen," and the second is like the "p" in "perish," rather than the "f" sound we are used to in English. The same is true for transliterated "t" and "th" and "tsa" and "tsha" sounds, where the added "h" creates only a more aspirated "t" or "s" sound. All "c" sounds in Tibetan are a hard "c," and all "g" sounds are a hard "g," though this is less guttural than in English and closer to a "k" sound. "U" never sounds like the "u" in "bug," but always like the "oo" in "look."

Finally, it is our sincere wish that readers will thoroughly enjoy the many nuances that comprise the first glimpse of this introductory book to the great epic of King Gesar of Ling.

Among the ranks of the greatest epics that exist in this world, may this serve as a literary treasure that informs the world more completely about the highly sophisticated great civilization of Tibet and the possibility of replicating to some degree the noble qualities of the enlightened society that the land of Ling came to be known for. May all be auspicious!

LAMA CHÖNAM, SANGYE KHANDRO, and JANE HAWES
Light of Berotsana Translation Group
Ashland, Oregon
Fall 2010

HISTORICAL INTRODUCTION

IN THIS HISTORICAL INTRODUCTION I have been asked to provide some background on the scope of this project and to help place the Gesar of Ling epic within a cultural, literary, and religious context. It is our hope that this will aid the readers in understanding the first three volumes of the epic presented here. Lama Chönam's far more detailed introduction provides a wealth of material regarding the epic itself and how it fits within the culture of Tibet. He also provides a detailed explication of the chapters and volumes presented in this translation. On behalf of the late Dr. Robin Kornman, who was unable to write this himself, here I will write in more general terms about epic literature, how the project developed over time, and a few remarks about the text itself. Some of this may be redundant and, for this, apologies are offered. Nonetheless, may the glory of the world increase through these efforts.

GESAR OF LING IN EPIC LITERATURE

The Gesar of Ling epic is the national oral epic for the country of Tibet, equivalent to the *Iliad* and the *Odyssey*. It is generally accepted by scholars that it is indeed the longest single piece of literature currently in the world canon, encompassing some 120 volumes and about 20 million words. There are a number of different accounts of the epic that span from Persia through Tibet and into China and India. The version presented here is the one most commonly referred to when the epic is studied in the present day. This was compiled by Gyurmed Thubten Jamyang Dragpa, a disciple of the great Mipham Jampel Gyepei Dorje (1846–1912),* who was actively

---

* This is Jamgön Ju Mipham (Mipham the Great), who wrote down the Gesar supplication as mind terma. The verses of this supplication are bolded lines at the end of each of the chapters of volume 3. His students compiled the woodblock version of the Gesar epic that has been translated here.

involved in the propagation of the Gesar epic as well as the notion of enlightened society. Mipham Rinpoche himself revealed mind treasures for the spiritual practice of Gesar as a wisdom embodiment including many protector and juniper smoke-offering prayers. Just as was true for the *Iliad* and the *Odyssey*, many early versions of this epic were sung by bards, having been composed orally, and then passed down by word of mouth. Just as, the tales we know as the Homeric epics were written down hundreds of years after the initial composition, likewise the epic of Gesar of Ling was sung and composed for centuries before the present versions were rendered into text. In keeping with the way of all great epics, the story of Gesar of Ling has passed back and forth between oral and written forms for centuries.

All epics share certain characteristics. There are nine generally accepted characteristics of the epic form, which include such things as humanity's interactions with deities, long lists and long speeches, and a heroine or hero who manifests the virtue of a civilization. The first recorded epic of which we are aware is that of Gilgamesh, thought to be a ruler of Sumeria circa 2700 B.C.E., which tells a somewhat convoluted and gruesome story that displays both the good and bad of those Sumerian times. The oldest written copy of the *Epic of Gilgamesh* comes from a library compiled in the seventh century B.C.E. In a similar way we can see that for most epics there is an oral tradition that exists for some time prior to its being set in stone, velum, papyrus, or paper.

Epics impart to the inhabitants of a land the information they need to live in harmony and to understand their place in the world. Whether it's the *Iliad*, the *Epic of Gilgamesh*, the Arthurian legend of the Lady of the Lake, the *Mahabharata*, or the great tales of Scandinavia, Native America, or Africa; they all impart cultural knowledge vital to their respective people. While the times and places may vary across the globe and across millennia, the basic characteristics of what epics *do* and how they do it are fairly constant.

For instance, among other things, the *Iliad* tells us how to make a feast and how to organize a battle. It also tells how to negotiate and what forms of rhetoric one should employ when making a speech in counsel. The *Iliad* shows how to settle matters in tribal meetings, how to lay waste to a town, and how to defend. It tells what to do in battle with a spear. It tells a warrior how he should act toward his colleagues in arms and toward the enemy. It taught all the things that a warrior would need to know, from personal grooming to the handling of horses.

Likewise, the Gesar epic contains information needed in order to inform native Tibetans of their cultural heritage. As Lama Chönam's introduction indicates, the epic has particular resonance for the people of eastern Tibet known as the Gologpas. Along with the oral tradition exemplified by the Gesar epic, this area of

Tibet has also given birth to many great teachers of the Tibetan Buddhist tradition, from the first seeds of Buddhism in this area in the eighth century C.E. up until the present day. While we in the West may think of nomadic people as somehow simple, the epic shows their civilization to be rich, profound, colorful, and sophisticated.

So what could be said about the Gesar epic that is unique, and why might we be interested? It certainly provides a glimpse into the civilization of the Tibetan people, and this in itself is of prime interest. It describes how knowledge and wisdom, in this case with some Buddhist trappings but actually universal, can be transmitted. It is an example of how the best qualities of being human, such as loyalty, compassion, and virtue, will triumph over evil, deception, and self-interest. This describes how an unsullied mind, awake and aware, frees one from the taint of confusion and ignorance and aids in one's journey to insight itself. Aside from this, the epic's use of proverb is unusually extensive and could represent an area of ongoing interest and study, completely worthy of being its own self-contained contemplative practice. While the use of proverbs is common in other epics, the Gesar epic stands out for the breadth and depth of its proverbs. Their importance to the Tibetan people as well as nomadic people in general cannot be overstated. The proverbs represent the major method by which the cultural, philosophical, and religious knowledge of Tibet is transmitted by the epic. All the proverbs are arguments by analogy. For instance, they may imply that "the timing of action is all-important" by saying, "If the rain has not moistened the crops, then what is the point of placing seeds there?" This is obvious to the farmer, but has broad application. Each of the proverbs may be understood on many levels and are vital to the culture. The elderly and the educated would use the proverbs both to teach as well as to sway public opinion. When important decisions were to be made, all the members of a tribe would gather and they would listen to the petitioners recount the proverbs that they thought germane to the discussion. In this way the group would move toward consensus.

The Historical Context

To get a flavor of the beginning of the Gesar epic, we will start with a quote:

> Formerly, during the lives of the three ancestral dharma kings, when the land of Tibet passed from Bön to Buddhism, in order to naturally pacify the envy of the vicious gods and demons of Tibet, Padma Tötreng [Lotus Skull Garland], the great mantra adept, bound them by oath. If he had managed to make them swear their oaths of fealty to the buddhadharma three times, then the dharma kings would have

been long-lived and their subjects would have enjoyed well-being and happiness. However, powerful demon ministers took control over the subjects and, faced with this opposition, Padma was only able to tame and bind the spirits of Tibet twice, not thrice. This caused war in the four directions and the auspicious coincidence of the glorious gateway, the perfect astrological conjunction, was missed. The foreign borderland demons wandered into central Tibet, and the dharma kings fell down to the level of commoners.

This description of the history of Tibet comes in the beginning of the first volume of the epic.

Within Tibet there were and, to some degree still are, two main religions. The religion that predominated prior to Buddhism is known as Bön and probably came from the western areas of Tibet, perhaps as an Indo-Iranian-Manichean blend of folk beliefs and shamanic culture. It is clear from more recent research that just as Buddhism incorporated beliefs from Hinduism in India and Bön in Tibet, so too Bön incorporated much from a well-established preexisting set of folk beliefs. In any case, the first wave of Buddhism in Tibet was instigated by the Tibetan king who invited the Abbott Śāntarakṣita and the Vajra Master Padmasambhava to Tibet to instruct the people in Buddhism. This occurred in the eighth century C.E. In a relatively short time Buddhism flowered and flourished widely. Then, during the reign of King Langdarma (802–842 C.E.), Buddhism in Tibet was suppressed such that eventually this evil king was assassinated by the *yogin* Lhalung Palgyi Dorje. Following the king's death, chaos ensued. The king left two concubines who fought over the territory, and very rapidly the lineage of Tibetan kings fell away and Tibet became what it had been before, a large land mass ruled by warlords, with bitter rivalries and a variety of political systems.

There was then a second (known now as the New Schools) wave of Indian teachers who reached Tibet in the twelfth century. The Gesar epic, which has versions from Mongolia in the north; China in the east; and Nepal, Sikkim, Bhutan, and India rimming the south, probably began as an oral tradition during this time. In most versions, and the one that is presented here, Gesar is nondual with the great Vajra Master of India, Padmasambhava. Padmasambhava, while known to be an historical personage, has also become part of the celestial realm of deities for Tibetan Buddhist practitioners. The story of Gesar of Ling is one of reestablishing Buddhism in Tibet by eradicating the perverted rulers and their followers who had encroached to extend throughout the four directional borderlands. It should be noted that, not too surprisingly, in the Bön version of the epic, Gesar is able to unify Tibet and establish the primacy of Bön. (The Bön that existed in the twelfth century in Tibet differed from Buddhism to a degree that is no longer true for present-day Bön practitioners.) Nor is it surprising that in the Mongol version a Gesar known as Gesar Khan is victorious. Nonetheless, for the vast majority of the Tibetans for whom this represents the national epic, it is an epic that proclaims not just the cultural heritage of Tibet but also the primacy of the Buddhist ideals in worship and warriorship.

According to the Gesar epic, the problem of the age was that the non-Buddhist and Buddhist aristocrats were at war with each other. Bön and Buddhism were in opposition, and the Bönpo native Tibetan deities did not support the state. During the first introduction of Buddhism into Tibet, Padmasambhava was able to tame these deities twice, but not the third time required for the establishment of a fully tamed utopian Buddhist state. Because that did not happen, there came to be tumult in the invisible world and the necessary glorious gateway was missed. This is a very technical term: a glorious gateway is a moment when the planets and karmic energies are aligned such that something great can be accomplished. But this was not to be, and hence the tale is told.

It is interesting and important to note that there is an invisible world to keep track of where the important energies flourish. This is not a question of being superstitious, because generally in order to succeed at something there must be a viable plan, enough resources, and some degree of organization. Nevertheless, if there is to be success then the forces of coincidence also have to be in one's favor. Having this kind of so-called good luck is a science in Tibetan Buddhism. Understanding local energies, whether this be called politics or spirit worship, is much the same. To get things done, our understanding of the environment in which we function is critical. Unbeknownst to most humans, there are in fact things that affect local spirits and determine our ability to succeed in the world. Whether we are aware of this or not, all humans interact with these energies on a daily basis.

So it was that the dharma kings of Tibet fell, and the land of Tibet lapsed into chaos. Throughout the whole world in general, and in particular in the land of Tibet, the people became oppressed by suffering. Unable to bear this, one of the many manifestations of the Buddha, Avalokiteśvara, supplicated another manifestation of the Buddha, Amitābha, for help with this problem. This marks the beginning of the epic, and according to this version of the epic, Avalokiteśvara, the bodhisattva of compassion, sees the discord and suffering in the world and goes to the Buddha Amitābha for help.

The first three volumes of the epic are completely devoted to Gesar, who is at this point known by the name Joru, as he acquires all the necessary articles and implements that were promised to him when it was determined that he would incarnate in the human realm to bring an end to suffering. He doesn't actually fight any wars during this time. He just takes rebirth in this world and grows up as a very unconventional boy who manages to acquire all of his necessities, one by one, in order to assume the golden throne of Ling. When he's completely possessed of all of the objects that he needs to carry out Avalokiteśvara's plan, then the war sagas of the epic will finally begin.

Concerning Reincarnation

The notion of reincarnation is central to Buddhism and Tibetan Buddhism in particular. In general, until attaining enlightenment all beings are reborn lifetime after lifetime for eons of time. Particular enlightened beings, known as *tulkus,* who are no longer subject to the round of endless rebirth, may decide to return to this world for the benefit of others. They, unlike the vast rest of us, will be able to direct and choose when and how they will be reborn. Concerning this notion of reincarnation, and the intentional incarnation of a tulku in particular, there are many conditions that are necessary to sustain this kind of rebirth, such as the circumstance of one's parents. In the case of Gesar it was important that his mother be a *nāginī,* not a human being. This was one of his many requirements. In fact most of the major enlightened beings all promised to reincarnate at the same time in order to help Gesar in one way or another. Thus his whole family, and all the mighty warriors, supernal maidens, and the like who surrounded him, were all incarnations of great saints from India and Tibet. Actually what we are witnessing is a cosmic plot, a cosmic complicity to affect the world and take advantage of the glorious gateway that had previously been missed.

The Gesar Translation Group and This Project

In 1991 Dr. Robin Kornman began to research the Gesar epic. At the time, Kornman was a Buddhist student of Chögyam Trungpa Rinpoche and had just completed his doctorate in linguistic study, and the epic became so central to his life and breath that he would pursue the research until his death in 2007. Chögyam Trungpa Rinpoche, whose lineage descends directly from the Mukpo clan of Ling, encouraged his students to study Gesar, and Chögyam Trungpa's son, Sakyong Mipham Rinpoche, is said to be a reincarnation of the Mipham who was fundamental to the compiling of the version of the epic that forms the basis of this translation. In 1991

Kornman met with R. A. Stein, a French professor who was probably the foremost Western scholar of Gesar at the time and who inspired a number of scholars who are carrying on his work. It was Kornman's plan for the current three volumes to be but a beginning of a much larger work that would see many translators and scholars working to render into accurate English an increasingly larger portion of the Gesar canon. Although he began the work more or less alone, in 1995 he began active collaboration with Lama Chönam and Sangye Khandro.

Kornman was born in New Orleans in 1947. He worked for his father, helping in construction projects most summers, during which time he came into contact with, we believe, the asbestos that led to his death in 2007 from disseminated peritoneal mesothelioma. Kornman was the first director of Trungpa Rinpoche's initial retreat center, then known as Tail of the Tiger, now Karme Chöling, in Barnet, Vermont. He was one of the founding members of the Nālandā Translation Group and also taught at Naropa University in Boulder, Colorado, eventually going back to school and obtaining his PhD from Princeton University. His doctoral dissertation was a comparative study of the Gesar of Ling epic. In 1993 he accepted a three-year fellowship with the University of Wisconsin at Milwaukee. There, as was his talent and want, he developed close friendships in academia as well as within the sangha and the community.

As part of his dissertation, Kornman had completed a rough translation of the first volume of the Gesar epic, using copies of woodblocks from the Tibetan that he received. After meeting Sangye Khandro in Halifax in 1995, he began the collaboration that included Lama Chönam and allowed for the three of them to complete the rough draft translation of the first three volumes over the next six years. He also began teaching a small number of students Tibetan, one of whom was Jane Hawes, who went on to become an important contributor to this translation.

Lama Chönam was born in 1964 in the Golog region of northeastern Tibet. He entered the Wayen Monastery at the age of fourteen, where he studied and received teachings from many important lamas in Tibet. Lama Chönam's root master was the great Khenpo Münsel, in whose presence he remained for many years. During this time he was fortunate to receive many of the traditional Great Perfection transmissions and practices in a retreat environment with his master. Lama Chönam left Tibet in 1990 to fulfill his hope of meeting His Holiness the Dalai Lama and making a pilgrimage in India and Nepal before returning home. After accomplishing that, he was invited to visit the United States, which has become his new home. Lama Chönam has a lifetime interest in the epic of Gesar, having read extensively within it but also as a child hearing the epic from the bards of his native land. In 1999, with Sangye Khandro he founded the Light of Berotsana Translation Group.

Sangye Khandro, born Nanci Gustafson, traveled to India in 1971 to meet His Holiness the Dalai Lama and study Tibetan Buddhism. She arrived in Dharamsala, India, shortly after the Library of Tibetan Works and Archives had opened its doors to Western students. For the next seven years she traveled and studied extensively in India and Nepal, becoming adept in the teachings as well as preparing herself to become one of the foremost translators of spoken Tibetan. In 1977 she met the Venerable Gyatrul Rinpoche, with whom she collaborated in establishing a number of Buddhist centers in California and Oregon under the auspices of Düdjom Rinpoche. She has offered oral translation for a veritable who's who of Tibetan teachers, including His Holiness Düdjom Rinpoche, His Holiness Penor Rinpoche, His Holiness Khenpo Jigmed Phuntsog Rinpoche, Khenchen Namdröl Rinpoche, Dungsei Thinley Norbu Rinpoche, and many others.

From 1995 to 1999 Lama Chönam and Sangye Khandro traveled to Milwaukee to work closely with Kornman for several months of each year, going through the three volumes that make up this text. The practice was to read the Tibetan aloud and go through the text word by word. All of the sessions were audiotaped. As many of the terms were specific to the Golog region of Tibet, having Lama Chönam (who hails from this region) in attendance was vital to the success of the project. After 2000, Kornman worked with a small group in Milwaukee—Jane Hawes, Julie Brefczynski-Lewis, and Elise Collet—editing the translation of the text. Following Robin Kornman's death, and with the aspiration to finish this project, Lama Chönam, Sangye Khandro, and Jane Hawes joined together to review and retranslate large portions of these three volumes.

Jane Hawes had become a student of Chögyam Trungpa Rinpoche in 1976. A practicing physician, she began to study Tibetan with Robin Kornman in the mid-2000s, collaborating with him on a number of translations but devoting most of her time to working with him on the epic. Jane was responsible for safeguarding all the tape recordings and original translations that were made by the three translators during those long years of research. In 2009 Jane joined the Light of Berotsana Translation Group. With the publication of this book, Lama Chönam, Sangye Khandro, and Jane Hawes intend to continue to translate the great sagas of the epic, and have already begun work on the fourth volume, which depicts the subjugation of the land of Düd, and the *māras*. It is their sincere aspiration that the contents of this epic will always serve as a beacon of hope for those who aspire to participate in an enlightened society that is uplifted and facing toward the direction of the Eastern Sun.

David Shapiro
Milwaukee, Wisconsin
Summer 2010

Translator's Introduction

AN INTRODUCTION TO
THE FIRST THREE VOLUMES OF THE EPIC

MANY SCHOLARS, far more learned and eloquent than I, have written commentaries and given explanations regarding the classic world epic *King Gesar of Ling*. Although unqualified to offer any new academic perspective, my intention is to impart to the reader a taste of my experience as a nomadic child born and reared in the land that was the kingdom of King Gesar and where his remarkable legacy is still felt. The snow land of Tibet is the country that King Gesar uplifted and guided through his enlightened activities, as his sacred feet walked the hills and valleys of the Golog region where I was born. The stories of Gesar are still extensively performed throughout Golog as dramas and operas. As a child I grew up watching these performances and singing the songs to the sheep and yak I was herding, as well as to my family around the evening campfire. In Golog, the epic is still flourishing as it has been for hundreds of years, like a mirror reflecting a time long gone by, but the sights and sounds of which can still be seen and heard on the high plateau, in the ruins of the heroes' castles, in the same mountains, rivers, and meadows where they lived, and in the customs and lifestyle of the people. The Golog dialect is still full of the same vocabulary, proverbs, parables, and phrases that were used in Gesar's time. This is why it is natural for someone like me to share this with the readers, since this is what shaped my early life in Golog and is as familiar to me as everyday speech.

In working with Dr. Robin Kornman and Sangye Khandro to translate these volumes, I was afforded the wonderful opportunity to put the language of my childhood to good use, by clarifying many of the ancient terms and phrases and attempting to explain the key points of the presentation.

From the outset of this project, I have been fully confident that the translation of these stories of the enlightened, compassionate warrior Gesar into the English language will contribute to a global understanding of basic human goodness and dignity. In these modern times many cultures are losing their indigenous roots, forgetting and even ignoring their own customs and the priceless wisdom and insight that were gleaned over centuries of time. It is our hope that by bringing this epic into English at this time in the world, the ancient Tibetan culture and customs will not only be conveyed but emulated and preserved. Robin, Sangye, and I worked together on this translation for several months a year from 1994 to 2000, with every intention to celebrate the publication of this work as a team of colleagues. However, just as the Buddhist teachings strongly remind us, all things are transient, and, sadly, Robin passed away from cancer in July of 2007. In the final years of his life, although plagued by illness and general poor health, Robin continued to teach Tibetan to a small group of students and together they began the process of editing this translation. The main student among them was Jane Hawes, who is responsible for compiling all of the material that we have worked so hard to produce in the aftermath of Robin's death. Without her efforts, this work would certainly have been lost. Jane has been a key component in the survival of this translation and has continued to work very hard to compile and help edit all three volumes of this book. Thanks also go to Julie Brefczynski-Lewis and Elise Collet for their help.

I offer here a concise overview of each of the epic's principal figures, in the hope that such a reference will serve as an introduction to the stunning cast encountered in the stories. This account regarding Gesar and his people is based on my own observation, on the stories I heard from my elders, and on my own limited understanding of the teachings I have received from accomplished masters and scholars. I have attempted to portray each character as I have come to know them through reading the epic and watching it performed many times from the time I was a child. I have also referred to descriptions in historical accounts as well as other sources. The family relationships between the characters are clarified to the extent that I could find confirmation of them. I conclude with a brief summary that outlines the plot of each of the three volumes of our book.

THE EPIC

Scholars in Asia and particularly in Tibet claim that this is the longest epic that exists in the world. There have been approximately 120 volumes of Gesar stories compiled in recent years that include 20 million words and 1.5 million lines of poetry. As for the epic's origin, its stories have been revealed as *terma* (spiritual treasure), composed by scholars, written down based on pure vision, and developed through the oral traditions of bards and storytellers. These are all considered authentic sources.

The style of writing in these stories is extemporaneous poetry: sometimes in verse, sometimes in prose, and sometimes a mingling of the two. The language is so clear and vibrant that each image appears before you as you read or hear it, as sharply as if it were being carved in stone before your eyes, while simultaneously sounding alive, flowing, and natural. The epic is filled with ancient proverbs that have become a natural part of the fabric of everyday dialogue in Tibet and particularly in Golog. Each proverb contains both spiritual and worldly examples, lessons, and advice. My grandmother had a proverb for every occasion and to accompany every scolding or lesson she gave me as a child. Many of these are the same proverbs found in the traditional songs of the epic.

The themes of all the Gesar stories can be synthesized into the following four categories:

The first universal theme describes how to properly engage with the "five sensory objects" (objects of the five senses), and the consequences of utilizing them improperly. For example, the stories demonstrate that too much desire or attachment to external objects will bring suffering. On the other hand, the epic demonstrates how one can be content with whatever one has, if one is able to recognize that the cause of our satisfaction is our previously accumulated virtuous actions based on positive thoughts. The epic demonstrates how one can appreciate and even look forward to whatever comes one's way by cultivating a sense of contentment and avoiding unnecessary depression. Through this, one can know how to enjoy what one has without bringing suffering to others based on one's own pride, jealousy, covetousness, and general discontent.

The second theme describes the exceptional skills for correctly engaging in military activity according to the philosophy of the ancient warriors. This includes having the correct intention and methods, such as knowing how to draw a bow, how to fight with a sword, how to engage with enemies, and how to defeat those who lack these skills. On an inner level, these instructions are meant to be interpreted as showing how to engage with one's personal negative emotions. Just as without expertise and bravery a warrior will fail, each of us will fail if we handle our negative emotions without this same kind of skill and courage.

The third theme describes how King Gesar brought benefit to his subjects, disciplining the rebellious and acting as a parent for the humble and weak, delivering peace and joy to the minds of all. This serenity gave them the opportunity to practice dharma and achieve ultimate happiness.

The fourth theme describes the results of his activities and the way his subjects flourished by both spiritual and worldly standards. In the context of their lives, they found happiness, merit, and longevity, riches and nobility, which enabled them to practice the dharma. Their spiritual progress is also recorded—how they became suitable recipients of dharma teachings, how their understanding and practice developed, and how they passed away and attained higher states of rebirth and the capacity to benefit others in their subsequent lifetimes.

THE MUKPO LINEAGE

In general there are numerous clans throughout Tibet, such as the Nam, Sa, Ah, Nyi, and Lha clans. King Gesar belonged to the Mukpo clan and its lineage, based on the paternal connection through his father.

The Mother Text of the Mukpo clan, a prophecy describing the succession of Mukpo kings, gives the following prediction: "Following Yemön Namkhai Gyalpo, after thirteen generations of the people of Ling have passed, there will be no son and the lineage would thereby be held by the daughter. At that time the elder brother Chatül will marry Tricham Dzeiden of the Drong clan and a son named Ratra Genpo will be born to them. He, Ratra Genpo, will become the first king of Dokham.* He will be followed by Kings Ritritsen† and Mutritsen. Three sons will be born to Mutritsen: Chöliphen, Lamaphen, and Chöphen Nagpo, these three. The son of Ser, the son of Om, and the son of Chang, these three, will found the Elder, Middle, and Younger tribes of Ling. The royal lineage of Dradül Bum, Thoglha Bum, and Chöla Bum will rule the eternal Mukpo clan. The sons of King Senglön will be the three: the sun—Sengchen of Ling—the moon, and the stars."

Commentaries explain and expand on the cryptic wording of the prophecy as follows.

Following Yemön Namkhai Gyalpo, after thirteen generations of the people of Ling have passed . . .

The first king of the clan was Yemön Namkhai Gyalpo, who was followed by thirteen kings, the throne passing from father to son. Sources do not clearly designate the clan as "Mukpo" at this point.

. . . there will be no son and the lineage would be held by the daughter. At that time the elder brother Chatül will marry Tricham Dzeiden of the Drong clan . . .

The thirteenth king had no son, and so the throne passed to the last king's elder brother, Chatül, who became the king. King Chatül's queen was Tricham

---

* The northeastern and eastern regions of the Tibetan plateau.

† *Ritritsen* is the archaic spelling for *Rutritsen*.

Dzeiden of the Drong clan, also known as the Dri clan. Their sons became the kings of the Ah and Lha clans, and also the leaders of the four clans called Karpo (white), Nagpo (black), Trawo (multicolored), and Mukpo (maroon).

. . . and a son named Ratra Genpo of the clan will be born to them. He will become the first king of Dokham.

Among these sons, the one called Ratra Genpo became king of the clan known from this point onward as "Mukpo." He was also the first king of the Dokham region.

. . . followed by Kings Ritritsen and Mutritsen.

Ratra Genpo had two sons, Ritritsen and Mutritsen. Following Ratra Genpo, the Mukpo throne passed to Mutritsen.

Three sons will be born to Mutritsen: Chöliphen, Lamaphen, and Chöphen Nagpo, these three.

Of Mutritsen's three sons, Chöliphen, Lamaphen, and Chöphen Nagpo, the Mukpo throne passed to the latter, Chöphen Nagpo.

The son of Ser, the son of Om, and the son of Chang, these three, will found the Elder, Middle, and Younger (Lesser) tribes of Ling.

Chöphen Nagpo had three wives: Serza, Omza, and Changmoza. Each bore a son, sometimes called Serbu, Ombu, and Changbu, or the "son of Ser," "son of Om," and "son of Chang," respectively. These three sons became the founders of the eighteen Mukpo tribes that comprised the Elder, Middle, and Lesser Lineages of Ling. Serza was Chöphen Nagpo's first wife; her son was named Lhayag Darkar, the elder. He founded the Mukpo tribes called the eight tribes of the elder brother Serpa of Upper Ling, also called the divine tribes of Ling's Elder Brother Lineage. Omza was the second wife; her son was named Trichang Pagyal, the middle. He founded the six Mukpo tribes of Ombu of Middle Ling, or the divine tribes of Ling's Middle Brother Lineage. Changmoza was the third wife; her son was named Dragyal Bum, the younger. He founded the four Mukpo tribes of Muchang of Lower Ling, or the divine tribes of Ling's Younger Brother Lineage.

The royal lineage of Dradül Bum, Thoglha Bum, and Chöla Bum will rule the eternal Mukpo clan.

Chöphen Nagpo's younger son, Dragyal Bum, was also called Dradül Bum. From him, the Mukpo throne passed to his son, Thoglha Bum, who in turn passed it on to his son, Chöla Bum. Chöla Bum had three wives: Rongza, Gaza, and Muza. Rongza's son became Chipön Rongtsha Tragen, Gesar's elder uncle, the chief of Ling; Gaza was the mother of Yu-gyal, who was killed in the battles with the armies of Hor; and Muza gave birth to King Senglön, Gesar's father.

> *The sons of King Senglön will be the three: the sun—Sengchen of Ling—the moon, and the stars.*

Senglön had three wives: Gyaza, the nāginī Yelga Dzeiden, and Rongza. Each bore a son: Gyaza, the first wife, bore the eldest son, named Gyatsha Zhalkar. Yelga Dzeiden bore the boy Joru, who became King Gesar, and Rongza bore the younger son, Rongtsha Marlep. When the Mother Text refers to Senglön's sons, "the sun—Sengchen of Ling" indicates King Gesar, and "the moon and the stars" refer to his two brothers. Thus the Mother Text traces the lineage from Yemön Namkhai Gyalpo, the first king of the clan, to King Gesar.

The succession of clan kings is summarized as follows:

Yemön Namkhai Gyalpo (first king of the clan)
—thirteen generations pass—
Chatül (elder brother of the previous king)
Ratra Genpo (hereafter the clan is known as "Mukpo")
Mutritsen
Chöphen Nagpo
Dragyal Bum (also called Changbu or Dradül Bum)
Thoglha Bum
Chöla Bum
Senglön
Gesar

King Gesar

The main character in the epic is the Lord of Ling, King Gesar, also called Sengchen Norbu Dradül.[*] Gesar was not an ordinary human being but rather a manifestation of the enlightened activity of all the buddhas, brought forth by the strength of their

---

[*] Great Lion Jewel Tamer of Enemies.

great compassion at a time of despair in the land of Tibet. At the request of an enlightened buddha, he emanated from the pure land to the world of humans, bringing vast benefit to this realm. Even to this day Gesar continues to manifest in this realm and in others, out of his compassion for all beings. Gesar was said to be the manifestation of the bodhisattva protectors of the three families, Mañjuśrī, Avalokiteśvara, and Vajrapāṇi, who are the embodiments of all the buddhas' wisdom, compassion, and power. Gesar's every action was motivated by those three principal enlightened qualities. He was the great master of the *vidyādharas* (awareness holders), nondual with Padmasambhava in nature and the great emissary of his enlightened activity; a great *sattva* on the *bhūmis*,* who entered this world clothed in human flesh, for the sole purpose of benefiting the world and sentient beings. King Gesar received initiation to enter this world from the five buddha families. When he manifested in the land of White Ling, he conquered many malicious kings and māras and from that time until now, he has manifested in whatever way is beneficial to removing obstacles that arise on the path to enlightenment. These days, for those who supplicate Gesar with faith and devotion, his blessings will certainly be felt. It has been prophesied that in the future (which is actually predicted to be sometime in the twenty-first century), when this world is overcome by barbarians who hold extreme and perverted religious views, this great vidyādhara hero, Gesar Norbu Dradül, will arise in the enlightened body of a sacred warrior general, the foremost Rigden king of Shambhala, Rigden Raudrachakrin, and, enveloped in the splendor of a hundred thousand suns, will once again return to defeat the hordes of māras in our world.†

Gesar's Manifestation

At the time of King Gesar's birth, Tibet was a land of turmoil and anguish. When the bodhisattva Avalokiteśvara asked Buddha Amitābha to help relieve the people's suffering, Amitābha replied that there were a king and queen in the pure land who would give birth to a great being to be named Thöpa Gawa [Joyful to Hear], who would then manifest in the human realm to bring an end to suffering. To set his enlightened activity in motion, Amitābha sent Avalokiteśvara to visit the great master Padmasambhava where he was dwelling in Cāmara, the southwest country

---

* This refers to a bodhisattva who has realized the third path of seeing and hence enters the grounds of bodhisattvahood beginning with the first *bhūmi*, or ground, which is called Extreme Joy. Having entered the grounds or *bhūmis*, rebirth in saṃsāra no longer occurs.

† Rigden Dragpo Chag-gyi Khorlocan, Wielder of the Iron Wheel (Tib. *rigs ldan drag po lcags kyi 'khor lo can*).

of the cannibals. Once there, Avalokiteśvara manifested as a cannibal cub and requested permission for an audience with Padmasambhava, who granted his request. Padmasambhava then blessed the king and queen in the pure land, and the prince Thöpa Gawa was born with many miraculous signs. Padmasambhava supplicated the five buddha families to grant empowerment to Thöpa Gawa, and instructed him to emanate in the human realm. In turn, he requested certain companions and conditions in order that his manifestation would be successful in the human realm, and he made the commitment to do as instructed.

In the human realm, Gesar's mother, a nāginī princess called Yelga Dzeiden, received a vision and prophecy from Padmasambhava in a dream, foretelling the birth of her son, a great being who would become king and save the people of Tibet and neighboring lands. Shortly after this prophecy, she became pregnant, and she had many conversations with the infant Joru (as Gesar was referred to as a child) while he was still in her womb. When the child was born, Padmasambhava appeared and made aspirations for his success and protection.

Gesar's Birth

Mipham Jampel Gyepei Dorje (Mipham Rinpoche) and other scholars such as Jigdral Yeshe Dorje (Düdjom Rinpoche) say King Gesar was born in the Earth Tiger year of the first Rabjung (the sixty-year cycle used in the Tibetan calendar), or the year 1038 C.E. Although scholars make many different assertions regarding his birthplace, these are generally divided into claims that he was born in Kham or in Golog. The *History of Amdo* [*mdo smad chos 'byung*] states that King Gesar was born in Golog. However, many other written accounts specifically name Kyidsö Yag-gi Khado, near Shechen Monastery in Kham, as the birthplace, and this claim is supported by great scholars such as Ju Mipham and the great treasure revealer Lerab Lingpa.

Gesar lived until the age of eighty-eight (Tibetan reckoning counts gestation in the womb as the first year of life when calculating age) and passed away in 1125 C.E., the Wood Serpent year, on the peak of Tukar Yidzhin Norbu, which lies before the great mountain Magyal Pomra in the Golog region of northeastern Tibet.

Gesar's Youth

As a boy, Joru was always up to mischief, testing everyone and everything. A skillful magician, he could manifest countless likenesses of himself simultaneously engaging in various activities. This caused great confusion, but ultimately led to benefit, as was the case with all of his actions. As instructed by Padmasambhava, from the age of six Joru cultivated a savage air: he wore an antelope hat with horns as a headdress, a makeshift cloak made of raw yak-skin, and crude horsehide boots. His countenance would alter as needed, sometimes splendid, other times hideous. He pretended to be a hunter, robber, murderer, and virtually every kind of villain. These disturbing appearances were displayed in order to spread his enlightened activity ever farther, since all his seeming misdeeds were later proved to be illusory. From the relative perspective, his enlightened activity was expressed as every kind of crime, but from the point of view of the ultimate, the young Joru never performed any action that brought true harm. The final straw to effect his exile was to pretend to kill some of King Trothung's men. Through this display of wickedness, Joru brought about his own banishment and thus was able to leave his birthplace and go to the Ma Valley, where he was destined to enact his principal enlightened deeds.

When Joru and his mother arrived, the Ma Valley was a wilderness inhabited only by wild animals. Merchants would pass through when traveling between India and China, but otherwise there were no humans to be seen. Joru took possession of the valley, and he and his mother lived on wild yams and Himalayan *pikas* (a type of rodent) that he killed with his slingshot. He used a magical white willow staff as a horse and lived as a demon-hunter, capturing passing merchants and forcing them to build castles in the valley.

At this time, the people of Ling lived in the Kham region. One winter a terrible blizzard blanketed the land and the people feared for their lives. The Ma Valley remained a paradise untouched by the snow. Joru's elder brother, Gyatsha Zhalkar, a hero of the Ling people, requested that the people be permitted to stay on Joru's land to wait out the winter. Joru agreed, and the people of Ling moved to the Ma Valley. Joru divided the land into thirty parcels and sang a beautiful song describing the qualities of each of his future thirty warriors as he granted them their piece of the land. Once the inhabitants of Ling had settled in their new home, the stage was set for all of Gesar's subsequent enlightened activity to manifest.

One night, Gesar's jealous uncle Trothung had a dream, a false prophecy that if a horse race were held to determine the rightful sovereign of the land, he would win it himself, thus gaining the throne of Ling and the coveted Princess Drugmo. Joru's brother, Gyatsha, insisted that Joru be allowed to join the contest. Joru won the race riding his magical horse, an emanation of Hayagrīva that only his mother and future wife were able to capture, based on their karmic connection.

GESAR'S REIGN

Once the race was won, Joru became the king of Ling. At that time his outer presence was completely transformed from the strange, wild demeanor he had displayed as a child into that of a great being. Gesar's form was breathtaking; his countenance was the most handsome of the handsome, so that all never tired of looking at his face. His enlightened body, speech, and mind were fully endowed with the energy of dralas and wermas.* His horse, too, appeared very differently. When first captured, the horse was awkward and graceless, its qualities hidden, but now the steed's true appearance suddenly emerged in all its glory, much to the surprise of the onlookers. Gesar himself now appeared as a king with charisma and authentic presence, a true sovereign of dharma, fit to rule, and he spoke with unconditional, heartfelt loving-kindness toward each of his subjects. He confidently proclaimed himself to be an incarnation of Padmasambhava, an emanation of the great enlightened ones, and declared that his objective was to benefit all sentient beings and protect and spread all teachings based on virtue and wholesomeness.

Further volumes tell of Gesar's exploits once he was king. For example, he traveled alone to conquer the northwest land of Düd (land of the demons) and liberated their king, Lutsen Gyalpo. The demon king's wife, Meza Bumkyid, gave Gesar a potion that caused amnesia, and he was trapped in Düd for nine years. While Gesar was away, the king of the northeastern land of Hor, Gurkar Gyalpo, invaded Ling, kidnapped Gesar's queen, and destroyed Gesar's palace. His army slaughtered many important warriors, including Gesar's brother, Gyatsha. Gurkar Gyalpo was a poor leader, arrogant and foolish, and he sent his armies to attack against the advice of his ministers, who rightfully feared the power of Ling. When Gesar recovered from the demon queen's potion and returned home, he revenged the attacks with many magical activities, pushing the people of Hor to the brink of defeat, and finally leading his army to conquer them. After that, Ling was never again successfully invaded.

The stories of Gesar are exciting in their own right as fine tales, but to understand them as they are intended, it is crucial to keep in mind that King Gesar's every word and deed was an expression of his ultimate wisdom, compassion, and power. Gesar was an enlightened being, sent by the buddhas and bodhisattvas at a time of crisis and terror to bring peace not only to the land of Ling but to the hearts and minds of humanity worldwide. This is particularly important to recall when considering the many stories of battle. The wars Gesar waged were not holy wars to overpower or convert countries of other faiths. He was not fighting to conquer

---

* Special protectors of Gesar, they guard and assist him and their presence increases his magnificence. See further explanations of drala and werma under "Gods and Demons" in this introduction.

others because of their color, race, religion, or politics. Gesar's every deed was motivated by compassion; his purpose always to help all beings discover the causes of true happiness and well-being. He possessed the power and skillful means of all the buddhas, so he could manifest in whatever way was necessary for that purpose. Although he is well-known for his combat, in fact he engaged in all kinds of activity depending on what was most effective for his purpose. Mipham Rinpoche explained that Gesar tamed his subjects—that is, those beings who by their own predilections could and would follow his teachings, not necessarily just those living in his kingdom—through the three activities of peaceful, enriching, and powerful methods. He tamed those who saw him as an enemy—that is, malevolent beings bent on harm and incapable of following his teachings or voluntarily enacting any virtue—through wrathful means.

Even the beings that he seemed to kill were not slain in an ordinary sense but, rather, by that appearance their harmful and malicious behavior was brought to an end and their consciousnesses were sent to higher states. This method was used on those whose habits of malice and wrongdoing were so strong that all other means were ineffective. Such beings pursued their own short-term interests single-mindedly, without any thought for others or even for their own long-term benefit. As a result they brought nothing but destruction and torment to all, themselves included, and were immune to any peaceful method of ending their madness. Whatever his display, it is certain that Gesar acted only from immeasurable loving-kindness, with infinite skillful methods so that his reign and his life, as recorded in the stories of the epic from start to finish, were the fulfillment of the buddhas' enlightened wisdom intent.

OTHER PRINCIPAL CHARACTERS

The scriptures leave no doubt that, like King Gesar, each of the main characters, male and female, came to this world of their own accord in order to bring benefit to the planet, rather than wandering in the world as ordinary beings compelled by their negative karma. Moreover, in their clairvoyant wisdom they already knew the plots of the epic before they transpired. But, seeing how Padmasambhava's deeds could most effectively manifest, and the lessons that needed to be taught and learned, they pretended to have no foreknowledge of events and feigned the deluded motivations of ordinary beings. In truth, they were always acting deliberately to support and display Padmasambhava's miraculous activity.

The women of the epic are the keys to its precious treasure. They are the matriarchs and maidens, known far and wide for their beauty and warmth, and said to be vidyādhara *ḍākinīs* of the four classes[*] who entered this world in the form of human women.

The Thirty Mighty Warriors of Ling were also sent by Padmasambhava as part of his miraculous display, and along with them were the seven great champions (the Seven Super Warriors), and the three mightiest (the Ultimate Warriors) who were Falcon, Eagle, and Wolf. All were said to be incarnations of the eighty *mahāsiddhas* of the noble land of India, and in the future they will manifest as the Rigden dharma kings in Shambhala. In the snow land of Tibet they were the warriors of Ling, who numbered thirty at the opening of the epic and grow to eighty as the story unfolds. Not only these warriors themselves but their horses and weapons are legendary, and their names are still well-known. Their mounts were magical steeds that could speak, traverse any terrain, and fly. They were manifestations of awakened beings, and the epic includes tales of them assisting their riders, even saving their lives. The warriors' weapons are also renowned. For example, Gesar gave a magical arrow to each of his warriors, which they could use in their darkest hour to save themselves or perform a great deed.

These archetypal warriors can be understood from both an outer and inner point of view. The outer warrior is exemplified throughout the epic as being fearless when it comes to subduing enemies and so forth. The inner warrior incorporates those same qualities and activities when the battle is joined with his own negativity rather than an external adversary. A warrior must have wisdom and skillful methods in order to be victorious. Likewise, these same qualities of wisdom and method are the only way to defeat one's own passions and mental afflictions. The warrior must be fearless and assured, ready to act without hesitation or hampered by doubts. Likewise, one must be ready to engage with mental poisons—our true foes that appear every day—and deal with them immediately and resolutely. Thus the warriors are still models for us today, as our battle with negative emotions is far from over.

King Senglön (Gesar's Father)

Senglön was born to King Chöla Bum and his third wife, Muza. In India he incarnated as the mahāsiddha Āryadeva and the Rishi Legjin, and it is said in Shambhala he will be the dharma king Zijid Thaye. He was light-skinned, his body

---

[*] The "four classes" of *ḍākinīs* are those born of space, born of mantra, born of sacred places, and wisdom classes.

well-proportioned, and he wore his salt-and-pepper hair and beard moderately long. He dressed in full battle regalia, perfectly fitted and studded with the finest jewels. He had a gentle heart and manner; his form blazed with majesty; his voice was as sweet as a flute, and his mind was like a mandala of clear light. He was famous for the accuracy of his arrow divinations. Respected by all, the richness of his merit and charisma made his body a castle for the dralas, a fortress for the wermas, and a life-force stone where the protectors dwelled. Senglön married Gyaza Lhakar Drönma,* and on an excellent day in the twelfth month of the Female Water Ox year, their son Gyatsha Zhalkar was born amid many wonderful signs.

Later, when Gog and Ling were at war, it was Senglön who received the girl called Gogza, who was the nāginī princess Yelga Dzeiden, as the first spoils of the battle. Their firstborn son was Joru, who grew up to be King Gesar. Senglön's third wife, Rongza, bore Gesar's younger brother, Rongtsha Marleb.

The Nāginī Princess (Gesar's Mother)

In order to bring the nāginī princess Yelga Dzeiden to the human realm, where she was destined to bear the child who would become King Gesar, Padmasambhava arranged for an invitation from her father, the *nāga* king Tsugna Rinchen. Padmasambhava first sent a plague to the nāga realm, and then through the influence of his magic, all the mirror divinations consulted by the nāga king revealed that Padmasambhava was the only master who could bring an end to the epidemic. Thus he came to the nāga realm at the king's invitation, conferred his blessing to end the plague, and accepted Tsugna Rinchen's youngest daughter, Yelga Dzeiden, as an offering along with other precious gifts.

This is the method by which Padmasambhava brought the nāginī princess to the middle realm of humans,† where he asked the king of Gog, Ralo Tönpa Gyaltsen, to care for her. Ralo Tönpa Gyaltsen raised her as his adopted daughter until she was grown. When Ling and Gog were at war, as karmic destiny took its course, she came into the hands of the Ling soldiers. At this time she also became known as "Gogza" or "Gogmo"—the girl of Gog. Senglön Gyalpo took her as his wife, and to them was born the divine child, Joru.

Yelga Dzeiden's physical beauty is elaborated upon in the epic when the

---

* Lhakar Drönma of China.

† It is common to refer to "the upper realm of gods," "the middle realm of humans," and "the lower realm of nāgas."

soldiers of Ling suddenly find her in the wild. The epic portrays her beauty to be so magnificent that all those who encountered her were awestruck. Her skin was luminous like the flowers on the shores of a lake or like the sun reflected off a lotus petal. Her eyes were clear and fine, her bearing as straight as a bamboo stalk in summer and as graceful as when it wafts in the breeze, her form as smooth and supple as a white silk scarf. The strands of her long, flowing hair were like silk. Her exquisite beauty brought joy to all.

Queen Drugmo (Gesar's Wife)

Drugmo's father was Kyalo Tönpa Gyaltsen, the wealthiest man in Ling and patron of many festivals. On the day of Drugmo's birth, a snow lion appeared, posed on a snow mountain, and a dragon roared in the sky; thus her name combined the two terms: Sengcham Drugmo, meaning Lion Sister Dragoness. She had both a sister and brother; Drugmo and her sister were considered to be emanations of White and Green Tārā. Drugmo constantly displayed all the qualities of White Tārā, proving that she was truly an emanation of this goddess and not just an ordinary person. Occasionally she displayed the characteristics of an ordinary woman, so that ordinary men and women could relate to her. In general, though, she is considered to be a superior model of the feminine principle, just as Gesar is considered the ultimate model of the masculine, and she is admired and emulated to this day.

At the horse race sponsored by Trothung to decide the ruler of Ling, Drugmo and a dowry of all the wealth and connections of her family was the prize. Drugmo was the loveliest of women, like a summer flower, sought after by all throughout the land. Her beauty and grace were known far beyond the borders of Ling. Her voice was sweet as a nightingale's, and her mind held all the wisdom and compassion of the goddess Tārā. When swathed in the silks and jewels of a queen, she was as magnificent as the multicolored peacock.

When Gesar was preparing to manifest in the human realm, he specified that he would need a queen who possessed the qualities of Drugmo. Gesar's relationship with the coveted Drugmo brought conflict and incited the jealousy of many kings who desired her hand in marriage. This in turn gave Gesar the opportunity to benefit those suitors in myriad ways. Drugmo was utterly loyal. Even when taken and imprisoned by Gurkar, the king of Hor, she never forgot nor betrayed her king or country. She never gave her heart to Gurkar, but instead she had him build a castle just like Gesar's to remind her of her homeland. Finally, although captive in Hor, she sent Gesar a letter carried by three cranes who were her *la-ja*, the birds of her life force. Although at first the birds meant nothing to him because of his amnesia, they skillfully caused Gesar to begin to remember his country and identity. In this and many ways, Drugmo was an important figure in many of the Gesar tales, not only as Gesar's wife but as a loyal citizen of her country.

Chipön Rongtsha Tragen (Gesar's Uncle)

The chief or *chipön*, named Rongtsha Tragen, was the son of Chöla Bum and his first wife, Rongza. Chipön Rongtsha Tragen was the reincarnation of the mahāsiddha Nāgārjuna and the paṇḍita Sergyi Dogcan from India. He was also prophesied to be the dharma king of Shambhala, Dawa Zangpo. The picture that comes to mind when reading of him is the image of an elder gentleman, a white hat upon his head, a spray of wrinkles across his brow, his hair and beard whiter than a conch, and his manner as warm and kind as the most loving of grandfathers. His majestic form was clothed in exquisite garments and adorned with jewelry. A genuine dharma practitioner, his diligence was such that his recitation of the six syllables OM MAṆI PADME HUNG/HŪṂ poured forth day and night like a river.

His characteristics are described in volume 2, here titled *Gesar's Birth and Childhood in the Land of Ling:*

> His wisdom is like the sky at dawn; his skillful compassion like the spring warmth that thaws both earth and water. His ethics are as straight as a ruler; he distinguishes true actions from false like splitting a shaft of bamboo. He puts the mighty under his yoke; like a mother and father he cares for the humble; he is head of the family, the ultimate authority consulted at gatherings and the commanding officer when defeating enemies. He belongs specifically to the younger brother lineage, but he is respected as the chief of the whole of Ling.

The epic also shows that this great being was universally respected and relied upon as the senior chief among Ling's leaders. Chipön married a maiden from Tibet, Metog Tashi-tso. They had four children: the older son was named Yuphen Tag-gyal, the middle son was Lenpa Chögyal, the younger son was Nangchung Yutag, and their daughter was called Lhamo Yudrön.

King Trothung (Gesar's Uncle)

While in the upper pure lands, before Gesar emanated into this world, he asked for a foil who would invoke his enlightened deeds. Consequently, his uncle manifested as a turncoat, a spiteful adversary, and a manipulative gossip who would play upon others' emotions. Trothung had a malicious mind and was jealous of Gesar from the beginning of the epic to the very end. According to the general descriptions found in the epic, Trothung's appearance had no trace of the greatness or splendor that marks the bearing of a leader, nor the fierce and assured manner of a hero; it showed only the traits of an old man. His dark face was filled with wrinkles; half of his long gray hair hung over his shoulders, the other half was pulled up in a knot; his beard hung down long and was streaked with white. His every thought, word, and deed were abrupt and inappropriate, and he could not sit still. He relished a high seat to lord over others and was a master of bragging and flattery. He was always conceited and proud, lustful and envious, pretentious, boastful, deceitful, and hypocritical. Because of these qualities, he was scorned by most everyone. Trothung appeared in this way in order for Gesar's miraculous activities to manifest, yet in actuality he was an incarnation of the Indian mahāsiddha Naropa. In Shambhala he will manifest as the dharma king Lhayi Wangpo. He is inseparable with the wisdom deity Hayagrīva, and as such, he came to be a dharma protector in both the Bön and Buddhist traditions.

Denma (Gesar's Chief Minister)

Even before Gesar became king, Tshazhang Denma Jangtra was an important man in Ling. During Gesar's reign, Denma was his greatest minister and was also the most famous archer in the land. He had dark skin and a hero's appearance. Through all the stories of the epic he was steadfast and noble and remained loyal to the end.

Gyatsha Zhalkar (Gesar's elder brother)

Senglön's first wife, Gyaza, bore Gyatsha Zhalkar, his first son. The name Zhalkar referred to the handsome appearance of his porcelain-like face. A mighty warrior swordsman, he was determined and unwavering once his mind was made up, and he was always loyal and affectionate to Gesar's mother and the young Joru. When Joru was banished, Gyatsha still stood up for his brother's right to be included at holidays and festivals. When Gesar was in the northern land of demons, Gyatsha led Ling in Gesar's stead, as the other rulers were too elderly. He fought the armies of Hor valiantly when they invaded Ling, never despairing. At his death he made the bitter wish: "May I take rebirth as a falcon, and whenever I kill a bird, may I feel satisfied as though I killed the enemies of Hor." Because of this aspiration, he was actually reborn as a falcon, and he again met his own son, who had grown to be a great warrior himself. Once the country of Hor was finally defeated Gyatsha felt satisfied, and it was then that Gesar guided him from his falcon rebirth to the state of liberation. Although later reborn in the pure land of Sukhāvatī, the volume describing Gyatsha's rebirth as a falcon and his exchanges with his son and with Gesar is a heartbreaking, cautionary tale about the dangers of hatred and vengeance.

GODS AND DEMONS

Throughout the epic one encounters the terms *drala, werma, windhorse,* and references to various gods and demons. It can be difficult to understand what these terms refer to, whether they are certain kinds of energy, formless beings, good and bad luck by other names, or something else altogether.

Drala and werma are ancient designations that mainly originate with the Gesar epic. The dralas and wermas are the protectors of Gesar and the people of Ling, and they assist in accomplishing enlightened deeds. Drala can sometimes be understood as a powerful and overwhelming energy. This affects each one of us in terms of how we function in our life. For instance if one is able to accomplish something truly extraordinary, the power or energy behind that accomplishment is called drala. Sometimes the term *drala* refers to an individual protector, such as Gesar's elder drala brother Dungkhyung Karpo [White-Conch Garuḍa], who was his personal bodyguard.

As for werma, there are said to be thirteen principle wermas, represented by the thirteen animals, as mentioned in the epic. Drala and werma also refer to local spirits, but the simplest way to understand them is through their function as the guardians or messengers of Gesar. For example, in the second volume of the epic, when Gesar's uncle Trothung hires a black magician to kill Joru, Joru invokes all the dralas and wermas to protect him, following which they all manifest as inconceivable legions of protectors to overwhelm the magician.

The dralas and wermas protect all of the warriors, not only Gesar. Moreover, the dralas and wermas naturally surround and assist anyone who has basic human dignity and goodness. According to ancient Tibetan beliefs, generally when a person is born, there are gods[*] or positive spirits who are simultaneously born with

---

[*] Gesar's three sibling protectors, Dungkhyung Karpo, Ludrül Ödtrung (or Ödchung, this name is spelled in different ways in the Tibetan text), and Thalei Ödtro, mentioned in volume 2, chapter 3, are not the same as these gods that accompany each ordinary human. They are called "sibling" because, like the personal gods mentioned here, they were born from his mother at the same time as his birth, but these three are Gesar's special protectors.

them as well as demons or negative spirits who are born with them as well. These spirit beings are formless, and their powers and numbers will vary according to each individual. If one has an abundance of previously accumulated merit, then the positive spirits will tend to be more numerous and powerful; whereas if the accumulations are predominantly negative, the negative spirits will follow suit. In this life if one accumulates great merit or great negativity, then the positive and negative spirits will increase or diminish accordingly.

There are five specific protector gods born with humans to reside on their body. These protectors are both visible and invisible. Invisibly, they manifest as good luck and success in one's life, and they grant protection from calamities and accidents. If visible their physical description is as follows:

Molha, the god of the female, appears as a young girl, white in color, holding a long-life arrow and a mirror, wearing a blue silk cloak and the skin of a female deer, adorned with many jewels. She is said to reside under the left arm and to accompany each person like their shadow. If the person believes in and practices basic dignity and goodness, she is said to help increase their *prajñā,* or wisdom.

Soglha, the god of the life force, appears as a young boy, white, holding a pennant spear and a lasso, wearing armor and riding a black horse. He dwells in the chest. For a person who is not spiritual, he may appear as a worldly spirit such as *düd* or *tsen*. For a dharma practitioner, he can appear as a protector.

Polha, the god of the male, appears as a man of middle age, white, holding a platter of gems, wearing a blue silk cloak and a white silk diadem, adorned with countless jewels. He dwells under the right arm. For a person not involved in buddhadharma, he may appear as an ancestral god; for a practitioner, he may appear as a protector sent from the lineage masters.

Yulha appears as a young boy, white, wearing armor, a shield, and holding weapons such as a bow and arrow. He rides a white horse and dwells on the crown of the head. Like Soglha, for a person who is not spiritual, he may appear as a worldly spirit, but for a dharma practitioner, he may appear as a protector.

Dralha also appears as a young boy, white, holding a pennant lance and lasso, and riding a white horse. He wears weapons at his waist and is adorned with a silk diadem and jewels. He dwells on the right shoulder. Like Soglha and Yulha, he appears either as a worldly spirit or a protector.

There are many categories of guardian spirits, such as guardians for the house, castle, farmland, domestic animals, entranceways, paths, ornaments, clothes, food, companions, family lineages, and prosperity. These spirits are not just based on ancient Tibetan culture; they are also mentioned in Buddhist scriptures.

The epic is steeped in the notion of lungta, or windhorse. The windhorse is the supreme steed carrying wish-fulfilling jewels, able to go anywhere freely without obstacle. The windhorse is gold in color and represents the energy of success. If life treats one well, one is confident, inspired, and everything is proceeding harmoniously, then it is said that one's windhorse is raised or uplifted. If everything is going wrong, if one's fortune takes a turn for the worse, then it is said that one's windhorse has diminished or been lost. In Tibet there are ceremonies to uplift windhorse energy. The power of windhorse is represented by four animals: the two mighty ones in space are the garuḍa and dragon; the two mighty ones on the earth are the snow lion and tiger. The red tiger represents bravery, the white snow lion represents magnificence, the green garuḍa represents uplifted energy, and the blue dragon represents renown. In order for windhorse to move freely, one must enliven the energy of these four.

This completes the character sketches.

GESAR PRACTICE

Various spiritual practices have been written using Gesar as the principal figure and source of blessings. According to Mipham Rinpoche and other great scholars and accomplished masters, Gesar can be practiced as the guru, the meditation deity, the dharma protector, or the wealth deity. When practicing Gesar as the guru, he is Guru Yidzhin Norbu, the Wish-Fulfilling Jewel. Through this practice one is able to realize the nature of mind to be inseparable with the guru and attain the supreme *siddhi*. When practicing Gesar as the meditation deity, all obstacles are removed, and the wisdom ḍākinīs such as Drugmo—Gesar's consort, an emanation of White Tārā—quicken one's attainment of siddhis. When practicing Gesar as a dharma protector or wealth deity, then the common siddhis such as the peaceful, enriching, powerful, and wrathful activities can be accomplished without obstacle.

One such protector practice is called the Gesar *lhasang*, or juniper smoke offering, in which the offering substances are poured onto a fire. In general, when making any such offering, four guests are invited: the Triple Gem, dharma protectors, the negative forces to which karmic debts are owed, and the objects of compassion (meaning the sentient beings of the six realms). Additionally, in the Gesar lhasang, from an outer perspective one invites Gesar and the warriors of Ling, who are understood on the inner level to be the dralas and wermas. On the innermost, or secret, level these are the enlightened beings, buddhas and bodhisattvas. Once the guests are invited, offerings are made of many sacred, medicinal, and beneficial substances, prepared according to instructions set down by authentic lineage masters. Delicious food and drink are offered, and inconceivable mental offerings are made simultaneously. The ritual is performed by burning the substances, and by the virtue of this offering, one's obstacles are removed and great merit is accumulated. This is one example of the versatility of Gesar practice.

Mipham Rinpoche composed many different versions of Gesar practices for specific purposes, such as rituals for protection, longevity, wealth, and all kinds of success. There are also Gesar practices to increase inner confidence, as well as those to summon richness and bring tranquility to the mind.

In general the warriors in the epic embody dignity, loyalty, humility, confidence, courage, and respect for self and others. Taking this as the example, anyone possessing these qualities will be capable of transforming any circumstance into a positive experience with beneficial results. The warriors demonstrated self-respect by treating their bodies, armor, and weapons as shrines to the dralas. They cared for these with reverence, not out of self-cherishing or vanity but rather for the potential they held to bring benefit to all. They had great courage and confidence without succumbing to pride or jealousy. If one wishes to engage in Gesar practice, these qualities must be valued and shown respect.

Diligence in such practice will bring benefit in worldly life, as well as the ability to radiate charisma and trustworthiness, a body that glows with splendor, speech that is potent and compelling, and a mind filled with altruism.

THE LEGACY OF GESAR

In Tibet, there are some who see Gesar as an enlightened being and a wisdom deity, while others are merely inspired by his story and take him and his warriors as ordinary role models—the little boys want to be Gesar and the girls want to be Queen Drugmo. Whether seen as a warrior or a buddha, however, he has been beloved and revered until this day. The traditions of Ling were never intentionally or systematically preserved, but the tales and characters of the epic are so inspiring that they have been naturally perpetuated, and thus the culture of White Ling has survived. Until now, its traditions have remained strong in Golog and other regions of Tibet, but modern culture is becoming so prevalent and influential that it remains to be seen if these customs and values will survive much longer. Many in the younger generation have had no opportunity to encounter the legacy of Gesar's wisdom, and lacking any real understanding of it, have no way to see how it could still be relevant in a modern context.

I have had the good fortune first to grow up with these traditions and then to live in America for many years. Based on this experience, to my understanding, Gesar's wisdom is not only relevant but invaluable to the modern way of life. The insight and reminders captured by the epic's proverbs will always be applicable whenever someone is faced with a personal dilemma and they will help to point out the right path when there is confusion. While the Gesar epic is still a living tradition, there remains the opportunity to apply this ancient wisdom and advice concerning basic human goodness to the complexities of modern worldly life. These noble qualities are developed between human beings, through direct and personal heart connections. If each one of us tries earnestly to cultivate these qualities, without pretense or hypocrisy, there is the chance for each of us to become like the heroes and heroines of Gesar's time. As a result, the peace and prosperity that would fill our world could be a rebirth of the glory of the land of White Ling, reawakening the inner wisdom of this millennium and spanning the continents of this world.

SUMMARY OF VOLUME ONE
Chapter One

At the time of King Gesar, Tibet was in chaos. The people's leaders were consumed by infighting, demonic forces grew ever stronger and more pernicious, and the Buddhist doctrine was waning. The bodhisattva of compassion, Ārya Avalokiteśvara, holds all beings with his compassion, and in particular he is the guardian protector of the snow land of Tibet. Therefore in this time of great suffering Avalokiteśvara supplicates Buddha Amitābha in the pure land of Sukhāvatī for his blessings and assistance.

Amitābha responds as follows: "In the higher pure lands is a divine prince named Demchog Karpo Ngangyag. His father is Ödden Kar; his mother is Mandā Lhadzei; his wife is Gyuma Lhadzei. He and his wife will give birth to a son, born from the compassionate light rays emanating from Buddha Akṣobhya's heart. This child will bring joy to all who hear of him, so he will be called Thöpa Gawa, Joyful to Hear. He will even have the capacity to uplift and bring joy to all who lay eyes upon him. If he comes to the southern continent of Jambudvīpa, the realm of the human beings, he will tame even those who are the most difficult to conquer. Take this message to Lotus Skull Garland, Guru Padmasambhava, who is presently residing on Cāmara, the southwest continent, the abode of the cannibals."

Avalokiteśvara manifests as a cannibal cub and travels to the southwest continent. Upon arrival he meets the seven-headed cannibal [*rākṣa*] minister, and has many humorous conversations with him. Finally he asks for an audience with the Guru Lotus Skull Garland, and the minister goes to request permission. When he returns, the cannibal cub is holding a beautiful flower. The minister wonders if indeed this visitor might be either god or demon, but as Lotus Skull Garland had said to grant him entrance, the minister lets the child in. Once the cub is inside the palace, the flower he is holding becomes a white light that dissolves into Lotus Skull Garland's heart. Through his wisdom intent, Avalokiteśvara supplicates and invokes Lotus Skull Garland, who smiles with such radiant joy that the minister is immediately liberated from that realm. Guru Lotus Skull Garland then grants Avalokiteśvara's request, and Avalokiteśvara returns to the Potala pure land.

Then Guru Lotus Skull Garland blesses the prince and princess in the higher pure lands to become the wisdom deities Hayagrīva and Vajravārāhī. In order to do this, first he invokes Samantabhadra, and from Samantabhadra's heart there emanates a five-pointed blue *vajra* marked with a HŪM syllable that dissolves into the crown of Prince Demchog Ngangyag, who feels that he himself becomes Hayagrīva and experiences ineffable bliss. Lotus Skull Garland then invokes the wisdom ḍākinī Dhātviśvarī, and from her heart emanates a sixteen-petaled red lotus marked with the syllable ĀH, which then dissolves into Princess Gyuma Lhadzei's crown. She experiences herself as the blissful Vajrayoginī. The magical child Thöpa Gawa is born to them, reciting the hundred-syllable mantra as he enters this world and taking his seat floating one cubit above an eight-petaled golden lotus, singing a dharma song that teaches the law of cause and result. Lotus Skull Garland knows that through his omniscience the moment for conferring empowerment has arrived, and from his five places emanates light to invoke the five buddha families and request them to grant empowerment to this sacred child.

Chapter Two

The great yogi Mahāsiddha Thangtong Gyalpo, who was not a Lingite,[*] has a dream in which Padmasambhava instructs him to travel to Ling. Waking, he journeys there as instructed. In Ling, the great chief, Rongtsha Tragen, has such a remarkable dream that he decides to proclaim it publicly. Thangtong Gyalpo is present when the dream is recounted, and he explains that the meaning of the dream indicates the impending birth of a great being.

Chapter Three

In the higher pure lands, the divine prince Thöpa Gawa receives Padmasambhava's command to manifest in the human realm in order to benefit beings. In reply, Thöpa

---

[*] A citizen of the land of Ling.

Gawa stipulates certain conditions to Padmasambhava, including the need for the location of his birth to be exact and the requirement that he have the correct companions—including an adversary who will test him at every turn and thereby invoke his surpassing qualities. Padmasambhava grants each request, and Thöpa Gawa then swears to manifest in the human realm and subdue the demons such as those from the borderland country of Hor. The benevolent protectors and spirits of the place all appear and pledge to assist him in accomplishing his deeds.

Chapter Four

Padmasambhava is invited to the nāga realm to cure an epidemic, which in fact he had secretly brought about, and the nāga king Tsugna Rinchen offers him many precious jewels in gratitude. But the great master refuses them, and instead requests to see Tsugna Rinchen's daughters, which causes an uproar among the nāgas. Padmasambhava accepts the king's youngest daughter, Yelga Dzeiden, as the offering for his assistance. At Padmasambhava's instruction, when Tsugna Rinchen asks what she would like to take with her, rather than the usual riches and jewels, she requests the precious scriptures of the nāga realms called *Lubum Poti Chu-drug* (*The One Hundred Thousand Prajñāpāramitā Verses in Sixteen Volumes*). This is an important version of the Prajñāpāramitā that is a principal treasure of the nāga realm. She also requests a dri* with inexhaustible milk, a magical tent made of such fine material that the stars could be seen through it, a bottomless golden urn of food, and a substance that produces an endless thirst-quenching nectar. Her father is reluctant to part with his most precious treasures, but as his daughter was departing for another realm, he sings a song granting her request and also presents her with many special wish-fulfilling nāga jewels. Padmasambhava then delivers her to the human realm and places her under the care of the king of Gog, Ralo Tönpa Gyaltsen.

SUMMARY OF VOLUME TWO
Chapter One

Chapter 1 begins with a brief history of the lineage of the Mukpo clan.

Since Chipön, the chief, is omniscient, he knows that the land of Ling is destined to tame the wild demons that are its enemies. To this end, he sings a long song

---

* A female wild ox; the yak is the male.

supplicating the buddhas and bodhisattvas to send a magical, divine child to accomplish this miraculous activity.

Gyatsha Zhalkar, Senglön's eldest son and one of the mightiest and most respected warriors of Ling, is invited to China by the emperor, his maternal grandfather. While he is gone, there are skirmishes between Ling and Gog. In one of these battles, Lenpa Chögyal, Chipön's middle son and Gyatsha's cousin, is killed in battle. When Gyatsha returns from China, he knows nothing of what has occurred. But upon hearing the news, he swears revenge. Although Chipön tries to dissuade him from renewing the fighting, saying Lenpa Chögyal had already been avenged, Gyatsha is unmoved and again the armies of Ling attack Gog. The troublemaker Trothung betrays Ling by sending a magical arrow with a letter warning the king of Gog that the Ling armies' attack is imminent, giving him enough time to escape. When the Ling army arrives, the king of Gog has already fled, but his adopted daughter, the nāginī Yelga Dzeiden, has not escaped with him. Magically, a very thick fog suddenly arises, and she is enveloped within it. Her special dri, carrying all her treasures from the nāga realm, runs away and the nāginī pursues her, first on horseback and then on foot, until finally she collapses in exhaustion and falls asleep. When she awakens the Ling army is already surrounding her.

Previously, when the Ling army set out, Senglön, Gesar's future father, performed an arrow divination that showed that the army of Ling would reap great treasures as the spoils of the campaign. However, King Trothung thought otherwise, as he had already secretly warned the king of Gog to flee, and so he told King Senglön that whatever treasures came to them that day would be Senglön's alone. That is the day they find Yelga Dzeiden in the forest. Her beauty and qualities are described in detail in the epic. They call her Gogza or Gogmo, "Girl of Gog," because they know her to be a daughter of the king of Gog, Ralo Tönpa Gyaltsen. When the soldiers of Ling interrogate her, asking, "Who are you? Where are the soldiers of Gog?" she tells them her own history but not the location of the army, as she will not betray her adopted clan.

Upon finding her, King Senglön claims her as rightfully his, since all the treasures of the day had been promised to him. Uncle Trothung now objects, wanting the girl for himself and so arguing that a girl is not to be a treasure. Nevertheless, the arbiter of Ling, Werma Lhadar, rules in favor of King Senglön, so Gogza is then destined to become Senglön's second wife. Returning with him to Ling, she rouses the jealousy of Senglön's first wife, Gyaza, and is forced by her to live in a little tent behind the king's main tent. Gyaza's son, Gyatsha Zhalkar, on the other hand, is very civil and courteous to Gogza because she was his first prize of war, and as such very precious to him.

Chapter Two

One day, Gogza aimlessly wanders to the shores of a lake. The reflections in the lake, the waves, and the sound of the water all remind her of the nāga realm and her parents and family. She is filled with longing for her homeland, and her eyes brim up with tears as she sings a song of yearning for her parents and for Padmasambhava. At that moment, her father, the nāga king, appears riding a gray steed. He sings to her an uplifting song of encouragement and advice, and gives her a wish-fulfilling jewel. Her body is filled with joy and her mind becomes so clear that she gains mastery over all appearances. Then she drifts off to sleep on the shore of the lake.

As she dreams, Padmasambhava appears to her, coming from the southwest, riding white clouds. He places a five-pointed golden vajra upon her crown and gives the following prophecy:

"A magical, divine child will be born to you, who will tame all dark forces, demons, and māras. He will be king of Tibet and conquer the four principal and eight lesser neighboring savage lands, becoming their sovereign and guru. When he is born, his first drink will be offered by your father, Tsugna Rinchen; his first garments will be offered by the *nyen* (spirits of the earth). You must be the first person to respond to him. Magyal Pomra (the local mountain spirit, actually a realized bodhisattva) will serve his first meal."

As prophesied, shortly thereafter she becomes pregnant, accompanied by many miraculous signs. She has numerous dialogues with the infant Joru during the pregnancy. At his birth, Padmasambhava sings a beautiful song of prayer for Joru to be guarded by the wermas and other protectors, and to have certain weapons, ministers, and so forth; in short, that he will have all that is necessary to accomplish his enlightened deeds.

Joru's elder brother, Gyatsha Zhalkar, rejoices in the birth of this precious child and consults with Chipön. He has noticed marvelous signs, for example that the infant Joru looks like a child of three months when he is actually only three days old. Gyatsha asks if any special ceremonies should be performed or steps should be taken for the safety and well-being of this remarkable child. Chipön replies that according to the Mother Text of the Mukpo clan, the child will be protected from all harm that might come to him. The chapter concludes with their dialogue.

Chapter Three

Trothung is jealous that his brother Senglön has such an exceptional child, and he tries to kill Joru through poison and black magic. First, Trothung pretends he is a benevolent uncle, fawning over the child, and tells Joru's mother he would like to give the child his first food from human hands. As the meal is heavily laced with poison, Trothung is sure the food will kill the boy immediately, but Joru does not die. Then Trothung negotiates with the black magician Amnye Gompa Raja to kill the child, promising to give him the inner treasures of Ling if he succeeds. The black magician tries to kill the infant, but clairvoyantly Joru already knows the plot. Joru knows that the time is right to tame Gompa Raja, so he asks his mother to bring him four pebbles, and he places the four pebbles around himself in the four directions. With these pebbles as their support, his protectors emanate armies of deities in all directions, guarding Joru from all harm or defeat. These protectors include his three sibling protectors, his older brother Dungkhyung Karpo, his younger brother Ludrül Ödchung [Nāga Serpent Little Light], [Sing] Cham Thalei Ötro [Sister Completely Luminous], and also Nyen Gedzo[*] and the nine supreme dralas.

Gompa Raja arrives and invokes demonic forces in his attempt to kill Joru, but Joru liberates Gompa Raja and the many demons and then emanates as Gompa Raja and pretends to kill the appearance of Joru. Still in the guise of Gompa Raja, he takes Joru's skin to Trothung and demands his payment, the promised inner treasures of Ling. Trothung gives the precious treasures to the Gompa Raja imposter, who is actually Joru. This is how Joru comes to possess the riches. The false Gompa Raja leaves Joru's skin behind as he departs, telling Trothung, "This skin is not dead yet."

After a moment, the skin moves and its eyes are clear and smiling. Trothung becomes frightened and begins to doubt that Joru has actually been killed. He goes to Gompa Raja's cave, which is blocked by a boulder and marked with a boundary sign. Peeking within, he sees the bag of Gompa Raja's pay and his staff leaning against the boulder. Trothung rejoices that Joru seems to really be dead, and Trothung then manifests as a rat to enter the cave. Once inside, he cannot find the bag or staff anywhere. Trothung thinks that perhaps he was unable to see them because he was in the form of a rat, so he transforms his head back into a human head, but his body remains as that of a rat. Looking around, the bag and staff are nowhere to be found, and everything inside there is just black and charred. At that moment, Joru appears and binds him with magic so that Trothung cannot transform back into a human body. Trothung apologizes profusely and makes exaggerated promises, begging to be released from Joru's magical spell.

---

[*] King of the nyen spirits and one of Joru's fathers.

Chapter Four

One night Padmasambhava, with oceans of ḍākinīs, appears in Joru's dream and gives him the following prophecy and advice:

"You must take over the Ma Valley and tame the cannibal demons with your miraculous powers. Make sure you alter the dreams, special indications, and divinations of Ling, which now all reveal you as a divine child, so that you will be forced out of Ling and can depart with your mother for the Ma Valley. The Ma Valley borders the demonic land of Hor and other countries that you must conquer. The deity of Magyal Pomra Mountain in the Ma Valley is the principal protector of Tibet. The Ma Valley itself is the heart of Tibet. Now it is a wilderness, and the wild pikas are the masters of the rivers and meadows there. The wealthy silk road route that passes through this region is constantly robbed by bandits from Hor. The roads there are all narrow and treacherous footpaths. There are no dogs, but the pikas will bite; there are no leopards, but the wolves will kill; you must take possession of that land and break faith with the people of Ling through your wild and unconventional conduct. Make sure the rumor spreads that your mother, Gogza, is a demoness, and that her son, Joru, is a cannibal cub. Continuously break the laws of White Ling, and bring down evil dreams and bad signs on the people. If you do, you will be banished from the land. This humiliation will allow your inner qualities to be revealed. The proverbs say: 'The inner qualities of the tigers in their prime* are revealed by the enemy.'"

Joru follows this prophetic advice and appears to commit many crimes, including murder and cannibalism. Finally, he casts a magical illusion so that the young girl, Drugmo—in fact, his future queen—thinks that she sees Gesar killing some of Uncle Trothung's men. She tells others of what she has seen, and as she is loved and respected by all, of course she is trusted as a witness. Trothung's men are actually just lost in the forest, but before they return, Joru and his mother are banished. This is the means through which Joru is able to leave the land of his birth, just as Padmasambhava has instructed.

Chapter Five

While the decision is being made to banish Joru and his mother, Joru's wild and criminal behavior causes Chipön to ponder carefully. "There is no doubt that Joru is the emanation of a great being, as told in the prophecies of the deities and ḍākinīs, but his recent conduct has violated the laws of White Ling. I do not know what his

---

* Meaning "young warriors."

true intention is, but it is certain that he is intent upon being unlawful. Moreover, since he is a divine child, it is inappropriate that ordinary regulations should apply to him. What am I to do? Previously, all the signs were encouraging, but this year, all dreams and prophecies are dire. I must consult the famous diviner, Moma Künshei Thigpo, whose mirror divinations are acutely accurate."

Then Chipön falls asleep, and before dawn, he dreams of a ḍākinī holding a long-life arrow, saying, "Although Joru's birthplace is excellent, if this divine child who has manifested as a human stays only in his homeland and is not able to take ownership of the Ma Valley, which is the place where he will tame the four māras, he will be of no benefit. He must go to the Ma Valley. To heal the broken laws of White Ling, do not tolerate his wild behavior but banish him! In three years, the Dza and Dri valleys will be covered in white silk [meaning snowdrifts], and the wild ass, starving, will even search the skies for food. During this time the Ma Valley will remain beautiful like a conch stupa, and adorned with great fertile fields like patches of five-colored silk."

The insightful Chipön understands the meaning of these poetic sentences and convenes the council of leaders in order to give the command to banish Joru to the Turquoise Valley of Lower Ma [Mamed Yulung Sumdo]. Even Joru's mother is now giving rise to doubt concerning Joru's behavior, since the illusion of his cannibalism and other atrocities are so convincing. Although the council agrees to the punishment, none wants to bear the news to Joru. In fact, Joru already knows of the decision, and Magyal Pomra, the protector, has already moved all of Joru's belongings to the Ma Valley, but outward appearances remain unchanged. In the council, Gyatsha offers to deliver the news himself, but then the minister Denma volunteers to go. When Denma arrives at Joru's camp, Joru has pitched a tent of human skin with tent ropes made of human intestines, surrounded by a fence of both human and horse corpses, some fresh and some decomposing. The scene is so atrocious that even the habits of the cannibals of Langkapuri were as nothing! Denma thinks, "It is tragic that the lineage of Chöphen Nagpo has come to this."

Then Denma begins to doubt. "People say he is a murderer, but no one has witnessed his killing. Although there are many corpses lying around here, there are no accounts of those who have been killed or gone missing. Perhaps this is just a magical illusion." Thinking in this way, suddenly his mind is filled with unshakable faith for Joru because of previous karmic connections. Thinking that he will wave to Joru using his sword, Denma stops himself because that would be disrespectful, as a sword is what is used to summon enemies. Likewise, a whip is used for horses, so that is also inappropriate. Finally he uses the flag from his helmet to gesture to Joru. The boy strolls over to him, while gnawing on a human arm.

1

Joru greets Denma warmly, and at that moment the corpses of humans and horses vanish like a mirage. In that instant all impure perceptions disappear, leaving only pure wisdom phenomena. Denma respectfully removes his weapons and armor and leaves them on the doorstep, but Joru gently chides him, saying, "Do not leave those there—they are the castle for the drala," and he carries them inside with his own hands. During their visit, Joru and Denma exchange songs and conversation, rekindling their strong and affectionate connection as inseparable friends. In conclusion, Joru tells Denma, "Now go back to Ling and I will follow after you. Tell them that although you were afraid to approach me, you delivered your message from a distance and I agreed to come to the council. For a time do not tell anyone what we have spoken of."

When Joru is banished and prepares to leave Ling, everyone forgets his crimes and their eyes fill with tears of sadness. Before his departure Joru tells Gyatsha Zhalkar, his older brother, "Don't worry. Everything is happening exactly as foreseen in the wisdom prophecies. Magyal Pomra has already made preparations to receive me, so I need neither companions nor provisions to accompany me." Joru and his mother leave Ling and travel to the Ma Valley, where they settle and live on wild yams and pikas that he kills with his slingshot. Joru lives like a hunter and a thief, capturing many merchants who travel between China, India, Hor, Ladakh, and other lands, and he forces them to build castles in the Ma Valley.

Chapter Six

One winter, the country of Ling is so severely buried under snow that everyone fears for their lives. In the Ma Valley, however, it is as warm as spring. It is decided that Gyatsha Zhalkar and five warriors will journey to Ma and request that Joru allow the Lingites to settle in Ma until the severe weather has passed. As they approach him, Joru sees them from a distance, and in order to humble them he pretends not to recognize them, but he shoots a stone from his slingshot that shatters a great boulder nearby. Its mighty sound frightens the warriors, and several of them faint. When Gyatsha identifies himself, Joru's attitude completely changes, and he then greets them hospitably. A lengthy exchange between Gyatsha and Joru follows, and they agree that the people of Ling should make the Ma Valley their home. Gyatsha takes the news back to Ling, and the people gather their belongings in preparation for the long journey. When they arrive in Ma, Joru sings a lengthy song, telling them of the qualities of the divine Ma Valley, and giving a section to each of the Thirty Warriors of Ling. In the song, he introduces himself as King Joru and describes himself thus: "Outwardly I am a lonely, wandering beggar boy. Inwardly, I am the castle for the dralas. Secretly, I am the embodiment of all victorious ones."

The people of Ling all praise him and tell one another, "What do you expect from a descendent of the great Mukpo lineage?" Gesar's uncle Trothung, however, is not so happy because Joru gives him the worst piece of property. Nevertheless, Trothung's son receives a fine estate, so Trothung's spirits are not entirely downcast.

The local spirits of the Ma Valley protect the people of Ling and nurture them so that the poor become rich and the lowly become mighty. At one point, Joru gathers the people together and reveals *terma*, spiritual treasures, from the lower Magyal Pomra Mountain. These include a golden Śākyamuni statue, an Avalokiteśvara statue made of conch, and a turquoise Tārā statue. He also reveals a conch horn, a drum, cymbals, and a flag, all for military—not ritual—use; and additionally, he reveals a key and map for accessing other treasures. All who witness this are moved by this miraculous display, and many favorable signs appear such as a rain of flowers falling from the sky, a tent of rainbows filling the air, and sweet smells rising up from the earth. After this auspicious event, the flourishing of Ling redoubles. Each warrior builds a castle on his territory, and the people enjoy prosperity and well-being.

Summary of Volume Three
Chapter One

Joru is so unique for two reasons. From the dharma perspective he is a manifestation of the buddhas and bodhisattvas; from a worldly perspective, he is the son of the gods, the earth spirits, and the subterranean beings, all three. From both perspectives, Joru's special manifestation makes him a kind of superhuman being. His enlightened activities, as well as his worldly display of magic, contribute to his unique gift to transform circumstances and benefit others.

As for Joru being the son of the gods, nyen, and nāgas, it can be explained that before he manifests in this realm, he is born in the upper pure lands as the son of the king of gods, and from there he intentionally takes rebirth in the human realm, so he remains a son of the gods, or a godling. He is a son of the nāgas, because his mother was a nāginī princess, and he is a son of the earth-spirit nyen, because his mother has a vision of the king of the nyen when he is conceived.

Joru is a son of the gods, nyen, and nāgas because throughout his life he is protected by all three kinds of spirits. At his birth, his three main protectors—a god, nyen, and nāga—enter this world at the same time that he does. These spirits are sometimes formless, but occasionally, when circumstances demand, they take on form. They are his constant companions and guardians who watch over him and the success of his enlightened activity.

During his first five years in this realm, Joru tames all the formless negative spirits in the Dri and Da valleys. Starting when he is six years old, through mischievous, wild, and reckless conduct he breaks faith with White Ling as instructed by Padmasambhava. When he is eight, he takes possession of the Ma Valley. While living there, the protector called Nenei (Auntie) Nammen Karmo, also known by many other names, appears to Joru riding a white snow lion and gives the following prophecy: "If you cannot take possession of the land of Ling this year, although you will still emanate many magical manifestations, the people will come to disparage you more and more. In the end the only sign of your accomplishment will be the suppression of your uncle. Today your steed runs with the wild horses of the north, the same age as yourself. If you fail to master him this year, his body will dissolve into a rainbow and then vanish. Your consort, Kyalo Sengcham Drugmo, was sent from the higher pure lands, and if she does not become yours this very year, she will marry the son of Tag-rong.* If you lose Drugmo, then you will miss the gateway of enlightened activity. Therefore make sure that tomorrow at dawn Trothung receives this false prophecy, ostensibly from the deity Hayagrīva: 'You must sponsor a gathering of the people of Ling and propose a horse race. The winner will win the status of king and the wealth of Ling's treasures, including Drugmo. The Turquoise Bird† will reach the finish line first, and Drugmo will be yours.'" She cautions him, "Joru, your steed must be captured by the lasso of great emptiness."‡

Then Joru thinks, "Until now, except for when I revealed myself to my mother at birth, no one has seen my true appearance. I have shown nothing but ragged clothes and an ugly body to all, like a lotus hidden in the mud. If this is all they ever see it will bring no benefit. The time has come to reveal my true form. In order for my steed to help me win the throne for a while longer I will continue to show them many kinds of unusual, wild behavior."

Then while Trothung is in strict retreat, practicing the deity Hayagrīva, Joru manifests to him as a raven, which Trothung takes to be an emanation of Hayagrīva, and the raven gives the prophecy instructed by Nammen Karmo. At first Trothung

---

* Referring to Trothung's son, Dongtsen.

† Trothung's son, Dongtsen's, horse.

‡ This last phrase is cryptic, but "great emptiness" often refers to the feminine—it means Joru's horse can only be captured by Drugmo.

doubts the prophecy, because Hayagrīva's prophecies had proved inaccurate in the past. However, the raven then vanishes by dissolving into Trothung's main statue of Hayagrīva on his shrine, at which point his doubts are dispelled, and he fully believes in the prophecy from that point onward.

Trothung sings a song to his wife, Denza, describing the raven's words. Denza tries to explain to Trothung that this seems like a trick of Joru's, not a genuine prophecy, but Trothung, spurred on by the dralas and wermas, refuses to listen as he is tortured by his lust for Drugmo.

Disregarding his wife's advice, he sends out messengers to gather all of Ling. Denza is disappointed, but she considers that her difficulties with her husband are the result of her own previously created karma. She quotes a famous proverb: "The karma of previous lives cannot be deflected; just as the lines and wrinkles on one's brow cannot be wiped away." As a result she helps her husband prepare for the horse race.

At the celebration, there is an exchange among the warriors, during which the principal warriors each sing a song offering their opinions. Led by Chipön, they all agree to hold the horse race, with the winner taking the wealth and throne of Ling, with Drugmo as his queen. They decide the time, location, distance, and other rules of the race.

Chapter Two

Gyatsha insists that Joru must be included in the horse race or he himself will not participate. All of the warriors agree that Joru should be invited. Then Chipön says that while anyone could carry the message to Joru where he stayed in the Lower Ma Valley, the protectors had specified that it must be Drugmo who extends the invitation. He instructs Gyatsha to pretend to be very upset with Drugmo. "Tell her that as she was the witness responsible for getting Joru banished, now, since the time has come for him to return to Ling, she must be the one to invite him back."

Drugmo goes to invite Joru, but there are many trials and obstacles on her path as Joru creates magical illusions to test her. Through these interchanges, Drugmo and Joru become further acquainted and establish an even stronger connection.

Chapter Three

Joru asks Drugmo to go into the mountains and capture the wild horse that is to be his steed. Drugmo sings a song, saying, "Unless Joru is a magician, I have no way of knowing how to find a lone horse in these mountains. Tell me where the horse is and what it looks like." Joru replies with a beautiful song describing the outer and inner qualities of his horse. Drugmo and Gogza, Joru's mother, go to capture the steed and, succeeding, they bring it back to Joru, singing songs of its divine qualities.

Chapter Four

Drugmo invites Joru back to Ling. On the road, Joru again displays many magical illusions, which serve to awaken Drugmo's good karma and merit and sever any doubt, misunderstanding, or incorrect views she may have. Consequently she gains unshakable confidence that Joru will become the ruler of Ling and hold the wealth of the Kyalo clan, including Drugmo herself. She offers him a golden saddle, bridle, and other precious treasures, and leads him from the Lower Ma Valley back to his tribe in Upper Ma. When Trothung sees Joru's horse, right away he wants the horse for himself, and he asks Joru to sell it to him. They have a humorous exchange in which Joru leads him on, asking for food, silk scarves, and other goods in order to make the sale possible. Trothung politely promises to give Joru all that he asks for.

Chapter Five

The warriors of Ling begin the great horse race, and Joru creeps surreptitiously around the fringes. Drugmo's cousin, Ne'uchung, has received a prophetic dream sent by the protectress Nammen Karmo, and she wants to announce that Joru will win the race. Drugmo feels that this dream must be accurate—because the signs she had when capturing Joru's horse and so forth all indicated Joru's victory as well. However, Trothung's daughter is upset by this exchange, as Trothung is certain that his own son will be the winner.

The chapter concludes with Drugmo singing an introduction to each warrior and their horse for the spectators.

Chapter Six

The verse at the opening of the chapter explains that during the horse race, Joru tames demons and destroys Trothung's lies. He tests the diviner, the physician, and so forth.

First Joru rides with the lowest beggar in the land, a hunchback named Gu-ru.*

---

* *Gu-ru* in this case is not the term of respect for a spiritual teacher, *guru*, but a Tibetan word that means "hunched one."

Joru tells him, "We are both beggars, so we should share whatever we receive. If I win the prize, I will share with you; if you win, you can share with me. What do you think?" Gu-ru, although poor, is proud, and he arrogantly replies, "I might not be rich if compared to rich men, but compared to the beggar Joru, I am a wealthy man." Then he flatters himself, boasting of his qualities and possessions, and concludes by saying, "I am not going to share anything with you."

Then Joru tests a doctor, pretending to be sick from exhaustion and malnutrition. The doctor examines him by reading his pulses through the lead-rope of Joru's horse. He concludes that Joru is completely free of any illness: "There is no trace of sickness in your body, within or without."

Next Joru tests a diviner, asking for a prediction of the outcome of the race. Joru says that he will not bother to run any farther if there is no hope of him winning. The diviner, however, sees some of Joru's true qualities. He uses a piece of string and ties it in knots relating to the sky, the earth, and the water, and concludes, "Your power is enough to cover the earth, just like the blue firmament. If you take your seat, you will be able to hold it. The foundation you establish will be as strong as the changeless earth itself. If you take the throne, you will be a valuable leader, and bring benefit to all beings. The rivers and streams naturally gather in the great ocean. Although the water disappears to far shores, it will naturally return.* There is no divination better than this. You must run the race!" Joru also teases his brother Gyatsha, by manifesting a magical appearance to provoke him and then reappearing in his ordinary form to taunt him.

Chapter Seven

For the remainder of the horse race, Joru tests and teases the other warriors. Then at one point the protectress Nenei Nammen Karmo, along with the rest of Gesar's principal guardians, appears to him and urges him on, saying, "Do not dawdle any longer, but run as fast as you can!" He has already passed Trothung's son, Dongtsen Nang-ngu Apel. Dongtsen Nang-ngu Apel's horse is captured by Gesar's dralas, who throw it down, but Dongtsen Nang-ngu Apel runs ahead on foot to try to claim the throne. The dralas stretch the distance to the throne so that Dongtsen Nang-ngu Apel is unable to reach it. Joru, racing at top speed, manifests many likenesses of himself—some already on the throne, some trying to kill Dongtsen Nang-ngu

---

* This refers to Joru gaining the prize, including Drugmo, but in the future losing her temporarily when he is trapped in the northern land of demons, and then reuniting with her once again.

Apel's horse, some elsewhere. Thus Joru wins the horse race and is enthroned on the golden throne of Ling. Once that occurs, the appearance of the wild boy Joru drops away, and his destined magnificence as King Gesar becomes evident for the first time in its exquisite splendor. He is given the name Gesar Norbu Dradül, and that is when the final conditions for the manifestation of his principal enlightened activities are complete. Music is heard, resounding throughout the land, although no human has touched a drum or horn. All the gods and humans gathered offer prayers in honor of the auspicious occasion.

LAMA CHÖNAM
with SANGYE KHANDRO and
SHASHIKALA REITZ
TASHI CHÖLING
Ashland, Oregon
Fall 2010

ACKNOWLEDGMENTS

IF THE ILLUSTRIOUS ROBIN KORNMAN (1947–2007) had not possessed the determination, genuine heart, and passion for anything concerning Gesar of Ling, this colossal endeavor would have never seen the light of day. We are grateful that our paths crossed serendipitously nearly two decades ago.

The threads that have intertwined in these modern times to bring Tibetan culture and spirituality to the West are many, and the torch of the maverick energy and piercing insight into Western mind of the Vidyādhara Chögyam Trungpa Rinpoche was singular. Rinpoche was Robin's root guru (spiritual guide) and his devotion for this great master was intense and constant. Not a day in our work would go by that Robin did not acknowledge his guru in one way or another. Hence we acknowledge the Vidyādhara Chögyam Trungpa Rinpoche as the guiding force behind this effort and the source from which this translation actually took birth. In addition, in the earlier years of his exhaustive research Robin had great admiration for and was inspired by the work and research compiled by Professor Rolf Stein, who, in 1956, published a partial translation into French of the first three volumes of the epic from the version known as the Lingtsang of Dege woodblock and subsequently wrote a treatise in French on the Gesar epic, titled *Recherches sur l'épopée et le barde au Tibet*.

Robin went on to write his own doctoral dissertation and rough-draft translation of the first volume based on Stein's work, supported by his professors and colleagues at Princeton University; also important was his time at the Sorbonne, where he worked with Samten Karmay, Tendzin Samphel, and many others.

His great friendship with Larry Mermelstein and other colleagues of the Nālandā Translation Committee was not only helpful but a precious treasure for Robin. We are grateful to the Buddhist and Shambhala communities of Milwaukee, Wisconsin, where many friends devoted their time to supporting Robin as well as Lama Chönam and Sangye Khandro during the early years of this work. Geoff Picus, Kathy Carter, Janis Bauer, and Ruth Lohlein were tireless helpers and companions. Some of these same people, and many others supported Robin through the difficult years of his illness that ensued. The companionship he had with his trusted friend Michael Sullivan and his friendships with Newcomb Greenleaf, Bill Hebbert, Paul Bankston, and Steven Shippee were particularly close.

David Shapiro, through his own scholarship as well as his connection with Robin, was able to construct the introduction presented here on behalf of Robin, extracted from the seeds of what Robin had written. In addition, David spent countless hours listening to the rough-draft translation, along with his daughter Hazel Shapiro, who offered useful suggestions. Lily Shapiro transcribed Robin's talks, which became the basis for David's introduction, and both daughters assisted with the technical logistics of collaborating from afar.

Without hesitation, Cam Kornman, Robin's sister, graciously facilitated the unobstructed completion of this project. The depth of their mutual love was evident in their support of each other.

We are indebted to Bill Karelis, who, after Robin's death, was the catalyst for ensuring that Lama Chönam, Sangye Khandro, and Jane Hawes were able to collaborate to finish this translation and bring this project to fruition.

Julie Brefczynski-Lewis and Elise Collet worked devotedly with Robin on the preliminary edit of our translation up until the time of his passing, and they also helped to reread the current version. Beyond that, the loving friendship that they maintained throughout their time with Robin was deep and genuine.

Alak Zenkar Rinpoche has graciously offered one of the prefaces to this manuscript as well as his wisdom and expertise in the field.

We are humbled and honored that His Holiness the Fourteenth Dalai Lama, Alak Zenkar Rinpoche, and Sakyong Mipham Rinpoche have added their important perspective and blessing to this publication. We are also fortunate to have the professional expertise and impeccable style of Shambhala Publications moving this along to completion. In particular, Emily Bower worked with tireless attention, her constantly fresh eye refining both the detail and the narrative whole. We appreciate the help of Dr. Peter Alan Roberts, who reviewed the Sanskrit terms. The work on this project has spanned decades, and during this process there have been countless individuals who have participated and contributed to this noble effort. We apologize for not being able to personally acknowledge everyone, but since you know who you are we wish to extend our deep gratitude to each and every one of you. Your efforts have not been forgotten in the pages of this book, and it is our sincere prayer that readers will derive knowledge, inspiration, and pleasure as they read about the life of this Great Being. We apologize for errors of content or any inabilities to portray the meaning accurately. It is our sincere aspiration that this epic may endure in the languages of this world and that we may continue to translate the important stories of Gesar's life for the future posterity of this ancient wisdom heritage and legacy. May all of our combined efforts bring great waves of benefit and well-being to all realms of the world.

In conclusion our gratitude goes to the patrons of the dharma and translation work who have allowed us the dignity and freedom to work on this translation for many years, devoting all of our time and energy to the offering and craft of translation. May the merit accumulated by everyone involved in this noble project be dedicated to the welfare and benefit of the Buddha's doctrine in this world, the long life of the lineage masters, and the happiness and liberation of all living beings. May the legacy of King Gesar of Ling continue to inspire the inhabitants of this world so that beings may awaken from their slumber of ignorance to increase and nourish their mind's true nature in the context of an enlightened society.

LAMA CHÖNAM, SANGYE KHANDRO, and JANE HAWES
Light of Berotsana Translation Group
Tashi Chöling
Ashland, Oregon
Fall 2010

VOLUME ONE

*The Events Leading
to Gesar's Incarnation
in the Land of Ling*[1]

Introductory verse by the Tibetan editor.[2]

OM SVASTI
From *dharmatā*,[3] your unceasing compassion gave rise to
The impartial awakened mind[4] which benefits beings.
Never abandoning that, you took the *vajra*-like oath,
The self-radiant one hundred points[5] of the fourfold
    manifestation of buddha activity.[6]

Once, when perverted ambitions piled high into a mountain
    of evil merit
And pride rose up to a rocky peak of haughty arrogance,
To show the teaching of cause and effect[7] you crushed it with
    this vajra.
Greatest of heroes, supreme being, jewel tamer of enemies,
    may you be victorious.

CHAPTER ONE

A white moon of compassion from the Noble Supreme One*
Dissolves into the heart center of Nangsid Zilnön [Who
    Quells Existence with Splendor].†
The five families of the victorious Buddhas‡
Grant empowerment to Thöpa Gawa [Joyful to Hear].§ 8

IN THIS TIME OF the five degeneracies of the dark age,9 it is difficult to liberate savage sentient beings from evil karma through the *sūtrayāna*, the causal vehicle of characteristics, alone. It is even difficult to ripen them through tantra, the fruition vehicle of the secret mantra.10

> *For their minds are dry as a piece of rock;*
> *If you do not carve its hard surface with a chisel,*
> *Even if you soak it in a stream, it will not give way.*
> *Even if you work it with butter and oil, it will not become flexible.*
> *They are too stiff to be bent by the teachings on this life and the next.*
> *They will not submit to the restraint of the monastic law.*

---

* Avalokiteśvara.

† One of the epithets of Guru Rinpoche, Padmasambhava.

‡ The five buddha families.

§ One of the epithets of Gesar.

Formerly, during the lives of the three ancestral dharma kings, when the land of Tibet passed from Bön to Buddhism, in order to naturally pacify[11] the envy of the vicious gods and demons of Tibet, Padma Tötreng [Lotus Skull Garland] the Mantra Holder bound them by oath. If he had managed to make them swear their oaths of fealty to the buddhadharma three times, then the dharma kings would have been long-lived and their subjects would have enjoyed bliss and happiness. However, powerful demon ministers took control over the subjects and, faced with this opposition, Padma was able to tame and bind the spirits of Tibet only twice, not thrice. This caused war in the four directions and the auspicious coincidence of the glorious gateway, the perfect astrological conjunction,[12] was missed. The foreign borderland demons wandered into central Tibet and the dharma kings fell down to the level of commoners.

The whole world in general and in particular the land of Tibet, indeed all lands, changed and became oppressed by suffering. The compassionate mind of the Noble Excellent Great Compassionate One could not bear this, and so he supplicated Amitābha, Lord of Sukhāvatī.[13]

[Avalokiteśvara supplicates Amitābha to intercede in Tibet.][14]

OṂ MAṆI PADME HŪṂ HRĪḤ
I bow to the refuge, chief of the vast pure realm,
Amitābha,[15] Lord of Sukhāvatī, in the west.
Although compassion is truly unbiased,
Look down on this impure place of *saṃsāra*.

In the ocean of saṃsāra's suffering,
You know how to kill the sea monster of sin.
How terrifying are the waves of the five poisons!
Minds blinded by obscurations
Circle endlessly in saṃsāra, how pitiful!
Please compassionately reveal supreme skillful means.[16]

With these words he reverently supplicated. The blessed one Amitābha answered with these words:

Good, good, O son of noble family;
For sentient beings confused by ignorance,
If they are not fortunate disciples, it is difficult to guide them.

Thus, if beings in the age of the five degeneracies
Have no iron ring of faith,[17]
Even the teacher who guides beings out of the three worlds
Has no way of catching them with the iron hook of
    compassion.

But in the divine buddha field of the thirty-three[18]
The father, the great god, Ödden Kar [White Luminosity]
And the supreme mother Mandā Lhadzei [Celestial Flower
    Divine Beauty]
Have a son, Demchog Karpo Ngangyag [White Supreme
    Bliss Good Nature].
He and Gyuma Lhadzei [Illusory Divine Beauty]
Will unite as *E* and *vam*[19] and give miraculous birth
Through their light rays of unfabricated compassion[20]
To the child Döndrub [Accomplisher of Benefit], an
    emanation of their blessings.[21]
He is Joyful to Hear and delightful to see.
If he were to transfer into a human body in Jambudvīpa,
That heroic bodhisattva would tame untamable disciples.
Sentient beings in the land of Tibet would experience bliss
    and happiness.
There is no doubt they would be liberated from birth in the
    lower realms.
Therefore, you must go to the continent of Cāmara.
Supplicate and repeat these words to Padma Tötreng.
Strive for the benefit of beings, supreme warrior of the mind.
Remember this, *E ma ho!* *

He graced and honored Avalokiteśvara with these words of prophecy and confirmation.

[Avalokiteśvara visits Padmasambhava to request that he cause the emanation of Gesar.]

---

* *E ma ho!* is a Tibetan exclamation of wonder and jubilation.

Then, in a single instant, Avalokiteśvara, the greatly compassionate Lord of Skillful Means, went to Padma Ödkyi Zhalyei Dechen Lhundrub kyi Potrang [Celestial Palace of Lotus Light—Spontaneously Present Exaltation] on the subcontinent of Cāmara. There he found a magnificently terrifying city of *rākṣasas*, a place so terrifying that it frightens even the death gods and makes the Lord of Life himself, Brahmā, withdraw. A land so terrifying that even the *vināyakas* shun it, not to mention ordinary men, who cannot even bear the sight of it.

In this place, in order to effect measureless benefit for beings, Avalokiteśvara manifested as a demon cub, wearing a crown made from mother of pearl, enveloped in a halo of glimmering white light. Arriving at the eastern gate of Jampei Künkyab Lingchen [Great Garden of All-Pervading Mercy],[22] there a demon minister rākṣasa with seven heads saw the child and said:

> What a wonder! What a sight I am seeing this morning!
> I would say you are a god, but you look like a demon rākṣasa cub.
> I would say you are a demon, but for your aura of light.
> Within the walls of Padma Barwei Rawa [Garden of
>   Blazing Lotuses],
> We sentient beings, confused by ignorance,
> Have never seen and would be lucky even to hear of
> The coming of such an unfamiliar child.
> What is the great aim, the great matter that caused you to
>   journey here alone like this?

Then he sang this song of interrogation:

> Lu Ala,[23] the song begins.
> Thala is the melody of the song.
> These are the demon lands of Cāmara,
> The country of the impure rākṣasas and demons
> And the pure land of the vidyādharas and ḍākinīs.
>
> This morning, young child, you suddenly arrived here.
> Where do you come from, what kind of place?
> What aim could you have that is of such great import?
>
> *If you do not have in mind great matters,*
> *Then there is no great reason* [don] *for coming so far.*

If you haven't been possessed by an evil spirit [gdon],
Why would you drown yourself in a river?
Only a very serious court case
Could put a wealthy man in jail.[24]

In Cāmara's Blood Lake of Sin[25]
The bite of the jaws of the cannibal demons is hotter than fire.
The reach of the arms of the cannibal demonesses is longer
    than a river.
The *tramens* on the hunt race around faster than the wind.

What's your reason for coming here?
Who are your father and mother, their race and religion?
Don't you keep any secrets, tell me straight out.

Honest speech brings success to the monastery.
Straight arrows strike the target yonder.
If your path is straight, the road between central Tibet and China is
    not long.[26]
One sign is enough for a superior man to understand.
If not, it is like whipping an old ox.

If that's what you need, then look to your precious life.
If you understand, I have explained my words.
If not, I'm not going to sing them again.

Thus he sang and the boy cub answered, "Oh yes, sir, I understand.[27]

If the secret pith of the proverb does not emerge,
Even though the meaning is profound the secret words will be mute.
If you can't have the results in your hands,
All those words are just bubbles of spit.
If earth and water do not burgeon in early spring
Then the southern turquoise dragon is just a silent venomous snake.[28]
In the sky Mount Meru is circled by the sun and the moon.
If they do not benefit the plains of the four continents
Then Meru is neither of benefit nor harm.
The sun and the moon would just spin like the heads of brainless dupes

And the people of the four continents would have no appreciation for
    the virtues of the sun and the moon.[29]

My cause, on the other hand, is great.[30]

The continents of black earth come to an edge[31]
But no one can find the measure of the white clouds above.
If my cause is great, I'll go to China and back in one day[32]
And I'll repeat my words again and again.

Of course, I have many stories I could tell, but only to the leader, majestic Padma Tötreng. Take me up the staircase to the imperial assembly hall of the Great Minister. There is no reason to casually explain this great cause to a public gathering. Just as the proverb says:

If you throw the six grains in a meadow, there will be no sprouts.
If you plant seeds in a plowed field, then you get results.

So the tale I must tell is like this," and he sang this song:

OM MAŅI PADME HŪM HRĪḤ
I supplicate the transcendent dharma.[33]
May I hold to the natural state of ultimate emptiness.

In case you do not recognize the likes of me,
I am the beloved child Künphen Nyinje [All-Benefiting
    Compassion].
My father is Jangsem Künkyab Gön [Compassionate
    Sovereign Lord].
My mother is Tongnyid Chödrön [Emptiness Dharma Torch].
This morning I came from the Plain of Great Bliss.
The goal I seek is the benefit of self and other;[34]
My destination is the isle of Cāmara;
My request is to master Skull Garland.
Thus, as the ancient proverb says:

Though merchandise from China is essential to central Tibet,
It is not that the farmers of central Tibet are lacking in wealth,

It is that this sustains the mental link between China and Tibet.
Though empowerments and teachings are essential between master
  and disciple,
Passing them down does not mean the teachings are not precious,
It is that this sustains the samaya link between aspiration and path.
Though the great minister is essential to the district and its chief,
It is not that without the minister the system is unable to function,
It is that this is the way the status of both the government and
  monasteries is displayed.

> The real meaning of my words I offer to you.
> Please intercede on behalf of my humble self.
> When you make your request to the leader, bare your heart.
> The extent of his compassion will depend on karma.

> My import is not small; it is of great importance.
> Of great import is the general welfare of beings.
> If it were unimportant, why would I have come?

Futile wandering in borderlands,
Buying famine itself,
Those who suffer not, yet throw themselves into deep gorges,
Have let their life force be carried away by demons.
The wealthy who carry their goods on their heads[35]
Are just asking for their wealth to be squandered.
The mighty who oppress the many
Will cast themselves down in self-humiliation.
The humble who presume to utter proud words
Will just close themselves off from receiving any benefit.[36]

Things such as these are indeed pointless.

> But into the hall of Lord Rākṣa Skull Garland
> I had no choice but to enter.
> May you deeply consider and seize me with your compassion.
> I offer this narrative story;
> Please let my words enter your mind and heart.

Thus he requested and the demon minister replied, "Hey, you![37] Since ancient times our demon king Rākṣa Skull Garland's royal lineage has had terribly strict rulers. Their law strikes hot as lightning bolts. Their sovereignty covers the country, vaster than the blue sky. Their clout is mightier than Rāhu.[38] What can a little gypsy kid the likes of you hope for? Even when we who are the interior ministers stand before such kings, we are just waiting to be punished even if we have done nothing wrong. They are ready to jump on us for no reason or arrest us for no real cause. They are ready to gobble up the flesh of a living man and gulp down the blood of a live horse. In this lineage there have been such men. This king's guts seem to have broadened and his mind, which is empty in nature yet full of mercy, unites all three temperaments: peaceful, wrathful, and relaxed.[39] In recent generations they have all been the same that way:

> *Like sleeves cut from the same pattern or beads chosen from the same*
> > *rosary.*
> *In the strictness of our monastic law and the law of the land*
> *'Roots and sticks are not to be mixed!'*[40]

I am ready to ask whether you will be well received. Otherwise we both will be like an old ox leaping into the river when it is thirsty, or an old cow heading for grass, or an old donkey driven by rain. No one has ever dared to informally barge in on him.

Generally when you visit a temple, you offer the guru there a white scarf. If you are able to greet him, what do you have as a presentation offering?"

Avalokiteśvara answered: "I have the thirty varieties of formal presentation offerings. If you want to count them, they are: as dharma the six-syllable MAṆI mantra, as path the six perfections along with the six objects of outer appearance, the six consciousnesses of inner knowing, and the six gates of the sense faculties that lie in between. Are these suitable presentation offerings?"[41]

When he had said this, the minister answered, "I can't really say if that will be acceptable.

> *The more the poor man values food,*
> *The more the rich man tightens his stomach for him.*
> *The more the rich man values a horse,*
> *The more stubborn-headed the merchant is on his selling price.*
> *The way it is, the dzomo of a poor person is like a horse,*
> *But for a great band of robbers it is nothing but a quick snack on the*
> > *road.*[42]

> *The jackal that usually eats horses*
> *Sometimes wonders 'perhaps this sheep would do?'*

Who knows what will be satisfactory as a presentation offering? At the same time I cannot say that these presentation offerings would not do.

> *The sacred symbol, the souvenir of a pilgrimage to Tsari Mountain,*
> *Is really nothing but a nine-node bamboo stick.*[43]
> *To import chao hsi tea,** *you must transport across hill and dale,*
> *But anybody with money can have a pinch of it if they want.*
> *Indeed the worth could then exceed a nugget of silver the size of a*
> *   horse's hoof.*

Are these things you bring of great value or tiny and insignificant?" The boy responded, "Indeed, they are not great, for this is just the precious jewel of being free and well-favored,[44] the two spans and four cubits of the human body. On the other hand, they are not meager, because if you possess the power of analysis, you can see that they are the inexhaustible provisions for this life and the next, the karmic wealth that fulfills all wishes in saṃsāra, the wish-fulfilling gem, so difficult to acquire."

[The demon minister continues] "But if you do not possess an analytical mind,[45] then these things are the anchor of the three poisons in the ocean of saṃsāra, the stick that drives us with happiness and sadness,[46] a sack full of filth. Well now, whoever you are, I will request that you be received into his presence. Wait here for a moment," he said, and he entered the palace.

[Padmasambhava and Avalokiteśvara finally meet, but in a mystical way.]

There on top of a wrathful seat of corpses,[47] on a dazzlingly beautiful throne of gold, sat Lotus Rākṣa Skull Garland [Padmasambhava] himself, his mind resting in meditation on the great nature of phenomena. Even though he already understood that Avalokiteśvara was waiting outside, Padmasambhava feigned ignorance and said to the great rākṣa minister with seven heads:

"Hey, you! This morning, who was that singing pointless songs, chanting

---

* Jasmine tea.

unceasing melodies, and repeating imbecilic words? What great purpose does he aim to attain? Who does he trust? To whom does he bow down?"

The minister thought to himself, "Even though he's sitting on his lordly throne, his bright eyes see the bridge outside."

> *It seems that the sun is traversing the sky,*
> *But its light pervades Jambudvīpa.*
> *It seems that the southern clouds* [48] *are piled in the sky,*
> *But they rain across the dense earth.*

He thought that Padmasambhava in his chamber had probably seen everything that had just happened outside and said to him, "Oh Precious Crest Jewel, in the varicolored hundred thousand demon villages of great bliss, at the eastern gate of the iron wall[49] named Jampei Künkyab Lingchen, a little boy who is not a human and not a demon, who is not a god, but has an aura of white light, has dropped in. He says that he has a matter of pith and importance to impart. Listen carefully and focus the silk scarf of your hearing. Please, Lord, direct your mind." With these words he prostrated three times and then sang this informative song:

> Lu Ala, sing the song this way.
> Above in the Ruby Palace,
> Amitābha of Uḍḍiyāna, know me!*
> May I and all sentient beings filling space
> Attain the state of a deathless awareness holder.
>
> Seated on top of a jeweled throne with a peaceful and
>   wrathful corpse[50]
> On a blazing lotus,
> Leader in this life, dear lord and chief, listen.
> Guide in the next life, O guru, listen,
> Buddha who benefits us in both this and future lives.
> This morning when the golden rays of the royal parasol[51]
> Struck the peak of [Zangdog] Pelri [Glorious Copper-
>   Colored Mountain],

---

* "Know me!" (Tib. *mkhyen*) is a salutation used when a disciple is invoking a deity, asking for its attention and blessing.

At the eastern gate of Jampei Künkyab Lingchen,
In the middle of the Plain of Great Bliss,
Appeared a beautiful little boy radiating light,
Embellished with garlands of light rays and rainbows.
He said his name is Künphen Nyinje.
He said his great purpose is the limitless benefit of beings
And that he must be presented directly to you, the leader of
    Cāmara.
He said there is no time to spare.

This great utterance of the field of generosity,
If not a skillful way of offering,
Is a sign that the guru is a learned master.
That purification of the cause of a succession of crimes,
If not extortion exacted by a minister,
Is the yoke oppressing the mighty chieftain.
The heat-covering storm clouds in the sky,
If not the devouring mouths of the eight classes,
Are the timely rain that helps to ripen the six grains.
The prayers of a humble beggar,
If not hunger's call for help,
Are the white silk scarf of the humble beggar's pure intentions.

Although I could not grasp his thought, I am still obliged to
    speak on his behalf.
This long presentation scarf of his formal request[52]
Is difficult for this minister to pass on to you.
The essential point in his request seems to be
That he would like permission to come before your golden
    throne.
Forgive this fool for filling the golden palace of your ears with
    this news,
However, if the affair is important, I have served your honor.
If you hear and understand my offering song,
Then please give your reply to what he has requested.[53]

Thus he requested and the magnificent Skull Garland Lotus answered: "Oh, Excellent! According to the examples in the proverbs:

To the guru who is a guide and a teacher,
Better abandonment of evil deeds than a hundred offerings.
To the chief whose sovereignty is vast,
Better the straight truth than a hundred presentation offerings.
When you begin to accumulate merit,
Better an auspicious connection[54] *than a hundred material*
  goods.

Today, in the Fire Monkey year, the eighth day of the first moon, on the day of the glorious gate of auspicious coincidence, whichever he is of the eight classes of beings, whether *lha*, nyen, *lu*, or human,* now quickly allow him to enter and stand before me."

Then the minister went out to the gate but the little boy had disappeared without a trace. There should have been some sign of him, but instead it was like the proverb:

No tracks of the bird in the sky;
No path of wind for the bird;
No prints of the mouse on the ground
No hiding hole for the mouse.

But straight ahead there was a golden lotus with eight petals; upon its stamen stood a white HRĪḤ. On the petals, the syllables OṂ MAṆI PADME HŪṂ HRĪḤ ĀḤ[55] were repeating their own sounds. He thought, "How strange. What shall I declare to the chief? How will I explain this to the ministers? What will I say to the servants? What will I proclaim to the people?" His mind flipped back and forth twelve times; he came up with at least twenty-five stratagems.[56] Finally he thought,

"Since the empty mind is inexhaustible,
There is no exhausting the intelligence of a great man.[57]
If you do not clamp down on your little tongue,
There is no end to the speech of learned ones.

---

* "Whether lha, nyen, lu, or human" (Tib. *lha, gnyan, klu, mi*)—that is, gods, nyen (mountain-dwelling spirits), nāgas (gods, mountain spirits, serpents, water-dwelling spirits), and humans—a traditional division of beings into four orders.

If you do not measure the step of your little feet,
There is no end to the length of a dirt path.
If it does not reach the blue water,
There is no end to the blazing red fire.

This time it is like:

A support without blessings,
Like the relics of a pig;[58]
A mumble without clarity,
Like a mute explaining the taste of brown sugar.[59]

Although it may be pointless to try to describe this with words, maybe I can carry it in my hands. I guess that person I saw this morning must have been some kind of magical emanation. So it seems that this flower here might be his magic. If that's so, then why not carry the flower in and place it before the king? Just this morning the king said a person with merit needs an auspicious connection.[60] And after all, the king gave me orders, saying, 'Whether it is a god or a demon, bring it in'. Since this thing is an intangible rainbow-like form, perhaps this is a magician's trick or a magician's basis for transformation.[61] Whether good or bad, I know that it is something miraculous!

Even though there is no one here to give his message to, I'll just have to take this thing that has appeared here inside and offer it."

This is a matter of pleasing the white snow mind and
Of what seems lovely to these colorful eyes.[62]

He thought it must be some kind of auspicious sign, so he picked up the flower and carried it to the door of Padmasambhava's [Skull Garland's] private chambers, called Self-Appearing Lotus. The flower in his hand turned into a white light the size of the moon and dissolved into the heart center of the demon king Rākṣa Skull Garland.

[Avalokiteśvara calls upon Padmasambhava to create the incarnation of Gesar from primordial ultimate mind.][63]

Then through the self-clarity of his wisdom intent, the Great Compassionate Avalokiteśvara sang this song, easily comprehended, which invokes the mind stream.[64]

OṂ MAṆI PADME HŪṂ HRĪḤ
From the pure land of the Blazing Lotus
Blessed One Amitābha, know me.
You who are supreme in the lotus family, Treasure of
    Omniscience,
Miraculous king, please heed me!

It is difficult to tame the wilderness land of Tibet.
In the kingdom of the land of snow,
Nine oath-breaking demon[65] kings and ministers uttered
    perverted aspiration prayers.
When they transferred from that life
They were reborn as:

The eastern demon [māra of the east], Southern Throne
    Tiger Eye,
The southern demon, Poison Tree of Sadam,
The western demon, Lutsen [Nāga Might] of the Mu clan,
The northern demon, Gurkar, White Tent The'u Rang Cub,[66]
Turquoise Peak[67] Luminous Child,
Earth Lord King Nyenrawa,
The Lion Demon Asê Khyilpa,
The barbarian Demon King Shingtri,
And the general demons of the world such as Black Bear, and
    so on.[68]
Each one of them is surrounded by an innumerable retinue,
The visible enemies and the invisible demonic forces
Who are to be the culprit leaders inflicting misery on the land
    of Tibet.
They will treat the teachings of cause and effect and the Rare
    and Precious Three Jewels with contempt.
They will lead all sentient beings down the path to the lower
    realms.
They will sow the seeds of the lowest possible realms.
Oh pity the ignorant beings in saṃsāra!
The great powerful one who tames the difficult to tame,
Great being, divine child, Joyful to Hear,
The primordially pure is self-liberated.[69]

May the five families of the victorious ones grant him
  empowerment.
May the protectors of the three families bless him.
As the *nirmāṇakāya* who tames the vicious,
It falls upon you to invoke your samaya.[70]
Therefore, protector of beings, don't be idle.

Thus he supplicated. And then Nangsid Zilnön [Lotus Skull Garland] smiled, his heart glad, and replied, "Good," and sang these words in a sweet melody:

Kye Ho! O supreme bodhisattva, very good!
Your striving for the benefit of beings is excellent.
In the limitless sky of your enlightened mind of *bodhicitta*
The white luminous moon of your compassion shines upon
  others.
The innumerable constellations are your aspiration prayers.
Your kindness eliminates the darkness of ignorance.[71]

Like the moon in the midst of the lunar mansions,
You are the child who binds the phenomenal world in
  servitude.
Great bodhisattva, hearing you brings rejoicing and
  liberation.
You are the lord who embodies the activity of all the buddhas.

All the victors are one in the space of wisdom.
The buddha nature of the *sugatas* pervades all sentient beings.
Accordingly, in order to liberate all unrealized saṃsāric
  beings,
The sugatas cannot help but fulfill their vows to benefit
  beings.
Protector, whatever you intend for others' benefit
Will come true for sentient beings.
May your practice of the perfection of aspiration be
  complete.[72]

In this way he prayed and confirmed the invocation of the sacred vow of all the sugatas of the ten directions. Even the demon minister of this *sambhogakāya* field of disciples was established in bliss through liberation upon the sight of that which is astonishing. Then the Great Compassionate One departed for Potala Mountain.

[Padma causes the birth of the future Gesar as the godling Thöpa Gawa, Joyful to Hear.]73

Later, on the holy day when the *ḍākas* and the *ḍākinīs* gather, the tenth day of the lunar month, deathless Lotus Skull Garland himself was surrounded by a vast assembly performing a tantric feast.* While he was dwelling in the *samādhi* of the all-pervading *dharmadhātu*, from the top of his head he emitted a green ray of light, which invoked the mind stream of the dharmadhātu Samantabhadra [Always Excellent]. Then, from the heart center of the dharmadhātu Samantabhadra, there emanated a five-pointed blue vajra marked in the center with the syllable HŪM.† It radiated out and went tothe garden Tsasum Gawa [Joyful Three Roots] and entered the top of the head of the godling Demchog Karpo Ngangyag. He experienced inexpressible bliss and had a vision in which he became the wrathful deity Heruka Hayagrīva, the Neighing Horse.74

From the heart center of Dhātviśvarī‡ Mother of Basic of Space emanated a red lotus with sixteen petals, the anthers marked with the syllable ĀḤ.§ It radiated light, which entered into the top of the head of Gyuma Lhadzei. An inexpressible meditation experience blazed within her, and she had a vision that she transformed into the Vajra Sow Vajravārāhī. Then Hayagrīva and Vajravārāhī joined in passionless union.75

The sound of their union of bliss and emptiness invoked the mindstreams of the sugatas of the ten directions. From the heart centers of the blessed ones, the victorious ones of the five families, various colored lights emanated in the ten directions, cleansing the obscurations of the five poisons of all sentient beings. The lights gathered back here and transformed into a crossed double vajra, the essence of the activity of all the *tathāgatas* of the ten directions.

That vajra entered into the crown of the head of Demchog Karpo, where it was melted by the fire of exaltation. Then that became the energy of wisdom wind

---

* Sanskrit, *gaṇacakra*.

† HŪM: the seed syllable of enlightened mind.

‡ Tib. *dbyings phyug ma*; Yingchugma.

§ ĀḤ: the seed syllable of enlightened speech.

(prajñā), which entered into the space[76] of Gyuma Lhadzei and was blessed as the nirmāṇakāya.[77] A moment later, the god child miraculously appeared in her lap, blazing with magnificent dignity and splendor. To see him brought liberation. To hear him brought joy. As soon as he was born he began to recite the sound of the hundred-syllable mantra.[78]

Upon an eight-petaled golden lotus he floated in the air in vajra posture the height of an arrow length. He raised up this song, which teaches the meaning of cause and fruition.[79]

> OṂ MAṆI PADME HŪṂ HRĪḤ
> From the pure land Akaniṣṭha,
> Bhagavat of the five families of the victorious ones, know me.
> For I and all sentient beings equal to space
> Please naturally pacify discursive thoughts of the five poisons.
> May we meet the wisdoms of the five *kāyas*.[80]
>
> If you see the sole essence of the *dharmakāya*,
> Buddhahood is delivered in the palm of your hand.
> Nevertheless, for ignorant sentient beings,
> Even if you explain it, it is difficult to understand.
>
> According to the interpretable meaning, if gods and humans
>   wish to be
> Protected from the fear of saṃsāra,
> They must seek refuge in the Three Rare and Supreme Ones
>   [Three Jewels: Buddha, Dharma, Sangha].
> If they wish to pacify suffering naturally in its own place
> Then they must generate bodhicitta, which holds others
>   dearer than self.
> Beings of the three lower realms, barbarians, and erring gods,
> Those of perverted views, inhabitants of lands without
>   dharma, and the mute:
> When you are free from the faults of these negative eight
>   states of being[81]
> And when you are born in the central land, with faculties
>   whole, with faith,
> Without reversed karma, inclined to virtue,[82]
> Then, if you do not practice the holy dharma,

What will happen when the one known as Yama comes?
Lord of Death, the sharp and swift,
He comes whether good or bad, to friend and foe alike.

The high ones famed as the sun and the moon
May seem to pervade the four continents with their rays,
Yet it is unheard of that they would eclipse planet Rāhu with
    their light.
Likewise the high kings should think on this.

The red rock cliffs are high and mighty.
Only the vulture can make its way to them.
Yet it is unheard of that they would beat their rival, the
    lightning meteoric iron.
Likewise the mighty unrivaled aristocracy should think on this.

In the third month of summer, tiny creatures cover the
    ground.
At harvest time one covering of frost destroys their precious
    lives.
Likewise the lowly and humble should think on this.

Generally, at first you are born in your dear mother's lap.
You are fed with soft food, the delicious three sweets.
You are dressed in soft clothes and silk brocade.
In the middle time, you are distracted by saṃsāric activities;
You turn the wheel of passion and aggression with friends
    and enemies.
If you are high up, that's not enough, for you fear that you
    may plunge;
If low, you will suffer from taxes, war, and forced labor.
Neither the strong nor the weak have protection from their
    inevitable end.
You suffer from fear of others' contempt.
If you are rich, you suffer because you can't sustain your
    livelihood.
If poor, you suffer by not being able to feed your face or
    clothe your back.

The suffering of human life is endless, and inexhaustible,
Tossed about on the wind of four hundred illnesses;
There are many ways to die from the onset of sudden
    obstacles.
When you are old, you can't bear up against sickness,
Your old body is like a dead tree on a river bank;
It is rare for someone to listen to the words of the aged.
The old mind gathers all the suffering of the world,
When finally you are struck by a long fatal illness[83]
All sweet and delicious flavors nauseate you,
Your soft warm bed becomes harder than stone,
You become fed up with taking beneficial medicines,
The sleep guardian[84] gets you angry,
Your grunts and groans are inexhaustible,
A day and a night take forever to pass,
Your spells and divinations reverse auspicious coincidence.[85]
Your life, so preciously guarded and pent within,
Even though you have pure dharmas; now it is too late to
    plant virtuous roots.[86]
For the stingy who held back generosity,
It is really too late to hope for help in the forty-nine days.[87]
On the day when death has finally come,
Taking medicine is like trying to drive a stake* into a stone;
On the day when you are facing Yama, Lord of Death,
Averting ceremonies are like using a torch made of water.

When the glorious gate of merit turns upside down,[88]
No matter how hard you work, all you get are blisters.

When vitality and windhorse are upside down,[89]
All worldly skills are like bubbles in water.
The castle of the dralas is turned away[90]
And this enemy fortress will take away one's life.
The mighty warrior whose heart was once brave
At the moment of death is a lump piled with earth.

---

* Phurba, an ancient dagger.

A rich man's avaricious inner stores[91]
Amount to a wooden stake of attachment driven into the
     ground.[92]
His whole life spent pursuing illusory food and clothes,
At the hour of his death, he is naked with empty hands.

Even the high king on his golden throne
Must pillow his head that day on cold earth,
And the queen with silken robes on her back
Burns in an oven, clothed in red flames.
Even the youthful tigers in their prime, with their six
     attributes of a warrior,
Are dragged on the ground by the king of birds,*
And the wise mothers and aunts
Are bound head to foot by the black rope.
In the Frightening Red Charnel Ground,
On the day when the pale corpse is hacked to pieces by the
     knife and the ax,
Alas! It is too late for regret.

The hot and cold of hell is unbearable.
The hungry ghosts are starving and parched.
The animals, mute and stupid, lose their freedom.
The warring jealous gods struggle and die by the knife.
And we gods of the higher realms,
Though spared illness and aging, are carried away by
     distractions.
Seven days before death the portents of the god's death arise;
The brightness of his lovely palaces fades,
His dear wife withdraws far away,
His garlands of sweet smelling flowers wither,
His body starts to stink and its light dims.
The negative experience of cause and effect blazes up in
     terrible suffering;

---

* The vulture.

Now even regret is merely cause for more suffering.[93]
All you heedless and crazy beings of the six realms
Do not wander; turn your awareness inward.
Lord gurus, determine to resolve the nature of mind.[94]
Imperial rulers, do not mistreat the law of cause and effect.
Mighty warriors, do not disturb the policy of the king.
Rich men, offer up and give down most generously.
Common people, do prostrations, circumambulations, and
    recite the *MANI* mantra.
Through a precious human life there is no virtue that cannot
    be accomplished.
Exert yourself with as much vigilance as possible.

I am Vajrasattva himself,
The primordially pure dharmadhātu Samantabhadra.
O beings pervaded by impure illusions,
Listen to this song's words and think through their actual
    meaning.[95]
Hold this jewel close.
If you do not understand, there is no way to explain it.[96]

Thus he proclaimed the great sound of dharma according to the minds and dialects of all animate and inanimate beings.

[Thöpa Gawa is empowered with the five Buddha families.][97]

At that time, on Zangdog Pelri in Cāmara, the Master, Lotus Skull Garland, knew that the time had come to confer empowerment on Thöpa Gawa. From his forehead, white rays of light invoked the mind stream of the Buddha Vairocana in Akaniṣṭha. From Padma's heart center, blue rays of light invoked the mind of Akṣobhya in Abhirati. From his navel, yellow rays of light evoked the mind stream of Ratnasambhava in the buddha field Pelden Palden [Endowed with Glory]. From his throat center, red rays of light invoked the mind stream of Amitābha in Sukhāvatī. From his secret center, green rays of light invoked Amoghasiddhi in the buddha field of Lerab Dzog [All-Accomplishing Activity]. Then Padmasambhava raised this song in order to supplicate for the fruition of the truth.

[Padma invokes the five Buddhas in order to empower Thöpa Gawa.]

OM
The perfectly pure five poisons are the five wisdoms.
I invoke the sacred oath [samaya] from unborn space.
The perfectly pure five elements are the five goddesses
Arising for the benefit of beings from unceasing space.
From the supreme method of the empty nature of
    phenomena.
Prajñā shines as the embodiment of compassion.
To this nirmāṇakāya who will guide beings,
Grant empowerment so that he may conquer the hordes of
    māras.
This is the ultimate song of self-luminosity.

According to common worldly proverbs:

It is a sorry guru who has neither empowerment nor textual
    transmission.
It is a sorry student who lacks the sacred vows of samaya.
It is a sorry ruler who has no supporters to honor and magnify him,
And sorry subjects who lack good manners.
Weapons which are neither sharp nor tempered,
Even if they have both handle and sheath, cannot handle the enemy.
If you have the main six herbal ingredients, but not the additives,[98]
Even if the medicine is pleasing and fragrant it will not heal.
A field which has not been worked
Will not bear fruit even if the six grains are sown.

So therefore let us enthrone, praise, and honor him.
Sever the life force of the enemy with the weapon of
    compassion,[99]
Heal the six realms with the medicine of blessings,
Spread enlightened activity through the field of disciples,
And pray that all sentient beings be liberated.
May there be the auspiciousness of the complete
    accomplishment of all wishes.

With these words he invoked the samaya vow of the compassionate minds [of
the five Buddhas and their consorts].

[Buddha Vairocana gives the empowerment of body and names the divine child.]

Then in Akaniṣṭha, from Vairocana's forehead, light rays streamed out in the ten directions. They purified the obscurations of ignorance of all sentient beings and gathered back here in the form of the syllable OM representing the enlightened body blessings of the sugatas of the ten directions. This became a white wheel with eight spokes. The wheel traveled in the realm of the mid-heavens to rest directly in front of the divine child. From it came the self-proclaiming sound resounding with these words:[100]

> OM
> From the self-appearing wisdom of dharmadhātu,
> At the moment of your birth, you are the lord of beings.
> You are the king who possesses various magical emanations.
> You dispel delusions from the deluded minds
> Of all confused sentient beings
> Who are pitifully unclear, befuddled by the eight confusions.[*]
> Through laziness, doubt, and delusion,
> And ignorance due to conceptual obscurations,
> Though free, they are still distracted by saṃsāric activities;
> Though well-favored, they are too lazy for dharma.
> When the time of death finally arrives:

> *Though the guru lacking dharma wears a golden hat,*
> *Shining to show his lofty rank,*
> *He will have trouble finding the path to the next life.*
> *The leader who lacks a gentle mind,*
> *Whose tyranny shows he is strong in the law,*
> *Will be punished by karma as he punishes others*
> *Like a man struck by a stone he throws in the air.*[101]
> *The disciple with no samaya,*
> *Whose open mind shows him to be learned,*[102]
> *Has empty talk which is nothing but a mist of spit.*

---

[*] This probably refers to the eight worldly dharmas, which are: praise and criticism, pleasure and pain, fame and disgrace, gain and loss.

The rich man with no generosity,
Though he has collected wealth through avarice,
At the time of death will be naked and empty-handed.
These are the characteristics of saṃsāra.

On this noble being is bestowed
The name Thöpa Gawa.
When the name of this Buddha, endowed with blessings,
Is heard it brings joy and exhausts negativity.
If this leader with vast sovereignty remains,
He will bring happiness to the kingdoms of the world.
May his presence defeat the enemies of the four directions.
May everyone who meets him be free from rebirth in the
    lower realms.
May everyone who sees him enter into the pure lands.
Buddha Abhiśinytsa OM*

After the wheel had uttered these words, it dissolved into the child's forehead. From this day on he was known as Thöpa Gawa [Joyful to Hear].

[Buddha Akṣobhya gives the empowerment of the enlightened mind of the Vajra Buddha family.]

Then, in the eastern pure land of Abhirati, from the heart center of Akṣobhya, light rays streamed forth. They purified the obscurations of aggression of all sentient beings and gathered back in the form of a blue five-pointed vajra, the embodiment of the mind blessings of the victorious ones, and then dissolved into the heart center of the divine child. As a result he mastered the treasury of samādhi. Then the entire assembly of the five buddha families holding jeweled vases filled with amṛta offered to bathe him, saying:

HŪṂ
From the great vajra space of emptiness
Flows the nectar of mirror-like wisdom.

---

* This is the mantra that confers empowerment. It ends with OM, the seed syllable of enlightened body.

May the weapons of vajra aggression
Conquer the hosts of enemies,
The poisons of the ignorant angry sentient beings of saṃsāra.

The guru who has no compassion,
Even though he exerts himself in mantra recitation,
Will still not become a buddha.
The ruler who has no loving kindness
May enforce the law, but will lose his districts.
The warrior who has no restraint,
Though hearty and brave, will die by the sword.

Therefore, in the savage minds of all sentient beings
May no sinister thoughts arise.
Supreme being, divine child, Thöpa Gawa,
Even though you are not obscured by the three poisons,
Still I will grant you the empowerment of the three kāyas.
May you spontaneously perform the buddha activity of
    pacifying.
Vajra Abhiśinytsa HŪṂ

Thus they bathed him with amṛta.

[Ratnasambhava confers the enlightened qualities empowerment of the Ratna Buddha family, dresses him as a king, and enthrones him.]

Again, in Pelden Palden, from the navel of Ratnasambhava, light rays streamed forth, purifying the obscurations of pride of all sentient beings. They gathered back as all the qualities and merit of the victorious ones in the form of a blazing jewel and dissolved into the navel of the divine child. He was then adorned by the bodhisattvas of the ten bhumis with priceless precious ornaments: jeweled crest ornaments; throat, shoulder, hand, leg, and ear ornaments; rings; long and short necklaces of crystal; divine clothes of *panyacalika* silk, and so forth, ornaments worthy of a great being. With all of these he was clothed and enthroned, as they raised this auspicious song:

TRAṂ
The precious wisdom of equanimity,
Perfectly purified pride is the wealth of the *ārya*.

29

Meritorious one, accumulator of all merit,
Great source of jewel wisdom, Ratnasambhava,[103]
As you are empowered in order to tame the difficult to tame,
Through your compassion please work for the welfare of beings.
Your compassion is like the sky,
May the auspiciousness of equanimity be present.
For disciples who are like the constellations,
May the auspiciousness of your boundless buddha activity be
    present.
For your life span like a vajra,
May the auspiciousness of indestructible deathlessness be
    present.
For the symbol of the stability of your vows to benefit beings,
May the auspiciousness of unchanging spontaneity be
    present.
By these beautiful ornaments, the precious jewel crown,
May the auspiciousness of exalted majesty be present.
By these earrings and rich golden necklaces,
May the auspiciousness of your sky-pervading fame be
    present.
By these fine, soft, and light vestments,
May the auspiciousness of conquering the hosts of māras be
    present.

Great being, precious Thöpa Gawa,
Although you are not attached to ordinary ornaments,
I empower you with the five precious noble qualities.*
May your buddha activity of enriching be spontaneously
    accomplished.
Ratna Abhiśinytsa TRAṂ

Thus he was enthroned with auspiciousness.

[Amitābha confers the enlightened speech empowerment of the Lotus
Buddha family.][104]

---

* Contentment, joy, forgiveness, compassion, mindfulness.

Again, in the Sukhāvatī pure land, from the throat center of Amitābha, light rays streamed forth, purifying the obscurations of desire of all sentient beings. They gathered back here as the blessings of the speech of all the sugatas in the form of a red lotus and dissolved into the throat center of the divine child. He was then empowered with the sixty branches of melodious speech. Furthermore, the support of the samaya of all tathāgatas,[105] a golden five-pointed vajra, descended from the sky into his hand:

> HRĪḤ
> Perfectly purified desire is the space of discerning wisdom.
> Great desire is exaltation free from attachment, Lord of Lotus
>   Speech,
> You are the supreme skillful means of connate wisdom.
> This vajra is the support for your sacred vows, your samaya.
> Until the ocean of saṃsāra is empty,
> You will liberate the ocean of sentient beings.
> Having realized the ocean of wisdom,
> May you perfect the ocean of aspiration.
>
> You empowered the imperial lha above,
> And will proclaim commands upon the middle nyen
> And open the treasury of the nāgas below[106]
> In the Wishing Land of Ling,* look after the benefit of
>   beings,
> The Black Düd and the Yellow Hor,[107]
> Those with form and those without, bind them all by oath.
>
> Although the bodhisattva who looks after the benefit of
>   beings
> Needs no encouragement to keep this samaya,
> Just as you promised to lead beings from saṃsāra,
> May you spontaneously accomplish the activity of
>   magnetizing.
> Padma Abhiśinytsa HRĪḤ

---

* (Tib. *gling mthong smon*). Literally, "seeing Wishing Ling," meaning Ling as "the land that, if you see it, you wish to be there." An epic epithet.

This song was pronounced throughout the mid-heavens.

[Amoghasiddhi empowers him with the enlightened activity of the Karma Buddha family.]

Again, in the All-Accomplishing Activity pure land, from the secret center of the Blessed One Amoghasiddhi, light rays streamed forth, purifying the obscurations of jealousy of all sentient beings. They dissolved into the secret center in the form of a green double vajra, the essence of the activity of all the sugatas. He accomplished mastery over all vast buddha activities. Furthermore, a silver bell descended into his left hand, representing the spontaneous accomplishment of all four buddha activities of the sugatas.

> ĀḤ
> Perfectly purified jealousy is Amoghasiddhi,
> The completely pure wisdom of all-accomplishing action.
> Great wrath is the great sound
> That quells the self-occurring sound of the five poisons
> And skillfully tames the disciples of the five corruptions.
> Powerful hero
> Who conquers the great mountain of conditioned existence,
> You who have perfected all buddha activity,
> From the great billowing clouds of your peaceful compassion
> The terrible lightning strikes flash
> And conquer the crags of the great sinners' pride.

The guru addicted to wealth,
If he is not conquered by the logic of the learned,[108]
Then his guts will be filled with empty quotes.
The ruler who is full of pride,
If karma does not fall right on him,
It will ripen as agony for the people and the land.[109]
The prideful youth, tiger in his prime, full of himself,
Unless a real warrior knocks him out,
Then his hollow bragging will roar like a thousand dragons.
The self-absorbed young woman,
If famine does not strike her down,
Then her self-centeredness will reach beyond the sky.

Therefore, in this time of the dark age,
The vindictive sentient beings
Be little cause and effect, and pile up perverted aspirations.
Let not your compassion abandon them but liberate them
    into the purelands.
Let a downpour of vajra weapons descend upon the
    skandhas.[110]
Seal their consciousnesses with this vajra of the dharma
    realm.
You, bodhisattva, are the embodiment of compassion.
Although your buddha activity is unfaltering,
May your wrathful buddha activity be spontaneously
    accomplished.
Karma Abhiśinytsa ĀḤ

Thus the abhiṣeka was conferred.

All the assemblies of great supreme wrathful deities enthroned him with the four empowerments.[111] Then the divine child Thöpa Gawa became full of learning, good qualities, splendor, and dignity unrivaled in the world.

This was the chapter on the birth by magical transformation and the conferral of empowerment. Composed in colloquial terms that are easy to understand, this is known as A Continuously Flowing Stream of Blessing.

CHAPTER TWO

Chipön Rongtsha Tragen[*]
Describes a dream to the assembly of White Ling.[112]
Thangtong Gyalpo [King of the Empty Plain] predicts that
    this dream
Is a sign of the birth of a supreme being.

[Chipön has an auspicious dream.]

IN THE MIDDLE LAND OF HUMANS,[113] in the northern part of the southern continent of Jambudvīpa, is a land called Dokham. It is part of the snow land of Tibet. It is a prosperous region, a land breathtaking to behold.[114] It is to the right of the Ma River in the area known as Lung Traphug Chogyei [Valley of Eighteen Falcon Caves]. There, in the universal mountain pass, in the left wing of Tratöd Namdzong [Upper Falcon Valley], is the great castle called Shar-ri Drugdzong [Eastern Mountain Dragon Fortress]. It is there in that fortress, in his chamber called Padma Nyishar [Lotus Sunrise], that the incarnation of the Mahāsiddha Kukurīpā, Chipön Rongtsha Tragen, the first born of the Thirty Mighty Warriors,[115] the first of the Thirty Skulls,[†] the most charismatic[‡] of all thirty, had a special dream vision

---

* Rongtsha Tragen is the chief of the Lesser Lineage.

† "Thirty Skulls" (Tib. *thod pa sum cu*): literally, "the thirty foreheads." This means that Chipön is principal among the Thirty Mighty Warriors.

‡ Charisma (Tib. *dbang thang* [pronounced *wang thang*]) authentic presence and field of power.

in the sleep of luminosity.[116] He dreamed that just as the golden sun rose from the eastern peak of Mount Magyal Pomra, its rays illuminated the land of Tibet. From the midst of the sun's rays a golden vajra descended upon the peak of Kyigyal Tagri [Tiger Mountain King of Joy], the home of the greatest *zodor** spirit in the middle land of Ling.

On the plain of Dalung [Moon Valley], the Tibetan gods of the chase were gathering. It was the day of the month when the silver moon[†] rose over Mönlam La [Aspiration Pass] and constellations sparkled above Ser-la [Golden Pass]. In the dream, a rainbow arched over Gedzo Mountain[‡] and ropes of its light rays extended to Mapham Lake where [Chipön's] youngest brother King Senglön [Lion Minister] stood holding aloft a parasol made of white silk on top and a rainbow-like fringe of red and green. It had a golden silk skirt and a golden handle, which he slowly turned.[117] The parasol extended across the world: west as far as the land of Panghol in Persia and east as far as Ding Ting Mountain in China, as far south as Rimam in India, and over to Yungtriwan in the country of Hor to the north.

Then, in the dream, upon an arch of white clouds from the southwestern sky came a lama wearing a lotus hat, riding a white lion, holding a vajra in his right hand and a *khaṭvāṅga* in his left. He was escorted by a red woman who wore bone ornaments.[118] Speaking in unison, they said, "Great chief, sleep not, but awake. At the first light of dawn, when the royal parasol of the sun rises over Potala Mountain,[§] if you wish the sun's rays to reveal Ling, then there is no benefit from a man's imprudent sleep. Listen, and do as we say." Then they sang this song:

> OM is the start of the song with the eight auspicious
>   meanings.
> ĀḤ is the unborn syllable.
> In the end the vow is sealed with HŪM.[119]
> May you accomplish the realm of the three kāyas.
> Listen, chief of the great tribe of Ling:

---

* A *zodor* is an epithet for a drala or a werma. A zodor can also be understood to be a local guardian spirit of the land.

† (Tib. *dngul gyi zla ba tshes*). The full moon.

‡ Named after a great nyen (or mountain spirit) called Gedzo.

§ Potala Mountain is the pure land of the bodhisattva of compassion, Avalokiteśvara. The physical location of this mountain in our world is in northeast China.

If you do not know the measure of your own sleep,
The slumber of your ignorance will be inexhaustible.
If you do not know the measure of your own superiority,
The crag of your pride will be irrepressible.
If you yourself are unable to be fulfilled,
Your greedy rich man's mind will never be satisfied.

Today, in the first summer month of the Fire Bird year,
On the eighth day of the waxing moon, at dawn,
The omens are not bad, they are good.
Starting with the high Elder Lineage, the order of the
    Garuḍa[120]
Through the Middle Lineage, the renowned rank of the
    Dragon,
And the Cadet Lineage, the brave and daring Lion Cubs,
Down to the common people, the order of the smile-striped
    Indian Tiger:[121]
Let these thirteen divine districts gather.
On the eighth day of the second month of summer
Gather everybody else, from the gurus above
Down to the lower classes below;
From the mighty kingdoms abroad
Down to the fathers and uncles of the rich local clans.
At daybreak when the sky begins to lighten,
Have them congregate on the divine plain in the white* land
    of Ma.
Up until the fifteenth day of the waxing moon,
Perform feast offerings and render praise to the dralas.
Led by golden wood and the turquoise juniper,
Erect thirteen smoke-offering altars, made of the best of woods.
Led by the drala windhorse flag,[122]
Hoist thirteen grand and auspicious flags.
Led by the practice of the great-cloaked Vaiśravaṇa,
Convene thirteen practice groups[123] to summon prosperity.[124]

---

* "White" refers to virtues or that which is positive in terms of karmic intention.

Led by the king full of merit,
Michen Gyalwa'i Lhundrub [Great Man Spontaneously
    Accomplished Victor],*
Lay out thirteen circular dancing grounds of good fortune.
Let the wealthy and prosperous mothers and aunts,
Led by Garza of Kyalo,
Raise thirteen songs of aspiration.
Led by granulated and brown sugar,
Arrange the thirteen delicacies made from dairy.
All this will surely bring good fortune to Tibet
And will build up Ling's field of authentic presence.

If you are about to enter the divine pure realm,
That's not the time to have loose faith.
If you are about to eat the feast offering which grants siddhi,
That's not the time to drool, O son of excellent father.
In the same way, on the day when you set out dishes for the great
    festival,
Don't be slack in your preparations, lineage holder of excellent family.

On the day when you serve beverages like tea and beer,
Don't let your knees tremble, O daughter of excellent mother.
On the day important guests dismount at your gate,
Don't fumble with your hands, O family of wise women.
On the day when the glorious gate of good fortune is in position,
Don't ruin the signs of this auspicious occasion, O lineage of honored men.

If you have understood, then wear this like golden earrings,
If not, all efforts have been in vain.
If that is how it is, then what's the point?[125]
May all auspicious wishes be fulfilled.

When the lama in the dream finished speaking, he dissolved into the western sky, and at the same moment Rongtsha Tragen awakened, happy and greatly rejoicing, with bliss dawning in his body and joy bursting in his heart. "Hey you!" he

---

* One of the Elders of Ling.

called and called to his servant Gaten Darlu [Joyful Doctrine Propagator], his voice sounding like the pounding of a small drum. He called out like the howling of a she-wolf, saying, "Hey! Gaten Darlu! Hey you, Tenpa Dargyei [Doctrine Increaser], my boy! Hey! Are your thumbs in your ears?"

They woke up and replied, "Oh my goodness! What could be the matter? This solid noble Chipön King, whose body usually moves slowly like a majestic elephant, whose speech flows slowly like the sound of a great river, whose mind moves slowly like the sun in springtime,[126] ordinarily he is majestic like Sumeru, the king of mountains and expansive just like the vast earth itself! But today he bleats like an old goat, and barks like an old dog, yelling 'Hey! Hey!' like the chopping of wood. His cursing[127] sounds like the hammering of a blacksmith!"

The servant thought, "What's wrong?" as he called out, "Yes, sir, yes, sir!" And with no time to pick up his belt, he clutched and gathered his robe like a thangka cloth,[128] trampling his hem underfoot, tripping forward like a pecking bird, his head bobbing as though bowing to the Jowo shrine.[129]

Going up into the castle, there he found Chipön neatly and fully dressed from head to toe, seated just next to the golden throne with his legs bent down like a Chinaman.[130] [The servant] thought, "Oh my goodness! Usually by dawn he has recited at least fifty-thousand of the six-syllable mantra,* the sutra of confession twenty-one times, sutra recitations, dedications and aspiration prayers, water offerings, smoke offerings, and numerous supplications. Until these are complete he never wanders from his square bed and never breaks out of the vajra posture. But today, seeing how preoccupied he seems,

> *When the avalanche falls down the white snow mountain*
> *And the snow lion seeks his prey on the plains,*
> *It is certain the wild game will be restless.*
>
> *When dark fog banks roll down the slope of the glaciers*
> *And the gentle showers of rain wish to fall,*
> *It is certain the sky will not be clear.*
>
> *When the dear chief arises from his golden throne,*
> *It is certain that the servants will be restless at their stations.*

---

* OṂ MAṆI PADME HŪṂ.

Now, what command has been given?" the servant wondered, and took his seat.

Then the chieftain said, "Hey there! Listen! This morning I had an especially sublime dream, unheard of in the three older generations of the Mukpo clan, as well as in the three younger generations of Ling!

> *The vast blue sky is hard to cover,*
> *The solid earth is hard to support.*

Could this dream vision I have had possibly come true for the black-haired Tibetans? Only a lama full of blessings, a leader full of authentic presence and charisma, or a rich man full of merit should hear of this—no one else shall be told! Perhaps we could invite Mahāsiddha Thangtong Gyalpo? On the other hand, considering the importance of this morning's dream, it seems that:

> *Without summoning the lama,*
> *Benefit for beings is there.*
> *Without practicing,*
> *The vision of the deity is there.*
> *Without arranging auspicious coincidence,*
> *The previously accumulated merit is there.*[131]

Now I must dispatch letters to both Michen Gyalwa'i Lhundrub and Kyalo Tönpa Gyaltsen [Teacher Victory Banner of Kyalo]. Brew me some tea and bring it here."

The servant thought, "What a relief, he had nothing heavy to say at all!" He went to the stove, where the fire burst forth of its own accord. There, within the copper pot Tashi Kyilwa [Swirling Auspiciousness], the jasmine tea Metog Yangdzin [Blossom Wealth Holder], was already boiling away. Awakening the chief cooks, who were close by, he seasoned the tea in the sparkling silver tea goblet with the refined essence of butter. Tempering it with white salt from the Northern Lake, he poured in milk of the third summer[132] to brighten its color. He asked the kitchen servant Sönam Yarpel [Increasing Merit] to light and bring the golden butter lamp. They both then went to the bedroom, and Chipön said,

"Hey you two, Tenpa Dargyei and Sönam Yarpel, offer the first portion of tea in the protector goblet for this morning's auspicious connection. Then it would be good to pour the tea and raise an offering song in praise of its qualities." It is as said,

This gateway of song which expresses bliss and happiness in free-
    flowing speech
Is the blessed start of auspicious coincidence and good fortune.[133]

Then the two servants made the first offering in the protector goblet. Shielding the offering with a decorated cloth made of auspicious material worthy to be offered to the gods, a scintillating Tashi Nyinmo Delek [Auspicious-by-Day] scarf,[134] they held up the golden lamp as well as the silver goblet and offered this petition in the form of a song on the auspiciousness of offering tea:

Ala is the beginning of the song
And Thala gives its melody.
The letter A* and the Mukpo clan,
Are both great before being praised.

The start of the song is adorned with A
Just as the Mukpo clan leads the lineages of men
And this auspicious first month of summer
Is led by the cuckoo's first song of good news.[135]

It is the first milk of the sublime prosperity animals,[136]
The month of the widely famed dragon,†
And the ripening of the six grains that grow.
Now is the start of happiness for the six tribes.

At the beginning of this song of good fortune,
See this butter lamp that dispels darkness:[137]
The vessel's exterior is made of gold.
This is a sign that the family lineage of the eight brothers of
    Serpa of Upper Ling[138]
Is as good as gold.
The lamp is filled with melted butter.

---

* "A" (pronounced *Ah*) is the primordial sound of emptiness and represents the source of all sound, including the Tibetan alphabet.

† This is the third month of the lunar calendar. The dragon is widely famed since his thunder is heard throughout the land.

This is a sign that the six tribes of Ombu's Middle Ling[139]
Are an overflowing lake of happiness and richness.
Its flame dispels the darkness.
This is a sign that the four districts of Muchang of Lower
    Ling[140]
Are blazing with merit like fire.[141]

This honorable offering within the silver goblet,
Chinese tea, is the best of the crops.
Glowing with quintessence of the third summer's milk,
Containing pure refined butter drawn from the nectar of
    floral grazing,
And for good savor, the white salt of the Northern Lake,
Its six excellent substances are augmented by the minor
    medicinal ingredients.[142]
It is warm, sweet, smooth, rich, and nutritious.
Excellent in smell and color, it restores the constitution.

This choice amṛta endowed with the eight noble qualities,
The select portion of tea, is offered to the gods,
The Rare and Precious Three Jewels exalted above the azure
    sky.
The second offering is made to the nyen in the middle,
Whose bliss, happiness, fame, and glory are as vast as the sky.
To the third offering we invite the nāgas below;
May wealth and prosperity fall like rain.
The fourth offering is to the ruler of the great district,
Who defeats with his splendor the four enemies in the four
    directions.

The azure firmament is the acme of the five elements.
This is the reason its covering is so vast.
Mukpo Dong is the head of all clans.
This is the reason its glory is exalted to the skies.
This Wishing Land of Ling is an enclosure of prosperity.
This is the reason that bliss and happiness gather here.
This white silk scarf is long and auspicious.
This is the reason that it creates a great fortunate connection.

This khata* marked with Tashi Nyinmo Delek.
Is the reason that happiness prevails evenly from beginning to
    end.

This district known as the six tribes of White Ling
Is exalted to the sky like the sun and moon,
With its lower districts sparkling like constellations,
Greatly renowned like the turquoise dragon.
May its sovereignty be equal to the vast covering of the sky
And its life force is like a vajra rock.
May its government be firmer than Sumeru, king of mountains.
May its windhorse flourish like the wish-fulfilling tree.
May its destiny† be as firm as the earth.
This offering song of good fortune,
May it accomplish all aspirations!

Having spoken, they filled the drinking vessel called Sönam Todir [Bulging Vase of Merit] and at that very moment in the southern sky the turquoise dragon roared. Then Chipön said, "Ah yes! The unarranged auspicious connection has arranged itself![143] This is the self-proclaimed sound[144] of the turquoise dragon!" He then enjoyed his tea.

[Letters reporting the dream are sent to the rich and powerful leaders of Ling.]

Then in the early light of the second dawn,‡ he told his secretary Sherab Gyamtso [Wisdom Ocean] to send a letter to both Michen Gyalwa'i Lhundrub and Tönpa Gyaltsen of Kyalo. First he dictated the letter to Michen:

> *To the honorable great chieftain who through the power of*
> *his merit has achieved and elevated station:*[145]

---

* Ceremonial scarf (Tib. *kha btags*).

† (Tib. *las dbang*). Literally, "the power of karma."

‡ There are three sessions or watches of the predawn to dawn period: the first, middle, and last sessions of dawn (Tib. *skya rengs dang po, skya rengs bar ma,* and *skya rengs tha ma*).

> You who from your ocean of white virtues
> Ripen to fruition like the golden sun, which rises to reside in
>   the sky of merit,
> Free from the blemish of water-drinking clouds,
> Know that I rejoice!
> For our part, here in the ocean of the land of Ling
> We have seen the birth of a lotus, an auspicious dream sign.
> If you want the petals of this amazing prophecy to open,
> Be timely in sending your garland of sun rays of
>   compassion.[146]
> This letter is like a melodious song which the mounted
>   courier will explain in detail.

Held high to indicate good fortune, the letter was wrapped in a bolt of golden treasury[147] brocade. On a virtuous month and day, the courier was instructed to take it from Yudrug Gying Dzong [Crouching Turquoise Dragon Fortress] to Ga'u Ser Dzong [Golden Amulet Fortress]. It contained a detailed narrative of what had transpired and the order to come.

[The letter to Kyalo Tönpa:]

To Tönpa Gyaltsen, whose virtues have manifested a white fruition:

From the milky ocean of your unceasing utterly white virtue,
The timely ripening of your excellence and aspirations is the lunar
    mansion.*
It increases my joy to hear that Rāhu is far from you at this time.
Here I am well. If you want the one-hundred petals of the
    kumuda flower†
Of White Ling to open under your white light of the moon,
    releasing the prophecy,
Do not miss this moment of fortunate connection.

This letter is like a melodious song which the messenger will narrate in detail.

---

* Lunar mansion or Lord of Constellations (Tib. *rgyu skar dbang*), is a poetic figure for the moon, which shines all the more beautifully because it is adorned with a surrounding retinue of stars.

† The kumuda flower is a water lily that opens in the moonlight.

Conveyed in a scarf decorated with the eight auspicious symbols, this was written on an excellent month and day in Yudrug Gying Dzong. The letter, sealed in command, was sent to his home, the six prosperous valleys of Nelchag, called Kyalo Wealthy Pasture Land.

Just when the tip of the sun's rays touched the eight provinces of Ser in Upper Ling, the six tribes of Ombu in Middle Ling, the four districts of Muchang in Lower Ling, the wealthy districts of Ga and Dru, the twelve myriarchies of Denma, the Kar and Nag chiliarchies, and the eighteen great wings of Tag-rong, like a flock of flapping birds scattering in all directions, notes were sent out to the people of Ling. The contents contained a directive to each individual: "On the morning of the fifteenth day, at the moment the mountains are wearing golden hats, you must converge at Nyida Khatröd [Conjoined Sun and Moon], the great gathering place of White Ling."

[Thangtong Gyalpo, the priest of Ling, visits Chipön.]

Chipön thought, "The chronicles have it that there is a guru *siddha* named Thangtong Gyalpo, a man whose compassion is higher than the sky and whose oral instructions are deeper than the ocean. He should be invited to Ling." But, because Thangtong was a wandering ascetic, the chief had no idea how to find him. At the very moment when he was wondering where to send the invitation, Padmasambhava appeared in the clear light sleep of Thangtong Gyalpo. He said, "Son of Noble Family, it would be greatly beneficial if you would go to Trakhar Namdzong [Falcon Castle Sky Fortress] and work for the benefit of beings in the Wishing Land of Ling." Thangtong Gyalpo set out according to this timely prophecy.[148] There, on the tenth day, just as the sun's rays struck the tips of the mountain peaks, he arrived at the gate of the castle Shar-ri Drugdzong. Then he sang this *dohā** of auspiciousness:

> Kind and gracious Lord Guru,
> Bestower of siddhis, yidam deity,
> Assembly of ḍākinīs, who dispel obstacles,
> From my heart, I supplicate you to be inseparable from me.
> Grant blessings so that I may accomplish my aims.

---

* (Tib. *mgur*). Spiritual hymn.

Alas! Listen, oh patron and chief!
Since it is difficult to find a free and well-favored birth in
    Jambudvīpa,
If one fails to accomplish the divine dharma[149] that brings
    stable bliss,
It will be like going to an island of precious jewels
And returning empty-handed.
What is the difference between a tight-fisted rich man
And a hungry ghost guarding a treasure?
Both are powerless to enjoy it—how pitiful!

If you cannot make offerings to the Three Jewels,
Partaking of your own wealth is like an old ox gulping down water.

Don't you see there is no beginning or end?
If you don't give alms to the needy,
Your food and wealth are like a tree rotting in water.
Don't you see that it will bear no fruit?

Generosity is the path of merit.
Through generosity, glory and fame will flourish.
Generosity is the virtue that brings peace.
Therefore, propagate that perfectly pure generosity.

I am an ascetic who wanders many lands.
Grant me a connection with the feast offering of food and
    drink,
And I will seal it with dedications and aspiration prayers.
The auspiciousness of the buddhas fills the sky;
May there be the auspiciousness of exalted status.
The auspiciousness of the holy dharma pervades the mid-
    heavens;
May there be the auspiciousness of its increasing field of
    power.
The auspiciousness of the sangha expands across the earth;
May there be the auspiciousness of their merit increasing.
May this offering of an auspicious dohā
Make a fortunate connection with the land of Ling!

[Chipön praises his visitor, but challenges him to prove he is a good lama.]

Thus he spoke. Then Chipön thought to himself, "There's a proverb which says,

> *If there is good karma in the morning, the way is easier.*
> *If there is a warrior, the weapon is sharper.*
> *If there is high status, the sovereignty is greater."*

He thought, "This may be the Mahāsiddha Thangtong Gyalpo singing a dohā at my door, but I'm not sure." Gazing through the bright window ornamented with gilded latticework, he saw a man with the plaited locks of a hermit mahāsiddha coming. His goatee was so long that it came down to the middle of his chest. He was wearing a sleeveless maroon robe and a blue meditation belt around his neck for a necklace. He wore a white cotton shawl and conch shell earrings, and held a bamboo cane in his hand. To see his face would bring delight, and to hear his voice would awaken faith.

Chipön said, "Now I am certain this is Thangtong Gyalpo!

> *By his six powers, turquoise mane, and maturity,*
> *He seems to be a white snow lion.*
> *I'm sure he can wander the white peaks of the snow mountains.*
>
> *The span of his six wings spreads so evenly,*
> *He seems to be a white-breasted vulture.*
> *I'm sure he can pierce the highest regions of the azure*
>   *firmament.*
>
> *By the six smiles complete on his body*
> *He seems to be a Bengal tiger, inscribed with designs.*
> *I am sure he can prowl the sandalwood forest."*

"In any case," he thought, "I should approach him and make some inquiries." So he said, "Oh Mahāsiddha, you've come! You must be tired!

> *If you don't liberate yourself through realization on the spot*
> *It will be difficult to benefit others with compassion.*

47

You who sang this melodious little dohā—what land do you come from? What do you have to tell us?" and Chipön sang this song:

> The beginning of the song is sung with Ala.
> Thala is the way the melody goes.
> Guru, yidam, and Three Jewels,
> Never parting, remain as my crown ornament.
>
> As I begin, this song is offered to you.
> May all my aims be accomplished according to the dharma.
> In case you don't recognize this place,
> This is the mountain pass of Traphug [Falcon Cave] in
>   Jambudvīpa.
>
> First, the hues of the late summer flowers,
> Second, the well-fed gleam of the grazing livestock,
> Third, the brilliant mind of Chipön;
> This is a colorful valley of happiness and good fortune.
>
> If you don't recognize what kind of man I am,
> I am the crest jewel of the six tribes,
> The golden toils of the chieftain's law;
> I am Chipön Rongtsha Tragen.
>
> So early this morning,
> O Mahāsiddha, from where did you come?
>
> First, with white conch shell earrings,
> Second, with a white walking stick of fine bamboo,
> Third, clothed in white cotton;
> You seem to have come from among the white gods.
>
> First, your blue plaited hair,
> Second, your blue mustache and goatee,
> Third, your blue meditation belt, worn like a necklace;
> You seem to have come from among the blue serpents.

First, your dark red complexion,
Second, your dark deerskin robe,
Third, your dark red skull cup;
You seem to have come from the clan of Mukpo.

How is your confidence in the view?
How is your experience in meditation?
How is the discipline of your conduct?
[Answer well, for] according to the traditions of worldly
    proverbs:

A lama without noble qualities,
Is like a seagull which just hovers over the ocean.
If his honor is not thick with the blessings of compassion,
Wearing his extra robes just serves to weigh him down.

The chieftain without sovereignty,
Is like a lion stuffed with straw.
Without authentic presence to sway the people,
His arrogant pride just serves to ridicule him before everyone.

A mighty one[150] *with no self-control*
Is like a donkey covered with leopard skin.[151]
If there is no accumulation of karmic power,
Vengeful forces could steal his life away.

A siddha without the view[152]
Is like the posture of empty armor.
Lacking control over channels and winds,
To be clad only in cotton just causes cracking oozing sores.[153]
Now, please answer me straightforwardly.
If the blessings of the lama are not limited,
Then will not the benefit to disciples be great?
If the chieftain is not weak in protecting life,
Will not his sovereignty cover all districts in the country?
If the exertions of daily life are not meager,

Then won't harvest and husbandry be good?
If sealing with dedication is not meager,
Whatever is offered as the gaṇacakra feast will be sufficient.[154]

If this song has fallen into error, I confess.
If this has all been foolish chatter, please forgive me.

[Thangtong Gyalpo answers Chipön's song point by point.]

Thus he requested and the Mahāsiddha answered,

On the great vast plain [*thang*] of my view,
I dwell as the Mahāsiddha king [*rgyal po*] of emptiness
    [*stong*].
Therefore I am known as Thangtong Gyalpo.
You, the powerful chief of the great districts,
While your great mouth consumes the people, their horses,
    and dzo,
You speak with fancy proverbs about the realization of the
    nature of the mind.[155]

A man with no table knife
Does not cut from another's delicious meat.

A man with no property
Does not try to take another's profits.

A man with no learning
Does not force his philosophy on others.

"Let me tell you about myself in metaphors," he said, and he sang this dohā:

OM May I see the very face of the dharmakāya!
ĀḤ May I accomplish the pure realm of the sambhogakāya!
HŪM May I achieve the nirmāṇakāya that benefits beings!

In case you don't know who I am,
On the center of the great bliss plain of the view,

I collect the taxes of coemergent emptiness,
Quell the mighty yoke of the five poisons,
Protect the weak from the reaches of saṃsāra.
That is why I am called Thangtong Gyalpo [King of the
    Empty Plain].
My view is vast and unbiased,
My meditation experience stable and still, and
My conduct free from the hope and fear of contrived rules.

[Thangtong Gyalpo describes Chipön:]

You are known far and wide by the name of Chipön,
Trustworthy elder of the world.
Even though you don't have four faces encircling your head,
Still your pleasing speech resembles the Vedic melody of
    Brahmā.*

These three saffron dharma robes
Are blessed with the teacher's noble qualities.
Where can there be anything greater than those blessings?
Imperial chief of this great district,
Through your accumulated merit, you were born as a king.
Where can greater authentic presence be found?

The Mighty One, feared by the entire kingdom,
Is considered by all to be like the Lord of Death.
If there were no karmic accumulations, what reason would
    there be to fear?
This illusory empty armor of the body
Is impermanent; since the flesh and bones will separate,
How can the fissured skin be worse than that?
Everything I have said is nothing but the sarcasm of my
    confusion, for;
If the guru does not consider the benefit of beings,
It is pointless to lead disciples to the pure realm.

---

* The aspect of the god Brahmā with four faces.

If husbandry is not accompanied with merit,
It is pointless to plow and sow the field.
If the patron has no faith when he makes offerings,
It is pointless to boast that merit has been accumulated.
I am not free to stay, but must depart.
Since life is impermanent and the time of death uncertain,
It is pointless to procrastinate in the face of the dharma of
    men.
You, great chief, take this to heart!

Having thus spoken, he began to make preparations to depart. Chipön then thought that no matter how he observed him, by the majestic splendor of his body, the melody of his speech, the high realization of his mind, the ruddy complexion of his face, and the long goatee of his chin, he could tell that he must be who he said he was, Thangtong Gyalpo, and therefore that he must have spoken the truth. He thought, "What joy! For the six tribes of Ling the merit is in full bloom like the first month of summer. Just as the cuckoo, the guest of spring, arrives without invitation and just as multitudes of beautiful golden flowers bloom without planting, just so, auspicious connections have lined up, this authentic presence has naturally gathered, and merit has come together perfectly."

Quickly, he went on to the silk treasury called Trinlung Chugmo [Wealthy Cloud Valley] and took the khata scarf called Padma Tongden [One-Thousand-Lotus-Fringed]. That day he didn't send his usual male servant on the commission nor did he send his usual female servant. It was so important that the dear chief himself became the servant. Just like the proverb:

> Using brocade as a hot pad rather than burning your hands
> Or using sandalwood as a poker without even having a second
>   thought.

Chipön himself approached the guru and held out the khata. Prostrating like a servant pumping bellows, he knelt down on his knees and sang this song:

If the song is led by Ala, it is free from birth and cessation.
Thala holds the meaning of the song.
Oh listen, Mahāsiddha Thangtong.
Toward a confused being such as myself,
Even the buddhas should not look down upon me.

You whose hearts are filled with love for sentient beings,
Please pull us forth from the ocean of existence.

This morning, in my confused perception,
I asked you many impertinent questions
Through this song of the magical deception of my mind.
Whatever vain frivolous words I spewed forth, please
    forgive me.
This white silk adorned with one thousand lotuses,
Not small in value, is prized in China and Tibet.
By this scarf may a dharma connection with the guru be
    made;
That is why this is called the white scarf of auspicious long-
    lived dharma.
This scarf will open the gate of the dear chieftain's law,
This scarf is the very key to the law.
This is no brag, but the very truth.

The royal parasol of the sun would not be a welcome guest
If it did not protect with its warm and gentle light,
For then its circling of the four continents would be pointless.

The clouds and rain would not be a welcome guest
If they did not moisten the rich dark earth below,
For then the dark southern clouds amassing would be
    pointless.

You, the Guru, would not be a welcome guest
If you did not convert the land of Ling to the dharma,
For then your being a siddha would be pointless.

Therefore, in Shar-ri Drugdzong,
The best would be if you could consider a three year retreat.
I, Chipön, would personally provide the provisions.
Second best would be for you to turn the dharma wheel here
    for three months.
I, myself, would request to be your patron and provider.
Or at the least, stay and take a three-day rest.

I will see to the preparations for the gaṇacakra feast.
Relax your mind and rest in meditation.
Letting go in the ground of mind's empty nature is best.
If you let go then the *ālaya*[156] will rest in its own place.
Letting the lofty southern clouds float slowly by is best.
If they are left as is then the timely rains will descend.
Letting the lowly rivers' waves roll slowly by is best.
If left as is then the ferry will cross with ease.
The restless have no marvelous qualities at all.
A restless chieftain will ruin the districts under his command.
A restless horse will throw down his rider.
A restless girl, who marries, ends up back home again.
A restless monk breaks his vows.
A restless merchant will suffer losses.

Before the mandala of the all-illuminating sun,*
What need for the firefly's tiny lamp?
Nevertheless, for the oral lineage's grandchildren
I've woven this advice[157] into a song.
You, the Mahāsiddha who omnisciently knows how to
   benefit others,
First of all, look on the face of this old man;
Secondly, consider the benefit of beings.
Don't go, stay here and care for the disciples of White Ling.
If there is confusion in my song, with regret, I confess it.
If my speech was frivolous, I beg your forgiveness.

With these words he urgently supplicated. Then the Mahāsiddha Thangtong Gyalpo thought, "The time has come to ripen the disciples and the prophecy is about to be spontaneously fulfilled." Knowing this, he then promised to stay in the upper and lower regions of Ling for three years to accomplish the benefit of beings. Then separate messengers were sent to Ga'u Ser Dzong and Kyalo's pasturelands, traveling continuously day and night.

[Michen receives a prophecy and Chipön's letter.]

---

* The "all-illuminating sun" refers to Thangtong Gyalpo.

54

Then Michen Gyalwa'i Lhundrub had a dream. In his dream a golden man wearing golden armor, a white helmet, and riding a golden horse, a man full of majesty and splendor, said, "I am the proprietor deity, the zodor Magyal Pomra. Don't sleep! Quickly arise and prepare yourself! Whether the common good fortune of the six tribes of Ling will be good or bad depends on you. Prepare to host a grand reception with pleasant conversation and abundant offerings."

The next day was the tenth lunar day, and when the sun warmed the sky, Michen completed the daily recitations and the feast and smoke offerings. Then in the great assembly hall he prepared the seating arrangement,* the banquet, and then gathered the people. It was then that suddenly somebody came up and said, "A messenger from Trakhar has just arrived at the front door." Recalling his dream, Michen said, "Quickly show him in."

The sealed letter was placed before him by the messenger, who thought, "Perhaps I should make prostrations to show respect, and since today is so auspicious, it is like the saying 'happiness should be led by a song.' Therefore without any other talk, I should offer this song that explains my purpose."

Oh excellent song, such a happy beginning!
Listen, for this is to be good news.
Are all of you here in the peak of good health?
Yesterday I came from Yudrug Gying Dzong
At the highest peak, the spiritual gathering place of Traphug,
Chipön's sovereignty reaches the sky.

In the Falcon upper foothills are eighteen great valleys
Where the villagers are as numerous as brilliant nighttime stars.
The cuckoo which comes from the south
Aims to light upon the crest of the juniper, the tree of the gods.
His good news, famed throughout the land of Tibet,
Will bring the many-colored blossoms of the three months of
    summer.
The white clouds that arrive from the south
Aim for the highest center of the azure firmament.
Their rainfall saturates the earth,
Ripening the six grains of the three months of autumn.

---

* (Tib. *gral*). A row of ceremonial seats, positioned in order of rank.

I, the messenger, have arrived from upper Trakhar,
With Ga'u Ser Dzong as my destination.
This important report made to the chieftain
References the political affairs of the six tribes of White Ling.
This from King Chipön Tragen:
"Yesterday on the eighth day of the waxing moon,
In the predawn hours, in the course of my clear light dream,
An especially wonderful prophetic dream arose.
Urgently go and present all the news
To the great chief, Gyalwa'i Lhundrub,
On this important occasion he must certainly accept my
    invitation and join me."

Your honor's immutable body is like the royal parasol of the sun.
Since it is important that it encircle the four continents,
If the land of the black-haired ones is allowed to darken,
Then one fears the royal parasol overhead has been harmed.

The great chieftain who sits on the golden throne
Must accomplish the important mission of traveling to the
    corners of the kingdom.
If the welfare of the many districts is ignored,
Then one fears the great chieftain has lost political control.

The rain clouds at the summit of the royal mountain
Must rain above the vast fields.
If the crops in the square field are not abundant,
Then one fears the supplication-offering to the zodor has
    been neglected.

You must get up now and quickly prepare to go.
If you ask where the young monk will go, it will be to central Tibet.
There he will settle with confidence his views on dharma
    philosophy.
This is the reason he wears the four-sided robe of a monk.[*]

---

[*] (Tib. *gzan*; pronounced *zen*). The large shawl that monks wear over their shoulders.

If you ask where the youthful tiger will go, it will be to China.
There he will bring the Chinese goods back to central Tibet.
This is the purpose for the great strength in his torso.

If you ask where the rich man goes, it will be to the
     marketplace.
There he will reap profits which will turn to greater wealth.
This is the purpose for pitching his four-cornered tent.

If you ask where the imperial dear chief goes, it will be to
     handle political affairs.
There he will skillfully hold the four corners of the kingdom.
This is the purpose of his vast intelligence.

This is not just being outspoken but is as things are.
This offering of song that you have heard;
I pray you will find true understanding in your heart.

Having said this, he gave a detailed account [of Chipön's dream and commands]. Michen thought, "These words are true," and promised to come, saying, "Well then! According to the proverbs of the world:

> *A great man,* * *a great mountain, a great lake, these three*
> *Should best remain properly in their place, without budging.*
>
> *If consumed by all the important political and secular obligations,*
> *The great chieftain will be taken away to the border lands.*
>
> *If the tremors of Meru are many,*
> *The nations and cities will be leveled.*
>
> *If the lake wells up to overflow its banks,*
> *The land will be torn with crevices.*

Unlike that, this is the cause for the political condition in the six tribes of Ling

---

* (Tib. *mi chen*). A pun on Michen's name.

to be stable. If the heads of the people of White Ling are to be elevated, if the honor of the name of the Mukpo tribe is to be famed, then I will go!"

He carefully examined the inner meaning of the contents of the letter that had been presented to him. He thought, "The dream I had last evening and the contents of Chipön's letter are secretly the same. In general, concerning King Uncle Chipön:

> Although the sun is warm, it's difficult for him to be
> overheated.
> Although the wind[158] is frigid, it's difficult for him to be
> chilled.
> Unless words have great meaning, they will not escape his
> mouth.
> Unless there is a point to his actions, he will not resolve his
> mind.

This could be a measure of great importance." Reflecting upon that he then said, "Today I must go. Let several of my servants also prepare to depart with me."

In a moment, the saddle and saddle blanket were placed upon his best riding horse, Gawa Trazur [Bright Blaze], along with the crupper and bridle. Tightening the girth straps, his four-square bodily presence could overwhelm the enemies of the four directions. All at once, the four parts to his wooden saddle frame could quell the four continents. Like the glorious dralas faring forth from their nests,[159] the chieftain, accompanied by eight servants, departed for Tratöd [Upper Falcon Valley].

[Kyalo Tönpa receives his letter.]

Likewise, back at the six highland slopes of Nelchag, Tönpa Gyaltsen of Kyalo* was sleeping inside of his great yak-hair tent called Tingshog Gung-gu [Azure Nine-Panels]. He dreamed that a white man wearing a silken turban appeared and said, "I am the *upāsaka* Gyogchen Dongra [Great Cannon Face]." He held in his hand a golden tray studded with jewels and he rode a divine yak called Gang-ri Gyingshei [Snow Mountain Majestic Knowledge]. He said "Wealthy Kyalo, don't sleep, but look outside! If you listen to the good news outside your door your own

---

* The wealthy Kyalo Tönpa Gyaltsen was Queen Drugmo's father and another great Elder of Ling.

wishes come true. It's up to you whether White Ling comes to turmoil or delight."

As soon as Tönpa Gyaltsen awoke from his dream, the guard dog,[160] Ngampa Drugdrak [Ferocious Roaring Dragon], began howling loudly like a leopard in its prime. Lunging and pulling his chain, he whipped around like a circling slingshot. Tönpa Gyaltsen quickly arose and called for his servant Dega Lhazang [Noble Divine Favorite of the People]. Looking outdoors, he saw that a messenger from Trakhar had arrived. He thought, "I wonder what news he's bringing? According to my dream, it's probably not bad."

He went inside, and at the fire-pit tea stove the fire naturally flared up on its own, and the tea began to boil of its own accord. Then Kyalo thought, "The way in which this red fire blazes, and the way in which this u-zi tea boils, shows that my dream and the auspicious connection of good fortune are in harmony. I am certain that this messenger brings with him the sweet sound of some good news."

> *If you see a snow lion's turquoise mane,*
> *Of course his six powers are complete.*
> *If you see the head of a makara,*
> *Of course you know that his body is adorned with a paisley design.*[161]

Thinking in this way, Kyalo questioned the messenger. The messenger made his report in detail, explaining how the prophecy had come to Chipön, how White Ling must gather together, and how, since Michen and Kyalo were the leaders of the auspicious connection, they had no choice but to meet together.[162] Then Kyalo answered, "Since this is so important, even though I am an old man, to reverse the command of His Majesty the King is like trying to hold back a landslide. When swift action is needed, it is meaningless for a servant to act like a boss." Saying that, as soon as the sky was bright, he mounted the steed Gugya Rachig [Select Unicorn] and together with two servants departed for Tratöd.

[The four leaders gather and perform ceremonies, and Chipön gives a long auspicious speech.]

Then, on the thirteenth day, the guru possessing blessings, Siddha Thangtong Gyalpo; the possessor of mighty activity, Michen Gyalwa'i Lhundrub; the possessor of the wealth of merit, Tönpa Gyaltsen; the possessor of vast intelligence, Chief Rongtsha Tragen—the guru and chieftains, these four, who are the four gates to enlightened activity, convened in the great assembly hall Tashi Ködlek [Auspicious Elegance] in Yudrug Gying Dzong.

They came together, sitting according to the order of precedence, and the banquet was properly set before them. They enjoyed fine tea and liquor. There were plates of the three sweets and numerous portions of meats and soft sweet cheese abundantly and respectfully served. As a symbol of their auspicious connection, King Chipön, Uncle of the Mukpo clan, presented to the guru and the two chieftains three scarves called Nyinmo Delek [Auspicious-by-Day], Tashi Drug Gorkha Tröd [Auspicious Intertwined Dragons], and Padma Lentsar Tongden [One-Thousand-Lotus-Fringed]. He offered before them a golden-tipped vajra and bell made from magical sky-meteorite metal, three bolts of royal brocade silk with the design of golden fish and dragons, and a golden vessel filled with ghee. Then Chipön said, "Siddha, guide of beings of the three realms; Chief who is exalted by strength gained through merit; Tönpa, whose wealth is the fruition of accumulated generosity: you who have the high-ranking seats of honor of the divine lineage, and those of you who are seated here, please listen. Let me briefly explain to you now by way of word, meaning, and song, these three, the reason and specific purpose for which you have come here.

In the sky above, the constellations are excellent and the eight-spoked wheel of interdependence* is pitched and, on the earth, the seats of happiness and prosperity are arranged like an auspicious eight-petaled lotus. In between, the excellent qualities of the great blessings that arise from the enlightened religious and secular activities are the curtains adorned with the eight auspicious symbols. With these auspicious words I begin.

Now, I could speak of many subjects here today for, according to ancient proverbs:

> *The way the outer vessel, the world, has come together;*
> *The modes of liberation of the inner inhabitants, sentient beings;*
> *The source of the Rare and Precious Three Jewels;*
> *The myths of the ancestral lineages,*

And so forth. Indeed, if I spoke of these many subjects here it would be like the ancient proverbs that say:

---

* When one gazes up into the heavens the sky appears to be like an eight-spoked wheel based on the geomancy of the mountains that reach into the sky. This indicates that the area has these signs of auspiciousness.

If the sky is vast, the stars are countless;
If the earth is vast, the six grains are countless;
If someone's knowledge is profound, they are a treasure of
    information.
The cosmic snow mountain of Kailash
Is the source of the great rivers.
This unmistaken paternal lineage of the [Mukpo] Dong
Is the source of the excellent ancient legends.

Although I am not claiming greatness, indeed these accounts of how the cosmos came to be are great and lengthy; as the proverb goes:

Declaring the greatness of the statue of divine Jowo
Would be like putting a lighted lamp up to the exalted umbrella of
    the sun.

In the same way lofty explanations are not necessary when addressing people of such high stations as all of you, gurus and chieftains. The rest who are gathered here today, seem in my eyes to be full of the same luck as those who learn noble qualities in monasteries. I'm an old man who is wasting your time. As the proverb goes:

No need to tell you what you already know.
No need to point out what you already see.

So now let me with auspicious words lay out the main body of this speech.

There must be a great purpose for a great mountain to shake.
There must be a great purpose to roll out the carpet of the great plain.

Yesterday, at dawn on the eighth day of the waxing moon, I dreamed about a prophecy so amazing that it seemed impossible such a thing could occur in this world between heaven and earth. If I explain it now, it would be like the proverb:

Anything is possible to dream in the spring;
Anything can grow in the summer fields.

On the other hand if I keep it secret, I could be punished by the imperial gods or the six tribes of Ling could be shrouded by obstacles and miss this chance, so perhaps I would regret such a decision. Now, with the clairvoyance of the all-knowing lama, the decisiveness of the vastly intelligent chieftain, and the merit of the wealthy patron, we must conduct a careful and detailed examination of the situation.

You who are seated above, in your presence, Chieftain and Lama, 'singing with empty words and paying homage with empty hands' is no way to show due respect to the greatness of this auspicious occasion. It is, for example, like the proverb:

> Although the yellow myrobalan seems small, it is still one of the six
> medicinal herbs.
> Although the flowers seem insignificant, they are still objects for
> offering."

So that it would not be empty, in the space in front of the great Mahāsiddha he placed the golden bell and a vajra made from magical sky-meteorite metal. In front of Michen he placed the three bolts of golden yellow dragon brocade. In front of Kyalo Tönpa he placed a golden vessel filled with ghee. Then, as a symbol of auspicious connection, he offered each one of them a scarf of good fortune.

Finally, he said, "It is my honor to bestow the gift of this melodious song on this auspicious occasion and to request the elegance of your attention. I ask the aristocracy of the elders who are seated here to kindly pay heed and attentively listen to this melodious song of offering."

Then Chipön interpreted the prophecy in his dream, raising the song that set out the reason for the gathering of the assembly of White Ling.

> The song begins with Lu Ala.
> Thala is the melody of the song.
> May the buddha, dharma, and sangha,
> Three Supreme Jewels, lead this song
> So that pure intentions may accord with the dharma.
> Today the astrological alignment is excellent.
> Even the royal parasol of the sun is cheerful and warm.
> On earth the time is right, for the fortunate connections have
>   come together.
> The auspicious ranks of guests are full of splendor.
> The song delights with joy and bliss!
> In case you don't recognize this song,

It is this uncle's song called Long-Lasting Bliss and
    Happiness.*

The sunlight of the three months of summer lasts long.
The happiness of the six tribes of White Ling lasts long.
The pleasure derived from Chipön's song lasts long.
From this comes the name of the song, Long-Lasting Bliss
    and Happiness.

In case you don't recognize this land,
These are the three upper slopes adorned with pure white
    snow;
This is the reason that the faces of the gods are white.
The three midsections of the valleys are adorned with striated
    slate rocks;
This is the reason the six upper districts flourish.
The three lower valleys are adorned by the pasture lands of
    the nāgas;
This is the reason the grazing herds increase and prosper.
The point of what I have to say is this:
You of the superior rank who sits aloft on the golden throne,
Gracious Guru, who gives guidance, please listen.
To the right, upon the silver throne,
Michen Gyalwa'i Lhundrub, listen.
To the left, upon a stack of brocade cushions,
Tönpa Gyaltsen of Kyalo, listen.
Yesterday, on the eighth day in the predawn,
In the course of the sleep of luminosity,
The sun shone on the peak of Magyal Pomra Mountain.
I dreamed that the sun rays revealed Tibet.
A vajra appeared in the center of the sun rays,
I dreamed that it descended onto the peak of Kyigyal
    Mountain
And that the thirteen gods of the chase
Were prostrating on the plain of Dalung.

---

* (Tib. *bde legs skyid ring mo*).

I dreamed that from Mönlam La
Waxed the silver moon.
I dreamed that from the golden pass of the Dru Valley
Blazed the ornament of the conch-colored star.*
I dreamed that the younger brother Senglön held in his right
    hand
A golden parasol with a handle of gold.
The top was white with red and green rainbow stripes,
And the four edges were covered with fringe.
Was this a positive dream or a negative dream?
Then, in the course of the sleep of luminosity,
A guru wearing the lotus hat riding upon a snow lion appeared.
He wielded a vajra and khaṭvāṇga in his hands.
He was led by a ḍākinī wearing bone ornaments.
She was red, holding a curved vajra blade and a skull.
In unison, they spoke to me and said,
"In the first month of summer, on the eighth day in the predawn,
The dream that you had was not negative, it was positive.
On the thirteenth there should be a gathering of the
    aristocracy.
On the eighth midsummer day until the fifteenth,
The six districts should gather in the divine land of Ma,
Perform a feast, a prosperity ritual, a smoke offering, and
    protector offering prayers.
Magnify the auspicious connection with song and dance!
Hurry, hurry!" They repeated this nine times.
Then I dreamed that they vanished into the southwestern sky.
Can dreams be trusted?
If so, now we must hurry!

When the foundation of the highest of castles is to be placed,
It is necessary to build a firm basis.

When the patterns of the irrigation ditches around the field are to be dug,
It is necessary to bring up the essence of the earth.

---

* (Tib. *dung gi skar*). Venus, "the morning star."

When the welding salt of a keen blacksmith is pounded in,
The knife must be sharp and strong.

When you are to cut out the pattern for comfortable clothes,
They must suit the body well.

Quickly consider what must be done.
Through hearing this song,
May the path of your ears bring you happiness and joy.
Consider the fruition of the meaning and deliver your
answer.
May this divine aristocratic assembly gathered here keep all of
this in mind.

[Thangtong Gyalpo lends his voice, confirming their understanding of the prophecy.]

Thus having sung, the Mahāsiddha Thangtong Gyalpo smiled and said, "Oh good! According to what I, this old monk, understand:

The way the royal parasol of the sun moves,
There is no way it could not rise at dawn.
I don't think it matters whether or not you see the morning star.

The way the mist envelops the lofty snow-patterned mountains,
There is no way that a pleasant rain could not fall.
I don't think it matters if the turquoise dragon roars or not.

The way the prophecies come from the imperial gods,
There is no way the auspicious connection will not come
together.
I don't think we need to rely on my omniscience as guru.

Nevertheless we should make an exception and closely examine the important matter of this prophecy.

If a ruler of a great district is distracted,
Rumors will run rife through the kingdom.

Half of the people will be divided by litigation and half of the
districts will be exiled.

If the scouts on the three passes are distracted,
Then even thorn bushes will rise up as enemies and
Half of the horses will be ripped to a bloody pulp.

If the mind of a great meditator is distracted,
Then phantasmic irruptions of gods and demons will go wild and
The meditator's empty cave will be filled with armies.[163]

It is just as these proverbs state." Then, having said that it is necessary to care-fully analyze the situation at this time, he entered a meditative state for a moment and again he spoke.

"That golden hat on the three lofty peaks of the mountains,
Except for the sun's rays, who else could place it there?
That cuckoo from the heartland of Mön in the south,*
Except for the three months of summer, when should his call
resound?

This dream in which the three excellencies converge, except for an auspicious connection, why would it be dreamed?

Today, this assembly has received such good news! Even if the hills and valleys are filled with gold, for a renunciate yogi like me it makes no difference. But today's good news has brought me a feeling of great joy." To express his feelings, Thangtong Gyalpo then sang this song, which deciphered the prophecy in the dream:

OM Although dharmadhātu is unborn,
ĀH Because of unobstructed love for beings,
HŪM I shall carefully decipher the prophecy about the
    incarnation.[164]
Listen, lord of the people of White Ling.
You are of the ancestral lineage of the gods of clear light,

---

* *Mön* may refer to Bhutan, Sikkim, or Nepal, or it may just be a general reference to southern borderlands that have a tropical climate.

The lineage of the mahāsiddhas,
And the lineage of the clever-minded learned ones.
Therefore, your dream is not deluded.

The sun rising from the peak of Magyal Mountain
And the light rays that reveal the land of Ling
Are a sign that the sun of wisdom and compassion
Will enrich the land of Ling with buddha activity.
That a golden vajra emanated from that
And descended on the peak of Kyigyal Mountain
Is a sign that a being who came from the divine
Will take birth on the apex of the crown of the head.
The thirteen gods of the chase making prostrations
Is a sign that they will come to greet the being who will be a
     protector of the land of Tibet.
The moon rising over Mönlam La
Is a sign that the elder uncle is a wrathful emanation.[165]
The sparkling morning star that ornaments the Ser La
Is a sign of the deeds of the Minister Denma.
Its rainbow shaft that penetrates Mount Gedzo
Is a sign that Gesar's father will emerge from the nyen.
Its cord of light that extends into Mapham Lake
Is a sign that his mother will emerge from the nāgas.
The silk umbrella held in the hand of Senglön
Is a sign that Senglön will be his earthly father.
The white crown of the parasol is a sign of pacifying buddha
     activity.
The red rainbow color is a sign of overcoming the three
     realms.
The green is a sign of wrathful buddha activity.
The yellow fringe is a sign of enriching the ten directions.
The golden handle of the parasol
Is a sign that his benefit for beings will be more valuable than
     gold.
That it completely covers the four directions
Is a sign that the four border countries will be quelled
     through splendor.
It is a sign that the four enemies will be stamped out and

That the wealth of the borderlands will be brought home
And the borderland demons will be bound by oath.
Not only that, but the guru, the masters,
And the ḍākinī Vajravārāhī;
If whatever they say is taken to heart,
Then White Ling and its pure aristocracy
Is a sign that among the eighteen kingdoms of our equals
We shall achieve a status that exceeds the sky.
That our mighty power will be unrivaled
Is a sign that our sovereignty will expand to quell all with our
    splendor.
So let's go now, don't blunder, but quickly act;
Try your best and don't fail!
Prepare now to convene the assembly of White Ling.
Hereafter, from today onward,
Whatever you wish will be accomplished in accordance with
    dharma.
This song of splendid auspiciousness,
May those of you seated here in this assembly, keep it in your
    hearts.[166]

Thus he sang. Then Michen Gyalwa'i Lhundrub felt overwhelmed with joy and exclaimed, "I'm so pleased! Furthermore, to hear news like this probably means that merit has been accumulated in previous lives. Could this even be true? Yet, could the merit that comes from the power of karma be enough to handle this? I fear not, for to quote from the proverbs of the people:

> *Without faith, blessings are difficult,*
> *Without merit, riches are difficult,*
> *Without farming, harvests are difficult,*
> *Without exertion, accomplishing a goal is difficult.*

This dream is probably a prophecy, and we need to take up whatever was said in it with vigor and enthusiasm. According to Chipön's dream and the prophecy of the Siddha, we should carefully consider and discuss what we need for the coming assembly of the six tribes of Ling. Then, we should supplicate and make offerings to the dralas in the Kaling Temple in Ma, perform prosperity practices and feast offerings, and, all together, celebrate this auspicious connection. Whatever preliminary rituals are necessary in order to accomplish our objective should be properly arranged. I think it is very important that we get to work on this with haste."

Then Kyalo also said, "Michen is right! There is little need for me to try to analyze the Siddha's prophecy any further. However we view the blessings of the divine gurus and the prophecies of the mother ḍākinīs, it is certain that their meaning is extremely important. Therefore you nobles of White Ling, great gathering of god-like mighty warriors and lineages of father and uncle family lines like the great Mount Meru, it is essential, concerning this great secular matter, that all of you do as the proverb states:

> *Those with minds should share your intelligence;*
> *Those who are wise should exercise discernment.*
> *Issues should be brought to the table;*
> *Final decisions should be made face to face."*

They continued for the rest of that morning and the next day with verbal consensus, mental concurrence, and equality of intention.

[The nobility of Ling and the greater masses of Ling gather.]

That second morning, between predawn and dawn they went to the valley entrance called Nyida Khatröd, and the inhabitants of Upper and Lower Ling gathered in a great assembly at Dephu Drug.* That great encampment had so many white tents pitched that it resembled a field of sparkling white wild flowers. The pillars of smoke competed with the southern clouds. The people's countenances were lustrous, their hats and clothes were in perfect order. It was like a field of multicolored flowers in the three months of summer. The horses' coats were lustrous and their gaits synchronized, like the ripening of the six grains in the three months of autumn. All of the tents were lined up in proper order. In the center the most special main tent was pitched, resembling a snow mountain whose pinnacle was studded with a golden hue like that of the rising sun. Within it they arranged a golden and silver throne, spread out tiger- and leopard-skin cushions, and arranged rows of brocade silk and silken cloth.

The rays of the sun pervaded all the mountains as the white conch of the civil law was blown, resounding far and wide. The leader Anu Zigphen of Tag-rong

---

* Place of the upper six districts.

presided over the Elder Lineage, which resembled a gathering of tigers with elegant coats. The Leader of a Hundred Sergyi Argham presided over the Middle Lineage, which resembled a perfect string of pearls, and the leader Chölu Darphen of Bumpa presided over the Cadet Lineage, which resembled a gathering of superlative arrows. Coming together they went inside the official tent, called Tongwa Kunmön [Fills with Admiration], where the capable mediator Dardzom of Muchang raised this song establishing the order of precedence of the assembly:

[A song by the mediator Dardzom calling the roll of the leaders of Ling and establishing the order or precedence.][167]

> The song begins with Lu Ala,
> Thala is the melody of the song.
> In the castle of rainbows, clouds, and light,
> Dwells the genyen spirit Dorje Luphen.
>
> Today for these auspicious seated ranks
> May the azure sky above be free from raging storms.
> Here in the gathering of Kyalo's celebration it is as the proverb goes:
>
> *The main aim in the monastery is*
> *More than performing one hundred great deeds.*
> *Just make sure you know your proper station.*
>
> You are high-ranking nobles
> Who sit in the row above.
> So, for you, it is not necessary to polish the white conch.
>
> Nevertheless, this younger generation of White Ling
> Must listen carefully and try to understand these proverbs.
>
> On the imperial level, the golden throne of the highest rank,
> The Guru who guides the Mahāsiddha is seated.
> On the silver throne that is placed to the right,
> Chipön Rongtsha Tragen is seated.
> Upon the beautiful conch throne that is placed to the left,
> Michen Gyalwa'i Lhundrub is seated.
> In the front row on the sandalwood throne,

Leader of a Hundred Sergyi Argham is seated.
On a soft cushion patterned brightly like the striped skin of a tigress,
Chief Tag-rong Zigphen is seated.
On a cushion spotted like the skin of a leopard,
The Mazhi [Four-Mothered] Chief Trogyal is seated.
On a comfortably arranged stack of round double cushions of
    panther skins,
The Leader of One Thousand [Chiliarch] Treltsei Shemchog
    [Supreme Knowledge], is seated.
Below on the righthand side, on a double brocade cushion,
Kyemchog Tharpa of Yadei is seated.
Below on the lefthand side, on a double brocade cushion,
Anu Chinglön Sengtren is seated.
In the middle, on a carpet,
Yuyag Gönpo Tongthub is seated.
To his left and right on double panther-skin cushions
Dongtsen, Darphen, and Ah-Gyal are seated.
In the next row, farther back on the right,
Pasel Lhashei Karpo is seated.
And to the left,
Lower Officer Nyibum of Serpa is seated.
Seated in front of the rows of the powerful Ga and the
    wealthy Dru clans are
Chökyong Bernag of Gadei and
Tönpa Gyaltsen of Kyalo.

On the seat of the leader of the thousands of inhabitants of
    the Denma clan
Sits the young minister, Maternal Uncle Jangtra.
Seated above is the representative of thousands of subjects,
Berkar Tharpa Gyaltsen.

After that, from the mighty warriors on down to the
Leaders of ten thousand, one thousand, one hundred, and ten,
Let the dignitaries and the elders be seated at the head of
    their rows,
And the humble and the young together below.
The reason for this order is as the proverb states:

> *A human being is distinguished by his head, neck, and shoulders,*
>   *these three;*
> *Herd beasts have horns, a back and a front, these three;*
> *The earth has mountains, plains, and geographic features, these three;*
> *Isn't that so?*

According to the rules of the monasteries, the elders are respected and the youngsters listen to them. Today, relax and sit quietly, for:

> *If there is a transgression of the ethical code,*
> *It is a matter of the dharma law of the guru.*
> *If there is a transgression of the hierarchy,*
> *It is a matter of the secular law of the chieftains.*

May the assembly gathered here in ranks listen and do as directed!

By that time, all the ranks, without any commotion, had quietly taken their seats. Then the u-zi tea was served from wooden buckets. Measures of tsampa* were served from wooden vessels. Drinks of beer† were served in pots. Quarters of marbled yak meat were served. Mounds of rich thüd were served all around. Plates containing the three sweets such as fruits and so forth were served. The servings and offerings were carefully apportioned to the ranks of this great celebration. Then, Uncle Chipön stood up at the head of the great main row.

[Chipön's speech to the greater assembly:]

"Oh, today the alignment of the constellations in the sky is an excellent omen and on earth the queen of the four seasons accommodates everything. In between, here all the people gathered are healthy, happy, and full of good fortune. This is a great gathering of the nobility of the six white tribes, starting from the guru, the leaders of men, the clergy,‡ and the inhabitants of the districts, the mighty, the

---

* *Tsampa* is roasted barley flour.

† (Tib. *skyems pa chang*). Tibetan *chang* is almost always beer, however the word can refer to any alcoholic beverage.

‡ Those who live in the monastery.

wealthy, and the youthful, these three, down to the humble leader of ten. In this assembly place of so many people, we must extensively and profoundly discuss all possible activities and the future of this extremely important endeavor. Accordingly, the prophesying of the gurus, the deliberations of the leaders of men, the advice of the elder generation, the bright intelligence of the youths in their prime, all must put forth their ideas now without reservation, rather than:

> *Saying one thing, while thinking another.*
> *Don't pound the black poison ax of selfishness*
> *On the solid gold boulder of our common welfare.*

Furthermore,

> *If you don't take three steps, a month's journey will never end.*
> *If you don't speak three words, there will be no outcome to a*
>   *discussion.*

I, Chipön, yesterday, in the predawn of the eighth day of the first month of summer, while dreaming, received several clear light prophecies. I myself must reach a decision about these prophecies for the general welfare of all:

> *When a lowly person's intelligence is limited,*
> *The great goal of the masses will be lost.*
>
> *When a mischievous horse is allowed to run free,*
> *The rider will be thrown to the ground.*
>
> *When three men are in perfect agreement,*
> *The laws of the land will be balanced.*
>
> *When the three hearthstones are put right,*
> *The hearth for the copper vessel will be stable.* *

---

* This refers to the way that tea is made in Tibet. The "foreheads" of three stones are placed in a tripod such that a pot can be balanced upon them. The nomads will then make a fire underneath, and this becomes their fire stove.

And so in keeping with these proverbs, the guru Thangtong Gyalpo, Michen Gyalwa'i Lhundrub, and Kyalo Tönpa Gyaltsen, these three, reached a harmonious decision and all the people were successfully gathered.

> *If innermost mind*[168] *is directed to the divine,*
> *The four successes will be more stable than a mountain.*
> *If the source of the waters is the snow mountain,*
> *It will flow until the end of the kalpa.*
> *If human nature originates from the Mukpo Dong,*
> *Then stability, splendor, and peace, these three, will converge.*
> *If mind's resolution originates from a prophecy,*
> *In the future there will be no regrets.*

I [Chipön] was thinking in this way when I asked Thangtong Gyalpo about my dream, and he had answered, 'This is not a dream, this is clear light. This is not delusive appearance, this is prophecy. This concerns the future of the black-haired Tibetans. This great purpose of the six tribes of Ling should not be ignored or postponed! This gathering of the six tribes must be excellent! Chipön must explain his dream, Kyalo must arrange the celebration, and Michen must make the final decision.' In keeping with that, since that is the way that my dream was and that is the way that Thangtong Gyalpo interpreted the prophecy, all of you in this great assembly who are of the nobility of the great tribes, listen with your ears, analyze, and keep this in mind!"

Thus he spoke. On this day, joined together like the sun and moon, the dream and the prophecy were conjoined as well. Then Chipön, the uncle of the Mukpo clan, sang this song:

> OṂ MAṆI PADME HŪṂ HRĪḤ
> Lu Ala is the unborn dharmadhātu.
> And Thala leads the unobstructed words of speech.
> I offer to the supreme teacher, the buddha worthy of
>   offerings,
> To the peaceful, passionless holy dharma,
> And to the sangha blazing with the glory of noble qualities.
> May the Three Supreme Jewels remain inseparably on the
>   crown of my head.[169]
> Today, in the castle of the dralas

May the three hundred and sixty mighty dralas[*]
Lead this cosmic song.[170]

If you don't recognize this place,
It is Nyida Khatröd in the land of Ma.
It is the place where both Ma and Yak valleys unite like the
    sun and moon,
Where the guru and chieftain are unified like the sun and
    moon,
Fathers and uncles are unified like garuḍas and dragons,
Sons and nephews unified like lions and tigers.
Here, where the two excellent ones are united like the sun
    and the moon,
The happiness and joy of the six tribes are united.

If you don't recognize the likes of me,
My father's conch lineage is the trunk of the tree.
On it blooms the golden flower of the son lineage;
Here the turquoise cuckoo of good news alights.

It seems that the dream, this sweet voice, and the meaning of
    the words originate there.
If you don't recognize a song such as this,
It is the good news that unites the noble Ling.
It is here that the dream and the prophecy are united.
At this great celebration we come together to sit in counsel,
The chiefs of the six tribes have gathered,
The people have gathered.
That being the case, right now it is time for the story.
Greetings, great gathering of the districts, listen!
The day before yesterday, on the eighth day of the waxing
    moon,
In the course of predawn luminosity,
The sun rose on the peak of Magyal Pomra.
There, the light of a golden vajra

---

[*] Refers to the drala retinue of the drala Nyentag Marpo.

Descended on the peak of Kyigyal Mountain.
On the plain of Dalung the gods of the chase assembled.
In Senglön's hand a golden parasol revolved.
I dreamed that its four edges were covered by fringe.
A rainbow shaft pierced Gedzo Mountain,
And light extended out to Lake Manasarovar.
From Mönlam La, the conch moon rose,
From Ser La, the morning star sparkled.
I dreamed that the sun, the moon, and the star, these three,
　　were united.

In the luminosity that occurred beforehand,
A lama, in the sky to the southwest,
Wearing a lotus hat came riding a lion,
Holding in his hands a vajra and a khaṭvāṅga
And guided by a woman who held a hooked knife and a skull.
In unison, they spoke these words to me.
"Great chief, sleep not, but awake.
The time of happiness in the six tribes is about to begin.
From the midsummer month on the fifteenth day of the
　　waxing moon,
Let the six tribes gather on the plain of Ma Valley
And offer a feast, drala and prosperity smoke offerings,
And joyfully celebrate with song and dance.
This will make a perfectly endowed auspicious connection."
I then dreamed that they went into the southwestern sky.
When I awakened my body and mind blazed with bliss and
　　warmth
And there was the Siddha Thangtong Gyalpo,
As if a boulder of pure gold had just rolled up to my doorstep.
I told him of my prophetic dream.
The good omen I told to these three, the guru, the chieftain,
　　and Michen.
They responded, "This dream is not bad, it is good."
The sun rising at the peak of Magyal Pomra
Is a sign that the gods are aligned with virtue.
The golden vajra descending on Kyigyal Mountain
Is a sign that the thirteen gods of the chase will come to greet

The emanation of the Buddha.
The golden parasol Senglön holds in his hand
Is a sign that he will hold the father lineage.[*]
The rainbow shaft piercing Gedzo and Lake Manasarovar
Is a sign that the father will be a nyen and the mother a
    nāginī.
That he is to be born the king of the Masang family[171]
Is a sign that he will suppress the four directions with his
    splendor.
Furthermore, if the instructions of the Lotus-Born Guru
And the ḍākinī Vajravārāhī are taken up,
Then White Ling's plans will be accomplished.
Therefore, all of you in this diverse assembly,
Having gathered here today for the great political goals of Ling,
Should take this golden key of our common objective
And place it in the hand of the one with sharp mindfulness
    and discrimination.

The general political goals,
Like a medicinal bush,
Will stimulate the minds of the wise ones.

If called, of course there is an answer.
If questioned, keep an open mind.

If fog does not clear the foothills,
The paths to the valley will not be open.
If gentle rains do not fall from the sky,
The six grains will not mature on the vast plains.

If the many don't offer up their opinions,
The learned will not come to resolution.

If a horse is not primed for a race,
The fastest steed will never get the ribbon.

---

[*] Senglön is destined to be the father of the future Gesar.

Therefore, each man's every thought should be revealed
And the lineage of fathers and uncles should finally decide.
Entrust your innermost mind to the Three Precious Jewels.
Keep this in your thoughts, great tribes of Ling!

Thus he sang and all of the members of the nobility in the assembly went on
and on with their discussions, like the proverb:

Each man, his own song; each bird, its own voice.

They became of one mind concerning their common future goal, and Gyalwa'i
Lhundrub said, "Today, there is no one left who has any doubt about the dream of
Chipön and the prophecy of the Mahāsiddha. As in the proverbs:

*Although the stars are greater in number, it is the moon which
    dispels the darkness.*
*Although the breadth of the valley is great, it is the bridge that
    brings the guests.*
*Although the reach of the river is long, the sovereignty of the ferry is
    greater.*

*The minds of men and the minds of gods are in harmony, so let the
    gods decide.*
If the minds of one hundred men are in harmony,
It is like the synchronized gait of one hundred horses.

In accord with yesterday's dream and prophecy, starting on the day of the waxing moon* in midsummer, let each of the inhabitants of Upper and Lower Ling pack
up their encampments and move them to here. From the eight golden provinces of
Upper Ling to the group of ruddy Ta'u people and from the eighteen great wings[†]
of Tag-rong to the tribe of Karnak Tongkor, all must gather here on the plain of Ma
Valley."

---

* The first day of a lunar month (Tib. *yar tshes*).

† Literally, "provinces" or "tribes."

[Michen distributes responsibility for performing the rituals of the great celebration among the community.]

As for the offering rituals to the Three Jewels and the Three Roots, the feast offering, and lofty praise to the dralas, juniper smoke offerings, protector supplications, summoning, accomplishing prosperity rituals, and the songs and dances of the celebration of auspicious connection and so forth, the individual duties and responsibilities for performing these ceremonies were delineated by song, sung with the melody known as Overwhelming the Great Gathering with Splendor,* by Michen Gyalwa'i Lhundrub.

> E the song is as vast as the space of the sky of existence.
> Thala is the unobstructed ground of the words.
> This is the land of Ling in Dokham greater Tibet.
> If you don't recognize it by name,
> It is Nyida Khatröd of Ling.
>
> Today, in this huge assembly, this ruddy crowd,
> From Kham, Amdo, and Ü-Tsang in central Tibet in the land
>   of four rivers,[172]
> From the land of the six ridges,[173] known to all,
> Gurus, leaders of men, nobles,
> And the clergy and laity of this great province, listen here.
> Today, because of a serendipitous natural connection,
> Although of many ranks, you are of one mind.
> Entrust your innermost mind to the Rare and Precious Three
>   Jewels
> And by listening, come to a decision.
>
> *The sky must indeed be a great vast pervasive covering,*
> *For the sun and moon dispel the darkness in all four continents.*[174]
> *A clear mind must be stable at the root,*
> *For the holy dharma, explained to the whole world, has spread here*
> *   in Tibet.*

---

* (Tib. *khrom chen zil gnon*).

Indeed the six tribes are broad and vast,
Like the Siddha and Chief, they are of one mind.

Now according to the meaning of the prophecy and the
  dreams.[175]
On the first day of the midsummer month, let us gather
The nobles of the assembly of White Ling
On the plain of Ma Valley.
Since you, Kyalo Tönpa Gyaltsen,
Are the patron possessing great merit,
You will sponsor this celebration.
All the gurus and siddhas
Will offer smoke, invoke and praise the dralas.

Michen, Zigphen, and Tharpa, make three,
Chipön, Trogyal, and Sengtren, make six,
Gyapön, Treltsei, and Yuyag, make nine,
Dongtsen, Margye, Darphen, and
Nyima Gyaltsen, these thirteen,
Representing the lands of Do, Ling, and Kham, these three,
And all the subjects with their horses must gather.
Likewise, bring along materials for the grain offering, the
  smoke offering, and the select offering.
And bring the windhorse flags, longevity arrow, and
  mountain offerings,
Armor, offering trophies for protectors, and animals saved
  from slaughter.[176]
Suit the mounted men with hats, clothes, and the six
  ornaments,
Together with helmets and shining armor.
The stallions should be well prepared in grooming and gait.
Likewise, the saddle, saddle blanket, and bridal ornaments
  should be well arranged.
Garza, Gyaza, Rongza, these three,
Ragza, Driza, and Draza
Dartsho, Chötrön, and Sönam, these women,
Peldzom, Derge, Yangzang, and so forth,
These are the thirteen ladies, mothers and aunts.

While the heroes dance, these heroines sing,
And a feast will be performed to promote the auspicious
 connection.

Make this assembly so great that
Even the sun and moon won't dare to circle above,
Mount Meru won't rest in the plain,
And demonic forces will be unable to bear it!
From the bottom of their hearts, the vindictive enemies will
 shrink in terror.
Your relatives will be filled with pride.
Prepare the auspicious connection and
Ensure that Ling will be undaunted by the enemies of the
 four directions.
Whatever this great human lineage is capable of doing,
Let this fame spread across a thousand districts.
If any individual does not publicize this,
Then he will be interrogated by the two laws.[177]
Here in this great assembly of the gathering of Ling,
Those of the nobility and the commoners must bear this in
 mind!

Having thus spoken, accordingly, this decree was transcribed and copies were distributed. The Guru, Chief, and the multitudes who gathered for this great assembly took the decree to heart and made their plans. Their hearts in agreement and minds in accord to accomplish the promise, they each dispersed to their own place.

CHAPTER THREE

Following the command of Master Lotus
The divine child Thöpa Gawa,
In order to conquer both the Hor and Düd,[178]
Took an oath to come to the land of humans.

IN THE CENTER OF TIBET, in the core of the six ranges, this divine child Thöpa Gawa was to become the eliminator of misery caused by demons and rākṣasas, the destined savior of the black-haired Tibetans, the yoke upon the Yellow Hor, and the one to subdue the evil Düd. Knowing that he must come as the divine prince of the Bumpa* clan, based on his previously generated bodhicitta, the time had come for him to tame the beings of his destiny. From the Lotus Light Palace of Cāmara, King Lotus Skull Garland opened the mandala of the Fearsome Great Glorious Hayagrīva. Here, seated in rows at the feast, were one hundred and eight vidyādharas, one hundred and eight ḍākas, and one hundred and eight ḍākinīs, including the vidyādhara of the gods, the Blooming Lotus Who Quells Existence with Splendor, and Thöpa Gawa, who was the one destined to tame the barbarians dwelling at the borderlands of the snow land of Tibet.

In order to invoke the timely samaya of Thöpa Gawa and the seventy-five glorious protectors,† the thirteen gods of the chase who guard Tibet, the Masang who are among the four classes of the great nyen, and the twenty-one genyen, along

---

* This is another name for the Mukpo clan.

† (Tib. *dpal mgon bdun cu rtsa gnyis*). These are Bön gods, native Tibetan deities.

with the vast assembly of gods and nāgas who take delight in aligning with virtue, he [Padmasambhava] sang this dohā proclaiming the crucial point of the vow they were to take.

[Padmasambhava enjoins Thöpa Gawa and a vast retinue of gods and spirits to go to Tibet to protect Buddhists from the attacks of demon kings.]

OM dharmapālas enact your samaya,
ĀH In the unborn empty dharmadhātu,
HŪM Compassionate dance magical emanation birth,
Vidyādhara Blossoming Display,* listen here!
Through the unsurpassable bodhicitta of the mahāyāna
And the not-to-be-transgressed vajra samaya,
The time has come to perform enlightened activity for the
    benefit of others.

In the great space dome[179] of the azure firmament,
The sun and the moon have no leisure to take their ease;
This makes it possible to have an east and west.
This is how the sunny and shady slopes got their names.[180]

Because of the increase and decrease of the external elements,
The grasses and medicinal herbs have no leisure to take their
    ease;
This makes it possible to have hot and cold.
This is how summer and winter got their names.

Because saṃsāric friends and enemies come from passion and
    aggression,
The people have no leisure to take their ease;
This makes it possible to have hope and fear.
This is how gods and demons got their names.

---

* This is the name that Thöpa Gawa is known by in heaven.

In the land of Tibet, the beings of the five degeneracies
Have no chance for happiness because of their previous karma.
But if you suppress the current circumstance of the Hor and
    the Düd,
Then you, Noble One, will benefit beings as a matter of course.

Therefore Vidyādhara Thöpa Gawa,
In order to guard those to be tamed in the land of Tibet,
Show them the self-nature of cause and effect.
In order to uplift the Supreme Three Jewels,
Go to the land of snow without delay.
All you gods of the chase and zodor, who guard those who are
    virtuous,
All you dralas stand by this man.
Wermas, keep company with his body.
Don't be idle! Support and befriend him without wavering.
Master the four enlightened activities.
Do not transgress your commitment. Samaya!

Then, child of the gods, Thöpa Gawa,
As the aspect of skillful means and compassion,
I will dispatch to accompany you now and in the future,
The *mudrā* of exaltation as your consort, samaya friends, and
    an assembly of heroines.*

Demolish the tangible enemies
At the four border regions and in the eighteen kingdoms,
Bind by oath the intangible demons and obstructing spirits,
Inspire those inclined to practice dharma,
Humble the sinners to remorsefully confess, and
Awaken recognition of cause and effect.
Don't be idle; don't be idle, son of noble family.
O dharma protectors and dralas who maintain virtue
And you child, keep this in your hearts.

---

* This references the companion ḍākinī who helps Gesar to be successful in conquering each
kingdom.

After he spoke, each of the guardians of virtue, the dralas, wermas, zodors, hunting gods, and tenmas individually took their oaths.

[Thöpa Gawa considers Padma's command, decides to obey, and frames his answer.][181]

Then the divine child Thöpa Gawa thought to himself, "Once the gracious *mahāguru*, who is the nature of the omniscient buddhas of the ten directions, has conferred his command, first of all, how can such a proclamation and samaya ever be opposed? Secondly, the benefit the guru brings to others also benefits himself." And, as the proverb goes:

> *All the fancy trappings*[182] *of saṃsāra are really just to put food on the*
> *   plate.*
> *When a boy is born, he benefits himself by working for others.*
> *When a horse is swift, he is victorious in the race.*
> *When a weapon is sharp, it cuts meat and crushes bones.*[183]

Thinking, "How could it not?" he said, "Oh yes, sir," and, as the proverb states:

> *When a guru speaks to disciples there's no talking back;*
> *The karma of those who do will ripen in hell for corrupting samaya.*
> *A worker never rebels against a master's command;*
> *Those that do end up in self-defeat, losing their necks and possessions.*
> *Shepherds cannot push a landslide back up the hill;*
> *If they could, their heads would crack.*

For as the proverbs tell us:

> *Without good reason, samaya must not be broken,*
> *Without benefit there is no reason to boast.*

"Although I have not broken your commands, O guru, nevertheless dear Chief, they seem heavy, for it is:

> *Like a tax laid on a beggar's son,*
> *Like the saddle bags heavily packed by your nephews*
> *In early spring when the cattle have no fat or strength.*[184]

In order to accomplish the great benefit of enlightened activity that you, Guru, command, I will require worldly support from humans, and spiritual blessings from the divine ones.[185] Just as:

> *Asses and deer depend on the mountain,*
> *And the great buck, the rack on his head.*
> *Otters and fish depend on the lake,*
> *And the undulating fish, their brows' dancing eyes.*[186]
> *The monastery depends on the guru,*
> *And the karmic result depends on his noble qualities.*
> *The soldier depends on the chieftain*
> *And his skills depend on the outer display.*

> *Though a boy is brave,*
> *He still needs a weapon to slay the enemy.*
> *Though the herd looks powerful,*
> *Whether or not a bull has the strength to carry burdens depends on*
> *   the grass.*
> *Even though empty words like the bark of a mastiff may be*
> *   impressive,*
> *There is no way they can please our loved ones.*
> *Even though empty-handed anger arises,*
> *There is no way this can kill the enemy.*[187]

Therefore:

> *The subjects below magnify the leader,*
> *Fine monks are an ornament to the guru,*
> *Good fortune is a catapult for wealth*
> *And weapons are what make the warrior capable.*

> *Since there is nothing left uncovered by the azure firmament*
> *The southern clouds have no need to be upset.*
> *Since there is nothing left unsupported by the earth's warmth,*
> *The zodor have no need to be jealous.*[188]

If my father, mother, paternal and maternal lineages, servants and subjects are not fully endowed, then even if I the divine child accept your command, don't you think it will be difficult to accomplish this noble goal?" In this way the divine child, Thöpa Gawa, presented his account of the situation and sang this song to Master Padmasambhava:

> The song begins with Ala.
> Thala shows the way the words are sung.
> From the unborn dharmadhātu pure land,
> Unobstructed five families of the victorious one, know me!
> The ignorance of the five poisons is pacified in its own
>   place.[189]
> May I meet self-awareness wisdom.
> Supremely kind unrivaled Lord of Dharma,
> Glorious Buddha Lotus Born,
> Do not lose your watchful eye of compassion
> But listen with your ear of great loving-kindness.
> I will work for the benefit of beings in the land of Tibet
> And tame the difficult to tame in the borderlands;
> No doubt there will be great hardship.
> I, the Powerful Blossoming Vidyādhara Nangsid Zilnön,
> Will stir saṃsāra from its quiver for the benefit of others.
>
> Nevertheless, if this single arrow of compassion
> Does not rely on the bow of skillful means,
> The target of the difficult to tame will be hard to hit.
> If the waves do not crest from the ocean below,
> Then pleasant rains will not fall from the azure firmament
>   above,
> Nor wet the deep soil of the pristine earth,
> And the six grains of the vast plain will not mature.
>
> If the flesh and blood of one's kind mother and father do not
>   come together,
> Then the divine child will never be transferred to a human
>   body.
> And if the good fortune of the black-haired Tibetans does
>   not coincide,
> Then I will not be able to benefit beings.

Even though an indestructible, deathless wisdom holder
Is not attached to blood, flesh, and bones,
The black-haired Tibetans can die for their patriarchal clan.
Although the southern clouds have no fear of falling
And the kingly eagle soars through the sky,
I need a father who descends from the nyen
And comes from an important family bloodline.

Self-awareness that fulfills all wishes
Is not attached to illusory wealth.
However, among the humans, who rival the high and
    disparage the low,
High rank and power depend on gaining material wealth.
A mountain rises up from dirt and stone,
While its height comes from its jutting crag.
I need a mother who comes from the nāgas,
Whose maternal lineage is endowed with wealth.

In this dharmatā of coemergent bliss and emptiness,
Although I am not attached to the deceptions of a worldly
    household,
I need a wife who is a wisdom ḍākinī,
Who is without the biased conduct of a worldly life,
And who is free from faults.

Although the six classes of sentient beings are not other than
This pure land of self-appearing great bliss,
In order to compassionately protect disciples,
I need a land that is endowed with splendor and glory.

In the magical wheel of self-radiance,
Although there is no shortage of ordinary attendants,
I need manifest subjects who will fully serve me
And accompany me when we tame the hordes of demons.

With the armor and weapons of patience and knowledge,
What need is there for an iron bow and sharp weapons?

But in order to purify the karmic ripening of the difficult to
    tame,
I will need a horse, and a warrior's armor and weapons.

If you cannot grant your blessings for this,
Although it is easy for me to make promises,
It will be difficult to fully accomplish the benefit of others.
Therefore Master, do not be idle; hold me with your
    compassion.

If there was any confusion in my song, I confess it.
If these have been idle words, I beg your forgiveness.

[Lotus Born seeks a birthplace for Gesar.][190]

Thus he sang, and Lotus Born sat leisurely contemplating for a moment, thinking, "Now, in order for this emanation to accomplish the welfare of beings, there is
no question that all these auspicious connections are indeed necessary for the spontaneous accomplishment of his enlightened activity." Then Padma first looked over
the snow land of Tibet, seeking, on behalf of the bodhisattva Thöpa Gawa, a zodor
endowed with glory and splendor and a place where the hero could reside.

In the upper* region of Ngari there are three areas: Purang, surrounded by
snow mountains; Gugey, surrounded by barren cliffs; and Mangyul, surrounded by
rivers. The four regions of central and western Tibet [Ü-Tsang] have the branch
areas of the right and central and the left and upper.

In the lower region† are the six mountain ranges of Mardza, Pombor, Tshawa,
Ngülda,‡ Markham, and Minyak. In that region are also four rivers,[191] along with
the four farms,[192] the four castles, and the four hidden lands. Although he gazed
over the entire land of Tibet, each one of these places was suitable in its own right
but still not perfect, as it was rare to find a single land endowed with every attribute
of the noble qualities.

Then he looked to see who would be the capable subjects inhabiting these

---

* (Tib. *stod*). Refers to the westerly direction. Ngari is the western section of Tibet.

† (Tib. *smad*). This refers to the easterly direction.

‡ Elsewhere this ridge is given as Zelmo.

places, and he saw that in the upper part [west] of Tibet, the region of Ngari, there were three lands divided into nine great wings: Purang, Mangyul, and Zangkar, these three; plus Li, Drusha, and Bey, making six; plus Zhangzhung and Upper and Lower Tri-te, making nine. Within the middle region, in the four regions of Ü-Tsang were: Tshalpa Gyama and Drigung, those two; and the twofold Yazang and Phagdru, making four altogether. In the northern land of Tag-lung there are the two: Lho and Drug. In Tsang there are the two, Lho and Ngari, plus Chang and Chumig, making four. Zhal-lu and Dramigung make two more, and between Ü-Tsang there was Yardrog. These are the thirteen myriarchies.[193] But even though Ü and Tsang and Ngari were dharma lands, they were not lands capable of sustaining the majestic splendor of the divine child Thöpa Gawa. These were not lands where taming of both form and formless wrathful beings would be likely to occur.

Below [to the east] are the six ridges of Dokham, which are divided into three sections: in Upper Ling were the regions known as the eight brothers of Ser; in Middle Ling, the six districts of Ombu; and in Lower Ling, the four divisions of Muchang.[194]

Within this area is the Prosperous Wealth Enclosure of the River Ma;[195] the country of Ling known as the Wishing Land of Ling; and the landmark of Dokham, called Kyidsö Nyima Rangshar [Self-Arising Sun of Happiness and Leisure].[196] Between Middle and Lower Ling is a land possessing all ten virtues: where authentic presence flourishes and where the subjects are capable of serving. It is there that the qualities of both place and subjects unite in perfection.

Gazing at the paternal and maternal families,[197] he saw the six clans of Tibet: in Drigung, the Kyura clan; in Taglung, the Gazi clan; in Sakya, the Khön clan; in Chögyal, the Nam clan; at Kyungpo, the Cha clan; and at Ne'u Dong, the divine, or Lha, clan. Although these were all highly regarded families, the land around them and the subjects to be tamed were incomplete and had not united.

From among the clans, Ga, Dru, Dong, these three; Sed, Mu, and Dong, these three; and Pel, Da, and Tra, these three, his paternal lineage was that of the Mukpo Dong. His father lineage was to descend from the Masang nyen. From among the three clans of Upper, Lower, and Middle Ling, the maternal lineage was that of the Muwa clan. The mother lineage was to descend from Changmoza,[198] the youngest of the three daughters of Dzagyal Dorje Phenchug. Changmoza had three sons:* her oldest son was King Chipön, the middle was King Trowo, and

---

* Literally, the Tibetan describes Changmoza as the mother of Chipön, Senglön, and Trothung, but we have taken this to refer to her as their matriarchal ancestor several generations back.

the youngest was King Senglön.[199] Senglön was of the family of great bodhisattvas with a peaceful heart and a gentle mind, excellent by nature and very open-
minded. His family lineage was excellent. The zodor here is the great, supreme
Nyen Gedzo, the principal protector of that family, and so, fitting to become Gesar's spiritual father.

However, his mother was not yet there, for she had to be of the race of the nāgas.
The nāgas are divided into four castes: the royal, the merchant, the brahman, and the
ordinary (that is, the commoners and the lower castes).[200] It would not do for his
mother to come from the caste of the common folk or the untouchables. Befitting
this role, from the kingdom of the pure nāgas, was the youngest of the daughters of the
nāga king, Tsugna Rinchen, called Metog Lhadzei [Flower Divine Beauty], a ḍākinī
who had attained the bodhisattva grounds. He knew that she would be summoned
by skillful means. His companion ḍākinī* from the pure land of Turquoise Leaf Array
would be an emanation of wrathful Tārā, called Light Rays of the Grimacing One,
and would manifest as the daughter of Kyalo.

The armor and weapons would be empowered by the nine brother dralas, and
the steed would be blessed by Hayagrīva, and so on. Thinking this, Padma knew all
would be spontaneously accomplished, and he then spoke, "Oh this is excellent.
Son of noble family, in order to tame those who are vicious and hard to tame in
the kingdom of the snow land of Tibet, I will reveal the details of the dependent
circumstances that will make all of this possible. Keep this in your mind!" He then
sang this song in the melody known as the Self-Proclamation of the Unobstructed
Vajra That Suppresses the Hosts of Māras through Splendor:

> OM Ami Dewanaye
> In the pure land of the five lights of self-appearance,
> Bhagavan, victorious one of the five families, know me.
> Purify the obscurations of the five poisons of all sentient
>   beings.
> May I encounter the self-nature of wisdom.
>
> Listen, son of fortunate family,
> Through your four activities of pacifying, enriching,
>   magnetizing, and destroying

---

* Gesar's wife will be an emanation of Tārā in wrathful form who will be born as the daughter of
the wealthy Kyalo Tönpa.

You must tame the field of disciples of the five degeneracies
With your companion acquired through the auspicious
    connection of skillful means,
In the place where you establish your kingdom with subjects
    capable of serving you,
Your father who created you, and the mother of your birth,
Your swift horse and solid armor,
Sharp weapons and brave warriors,
You will have the skillful means and compassion necessary to
    tame the difficult to tame.
If you cannot tame them through magnetizing and
    destroying,
Innumerable accumulations of negativities and bad karma
    will occur.
Then even the buddhas would have trouble saving them.
For this reason you must develop your army of dynamic
    power.
Therefore, divine child Thöpa Gawa,
In the three regions of upper Ngari
The highland is encircled by the holy dharma,
Gugey is circled by the swastika* shamans of Bön,
And Purang is encircled by the nectar of healing herbs.
These are the regions of upper Ngari.

In the middle land of Ü-Tsang are the four regions.
In Ü are the regions of the center, Üru, and the left, Yönru;
In Tsang the right region, Yeru, and the branch, Ru-lag;
These are the four regions of the land of Tibet.[201]

Below† are the six mountain ranges of Dokham:
Madza, Pombor, Tshawa,
Ngülda, Markham, and Minyak;
And the four rivers: Dri, Da, Ma, and Ngülchu.

---

* In the Tibetan religion known as Bön, the swastika, an ancient Indian symbol for the sun, is used roughly as an equivalent of the Buddhist and Hindu tantric scepter, the vajra.

† To the east.

These are the four rivers and six mountain ranges of Dokham;
These are the many regions of the land of Tibet.
Similarly, it is the place that can contain the activity of the
    Great Being [Gesar]
And the classes of the humans and the divine.
In the area of the Dri and Da [Rivers] in the Zelmo mountain
    ranges,[*]
In the Wishing Land of the enclosure of prosperity
Is the immutable landmark
That indicates all the signs of happiness and ease in the land
    of Tibet,
Kyidsö, where the upper country of happiness and the lower
    area of leisure[202] conjoin.

As the sign of the union of skillful means and wisdom,
There are two rocks resembling the feathers of an arrow;
That is a sign of the increasing buddha activity of both
    temporal and spiritual traditions.
There are two grassy meadows that resemble unfolded mats of
    wool;
That is a sign of perfecting the benefit of self and other.
There are two identical rivers resembling a pair;
That is a sign that all wishes will be spontaneously
    accomplished.
In front is Mönlam Dragkar [White Boulder Aspiration
    Prayer Mountain];[203]
That is the place where you will establish your kingdom called
    Wishing Ling.
Your incarnation will be revealed there
And your capable subjects' authentic presence will flourish.
These are the six tribes in the divine white districts.
Your father's lineage descends from the Masang nyen;
The paternal lineage is protected by the zodor Gedzo;
This is why it is the divine ancestral lineage.

---

[*] Zelmo is a mountain range in Dokham.

Your mother is one of the treasures of the nāgas,
The daughter of Tsugna Rinchen,
Nāginī Metog Lhadzei by name;
By skillful means she will be summoned to the land of Tibet
To be the supreme mother of your birth,
And Tārā will be invited from her pure land of Turquoise
     Leaf Array
To be your wisdom companion.

Your horse, equipped with all the armor of the dralas,
Will be an emanation of the Supreme Victorious Horse
     Hayagrīva.

Through various skillful means you will tame the
     wanderers.
So, Great One, do not allow your enlightened intent to
     weaken.
I will provide the auspicious connections for this enlightened
     activity to occur.
Don't be idle; don't be idle, child of noble family.

The cherished guru wearing the bordered skirt of ordination
Who does not shy from the practice of the teachings on sutra and
     tantra,
Must have the scholarship of someone with vast qualities.
Just wearing a four-sided robe will not earn him due respect.

Young warriors, youthful tigers in their prime, with ivory rings
     adorning their hair,
If they are not known for their courage,
Then they may as well break their sharp weapons on a stone,
For the fancy sword in its ornamental sheath can't think for itself.

The young maiden dressed in brocade silk, turquoise, and silver,
If she is not known for her good character,
Then the outer beauty of her in-law's home may be lost over a cup of
     tea or a glass of beer.
Just washing her face won't make her popular with those people.

Therefore divine child Thöpa Gawa,
In the region of the world known as Tibet,
When you, Great One, protect the welfare of beings,
The buddhas and bodhisattvas will be your personal
    guardians;
The yidams and ḍākinīs will stand behind you;
The dharmapāla protectors will be your companions;
The hunting gods and guardians of virtue will support your
    enlightened deeds.
Concerning your divine calling to guard the world,
I will gradually give the prophecies and the mandate to enact
    your deeds.

For the sake of the sentient beings at the borderlands of
    Tibet,
Don't let your compassion decline, O son of noble family.
In order to tame the evil forces of the five degeneracies,
Do not allow your strength to decline, O heart son.
Divine child hold this in your mind.

Thus he spoke, and then the divine child Thöpa Gawa, in order to place the kings of the dark side as well as their kingdoms in the state of buddhahood, generated the courage of the mind of enlightenment and thought: "Even if they secure in their minds but a single virtue, until they completely enter the path of awakening, I will remain patient with them even if they hack my heart into a thousand pieces. May it be so! O yes! Sublime and constant source of refuge, kind precious king of dharma, I the divine child Thöpa Gawa will do as the proverb says:

> *If the sins of saṃsāra were not great,*
> *Then the bottom of hell would not be deep.*
> *If hell's bottom were not deep,*
> *The blessings of the Buddha would not be seen.*
>
> *If the hordes of enemies were not a dense crowd,*
> *Then how could we distinguish the heroes?*
> *If we cannot distinguish the heroes,*
> *Then how can we know if the weapons are sharp?*

If the plain is not smooth,
The racehorse cannot run the course.
If the racehorse does not run the course,
How can we tell who is fastest?

In order to place yokes on the necks of the hordes of māras and exalt the side of virtue, purify the sinners' ripening karma, and uplift the minds of those who practice dharma, you must reveal the actual form of cause and effect. If one accumulates virtue the result is happiness, and if one accumulates nonvirtue that is the basis for suffering. So in order to gain certainty with karmic causes and results in this lifetime, I willingly accept whatever you command of me!

These sinners with negative karma, the Hor, the Düd, and others, who have never even heard the word 'dharma,' are the objects of compassion. If I am able to give them the opportunity to recognize the true nature of cause and result, then perhaps some of them will realize the fruition of buddhahood. If I am unsuccessful, then even though my heart is hacked to pieces, I the divine child Thöpa Gawa will never forsake my vow to benefit others. I will place my own life on the line and with you my Guru as witness, I make this commitment from the depths of my heart. May the root of this be dedicated to those who have been my mothers, all sentient beings limitless as space, including all living creatures down to the tiniest insect. Before you, the embodiment of the sugatas of the ten directions, I offer the mandala of the awakened mind (bodhicitta) of the dharmadhātu. Take hold of me with your great loving-kindness; without wandering from your state of enlightened awareness, listen to this song which I, the divine child Thöpa Gawa, offer to you, O Lotus Born."

> OṂ MAṆI PADME HŪṂ
> OṂ The mandala of the dharmadhātu adorned by awareness;
> ĀḤ The mandala of my body adorned by sense faculties;
> HŪṂ The jeweled mandala adorned by gold and turquoise.
> The embodiment of the dharmakāya and sambhogakāya,
> Nirmanakāya, Lord Padmasambhava, to you I make this
>   offering.
> May I and all sentient beings pervading space
> Attain the fruition of buddhahood.
>
> I, the supreme being, am the vidyādhara Thöpa Gawa.

That lion cub on the peak of the snow mountains,
If his claws do not overcome with their splendor,
Then his six powers[204] are of little benefit.

That roaring dragon dwelling amidst the southern clouds,
If his harmonious roar does not pervade the entire kingdom,
Then the wishing-jewel[205] he holds in his claws is of little benefit.

That king of all birds, the garuḍa, atop the wish-granting tree,
If he cannot surge to the pinnacle of the world,
Then the spread of his feathered wings is of little benefit.

> The sentient beings of Tibet in this time of the five
> degeneracies
> And the black hordes of the samaya violators, the Hor and
> the Düd,
> Those who are my destined disciples seem to be quite coarse.

If a tempered iron chisel cannot carve a stone,
Then a chisel of pure gold will not do the trick.
If the deadly poison does not burn terribly,
Then the peacock's fan will have no luster.[206]

> If the root of the five poisons is not determined,
> Then the wisdoms of the five kāyas will not be seen.
> The true color of the dear divine guru is revealed through the
> godly demons.
> The true color of a heroic boy is revealed by his enemies.
> The true color of a young girl is revealed by her vanity.
> The color of polished silver is revealed by the tarbu berry.[207]
> If the enemies of the teachings are not annihilated,[208]
> Then protectors of the doctrine will not be exalted.
> If the harm-doers are not cut off at the root,
> Then those who are excellent cannot be identified.
> If their evil karma does not ripen upon them,
> The people will not remember to be virtuous.
> Therefore I will accomplish whatever you have commanded
> through enlightened activity.

Through peaceful and wrathful skillful means and
    compassion
May the sinners of the dark side with evil karma,
Those who have a karmic connection to me, be it good or
    bad,
Have the opportunity to recognize the truth of cause and
    result.
In the future may they continue to be born as my disciples;
Ultimately may they attain the fruition of buddhahood.
Stirring saṃsāra from the depths,
May the benefit of others be accomplished through the
    flourishing of enlightened deeds.

In this way, I offer the root of all this perfectly pure virtue
Before you, the embodiment of the sugatas,
Supremely kind Lotus Born.
I offer all this as a mandala for the benefit of beings limitless
    as space.
Please accept this with your great loving-kindness.
May I, the divine child Thöpa Gawa,
Take my human body in the land of Tibet.
The time has come for me to tame those who are unruly with
    skillful means.
Whatever positive or negative signs, dreams, prophecies,
And so forth there may be,
Please teach me the unknown and reveal the unseen.
In accord with your word, I offer this samaya prayer.
Clearly hear this song of offering,
Sublime source of refuge, and hold this in your heart.

Thus he sang, and then Lotus Skull Garland Who Quells Existence with Splendor, along with his retinue of ḍākas and ḍākinīs, wisdom holders, dharmapālas, guardians of virtue, and gods of the chase, delighted in the feast offering of exaltation, after which they departed to their own abodes.

CHAPTER FOUR

Master Lotus Born is invited to the land of the nāgas
To cure an epidemic.
To repay his kindness the nāga king Tsugna Rinchen
  [Precious Jewel at the Crown]
Sends Metog Lhadzei to the human realm.

[Padma decides to intentionally pollute the seas for the greater benefit.]

THEN THE DIVINE CHILD Thöpa Gawa, the destined deity of the land of Tibet in Jambudvīpa, was to take birth in the middle land of humans. He would be
brought into the world by his father, the Masang nyen Gedzo, and his mother, the
nāginī Yelga Dzeiden* [Lovely Branch]. In order to tame the nonhuman race of
māras of the lands of the four directions, it is as the proverb says:

> *Only poison will cure illness brought on by poison;*
> *If you want to cut iron, only iron will do.*

Therefore he must become like the race of those to be tamed.

It was crucial that the divine child be born as the son of a nāga and a nyen.
Therefore, according to his previous vow, Guru Lotus Born considered what skillful

---

* This is yet another name for the nāginī, Metog Lhadzei.

means he would use to summon the nāga daughter. Then he cursed the nāgas, projected incantations into certain substances, stuffed them into the left horn of a black dzo, covered the opening, and threw it into Lake Manasarovar.[209] At that moment there was a great roaring sound, and the foul disease of this curse began to spread throughout the underwater kingdom of the nāgas.[210]

[The nāgas convene to discuss the epidemic. The nāga king decides to invite the diviner god Dorje Ngangkar (White Vajra) to do a divination to discover the cause of the epidemic.]

The nāgas had no idea what had caused this condition or how to effect a cure. All the nāgas were frightened and terrified, and all their leaders gathered before the nāga king Tsugna Rinchen. With one voice of lament, they presented the words of this request. In order to easily understand the hidden meaning, they made their request and he answered every question within a single song.

> OM MAṆI PADME HŪM
> Alas! Alas! They wept.
> We don't usually begin this way.[211]
> But how, when we are as miserable as this,
> Can we fashion a song of happiness, hope, and wonder?
> Instead, we will heal our minds with a song of complaint.
>
> Seated on your unchanging jeweled throne,
> O nāga king Tsugna Rinchen
> We entreat your undivided attention.
> Listen to us with the silken scarf of your ears.
>
> On the night before last,
> Passing through the sky to the land of the nāgas,
> From a mass of fire came a bolt of poison
> And such a tempest that the oceans almost mingled with the
>   earth;
> The bolt nearly dried up the ocean
> As it descended into the heart of the nāga kingdoms.
>
> From that ill-omened moment on,
> The nāga kingdom has been filled with disease

Caused by previous karma and sudden conditions.
What have we done wrong and how can we cure this?

Alas! The ignorance of saṃsāra, how sad:

A healthy body full of vitality
Will never be appreciated until it experiences illness and grief;
A happy human life full of leisure
Will never be appreciated until the moment of death.
Unless [we are] crushed by conditions,
We never appreciate the kindness of the guru;
Unless sudden disputes occur,
We never appreciate the dear chief's protection;
Unless our own mouths water from hunger,
We never appreciate a poor man's need to hoard.

These are our regrets in this aftermath.
Now what shall we do? What is best, O Precious One?

Listen to the words of our account as
We entreat you to examine our predicament, and reply.
This is the respectful request that we nāga subjects submit to you.

Then the nāga king Tsugna Rinchen answered. "Oh, I understand, I understand, oh dear, oh dear, oh my goodness!"

If there is no roost, the bird does not land.[212]
Without the bird's sudden flight, a horse has no cause to bolt.
And if the horse does not bolt, why would the rider's head crack?[213]

In the land of humans in Jambudvīpa, there must be a black magician performing magical feats. Otherwise, there's no reason for this to have happened. Therefore, as it says in the ancient proverbs:

When it's time to chant the teaching, the lama's voice is lost;
When it's time to give, the patron's hands are cramped;
When it's time to run, the hamstrings of the horse quiver,
When it's time to hunt, the hound is short of breath.

We of the nāga race are supposed to have clairvoyant powers,
Why can we not see through this darkness?
Why could we not foresee this problem?
Let all diviners perform divinations
And all you astrologers draw up your charts.
Let humans supplicate the gods
And the gods give them healing rituals to perform.

In the highland pass of Marshöd
Dwells Dorje Ngangyag* of the Mar Valley.
He is a master of divination and prophetic rites
And he is a great friend to the noble caste of the nāgas,
Call on him, the prognosticator, for all you need.
Moreover, the nāgas of our five provinces
Should discuss a plan and consult with one another.
If you have understood what you have heard, it is helpful for
    your mind.
If you don't like this, then you don't need to listen.
Bear this in mind, nāga subjects!

[A nāga child is dispatched to request the divination. Padma secretly suborns the diviner to perjury.]

Thus it was said, and everyone in the kingdom agreed to summon the divination master. They decided to send a young nāga child named Nangwa Ziden [Majestic Appearance] to Marshöd Shelkar Lhadrag [Lower Valley of Mar Crystal Divine Crag] to call on the diviner god. Meanwhile, Lotus Skull Garland, bringing down a veil of obscurity on the nāgas, entreated the diviner god Dorje Ngangkar to fulfill his aims, saying, "The nāga king Tsugna Rinchen is dispatching somebody to summon you, Dorje Ngangkar. When he comes, tell him that the only way to cure the nāga illness is to summon the Mantra Holder Rākṣa Skull Garland and, in particular, that everyone must willingly obey his command or not only will there be no benefit, the entire nāga kingdom will be in danger of extinction. As the proverb of the wise ones states:

---

* This is another name for the diviner Dorje Ngangkar [White Vajra], and could be said to mean something similar, such as Vajra Domain.

The six curing medicines will cure with the minor ingredients;
The piercing bamboo arrow is sped by its feathers;
The plow works by extending its iron teeth."

After Lotus Skull Garland spoke, the divination god promised to obey his command. Then, the nāga child Nangwa Ziden instantly arrived in the highland valley through magical powers. Offering the divination god Dorje Ngangkar a radiant crystal jewel with one eye, he said, "Master of the divination ceremonies of the phenomenal world, with clairvoyant powers like a king, you possess the divine eye that knows all. We of the pure kingdom of the nāgas have been struck by eighteen different maladies, many of which were previously unknown. Why did this happen? What have we done wrong? We don't know what will help us or what medicines will restore us. The king of the nāgas, Tsugna Rinchen, has sent me to quickly come here with these tidings in order to invite you, the famous and renowned diviner Dorje Ngangkar, to come from Jambudvīpa, the country of the nyen. Please listen attentively, and accept our invitation." So saying, the nāga child Nangwa Ziden then offered this song to the diviner god Dorje Ngangkar:

> The song begins with Ala.
> Thala brings the melody along.
> In the clear and luminous crystal castle,
> Within a tent of rainbow clouds of light,
> On a throne of precious gems,
> Master of divination in the phenomenal world,
> Dorje Ngangkar, please listen to me.
>
> In case you don't recognize me,
> I am the nāga child Nangwa Ödden[*]
> From the exalted treasure gate of the water-dwelling nāgas.

According to the ancient proverbs:

Dawn cannot help but break,
Led by the royal parasol of the sun. This is the reason darkness is
*   dispelled.*[214]

---

[*] This is another name for the nāga child Nangwa Ziden.

The dove cannot help but coo
When the royal bird, the cuckoo, is the messenger.*
This is the reason the earth and water warm.

The humble servant cannot help but rush around
When the chief who sits on high gives orders.
This is the reason there is such urgency.

In the kingdom of the water-dwelling nāgas
Unimaginable evil omens and unwelcomed diseases
    previously unknown
Have suddenly emerged!
Please explain what has happened, and why.
Diviner, we urgently entreat you to come and help.
You the white snow mountain god and we the cool nāgas
Are counted as relatives and numbered as friends.
We keep face by upholding these oaths.
Therefore make haste in these matters of great importance.

If a small spark of fire is not extinguished,
When the flames consume the mountains and valleys it is too late.
If the canals are not built when the water is low,
When the floods breach the banks it is too late.

You diviner, please hold this in your mind."

[The diviner then departs for the nāga land, where the king formally requests the divination.]

Then the divination god Dorje Ngangkar thought, "Just yesterday[215] I promised Ācārya Padmasambhava to follow his vile plan. It is as the proverbs say:

A deed promised must be swiftly taken up,
Lest it slip away."

---

* The cuckoo bird appears after winter to indicate that spring has arrived.

With this thought in mind, the diviner said, "Oh yes. Although the middle nyens and the lower nāgas are blood relatives,[216] they have harmony as well as discord[217] and when enemies converge, they will unite to face them, just as:

> *There are many varieties of herbs and grasses that grow from the*
> *ground,[218]*
> *Yet when the winds blow, the tips of their blades will bend in the*
> *same direction.*
> *There are various constellations that appear in the sky,*
> *Yet when the sun rises, they will fade away together.*

Thinking along these lines, there's no way for me to say 'I cannot go.'" He loaded three hundred and sixty divination threads; one thousand five hundred divination sticks; one hundred and fifty divination stones; thirty-two divination arrows; a three-thousand six hundred square divination board; and the divination text onto the backs of fifty mules and set out with the nāga child Nangwa Ödden as his companion. Eventually they arrived at Sidpa Yutso [Cosmic Turquoise Lake], the domain of the nāgas.

There the nāga king Tsugna Rinchen offered Dorje Ngangkar the jewel Ting-öd Münsel [Blue Light That Dispels Darkness] and his moonstone rosary called Chusel Tsanei Künjom [Water Crystals Curing All Fevers] as he offered this song:

> ᴇ If this is sung from the secret pathway of the throat,
> The story of words will emerge of its own accord.
> Listen, Dorje Ngangkar, master in phenomenal existence,
> Principal diviner, astrologer and mirror diviner,
> According to the ancient proverbs:

> *Although the shaft of the arrow may be fine and straight,*
> *If it is not ornamented with the feathers of a white vulture*
> *It is difficult to shoot straight on the paths of the wind.*
> *Of course the story is enticing when put to words,*
> *But if the mind does not extract the meaning*
> *It is difficult to discern the main point.*

> Just before midnight on the night before last,
> Across the ocean path of the nāga country,
> A poisonous dagger emitting pestilential vapors, and

Causing a tempest that nearly combined the earth and water,
Fell in the very heart of the land of nāgas.
From that day onward
The kingdom of the nāgas became afflicted with deadly
  disease;[219]
Eighteen types of illness are blazing like fire.
We are far from knowing what measures to take to remedy
  our situation.
According to the ancient proverbs, it states:

The frost that comes between autumn and winter;
Is it really a great sign,
Or is it simply the fact that bad times are approaching?

A great river that runs between shade and sun;
Is it really raging with contention,
Or simply surging in its course through the valley?

In the vast sky of the azure firmament,
The lone royal parasol of the sun has become lost.
If it did not divide the golden sphere of the moon,
How could we distinguish the white waxing and the red waning?

In the northern plains of Achen
A lone traveler has become lost.
If the constellation of the Pleiades failed to appear,
How could he distinguish east from west?

In the nāga domain, the treasure gate of the cool lakes,
Tsugna Rinchen has become lost.
If the prognosticator does not give his predictions,
There's no way of knowing what healing rituals should be
  performed.

Therefore, diviner, we entreat you to decode the divination.
Please tie the knots in the divination cords.
Arrange the sections of the divination charts
And spread your divination stones on the ground.

Arrange the divine arrows in their rows and
We will prepare whatever materials may be necessary.
Accordingly, please tell us what you need.
Diviner, bear this in mind.
Thus he sang.

[The diviner strategizes in advance the complex construction of his false divination, performs the ceremonies, and delivers the prognostication that they must hire Padmasambhava at all cost.]

Then the diviner god Dorje Ngangkar thought to himself,

"A clever man who spins a web of lies
Must review his tricky thoughts three times over,
Or there is no way a good thinker will accept his stories.

A white vulture with wings of wind
Must circle three times in the highest path of the birds,
Or there is no way to land on the earth.

It must be like that." Then he said, "In order to do divinations for the king of the nāgas, for the illness of the nāga population at large, and for important affairs in general, the supporting materials, practice materials, and bases for offerings must be abundant. If not, I need hardly say how dangerous and great this epidemic could become. The stainless, divine white divination ground,* the thirteen golden grooved[220] divine arrows, the fifty varieties of precious jewels, the collar bone of a white vulture, the right leg of a white ewe, the untarnished crystal mirror; these things must be prepared. Later I will be able to tell you what is necessary based on the outcome of the divination."[221]

Immediately they arranged all the necessary materials before him. Then the diviner Dorje Ngangkar placed the stainless white basis for divination in front of himself. It was ornamented with the thirteen golden grooved divine arrows. The collarbone of a white vulture and the right leg of a white ewe were placed upon it. He fastened the untarnished crystal mirror upon that, spread the fifty varieties

---

* The "divination ground," or basis (Tib. *lha gzhi*), is a cloth or a board upon which the divination materials are laid or cast.

of precious jewels on that basis, and arranged the three-hundred-and-sixty-square divination board and also the one thousand five hundred garuḍa sticks, three hundred and sixty knotted threads, as well as the thirty-two divine arrows. He rubbed his hands together, pressing hard for a powerful and clear indication, and broke into this song:

So! [222] From the upper glorious spirit castle,
The divination master of the phenomenal world,
Son of Yel, Thor, and Dar, these three,[223]
Ancestors of divination, dralas of the phenomenal world: *So!*
Masang nyen, master of the azure firmament: *So!*
Sidpa Kunshei Thangpa [Knower of Existence Who Dwells
　　on the Plains]: *So!*
Be the guides of the divination I make here today.

Dark fog obscures the divination.
Hidden turmoil obstructs the divination.
Clear the obstruction of delusion causing stupidity and
　　dullness.
Clear the covering that is like clouds from above.
Clear the covering that is like fog from below.
Clear the clouds that are like dust in the middle.
Uncovered, it will be clearer than a radiant and luminous
　　crystal
And polishing will make it more beautiful than the finest
　　turquoise.

I perform this illuminating divination today
Because the kingdom of the pure nāgas
Is oppressed by impure obscurations.
To begin with, how has this occurred?
Secondly what are the conditions?
Finally, what will happen?
What can be done to remedy this?
Clearly reveal all answers, hiding and obscuring nothing as well!

[Then the diviner Dorje Ngangkar gives the results of the bogus divination.]

Oh my goodness! This divination is disturbing.
The beginning of the divination is good, but overall it is very
    heavy.
The future may look up, but right now there is a decline.
Even so, perhaps the healing ceremonies will work, although
These bad omens seem impossible and the diseases incurable!
In the kingdoms of the nāgas this
First came about from the land of humans
When the king of Tibet, Trisong Deutsen,
Invited the Master [Padma] and erected the temple.
Unable to tame the minds of the nāgas,
It seems they broke Padma's command and this punishment is
    the result.
And furthermore, we are all plagued by demonic forces that
    disturb the hearth and cause baneful smoke infections.
If remedies are not performed soon,
The kingdom of the nāgas will surely be emptied.

The remedy to cure this must come from the human land of
    Jambudvīpa
Where there is a guru who cleanses such foul pollution.
If you are unable to invite this Guru Padma to come here,
Then remedy and hope are both exhausted.
According to the tradition of the ancient Tibetan sayings:

When it comes to life itself, don't be stingy with possessions;
When it comes to possessions, don't be careless;
When it comes to care-taking, be zealous in your exertion.

If the enemy does not suddenly fall upon you,
Hearing scary stories of the enemy's approach is just sweet
    conversation.

If a long dispute does not turn into the price of blood revenge,
Then the exchange of harsh words can terminate the demonic forces.

Nāga king, bear this in mind."

[The nāga king convenes an assembly to decide how to act on the divination.]

Thus he sang, and then the nāga king Tsugna Rinchen thought,

> *One life's accumulation of wealth and property*
> *May serve to feed and clothe one man.*
> *But if this fails to benefit the obsession with the cherished life itself,*
> *One day it will be an impermanent illusion.*

Then he said: "Oh, good, so be it, kind prognosticator.

> *Whoever benefits us is kin; whoever harms us is foe.*
> *The response to benefit is kindness; the response to evil is harm.*
> *A man who doesn't know this is the worst of the worst.*

For your great kindness, prognosticator, I offer thirteen mule packs of precious gems." Then he was escorted home with his offerings.

The next day, nāgas from the royal and merchant caste down to the commoners and untouchables all convened on the Turquoise Meadow.*

"Now just as the diviner said yesterday,224 we have no choice but to invite Guru Padma. However, none of us have ever seen or met him before. It would be difficult for the nāga nobility to go to him. Is there anyone who would undertake the task of inviting him?"

The son of the black-throated nāga commoners, the nāga child Yerpa'i Trin-ga [Cloud Lover of Yerpa] said, "I will call on the greatly kind Master [Padmasambhava] and try to get him to make a solemn vow [to come]. I will see if I can obtain the transmission of the profound samaya. It is easier to send a little kid, so it has fallen to me to go." Everybody who met there was in agreement about this. [Then Tsugna Richen said:]

"You, the nāga child, Yerpa'i Trin-ga:

> *A man dispatched and an arrow unloosed*
> *Should go where they're sent and land where they're aimed.*

---

* This is the same place as the Blue Turquoise Plain of Ne'u Seng.

If we have the karma for the Lotus Guru from Uḍḍiyāṇa to
    come to us,
Whatever needs to be done will be placed in his hands.
Whatever he says we will promise to do.

For as the ancient proverbs say:

If the valley's little stream is never dry
Then the melting of the great snow mountain is said to be never-
    ending.

If the flower is not destroyed by the frost,
Then even if the herbs are lost, it is said there is no regret."

[The nāga child is dispatched and meets with Padma.]

A wish-granting lapis vase and a cooling jewel that prevents fire were sent along with him as presentation gifts. Then the guru Lotus Born, knowing that the nāgas were inviting him, in an instant magically went to Ma Dentig Padma Shelphug [Lotus Crystal Cave of Ma Dentig], where he stayed. Through Padma's blessings, even the nāga child Yerpa'i Trin-ga knew where to find him. The moment the child arrived in Ma Padma Shelphug, the Master pretended not to know him, and said, "You, young boy wearing silken clothes, with a clockwise swirling conch on the top of your head wrapped in a blue water-silk turban, mounted on a long-horned female antelope, holding in your hand a jewel and a vase: from which of the three races do you come: the gods, the nyen, or the nāgas, and for what reason have you come here?"

The nāga dismounted from the antelope, and the lapis wish-fulfilling vase and the cooling gem that prevents fire were offered up before the guru. Then respectfully prostrating, the child said, "O undeceiving protector of this and all future lifetimes, I have come from the subterranean nāga realms, sent by the king Tsugna Rinchen to tell you our story." Then he offered this song:

OM This is the beginning of the auspicious song.
Embodiment of the dharmakāya and the sambhogakāya,
Lord nirmāṇakāya Lotus Born, I bow down to you.
Please cleanse all impure obscurations.
Of course you know all about a person like me.

I am a boy from the untouchable class of nāgas,
Impure, as I was born of the family of animals,[225]
Pure, as I now see the lord Lotus Born.
Sent by the nāga king Tsugna Rinchen,
I am a just a courier, a messenger.
This inexhaustible wish-fulfilling lapis vase
And cooling fire-preventing jewel
Are the mandala presentation offerings he has sent to you.
All of us in the pure kingdom of nāgas
Have been stricken by the obscurations of miasma and
    pollution;
Many types of incurable diseases have arisen.
The prognosticator Dorje Ngangkar from Mar Valley
Received negative divinations and disturbing predictions,
He said that the only remedy for this is to invite the Lotus
    Born Guru
From the land of the humans in Jambudvīpa.
Otherwise the kingdom of the nāgas will empty.
According to the ancient proverbs which state:

Whatever the divine guru intends, he intends for the benefit of
    others.
In order to turn the six classes of beings to the dharma
The guru meditates on love and compassion.

Whatever a rich man intends wants, he intends for his own
    benefit.
In order to be successful in one's own business
A person aims to secure profit.

The purpose in craft of carpenters and blacksmiths is for tasty food.
In order to always have meat to eat and liquor to drink
Craftsmen work to be clever with their hands.

Forgive my importunity, but this is how it is.
You, Guru, please make haste and come.
Free the race of nāgas from illness
And establish the nāga realm in well-being.

Whatever load you lay upon us we shall carry,
Whatever you propose we will completely embrace.
This request comes from all the five castes of nāgas;
I swore to present it before you;
Don't disappoint me with your response.
Lord Guru, bear this in mind.

Thus he requested, and the Guru spoke, "I am here at the command of Avalokiteśvara.[226] He can see many things with his thousand eyes. He can guide many beings with his thousand arms. When it comes to guiding sentient beings in the three worlds, just one or two make the difference between many or few. If you think you need help, rather than waste your time in senseless speech, chant MAṆI mantras. Better to stamp out *tsatsas* than to have idle hands. Better to meditate on bodhicitta than to have a distracted mind. I will stay settled in this sacred place, for:

> *The guru who pursues*[227] *material gain,*
> *Scurrying around here and there, meets with sin.*
>
> *A selfish person*
> *Full of activities, meets with conflict.*
>
> *A rich person who is discontented,*
> *Carrying many wares to market, encounters enemies.*

That being so, these proverbs point out that one should not wander here and there. Furthermore, with respect to benefit for others, from the highest peak of existence down to the lowest hell, we must make unbiased prayers that include all beings in all directions by thinking that all sentient beings throughout space have been our mothers and fathers. Otherwise we would be like a beggar without food who tries to fill his cup wherever he goes. The inner message of this account should be understood as follows," and he sang this sacred song:

> OM May the immutable resting place of the dharmakāya be
>   achieved.
> ĀH May the pure realm of the sambhogakāya be
>   accomplished.
> HŪM May the nirmāṇakāya which benefits others be
>   accomplished.

May I and all limitless sentient beings
Be established in the state of buddhahood.
Now then, nāga child listen here:

The mere title guru doesn't make a guru.
Just saying other's benefit doesn't make it other's benefit.
It is through realization that the mind is set free.
Attachment and ego-clinging must be cut.

Just finding a needle and thread, and then supplicating the
    wealth god,[228]
Just losing one's shoelaces, and then calling on the oath-
    bound protectors,[229]
Calling the acquisition of material goods the benefit of
    others;
Are all just acts of outer ego-clinging.

Not seeing one's own faults, yet proclaiming those of others,
Being biased about religion and individuals,
Calling a philosophical tenet that which is really only
    meditation based on passion and aggression;[230]
Are all just acts of inner ego-clinging.

When meditating, to materialize the generation stage,
When practicing, to arouse compassion with a biased mind,
When training in the completion stage, to have a focal
    point;[231]
Are all just acts of secret self-grasping.

If craving for wealth and material objects can be
    abandoned,
Then half of the path is accomplished!
Seeking food, clothing, patrons, and fame,
There is no greater demon than that!

The one under the golden hat has a high view,
But inside the brocade on his back is a show-off meditator.
In the presence of patrons, he becomes careful of his conduct;

Surrounded by wealth and endowments, his ability to benefit
    others vanishes.
Still it is said that this is the brainless guru's enlightened
    activity.
The day conditions ripen to bring the Lord of Death,
It is too late for strong remorse.[232]

I, a lowly little monk, asleep in my rat hole,
Have no hope of receiving wealth or extensive offerings
    from the nāgas,
Still, it seems I must go to the land of the nāgas.
Although I have no expectation for ordinary material
    wealth,
You will have to make many promises difficult to keep.
If you agree to this, then of course this guru will go.[233]

If a great mountain is invited as the guest,
There must be a great plain to be its host.
Without that, why should the great mountain move?
If the broad river must pass through a narrow channel
There must be a golden canal to be its conduit.
Without that there's no way for the golden river to flow.[234]

Nāga child keep this in your mind."

He answered, "I, a nāga child, came to the land of humans to accomplish a high mission. If I cannot succeed in my purpose, then the high promise I made will be meaningless.

If the young tiger with his threefold panoply*
Does not get the great buck's rack,
Then it is meaningless for him to wear his hunting garb.†

---

* Arrow, lance, and sword.

† Hunters' accoutrements such as ivory rings for their braided hair, ivory bracelets, and thumb rings.

If the mothers and maidens carrying gilded pails
Do not get the pure mountain water,
Then it is pointless for them to carry their silver ladles.

Guru, please come! All the castes of the nāgas from the nobility above to the commoners and untouchables below are of one mind, one counsel, one determination, and one voice, and as one community extend to you this invitation. In general, we are not like the class of humans, so we don't have the custom to first make a decision and later change our minds. What the leader decides, the servant enacts. With us it's not the case that the servant has the power of command, because the command is spoken only once by the king."

Then he began prostrating fervently, his hands pumping like bellows, whoosh, whoosh. Begging with thumbs sticking out as though beating a little drum and moving up and down, he looked like a man furiously bowing a biwa.*

Then the Precious Master said, "Well now, you go on ahead of me and carefully make your report. I will follow after."

Now that it was decided that he would come, the nāga child Yerpa'i Trin-ga went back to the nāga king Tsugna Rinchen to report as follows: "This guru Master Padma may be as famous as the turquoise dragon, but he's as feeble and unlucky as a flame in the wind. His name is great, like a white snow-lioness, but if you get near him you see he's like a mangy dog. Well, he is just like a little white-faced monk and seems a bit stupid, but if he can cure the nāgas' diseases, then we have him now. On the other hand, as the proverbs say:

Don't debate a stupid man.
Don't play with nettles with your hands.
Don't bargain with a stubborn man.

Personally, I didn't really get to know him. He insisted that we make impossible, impractical promises. When he spoke formally, he spoke about cause and result, but whenever he made conversation, he was a man who was trying to make a deal. Think about it: if he fails to benefit us, we'll have more complaints than we can count. In any case, whatever he does, I've placed all our trust in his hands and promised to do whatever he says. You had better start making preparations."

---

* A *biwa* is a Chinese bowed instrument.

Then the nāga king asked, "Did he mention if there were any articles we need to acquire?"

"No, he didn't say anything. But he said that when you invite a great mountain, you must lay out a great plain or that when you want to guide a swollen river, you need to make a golden canal for it to pass through. He also said these diseases are dangerous."

Then some other nāgas replied, "To put an end to the illness in this great district:

As long as the great buck doesn't roll off the mountain cliff,
He can go wherever he wants.[235]

As long as the snow on the upper highland is not melted by the sun,
Then the colorful snowy crags can always appear.

As long as the fish and otter do not end up on dry land,
Then we can do whatever we want with the river and the river bank.

The wealth that we lack is not difficult to acquire. So let's do what he says with what we have."

[Padma and Tsugna Rinchen bargain over Padma's fee.][236]

Then Guru Master Padma through his magical powers instantly arrived at the upper treasure gate of Lake Manasarovar in the land of the nāgas at Sidpa Yutso. There some of the sick nāgas were crawling on their right sides, sighing and groaning in pain; those crawling on their left sides were screaming cries of anguish. Some of the nāga serpents were lying spread on their backs shivering with their tails flopping back and forth, as they cried out in misery.

In the nāga castle on Bendril Yutsei [Lapis Turquoise Peak], the nāga prince Legpa Charbeb [Excellent Rainfall] was afflicted with disease and writhed to and fro like an undulating fish. There they invited the Precious Master to be seated on a golden throne within the palace. The nāga king Tsugna Rinchen brought him a red pearl plate loaded with varieties of luscious ripe fruits and, carrying the precious vase that destroys poison, served the ambrosial tea of the quintessence of medicine. He said, "Gracious One, sole protector in this and future lifetimes, welcome! Are you exhausted from your journey?[237] Gracious nirmāṇakāya! Listen; oh listen to the long white scarf of our speech as I offer this song, which is an account of the true story of what has happened here."[238]

OṂ MAṆI PADME HŪṂ HRĪH
I bow down to the gracious Lord of Dharma,
The guru who is the heart of all the buddhas,
Who sounds the ambrosial melody of the sacred dharma,
Who, as the nirmāṇakāya, is the embodiment of the sangha.

The select offering of the three sweets from the quintessence
    of trees*
Filling a plate made of red pearl,
And within the precious vase that destroys poison
Is the offering tea called quintessence of medicine.
With reverence I offer these, please lovingly accept them.

Just as the sun in the lofty firmament
Nourishes the lotus in the mud,
We in the realms of pretas and animals
Ask you please to look down on us with your eyes of
    compassion.

Here in our pure nāga kingdom
Although the hunters have not scared off the mountain nyen,
The zodor's hailstorm[239] is increasingly destructive.
Although the nyen have not struck the nāgas with an
    avalanche,
The sores and tumors on their limbs multiply.
Although our offerings in temples have not ceased,
The dharma protectors become increasingly irritable.[240]

Just before midnight several days ago,
Pestilential vapors descended into the heart of the nāga land.
Unbelievable bad omens ensued and from that time on
The pure land of the nāgas has been afflicted with obscuring
    pollution.
All sorts of incurable diseases have arisen.

---

* (Tib. *shing bcud*). A classical metonym for fruit.

The prognosticator Dorje Ngangkar said,
"If you don't obtain Master Lotus,
The country of the nāgas will become nameless.

If you don't dig with a hard rock,
Then you won't reach the treasure that is deeply buried.

If he doesn't go to the steep face of the mountain,
Then the hunter won't reach the prize of the meat.

If your precious treasure is not handed over for ransom[241]
Then you won't be able to buy your cherished life."

He [the diviner] cautioned us not to be attached to our wealth and valuables. So, Guru, that is why we have invited you.

If the warmth and gentleness of the sun abound,
There is no regret when the southern clouds disperse.

If the land of the nāgas is restored to well-being,
Then there is no regret if the prosperity of the nāgas is
     dispersed.
Whatever command you give us and whatever path you send
     us upon,
Whatever is to happen, it is in your hands now.
You who have listened to this song of offering,
Please keep this meaning close to your heart.

Thus he requested, and Master Padma said: "According to the proverbs of worldly existence, if need be, then:

To climb high up to the sky, hoist a ladder;
To enter the dense earth, tunnel down deep;
To carve hard rock, use a chisel;
To cross a flowing river, use a boat or a bridge.

And, as the proverb says, there are methods for curing the pain of illness:

The medicine that restores the internal organs,
The offered substances that please the godly demons,
The rites that banish the great demonic forces.

Although there are many considerations and techniques, given the way that these unlikely evil omens came to the land of the nāgas, the way that these incurable illnesses multiplied, and the way that the diviner had negative signs, wherever one looks:

The patron's obstacles are great,
The puja master is pitiful.

Therefore, as the proverb says:

If you try to help others there is obviously some danger for oneself,

Thus, wherever I point my finger, that is my offering. Just like:

Whatever makes a beggar's mouth water,
Whatever a poor man's stomach can take,
That is the extent of what you should prepare.

Will you give me whatever I say I want and keep track of it?"

The nāga king and all the ministers thought, "What the messenger told us yesterday is certainly true. He's the kind of man who

Grabs the tongue before the head is cooked,
Scoops out the noodles before slurping the broth.
Cranes his neck even before he yells out, 'Ki!'[242]

Whether good or bad,

If difficult feats are rare,
Then any rarity must certainly be expensive."

Then the nāga king said, "Well,

Before a conversation one should say, 'Ki!' and 'So!'
Before eating food one should make an offering.
Before the horse race is the time to place the bet.

So, whatever you command of us, we will do it." They then took a solemn oath.

Then Padmasambhava replied, "Well, now then, as many as possible of the varieties of medicinal plants, pure water, and healing medicines; yellow gold, creamy silver, red copper, blue turquoise, and clear crystal, a vase encrusted with these five gems and adorned with sprigs of *kuśa* grass; a mighty lion, a wish-fulfilling cow, a nourishing dri, a crystal-egg sheep, and the milk of a long-lived goat; a stainless white divination board, a white clockwise-swirling divine conch, a divine white offering cake with blown petals, a white triple-notched white divination arrow—all this I need for my preparations.[243]

Early tomorrow morning on the Turquoise Plain Ne'u Seng[*] bring together all the ailing nāgas of the five castes."

[Padma's ceremony of purification.][244]

The nāgas assembled all the necessary articles for the ceremony, and early the next morning on the Turquoise Plain Ne'u Seng, all the ailing nāgas came: the crippled were carried, the blind were led, and the chronically ill were helped along. The invalids were carried on stretchers. Some were carried by their family custodians. Those without guardians dragged themselves along. The Master set up the mandala of Ārya Siṃhanāda.[†] With *dharaṇīs*[‡] and mantras he blessed all the smoke-offering substances that purify pollution, and with the milk of the five sorts of livestock he filled the vase of five jewels to the brim and enhanced it with medicinal ambrosia. He made smoke from the excellent plants and herbs and sprinkled and dispersed the five kinds of purifying water by waving the kuśa grass, as he sang this song of the smoke offering that purifies obscurations.

---

[*] A *ne'u* is a lush green meadow.

[†] Ārya Siṃhanādais is actually a manifestation of Padmasambhava as a wrathful deity with a lion's head. The name means "Lion's Roar."

[‡] A dharaṇī (Tib. *gzungs*) is a mantric formula. Such incantations hold many powers and hence the term means to "hold or sustain."

OṂ ĀḤ SENGHANATHA HŪṂ
I supplicate the Three Rare and Supreme Jewels of Refuge.
The illness of the five poisons, whose essence is ignorance,
Is cured by the medicine of the wisdom of self-awareness.
May the five kāyas spontaneously occur.

Outwardly, the three: wind, phlegm, and bile,
Inwardly the three: heat, cold, and agitation,
Secretly passion, aggression, and delusion, these three as well:
When they arise, they arise from the expanse of the mind.
And when they dissolve, they dissolve into the expanse of
    space.
The outer four elements are the father of poisons.
The inner four elements are the mother of poisons.
The Three Rare and Supreme are free from poisons.
By the truth of these authentic words,
The three poisons dissolve into the four elements.

The golden vase is filled with the milk of a snow lioness,
The water of equanimity, an aspect of Ratnasambhava.*
May it wash away the obscuration of pride of the nāga
    nobility.

The silver vase is filled with the milk of the wish-fulfilling
    cow,
The water of emptiness, an aspect of Akṣobhya.
May it wash away the obscuration of anger of the royal caste
    of nāgas.

The copper vase is filled with the milk of the nourishing dri,
The water of discriminating wisdom, an aspect of Amitābha.
May it wash away the obscuration of passion of the brahman
    caste.

---

* For the identification of this and the following four Buddhas, see "buddha families, five" in the
glossary.

This crystal vase is filled with the milk of the prosperity
    sheep,
The water of the mirror-like wisdom, an aspect of Vairocana.
May it wash away the obscuration of delusion from the
    untouchable nāga caste.

This turquoise vase is filled with the milk of the longevity
    goat,
The water of all-accomplishing action, an aspect of
    Amoghasiddhi.
May it wash away the obscuration of jealousy from the nāga
    commoners.

This wisdom water, the essence of the five buddha families,
Cleanses the five poisons of the five castes of nāgas.
May the unclean and impure become pure.

Azaleas with conch-shaped flowers,
Mugwort with golden cord-like stems,
Tamarisk with copper-colored burls,
Juniper with turquoise-colored leaves,
The nyatri shrub with coral-colored catkins:
May the smoke from these five different trees
Clear away the veil of samaya violation from the five castes of
    nāgas.
Wash, wash, wash them clean.
Cleanse, cleanse, cleanse the corruption of broken vows.
Drive away, drive away, drive away the obscurations of the
    demonic forces.
Draw near, draw near, draw near us, O essence of long life.

May the pure kingdoms of the nāgas
Be free from sickness as if they gained the bodies of gods;
Be free from old age, as if they gained the body of a fifteen-
    year-old.
May they be sheltered by the protecting deities.
From this day onward
May all nāga castes be liberated from disease.

In the Tibetan land of Jambudvīpa,
May the rains come in a timely manner
And may the crops and livestock always be excellent.
May human and animal diseases be prevented
And may the entire nāga realm be established in well-being.
May there be fully endowed auspiciousness.

Thus he prayed. As soon as he had finished his purification and smoke offering, all the ailing nāgas were immediately cured of their diseases. The crippled danced, the mute broke into song, the blind saw the face of the guru, and the deaf heard the dharma. From that day onward, all the nāgas became more radiantly splendid than ever before, and the nāga king Tsugna Rinchen sang this song called Amazing Happiness!

A happy song, even happier, the nāga realm is happy.
This melodious song brings joy to some and happiness to others,
The song is offered to this greatly kind Guru.
We offer because the Guru came to fulfill our wishes.
We are happy because he came to accomplish what he
    accomplished.
We are happy because we are free from deadly disease.
We are happy for the nāga land is established in well-being
    once again.

Today I sing this song of amazement to express our happiness
    and well-being
I can't help but sing this song of marvel!
On the Turquoise Plain Ne'u Seng in the land of nāgas
The crippled are dancing clickity-click.
The mute are singing tra-la-la.
The eyes of the blind can see his face flashing.
The deaf hear the dharma ever so clearly.
This means we nāgas have been freed from disease.
Not only did the crippled recover, but they thought to dance.
Not only did the mutes' voices open, but they broke into song.
Not only did the eyes of the blind open, but they saw the face
    of the deity.
Not only did the deaf recover, but they heard the sacred dharma.

Not only were the nāgas cured of illness, but their bodies are
    resplendent.
Ah great happiness, as the worldly proverbs state:

When there's that much happiness, are they giddy?—nothing but!
Even when they're deep under in sleep, they belt out songs.

When the stomach is full, does a person talk?—nothing but!
They talk about how hard honey candy hurts the liver.

When people are rich, are they active?—nothing but!
They go all about in their pearl-encrusted Mongolian boots tied with
    rainbow laces.

In the pure kingdoms of the nāgas
Do we know whose kindness has brought this happiness?

That the six fruits ripen in the fields of the lower great plains
Is due to the noble kindness of the wealthy southern clouds.
For, if the sweet rain does not fall,
The turquoise-green crops will not burgeon.

That the upper mountains are lifted up to exalted height
Is due to the noble kindness of the snow mountain range.
If the mountain pass is not blocked by a snow mass,
Then the notch in the crags can be easily found.

That the lower plateaus do not lessen but grow with blooms
Is due to the noble kindness of the blue turquoise lake.
If the source of water does not reach the lake
Then the spring that perishes in winter will come back to life
    in summer.

That the five classes of nāgas have been cured of disease
Is due to the blessings of Guru Lotus Born.
If the Guru had not performed this cleansing and smoke
    offering,
Then what would have become of the kingdom of the nāgas?

Your great kindness, O Nirmāṇakāya,
Could not be repaid in ages of time.
From now on, whatever you say, we answer, "Yes."
Whatever you want, we offer it.
Lord Guru, please keep this in your heart.

Thus he spoke, and then the rest of the nāgas said that indeed it had been just yesterday that he had committed to doing whatever was necessary and had struck a bargain about what he would give. Citing sayings about the way one should make offerings they said, "Now we must repay the full measure of his kindness."

It's easy for a poor man to make promises.
It's not that he is arrogant
But he must do what he can to save face.

It's easy for the rich to promise contributions.
It's not that they are without avarice
Since they still fear that their herds will diminish.

When the delicious meat is being eaten, it tastes great;
When it's time to pay for the meat, it hurts.
When you're drinking liquor, it's delicious;
When you're vomiting bile, it's bitter.

Having quoted these proverbs, they said, "I wonder what the Guru will say?" Some said, "He may say that he wants us to offer the jewel Ting-öd Zibar [Deep Blue Blazing Splendor]."* Some said, "He'll say he wants the seahorse Ziwang Phurshei [Splendid Stride Flying Knowledge]." Some said, "He'll say he wants the precious stole called Drojam Phagpa Rinchen [Soft Precious Skin]." Some said, "The waterproof shoes called Chulam Samtsei [Freedom to Walk]." Some said, "He'll ask for the little crystal vase Chuchüd Shel [Water Quintessence Crystal]." Some said, "He'll ask for the turquoise branch Shing Chüd [Wood Quintessence]." Some said, "It will be the armor Yamed Beṇḍrilya [Rustless Lapis]." Some said, "The antidote

---

* This refers to the same jewel previously called Ting-öd Münsel [Blue Light That Dispels Darkness].

to poison, Dugkyöb Dugzil Zhuntig [Crystal Dew Poison Curing Potent Drop]." Some said, "The febrifuge Tsenden Trulgi Nyinpo [Cooling Sandalwood Serpent Essence]."

"If he does indeed want each and every one of all of the nine various offerings, then since he's been so kind, what else can we do?"

Some said, "Instead of waiting for him to say what he wants, let's just give him one massive donation right now."

All agreed, and the following morning, on the Turquoise Plain Ne'u Seng, they arranged a golden throne beautified with inlaid turquoise, brass lotus petals, groups of emeralds in designs, and hanging ropes of variegated pearls. On that throne the Great Master took his seat, and they piled before him the thirteen precious jewels that fulfill all needs and desires. The poor were shocked when they saw the wealth, just as cowards are shocked by seeing hordes of soldiers, the starving are shocked by the sight of food, and the foolish are shocked by conflict.

The nāga Migön Karpo [Kind Protector of Humanity], holding his mala of *amra bhanga* seed,* said, "Supremely kind guide of all beings, precious dharma king of the three realms, please lend me your ears. It is not necessary for me to go into detail about what is happening here at this time, as the proverb states:

> *The inimitable guru Nāgārjunagarbha,*
> *Inimitable patron Tsugna Rinchen,*
> *Inimitable palace Lapis Turquoise Peak,*
> *Inimitable caste of nāgas, the White Royal Caste.*

From ancient times until now, our refuge in the Three Jewels has been constant. The pure realm of perfect virtues has not been perverted. The golden cord of samaya has not been severed. In the same way, from the time of Padma Wangchen [Lotus Great Power] down to happy great nāga king Nanda, the patron and guru are like an old icon that need not be explained anew. Like the deity received when you toss the flower in the mandala,[245] you, Guru Lotus Born, have freed the general nāga population from disease. Considering the measure of your great kindness in creating such well-being in our nāga dispositions, you are not unworthy of receiving offerings filling the three chiliocosms. Furthermore,

---

* There is no seed by this name in Sanskrit. Generally, *amra* is "mango," but it is hard to imagine that the serpent prince's mala (string of prayer beads, like a rosary) had 108 huge mango seeds on it.

No matter how small the flower, it is an offering material.
No matter how small the myrabolan, it is one of the six superior
    medicines.

These offerings are presented to you; please accept them with your great love and
without allowing your awareness to wander, please listen," he said as he sang this song:

> Lu Ala Lu the song is sung in this way.
> Three Refuges and Three Roots,
> Please remain inseparably as the crown ornament of my head;
> This offering of song is first presented to that spot.
> May I achieve all my aspirations in this and future lives.
> Supremely kind Guru Lotus Born
> Listen here for a moment to my song.

> *The great kindness of the royal parasol is like that of parents,*
> *Its radiance alone nourishes the four continents;*
> *That kindness is as kind as the eyes in your forehead.*
> *The great kindness of the southern clouds is like that of parents,*
> *Their gentle rain alone nourishes the dense earth;*
> *That kindness is like the utterance of your tongue.*

> Guru who is greatly kind like parents,
> It is your blessings alone that restored the country of nāgas;
> That kindness is like your heart that sits in your chest.

> An eon of time could not repay your kindness.
> Even if we were to fill the three thousand myriads of universes
>   with gems
> Actually presented to the Rare and Precious Three Jewels,
> It would be just an indication of our gratitude.
> Because of your activities, the nāgas[246] have well-being.
> So as not to be empty-handed in repaying your kindness,
> The thirteen precious jewels that fulfill all needs and desires,
> The thirteen jewels that dispel darkness,
> The thirteen jewels that reduce fever,
> And eighty mule packs of precious stones,
> Fifteen great liters of pure gold dust,

Along with a garland of precious mango seeds;
All this we offer with faith; please accept it with pleasure.

Without forsaking your compassion, lovingly protect
All pure kingdoms of the nāgas.
And from this day onward,
This gathering of faithful patrons
Will be connected to the root and lineage guru by samaya.
May both guru and sponsor, paired like the sun and moon,
In the sky of the accumulation of the two merits,
Be inseparably connected.
In the space of your wisdom intent do not disdain
This song of offering that your ears have heard, but accept it
    with your compassion.
May auspicious well-being and goodness prevail.

Thus he supplicated, but the Guru's face became black as gathering clouds, his eyes flashing like lightning, and he grimaced, while his nose wrinkled like waves of water, and he said, "You of the different nāga casts:

Not repaying the master's kindness, the guard dog steals the butter.
The hunter profits by the stag's rack, [but the stag dies].
No better recompense than rubbing oil into a rock.
No doubt, if you remove the bridge after you've crossed the river,
Wouldn't you need to look back to see if there is a boat?

You won't accomplish what you really desire with the value of your jewels. I am a guru who has the power to kill or cure."

All the nāgas were shocked. "Now we cannot back down from the words that escaped our mouths yesterday. Once the arrow has escaped the bow, it is foolish to think we can pull it back," they thought. "From now on, we will consider no offering suitable unless the Precious Guru himself requests it. We swear this on the *One Hundred Thousand Verses* of the nāgas.

Then the Guru said, "Well, then, ask the nāga princess Lady Demkar Lhamo [Undulating White Goddess] to come here. I have something private to tell her."

Everybody went, "Oh my, what did the Guru say? Now, he's not going to kill nāga princess Demkar Lhamo, is he?! The anxiety of the Chinese and we nāgas is the same. A lama like this is capable of doing anything, isn't he? And yet, what other choice do we have at this moment?"

The nāga queen Demkar Lhamo was brought before the Guru, and he asked everyone to get out. All the nāgas went outside; the foolish ones were trying to stop giggling, and the clever ones were making hand signals to each other.

The Guru said to the nāga queen Demkar Lhamo, "Your family's offering to repay my great kindness is certainly a poor excuse for a gift. Even though among these offering substances there are many delicacies, things beautiful to behold, or pleasing to hear, there's not a single thing that I want. Multicolored precious stones, yellow sand, all of this, even if it were just lying around on a vast plain that belonged to no one, I wouldn't have reason to touch it. What would I want with it? I can't eat it, because I can't chew it. I can't wear it, because it won't cover me. If I were to wear it like jewelry, it would just weigh me down.

Now, the key point of eighty words is just like the four girth straps that hold a big yak saddle on. What I'm getting at is this: I have heard that you have several famous young girls among you. I want you to bring them here.

> *With my fine little eyes I will see who is fairest.*
> *My white snow mountain mind will see who I like best.*

Will you offer one to me?"

Then the nāga queen became so embarrassed, her face could not contain it, and she broke out in a sweat, saying, "Yes, sir, yes, sir," while she slowly backed away from him.

Meanwhile all the other nāgas were saying, "Do you think there is any way to ask the nāga queen what offerings to begin making?" A dull-minded nāga from the untouchable caste replied, "If there is a way for the Guru to invite her, then why can't we find a way to ask her?"

Then she came outside, but she felt awkward saying what the Guru had commanded. She nervously paced back and forth, weaving among the ranks of nāgas. The rest of the nāgas, not knowing what to ask, just stared at each other like a person stunned when he suddenly sees a scarecrow. Then the dull-minded untouchable called Ngogüd [Wild Face] audaciously stepped out from the ranks and, looking back and forth, said: "Well, precious queen, has a decision been made about the offering?" And everybody burst into laughter.[247]

Then the queen blushed and, not knowing how to say it, scribbled a note and placed it before the nāga king, who slapped his hands and thought, "Alas, how unfortunate! That stupid guru is intent on disgracing himself." He then announced the contents of the note and that the offering to Padmasambhava would be the nāga maiden of his choice, and he said, "Bring the three girls here."

Some nāgas laughed in amazement, while others, not surprised at all, tried to hold back their laughter. As it is said:

Outwardly approving; inwardly concealing your disgust.

The nāgas all thought, "It's not as if what we are offering is not great. After all, we haven't gone back on our promise of the nine jewels of the nāgas. It's not as if the consequence is insignificant. The eldest daughter, Gödchung Karmo [Little White Vulture], has already been promised to Garkhen [Dancer], the son of the queen of the Yākśas. The middle daughter is Khatsar Lumo-tso [Amazing Wondrous Appearance Nāginī Lake], who has promised to go to the Chinese Hamipaṭa. The youngest is Lenyu Khatam Do-to [Stupid Mute Stone Target],* and he certainly won't choose her. In any case, the Guru has been very gracious to us, and without that there is no way we would have even considered giving a nāga princess to the inhabitants of Tibet. Now, against our will, we are forced to follow through on our promise and give him his choice of the three. Do you think we should first ask each one of them what they think? Or, if not, don't you think we should at least tell them what is really going on?"

Then the nāga king Tsugna Rinchen said to his three daughters, "Because of the great kindness of our Guru, we have already promised him whatever he asks for. Even though we have offered eighty mule packs of jewels and fifteen liters of gold dust, he has said that we must offer him one of you three. Now, as it turns out, the eldest and the middle of you have already been promised elsewhere. But,

> *Just as one turns to the warmth of the sun,*
> *Whoever shows great kindness must be rewarded.*

We have no choice but to return his kindness, so the three of you must go to him."

Then the intelligent nāga ministers said, "Now, this Guru of ours:

---

* This third and youngest daughter is actually Metog Lhadzei, but the people knew her by this other name as well. It is to show her insignificance among the three daughters.

Has a long neck like that of the white vultures
That will surely land upon the corpses of the dead animals.
His arms are long like the limbs of the leopards
That will surely snatch and devour a dead dog's body.

Why not ask him to choose not only from just these three nāga daughters but also from among those other girls, who are not only beautiful to look at but are from a good family?

Although freshly cooked white rice is a popular dish,
The wild sweet potato is sweeter than a chunk of brown sugar.

Look at the way this pale-faced Guru treated precious stones and gold dust as though it was just pebbles and sand. The monk with the white face has the fault of being overly excited like:

An arrogant girl is faulted for going crazy over men,
A horse in a frenzy is faulted for being untamed."

"Who knows who he is going to choose," they said.

Then everyone agreed to show him the [rest of the] maidens: one from the royal caste of the nāgas named Dziden Drön [Lamp of Splendor], a maiden of the brahman caste called Metog-tso [Flower Lake], a maiden of the commoner's caste called Lhadzei Kyid [Happy Lovely Goddess], and a nāga maiden of the untouchable caste called Yu-chung Men [Little Turquoise Maid]. All these seven girls were daughters of the nāga king or his ministers. On their heads they wore piled up the jewels that grant all wishes and needs, and on their backs they wore silken brocade robes. Their bodies were slim and straight like bamboo shoots in the spring, their faces as pretty as summer flowers, and their complexions fair as the youthful autumn moon. The youngest among them, Metog Lhadzei, stood out from the others. She was slightly darker[248] and shorter than the rest.

There was much commotion as the nāgas all said, "We must go and see what the guru will do now!" The girls arrived before the Guru, acting afraid and pretending to be scared, tilting and bobbing their heads. They couldn't stand still, and one seemed to be scratching her head continually. The Guru rolled his head from one side to the other, his rooster eyes darting around. Finally he saw Metog Lhadzei and said, "Of the last two girls in the line, the final one is swarthy and meek, and even though she is not the most divine, she is lovely to my fine eyes and pleasing to the snow mountain of my mind. She is the one I like." Then, just as the proverb says:

> *If something's outrageous, then even the monks in their rows will*
> *   laugh;*
> *If you're too full, you will vomit into your own bowl.*

Everybody doubled over in laughter; old women's chests heaved, and babies almost passed out laughing. Their sides ached from belly laughs; their eyes stung with each giggle. As the proverb says:

> *It's not hard to make a choice;*
> *But it's a shame to have made the wrong choice.*

And they all thought, "That's for sure." Then the Guru said, "Well, are you going to offer her to me or not?"

And the king replied, "O yes, sir:

> *The coracle's in the water;*
> *The arrow's in the bow;*
> *The foot's in the stirrup."*

Then the guru said to the girl, "Tell your father that you will need to prepare to bring the tent called Yudra Ting Gung-gu [Blue Turquoise Yak-Hair Tent in Nine Partitions], the sixteen-volume nāga's *One Hundred Thousand Verse Wisdom Sutra,* the cattle of the nāgas, and the female yak, the dri, with three turquoise horns. You had better repeat this [to your father]. And also bring the Cintamaṇi That Dispels Poverty;* the Jewel That Quenches Thirst, which is the essence of the snow mountain; and the Small Maroon Golden Urn that is the quintessence of food. Do not ask for anything other than these."

Then everyone returned to their homes, and the nāga maiden Metog Lhadzei sang this song to her father, the nāga king Tsugna Rinchen.

> I have no choice but to sing this song,
> But whether it is melodious or not is up to me.

---

* Sanskrit, wish-fulfilling jewel.

You in the golden throne above,
My dear father Tsugna Rinchen,
There is no birth without a father and mother;
Rarer than that is a father with a loving mind.
In the next life it is difficult to find the sacred dharma;
Rarer still is a dharma endowed with blessings.

The idiot race of red-faced meat-eating Tibetans
Do not clearly distinguish between dirty and clean.
I fear going to such as a land as that
More than death, but it is inscribed on my skull.
Although my heart aches with despair, this is the command
    of my parents.
Thinking this repays their gift of my body, I soothe my mind.
According to the tradition of worldly proverbs:

A traveler on a long journey should be bedecked with goods.
Without such wealth, one would be a beggar in borderlands.

The arrow shot at long-range should be bedecked with feathers.
Without feathers, it's just a notched bamboo stick.

The bride sent far away, should be bedecked with gifts.
Without gifts, she's just a lonely barefoot stray.[249]

Since the land to which I must go is far from my father's
    home,
I need the tent called Yudra Ting Gung-gu.
Since this guiding guru is very strict,
I need the sixteen-volume nāga's *One Hundred Thousand*
    Verse Wisdom Sutra.
Because the borderland of the black-haired ones has declined
    in prosperity,
I need the wealth of the nāgas, the dri with prosperity horns.
I need the Cintamaṇi as my portion of our wealth.

I need the Small Maroon Golden Urn, my portion of our
    victuals.*
Since those dry mountains are far from the moisture of our
    ocean,
I need the Jewel That Quenches Thirst, the essence of the
    snow mountain.
Warm clothing and pleasing speech,
Loving counsels and kind advice; all these things I need from
    you.
Although this maiden girl's mind is grieving,
I do not dare to oppose the command of my kind parents.
In the territory of Tibet in Jambudvīpa,
If there is happiness, it is due to the kindness of the Rare and
    Precious Three Jewels;
If there is suffering, it is through the power of previously
    accumulated karma.
I will never forget the kindness of you, my parents; I will keep
    you in my heart.
Do not forget me, your daughter; please hold me close in
    your heart.
If I am in need, there is a root family, there is a lord.
If I am not in need, then my happiness is my own merit.
You, my parents, please keep this in your hearts.

Thus she sang, and the nāga king Tsugna Rinchen said, "Our nāga kingdom has been reestablished in well-being. To repay your kindness in having cured all the nāgas of illness, we have no choice but to offer you, our daughter, to Guru Lotus Born. As the proverb says:

The maiden girl doesn't stay in her family home.
The vulture doesn't stay in his nest to die.
It's a woman's fate to abandon her [father's] home.
It's a young tiger's honor to fall and die in battle.

---

* For the urn can produce food magically.

You are my own flesh and bones and beloved to me, but I would cut off my own head and ears before being shamefully disloyal. Of course you must go laden with your dowry of jewels and clothing. The common treasures and wealth of the nāgas are not just handed over to others, but since you are my cherished daughter and your groom's home is so far away, I must give you everything you have asked for."

For this reason, on the following morning the king offered his daughter Metog Lhadzei to Uḍḍiyāna Padma and made ready her dowry of the sixteen volume nāga's *One Hundred Thousand Verse Wisdom Sutra*, the tent called Yudra Ting Gung-gu, the wealth of the nāgas, the dri with prosperity horns, the Small Maroon Golden Urn for her share of victuals, the Jewel That Quenches Thirst as the essence of the snow mountains, and many valuables including the jewel of the nāgas that fulfills all needs and desires. Then he sang this song:

> I, the nāga king Tsugna Rinchen,
> Am the crest jewel of all the nāga castes,
> The great sovereign of the underworld of Jambudvīpa.
> No one else governs here.
> Listen Uḍḍiyāna Padmasambhava,
> The initial reason for your coming here
> Was because our nāga kingdom was afflicted with impossible
> illnesses.
>
> First, delusion in the minds of the nāgas,
> Second, due to terrible fierce wrath and aggression,
> In the end we were brought down by our own imperial
> passion and desire.
> On the brink of being motivated by jealousy
> And in the clutches of the demonic forces of pride,
> We invited your skillful means to cure us.
> Knowing in your heart the benefit of beings, you came gladly
> And looked upon our entire nāga kingdom with your
> compassion.
> With the supreme medicine of the five wisdoms,
> You cured us of the illnesses of the five poisons.
> With clouds of smoke from the five types of trees
> You utterly cleansed our impure corruptions and
> obscurations.

I supplicate you, Lord of Great Kindness.
In particular, in order to repay your kindness,
Although I offered an abundance of five varieties of jewels,
You were not pleased with illusory wealth.
Since you see the nāga girl as a disciple who will benefit
     beings,
I offer her to you in accordance with your wishes.
This dowry portion of precious wealth,
The nāga tent called Yudra Ting Gung-gu,
The wealth of the nāgas, the dri with wealth-energy horns,
And the nāga's sixteen-volume *One Hundred Thousand Verse
     Wisdom Sutra**
Are indispensable to me; nevertheless I will send them with
     her as her dowry.

How can this offering be the end?
According to the worldly proverbs:

The guru who is the guide of beings,
If he does not continuously care for his students,
*Conferring a few empowerments alone will not deliver them
     buddhahood.*

The chieftain who rules over a vast area,
If he does not continuously advise his subjects,
*Hearing just a few of his words will not please their minds and is not
     something they can depend on.*

The day that the kind parents give their daughter away,
If the paternal family she leaves behind does not always watch
     out for her,
Just giving her a few material possessions will not bring her
     satisfaction.

---

* There are both twelve- and sixteen-volume versions of the collection of Prajñāpāramitā texts. This accounts for the variation in references in the epic; both are correct.

The first stroke of good fortune came from the nāgas
When we of the nāga kingdom were freed from disease.
May the prosperity and good fortune of the nāgas be given to
    the humans.
The second stroke of good fortune will come from the nyen
When the drala nyen is born in the family of humans in
    Tibet.[250]
May there be the auspiciousness of reversing the army of
    barbarians.
The third stroke of good fortune will come from Ling.
When bliss and happiness are established and spread in
    Multicolored Ling.
May there be the auspiciousness of the happiness of holding
    the celestial cord.[251]

May the sun of auspiciousness shine;
May the white moon of auspiciousness dawn;
May the auspicious banner cover the peak of existence.
May the white conch of auspiciousness resound
In the land of snow in the southern region of Jambudvīpa.
May the auspiciousness of happiness commence.
May the covering sky continue to cover;
May the supporting earth continue to support;
May it come about that Tibet is a source of hope.
May all aspirations be fulfilled!

If you understand the song, keep it in the core of your heart.
If you don't understand it, there is no way to explain it.
May you keep this in your heart just as it is.

Thus he sang, and the special connection was made. Guru Uḍḍiyāna Padma
expressed his pleasure as the proverb says:

If the guru is pleased by the offering, the blessings will be all the
    greater;
If the girl is happy with the dowry, then her father's repute is all the
    greater;
If the servant is happy with his food, his "Yes sirs" will be all the more.

Just like that, Padma had blessed them by putting an end to the illness of the nāgas so that it would not recur. There would no longer be any droughts or sandstorms, nor harm derived through delusion. Although it was difficult for the patron and guru to separate, nevertheless, the king escorted Padma off on his way and through his miraculous powers Padma took the nāga wealth and the king's daughter along with him out of the ocean.

Then after a while, he thought to himself, "I had better find a lord for this maiden," and he burst forth with this song:

> NAMO BUDDHA BODHISATTVA
> From the Akaniṣṭha great bliss dharmadhātu pure land,
> Is the unerring refuge dharmakāya Samantabhadra.
> I supplicate you to reveal the unobstructed display of
>   awareness.
> I am the glorious Lotus Born.
> Nāga woman Yelga Dzeiden
> Listen, here is my question.
> Although I arise, I arise from within the unborn,
> Although I go, I go back into the unborn
> I have no reason to remain here.
> So now, for a while you may choose which land to inhabit,
> Which king, which leader, which family and master;
> Whatever you want, choose, and I'll ask for you.
> Meanwhile I will make the arrangements for your future
>   family,
> You will stay there for three years.
> At that time I will send the keeper of the prophesy to you.
> Whatever you wish now, speak up clearly.

Thus he sang the song, and she had no idea how to respond. Then the Guru went on to say, "I will receive an indication of the auspicious connection that you have with your future country." He removed his hat and flung it up into the sky, and it landed on the roof of the tent of Tönpa Gyaltsen of the Gog Ralo paternal clan, encircled by masses of rainbow light rays. Tönpa Gyaltsen saw this and thought, "Could this be a good sign?" He picked up the hat and placed it on his shrine as an object of devotion. Through his miraculous powers the Guru then arrived at the door of Gog Ralo Tönpa Gyaltsen. That very night, Tönpa Gyaltsen had a prophetic dream in which a white man surrounded by rays of light gave him a vase filled with nectar and said, "Early tomorrow morning, go and see who has arrived at your doorstep and whatever is told to you, promise to do it. If so there will be great siddhi." Then he vanished from sight.

When he awoke he donned his clothes and shoes and went to see who would be at the door. In no time at all, a guru wearing the lotus hat and a beautiful girl leading a dri laden with her belongings arrived there. Wondering, "What's this all about," Tönpa Gyaltsen was astonished, because by the sight of his lotus hat the man at the door seemed to be a guru, but he looked like an ordinary man since he was leading a girl. Tönpa thought, "Perhaps this is what was predicted last evening." In any case, thinking he wanted to question them, Tönpa Gyaltsen stooped down to greet them: "Well, well-accomplished yogin with consort, where have you been and where are you going? What are the provisions that you carry on the back of this dri? Come on in, take a seat, and let's have a talk."

The Guru replied, "Ah yes, I have come from the continent of Cāmara and I'm planning to return there as well. I will depart to mingle awareness with the space of great bliss. I will depart to meditate on the wondrous bodhicitta, and I will depart to accomplish the profound benefit of others. I came here to see you, Tönpa Gyaltsen." With the Guru having said that, at that moment the messengers of [the Guru's] compassion overcame [Tönpa Gyaltsen's] three gates* and suddenly he remembered last night's dream and became filled with devotion and pure view toward the Guru. He offered him tea, liquor, and tsampa mixed with butter and, showing boundless respect and devotion, requested protection and blessings. Then Uḍḍiyāna Guru Padmasambhava said, "Listen Gog Ralo Tönpa Gyaltsen, if my coming here does not achieve the benefit of beings, there's no point in calling me a guru. If a monk dharma practitioner does not abandon the lower realms, then it is disheartening to have entered the path of the profound dharma. If a great meditator cannot traverse the bardo, then his meditation experience is like a bubble in water. Now the main reason for coming here is as follows and, having spoken, he raised this dohā:

NAMO RATNA BUDDHA DHARMAYE
Buddha Amitābha who abides in the pure land of Akaniṣṭha,
With your undistracted enlightened mind consider the
  welfare of all beings.
Lead them on the path to the land of Sukhāvatī.
I am the guru Uḍḍiyāna Lotus Born.

---

* Body, speech, and mind.

First I came from the continent of Cāmara.
I came for the benefit of the beings of the three realms.
Second I went to the country of the nāgas for the benefit of
    beings
And saved them from the fear of the suffering of disease.
They expressed their gratitude by offering me this nāginī maiden.
Finally I came to Gog.
This is the specific purpose of the interdependent
    connections:
This nāginī Yelga Dzeiden
Is to be your stepdaughter, Ralo Tönpa;
This Turquoise Tent in Nine Partitions
Is to be your prized treasure;
This sixteen-volume nāga's *One Hundred Thousand Verse
    Wisdom Sutra*
Is your object of devotion, Ralo Tönpa;
This nāga beast dri with turquoise horns
Is the wealth of your livestock.
Don't let the children pick these flowers that have sprung
    forth in the field,
Offer them to the gods.
Receive these blessings, for they have great potential.
Do not trade away these treasures of the wealth of the
    precious earth for profit;
Keep them well and gradually realization will come to you.
This nāginī maiden, Yelga Dzeiden,
Do not betroth her to another, but keep her as your daughter
    for a long time.

Ralo, you will rise in status.
The district of Gog will expand and increase.
Son of noble family, whatever you desire will occur.
I cannot stay, for I must depart for the continent of Cāmara.
If I don't go, all the rākṣas will be out of control.
Don't waver! This is my heartfelt advice.
When her true lord comes to claim her,
That is the time that the wealth, the man, and the maiden
    should be joined.

Until then, her happiness and sorrow are your responsibility.
If you understand the meaning of this song, you will know
    the purpose of all of this.
If you don't understand the song, there's nothing to explain.
Ralo Tönpa keep this in your heart.

Thus he sang, and Ralo Tönpa Gyaltsen said, "Oh yes, sir, as the proverb states:

The merit of the colorful meadow
Magnetizes the rain without invitation.
The merit of the third month of spring
Magnetizes the cuckoo without invitation.
The merit of the irrigation ditches in the field
Magnetizes the southern clouds without invitation.

The merit of Ralo Tönpa magnetizes the uninvited companion, the nāginī maiden. This is how it has come to be. Listen, O listen to this song." So saying, he [Ralo Tönpa Gyaltsen] offered this song:

Ala leads the song through the mind stream of bodhicitta.
Thala carries the path to liberation.
I am Ralo Tönpa Gyaltsen,
Ralo the head of all clans;
The country of Gog is the origin of all counties.
Greatly kind Lord Guru,
I take refuge in you; hold me with your compassion
In this life, the next, and the bardo, these three.
You are my source of hope, O nirmāṇakāya.
If you don't fulfill my hopes, but break your promise,
It will look like you, Guru, have abandoned saṃsāra
While the undesired Lord of Death makes great obstacles.
It will look like the husband has left for the mountain
    hermitage
While the mistress of the house is left behind, full of agitation.
It will look like the animals are grazing in higher pastures
While they are only pulling hard against their nose rings.
Although I shouldn't be so bold as to speak like this, this is
    how it is.

Therefore, I will make this nāga woman Dzeiden Ma
The princess of the one thousand householders of the Ralo
clan.
I will make the sacred dharma my object of worship.
We will care for this dri, the most cherished of all beasts.
How could anyone dare to break the guru's command?
If the disciple breaks the guru's command, then
The samaya connection will be the cause for the hell realm.*
If a servant breaks the command of his leader,
He loses his chance for food and clothing.
If children break the command of their parents,
Then they waste the kindness with which the parents cared
for them.
I will ensure that her happiness is immutable, like an armored
goddess.252
I will make sure her happiness is immutable.
I won't let her be unhappy; I'll care for her like my own
parents.
In the future when the guru returns,
All the goods, the articles and possessions I will convey to
their owner.
I swear on the Three Jewels to the truth of this.
If this oath is broken, may there be no liberation for me.
If you have understood, then please accept this offering of
song.
If you don't understand this, there is no way to explain it.

Thus he spoke and the Guru himself replied, "So be it. As for me:

If I entrust my possessions to someone, it would be to my disciples;
If I entrust my son, it's to someone with a loving mind;
If I entrust my victuals, it would be to a person who has a sense of
shame.

---

* Generally the pure samaya connection is the cause for liberation, but if this connection is defiled,
it will be the cause for rebirth in the lower realms.

The happiness and sorrow of this girl depends on you and this is what you need to know. I have nothing else to say." Saying this he departed along with a ray of white light into the southwestern sky.

The nāga maiden remained in the land of Gog for two years and five months. Finally, from the divine realm of the thirty-three, the divine child Thöpa Gawa knew that the time had come to accomplish the benefit of beings, and he passed from that divine realm.

Now the story of the way that he took birth in the land of humans in Jambudvīpa will follow in the sequel. The account up to here is called *The Divine Land of Ling, the Nine-Squared Divination Board.** Since it is an auspicious coincidence and the original spiritual and historical account, the blessings it carries with it are profound. The first biographical account is now complete.

> From the vast ocean of this protector's biography,
> This drop of purifying water of the nectar of excellent
>   explanations has been sprinkled
> On the tip of the kuśa grass blade of faith, exertion, and analysis
> As an offering of the pure water of enjoyment to the buddhas
>   and their heirs.
> By the virtue accumulated through this effort, may all
>   sentient beings
> Utterly destroy the māras of perverted understanding—
>   self-perception arising as the enemy—
> With the weapon of the primordial wisdom vajra,
> And may they achieve the invincible state of innate
>   fearlessness.

Of the many accounts of his life, this one is so genuine that many scholars and accomplished practitioners recommended it be carved into a woodblock. Accordingly it was carved and printed in the kingdom of Ling.

May excellent virtue increase!

SARVA MAṄGALAM

---

* *The Events Leading to Gesar's Incarnation in the Land of Ling*, volume 1 of this edition.

This epic was carved in Derge Lingtsang into woodblocks and the print taken from that became the original which was the basis for this typewritten version produced by Thubten Nyima [Alak Zenkar Rinpoche] and others who corrected, edited, and arranged the chapters.

VOLUME TWO

*Gesar's Birth and Childhood
in the Land of Ling*

PROLOGUE

THIS VOLUME WAS TAKEN from the woodblocks of the Ling family in Derge and is among the numerous biographical accounts of the Great Lion Being* of Jambudvīpa. The original is titled *Trung Ling* [*The Birth in Ling*], and is also known as *Metog Rawa* [*The Flower Garden*]; it also includes "Ma Sa Zung" [The Settling of Ma], which is sometimes called "Darkar Düdpa" [The Knotted White Scarf]. Using the woodblocks as the original, these books were typewritten, edited, corrected, and arranged by Thubten Nyima and others.

> NAMO GURU MAHĀ SENGHA MAṆI RĀJAYE†
> Although you are fully awakened, until the realms of beings
>   are emptied
> You will continue to spontaneously manifest countless
>   magical emanations
> To place limitless sentient beings in the state of the four
>   kāyas—
> O Buddha Śākya Sengei‡
>   protect us!
>
> The treasury, profound and tranquil like nectar,
> Is called the dharma of sutra, *vinaya*, and *abhidharma*

---

* Great Lion Being is an epithet for Gesar.

† A Sanskrit mantra meaning "I bow to the Great Lion Jewel King."

‡ Śākya Sengei means Lion of the Śākya and is the name of one of the eight aspects of Padmasambhava. In this form he appears as a Buddhist monk.

And is the wish-fulfilling power of *śila*, samādhi, and prajñā—
May the precious jewel of the sacred dharma that bestows
    supreme liberation be victorious!

Through the sharp weapon of prajñā that realizes selflessness
The mountain of the view of materialism[1] is utterly destroyed
And the continuity of the suffering of saṃsāra is severed—
Sovereign with the throne of the view, supreme assembly of
    āryas protect us!

To Padmākara* from the island in the lake of the Sindhu
    River,[2]
To the flower of the god Brahmā of the snow land of Tibet,
And to the Rigden Raudrachakrin from the north,
Who are indivisible from Gesar Jewel Tamer of Beings,[3]
    I bow down.

Your biography is like an ocean of milk
From which this drop on the tip of a kuśa grass blade of
    discernment
Is given as offering nectar to please the buddhas and their
    heirs
And sprinkled to dispel the torment of perverted views.

Eternally pervading and spontaneously present,
This single biography manifests in myriad ways.
When the sublime ones are presented from an ordinary
    perspective
The ripening karma is like the story of the nāga Ehle'i Dab.[4]
Nevertheless, the rūpakāya,[5] like the full moon in the sky,
Distinctly appears in the water vessels of beings' minds
    according to their own devotion and longing.
I have no interest in analyzing whether this is right or wrong;
Whatever appears to one's mind is the object of one's
    devotion.

---

* Lotus Born, an epithet of Padmasambhava.

Therefore, in the land of lapis lazuli called Thong Mön
    [Aspiration Upon Sight]
Where his fame is as astonishing as the god Indra,
The glory of his incarnation is so great that his biography is
    undiminished,
As clear as if carved in stone.

Therefore in Dzamling is this Great Lion among Men,
The account of whose birth is renowned throughout Ling.
The myriad flower-like arrangements of his miraculous
    emanations
Are resplendent here, like viewing the beauty of a delightful
    garden.

Having begun this biography with these words of auspiciousness, now concerning the enlightened deeds of the Vajra Lake-Born Lord of the Victorious Ones,* in order to tame the unruly in need of taming in the land of Tibet, he [the Vajra Master] actually appeared and sent forth emanations, instantaneously as well as gradually manifesting to enact the welfare of beings in multitudes of ways. Such spontaneous and effortless enlightened activity is the nature of all the victorious ones. It is proclaimed here that this account of the life of the Supreme Being of Jambudvīpa, Jewel Tamer of Beings, is in accordance with previous authentic historical accounts.[6] The first part of the epic of Gesar can be divided into these three volumes: (1) *The Divine Land of Ling: The Nine-Squared Divination Board*, (2) *The Birth in Ling: The Flower Garden*, continuing with *The Settling of Ma: The Knotted White Scarf*, and (3) *The Horse Race: The Sevenfold Jewel*.[7] Here is the story of his birth, explaining how he, a child, performed the benefit of formless beings in Dza, Dri, and Ma. The next part details how he engaged in fearless yogic conduct to settle the land of Ma, and the final account describes how he became the golden throne-holder of White Ling by manifesting his rūpakāya along with his miraculous manifestations.

---

* An epithet for Padmasambhava

CHAPTER ONE

While Gyatsha Zhalkar* was drawing up an army to send to Gog,
Trothung magically sent a secret message.
Senglön performed a clairvoyant arrow divination
And received Gogza† in gratitude as his share of the spoils.

FIRST AMONG THE RETINUE of hundreds of thousands of enlightened beings
surrounding the dharma king Indrabodhi was Padmasambhava, an emanation of
Amitābha. King Indrabodhi and his entourage were all emanations from the same
undifferentiated source. Through aspiration prayers and arousing bodhicitta, for
the noble families the time had come to tame the māras and cannibal demons of Tibet, and resounding as self-arising formless sound from the sky was this song, which
invokes the enlightened mindstreams [of all the sages]:

> E MA HO
> Unborn primordially empty dharmadhātu,
> Unobstructed ground for the arising of phenomena,
> The strength of emptiness free from the extremes of existing
>   or not,
> Listen to this song, a self-arising spontaneously present song.

---

* Gyatsha Zhalkar is the nephew of the Emperor of China and is Gesar's elder half-brother.

† Because she lived with Ralo of Gog upon arriving in the human land, the nāga princess is referred
to as Gogza, the girl from the Gog clan.

Without considering the six grains of the three months of autumn,
Why toil in the fields in the three months of spring?
Without considering the abundance of the plunder,
Why wave your arms to summon enemies and disputes?
Without considering the benefit of others,
Why single-pointedly practice to try to accomplish enlightenment?

Failing to know the minds of those to be tamed, one is not a buddha.
Failing to fulfill the welfare of others is not the sacred dharma.
Failing to lead others to liberation is not the sangha.

> Therefore, in the snow land of Tibet,
> The field of the Great Compassionate One Avalokiteśvara—
> Although the sun of dharma arises,
> The classes of māras threaten to eclipse it
> Through the perverted aspirations of the nine samaya-
>   violating demon brothers.

> If the dark side is not annihilated at its very root,
> The country of Tibet will become a land of darkness
> And sentient beings will be led to the hells below.
> In order for the king and ministers
> To tame these hordes of māras,
> The king should be like a *cakravartin* ruler,
> His outer ministers must abide in the borderlands,
> And his inner ministers must abide close to him.
> Then, the object of veneration Sergyi Dogcan [Golden-Faced
>   One]
> Will emanate as the elder uncle, the senior advisor [of Gesar].*
> The Brahman Halikapa
> Will emanate as the father† of the paternal lineage of the
>   Mukpo clan.
> The general of unrivaled warriorship

---

* Chipön Rongtsha Tragen.

† Senglön.

Will emanate as the older brother,* like a tiger in his prime.
The others, outer and inner ministers,
Will emanate in the forms of a harmonious brotherhood.
The time to benefit others has arrived.
Without distraction keep this in the core of your heart.

Thus the sound of this song invokes the mindstreams of the bodhisattvas.†

Among the royal ancestors of the Mukpo Dong clan, Chöphen Nagpo [Dharma Benefit Black] had three wives: Serza, Omza, and Changza, each of whom bore three sons. The son of Ser was Lhayag Darkar [Good Divine White Silk], the son of Om was Trichang Pagyal [Wolf Throne Victorious Warrior], and the son of Chang was Dragyal Bum-me [Victorious over Enemies Hundred Thousand Flames]. The lineages descending from these three became the Greater, Lesser, and Middle Lineages of the Mukpos.

From the Lesser Lineage came the son of King Dragyal Bum-me, Thoglha Bum [Lightning God Hundred Thousand]. In turn Thoglha Bum's son was Chöla Bum [For the Dharma Hundred Thousand]. Chöla Bum had three wives. They were Rongza, Gaza, and Muza, these three. Rongza's son was an incarnation of the Paṇḍita Sergyi Dogcan, born as Chief [Chipön] Rongtsha Tragen.

His intelligence and knowledge[8] were as bright as day,
His skill and compassion were like the springtime warmth of
    earth and water,
His commands were straightforward like lines drawn with a ruler,
He could distinguish true from false actions like splitting
    bamboo.
Unruly strong men he could yoke and suppress,
Like a parent he protected the weak and humble.
Of the brethren he was the chief,
At meetings his was the final[9] word,
When taming the enemies he was the general of all
    bandits.[10]

---

* Gyatsha Zhalkar.

† Gesar and so forth.

Although he was born in the clan of the Lesser Lineage, he was respected as the principal chieftain of all of Ling.

To Gaza was born a son, Yu-gyal [Turquoise King], who, while warring with Hor, was lost to the Hor in battle. To Muza was born an emanation of the Brahmin Legjin.* He was named Senglön [Lion Minister]. At birth he was:

> Outwardly gentle like a white silk scarf,
> Inwardly gentle like white butter pills,†
> A gentle warmth like that of the springtime sun.
> His mind was loose and relaxed like a knot in a scarf,
> His body was a heap of splendor, and
> His speech like a majestic melodious reed.
> He mastered the magical luminosity of enlightened mind.
> He was born as a fortress of many dralas,
> As a copper castle surrounded by wermas, and
> As a life stone that the samaya-bound protectors take as their
>   support.

Chipön married a Tibetan girl named Metog Tashi-tso [Flower Auspicious Lake]. Their eldest son was Yuphen Tag-gyal [Turquoise Benefit Tiger King], their middle son was Lenpa Chögyal [Simple-Minded Dharma King], and their youngest son was Nangchung Yutag [Sweet Youth Turquoise Tiger]. They had one daughter Lhamo Yudrön [Goddess Turquoise Torch], making four children.

Senglön wed a Chinese girl, Lhakar Drönma [Divine White Torch]. In the year of the Female Water Ox during the twelfth month‡ their son was born.

> His face was like the moon,
> His mind as vast as the sky.
> All of his actions were dharma activity.
> He was a bitter thorn-bush to his enemies,

---

* The Brahmin Legjin could have been the teacher of Thönmi Sambhota, who was the founder of the Tibetan literary language.

† A lump of freshly churned white butter often given to nomadic children as a treat.

‡ "Twelfth month" (Tib. *rgyal zla ba*). Literally, the "Royal Moon"; that is, when the moon is in the eighth constellation, mid-winter.

And a white silken scarf to his friends.
As a warrior he was a ferocious tigress.
He was like a falcon,[11] expert in the six skills of a warrior.

Everyone in his family called him Zhal-lu Nyima Rangshar [Face of the Self-Arising Sun]. Outside he was given the name Bumpa Gyatsha Zhalkar [Chinese Nephew White Face of the Bum Family].

For thirteen days the gurus did long-life and prosperity ceremonies, and the fathers and uncles made aspiration prayers, while the mothers and aunts danced and sang to celebrate his birth.

The name of the Greater Lineage's leader was Lhabu Namkha Sengzhal [Prince Sky-Lion Face]. The leader of the Middle Lineage was Lingchen Tharpa Sönam [Great Ling Meritorious Liberation] and the leader of the Lesser Lineage was Chipön. These three leaders offered an Auspicious-by-Day scarf to the neck of Zhal-lu. Then Chipön said, "O great gathering of divine subjects! Among merits this is the first sign of the spread of authentic presence, the field of power. Among dreams this is the first time that dreams have come true, and this is the first time to tame the enemies of the four directions. Now listen without distraction to the silk scarf of this song." And then the three leaders sang:

Ala Thala Thala the song is sung.
The song is offered to the great god Brahmā,
Offered to the local deity Magyal Pomra,[12]
To the strict and mighty zodor Gedzo,
And to the god of great ones, Nyentag Marpo [Red
    Mountain Tiger].

May their great sovereignty spread across the sky;
May the great vessel of the earth hold this all.
In case you don't recognize this place,
It is Kyidsö Yag-gi Khado [Conjunction of Happiness and
    Leisure],
The gathering place called Tagthang Tramo [Colorful Tiger
    Plain].
Inside the great four-cornered yak hair tent
Is a place of joyful reunions.
If you don't know the likes of me—
I am the king chief of the Rong clan;

My partners in this song are the leaders of the Greater and
    Middle Lineages.
We three brother leaders offer this song.

Today the stars in the sky are excellent;
On earth the time is right and the signs are excellent.
At this time when the three excellent signs converge
We must celebrate the birth of the leader of Mupa, Zhalkar;
The people of White Ling must perform song and dance.
May the gods and gurus perform longevity, prosperity, and
    purification rituals,
May the mothers and aunts make excellent aspiration
    prayers, and
May the fathers and brothers be open-minded with skillful
    means.
According to the sayings passed on by ancient Tibetans:

If you supplicate, honor, and make offerings
To the gods, jewels, and dear leaders, these three,
All your needs and wishes will be fulfilled.
If you diligently accomplish trade, husbandry, and taming your
    enemies, these three,
Then prosperity will come.
Horses, spouses, and homes, these three,
To adorn them and keep them clean is for your own good.

It has been a custom in the land of Ling
From the time of Ling Chöphen[13] Nagpo until now,
When the enemy came, we hoisted our spears as one,
When goods came, it was a custom to portion them with the
    tip of a knife and share.

The gifts for the birth celebration from the Greater Lineage
    of the Serpa are:
Ten coins of yellow gold,
Golden armor replete with silken ruffles,
A golden helmet with a golden silken victory standard,

A sword with a golden guard,
A golden horse named Serja Dingdrö [Soaring Golden Bird
     Gait],
A golden saddle with a golden bridle, and a gold crupper,
All adorned with silken yellow scarves of auspiciousness;
These are the ninefold offerings of yellow gold.

The gifts for the birth celebration from the Middle Lineage of
     Ombu are:
A stupa as white as a conch,
A clockwise-turning melodious conch,
Conch armor and a golden flowing robe,
A conch helmet adorned with a white silk topknot,
The sword Sampa Regchöd [Severs with a Thought]
With a guard of refined white silver,
The horse with a Mongolian gait Dawa'i Dogcan [White
     Moon Color].
A silver saddle, silver bridle, and silver crupper
Including the white scarf Auspicious-by-Day;
These are the ninefold offerings of white conch.

I, the chieftain of the Mu family of the Lesser Lineage,
Offer white turquoise[14] that resembles a drop of milk,
Turquoise armor called Dzari Thogkheb [Crag Mountain
     Meteorite-Proof],
A turquoise helmet called Namkha Lebchen [Vast as the Sky],
Adorned with silk flags called Trinlang Mö [Rich like
     Massing Clouds],
The ancestral wealth of Jurlha Bön [Coral Divine Chief] of
     Jang
The chestnut steed with a turquoise-beaded mane and saddle
     adorned with turquoise,
With matching turquoise bridle and crupper,
With the sword Shapho Dumchöd [Dresses a Deer],
Blue silken hand guard tie,
Including the inner scarf from the fish[15] Trawa Kha
     [Sparkling Mouth];[16]

These are the ninefold offerings of turquoise blue
Offered by the family of the Lesser Lineage for the birthday
  celebration.

Then, although the subjects of the six tribes of Ling,
Are divided into the Middle, Lesser, and Greater Lineages,
Despite their names, one is not greater than the other in
  status or achievement.
In the ancestral lineage of Chöphen Nagpo
They were named so according to which of [their founding
  mothers] was first born,[17]
And they all come from the same paternal tribe.
These three golden flowers of the royal family
Are like a single vase placed on the crown of the head.*
Whatever words they speak are like amṛta on the tongue,
Whatever actions they perform are for the general
  governance of the six districts.
According to the ancient sayings of the Tibetans:

In order to keep the square walls of a monastic college,
The holder of the vase and the sutras and tantras
Will be the one who is learned in the experience of the three trainings.

When the exalted leader upholds the law of the land,
The holder of the golden throne and status
Will be the one who has vast knowledge, authentic presence, and
  political savvy.

Therefore, we of the lineage of the white snow lion—
It is better that our turquoise manes inhabit the snow
  mountains;
We never thought to wander to the bustling town.
We descendants of the lineage of the turquoise dragon—
It is better that our roar dwells in the thundering clouds;
We never thought to wander through foreign lands.

---

* The ceremony of tantric initiation involves touching a blessed vase to the initiate's head.

So it is with the lineage sons of the Mukpo clan—
It is better that we place yokes upon the enemy;
We never thought that our own goal would not be
    accomplished.

Nevertheless:

The royal parasol of the sun
Gives warmth to the four continents.
Yet still, if the conch moon did not rise in the sky,
Who could find their way in the pitch black of night?
Although the stars sparkle, they would be of no help.

Thus, the twelve countries of Jambudvīpa
And the four borderlands that are the māra kingdoms
Will be tamed by one who is sent from divine White Ling.
When the warriors with form, the adversaries,
And the champions of the enemy gather for battle,
The three great chieftains of Ling will rise up like the sun.
Then, placing a yoke upon the formless obstructing spirits,
The demon harrying from behind,[18] and on the gods,
    rākṣasas, and ghosts,
He, though not human, will magically appear as a human boy.
First, he will be the one the imperial gods bow to,
Secondly, he is the one the body gods circumambulate,
Third, the one to whom the nāga Tsugna makes offerings,
And fourth, he is the one whose body has achieved
    miraculous powers.
May he be born as an ornament to White Ling.

Where in the lineage of the three brothers of Mukpo Dong
He will be born, was set down long ago.
All this is the fervent wish of Ling,
And this wish has burst from our mouths
As both an exclamation and a prophecy.
By the truth of these words of excellent auspicious
    coincidence
May the golden sun of the lineage of chieftains

Cover the sky with its great sovereignty.
May the great vessel of the earth hold this all.
May whatever song is sung turn to the dharma.
May these words be full of genuine meaning!
If the song has caused confusion, we confess the fault.
If the words have been but meaningless chatter, we beg your
    forgiveness.
May the six districts of Ling hold this in their hearts.

[Gyatsha Zhalkar visits the Emperor of China.]

Then Upper, Middle, and Lower Ling celebrated the birth with abundant song and dance. As for Zhalkar, in one month's time he grew more than other children would grow in a year. When Zhalkar came of age, the Emperor of China invited his three nephews to a feast: the son of Sadam of Jang, named Nyitri Karchen [Twenty Thousand Great Stars], the son of Achen of Hor, Lhabu Legpa [Excellent Prince], and the dear Zhalkar himself, the son of the Bumpa clan. He gave each of them the inner wealth from the natural resources of his own country. As principal gifts each one received a horse, a sword, and armor. Including gold, silver, tea, silk and so forth, about a hundred gifts were bestowed. Then he said, "O my three dear nephews, may your wishes be fulfilled! Listen to the white scarf of this song without distraction. Do not forget the fruit of this meaning—hold it in your minds. Here are three words of completely flawless advice." Saying that he broke into song:

Ala is the way the song begins,
Thala is the sound of the melody.
Undeceiving Refuge, Rare and Precious Three Jewels,
Abide inseparably as my crown ornament.

In case you don't know what place this is,
This is Trülgyi Potrang [The Magic Palace] of the Emperor of
    China.
In case you don't know the likes of me,
In the vast azure firmament
And on the face of the dense earth,
I am the ruler of China.
Now, listen closely to what I say.
The well-known proverbs of the ancients teach:

164

Mount Meru, the ocean, and a great leader, these three—
It is preferred that they be firm and unmoving.
Conversation, counsel, and arrows, these three—
It is preferred that they be straight, not crooked or bent.
Lawsuits, bows, and lassos, these three—
It is preferred that they bend wherever they are stretched.

It is possible that there will be turmoil and battle between the
    great countries,
But great leaders should be a single stable fortress.
The paternal lineage of the Chinese is whiter than conch;
Do not cut or carve this, for it is [precious] like gold.
The three horses, Pheasant, Peacock, and Duck,
Are the prosperity of the eastern country of China.
These will be the horses beneath you, my three nephews.

First the conch armor called Karmo Lhazang [Pure
    Benevolent God],
Second the turquoise armor called Bumgyal Tongthub [One
    Hundred Thousand Victories and a Thousand Defeats],
Third, armor of meteoric iron called Dzari Thogthub [Slate
    Mountain Lightning Proof]—
These weapons were magically forged by the eight orders of
    nonhumans
And are the life fortress that cannot be pierced by any swords.
Oh my three dear ones, Zhal, Nyitri, and dear little Lha,
I give you this armor as your companion for life;
May it make your bodies invincible.

East of China, so as to make this auspicious armor
Three cranes were fed with iron dust;
The iron dust that they vomited
Was forged at the first pale light of dawn by a rākṣa
    blacksmith
Into the sword Guzi Namkha Kyareng [Skydawn].
Made from masculine metal, like the male wrathful ones,
Feminine metal, like the laughter of the female wrathful ones,
And metal like that of their offspring, like shooting stars,[19]

165

With patterns on the blade like banking southern clouds.
Wielding it, it outshines the eight classes of gods with its
    splendor.
Striking with it crushes boulders to dust.
Jang Nyitri Karchen, I offer this to you.

The iron dust that the birds shat out
The blacksmith of the king of the tsen spirits, Yamshüd,[*]
In the obscure darkness of night forged into the sword
Azi Dugral Barwa [Blazing Poison Slasher].
The nape of the sword is as radiant as dawn,
The belly of the blade is as dark as nightfall,
The patterns on the blade swirl like the ocean.
Hard, tempered iron like an angry rākṣa,
Malleable iron like a tied knot.
Striking, it eats the enemy's flesh.
Lhabu Legpa of Hor, I offer this to you.

The iron still left in the birds' stomachs,
Even as the morning star shone
The blacksmith of the *the'u rang*[†] magically forged into
    another sword—
Striking molten bell metal
And forging molten bronze
Tempered in crocodile blood.
Dralas surround the nape of this sword,
Teeming and ready to act.
*Gandharva*s throng the dark razor edge of the blade,
They gather so densely that their groaning can be heard.
Patterns swirl on the blade like the ocean,
Their pounded imprint like swelling waves.
It is said that if you strike a great river
With this wind sword,[20] it will reverse the river's flow.

---

[*] Yamshüd is the king of the tsen.

[†] The *the'u rang* are spirits who support gamblers.

When it was in the country of China,
It was known as Tongtse Zilnön [Splendidly Quelling a
Thousand Sword Tips].
This is the sword of your heritage, Chief Zhal-lu of Ling.

Here are various types of gold, silver, and silk,
Varieties of tea and so forth which I offer—
Offerings by the hundreds to each one of you in celebration.
These [offerings] are to show my appreciation at meeting my
nephews.

To be a high leader of the great districts
You must bring down the mighty and
Like a parent, protect the humble and weak.
Like split bamboo, your actions discern truth from falsity.
Be open-minded like the expanse of space,
With upāya and prajñā like the rising sun;
Then your plan will be gentle like the earth and water in
spring.[*]
Goals will not be accomplished solely by persistence.
If you can't defeat the enemy and he overcomes you,
Then you will be unable to protect those who are weak.
If you only think of gaining wealth
Then you will never have a reputation for honest justice.
According to ancient Tibetan proverbs:

On nine round trips to China with the white garuḍa dzo,[†]
Although there is no intention to wound its back with a heavy burden,
That's the likely outcome if business is profitable.

Riding your steed nine roundtrips to steal,
Although there is no intention to whip its buttocks,
That's the likely outcome if you are after a pretty penny.

---

[*] In the wintertime the earth and water is frozen, so here he is emphasizing the fluidity and gentleness of the newly born earth and the flowing water of springtime.

[†] This means the best of all the dzo—like the greatest steed.

Swearing oaths of friendship nine times,
Although there is no intention to hurt each other's feelings with evil
words,
That's the likely outcome if the mind is stirred to anger.

Heart essence of China, my three nephews,
You are close relatives so don't think to bicker.
But if there is strife between the great countries, that's the
likely outcome.
With unwavering minds, keep this in your heart.
It's pointless for three brothers to show a hostile face to one
another.
Let all three brother swords remain sheathed together,
Always corral the three brothers' horses together,
For this promotes the dignity of the pure maternal lineage.

No doubt the great garuḍas are powerful,
But it is unthinkable that they would bare their claws and fight up
in space
For they think only of the dignity of the king of birds.

No doubt the three strengths of the white snow lion are fully
matured,
But it is unthinkable that they would fight down on the earth
For they think only of the dignity of the wild beasts.

If you understand this, it is treacle to the ear;
If you don't, there is no explanation for this song.
Three princes, keep this in mind.

After he spoke, everyone was filled with measureless delight. Then the three princes with their ministers, retinue, horses, mules, and the like safely returned to their own places.

[Gyatsha Zhalkar learns of the death of Lenpa Chögyal.]

While Gyatsha of Bumpa had been traveling from colorful White Ling to China, war had broken out between Gog and Ling. Eighteen paternal clans of Gog were destroyed by Ling. In the end Chipön's own son, Lenpa Chögyal, was lost to Gog. For some time they kept this secret from Gyatsha. One day Gyatsha went hunting and, near the spring Karmo Bumkhyil [White Spring of Myriad Swirls], he killed a deer. Just then two wandering villagers from Ling, a mother and son, showed up. The mother realized who he was and said, "Hey, you must be Gyatsha. How wonderful! With you White Ling has everything; without you there is nothing. It's really true. Last year without Gyatsha, Gog and Ling fought, and even though Ling destroyed eighteen patriarchal clans of Gog, what was the point, since Lenpa Chögyal, Chipön's cherished heart-son was killed? Even now, in the districts of White Ling they are saying that you, Gyatsha, will take revenge. Since I happen to be here in your honor's presence, kind leader, won't you please give me a share of this meat you've just killed?" He gave her whatever meat she wanted and carefully asked her questions. She spoke without concealing anything.

Anguish pierced Zhalkar's heart, and instantly he went to the Falcon Fortress to see Chipön, saying, "O King Uncle Chipön, sir. In the first place, how regretful it is to lack the ability to guard one's own kind; in the second place, to be and to act lewd and brainless; and third, indulging in the practice of thievery, keeping this secret to yourself while it is spoken of by the rest of the world.[21] It seems that this is really the way things are," he said, and then broke into this short warrior's song:

> The song is Ala Thala Thala.
> Thala is the melody.
> I bow at the feet of the refuge, the Oceanic Victorious One.
> In case you don't recognize this place,
> It is the wealthy Trakhar Namdzong.
> In case you don't recognize the likes of me,
> I am Gyatsha Zhalkar of Bumpa.
> I am a maternal nephew of the leader, the Emperor of China.
>
> Now then, King Chipön, sir,
> They say your great intelligence is like the dawn sky.
> But look at you—you're more like the dusk than the dawn.
> According to the ancient proverbs of the elders:

If the minister is corrupt, it should be discussed with the chief.
When at war, if somebody is lost to the enemy, a full account should
    be reported to the warriors.
If there's been a robbery, then call out for a clever lad.

169

These are three instances where it is good to speak out.
But man, you have stayed silent to hide your faults
And the words of a beggar woman have shamed me with her
    chiding.[22]

My older cousin Lenpa Chögyal—
When I think of him now, the winds of my heart grow angry.
First of all, a meaningless battle with Gog,
Second, allowing intermarriage with Hor.
It started with the evil shadow of Yellow Hor
And the ill-omened daughter of Künga [All Joyous];
These two brought the downfall of my elder cousin.
Künga's daughter, Zima-tso [Ocean Froth],
Must be sent back to Hor with her tears.[23]
I will not allow her to remain in White Ling.

My elder cousin was lost to Gog:
I, Gyatsha, will be his avenger.
I am Zhalkar, like a white snow lion;
The six skills of a warrior are my luxuriant turquoise mane.
To eat the red meat of my enemy like a hunter eats his game
I do not need the help of a carnivorous fox.
I am Gyatsha, like a tiger in its prime;
My body shining with its armor and weapons are its six
    smiles.
To drink the heart's blood of the enemy ponies
I do not need a platoon of spotted leopards.

I'll tarry no longer, but go to the land of Upper Gog,
First to take ninefold revenge,[24]
Second, to drink more of the heart's blood of the enemy,
And third to see to it that the land of Gog is no more.
Failing this, I, Gyatsha, will be merely a corpse.
If you understand this speech, it is sweet to your ears;
If you don't, there is no way to explain it.
Chipön keep this in your mind.

[Chipön counsels Zhalkar to moderation.][25]

As soon as he had finished, Gyatsha decided to set off for Gog by himself without further discussion. Chipön thought that it was better not to go to war at this time, but he could not manage to convince Zhalkar. He wondered how Zhalkar could possibly go there alone and decided he had better speak with him about this. So Chipön sang this song about the previous events and preparations the warriors must make for the coming battle:

> I can't help but sing this song;
> If I don't sing it, there's nothing left to do.
> When happy, this is a marvelous song for drinking tea and
>   liquor;
> When sad, it is a song to uplift the spirits.
> Unfailing Three Jewels of Refuge and
> Worldly zodors of White Ling,
> Come here today to befriend Chipön.
> Precious jewel of the divine lineage of Bumpa,
> With a relaxed mind, please listen to what I have to say.
>
> Last year, we clashed with Gog about land and people
> And, since we reached neither treaty nor accord
> The result was war between Gog and Ling.
> Three men could wait no longer:
> The chieftain Zigpen of Tag-rong,
> Chipön's son Lenpa Chögyal, and the
> Maternal Uncle Denma Jangtra
> Left for the upper land of Gog
> And destroyed the eighteen father tribes of Gog,
> But the benefit was little for in the end
> Lenpa Chögyal was slain.
>
> Hence, Ling has had its ninefold revenge;
> The lives of all the men were taken
> And Gog became a land of widows.
>
> But the community of Ralo Tönpa
> Had been concealed by gods, nāgas, and nyens, and
> Overlooked by Ling, they had been forgotten.
> Still the thought of defeating him doesn't fit in my mind,

For their protector and refuge is known as Padma Uḍḍiyāṇa,
Their guardian is the nāga king Tsugna Rinchen,
And nāga Tsugna's own daughter is in Gog.

So this is what I, Chipön, think:
In the Mother Text of the Mukpo clan it is said:

That jewel within the ocean
Will be taken by the mouse from the pinnacle of the victory banner.
Whatever positive qualities are desired will be accomplished.[26]

Thus it is said.
If you analyze this, isn't it about the present situation?
Last year during the turmoil of battle we:

Raised a really long club,
But only smacked a really short mutt.
This unwanted year of famine
Fell upon those who are weak, unfortunate, and suffering.

The kinsmen of Ling put their heads together,
But I, Chipön, was without my son.
According to the ancient proverbs:

Even if the feathers of the king of birds fall out,
Don't think that the white crag will change.
Even if the golden-eyed fish is caught on a hook,
Don't think the ocean will swell or ebb.
Even if in battle you lose a loved one, who is as precious as your own eyes,
Don't think to take revenge your whole life.

Knowing I'm sonless does not make me sad
Because my maternal nephew Gyatsha is alive and well.
I have no thought to seek revenge.
I swear this is true on the ancestral *One Hundred Thousand*
    Verse Scripture.
Let me tell you my darkest secrets:

First, the daughter of the nāga king Tsugna,
Second, the dri with prosperity horns,
Third, the little blue nine-partitioned tent,
Fourth, the twelve scriptures of the nāgas' *One Hundred
    Thousand Verses*—
The inner treasures of the underwater nāgas—
Are now the inner wealth of Ralo Tönpa.
I wonder if Ling will have dominion over these four.
When that happens, whatever we wish will be fulfilled.
When the year of the Mouse begins
I think the prophecy will have come to pass.
Treasure these words as the jewel within your collar.
If you go, there's no reason for you to go alone.
Let us all go shoulder to shoulder with Zigphen of Tag-rong,
And with Denma bringing up the rear guard.
Go with an army seventy-thousand strong.
You must bring together the heads and necks of your kinsmen.
To the divine country god zodor
Make offerings, praise with smoke and windhorse.
Dear leader Zhalkar, this is your first raid;
Perhaps without fighting you may be victorious.
If you understand these words, they're sweet to your ear.
If not, there is no way to explain it.
Leader Zhalkar, keep this in your heart.

Then the uncles and nephews had a productive discussion. The very next morning, messages and messengers were sent forth like falling snow to the upper, lower, and middle regions of Ling. The Brethren decided among themselves that they would dispatch an army of seventy thousand to Gog. Three days later, at the crack of dawn, assembling at Tagthang Tramo, they gathered in a state of perfect readiness.

[Trothung forewarns Ralo Tönpa Gyaltsen.]

Then Trothung thought: "This Bumpa Zhal-lu[*] is the very one who is skillful

---

[*] The addition of the syllable "lu" to a name is a term of endearment, and so Bumpa Zhal-lu means "dear Zhalkar of Bumpa."

at holding a white snow lion by its claws and a tiger in its prime by the tips of its ears. If the Brethren and his comrades-in-arms follow him to Gog, then the land of Gog will be no more; they will utterly annihilate it. This daughter of nāga Tsugna as well as their wealth will be our spoils. Zhal-lu will become legendary throughout Tibet. Even though all the treasures we capture will become the general property of Ling, surely the daughter would come to belong to the Lesser Lineage. I must do something about this.

Therefore, I'll do them the great favor of sending a messenger pigeon. Afterward, exercising my skill, I will ask them to give the nāga princess to Tag-rong, where she will be my portion and personal possession. Along with her I will certainly acquire some of the wealth of the nāgas. Even if that doesn't work out, the nāga Tsugna Rinchen is still her father, so what could be better than that?"

And so, he got himself a golden arrow, wrote this letter, blessed it with the mantra for speed travel and attached it to the neck of the arrow, releasing it from the bowstring.

Respectfully presented to Ralo Tönpa Gyaltsen of Gog,
From Trothung, the Chief of Tag-rong:

> Seeking vengeance for the death of Chipön's son last year, Bumpa Zhalkar, leading seven armies of ten thousand mighty warriors each, has decided to attack you the day after tomorrow. Fighting them off is beyond hope. Therefore by nightfall it is vital for you to escape and hide in a safe place.
>
> Now I have done you a great favor. Afterward, if I have a little hope, don't forget to honor it.

[Ralo Tönpa receives Trothung's letter and makes his escape, but the nāga princess wanders away.]

Then he [Trothung] invoked and enjoined the arrow to land on the top of Ralo's tent. He shot it from the peak of Gedzo Rimar [Red Mountain of the Spirit-Lord Gedzo] and, with a crackling sound, the arrow struck the top of the tent. Ralo Tönpa quickly read the letter tied to the neck of that arrow, and, understanding its meaning, he immediately sent messengers and messages throughout the land of Gog. The entire country of Gog including its army fled, but the mules and yaks were unable to carry the turquoise tent and the *One Hundred*

Thousand Verse Scripture. They just managed to lift the nāga treasure onto the back of the dri with wealth horns. That very night they started out and headed for the Ma Valley, which borders the country of Hor. While they were making their nightfall escape, the dri carrying the nāga treasure turned around and went back in the other direction on the path. The nāga daughter saw this, but no one else did. Because the moment of destiny had come, although the nāginī was riding a horse, she dismounted and, feeling more inclined to walk, tracked the dri on foot. She was unable catch the dri, but her horse got loose and went back the other way, following the clan. Although she called back to them, by the power of karma, no one could hear her. Alone, she followed after the dri along the banks of the empty Ma Valley, and, when she stopped, the dri would stop as well. Whether she went quickly or slowly, the dri would do the same, and so she couldn't quite catch up with it. Continually falling just short of catching it, she wandered wherever the dri went. The path they took wandered about aimlessly. During that time it never even occurred to her that she might be suffering from hunger, thirst, pain, and exhaustion.

> [The Ling army, finding nothing in Gog, starts to return home. But Chipön stops them and Senglön does an arrow divination to determine their next move.][27]

Meanwhile the Ling army, its armor and weapons flashing, had arrived in the country of Gog. The land of Gog was empty; nothing was left except their seats and beds. The Ling soldiers gathered for a meeting and Zhalkar, Sengtag [Adom], and the like, all the young warriors, were sent on reconnaissance to find out where the people of Gog had gone.

Some soldiers said, "We don't know where they went. All we soldiers are going to do is tire ourselves out to no end. Why don't we just go back?"

Then Chipön replied, "Even though we're following them for just a little silver, wherever the soldiers of the White Ling go, they never return empty-handed. How could we possibly leave without a victory? So let's have Senglön do a divination and base our decision on that."

Then Senglön performed an arrow divination:

> If we go as far as the time it takes to have a tea break,
> Beauty will be nectar to the eyes,
> The essence of the nectar will be inexhaustible,

And the treasure that fulfills all needs and desires will be ours;
Without fighting it will fall into our hands.
We will not slide our swords from their sheaths
Nor carry an arrow notched into its bow, but
Victory will be achieved by karma itself.

He said this respectfully informing them of the outcome of the divination.

Then Trothung thought, "This present divination is amazing. It must be a sign that all of this will eventually come round to Tag-rong. However it is certain that today there will be no victory." He wondered whether he ought to accuse Senglön of making an inaccurate divination and said, "Okay, as I have the feeling that the victory in this empty land could occur without even notching the arrow in the bow or sliding the swords from their sheaths, I bestow to you, Senglön, the plunder itself as the gift for this divination today."

Chipön said, "Okay, if that is the chieftain of Tag-rong's decision today, then let it be that way. Now let's make the tea and perform a smoke offering [lhasang], and then go."

[Sengtag Adom performs a lhasang.]

They went out to gather juniper for the smoke offering. Previously Ralo Tönpa's guru, Dorje Gyaltsen, had predicted that in this year his wealth would be taken away and enemies would come, and so he needed to make many smoke offerings and accumulate appeasement and fulfilling offerings to the dralas. He had prepared enough offerings for about a hundred yak saddle bags with varieties of woods, rhododendrons, juniper, tamarisk [ombu], and frankincense. The soldiers of Ling gathered it all up and performed a smoke offering that filled all of space.

Chipön said, "Today the connection is excellent, because this is the first raid of the warrior Gyatsha and because it is Mikyong Karpo [Kind Guardian of Humanity]* who invokes the gods—the warrior who is a castle and a support[28] around which the dralas of White Ling gather. Let him raise a song so that the dralas may land on the body. Let the other mighty warriors, wearing their threefold panoply, raise aloft in their hands their arrows and spears and stand at attention."

Then the warrior Sengtag Adom, a man in white with a white horse, carrying a white pennant, wearing a white helmet and white armor, with his white cape

---

* Mikyong Karpo is also known as Sengtag Adom.

covering his back, holding a white lance banner, a white standard, and divine white lasso, adorned with these nine whites—white as though they had emerged from the white gods themselves—raised this song like a crouching snow lion:

> The song begins with Ala Ala Ala.
> Thala gives the melody.
> May the refuge, the Rare and Supreme Three Jewels,
> Remain inseparable as my crown ornament.
>
> If you don't recognize this place,
> It has degraded into an empty plain of the vile enemy.
> It is the degraded wasteland of the evil enemy,
> A place vanquished by White Ling, as well as
> The homeland of Gog Ralo Tönpa.
> In case you don't recognize the likes of me,
> I am Sengtag Adom, a wolf among men,
> From the Maroon* Palace of Kyutri [Twisted Sash].
> This horse is Tong-ri Wangdzöd [Thousand Mountains
>   Treasury of Wealth].
> I am the magical son of Machen Pomra in the East,
> The heart son of the god, White Brahmā.
>
> Today is the day of auspiciousness;
> We make a smoke offering[29] to please the gods of refuge.
> First from the sunny side of the valley, we gather the juniper,
> Then from the shady side the rhododendrons,
> And from between them the white tamarisk—
> Renowned as the three trees of deathless amṛta.
> Buddhalocana is the hearth for burning.
> Māmakī is the water we sprinkle.
> We melt with the power of Pāṇḍaravāsinī.
> We summon with the wind of Samayatārā.[30]
> It blazes up in the expanse of the space of Ākāśadhātvīśvarī.

---

* "Maroon" here is *smug po* and could simply be the name of the Mukpo clan.

The clouds of smoke are the self-appearance of emptiness,
The spring brings forth all that is desired as spontaneous
  presence.
By making this smoke offering of the amṛta of empty
  appearances,
May the dharmakāya great Vajradhara,
The sambhogakāya five buddha families,
And the nirmanakāya three protectors,
These, the three meditation deities of White Ling, be
  cleansed.

First, Guru Padmasambhava,
Second, Langchen Pelgyi Sengei [Lion of Splendor of the
  Great Lang Clan],
And third, Langtön Changchub Drenpa [Awakened Guide
  Leader of the Lang Clan]*—
May these three gurus of Ling be cleansed.

Ḍākinī Yeshe Tsogyal [Wisdom Lake Queen],
The only mother Drubpa'i Gyalmo [Queen of Siddhi],
And Aunt Gung-men Gyalmo [Sky Goddess],
May these three aunts of Ling be cleansed.

The great god [mahādeva] White Brahmā,
Lord of the nyen, Zurphüd Ngapa [Five Knotted Locks of
  Hair],
And the nāga king Tsugna Rinchen,
May these three deities that protect White Ling be cleansed.

The drala Nyentag Marpo,
Samaya-bound Vajrasadhu, and
Life lord of the three worlds, Pehar—
May these three protectors who uphold the ancestral heritage
  be cleansed.

---

* These two lamas were very important for the Gesar epic and its place in the historical chronicles of Tibet.

The dralas who abide on the top of the white helmet
Surrounding the pennant headdress like vulture feathers,
The dralas who rest on the black armor
Surrounding the cape like the eight auspicious symbols,
The dralas who alight on the shield,
Surrounding the shield and its perimeter,
On the pale colored handle of the lance,
On the single-notched straight arrow,
On the bowstring and the blade of the sword;
May these dralas that surround with the wind force of a
    magical slingshot be cleansed.

Powerful vow-breaking enemies—
Dralas who deliver them into our hands, who conquer and
    control them,
Who kill just by a touch of their weapons;
May these three kindred protector dralas be cleansed.

Invisible, impenetrable enemy—
One's own fearless life the tent of protection;
May these three kindred preserver dralas be cleansed.

Increasing eloquence, prosperity, and
All-victorious windhorse;
May the three kindred abundance dralas be cleansed.

The noble steed's fancy baubles and trappings,
Its four hooves like wheels of wind,
And downy vulture feathers protruding from the tips of its ears;
May the worldly riding horse dralas be cleansed.

May the wermas who fill the heavens be cleansed.
May the dralas who fill intermediate space be cleansed.

Flapping silk scarves fill the sky,
Swirling white clouds of dralas,
Humankind filling intermediate space
Shouting *ki!* and *so!* like a dragon's roar.

The face of the vast earth is covered with horses.
A steady downpour of the rain of siddhis
Leaves us free from any doubt that the six grains will be
    abundant.
Therefore this white day
Is the first raid of Chieftain Gyatsha.

The vindictive enemy cannot bear the splendor of his
    presence;
See how they fled into the depths of the black earth.
After the evil enemy is driven underground,
May myriad rewards fall into our hands.
First the dharmic wealth of the gods above—
May we today inherit that as our spoils.
Second the increasing wealth of the humans in the middle—
May that be portioned to us today as our share of the spoils.
Third the inexhaustible wealth and riches of the nāgas
    below—
Today may we each receive our portion of that plunder.

All of White Ling is equally provided with lha.[31]
The aims of the white lha will be fulfilled.
May White Ling be adorned with myriad colorful rewards.
May the account of this prevail throughout Jambudvīpa.
May whatever we wish for be spontaneously acquired.
May the sparkling spoils arrive in our hands.
If we soldiers must wander for a year,
We must be prepared to do so even if this means we must
    circle Jambudvīpa.
May all that I pray for come to pass.
If you understand this song, it will be sweet to your ears.
If not, there is no way to explain it.
Brethren of Ling keep this in your mind.

Thus he spoke.

Then, as they rode off, they shouted in unison the warrior cry of *ki! ki! so! so!* and *lha gyal lo!* Most of them, agreeing with Sengtag's song, thought they would try to pursue Ralo Tönpa's group. Meanwhile, Gogza,[32] who was still running after the dri, decided to give up, but, although she wanted to rest, she was unable to find a comfortable place to do so in this desolate land. After a little while she felt so sad that tears uncontrollably welled up in her eyes. She was so tired that she fell asleep and dreamed of a young boy who was wearing silken garments. He gave her a turquoise pail full of milk along with this message: "This comes from your sister. Now go chase that dri again, for the time has come when your wanderings in the country of humans will accomplish the benefit of beings." And she awoke from the dream.

The little boy was nowhere to be found, but the turquoise pail full of milk was sitting in front of her. Knowing that it had come from her family to quench her thirst, she carried it along, drinking from it as she went. Running in the footsteps of the dri, she came to the flourishing valley of the land of Gog, just as the Ling army was meeting. The Ling soldiers saw her and thought:

> Her beauty was wonderful beyond imagining.
> Her radiant complexion was like a lotus blooming in a
>   lake,
> Like a lotus struck by the rays of the sun.
> Her twinkling eyes were like honeybees
> Buzzing on the shore of the lake.
> Her straight body was like summer bamboo,
> As if its leaves were blown by the wind.
> Her body was soft and gentle like white Chinese silk,
> As if the silk had been melted and poured into a mold.
> Her long flowing hair was like combed silk threads,
> Shining as if the silken threads had been painted with liquid
>   glass.
> This is how she appeared as she approached them.

The Mazhi Chieftain Trothung of Dong said, "Heh! Dazzling maiden from valley yonder, in your haste you have come upon [the army of] White Ling. These armed soldiers, the cousins and brothers of White Ling, are going to descend on the enemy people of Gog. Tell us how to receive the numerous rewards of our raiding. What's your story, girl?"

The girl thought, "How can I possibly hand over the people of Gog? On the other hand, I really have no choice but to tell my own story. Here in this empty place I might as well just tell them the truth. What's the point in keeping anything secret from them?[33] Anyway, because this is my previous karma there is no reason to be afraid."

Then the girl sang this song with the tremulous melody of the cuckoo bird:

> The song begins Ala Ala Ala.
> Thala leads the melody of the song.
> Protector guru Uḍḍiyāṇa Padma,
> The magnificent splendor of your presence inspires my song.
> May your speech, these words of truth, be voiced in this
>   melody of Brahmā.
> Look upon me with your omniscient enlightened mind and
>   grant your blessings.
>
> In case you don't recognize this place,
> It is the flourishing valley of the Land of Gog.
> In case you don't know who I am,
> When I was unstained by habitual patterns
> I was the Buddha Ḍākinī.
> Now during this life
> In the happy land of the underwater nāgas,
> I am the princess of the nāga king Tsugna Rinchen.
> I am the youngest of the three royal princesses,
> The nāginī called Yelga Dzeiden.
> I am the empowerment gift of the divine Orgyen Padma.
> I was presented to the family of Ralo of Gog,
> Given into their keeping, but not for my whole life.
> I was told that whenever the time is right, my master will
>   arrive.
> For some time I have lived as Ralo's daughter.
> During this time great change has come to the people of Gog,
> I do not know where the families have journeyed.
> It is said that they have gone to a boundless northern
>   wasteland.
>
> As for this girl's nāga treasure, first there is the dri,
> Second, the nine-partitioned azure tent,

Finally, the twelve volumes of the nāgas' *One Hundred*
    Thousand Verse Scripture.
The pack animals could not bear the burden;
We just managed to load everything onto the dri.
Like malefactors, we had to travel by night.
The dri carrying the treasure of the nāgas turned around and
    ran home,
But only this girl noticed it.
The jewel that my father, Tsugna, gave—
Entrusted with it I ran in quick pursuit.
I thought I could catch up with her and get close
So I dismounted my steed and ended up running on foot.
Unable to catch her, I lost my way and wandered here.
If the gods have led me here, look on me with compassion.
If the demons have led me here, then there's no escape.
Now as the proverbs of the ancients say:

As for parents, spouse, and mother-in-law, these three—
Your past life determines what your arrangements will be.

Pain and pleasure, good and ill, your fortune, these three—
Aren't they designs drawn by your own karma?

Aren't the local customs like this?—
If the divine guru who wears the dharma robe of silk
Does not inwardly determine the nature of mind,
His outer saffron robes are like a golden goose,
As though he has been forced to merely endure a relative body.
But the black offerings he receives, the cornerstone of hell, *
Are regretted far too late in the future.

If the imperial chieftain who sits on the golden throne
Does not himself take to heart the laws of the land,

---

* Black offerings (Tib. *dkor nag*) are probably religious offerings to the Three Jewels, which this monk appropriates to his own benefit, thus planting a karmic seed of rebirth in hell.

Then his ministers, servants, and subjects are an ever-turning wheel
    of deception.
It seems the status he has achieved is utterly crucial.
What a shame to be mistaken about the truth or falsity of karma!
When it ripens upon the head of the chieftain himself, it is far too late.
If the girl who wears gold and turquoise ornaments
Doesn't know how to keep the rich household,
Then she must continuously deceive and turn the wheel of fornication
Carrying the burden of uncomfortable shame.
Later when aged, if she returns back home
It will be a shock to everyone.

    These sayings are well known of old.
    This girl thinks that these words hold truth.
    The lord guru Uḍḍiyāṇa Padma
    Said that he needed me, the nāginī;
    My father Tsugna had no choice but to offer me.
    The day that nāginī and father were separated,
    From that moment on, all the excellent words of the divine
        guru meant nothing
    Because all he ever uttered were sermons.
    Now except for yearning to return back home to the nāga
        realm,
    This girl has no place to go!
    Oops, what have I said, I'm just teasing.

    Earlier this morning
    While I was in a state of foggy sleep,
    A boy with a turquoise topknot
    Wearing blue water-silk garments
    Gave me a precious turquoise pail
    Filled to the brim with milk to quench my thirst.
    He told this girl to chase after the dri
    And the reasons the divine Padma brought me here would be
        accomplished.
    Outwardly the radiance of the jewel has not declined,
    Inwardly the amṛta has not dried up.
    Now don't leave the dri there, but let her come here.

Until my body crumbles, I will follow that dri;
The crumbling of my body will be the cause of accomplishing
    benefit to beings.
This is not just a girl's stubborn decision!
If you understand these words, it is sweet to your ears.
If you do not, there is no way to explain it.
Cousins and uncles of Ling, bear this in mind.

The very determined girl prepared to follow where the dri had gone. Then Chipön said, "Now White Ling has accomplished the aim of its raid. There won't be a plunder to surpass this. The words of truth of the warrior Sengtag have come to pass, and the imperial gods have bestowed siddhis. Now we can return to the highlands of White Ling. These spoils will be the ornament of the world [Jambudvīpa]."

He spoke, and then Senglön said, "Uncle promised today's plunder to me as the prize of the divination. She belongs to me."

Then Trothung said, "The girl is not loot. It is not the custom to call something found in an empty place 'booty.' In any case, I saw her first."

It was then that the great arbiter Werma Lhadar [Divine Banner] said, "Since this is the innermost treasure of Ralo Tönpa, it is called booty, and is determined by its value. So, Senglön is right."

A slip of the tongue can't be recanted by a horse.
An arrow released by the thumb can't be drawn back by the hand.

"Isn't it like that? However, let the twelve-volume *One Hundred Thousand Verse Scripture* and the nine-partitioned azure tent of the nāgas be the general wealth of White Ling. The girl and the dri, according to Uncle, are the prize for the divination, so they go to Senglön."

All the Brethren said, "Good plan. So be it." So Trothung was left with no choice. And then, just as before, the nāga scriptures and nāga tent were carried on the backs of horses and mules, and the dri led, but this time to White Ling. Even the girl was satisfied with the outcome.

They were going to mount the girl on her horse, but there was no saddle. When they said, "What do we do?" she replied, "Once last summer, when I went out for a stroll,[34] there was a white boy standing next to that white crag over there. He gave me a golden saddle, a turquoise halter and crupper, and said to me, 'You must not take this anywhere or tell anyone. The time will come when you will need these. Until then, leave it here and I will stand guard.' So I placed them in a cave in that crag, and I forgot until now. I wonder if these things are still there. Since they were given to me either by my guru or my father's family, I think they are."

Several brawny men went to look for it, but saw nothing. Chipön said, "Girl, you should go. It will be there. And whoever wants to accompany her should go along, too." She went into the cave, and the golden saddle was sitting right there. Then they all knew for certain that she was the nāginī. Overwhelmed with joy and happiness, the Brethren called to the gods, shouting *ki!* and *so!* and they slowly returned to Ling.

The minute the girl arrived in the tent of Gyaza, the abode became a mass of light. The girl was wondrously beautiful, and wherever you looked, around her there were auspicious signs.

Gyaza thought, "She's going to overcome me." In her jealousy she was a bit annoyed.

Then Chipön thought, "I guess that since Gyaza's race is Chinese she must suffer the fault of great jealousy, which goes along with being Chinese. If this girl stays with us in our kingdom, then the intentions of the divine gurus and the prophecies of the ḍākinīs and all the signs and dreams that have come day and night seem to indicate that a divine child will be born here in White Ling. It seems that this nāginī will be his powerful mother. If he and Zhalkar are brothers together in the same house, it is predicted that both of them will have long life and good fortune. On the other hand, if they go their separate ways, it's hard to say if Zhalkar's life will be long enough to reach its appointed end. I don't think I dare say this. It's like the saying:

> *Why count on winnings that haven't come about?*
> *It is as pointless as naming your child before it is born.*

What's the use? Gyaza is not especially thoughtful; she won't listen," he thought and just let it go for a while.

Gyaza herself said, "There is no way I will allow myself to be in her thrall."

Since the girl's nāga tent had passed into the common property of Ling, Senglön thought, "I will set up a charming little tent for her [the nāginī] and all her needs will be supplied. Only she will be allowed to drink the milk of her dri, and only she will be in charge of it. Since she is a wisdom ḍākinī,* no matter what is done, she will only feel joyful."

---

* A wisdom ḍākinī is the embodiment of an absolute principle and thus already innately enlightened.

Chipön resolved the matter in this way: The nāginī would not be allowed to go anywhere except to the tents belonging to Gyaza's household. Senglön must keep his marriage to Gyaza as before, and the nāginī should not be given the power to control the Gyaza household wealth. And as far as the house and livestock were concerned, Gyaza was to determine the nāginī's fair share and distribute it as she would. Based on this, Gyaza gave her four animals—a mare, a dzomo, a dri, and a ewe. As this was an auspicious connection, the place came to be called Yang Rawa Go-zhi [The Four-Gated Prosperity Corral].

Gyatsha Zhalkar said, "Even though we can't be sure whether this girl is good or bad,[35] she is my first reward. Besides, all the other signs and connections have been positive; it's quite all right for me to keep her for myself. My mother may have thrown her out now, but later she will realize to her regret that it is no different than sending her own son away. It is too bad, for this diminishes the auspicious connection."

His heart was in great turmoil. He said, "I will not cast the girl away." He was purple with anger, and when he spoke these words he was standing beside Gyaza's tent looking like a rhinoceros horn. From that time on the nāginī's little tent was called Tritse Seru Tag-khama [Little Rhino Tent at the Back],[36] and everyone came to know it as that. For the three days that followed Gyatsha was sick with heart-wind,[*] in the chest and during that time did not utter a single word.

The people of Ling began to call the girl Gogza Lhamo,[†] which they shortened to Gogmo [Gog Lady]. Because Gogmo's dri gave an inexhaustible supply of milk morning, noon, and night, this saying became familiar:

> *The white dri of prosperity*
> *Has a hundred and three udders,*
> *But only Gogmo can milk it*
> *And only the turquoise pail can contain the milk.*

The nāginī stayed there next to Gyaza's tent for several months, and one night she dreamed of a guru who said, "Just below where your tent is pitched, there is a frog-shaped boulder. Move your dwelling in front of it." She told Senglön she had had this dream, and he said, "Do it, but keep the dream secret."

The next morning Senglön said, "Let's move this little tent of Gogmo close to

---

[*] Heart-wind (Tib. *snying rlung*) means "depression."

[†] Meaning "goddess wife from Gog."

the canyon, because I don't like it above our own tent." So they moved it in front of the frog-like boulder, near Chumig Nagring [Long Black Spring] of Nāga Tsugna.

While she was staying there, Gyatsha himself gave her whatever provisions she needed. Without ever going to seek permission from either his mother or his father, he took it upon himself to give things whenever she required them. And Gyaza did not dare say a thing. Gogmo was happier than Gyaza. Content with her little tent and small portion of wealth, she lived a blessed life.

Chipön thought, "If Gyatsha is not the best around, then who is? Whatever I, Chipön, have desired, he has brought about. He is a warrior complete in the six powers, with vast knowledge. He can do anything at any time without errors, accomplishing things perfectly whenever necessary." Thinking, "How wonderful he is!" his spirits soared.

Gogmo, too, offered Gyatsha choice portions of dri milk and curd. Her mind became quite attached to him, and she loved him as though he was her own son, and he cherished her no differently than Gyaza. As is said in the famous proverb:

If a son is noble there will be happiness from within and without.

Thus it was.

[*Note from the original editor of the Derge Ling wood block edition:*]

Although there are various divergences concerning the biography, it is not necessary for biographies of the Noble Ones to be exactly the same. Aside from this version, most of the literature found about the *Trung Ling* [*The Birth in Ling*] is actually incorrect. Rather than spending time refuting those errors and creating more pages, I will just let it be as it is.[37]

CHAPTER TWO

To the nāga princess Gogza
Is born Gesar Norbu Dradül.
He bands together with the dralas and wermas
And for a period of time he is called Joru.

ONE DAY THE GIRL WENT for a stroll by the edge of the lake. The lake was cool
and refreshing with its garlands of waves that came slowly washing in with a gentle
splashing sound. The variegated flowers on the green meadows were so vivid and
bright that at first she felt astonishment. Then, remembering the nāgas, she saw the
prosperity of the nāga realm, her mother, father, and all her relatives as though they
had appeared before her. In this mood she called to the nāgas with a sad song in the
melody River Slowly Flowing.

Helpless but to sing a few songs,
I must sing these or do nothing at all.
If happy, this is a joking song of joy.
If sad, this will uplift the mind.

I take refuge in the guru, yidam, and the Rare and Precious
    Three Jewels.
Remain inseparable as my crown ornament.

This place is Yagnyi Katröd;
I am the nāginī Yelga Dzeiden.

Dear blue lake with pleasing splashing sound,
Perhaps you are a messenger of the nāga king Tsugna.
Listen, for I have something to tell you.

In the azure firmament of this borderless sky of darkness,
The way the imperial sun benefits beings
Is to establish them in bliss by illuminating the four
        continents.
Above us the sun and moon encircle the land that is theirs,
Never separate from happy celebration with close kinsmen.

In the middle land of men, happiness appears
When the dear imperial chief leads his subjects to joy.
The laws of the land are enforced by the minister.
The chief who occupies the precious golden throne
Is never without the respect and veneration of his kinsmen.

From below, the princess of the subterranean nāgas
Has come to the human realm
To accomplish the benefit of beings in the six mountain
        ranges of Tibet.
My benefit for beings amounts to nothing— like the
        daughter of a barren woman;
I, the nāginī, am like a stray dog in the wilderness.
I've left my father's family behind in the depths of the ocean.
Did you understand this, O Golden King of the River?*

When the divine guru teaches dharma, he is full of clever
        words.
He says, "All wealth is impermanent like bubbles on water."
He says, "All friends are impermanent like birds on a branch."
He says, "Life is impermanent like a display of lightning."
His words don't fit with his actions.
Whether he's pleased or not depends on the size of the offering;

---

* Yelga Dzeiden's metaphor for her father.

Whether he scolds or not depends on the students' good
    looks.
Wealth and material possessions are for his own pleasure—
Look how his honorable hands tie the knot of avarice.
When the dear chieftain dispenses law, he's full of clever
    words.
He says it's for the happiness of the lower classes.
He says craving the wealth of others is not permitted.
He says the dishonest will be punished by the law.
His words don't fit his actions.
Inflicting suffering and famine on his subjects,
For the rich, penalties are just a painting;
If the previous secret payoff is significant,
Then look and see how an evil person escapes from the law.

My father Tsugna can say whatever he wants.
He said all three sisters are equally precious.
He said he would come to me from any distance.
He said "My daughter, I will make you happy."
Kind father, you don't stand by your words.
Father Tsugna, since you've forgotten me three years has
    passed.
It's been three years since I've heard our nāga language.
In the human land above I have neither kith nor kin.
The nāginī has neither protector nor possessions.
Did you understand that, O Golden King of the River?

The unborn and unceasing azure firmament
Is said to be one with the guru's mind.
Since this is true, here is my message to you:

The realization and conduct of the best guru
From the milky ocean of the sutras and the tantras
Churns the buttery essence of the dharma's view and
    meditation,
Which is mingled, so they say, with the core of his mind.
They never say that once mingled it becomes separated again.

The meditative practice of the mediocre guru—
Playing the harmonious cords of the scriptural canon,
He sings the sweet devotional words of dharma to others,
But only occasionally does he practice himself.
The righteous conduct of the inferior guru
Who deceptively takes valuable wealth from the unpleasant
   city of suffering,
Benefits no one and loses it to the thieves,
Bringing him both public ridicule and private torment.

The regret of the patron who cherishes his wealth,
The regret of the guru who can't hold on to it,
And the dissension caused by vain regret—
How surprising to think that these are ways to benefit beings.
Oops, not supposed to say that, I was just teasing.

In this lifetime, if you want to have companions
Only the dear chief can offer you protection.
In the next life, if you want to head toward liberation
Only the guru can save you.
My body, this arm-span triangle of flesh—
Only my parents can make it complete.

Now for the honest truth in the words of my song,
If you can see me, O guru, grant me your blessings.
If you can see me, O parents, give your support.
If not, from this day onward
This girl is on her own.
Neither the guru's words nor his prophecies
Have I ever transgressed, in letter or in spirit.
But if this song has erred, I fully confess it.
If my words seem frivolous, I beg your forgiveness.

Thus she sang. She sat there, weeping, when suddenly her father, the nāga king Tsugna Rinchen, appeared before her, rising up from the lake in the guise of a blue man on a blue horse.

"Daughter, don't be so very distraught. It is not that the guru and I didn't see you. I miss you so much, how could I possibly forget you? Nonetheless, here's my advice on the situation," and he broke into song.

> The song begins with Ala Ala Ala.
> Thala is the melody of the song.
> The place is the spring of the nāgas
> And I am Tsugna Rinchen.
>
> The sun and moon that ornament the space above
> Seem to illuminate the four continents,
> But the pointless impositions of the one who inflicts
>   punishment,
> Rāhu, causes suffering anew;
> If they are oblivious to this, they will be happy.
>
> The imperial chief who sits on the golden throne
> May be respected by his ministers, who are never far,
> But if the myriad masses, beggars, and dogs are unhappy,
> This will cause him suffering anew;
> If he is oblivious to this, he will be happy.
>
> The divine guru, who mixes appearance and mind,
> His every action is for the benefit of beings.
> The imperial chieftain, who has gathered the power of karma,
> Every law he enforces is for the subjects.
> Did you understand, O long-lived daughter?
>
> As the sayings of the ancients proclaim:

Though the sun and moon both appear in the azure firmament,
The blue sky does not favor one over the other.
While the golden rays shed by the sun encircle the four continents;
The darkness of night falls as the moon wanes—
For the sun and moon each have their own karmic mandate.[38]

Though the rocky mountains and meadows coexist on the dense
    earth,

The colors in the meadows transform from summer to autumn,
Yet the white crags of the mountains are unchanging from summer to
  winter.
It's not that the dense earth is showing favoritism to the meadow—
That is the karmic mandate of the mountains and meadow.

   I, nāga Tsugna, have three daughters.
The guru ordered me to send him the youngest,
While the middle and eldest stay at home.
Father Tsugna had no choice in the matter.
That, girl, is your own karmic mandate.

That's the way it is, and likewise:

The monk in his glittering silken dharma robe,
Pleasing his mouth, tastes the select portion and
Pleasing his rear, delights on the comfortable seat of a golden
  throne.
Then when he thinks that this is not happiness, but great
  suffering,
He seeks certain bliss in the skirts of a girl,
Once more confusing pleasure with pain, another spin of his
  hapless brain.[39]

The youthful tiger with his poisonous threefold panoply
Despite his parents' hoard in the inner chamber
And the farm, fields, and his status in his family,
Still thinking his wealth is as insubstantial as frost on a stone,
He seeks certain value in a stolen goat carcass,
Confusing well-being with pain, another spin of his hapless
  brain.

A maiden's mandate is to move to the groom's home.
That you go there is Padma's prophecy.
I, Tsugna, was required to give whatever dowry was
  mandated.
You must face toward the Wishing Land of Ling.
Although Mother Gyaza did not take to you,

The warrior Zhal-lu cared for you like a mother.
You think, "This is not happiness, I'm oppressed with pain:
Certain happiness is to wander to a foreign land."
Maiden this is just another spin of your hapless brain.

Oops, not supposed to say that! I was just teasing.
My jewel, which fulfills each and every desire,
That which fulfills all wishes and the abundance of all that is
    necessary—
Until a son is born who can surely handle this
Keep this inseparable from your body.
Even though I, the nāga king, possess enough wealth
To easily fill the mountains and valleys with jewels,
Until the time comes, there is nothing to be done.

Vast and great sovereignty comes of its own accord.
Until then, follow the words of the guru.
As for me, Tsugna, my thoughts are always with you; I will
    always come.
Before long, your happiness will begin.
If you understand my words, it is sweet to your ears.
If not, there is no way to explain it.
Girl, you must keep this in your mind.

Having sung this, he gave her the jewel and vanished into the water. After that, even the girl's body was ablaze with bliss and her mind, in a state of radiant awareness, could master all appearances. Completely relaxing in this state of bliss and emptiness, she fell asleep. Then she dreamed that from the southwest came a white cloud that floated up in the space before her. Riding on the cloud was Guru Orgyen Padma. He placed a golden five-pointed vajra on the top of her head and sang this prophecy in the melody of Brahmā:

Kye! Listen fortunate girl.
The guru, yidam, and ḍākinī, these three,
If understood, are the self-manifestation of wisdom.
Bliss, suffering, and equanimity, these three,
If understood, are the self-appearance of emptiness.
The appearance of place, designations, and body, these three,

If realized, are confused habitual patterns.
The mind that fixates on enemies, friends, and neutrals,
If recognized, is strong grasping toward habitual fixation.
This mental pattern of confused thought,
If examined, is like the appearance of a rainbow in the sky.
This empty essence of the nature of mind,
If realized, is the dharmakāya buddha.
Nature, intrinsic nature, and compassion, these three
Are the spontaneous three kāyas.
If you seek these elsewhere, not knowing them as your own,
You may roam the three myriad universes, and never find them.
Therefore, here are some examples.

In this ocean of saṃsāra's suffering
If there is a guide to freedom,
Then traveling the way of liberation will not be difficult.
If you have the courage of the oral instructions that point out
The unreal illusion of this phenomenal world,
Then whatever happens is the true divine dharma.
You, girl, from here on will be separated from your father,
But I will never be separate from you for a moment.
Whatever thoughts occur in your mind are the actual nature
    of phenomena
And whatever you do becomes the action of the six pāramitās.
Therefore, tomorrow morning
In the year of the Ox on the eighth day of the waxing moon
    during the final month of spring,
On this auspicious conjunction of the excellent time and holy
    day,
It will finally come to pass that a nonhuman prince, a magical
    child,
Will enter a womb.
He will be the slayer who tames the dark side.
He will be the general lord of the black-haired Tibetans.
He will become the yoke of both Düd and Hor.
The four great fortresses and the eight minor fortresses, and
The twelve bordering kingdoms of Ling

Will have as their chief a guru who guides them.
Until the time is right, the garuḍa,[40] king of the birds
Will not break out from his egg.
There is nothing to be gained from its rushing to be born,
For when it hatches, its six wings will be fully matured.

Your son will have a supreme indestructible vajra body.
For him a mother's concern with protection, frugality, and
    modesty, these three,
Are merely the mother's superstitious thoughts.[41]
Ceremonies of uplifting, respecting, and celebrating, these
    three—
Until the time arrives just let them be.[42]
The first butter to the palate[43] will be the long-life water given
    by Padma,
The first drink will be served by Tsugna,
The nyen will dress him in his first clothing,[44]
The response to his first nectar of enlightened speech will
    come from his mother,
The first food he is served will be offered by Machen Pomra.
His first taming of the enemy will be in the sky.

Don't forget these sayings, keep them in mind.
O nāginī, you must keep these in your mind.

After that song, the girl awoke from her sleep. Bliss pervaded her body, and she thought, "Those were wonderful dreams." She revered the Guru Padma Lotus Born as never before and sat there, tears streaming down her face.

On the evening of the eighth day of the last month of spring, while sleeping with her husband, Senglön, she dreamed of a handsome and charming golden man in golden armor who came and slept with her. She felt such love and longing that she could not bear to part from him.

The next morning just before dawn she dreamed that a vajra like the five-pointed one that the guru had placed on her head was blazing with unbearably splendid light rays and rainbows. It dissolved into the top of her head, and as she dreamed her body glowed with bliss and warmth. When she awoke, her body and mind experienced joy and bliss as never before. For many days she had no regard for ordinary food and clothing. In that dream of hers the man wearing golden armor was the nyen Gedzo. The honorable Masang Norbu Dradül,[45] who, like the sun and its rays, was never separate from the dralas and wermas, had blessed the immeasurable palace of the nāginī's womb,[46] and for nine months and eight days he stayed there delighting in the unconditioned bliss of the samādhi of spontaneous great equanimity.[47] During that period, the mother Gogmo was guarded and protected through the six watches of the day and night by the lord of the thirteen gods of the chase, the twelve tenma who protect Tibet, the glorious lord of the pure gods, and others: some coming in person, some sending their representatives. Some people heard songs in the night coming from her little tent. Some in the darkest part of the night could see just the little tent, which alone was not obscured.

Then Zhalkar dreamed that in Gogmo's tent there was a precious throne on which was a golden vajra, blessed by Padmasambhava and blazing with light. Similarly, Chipön and the others had many amazing signs and dreams. In one dream, a tree was growing from Trothung's neck, and so many fruits and flowers grew from it that he bowed under the weight and could not stand up. There was a thousand-petaled poisonous flower in Trothung's home, while a rain of jewels filled Upper, Lower, and Middle Ling. These were the sorts of dreams people had. Although there had been some uneasiness about the first dream, the later dream about the poisonous flower was a sign of Trothung's amazing son Aten, because he came to be renowned as Aten Dug-gi Metog [Stable Poisonous Flower].

Although the meaning of the appearances in these dreams could not be perfectly determined, they did seem to indicate that ultimately, although Trothung's intentions were bad and full of deceptive trickeries, in the end this would support and energize the activities that would be helpful to the young Joru.

In the Tiger year during the twelfth month on the fifteenth day, unlike ever before, her body like flower down became blissful, so light, and utterly loose and relaxed. Her mind became unobstructed and unimpeded both from without and within. At the very moment when the sun rose, led by white light that dawned from the crown of her head like the moon, there suddenly appeared a man as white as a conch with the head of a garuḍa, holding a spear with a white silken pennant, saying, "Mother, I am your firstborn son. I will not achieve the benefit of beings with a corporeal body. I am the guardian who resides upon his white helmet and, as for the retinue, they are the encircling garuḍa feather pennants. If you offer, then offer me the three sweet substances. I am the elder brother Dungkhyung Karpo

[White-Conch Garuḍa]. I will never be separate from the Great One [Gesar]." Saying this, he remained in space like a shimmering colorful rainbow.

At that moment, before coming to the middle land of humans from within the belly of his mother, the divine child Thöpa Gawa spoke his first words in the form of this dohā:

> It's Ala Ala Ala.
> Thala leads the melody of the song.
> May this song be supported by the five buddha families
> And led by the motherly ḍākinīs.
> Guru, yidam, ḍākinī
> Remain inseparable from my crown *cakra** of great bliss.
> In case you don't know what this place is,
> In the body, chakras, and channels of my kind mother
> It is the heart chakra of truth.
> This is the vast and pure sacred country
> And the excellent companions are the ḍākas and ḍākinīs.
> In case you don't know the likes of me
> I am the divine boy Thöpa Gawa,
> The son of the human land of Jambudvīpa.
> I have the freedom to go wherever I want.
> So listen. I've got something to say.
>
> It is thought that the southern turquoise dragon is born with
>   power and magic that
> Fill the pathways of the empty sky with its roar.
> If the white clouds do not adorn the sky,
> Just a naked dragon is an ominous sign.
>
> It is thought that the powerful wheel of the white lioness
> Can suppress the wild animals with her might.
> If the white mountains are not covered by a blanket of snow,
> It is said that the plain-prowling lioness is mistaken for
>   a dog.

---

* Henceforth, the term *cakra* will be anglicized as *chakra*.

I, the divine child, have been dispatched on this mission from
the god realm
To overcome the southern continent of Jambudvīpa.

If I am not furnished with mighty ministers with authentic
presence,
They will insult me and say, "This companionless leader is a
vagrant beggar boy."
When the divine guru embarks for the benefit of beings,
If he lacks a retinue and a field of disciples,
Then there's no way that the crop of benefit for beings will
mature.
If there is no benefit for others, that is not a guru.

The imperial chieftain can establish his subjects in well-being,
Yet if the districts, ministers, and subjects are without a lawful
government,
Then who will the secular laws apply to?
If there are no subjects, no one can be designated "chieftain."

When a maiden leaves her home for another,
If there is no worldly wealth of a dowry,
How can the descendants of her sons and nephews ever
prosper?
Even though they may say she is happy, she is a mere beggar
with some food.

I, the godling, have been dispatched as a leader in the land of
humans.
First, there must be a place where the great leader's
sovereignty can be established,
Second, there must be ministers who accomplish whatever is
commanded of them,
Third, citizens who abide by the law of the ten virtues,
Fourth, at all times and in all situations, relatives who care for me,
Fifth, a treasury that grants me whatever I will need.
Mother, tell me just how great or small all these will come to be.
If these five easily come together,

Then I the divine child will not stay in the god's realm but
    will come [to this land].
If they don't come together, then I must consider the choices.
At the time when I come,
First the crown chakra of great bliss,
Second the throat chakra of abundance,
Third the heart chakra of dharma
Fourth the navel chakra of emanation,
Fifth the secret chakra that holds bliss,
Mother, tell me, from which [chakra] shall I emerge?
If you understand this song, it's sweet to your ears.
If not, there is no way to explain it.
Kind mother keep this in your mind.

By listening to the self-resounding unobstructed vajra, like the peahen that hears the sound of the summer drum,[*] she was filled with immeasurable ecstasy, and in that state she offered this song that will open the treasure of interdependent enlightened activity, the song called Gogmo's Song of Happiness in Six Melodious Waves.

The song is Ala Ala Ala.
Thala leads the melody of the song.

I take refuge in the guru, yidam, and ḍākinī, these three.
May the guru adorn the crown of my head.
May the yidam accompany my body like my shadow.
And may the motherly ḍākinīs assist me.
This place is Kyidsö Yag-gi Khado
Where two rivers run like a double-belted sash,
Where two rock mountains align like feathers on an arrow,
Where two meadows spread like woolen cushions.
Close to the rock that resembles a frog
Is the outer gateway to the treasure of the nāga king Tsugna.
This is the place where I received the prophecy of the divine
    Padma.

---

[*] Dragon's roar.

In case you don't recognize me,
I am Tsugna Rinchen's daughter,
The empowerment prize of Uḍḍiyāna Padma.
I am Chief Senglön's cook.
Listen here, O son of the gods.

In the imperial play of the exalted sky clouds
From the light palace of the royal parasol of the sun,
When the dazzling golden rays rise over the eastern
    mountains,
There is no thought or worry whether there are subjects to
    warm or not.

From the treasure gateway of the treasure of the subterranean
    nāgas
Comes the jewel that fulfills every desire.
When wealth and prosperity fall like rain,
There has never been an account of a person not there to
    need it.

In the middle land of humans where fields are irrigated,
Ears of excellent grain are plentiful.
The day they adorn the lustrous and glowing field,
It's unheard of that a reaper wouldn't come.

The southern turquoise dragon is the mother of clouds.
Without the clouds, there's no reason for the turquoise
    dragon to come.
It's unheard of that a naked dragon would be burned by the sun.

The white lioness's homeland is the snow mountain.
If there's no snow mountain, how can she make a den for her
    cubs?
It's unheard of that the turquoise-maned snow lioness would
    be seen wandering in the marketplace.

If the chieftain has vast sovereignty, authentic presence, and a
    treasure of wealth,

Then the leaders, warriors, and subjects will naturally
    surround him.
If they don't flock to him, how can you say he's a chieftain?
Whether you say there are many or few subjects and ministers
Depends on the greatness of the imperial chieftain's
    sovereignty.
Whether you say that his retinue of disciples is many or few
Depends on the greatness of the divine guru's compassion.

Whether you can say that the saṃsāric homestead is
    prosperous or not
Depends on the degree of merit of the girl herself.
Have you understood this, divine baby of Gogmo?
According to the famous proverbs of the ancients:

When the geese fly north
If the strength of their fully developed wings does not become
    exhausted,
Then the boundless northern lakes won't turn anyone away.

If the golden-eyed fish are swimming happily,
If the strength of their supple undulating bodies does not become
    exhausted,
There will be no end to the depths of the bottomless ocean.

When the cuckoo bird comes to Tibet
If its stomach has the power to digest the essence,
The berries of the juniper tree are inexhaustible.

If you have indeed been sent by the gods to be our sovereign
    chieftain,
Then the ministers and subjects will be as numerous as blades
    of grass on the earth.
If the authentic presence of your actions is vast enough to
    cover this,
Then there is no limit to the number of your subjects in the
    southern continent.
Those words sang it like it is.

If I were to inform you about the place where you will reside:
It is the karmic land of southern Jambudvīpa.
To the east is the country of China as though reflected in a
    mirror.
To the south is the country of India arranged like a ledger.
To the west is the country of Persia, resembling a stack of
    scriptures.
To the north is the country of Gesar, resembling an
    arrangement of offerings.
In the center of these four countries lies Tibet.
In the upper region there are the three districts of Ngari,
In the middle are the four tribes of Ü-Tsang
And below are the six districts of Dokham.
There are four great rivers in the six districts.
Between the River Da and the River Dri
Is the center of Dokham.
The mountain behind is Gödpo Lhatsei [Haughty Mountain
    Peak],
The mountain in front is Rizhi Ta-nag [Four-Peaked Black
    Horse],
The mountain to the right is Dragngön Yutsei [Blue Crag
    Turquoise Peak],
The mountain to the left is Dzadong Ngurpa [Jagged
    Mountain Ridge].
The sky is pitched above, like an eight-spoked wheel,
The land is elegantly arranged, like an eight-petaled lotus,
And encircled by auspicious symbols.
For your ministers, who will accomplish your every desire,
There will be the Thirty Mighty Warriors of White Ling
Who are emanations of the Thirty Mahāsiddhas of India,
And the Seven Super Warriors,
Who are emanations of the Seven Paṇḍits of India.
And the Three Ultimate Warriors,
Falcon, Eagle, and Wolf,
Who are emanations of Three Holy Men of India.

Now to explain the population:
In Upper Ling there will be the eight brothers of Serpa,

In Middle Ling there will be the people of the six districts of
    Ombu,
And in Lower Ling those of the four districts of Muchang.
There are also the six tribes of Gapa Rinchen,[*]
Minister Denma[†] on both the sunny and shady sides of the
    river,
The red tribe of Ta'u,
And to the right will be the wealthy subjects of both Dru and
    Kyalo.
All together there are some twelve myriarchies of Ling.

Now concerning your family and relatives:
Your paternal uncle will be King Chipön,
Your older brother, Gyatsha Zhalkar,
Your worldly father, King Senglön
And your maternal uncle, Tsugna Rinchen.
For the wealth treasury of prosperity:
First, there will be the tea treasure of China in the east.
Second the silk treasure of Mi-nub in the south.
Third, the jewel treasure of Persia in the west,
And fourth, the coral treasure in the wilderness of the north.
They are called the great fortresses in the four directions of
    Tibet.
There are four minor subsidiary fortresses,
Along with four independent small fortresses.
If you know how to open the doors to these twelve fortresses,
    you will find they are filled with treasures.
Your mother will have the wealth that fills the mountains and
    valleys,
A source of wealth like an overflowing treasury,
This jewel given by Nāga Tsugna
Is called the Powerful King of Wish-Fulfilling Jewels.

---

[*] The tribal leader.

[†] Who rules the people.

When you're in the market for a fine, mature horse
Don't give a price until you've looked it in the mouth.
Once you've decided and it's all saddled up,
Even if the horse is toothless, you'll nevertheless have to say "All right."

When the bride departs for her new home,
Make sure to decide if the destination is good or bad before she goes.
Once bedecked and across the threshold,
Even if there were a choice, it would be too late.

Therefore, divine son, magical child,
When you came to accomplish the benefit of beings in the
    middle land of humans
I personally hadn't intended to be your mother; you were able
    to choose.
But after nine months in my belly,
It will be too late to question your choice.
Oops, I didn't mean that, just teasing!

My throat, my heart, my navel, these three
Are the immovable chakras and channels.
Both the chakras of the crown and the secret place
Are the entrance ways for coming and going.
Come through the crown down to the bliss-holding chakra
And there will be the auspicious connection of good fortune.
The five chakra channels are neither good nor bad.
The guru's blessings are all-pervasive.
The dralas are massing like cloud banks.
Werma are pouring down like rain.
The dharmapālas are flashing like lightning bolts.
The ḍākinīs dance, swaying to and fro.
Stay no more; prepare to come, divine child.
The long-life water of the Lotus Born of Uḍḍiyāṇa
And the amṛta of Drubpa'i Gyalmo await you.
May the four māras be bound by oath,
May the people of the four borderlands become your subjects.
May your life reach its limit,
May you overcome the three realms,

May you suppress with your splendor the three worlds,
May the imperial gods accomplish the benefit of beings,
May the motherly ḍākinīs accomplish their words of truth,
May whatever prayers you make be accomplished.
If this song has caused confusion, I openly confess it.
If it has been but idle talk, please forgive me.
Godling, please keep this in your mind.

When she finished offering that song, a child who seemed to be three years old, who was so bewitching that you could not have your fill of gazing at him, appeared from her secret place. His eyes were wide open, and she made not the slightest moan of pain.

He got into her lap, and at that very moment Guru Rinpoche gave him empowerment. Then he gave him long-life water, just as a newborn colt is given its first butter for the palate. He clothed his body in indestructible vajra armor. As symbolic food and drink, Nāga Tsugna then presented him the amṛta of long life, and Magyal Pomra offered him a ritual cake of one hundred tastes. Lord of Nyen Gedzo offered him colorful silk and clothing that completely covered his body.

And after that, from Gogmo's heart center within an egglike orb of blue light, appeared an infant with a human body and a snake's head. Presently, he said these words, "I am the third-born son destined for kindness. I am without a corporeal body to accomplish the benefit of beings, but I will be the guardian on his white armor. I am the younger brother Ludrül Ödchung* [Nāga Serpent Little Light]. My retinue is the silken cape that drapes over the armor. When you are offering to me, offer the selection portion of the three whites. I am the body god who never leaves the great being's side." Saying this, he remained in space as a radiant colorful light.

Then from Gogmo's navel, led by rainbow light rays, a beautiful girl of white emerged wearing clothing of vulture feathers. [She said], "Mother, I am your fourth child. I do not have a body of flesh and blood. I am the drala that accompanies the noble steed. I will be [Gesar's] sister Thalei Ödkar [Completely Luminous]. When you offer to me, offer tea and turquoise. My retinue is at the ear tip of the horse, Noble Mount, resembling the finest vulture feathers. I am the spy lamp that illuminates the situation. I am the body god that never parts from the Great One." Having spoken, she remained in the middle space. At that moment, the guru Lotus Born spoke the words of truth as prayers for auspiciousness by singing this song:

---

* The spelling of this name is also rendered as Ödtrung in the original Tibetan text.

NAMO GURU MAÑJUŚRĪYE

This godling who has taken birth in the land of humans,
The great loving Lokeśvara,*
He of unimpeded superior knowledge, Mañjuśrī,
And the powerful Lord of the Secret, Vajrapāṇi,
Are inseparable from his self-existing mind.
They will be symbolized by his rosary of jewels,
The mirror, a mansion of light that clearly reflects existence,
And the five-pointed crystal vajra;
These three spontaneously will adorn his body.
May there be the auspiciousness of bliss in Jambudvīpa.

So that he will be able to benefit beings with his body,
There will be the nine faults of the demons with perverted
    aspirations.
So that the element of fire cannot harm him
There will be the fire deity called Gyatag Marpo [Royal Red
    Tiger],
And his further emanation, the werma Tigress.
For the water element, there will be the wind god Yudrug
    [Turquoise Dragon],
And his further emanation, the werma Sergyi Nya [Golden
    Fish].
For the wood element, there is wind god Garuḍa King of Birds
And his further emanation, Khelkar Lag [White-Breasted
    Eagle].
For the iron element, the wind god Sengchen [Great Lion],
And his further emanation, werma Sengei Kar [White Snow
    Lion].
For crossing the plain of fire or a raging river,
There will be the king of winds, Tornado, and the weapons of
    the four demons.
His protectors will be these eight wind gods and wermas.
May they accompany the body of this Great One.
And may the auspiciousness of bliss pervade Jambudvīpa.

---

* Avalokiteśvara.

The wermas who protect him from noxious poison
Will be Kyilrog Sertrül [Coiled Friend Golden Snake].
And the food god Changthang Nönpo [Youthful Blue
    Wolf].
Along with Dungtra Horpa [White Horpa] who speeds
    ahead.
The gods who clear the murk of fog both day and night,
Will be the daytime shepherd Tangkar Gödpo [Strong White
    Vulture] and
The nighttime shepherd Ugpa Serpo [Golden Owl].
With the intelligent Ribong Karlu [Little White Rabbit],
The courageous Dredmo Sogkar [White-Shouldered
    Grizzly],
The disease curing werma, Lawa Rog [Black Musk Deer],
The wind power that prevents the reach of the demons' lasso,
    and
The werma Onager Khakar Kyangtang [Asian Wild Ass
    White Muzzle].
These are the nine wermas who protect from
Poison, black magic curses, and binding lassos.
May they accompany the body of the Great One
May the auspiciousness of bliss pervade Jambudvīpa.

First, the white helmet with silken pennants and garuḍa
    feathers,
Second, the black armor that deflects lightning bolts,
Third, the indestructible long life clothes of bliss-emptiness,
Fourth is the amulet, the life-force stone of the wrathful
    ḍākinī mamos,[*]
Fifth is the ḍākinī's silken activity sash,
Sixth is the red shield of six spokes,
Seventh, the Mongolian boots that splendidly suppress the
    godly demons,
Eighth, the tiger-skin quiver, a castle for the dralas.
Ninth, a leopard-skin quiver that is the castle of the wermas;

---

[*] Female demons.

These are the nine accoutrements that are the work of the
    eight classes of haughty ones.
May they accompany the body of the Great One.
May the auspiciousness of bliss pervade Jambudvīpa.

First, the sword Tabpa Lenme [Strikes without Riposte]
Second, the spear Khamsum Dradül [Quells the Enemies of
    the Three Realms].
Third, the lasso Trülnag Domgu [Black Snake of Nine
    Spans],
Fourth, the bow Ragöd Khyilpa [Curving Wild Horn],
Fifth, the ninety-nine divination arrows that support the
    gods,
Sixth, the slingshot Phawang Tongkhor [Slings a Thousand
    Boulders],
Seventh, the ax Dorje Dragchöd [Cuts Rocks like Vajras],
Eighth, the knife Shelgyi Drichung [Crystal Little Knife],
Ninth, the life stone Damcen Chagpa [Attracts the Oath-
    Bound Protectors].
These are the nine self-existing weapons of the dralas
Which sever the life force of all enemies so that they will
    never escape.
May they accompany the body of the Great One.
May the auspiciousness of bliss pervade Jambudvīpa.

That Noble Mount from the land of Orgyen
Is still in the belly of its Wild Ass mother.
In order to capture him with the magical lasso
And through the power of the truth of the ḍākinī's words,
May this horse become the karmic horse of the Great One.
May the auspiciousness of bliss pervade Jambudvīpa.

The companions who will help the divine child to perform
    his enlightened activities will be:
The flower he carries as his ornament, Sengcham Drugmo
    [Lion Sister Dragoness];
His divine arrow of good fortune from Chödrön [Dharma
    Torch];

Adorned with the five-colored silk from Bumkyid [Full of
    Happiness]; and
The beautiful mirror attached to it from Küntar [Total
    Freedom].
May they[48] unite in the hand of the Great One.
May the auspiciousness of bliss pervade Jambudvīpa.

The valley of Makhog, the great lion's stomach,
Connects in the upper part with the land of India
And in the lower part with the country of China.
There is no earth lord who is an embodied human;
The intangible spirits own this land.
When he reaches seven years of age,
Engaging in a hidden manner, through uncontrived yogic
    activity
May he take charge of this ownerless land
And bind the formless by oath.
May the auspiciousness of bliss pervade Jambudvīpa.

The golden arrow Samdrub [Fulfills All Wishes],
The longevity arrow of Drubpa Gyalmo,[*]
Including the arrow Namcag Gönpola [Meteorite Life Force
    of Mahākāla],
The thirty gold-notched divine arrows, and
The fifty divine arrows of Jambudvīpa
Are the Great One's board of eighty ministers.
May they become the ornaments of his bow of enlightened
    activity.
May the auspiciousness of bliss pervade Jambudvīpa.

That flying māra arrow for the forehead of King Lutsen,
May it join the divine arrows in the quiver.
May the horse of Gurkar's shoulder
Be under the immutable golden saddle.[49]

---

[*] In the original Tibetan text, this name is sometimes rendered as Drubpa'i.

May the heart lake of King Sadam*
Be the castle for the drala Sergyi Nya [Golden Fish].
May the great white wing feathers of the garuḍa Shingtri
Become the white feathers that adorn his divine arrow.
May the four demons be bound by oath.
May the four borderlands turn to the dharma.
May the auspiciousness of bliss pervade Jambudvīpa.

The four great fortresses and the eight lesser ones
Are the twelve gateways to their kingdoms.
May they be opened by the Magical Great One [Gesar].
May he bring the wealth of the borderlands to Tibet.
May those kingdoms of demons become his divine subjects.
May the auspiciousness of bliss pervade Jambudvīpa.

When the Great One has completely accomplished the
    benefit of others,
May he, along with the three ministers who originally joined
    him in his aspiration prayers,
Depart from the upper treasure gate of Sheldrag [Crystal
    Rock] and,
Without leaving their bodies, may they join the ranks of the
    vidyādharas.
May the auspiciousness of bliss pervade Jambudvīpa.

In the future, until the end of this eon,
May he be a wealth god for all those who practice correct
    dharma.
May he become a jewel that fulfills whatever others wish for.
This emanation of me, Padma,
Although emanation and emanator are inseparable,
May he be the greater emanation that benefits others.
May whatever aspiration prayers I have made, be
    accomplished.
And may auspicious bliss prevail in Jambudvīpa.

---

* King Sadam is the king of Jang, one of the borderlands to be defeated in a future epic.

Thus he sang, and from the gods came a symphony of music, a rainfall of flowers, and a dome of rainbow light. Guru Rinpoche conferred upon the divine child the name Supreme Being of Jambudvīpa, Gesar Norbu Dradül. For a while amazing and astonishing phenomena occurred, but everyone there was sworn to secrecy, and they remained, from then on, with that seal upon them.

At that time the three iron falcon brothers, who are the life force of all classes of māras, were dwelling in their nest on Mount Meru. Sometimes their bodies were so huge that they had the power to shake the earth. Other times they became the size of thumbs, for they were the support of the black māras' life essence. Every day they roamed around Jambudvīpa creating obstacles to the life span and life essence of dharma practitioners. While the ordinary people could not normally see them, at that time all the dralas and wermas of the side of virtue were summoning them to appear in the middle space of the sky. Powerless to escape, they circled there high in the sky in great rings. Knowing that the time had come to tame them, at that moment the Great Being received a magical bow and arrow and shot an arrow into the sky. Naked, he sat there on a boulder as the corpses of the three falcons fell to the earth. Still to this day the face of the stone is plainly imprinted with the impression of a three-year-old child's thighs and buttocks. It became known that, in less than a day's time of being in this world, he had tamed the three black falcon brothers.

On that same day all four of the nāginī's animals gave birth. The horse had a colt; the dri had a dri calf; the dzo had a calf; and the ewe gave birth to a lamb. At the same time, a dragon thundered in the sky, a rain of flowers fell, tents of rainbow light appeared, and many other astonishing signs occurred. In particular, there were rainbow clouds that appeared, connecting to the top of Gogmo's tent. Gyaza became suspicious and went over by Gogmo to take a look. An enchanting boy had just been born and was sitting on her lap. Even though Gyaza's mind vacillated between joy and sorrow, she said, "Let us bring him to Zhalkar," and she carried the baby with Gogmo following behind her. When Zhalkar saw the boy, he felt immeasurable joy and asked, "What's this?"

Gyaza said, "Gogmo has given birth to this child. But who knows whether he will bring us benefit or harm."

Zhal-lu took the boy on his lap, "Ah, what joy! Now all my wishes are fulfilled. May all the buddha activity of this younger brother be perfectly accomplished! Although he was born just today, he has already reached the physical maturity of a three-year-old. In the lineage of Mukpo Dong, we have had child emanations of nonhumans before. They were suckled with the richest milk of the white snow lioness, and enfolded under the wings of white vultures. Here is another one like them. This child is like the garuḍa, who hatches from his egg already perfectly complete in

213

all the six skills of a warrior. Such perfection will be ours as well; there is no doubt that whatever we two brothers do will bring us success on the path of our lives. Furthermore, as is said,

> Two brothers together are the hammer of the enemy,
> Two mares together are the seed of wealth,
> And two wives together are the ground and source of rumor.

Right now I must offer him some clothing and pure clean foods of the three whites," he said. He touched his head to the head of the child and put him down. The child sat up utterly alert, showing immeasurable love toward Gyatsha. "For the time being, I will call my younger brother 'Joru' because he is so alert." Then they offered him food of the three white substances as well as soft and comfortable silken garments that suited him well.

Gyatsha felt very content as he spoke to Gogmo, saying, "You must take especially good care of him. But in any case, the signs and indications are clear—no one will be able to make obstacles for him; even my dreams have been excellent.

Now I must meet with Chipön. According to our custom, the whole of Ling at large should celebrate his birthday party with songs, dances, and so on. Throughout Upper, Lower, and Middle Ling, whenever one of the three lineages of chieftains has a child, there is always a birthday celebration. But this situation is different from the others. Rather than follow the custom of the land, we should perform our observances at just the right time.

Girl, your coming to the land of humans has achieved its goal. If you have dreams or any other sign about what is necessary for the child, you must tell me." Saying that, he took Gogmo and her baby back to her tent.

[Meanwhile Trothung was having a bad time.] For two nights he had many nightmares. Then he heard the story of how Gogmo had given birth to a son. He sat there thinking about this and became quite uneasy.

Then Zhalkar and his body guard Midar Tag-lu [Full-Fledged Tiger] went before Chipön. Chipön and Gyatsha conferred for many hours, after which Gyatsha offered this song recounting the events that had occurred.

> The song is Ala Ala Ala,
> And Thala is the sound of the melody.
> All you guardians of the lore of the ancestral lineage:
> The chief drala Nyentag,
> The zodor Magyal Pomra,

Auntie Nammen Karmo [White Sky Goddess], and so on,
Lead Zhalkar today as he sings his song.
This place is Trakhar Namdzong
And I am dear little Zhalkar.
Today the situation is just like this:

The toil of the three months of spring
Delights the mind with the ripening of the grain.
The good ears of grain of the three months of fall
Adorn the field like sparkling gold.

Not knowing when to harvest, uncertainty arises.
So it is you I ask, the astrologer who knows the three times.

The practice of the two stages of the path, generation and
    completion,
Delights the mind with the common and supreme siddhis.
When your practice is perfect and you see the deity's face,
Not knowing what to say in supplication, uncertainties arise.
So it is you I ask, the guru who has perfected the path.

My first booty was the mother nāginī.
Thinking she would give birth to a divine child, we prayed,
And on the full moon day an astonishing divine son was born
Who already had the fully developed body of a three-year-old.
First of all, what rituals are necessary for him?
Second, should there be an enthronement to establish his
    reputation?
And especially, third, how should he be taken care of and
    brought up?
I haven't been able to decide what to do concerning these
    three matters.
Therefore, in my opinion,
This tribal lineage is like a white snow lion;
The turquoise mane of our karma and authentic presence
Will naturally surround him.
If the closest ministers and relatives, who are like the snow
    mountains, do not revere him,

And if the snow lion becomes disheartened,
Then the snow mountain will be full of regret.

This tribal lineage is like a brightly striped tiger;
The tiger's six smiles, the magical feats of the warrior,
Will naturally surround him.
If the fathers, uncles, and the jungle do not sustain him,
The tiger will be disheartened, and the jungle will be full of
    regret.

By the spiritual and worldly lore of the younger tribal lineage
    of the Bumpa clan,
The authentic presence of the divine child's holy person
Naturally surrounds him.
I, his older brother, will respect him as the greatest of chiefs.
If he thinks this won't happen, then I, the older brother, will
    be full of regret.

Among the precious jewels in the depths of the ocean below
Is the auspicious substance, the white conch that swirls to the
    right.
If recognized, it is worn as the crown ornament;
If not, then sadly it is passed around in the marketplace.

From the jewel treasure gate of the craggy middle world,
The yellow gold naturally forms elegant earrings.
If you understand this, [you understand that] these are the
    goods of the nonhuman spirits;
Not understanding this, you will regret it if it is melted and
    hammered.

This fortunate son of the father Senglön, Gogmo's child,
If we give it some thought, has been sent from the upper
    realm of the divine.
He is the heart essence of me, this leader of Bumpa.
If the fathers and uncles of Ling disdain him, the Bumpa clan
    will regret it.

216

Even if White Ling in general does not honor him,
I of the Bumpa clan intend to enthrone him
And make him the leader of the Lesser Lineage of Ling.
I, Zhalkar, will take the first seat as his minister.
So that he will develop vast learning in all intellectual subjects
You, Chipön, without appointment, are naturally the one
    responsible to teach him.
Within the clan of Bumpa, the one who qualifies as his
    personal minister
Is Tshazhang Denma Jangtra [Uncle Northern Light], the son
    of the Den clan.
Not only that, he will have all the uncles and brothers of the
    Lesser Lineage
Who are perfect warriors, like sacks full of spears.
Not only should he be the high lord of White Ling,
But I think he could place the whole southern continent of
    Jambudvīpa beneath his lordship.
Am I right, Chipön? Think it over.
If you have understood my words, they are sweet to your ears.
If not, there is no way to explain it.
Chipön, keep this in your heart.

Then King Chipön, the Uncle of Mukpo Dong, gave this much consideration, after which he offered to Zhalkar this song, which explains the predictions of the past accounts and gives counsel for the future.

The song begins with Ala Ala Ala.
Thala leads the melody of the song.
Buddha is my crown ornament.
The precious dharma is the ambrosia for my mind.
The sangha is the field to which I direct my faith.
Please be with me inseparably as I sing this song.
This place is known as Chipön's Falcon Castle, Trakhar.
Listen, Zhalkar to what I, Chipön, sing.
Even though I say "listen," this is not an offering of the
    dharma.
Nevertheless, it is a perfectly correct account of events.

First, there are the original manuscripts of the Dong
  civilization.
Second, there is the prophecy of the divine Uḍḍiyāna Padma.
Third, there are the deluded dreams that I, Chipön, have had.
Fourth, the signs of fortunate connection between the outer
  universe and its inhabitants.
When these four merge at once,
The divine child arises by the power of this merit.
However, according to the ancient proverbs of the past:

Even though the most delicious food is ghee,
No one has ever heard of a starved stomach that could digest it.
The mask of the awesome protector deities
Will not bring wonder to an immature child.
The essence of refined yellow gold
Will not gild the surface of a stone or a horn.

This son, who has been bestowed by the imperial gods above,
If only his close relatives place him in a high position,
Then all others will not show him respect.
That lotus that is born from the filthy mire,
If left until its form is fully developed,
On the day that it blooms with an astonishing smile
There is no need to clean off the mud;
The lotus never forgets its earthly beginnings.
Those cloud banks over the endless ocean,
Let them be until they billow white.
One day they will completely fill the sky,
Never needing to turn to the great rivers for help.
The clouds of the ocean will never forget where they came
  from.

That divine child of the nāginī Gogmo from the Dong,
Until the day that he can master the golden throne through
  his miraculous powers,
We do not have to show him respect; if we just leave him
  alone,
He will surpass even the mightiest

Without needing the fathers and uncles to assist him.
He must not forget his father's clan, the Lesser Lineage of
    Dong;
Moreover, having promoted the significance of the Lesser
    Lineage and the united inner ranks of the mighty warriors,
    chieftain, and ministers,
We never considered that we would be unable to accomplish
    our actions.
Since Mother Gogmo came to the Lesser Lineage
We have already achieved a freedom and political power that
    reaches to the four corners.
As long as fearless confidence is achieved in full measure,
Then even if our activities are delayed, why be afraid?

If with an unstable mind you drink the water of a coward's speech,
There is no choice but to engage in frantic activity.

Not only that, but the original documents of the Dong say:

"From the lair of the tiger, the six demons are subdued.
Riding the dragon, the six grains are received.
In the seventh year the Tigress* will wander as a vagrant in the
    nomad's land of the northern reaches
And become the lord of the castle.
In the twelfth year he will summon the ornament of his horse
    by lasso;
The prize will be secured like the sun rising from the peak of
    the eastern mountain.
Until then keep the blue steel in its sheath."

These are the words of the unmistaken prophecy.
Don't let these words escape your lips.
No one else knows this but I, Chipön.
Until the son reaches age twelve,

---

* Here Gesar is referred to as a tigress because he was born in is the year of the Tiger. Some accounts of the epic say that he went to the land of Ma [Golog] when he was seven years of age.

Aside from going along with whatever he does,
We should not counsel him with other advice.
Even if he calls forth the classes of enemies and demons,
Even if he reverses earth and sky, there will be no problem.
Of course you love him with all your heart, Chief Zhalkar.

I, this old man, am now content.
Chief Zhalkar and your brother, remain on your golden
    thrones.
I, your uncle, will shepherd your intentions.
Minister Denma will be the leader of the troops.
The mighty warriors of Ling will line up before you precisely
    like rows of tigresses.
Karma such as this is the gift of the past.
Before long the sun of happiness will dawn.
Were you listening, Zhalkar, son of the gods?
Bumpa chief, hold this in your heart.

When Chipön had finished speaking, Zhalkar slowly and carefully considered
the outer and inner meaning of this advice and, in a state of delight, returned home.

CHAPTER THREE

Trothung, evil-minded, becomes jealous and
Tries to slay Joru with poison and magic.
But instead, Joru
Tames Amnye Gompa Raja.

THEN KING TROTHUNG THOUGHT, "In my dreams this year, the signs for the
fortune of Tibet at large have appeared both good and bad. Among those signs, the
ones for Tag-rong* were nothing but bad. In the tribal lineage of Chöphen Nagpo,
starting with Lhag Yagdar [Increasing Excellence] of Ser, there have been nine sons,
like tigresses, who have descended as the Elder Lineage. Now, of the three lineages
of Ling, the Elder, Middle, and Lesser, there is just a single government with no personal leader who rules. But now, since the birth of Zhalkar of Bumpa of the Lesser
Lineage, the might of his paternal lineage has increased in power. The three brothers, Zhalkar, Nyibum of Ser† [the Elder Lineage], and Anu Paseng [Courageous
Youthful Lion] of the Middle Lineage, always back each other up. Because Chipön
is so deceptive, and the other two brothers are too young, they both willingly follow
whatever Bumpa [Zhalkar] says. Actually, it's as if they don't know how to be lords
of their own domains. Now, this boy just born to Gogmo is the son of Senglön, the
grandson of the nāga Tsugna, and the nephew of Gödcham Karmo [White Vulture

---

* His own tribe.

† This is a short form of Nyibum Daryag of Serpa.

Lady]. Even his mother can invoke the gods and summon the nāgas. His father is important; his mother is great. As if that's not enough, she says that she belongs to Guru Uḍḍiyāna Padma. Whatever the case may be, I can't tell for sure but it seems that this is a boy who seems to be half-human and half-demon. It's uncertain what is to come of this! Therefore, if we want to do away with him now, there seems to be a way to do that."

Three days later, in the morning, Uncle Trothung of Tag-rong mounted his horse Gu-gu Rogdzong [Black Fortress]. He brought along with him balls of white butter and honey cakes and many other sweet delicacies, all of which possessed the strong poison called Yumo Gug-gyel [Fells a Doe in Flight]. Having planted the poison in this way, he took it to offer as the child's first butter to the mouth.* He went to see both Mother Gogmo and her son at Gogmo's tent, where both valleys of Ci and Sug merge,† and he said, "Oh, what joy! Oh, Gogmo has a boy. He is Uncle's nephew. Only three days have gone by, but already he seems to be three years old. Without a doubt, he is a son of the Mukpo Dong lineage. If his uncle gives him his first solid food, this will increase his authentic presence. Where is that deceiving, rotten-minded Chipön when we need him? As the proverb says:

> *When you're cold, your clothes have no weight;*
> *When you're starving, your food has no nutrition.*

Uncle didn't know about this [birth] until today. So now, on behalf of the Tag-rong clan, I must make this offering of the pure first solid food." He gave him the butter balls, cakes, and so on, and the child ate every morsel. The food that Trothung gave him was so sweet and rich that even an adult could not have digested it, much less a child. Then he thought, "He surely will die now." But Joru pushed all the poison out of his fingertips as he expelled his prāṇa.‡ Trothung thought, "This poison cannot harm him because his mother is a nāginī, and, since the bodies of nāgas are a mass of poison, it seems that poison cannot harm poison. In the valley of Ciphu Drag-nag [Upper Black Crag],§ there is a shaman [Bön] black magician of Zhangzhung, who

---

* First solid food.

† This is another name for the valley known as Kyidsö Yag-gi Khado.

‡ Sanskrit, vital winds.

§ Where the Ci and Sug valleys meet.

transgressed the command of the teacher Shenrab* and who uses the meditation and liturgies of his religion only for black magic. His name is Amnye Gompa Raja [Grandfather Meditation Prince]. He has perverted views about the dharma of Padma. He is totally habituated to a wrong approach to generation stage practice, so that the entire dark side of the eight classes has befriended him. In the daytime, with his black magic, he would take the lives of both Buddhist and Bönpo practitioners. And in the evening, gathering with the mamos, he would rob ordinary beings of their lives. I used to rely on his help, and he would do away with all my enemies. So now it will be easy for me to send for him." Thinking that all other schemes had been exhausted, he said to Mother Gogmo, "It would be difficult for even the great covering of the sky to cover this boy. It would be difficult for even the great solid ground of the earth to hold him. You haven't done any sort of long-life ceremonies for him, and so you really must invite a guru to confer the longevity empowerments. As for the offerings, I'll take care of them. Make preparations by laying a clean cushion in this house." He said that and went to the valley of Ciphu Drag-nag. Amnye that very night had many disturbing dreams, and so he was sitting there diligently doing reversal practices. Tag-rong Trothung made three prostrations to the guru Amnye Gompa Raja and sang this song about the reason why it was necessary to liberate the boy Joru by slaying him:

> The song begins with Ala Ala Ala,
> Thala is the melody of the song.
> O founding teacher of the Bön, Shenrab, look upon me.
> Wondrous Bön Taglha Mebar [Blazing Tiger God],† look
>   upon me.
> Machig Sidpa'i Gyalmo [Sole Mother Queen of Existence],
>   look upon me.
> Assist me, Tag-rong, in singing this song.
> In case you don't recognize this place,
> It is the lower valley of Ciphu Drag-nag
> And this is the practice cave of Amnye Gompa.
> If you don't know who I am,
> I am Mazhi Trothung of Tag-rong,
> I am the shepherd of the people of the poisonous boiling lake,

---

* Shenrab is the founder of the Bön lineage, which was the original teaching being practiced in ancient Tibet. He is to the Bön as Śākyamuni is to the Buddhists.

† (Tib. *stag lha me 'bar*). One of the protector deities of the Bön.

I am the patron of the enduring Bön.
Now let me tell you how it is.
In White Ling, a land filled with the six grains,
Grows the bud of the most deadly poison, the poisonous *hala* reed.[50]
This is such a bad omen that, even if you cut it away, it cannot
    be eradicated,
Therefore I can only look to you [Amnye Gompa], the
    sharpest among sickles.

The vast plain of White Ling is filled with tigresses,
But this one is ominous for it has a hairless tail nine arm
    spans in length.
It is such a bad omen that, even if you chase it, it can't be
    caught.
That is why you are the crucial arrow that will stop him in
    his tracks.

In White Ling, a land filled with the divine lineage,
It is strange for there to be a bastard demon child such as this!
I even gave him black poison and he didn't die.
Now, it's only up to you to slay him with the power of your
    black magic.

It seems that the white prosperity sheep are freely grazing
    here and there,
But wolves have their dens on all the high mountains.
If someone doesn't splatter the wolf cubs' blood and
    brains,
It is certain that the sheep will never be at ease.

On the patterned village fields,
The green ears of grains are scattered about
But clouds, filled with hail, have their dens in the high
    skies.
If the eight classes are not bound by oath,
The five types of grain will never be at ease.

In this the colorful land of Ling,
Both I, Chieftain Tag-rong, and you, patron and guru, are
　　higher than the sky;
This yoke is pulling us down from our high position.
Unless we can permanently crush the enemy Joru,
We gurus and chieftains will never be at ease with his
　　troublemaking.
Do you understand, honorable Gompa Raja?
From the very day this boy Joru was born,
He said that he wanted to kill the Bönpo
And that he was the murderer who could slay you.
He said that he would certainly bring trouble to Chieftain Trothung
And that he must take control of the district of Tang-rong.
He said that sorcery, thievery, and seduction, these three,
Led the country into misery and suffering,
And so he would not stay where he was, but that he would go
　　to Ciphu
To take your head and arms, Amnye.

It is only thanks to dear warrior Zhal-lu that Joru has been
　　delayed and distracted thus far.
These words of mine are not baseless; they are the words of
　　Gyaza herself.
I couldn't just sit through all of this, so I came here today.
If we kill the enemy Joru today,
First of all, it accomplishes the guru's aims;
Secondly, it accomplishes the aims of Tag-rong.

It's easy to extinguish a fire when it's small.
You don't even need water; it can be snuffed with your thumb.
It's easy to subjugate an enemy when he is small.
You don't even need weapons; you can just wrap him in clothes.

Through my cunning ruse, I've already got him fooled.
They are actually inviting the guru to bestow long-life
　　empowerment and bathe him.

You must place the black magic torma* upon his crown,
You must put the black magic substances into his mouth,
And you must be the one to sever the stream of his life.
You mustn't stay here now, quickly depart.
The innermost wealth of the Tag-rong clan
Is the prosperity jewel called Phetse Nu-gu [Nine-Edged
     Little Sack],
Which is the work of the nonhuman godly demons.
It is a treasure source of all that is desirable
And a jewel that fulfills all desires.
It is the gift of prosperity and wealth
Given to Chöphen Nagpo of Dong by Magyal Pomra.
Once the guru fulfills the purpose of beings
And after your work in this world for others is complete,
Then we shall present this to you.
When the guru's work in this world is done,
The personal wealth of Tag-rong will become ours again.
This treasure of prosperity is no small thing;
It is presented as an offering to you to fulfill a greater purpose,
And both guru and chieftain will share in this gain.

These words and this presentation
Must be the inner jewel of conversation that's kept "under the
     collar."
On the day of Joru's demise,
Guru, you must come to the house of Tag-rong.
We will rejoice with song and dance
Then guru, the prosperity treasure will be yours.
If you understood this, it is sweet to your ears,
If not there's no connection to this song.
Amnye, please keep this in your mind.

Thus he offered this song full of lies and deceit. The guru gave it a lot of
thought, and then he said, "Sometime back I began having signs both day and night,
and not only that, these signs have accelerated over the last three days. If I analyze

---

* Offering cake.

last night's dream, there is no question that some strange demon has been sent on a mission to murder me. Since only three days have gone by since he was born, no matter what he tries to do, his power has not yet matured, and his windhorse has not reached its full measure. With my black magic even rocks that are like vajras can be destroyed, and it is even powerful enough to bring the turquoise dragon of the south down to the plains. There's nothing I won't be able to do, but as for the gift of the Tag-rong, I must accept it since the power of my evil mantras is so coveted." Then he thought, "If I don't complain to him about how difficult this feat is, and that he should be grateful for the favor, then he may not appreciate it."

So Amnye said, "Oh, yes, Chieftain Tag-rong, sir, it seems that this lowly servant must honor the command of the dear chieftain. If this job were a burden too heavy to bear, then your servant could not do it, and all hope would be lost. It seems the connection between guru and student is extremely profound for, if the samayas that have been proclaimed could not be kept, then the dharma would not be accomplished, and hell would be reinforced." Saying this he raised this song:

> Ala Ala Ala begins the song.
> Thala leads the melody of the song.
> Rāhu, nāga, tsen, demons, mamos, and so forth—
> Powerful haughty spirits of the eight classes, look upon me.
> This place is Ciphu Drag-nag.
> This is the place where tsen and mamos bestow siddhis.
> This is the place where the'u rang demons were bound by
>   oath.
> And this is my, Amnye Gompa's, practice cave.
> Now listen, Chieftain Tag-rong,
> And I will tell you the way things are.
>
> The divine guru, wearing the golden hat,
> Seem to be gazing in space with his sparkling eyes,
> But there is a mass of darkness in his heart, focused on the
>   valuable wealth.
> You can't tell by looking, but if you check you will know.
> Those bound by marriage, tied together by their vows,
> Seem like dry, lifeless bodies lying in one bed,
> While the dark side of their minds is lost to the face of their
>   lover.
> You can't tell by checking, but if you listen you will know.

The ax of the law of the dear imperial chieftain,
Thought to be the pleasing speech of his country's customs
    and laws,
Lands the negotiations and the victories into the hands of the
    wealthy.
You can't tell by listening, but if you look closely you will see.

According to the speech of the Mazhi King of Dong,
You say that you, the chieftain, have come here for the
    purpose of Amnye,
But your mind is focused on the politics of Tag-rong.
By listening I couldn't know, but I could tell by the offering.
This boy Joru, the son of Mother Gogmo
Even if he is my murderer, I, Amnye,
Am not going to just walk up to the doorstep of the rākṣasas
    to end my life.[51]
I, Amnye, will be the one man who can escape,
For my guides are both the demons and the cannibal demons,
And my friends the tsen and mamos keep me company.
Before I know if I'm going to get the valuable wealth,
What's the point in exposing the target of my precious life?
Chieftain Trothung, keep the likes of that in your heart.

Then Trothung started prostrating profusely and said to the guru, "Between sky and earth, it's impossible that your black magic would not be effective. By all means, come today and kill Joru, and I will definitely give you the Nine-Edged Prosperity Sack. Not only that, I swear on the *One Hundred Thousand Verse Wisdom Sūtra* of our fathers that the whole province of Tag-rong Dugtso Marpo [Tag-rong Red Poison Lake] will definitely support you all year round."

And then the guru replied, "Yes, well, all right then, I'll just go right away and go ahead with your orders. This very night I will see if I can kill Joru, and tomorrow I will come to the tent of the Tag-rong family." He also reminded him by adding, "Don't forget to repay my kindness."

Trothung said, "Oh, yes, sir, yes, sir."

Then Trothung returned to Gogmo's place and reported, "Today I was planning to go and see Lama Künga. But on my way passing through the lower valley of Ciphu Drag-nag, I met Amnye on the path. I asked him to do a divination, and he said that there is an obstacle that will last for three days and that, since Zhalkar and

Gyaza had shown him great kindness, he felt he should protect them during this time. At the same time I requested him to give the long-life abhiṣeka."

Then Trothung thought, "It's best that I leave now and stay away for three days, but not longer," and he hastily ran away.

At this time Joru did not yet have the actual support for the dralas such as the armor, helmets, weapons, and so forth, so he asked his mother, saying, "Mother, today the time has come for me to subjugate Amnye Gompa Raja. Could you please bring me four little pebbles?" She put four pebbles in his hand. He put one in front, one in back, and one to the right and the left. He visualized the pebbles as supports for the individual dralas, elder brother Dungkhyung Karpo, younger brother Ludrül Ödtrung, sister Thalei Ödtro, and Lord Nyen Gedzo, along with the nine brethren who were the best of the dralas, and the nine hundred conch-armored ones. The drala deities then dissolved into the pebbles and resided there.

Around about that time, Amnye Gompa Raja departed from his practice cave and arrived at a distance about three fields of vision away. When Amnye shouted *phat!* the first time, all the gods in the sky disappeared but, because Elder Brother White-Conch Garuḍa, surrounded by the armored nine-hundred conch dralas, abided as one with the pebble, Joru was unharmed. Again, as Amnye got one field closer he shouted another *phat!* and all the nāgas below him disappeared. But the younger brother with his retinue of nine hundred remained firm. On seeing the tent, Amnye shouted another *phat!* and all the nyen in the middle realm were dispelled. However, Gedzo and his retinue of three hundred and sixty remained firm. At that time, Joru focused his mind and called to the gods, and all the dralas returned like a flurry of snow. There was a swirling blizzard of dharmapālas, and everywhere wermas appeared like flashing lightning bolts. At the moment that the heretic Gompa Raja arrived at the door, Joru quickly ran, scooping up the four pebbles, and threw them. According to Amnye, there was a man in white with nine hundred conch-armored ones, a man in blue with nine hundred turquoise-armored ones, a man in yellow with three hundred and sixty golden-armored ones, and an army of ḍākinīs nine hundred strong chasing him. Without looking back he fled as fast as he could.[*]

Meanwhile Joru had sent an emanation to the heretic's meditation cave, which went in and evaporated the spring and did away with any provisions. Another emanation pursued Amnye, who ran a bit faster and arrived at the river bank, where he

---

[*] Concerning this account, some of the points are missing from the woodblock text, so the translators have supplemented the story by drawing from other versions of the epic.

pulled back his magician's shade.* To this day that river bank is known as the river bank of the man who wore the Black Bear Shade [*domra*].

Then Amnye saw that an army was approaching, so he thought, "I must throw the main torma to drive away the army." Thinking that, he went into his practice cave. At that very moment Joru, through his magic, sealed off the door to the cave with a huge boulder the size of a yak, so that there was no place at all for Amnye to go. The perverted heretic Bönpo said,

> Joru, you demon cub, naughty boy,
> Listen with your ears and watch with your eyes.
> At a distance—magic; close up—needles.
> We will see who is the best at knives and needles.
> Great loving one Garab Wangchuk† [Powerful One of
>   Extreme Joy], look upon me.
> Sole Mother, Sidpa'i Gyalmo, look on me.
> Düdmo Trag-gi Relpa [Bloody Single-Tress Demon Woman],
>   look upon me.
> Sog Düd [Life-Essence Demon], brothers, sisters and the rest,
> All the dralas to whom I continually make offerings,
> Dharmapāla guardians, be not meager in power.
> Eight classes of the dark side, don't be idle!

Saying this, he threw the great torma that had taken a day to empower. It hit the boulder and made it tremble. Then he took a torma that had taken a month to empower, and, intensely uttering his cursing incantations, he forcefully called upon the truth of his refuge and flung the torma so that it fractured the boulder, bringing down a torrent of meteorites, hail, and sparks outside of the cave. Joru assumed the form of Zilnön Padma Dragpo [Wrathful Lotus Who Quells with Splendor]. "Damn," Amnye thought, "I still can't beat him." Then, as Amnye threw the torma that had been empowered for a year, Joru, visualizing the cave as a meteorite abode without fissures, forced the haughty worldly protectors inside and rendered them

---

* Called a *domra* (Tib. *dom ra*), "black bear shade," this is a kind of hairpiece that exorcists would wear so that they could more easily see the demons and other intangible phenomena. Elders in Tibet would wear it, thinking it beneficial for their vision.

† Garab Wangchuk is the lord of one of the desire god realms known as Shentrül Wangchuk. These gods openly partake of the wealth that emanates from others.

powerless to escape. Because of the godly demons and the splendid torma's fire and wind,[52] they could not escape; the power and strength of the guardians that accompanied the flying torma turned back on them, and so completely destroyed Amnye that his body was scattered like dust particles.

At that time all the haughty worldly ones offered their life essence and promised to protect the Buddha's doctrine and they swore never to harm living beings again. Amnye's consciousness was separated from the murderous death spirits and led to the pure realm. Through his miraculous powers, Joru entered the cave and incinerated all the perverted black magic practice materials. As for Bloody Single-Tress Demon Woman and Life-Essence Demon, this brother and sister, he made a prayer that they would become the weapons that guard the doctrines of Buddhists and Bönpo and installed each one of them as a terma guardian. One emanation of Joru was still there with Gogmo. The people who were there had seen Gompa Raja run off, and most of them were wondering what was going to happen, but the mother knew that yesterday Amnye had seen that this boy had three eyes and that that was why he had fled. It became well known that, although he was only three days old, Gesar had tamed Amnye Gompa Raja.

The next day Gesar woke up early. He said to his mother, "Today I have an important matter that must be settled. Not only that, my protectors, such as the drala brothers and sisters, have already tamed Amnye, so today I must go to his deserted residence and gather up what remains." Then he left.

The mother thought, "The guru had told me that I did not have to take precautions in guarding him." Besides that she thought, "He's just a magical emanation, so whatever he does is fine." And so she sat there without any anxiety. That day early in the morning Joru went to the encampment of Tag-rong and emanated himself to appear just like Amnye Gompa Raja, and at the entrance to his tent he sang this song to Tag-rong Trothung:

> It's Ala Ala Ala,
> And Thala leads the melody.
> All you most powerful protectors of the dark side
> Help Amnye today to sing this song.
> If you don't recognize this place,
> It's the midlands of Trothung's campground.
> If you don't recognize me,
> I'm Gompa Raja.
> I'm the butcher who killed the demon Joru.
> Listen here, it's like this.

That demon child called Joru—
Is he the messenger of divine Padma?
I heard that he is the lineage son of the nyen Gedzo
And the grandson of the nāga Tsugna.
They say he is unrivalled,
Yet you Tag-rong have such great merit
And I have such great power and ability
That I have cut the cord of his red life-essence.
Last night, during the middle watch
I received an offering to pray for the deceased.
So I went there and flayed his skin
And threw his corpse in the rushing river.
His head was the skin of a god,
His waist was the skin of a nyen,
His legs were the skin of the cold-blooded nāgas,
And his hands were the skin of humans.
Skin like this is of great value.
Without the favor of the great merit of Tag-rong
And the greatness of Amnye's power and black magic
It is unthinkable that this would have fallen into our hands.
When the fine particles
Of Amnye Gompa Raja's body dissipate,
The owner of these skins will be none other than you, Tag-
    rong.
Crown the pinnacle of your castle with this human-skin
    victory banner.
In the carefree and mighty province of Tag-rong,
The people are suppressed by Chieftain Trothung, the one
    who holds control.
You, a headstrong chief, will destroy yourself as you defeat
    others
If you can't raise your head beyond your fortress, Phorog
    [Raven Heart].
In this headstrong fortress, the pillar between earth and sky,
You can't raise your head, but you can hoist Joru's [skin]
    victory banner.
That Joru, nasty son of Gogmo,

Although he possessed the power of a thousand godly
   demons,
First of all, he had nothing but white intentions toward me,
   Amnye,
Second, he did nothing against Chief Trothung,
Third, he always intended to repay the kindness of the fathers
   and uncles.
For these three reasons, when I cut his throat, he bled milk.
I regret that I killed this one who was innocent.
Even though I regret it, it was at your command, King Tro of
   Tag-rong.
The reason you gave that kind of command is that
This day is ruled by the constellation Rohiṇī;
It's actually a Rohiṇī Saturday.
Right now you must hand over the prosperity sack to me,
But that alone is not enough.
Although you, Tag-rong, are a garrulous man,
The one being you shouldn't have said to kill was the magical
   child—
That younger brother of warrior Zhal-lu who you told me to
   kill.
And the one thing you should never offer is the empty sack
   you are offering—
That empty sack belongs in the hands of a beggar.

That gift horse without incisors,
Although it is toothless, still you must accept it.

So you, chieftain of Tag-rong,
You own a dung sack and a club.
That bag and club are suitable for a beggar;
Now is the time to give them to me, this lowly one.
Chief Tag-rong, these things are beneath you.
If not that, then give me the wealth treasure of the national flag
And the seal of Mukpo Dong;
Then you can keep your hobo's bag and stick.
If you can't choose which one to give me,

Then I'll throw my three-day torma at you.
And I'll tell Chieftain Zhalkar everything!
What is your fancy, Trothung? Bear this in mind.

While he was saying that, Trothung recognized that the skin of Joru was hanging over the shoulder [of the imposter Amnye]. The Tag-rong family had a white willow staff that had been given to the Bönpo sage from Zhangzhung by a sky the'u rang.* As the innermost treasure of the godly demons empowered with the words of truth, it was a support for the siddhi of speed-walking and had the power to come and go on its own. Now the time had come that it was necessary for Joru to possess this. The stick and the support of prosperity, a long-life arrow, were tied to a sandalwood post. It was well-known that no one at all was allowed to touch them.

Trothung thought, "Joru's been killed. Though Amnye seems more controlling than before, I really don't blame him for that because I did weave some tales between him and Joru. Now he said I must give him both the prosperity bag and the staff! That is taking things too far! I have committed to give the prosperity sack, so there's no way to renege, but I didn't say I would give the staff, too. So there must be a way to get out of this. As for the national flag and the seal, how could I think of giving them? Furthermore, as the proverb states:

Power in another's hand,
Is like your own hair caught in a tree branch.

It's a way of saying, 'I'm done for.' If Gyatsha and Chipön hear of this, not to mention my wife Denza and my son Aten, and so on, it's certain they will have nothing good to say. So for a while I'll have to say that I'll give him whatever he wants; there's nothing else to do. But before long this guru will grow old; already today he is different from usual. Who knows, maybe it is the black magic of the gods of Ling that has affected him. If that's the case, then he won't last long.[53] When he dies, then Tag-rong's own wealth will come back into its owner's hands. Until then, if I pretend that Tag-rong and Amnye, patron and patronized, are as one, then that's the key point for making sure that the wealth is not lost into another's hands. Therefore,

---

* Here, *the'u rang* refers to a demon who was the main protector of King Gurkar of Hor. There are three levels of the demon: those that relate to the sky, the intermittent space, and the earth. In that order their colors are white, yellow, and black.

since he's only one single man on his own, whatever I do, it will surely work out." He thought things over at great length and then he said,

"Gracious Gompa Raja, sir, since you have accomplished whatever I asked of you earlier, Tag-rong and I can offer you the nine-edged sack and all necessary articles. The thing which is called 'the Bönpo guru's staff' will be no good for you, since it is the support for Tag-rong's innermost deity, Hayagrīva. If you take it, it will be no good either for patron or the guru. Instead of that, I'll give you however much gold and silver you desire."

Amnye replied, "Okay, so be it. I don't want the sack. You can keep both of them, but give me the flag and the seal. Now, out of friendliness, I did you the kindness of affording you a choice between your treasures. Moreover, since this Joru is the inner jewel of White Ling, the younger brother of the chieftain of Bumpa, and since he quells the demons of the dark side, how can these things I ask for possibly suffice as the fee for committing the sin of such a murder? Throughout all this my only thought has been of our old friendship, our familiarity, and the promise of our long-term connection. If I carefully report the details of what has happened here to Gyatsha, Chipön, Sengtag, and, not to mention, the chieftains of the Elder and Middle Lineages of Ling, then it wouldn't take them even a single day to destroy you, Tag-rong, without a trace remaining. Besides that, I worry about the turmoil that this will create among the brothers and the cousins, and I have been contemplating the repercussions for the future. Not only that, because you, Tag-rong, are the main person who will take care of my corpse and any legal actions, and even this victory banner of Joru's, I thought this would benefit you, since I am only thinking about your long-term welfare. It's important for you to give this careful thought. If you have something to give me, present it now. If you don't, then I have no choice but to leave and then respond with a double dose of black magic!" He started to leave, saying, "This situation is impossible just like the proverb:

> *The business is over,*
> *But the price is yet to be discussed."*

Then a frightened Trothung replied, "Don't do that! I can make the offering. How can there be angry minds between guru and patron?" and he quickly made the offering. "Now Lama, this is my special wealth I'm giving you, don't let anyone see it. Keep it until it is no longer of use to you. And when the day comes that the benefit of beings has been accomplished, please see that it's returned to me."

"All right, I won't tell anyone else about this, but Joru has already heard everything, for his skin that I am wearing is still alive. It makes no difference whether you or I keep these things; the day will come when I'll return them to you. Until then, from time to time I'll bring them over to your place," he [Amnye] said.

Then Trothung looked at Joru's skin hanging over Amnye's shoulder and noticed that the eyes were winking and the lips smacking. Just at that moment Amnye got up, turned around, ran off, and completely disappeared. Trothung sat there feeling uneasy and full of doubt.

At that very moment Joru appeared before his mother. Several days later, Joru said to his mother, "Today my mind feels clearer than ever before, and I feel such delight!" At that very moment Auntie Nammen Karmo manifested as a turquoise bee and, with the buzzing melody of a bee, she sang these words of prophecy:

> I supplicate the gurus.
> The motherly aunt's prophecy is like this—
> This chieftain of Tag-rong, Trothung,
> When you observe him, his intentions seem evil,
> But whatever he does will be helpful for Joru.
> His incarnation is high; still he has great obscuration from
>   the womb.
> For example, the perverted damsi*
> Have entered Tag-rong's heart;
> If you can't free him from possession by the damsi,
> The troops of White Ling will stir up internal strife.
> Even if you feel no need to fear the army,
> If there is internal struggle in Ling, the uncles and cousins
>   will destroy themselves.
> It will be difficult for them to find a common ground.
> So now you must go straight to the upper Kyid [Happiness]
>   Valley
> And, pretending that the heretic black magician Gompa has
>   died,
> Put the prosperity bag and the staff in a place where Trothung
>   can see it
> And, pretending that the boulder is the boundary marker of
>   his retreat,

---

* A *damsi* is a demon who corrupts the words of honor of mantra practitioners.

Be sure it has a hole large enough for a rat to pass.
Right now Trothung is on his way there;
Through a magical spell he will enter the cave as a rat.
Once he gets in bless him so that there is no possibility that
    the spell will be broken,
Then, let him disgorge the demonic possession.
This is not the right time for him to take
The pill that erases all memories.
Until he swears by drinking the water of oath
That he will not deploy the army,
Do not let him go!
His actions are two-faced like a ḍamaru,* but,
When you open the gates of the twelve fortresses, he will be
    useful.
My son Joru, keep this in the core of your heart.

He heard what she had sung, and, arriving at Ciphu through his magical powers, Joru instantly perched on a rock, manifesting as a falcon. Meanwhile Trothung
was lost in thought: "What could have happened to Amnye yesterday? Amnye
doesn't have those kinds of miraculous abilities. And what really has happened to
Joru? We've had no news of him. I don't know if Joru has miraculous abilities or
not." These thoughts made him feel uncomfortable. He decided that he must go
and see what had happened to Amnye, and so he left for Ciphu. Arriving there, he
saw that there was blue smoke billowing above the meditation cave, and he thought
that Amnye was inside. He went to the entrance of the cave and saw that a great
boulder closed the entrance to the door and served as a retreat marker as well and,
when he looked more closely at the boulder, there were two small holes that seemed
to have been made by a stick. Slyly peeking in through one of the holes, he could
clearly see everything within the cave. Amnye Gompa Raja was dead; his head was
hanging down and his black hair was disheveled. He recognized the staff and the
prosperity bag leaning against the wall on the rock face behind him and he became
overjoyed as he thought, "This is the best possible outcome." Immediately he transformed into a little rat and went into the cave through the hole, but the stick and
bag were nowhere to be found. Thinking, "This must be some kind of power of the

---

* A *ḍamaru* is a two-sided ritual hand drum; it is rotated back and forth with the hand, causing
beads tied on strings to strike the two drum faces.

words of truth,[*] because I have the body of a rat but I cannot see with my rat's eyes," he removed his rat head, and his own head appeared on the rat body.

He looked all around the cave and saw the remains of a fire and a flood, but the articles, the corpse, and all the rest were nowhere to be seen. At that instant, Joru destroyed the illusion, blessed him so that his magic could be annulled, and Trothung was wrought with fear. "Oh no! It seems that I've been done in by a demon!" he proclaimed. "I'd better get out of here," he thought. He cast a spell to transform his head back into a rat head, but the spell failed and his head would not fit through the hole, even though his body would. He didn't know what to do. He even prayed to Hayagrīva, but he still couldn't free himself. Finally, he forced his rat body out through the hole to the other side, but his human head just would not fit. At that very moment Joru arrived at the entrance to the cave.

Joru said, "This is the cave where the demon Gompa Raja was tamed; it has been made so that even the formless ghosts are not allowed in, much less those who have form. Today there's a footprint. Whether it was a god or a demon, I'm certain that it got inside." He rolled the boulder back just enough to allow a rat to pass. He went inside and exclaimed, "Hey, there's a bearded man's head here. This demon is certainly the devouring demon. I'm going to have to liberate this spirit as never before." He picked up the staff and whirled it around above his head. Trothung was petrified, and his mouth began to tremble like leaves blown by the wind. "O dear sweet precious Joru! You are not a man; you're a divine son of the gods! The gods, the guru, and the yidams, all three, although they may become wrathful, they do not hold on to it. Don't kill me; I am Tag-rong Trothung. I have overstepped my bounds and made a huge mistake and through my magical powers transformed my own head, so that now I can't annul the spell. My body can get through, but my head is stuck. Therefore, the fact that you, dear Joru, have come here is a sign that Uncle still has great merit. Save me, save me. Protect my life and save me! I promise to accept whatever you say."

Then Joru said, "Oh no! It seems that you are possessed and trembling and that the murderous death spirit has turned on you. If I had come just a little bit later, Uncle, you would have been dead by now. That would have made me very sad. It is as the proverb says:

---

[*] Accomplished masters have invoked certain prayers so that they will always come true. The words of truth are uttered by those buddhas and bodhisattvas who have this kind of power.

Sons and nephews without fathers and uncles
May be strong, but it is said that they are like a tigress wandering an
   empty plain.
The people will use the six-smiled one as a target for their stones.

That's what they say. Now come here," he said, and Trothung tried to pull himself back into the cave, but the rat part of his body was stuck, and he could not get free at all.

Joru then said, "All the murderous devouring demons are on your waist, because otherwise if a rat's body can get out that hole, why couldn't it get back in?" Telling him that he should pray one-pointedly to his chosen deity, Hayagrīva, Gesar placed his right hand on Trothung's head and mentally invoked the deities as he entered into a penetrating samādhi to remove the demonic possession of Trothung's body. Trothung vomited a two-headed black serpent, and Joru killed the snake while leading its consciousness to the pure realm. At that very instant Trothung easily entered back into the cave.

"The magic has been annulled, Uncle, but nevertheless you must go. I am also leaving," Joru said, and he went down the road a little bit. Trothung, fearing that there was no way that the spell had been broken, called after him several times, "Joru, Joru!"

Joru said, "What?" and came back.

"Nephew Joru, please put an end to this magic, and I will obey your every command."

"I cannot annul magic," Joru feigned. "However, your own head is attached to a rat's corpse, Trothung. If we cut it off and then throw away the corpse, Uncle, your real head could be put back on your body, wherever that is."

Trothung said, "How can I dare do that? This rat's body, though illusory, is the sole support of your uncle's body. Please try to think of some other method than that."

For a little while Joru pretended to be thinking. Then he said, "Right, Uncle, your intentions toward White Ling were particularly evil. Your inability to annul the magic must be the retribution for that. These days even though you take great pride in the strength of the mighty troops of Tag-rong, this pride cannot defeat the outer enemies, and it might even be the cause for inner turmoil among the cousins and brothers. Not only that, if necessary I, Joru alone, could easily wipe out the army of Tag-rong, down to the last man. If obstacles befall the life spans of Zigphen, Nya-tsha, Dongtsen, and others, I would feel remorse as if that had happened to my own elder brother, Zhalkar. You, Trothung, are a man who will stop at nothing, but your treachery in White Ling has been in vain. You must swear not to incite the armies to internal warfare. If you promise from your heart, then it's possible that this magic can be annulled. Trothung replied, "Yes, you're right. I am willing to both promise and swear."

He crouched beneath the cane and swore three times not to incite his troops to internal combat with either the Elder, Middle, or Lesser Lineages. The witness to the first swearing was Hayagrīva, to the second was Taglha Mebar, and to the third was the *One Hundred Thousand Verse Prajñāpāramitā* of Ling. At that very instant Trothung's body was blessed and he was restored to his former state, and Joru instantly departed.

When Trothung was going out, he dislodged the boulder, and this can still be seen down to the present day. Trothung saw that Joru had the staff, but he sat there not able to decide whether the problems he had had in the cave were because of Joru's magic or the death spirits that killed Amnye. "Although Joru knows everything that happened, if he is going to always be like that, then he's really a good person. Even though I have lost my most precious possessions, he hasn't told Gyatsha, Chipön, and the others about it," he thought, feeling quite content. From that time until Joru reached his fifth year, Trothung knew that he could not do anything against him, so it became well known that for that period of time Trothung did not engage in any evil or deceptive ways. During that period the formless beings of the Dza and Dri valleys were all bound by oath and placed under command. Their numbers were impossible to count.

Even before he reached five years of age, Joru accomplished the benefit of formless beings. Outwardly he had the appearance of a child and became well known for his inconceivable miraculous acts.

This completes the episode of the wondrous epic of *The Birth in Ling* called *The Flower Garden*.

CHAPTER FOUR

In keeping with the prophecy of Uḍḍiyāna Padma,
Joru makes the Ma Valley his domain
And subjugates the demons and rākṣasas through the force of
　his miraculous powers.
All the diviners of Ling have ominous dreams.

NOW THE STORY OF the settling of Ma, called *The Knotted White Scarf*, will be told. In the Male Water Horse year in the predawn of the fifteenth morning of the month of December in a state where dream mingles with clear light, Joru had a vision of Guru Uḍḍiyāna Padma along with his ocean-like retinue of ḍākas and ḍākinīs, as though he were actually meeting him, and with one voice they sang this song of prophecies to Joru:

The song begins with Ala Ala Ala.
Thala leads the melody of the song.
Now then Joru, son of the gods,
Listen and I will tell you the way things are.

The chick of the garuḍa, the king of all birds,
Has the power of the treasury of wind in the quills of its feathers.
If it could not pass through the highest reaches of space,
Then whether or not the garuḍa has six wings would matter not.

When the species of snow lions are in their prime,
The three skills of the turquoise mane are naturally matured.
If they could not reach the peak of the snow mountain,
Then it would matter not whether the three skills were mature.[54]

When the divine child comes to the land of human beings,
The signs of his miraculous powers and accomplishments are
　　unimpeded.
If he could not magnetize Jambudvīpa
Then it would matter not whether he had the signs of
　　accomplishment.

First, China with its white-leafed trees,
Second, India the country of rice,
And third, Tibet with its seeds of ram grass;[55]
Because of the quality of the earth, such diverse things grow
　　in these different lands.

First, the form of an innocent child,
Second, a sixteen-year-old youth,
Third, an eighty-year-old man with a wrinkled forehead;
Because of the quality of the ages, people change over time.

First, through meditation, buddhahood is attained,
Second, through virtue, the two accumulations are perfected,
Third, through sin, you continue to wander in saṃsāra;
These are the qualities of each individual's karmic actions.

First, the first spark that comes from stone and iron,
Second, the harvest that comes from seed and sprout,
Third, the karmic result of good and evil deeds;
The way that this occurs is due to infallible interdependency.

Therefore, this is the place of your birth;
The Ma Valley is the place where you will live.
The upper mountain range of Ma connects with the country
　　of India
Making the lineages of spiritual wealth of India close at hand.

The Lower Ma Valley connects with the country of China
Making the fall of the tea commerce of China close at hand.
To the east, Dzachen Khujug [Great Cuckoo Crag]
Is the path traveled by the bandits of Yellow Hor.
Joining with the Yak Mountain pass,
It makes a short path to the land of the Yellow Hor.
To the north, beyond the great marshlands of Ma,
Are the nomadic encampments of the Black Düd.
It is the fatherland of Atag Lumo,[56]
A place connected to the district of Chieftain Adrak.
It is also where the paths of the nāgas and the tsen cross.
The white salt lake of Dawu
Is the personal seat of Sadam of Jang.
It is next to the valley land of Ma
And is the place over which Jang and Ling will wage war.
There the Ma River coils like a turquoise dragon,
And the Hor River seems be strengthening it.

Zodor Magyal Pomra
Is the principle guardian of the land of Tibet.
The mind-pleasing mandala of the Ma Valley
Is the jewel essence of the land of Dokham.
The wealth of Persia, India, China, and Mongolia,[57]
The farmlands of Ati, and the limitless northern plains
All come together to converge like a cross.
You have no choice but to take possession of these lands.
If all six tribes of Ling were to go there, they still could not
    take that land.
Right now the ghosts are the lords of that place
And the lords of grass are nothing but the wild asses and yaks.
On the shady side of the valley of Nag-gyal Chugmo
    [Wealthy Queen of the Forest],[58]
The five classes of wild animals have laid claim there.
On the sunny side of the six mountains of the Khenpa [Sage]
    Valley,
Famine-creating rodents are the lords of the grass and water.
When merchants travel this route with their great
    possessions,

All their goods are stolen by the Yellow Hor brigades.
A lone person walks this path in fear
For, although there are no dogs, the rats will bite into his calf.
Who needs leopards? The wolves will kill you just fine.
All these creatures are befriended by ghosts;
You, the great one, must conquer those lands.
In order to get the people of White Ling to lose faith in you,
Joru, your behavior must be outrageous.
Make sure the rumor will spread that your mother Gogmo is
    a rākṣasi
And that you, boy Joru, are a rākṣa child.
Then you must break the laws of White Ling
And cause the people of the six districts to have bad signs in
    their dreams.
It will come to pass that Joru will be banished from Ling.
Their scorn will increase the inner qualities of the divine child.

The inner strength of young braves is revealed through their enemies.
A young maiden's inner strength comes from her self-esteem.

When the moon is waxing in the year of the Wood Monkey
You will take possession of the Sa-nag Lungdo [Black Earth
    Valley] in Lower Ma.[59]
You will have the blessings of the gods and gurus,
You will be accompanied by the motherly ḍākinīs,
You will be befriended by the dharmapālas.
In the Padma Valley, the excellent land of Ma,
During the excellent time of the waxing moon of the Wood
    Monkey
The excellent karma of your miraculous powers will turn
    things around.
The excellent districts of the six tribes will naturally come to
    you.
The excellent auspicious connection will be celebrated.
The excellent predictions will gradually come to pass.

Thus he sang and then vanished from sight. At the same time, because Mother
Gogmo was indeed a wisdom ḍākinī, she clearly heard the actual sounds of the

excellent lotus valley of Ma, smelled the sweet fragrances, and saw the flowers showering down. Having mastered this immaculate samādhi, she sat there in great delight.

One day, Joru said to his mother, "Mother, I need a hat for my head, shoes for my feet, and fine clothes for my back. I won't be satisfied with anything but exactly what I require. So, as they say,

> *Once a boy is born, he will learn to provide for himself.*
> *Once there is karma, the necessary wealth will be 'there for the*
>   *taking.'"*

Having said that, he left, riding his white willow staff. First he went to Seyu Mountain and killed the three antelope kindred famine demons, making himself an unsightly pointed hat made from the head of an antelope buck. That night he went down among the ropes of Chipön's yak-hitching corral, stealing and killing seven yak calves that were afflicted by the epidemic demon. Although they were unsightly when worn, he took the untanned hides of the calves and wore them as clothing with the tails still attached. In the middle of the night, he went down among the ropes of Trothung's horse-hitching corral, stealing and killing the horse demon colt with the white blaze down to its muzzle. For shoes, he donned unsightly rawhide boots made from this horsehide, sewing their soles together with straw. This is how he got himself a hat, clothes, and shoes as he bound these three demons by oath.

Then one day in Menlung Chugmo Ci [Wealthy Herbal Valley of Ci], Joru was digging in the ground as if he was searching for a pika, and while digging he said to himself, "When I, Joru, unearth the pikas, their burrows will collapse," and just then as he dug, the cavern caved in and nine terrible pika thief demons were buried. Then Joru said to his mother,

> *"Being able to make your own decisions*
> *Is more empowering than receiving a hundred golden letters from*
>   *the imperial chieftain.*
> *Having personal freedom*
> *Brings greater happiness than assuming a thousand golden thrones.*

Let's not stay under the rule of the chieftain of Bumpa. Since I, Joru, have no chieftain above me, I do not have to consult anyone about what I do or what I need. Since I have no subjects beneath me, even if the entire surface of the earth were to become my enemy, I would have no fear. Since I have no relatives around me, I don't have to waste any effort flattering them with sweet talk. Mother, since you and I have no worldly status, don't give a thought to what has happened in the past or what will happen in the future. If we go somewhere where the weather is fine and the land is pleasant, we ourselves, as mother and son, won't need to worry about our own survival. Let's not stay here any longer," he said, and they decided to leave. She said, "Are we going to the Ma Valley? If so, then I know how to get there." He replied, "Let's go to the lower valley of Drülgo [Snake Head], where it is warm and the wild yams are sweet."

Then they left.

Beyond the Dza River was Sinmo Buzen [Cannibal Demoness Child Eater]. Joru thought it was time to tame that demon, so he forcefully tied up the muzzle of his unbroken colt and at the ford in the river he crossed the Dza where Sinmo Buzen was devouring the corpses of four or five children. Joru said, "Sister, Demoness, may your life last for one hundred years! Give me some fire, and I'll show you a trick."

She gave him some fire and said, "What trick do you have to show?"

He said, "If you stay in this place, except for a few children, you won't get much to eat. But if you go to the other side of the river, you'll find there are plenty."

"What's the best way to get over there?" she asked.

Saying, "I will show you," Joru wrapped the tail of the little colt around her neck, and said, "Now follow me." When they got to the middle of the river, suddenly Joru turned the colt upstream and the demoness' neck snapped, and she was tamed on the spot.

As they journeyed farther on to lower Drülgo Valley, like a falcon pursuing a small bird, Joru met up with the demon Khase Rulu [Gray Beard], who was out on his haunting hour as the spirit who takes whomever he encounters and carries them away in the river. Recognizing that the time had come to tame him, Joru said to his mother, "Mother, you go behind me. I'm going to see what the road is like," and he went on ahead of her. There he found the demon with his mouth gaping open, and he silently prayed to the gods. Taking the leather lasso that was tied to his waist, eighty arm spans in length and with an iron hook, he threw it so that the hook caught the demon's heart, and he yanked it out, slaying him. He offered the flesh and blood to all the dralas and wermas, transferring the demon's consciousness to the pure realm.

After that they remained in lower Drülgo Valley. Through his power of speed-walking he caught a buck on a mountain slope and took the rack as his trophy. He killed an antelope buck with a stone and caught a wild mule with a lasso. He rounded up all the wild animals that were freely grazing on the slopes and built walls with their flesh. He made corrals with their heads and swirling lakes with their blood.

He captured as his prisoners all the travelers who passed through that desolate valley. He ate human flesh as his vittles. He quenched his thirst with human blood and spread out human skin as his seat. He stacked human corpses everywhere—all around on the plains. Seeing this, even the godly demons had their spirits broken, and the cannibal demons became nauseated. Furthermore, the way that he lived there had the power to terrify the eight classes.

For a year and a half he stayed there in lower Drülgo Valley, preventing travelers from passing through that area. By that time the Ling lamas, diviners, astrologers, fathers, uncles, brothers, and so forth all had been sent ominous dreams by the dralas and wermas. Everyone shared the same dream that Joru was bent on causing harm. They all thought that Joru, the divine child, had now turned out to be a demon. They began saying things like, "He's robbing all beings of their welfare and happiness, destroying the teachings of the Buddha, eating whatever flesh he sees, and he has become an actual red-faced cannibal."

Although they gossiped in this way, no one at all had the courage to stand up to him. It was then that seven hunters from the clan of Tag-rong went out on a deer hunt. They were unable to kill any deer, so they decided to stay in the woody[60] crags of Go-tsang [Eagle's Nest] overnight. Instantly Joru invoked a black horseman from Eagle's Nest to come before him, commanding him to detain the hunters of Tag-rong for three months. For that time he blessed the men and their horses so that they would not starve. Through his magical powers Joru made it look as if he had killed the hunters and horses and put their corpses outside. A search party was dispatched to reach some conclusion about what had happened to the Tag-rong hunters. After searching the mountains, they saw and identified the corpses of the men and their horses. It was said that everyone accused Joru of devouring them, but no one had the guts to approach him.

CHAPTER FIVE

Just as the ḍākinī had prophesied,
Chipön convened the great assembly of White Ling.
At the junction of the Turquoise Valley [Yulung Sumdo] of
  Lower Ma
The command to expel Joru was proclaimed.

THEN CHIPÖN, THE KING OF THE MUKPO DONG, thought at great length,
"This Joru has been foretold by the gods, lamas, and mother ḍākinīs and, wherever
you examined the signs in the middle regions, there was no doubt that he was an
emanation who was capable of quelling the four māras through his splendor. As it is
now his actions seem mainly intended to destroy the internal order of White Ling.
Whatever the case, if he has some other aim in mind, I can't figure it out or find a
good reason. If we allow him to continue on like this, the law and order of White
Ling will be undone. If the law is imposed upon him, he certainly will not listen and
not only that, since it is undeniable that he is of a divine lineage, it's not proper for
the law to punish him. So whatever he does, whether for good or for evil, we have
no choice but to ignore him.

Since the beginning of this year there have been many ominous dreams. Even
those seem to be a magical deception coming from either the gods or demons. No
one has the power to determine whether this is for good or for evil." Thinking, "If
we ask the diviner Künshei Thigpo [All-Knowing Accurate One] to do a divination . . . ," he suddenly drifted off to sleep, as he was lost in so many thoughts.

Toward dawn in his dream, a ḍākinī holding a bow and arrow and riding a
white snow lion came and sang this prophetic dohā:

NAMO BUDDHA DHARMA SANGHA
Leader who holds the golden gilded throne,
Lord of Mukpo Dong King Chipön, listen.

The king of birds, the garuḍa chick
May have been captured in the home for a while,
But when the time comes for its six wings to play with the
  wind,
It must reach the top of the wish-fulfilling tree,
Or there is a risk that it may reduce the house to rubble.

That jewel on the head of the poisonous snake
May have been found by a beggar,
But the riches that are the source of everything desirable
And a person with great merit must unite.
There is a risk that a beggar is incapable of handling a jewel.

When a divine child manifests as a human,
It may be that the land of his birth is excellent,
But he must take possession of Ma Valley,
The place where the four māras are to be bound by oath,
Or there is a risk that just holding onto his homeland will be
  useless.

Not only that, in the area between the Dza and Dri rivers,
The path is too narrow for the strong and mighty great
  elephant,
The distance too short for the steed Changshei [Knowing
  Steed] galloping like the wind,
And the distance too great for subjugating Hor and Düd.

All the bad signs and inauspicious connections
Are the enlightened activities of the dralas on the side of
  virtue.
The punishment for allegedly killing the hunters of Tag-rong
And the way to restore order to White Ling
Is to exile Joru.

Within three years
The area between the Dza and Dri rivers will be covered by
    white ice,
And all the wild mules will turn their blaze toward the sky in
    hunger,
The white-conch stupa of the Ma Valley
Will be adorned by the five-colored scarf of greater *rong*.[61]
If you understand this, keep it in the center of your heart.
If not, the words are sealed by the vajra.

Thus she sang, and he awakened from his sleep. Considering the main points of the prophecy, he felt that he understood the general idea and was quite pleased. Meanwhile, the chief of Tag-rong sent Tharpa Zorna [Hook-Nosed Tharpa] of Akhöd to Chipön's place. Upon his arrival, he recounted the details, saying, "The six provinces of Ling have no choice but to now unite. Both Mother Gogmo and her son seem to have been possessed by a cannibal demon. First they stole and killed Tag-rong's horses, and then they ate all seven of the horses and hunters. Since we can identify the men's armor and weapons and the horses' heads, we know that they are in Drülgo Valley. Not only that but, at Yongdzom [Gathering All] Mountain Pass, Sengcham Drugmo of Kyalo and her attendant both saw Joru forcing the seven hunters whom he had bound by the wrists to go ahead of him as he beat them with a whip of thorns."

Chipön replied, "Oh dear! Could it possibly be true that he committed such crimes? This Joru is the younger brother of the hero Gyatsha and the nephew of the nāga Tsugna. He is of the royal lineage of Mukpo Dong. If there is any reason to mention these things, of course go ahead. It is as the proverb says:

> *A man who guzzles the ocean*
> *Needs a stomach the size of the sky.*
> *A man who hoists Mount Meru on his shoulder*
> *Needs strength and might like the earth itself.*

Nevertheless, I think we should leave well enough alone, for as is said:

> *Don't race with the tsen;*
> *Don't throw dice with the māras;*
> *Don't get too close with nāgas."*

Chipön thought it might be better to leave well enough alone. "In any case, if Joru and his mother have become cannibal demons, the person who will be able to tame them must have exceptional skills, the signs of accomplishment, and the brave heart of a hero. No matter where you look, you will find no one who qualifies as a chief like Uncle Trothung.

Even before, when it came time to tame the rākṣasa Khesei Relpa,* it was Uncle who was the victor, who subjugated the enemy, and the one who gained the prize of victory; in fact in every single situation if it is necessary to tame any demon then there is no one who can do it except for Uncle [Trothung] himself.

So now according to the command of Tag-rong, tomorrow on the morning of the eighth day, tell all the people of the six districts of Ling, without respect to their stations, to gather at the great assembly ground of Tagthang Tramo." And he sent the messenger [Tharpa Zorna] back.

Soon after, messengers were sent out to individuals requiring that, without regard to their station, all people must gather on the eighth day. Chipön himself went before Gyatsha Zhalkar and carefully recounted how he had received predictions, as well as the outer and inner events thathad occurred. The meeting between them was sealed in strict secrecy.

Then on the eighth day, just as the mountain peak donned its golden hat, from the highest Tag-rong to the lowest Gu-ru of the Khyishi clan, from the eldest, Chipön, down to the youngest one, Nang-ngu,† everyone gathered. Trothung thought, "They're going to tell me to go and tame Joru," and he lost all courage and was filled with terror. As he sat there, his mind became gentler than a scarf, and his body became looser than cotton wool.

Then Chipön said, "These ruddy-faced people from the six provinces of Ling are 'settled like yogurt but stirred like blood,' with no choice but to gather. Since this was Uncle's command, and we had no choice but to gather, can any of you tell me what this is all about? What is your problem with Gogmo's Joru?[62] Is he 'a past disease or a future battle'?"

Uncle [Trothung] replied, "Uncle Chipön, dear nephew Gyatsha, and all who have gathered, I address you. I, Chief Tag-rong, have given serious consideration to the general political situation of White Ling and in particular the integrity of the Bumpa clan and not only that, Joru's personal situation. By no means have I found

---

* Another name for the spirit Kha-se.

† This is Yutag, the youngest of the Thirty Mighty Warriors. The youngest might be six or seven years old.

any peace of mind. This year the dreams and predictions have also been perverted. Concerning Joru, it is as the proverb goes:

> *Even though there is no pain in the body, there is still pain in the mind.*

I thought perhaps this is a case of illness through demonic possession. We must decide:

> *Which ritual will relieve the demonic forces and which medicine will cure the illness.*

Awhile back, Kyalo Sengcham Drugmo and Gochöd Yogpo Pagyal [Practical Servant Victorious Warrior]* both say they saw seven hunters from the locale of Tag-rong being driven across Yangdzom⁶³ Gyajei [Emperor] Mountain Pass by Joru. Not only that, I have been sent news of reports that have been spreading about the situation, claiming that in Drülgo Valley, close to where Joru and his mother are staying, the hunters' heads and the like have been identified. However I have had no complaints about Joru."

He spoke as if his words were entirely sincere. Then Chipön, Gyatsha, and the others all agreed to consult divinations and astrology. After the divinations and casting of astrological charts were most carefully performed, they were told that the outcome in all cases was the same: White Ling would never be at peace unless this Joru was sent away. Gyatsha felt a bit uncomfortable with this, but Chipön went on to say, "Oh listen, you the people of divine White Ling. I, Chipön, have this to say to you," and he offered this song:

> It's Ala Ala Ala.
> It's Thala Thala Thala.
> To the guru, the embodiment of all refuge,
> With undivided respect I supplicate you.
> In case you don't recognize this place,
> It is Tagthang Tramo.
> Listen to me, Chieftain Rongtsha.
> The profound dharma is the swift path of secret mantra

---

* This is Drugmo's attendant.

But without trust it is like the quick path to hell.
The delicious foods are meat, butter, and molasses—
But in poor health can cause life-threatening illness.
This magical child from the gods above us,
The boy Joru has come to harm Ling.
It seems as though White Ling's merit is exhausted.
Oops. I shouldn't say that! I was just teasing.
The profound dharma, the guru's oral instructions—
Once all doubt about the meaning is severed, it is even more
    profound.
The best of wealth, the gold of the Jambu River—
Once refined in red fire, it becomes even better.
Boys and nephews, with the courage of a tiger—
Once they encounter the wild beast enemy, are even more
    heroic.
Fathers and uncles who are like Meru, the king of
    mountains—
Once they encounter good or bad, are even more solid.
The warriors of the lineage of the clan of Mukpo Dong—
Once the enemy descends upon them, are fiercer than before.
If the child Joru brings harm to Ling,
Let's send him to whatever place will make him happier.

When heat and moisture unite on the square plain,
Whatever you do helps the green grass to grow.
When life flourishes like the rising patterns within a skullcup[64]
Whatever harm is inflicted will become beneficial.

When the sons and nephews abound in bravery and skill,
If there are many enemies, the booty is a father's bountiful field.
Did you understand this, people of the six provinces of Ling?

It's important not to bend the principles of the integrity of
    the law.
It's important not to belittle the river-like source of these
    reports.
Those fourteen, the men and horses of Tag-rong,
Seem to have been murdered by Joru

And Drugmo's testimony is sufficient.
The punishment for breaking these laws
Is to expel the boy Joru from Ling.
Blowing the conch, a hundred fatherly gurus will drive him away.
One hundred tigers in their prime will drive him with arrows.
One hundred maidens will throw handfuls of ashes.
Those fourteen, the men and horses of Tag-rong,
If they have not fallen to the hands of Joru,
If that becomes clear later, then Drugmo must confess and
    purify.
But still the negative predictions, divinations, and astrology,
As well as the ominous dreams of all the uncles and nephews,
Are a collective karma that cannot be affirmed or denied.
No matter how bad he [Joru] has been, there is no way to
    impose punishment.

A daughter with an unsightly harelip
Although displeasing, she cannot just be flung away.
A penniless beggar possessed by famine spirits,
Although better that he did not exist, there's no way to get rid of him.
The unsightly fellow with a wart growing over his eye
Would like to cut it out, but it's on his pupil.

If Joru of the family lineage of Mukpo Dong,
Had not committed the crime of breaking our law,
Even though the divination is ominous, we couldn't just
    exile him.
Now let Gyatsha Zhalkar
Gather whatever provisions he has for his younger brother's
    journey to the borderlands.
From this gathering place of Tagthang Tramo
Joru will be summoned by a messenger.
So who among the family members will be the courier?
Come forward now and proclaim yourselves.
Six provinces of Ling, bear this in mind.

Everyone agreed with what he had said. Then Trothung replied, "If he's going to
be expelled, let it be down through Black Crag Mountain in the land of famine spirits."

Zhalkar said, "My poor little brother, when I think that he is to be banished it distresses me. If we must exile him, then perhaps it's better for me to accompany him. Nevertheless because of the strict orders given by my family and especially my uncle Chipön, there is no choice but to follow their decision. Although no one place of exile is better or worse than another, let's send him up to Ci Yangdzom Nyima Sharyag [Meet Again like a Beautiful Sunrise]." Everyone agreed and the decision was made.

By that time Magyal Pomra was coming to welcome Joru and escort him along with all of his personal articles to the Ma Valley. But he [Joru] remained, sitting as he had been previously, in his magical disguise. Since Mother Gogmo was a nāginī, the sight of Gesar cooking and eating human flesh and blood was repulsive to her. Sometimes she thought this was a magical illusion, but other times she thought he really was eating and drinking flesh and blood and had nagging doubts and suspicions about her son.

Meanwhile back in Ling, they were still trying to decide who would go to Joru, but no one had the guts to stand up and volunteer. Then Zhalkar said, "If all you family members are too gutless to go, don't worry, I can go to summon my younger brother," and he got ready to go.

It was then that Minister Denma Jangtra thought, "By the power of my previous karma, I am a destined minister of White Ling. For the chief to go as the messenger and the servant to guard the golden throne is not the proper way," he thought, saying, "Precious Zhalkar of Bumpa, do not depart; stay as the ornament of your golden throne. It's Denma's turn to be the man to go." And saying this he mounted his great steed Ngültrug Denpa [Silver Colt] and departed like a bolt of lightning. Then Denma arrived in Drülgo Valley and looked around. As he looked up he saw that someone had pitched tents of human skin, held down by ropes of intestines. Fresh and rotting human corpses and horse corpses were stacked into a fence. He realized that to dwell there would be even more frightening than the land of the rākṣasas on Lankapuri.*

At first Denma thought, "How sad that Chöphen Nagpo's lineage of Mukpo Dong has come to this." On second thought, it came to his mind that if he [Joru] were to devour all the people of Ling in one fell swoop and pile up their flesh and bones, it still wouldn't come to this. "Except for the fourteen men and horses from Tag-rong, there has been no word of others who have been eaten, so it is unclear whether they are dead or alive, yet there are rumors that say he has consumed

---

* Lankapuri is another name for Cāmara, the island of rākṣasas.

everyone. If that were the case, it wouldn't make sense for the rest of us to have been spared. There's no truth to this gossip. It's impossible that there could be this owner-less mass of human and horse corpses." Suddenly he realized, without a doubt in his mind, that this had to be either a magical illusion or an emanation. Then through the power of his previous prayers and karmic connections, his mind welled forth with unconditioned, irreversible faith and devotion.

Denma dismounted and sat there for a short while. Soon after, Joru walked up to him gnawing on a human arm. Denma thought, "I should draw my sword and wave it to beckon him to come. But wait, what am I thinking? My sword Jangpa Yumar [Devouring Red-Handled] does not show itself except to the enemy. How could I have even considered showing it to someone like the child Joru?" Then he thought, "How about if I motion to him with my whip?" And he stopped himself again, thinking, "A whip is not a suitable implement for calling a chieftain; it is only used to drive horses. Since it's a suitable attribute for gurus and leaders, there is nothing more worthy to wave to him than the plumed silken pennant on the top of my helmet."

So he waved his helmet with white plumed silken pennants, and Joru came down to him, saying, "Oh my, Tshazhang Denma Jangtra has arrived:

> *If a great cause and a person with great expectations*
> *Are brought together, there is good fortune.*
> *To a superior person this seems natural;*
> *To a mediocre person this seems to require effort;*
> *To an inferior person this seems elusive.*

This seems to be the case here." He rose quickly, ran over, and, taking his horse by the reins, approached. As he came closer, the horse corpses and all the rest vanished like a mirage; Denma no longer perceived impure appearances but instead only the manifestation of the true nature of reality and enlightened bodies. Then Denma removed his armor and weapons and placed them at the entrance to the door. Joru said, "Don't do that. Your armor and weapons are the castle support for the dralas. Upon each one of them rests a specific deity," and he brought them all inside.

Then Denma entered the household, which was permeated with a delightful fragrance. It was cozy and cheerful within, making the mind joyful and awareness clear. Denma sat there, filled with fervent regard and faith. On that day, the special auspicious connection of chief and minister meeting face to face was properly sealed. Then Denma offered a great celebration of many celestial delicacies. Joru gave a spontaneous discourse in which he explained the origin of the Mukpo Dong and gave many prophecies that would be indispensable one day. He also gave him a glimpse of his wisdom kāya as Gesar. Denma himself made many prayers that for this and the succession of all lifetimes that king and minister would be inseparable. He then sang this song recounting the events that led to his visit:

> Ala Ala Ala begins the song.
> Thala is the song's melody.
> May the enlightened bodies of the refuges of guru, yidam,
>   and the Three Jewels
> Remain inseparable as my crown ornament.
> In case you don't recognize these lands,
> The ever-flowing Dza River courses down on the right
> And a mountain shaped like a snake's head appears on the
>   left,
> For this is the manifest cannibal demon continent of Chief
>   Joru.
> In case you don't recognize me,
> I am Tshazhang Denma Jangtra.
> I am the humble minister of the lesser lineage of Mu.
> Well then, honorable divine child Joru,
> Listen and I will tell you the way things are.
>
> While the people of southern Jambudvīpa are enjoying their
>   sleep,
> Sun, stay not in the firmament, but head for the western
>   mountain.
> Don't be late, for the darkness is coming behind you.
>
> While the people of the three continents to the west are
>   astonished and jubilant,
> Golden radiant sun, shine over all.
> Don't be late, for the dawn is coming to greet you.
>
> The three months of winter are imbued with hardship
> When greenery and flowers do not stay, but return to the soil.
> Don't delay, for the frost is pursuing you.

The three months of summer are endowed with well-being
When the colorful radiance of the smiling lotus is revealed.
The sweet rains usher in the summer season.
They say the six provinces of Ling are like a white paper
    flower
Ruined by Chief Joru's rain.
The rain-stopping wizard is Chipön—
He stops the rain, not for a lifetime but just for a day.
If rain failed to fall for a whole lifetime,
The grains of the six provinces of Ling would have no way to ripen.
Have you understood, O divine son of Gogmo?

If you know how to think about it, these phenomena are
    wondrous.
If you know how to see it, it's like a spontaneous spectacle.
First, the rainbow between the sun and rain,
Second, the mirage between the heat and moisture,
And third, the human corpses between emanation and
    transformation,
If recognized, are neither good nor ill.
If not, that illusion will be held as real.

The rain of subterranean cold-blooded nāgas—
They say that when called, it is by the dragon's roar
And when it comes, it is adorned with the appearance of
    white clouds.

In the upper land of the gods are the zodors of existence.
They say that when called, it is by the auspicious conch
And when they come, they confer the siddhis of happiness
    and well being.

In the middle realm of humans this divine child Joru,
They say that when called, it is by the cabinet minister
    Denma
And when he comes, he opens the gate to the treasury of
    magical transformations.

To the child who understands this talk, one sign is enough.
If not, I'll not repeat my words again.
Divine son, keep this in your mind.

After he sang the song, they [sat down] and had a long conversation. The awakened one, joyful Joru, offered the minister Denma this narrative song with the melody Nine Swirls of a White Conch:

The song is Ala Ala Ala.
Thala gives the melody of the song.
The dharmakāya teacher Samantabhadra,
The sambhogakāya teacher Vajrasattva,
The nirmanakāya teacher Śākyamuni—
May the embodiment of these three, Padmasambhava, look
  upon me.
In the ravine of the powerful land of Snake Head,
I am the powerful man who is known as King Joru.
Uḍḍiyāna Padma is my elector.
My spirit father is the nyen Lord Gedzo.
I am the nephew of Tsugna Rinchen.
I am the younger brother of dear Zhal-lu of Bumpa.
Now then, Tshazhang Denma Jangtra
Listen and I will tell you the way things are.

Even if the sun does not want to set,
The dark shadow is free do whatever it wants.
And even though the heat and moisture of summer doesn't
  want to pass,
The frost to come is free to do whatever it wants.

If the sun in the sky does not want to set in the west
The dark shadow cannot be free to do whatever it wants.
If the heat and moisture of summer do not want to pass,
The early frost cannot be free to appear.

Joru brings rainfall that harms
The white paper flowers of the six provinces of Ling,

But look, before long they could be blanketed with snow.
Whoever stops that is the best wizard of all.

In the southern vast plain [of Jambudvīpa] the bird that lives
    in the bamboo
Can't help but fly north in the summer;
The heat of the great farmlands will spoil its eggs.
With that in mind the king of birds takes flight to the north.
If I, Joru, don't want to go,
The six provinces of Ling will find it difficult to expel me.

I am a chick of the garuḍa king of birds.
When I reach the highest path in flight,
There will be no one in Ling with the six wings to follow me.
I am boy of the lineage of the white snow lion.
When I hold my home ground on the peak of Mount Kailash
Even though they intend to exile me, there will be no one
    who can slice a path in the white snow.
To subjugate the hosts of māras, this boy Joru
Was sent here by the imperial gods on high.
I cannot accomplish this purpose by staying where the
    weather is warm.
Therefore all those signs and dreams,
Whatever appears is the magical display of the gods,
Banishment is the way Brahmā shows me the path,
The black magic curses are the enlightened activity of Gedzo,
The punishment of my faults is Tsugna's support along the
    way.
As is said of old:

If you cross over the treacherous crag,
You'll arrive at the flat plain.

As they say:

If you do not take the path of a miserable mind,
Then how can you encounter the wealth of mental joy?

Whenever I go it is with the gods,
Wherever I go is my home,
Whatever I do is for the buddha doctrine.
This boy Joru is like a great swollen river—
One day golden fish of the six provinces of Ling will naturally
    swim here.
This child Joru is like an alpine greensward—
One day the deer and wild horses of the father and uncle
    ministers will naturally graze here.
In this excellent place, the colorful land of Ma,
The eternally blossoming lotus Joru
Will be the best hive for the bees of the six provinces of Ling.

Ma Pomra has come to receive me;
The nyen Kulha [Gedzo] is here to befriend me;
My escort nāga Tsugna has made every arrangement.
I will stay here no longer but will go to the heartland of Ma.
Before long, we, chieftain and minister, will meet again.
If you understood this discourse, it is sweet to your ears.
If you did not, there is no way to explain it.

When he had finished, for Denma Jangtra King of Tshazhang it was as though from the stainless space of his unwavering mind the sun of uncontrived faith and devotion arose. He prayed to be able to unceasingly serve the enlightened activities of his station as minister of Denma until Chief Joru's taming of beings was complete. As Denma was preparing to leave, Joru said, "Minister Denma, you go on ahead and say to the others 'I didn't dare get close to Joru, but I yelled out to him what you had said.' It is crucial that what happened here between us for a period of time must not be heard by anyone either outside or within Ling." Instantly Denma arrived back at the encampment of Ling and said, "Joru is truly a cannibal. I didn't dare to go close to him, but you can rely on me that I yelled out all your messages clearly. I heard him say he will come tomorrow."

Everyone said, "O Denma, you've returned to us safely," and they rejoiced immeasurably.

Then some Lingites thought, "Joru's coming to devour us." Others said, "With a gathering this large, what harm can come of it?"

Trothung, a little afraid, thought, "He may not eat everyone, but who knows, he might consume a few of us. Furthermore, between me and him there still exists a subtle grudge. I started this feud; I'm not sure now what Joru's going to do." He spoke up, "Everybody should put on armor, take up weapons, and stay in a state of warlike readiness."

Zhalkar replied, "What's the reason for that? Gesar is already being punished enough for his crimes against Tag-rong by being exiled from the land. What more do you want? Chipön, would you sing a song reminding us of the reason we're here? Concerning this idea that a hundred girls would hold ashes to throw at him—well think about it, first of all there's no question that he is a true son of the Mukpo Dong paternal lineage. Secondly, without a doubt he is a nephew of the nāga Tsugna. And thirdly, he is my own heartfelt younger brother. As if that's not enough, wasn't his mother Gogmo at the outset part of my spoils? So, to throw ashes on both of them is unacceptable as it degrades the dignity of the dralas. So that we don't contradict the previous ruling of White Ling and, given that tsampa is the ashes of barley, then let them be driven away with a hundred fists of tsampa instead."

Having heard this, everyone proclaimed, "Fine! Fine!" their minds and mouths in accord. Everybody stayed there waiting for Joru. Then Joru, with his unsightly antelope hat on his head and his ugly dried calfhide coat and hideous horsehide boots with matted straw soles laced with a single strand of horsetail, came riding his white willow staff. Mother Gogmo was more resplendent than ever before, riding her gray mare with a white blaze, adorned with a saddle that looked like the rising sun. She was leading a roan bay horse and holding a longevity arrow with a white silken pennant. That day the time had come to magnetize the life force and minds of the inhabitants of White Ling. Merely by seeing Gogmo and her son, their minds were irresistibly transformed, and they said, "Oh, look how sweet Joru is and how beautiful Gogmo is!" Riveted, they stared at Joru without blinking. The tribe's Uncle King, Chipön, thought, "If with all my heart I impose the words of law on this nonhuman, divine child, Joru, it will only cause the corruption of my samaya. Instead if I speak according to the prophecy there is no doubt that this will serve to open the gateway to the auspicious connection and enlightened activity." And so, thinking that the time had come to speak without hesitation, he began: "Well then! Great inhabitants of this divine White Ling and Joru of the divine lineage of the Bumpa family, listen here! I, Chipön, have this to say," and he sang with the melody called the Long and Solemn Song:

> The song begins with Ala Ala Ala.
> Thala leads the melody of the song.
> At the crystal mountain of the snow-capped peaks
> I offer to the local deity Magyal Pomra.

At the copper castle palace of the red crag
I offer to the king of the dralas Nyentag Marpo.
At the tent of clouds in the upper firmament
I offer to Manenei Nammen Karmo.
May the lore and secular power of White Ling increase.

In this place Kyidsö Yag-gi Khado
Is the gathering place called Tagthang Tramo.
If you don't recognize me,
I am Uncle King Chipön of Dong.
This is my sincere Long and Solemn Song.
And here is a genuine account of how it is.

The strong and solid four-sided castle built of stone
Beautified by its juniper-timbered roof
And not only that, adorned with the golden pinnacle—
We think this is a mighty fortress that will protect us for a
    lifetime,
But if there is an earthquake, it will be the hammer that
    smashes us.
Whatever karma you collect is like dirt piled upon you.
A bride-to-be is acquired by giving the treasured articles,[*]
The station of her in-laws is placed in her hands,
And not only that, their minds and hearts are tied like a
    knotted scarf.[65]
We think this one companion will last for a lifetime,
But if she's shameless she turns her whoring face to another
    man;
Her earnings are the bribery of her ass.
We think that by physically sustaining and nurturing our sons
    and nephews
Our children will be successful in worldly ways,
And not only that, we value them like our own precious lives.
If a boy makes good, it's expected that he will hold his father's
    seat,

---

[*] Gold, silver, silk, horses, yaks.

But if a boy turns out wrong, he is charged as the thief of his
    father's estate
And once he grows up he may end up just beating his parents
    with a club.

The boy Joru is the honorable nephew of Tsugna
And we had hoped he would be the ornament of the golden
    throne of White Ling,
And not only that, he's the essence of Zhalkar's heart.
In an ideal world, he would have grown up to be the hammer
    that that strikes the enemy,
But something went awry, for he killed the hunters of Tag-
    rong.
If his thieving hands have stolen the horses, his boots will tell.
These wrongdoings must be punished—
Massacring the wild animals roaming the mountain passes
Imprisoning the travelers passing through the valleys,
Eating human flesh and drinking human blood—
What he has done amounts to disturbing the gods of Ling—
That came clear in the divinations, prophecies, and charts.
Therefore we decided that we must expel Joru.

I, Chipön, will "decide for a hundred."
It's just as the proverb says:

If from the exalted imperial palace of the divine ones
The gods and dharma protectors were banished to the land of
    demons,
Then the dying will await their karmic destiny alone.

If from the subterranean land of the cold-blooded nāgas
Nāga Dungkyong [Nāga White-Conch Guardian] was forced to
    ascend,
Then the irrigated fields will await their karmic destiny alone.

If from this middle land of humans, the sight of which fulfills
    all wishes,
The boy Joru was banished to the north,

Then the fathers and uncles will await their karmic destiny
   alone.

Did you understand this, divine son Joru?
It is impossible to avoid timely karma.
Even soft mushrooms can emerge from a hard unyielding
   meadow,
And if the time is not right, even an iron stake can break
   [striking the ground].
Today in Min-drug Dawa [early winter][66]
On the fifteenth day of the broad pathway of the gods,
You can tell it's the right time by the conch moon in the sky,
By the twinkling Pleiades converging like friends offering
   consolation, and
By the lamp that dispels darkness [called]
The mandala of the royal parasol of the shining sun.
At the virtuous time when these three unite,
Likewise Gogmo and her son are united, and together
Depart from Yongdzom Nyima Shar-yag [Great Eastern Sun
   that Completely Unites]
With the aspiration prayer that we will meet again.
The punishment for an ostracized man
Is to be driven out by one hundred father gurus blowing the
   conch,
By one hundred tigers in their prime letting loose their
   arrows,
And by one hundred maidens throwing handfuls of ashes.

Don't lose heart; take these bad signs as your good luck.
These handfuls of ashes strike the heart of Zhalkar.
Tsampa is the ash of barley—
These hundred handfuls of tsampa will drive you out.
Whatever you need you must take from Zhalkar;
We'll escort you wherever you wish to go.
If you understand this song, it is sweet to your ears,
If you don't understand it, there is no way to explain it.

Thus he sang, and the minds and life force of all the inhabitants of Ling were magnetized; as a result nearly everyone forgot their fearful memories of what he had done in the past, and instead they felt deeply attached to Joru. So they all sat there, their eyes welling with tears.

Zhalkar had perfectly arranged for all the horses, yaks, provisions, and whatever was necessary, including the escort. Then Joru whispered to Zhalkar, "My leaving indicates that the time has come to fulfill the divine prophecy. After I'm gone, please don't be worried about me. I don't need any escorts and provisions for my trip today, since already yesterday Magyal Pomra and the virtuous zodors of the land of Ma came to receive me."

Joru leaned on his staff and said, "Well then, great inhabitants of the divine land of Ling, although I, Joru, have done nothing, even though you wish to paint a picture of my faults and shortcomings, in truth here is how it really happened," and he sang this song:

> The song begins with Ala.
> Thala leads the melody of the song.
> The great god White Brahmā
> And the lord of the nyen, Gedzo, the god of power,
> The wealth god Tsugna Rinchen,
> And all the virtuous gods inspire me to sing this song.
> Oh, you people of the six districts of Ling,
> Listen, for I have a few things to tell you.
> Appearances are not true, but an illusion
> And it's difficult for the outer and the inner to match.
> Although the outer may seem good, it is false in three ways:
> The sheen of a peacock's feathers may look good on the
>   outside,
> But the peacock is unclean on the inside, filled with poison;
> A coward's armor and weapon may look good on the outside,
> But inside he is gutless as though filled with the mind of a
>   fox;
> The face of a bedecked beauty may be lovely on the outside,
> But on the inside she is as phony as a bogus treasure.
> Although harsh on the outside, there are three things that
>   inwardly are pleasing:
> Outwardly rough, the conduct of a *chöd* practitioner[67]
> Is inwardly loving and compassionate;
> Outwardly harsh, the advice of fathers and uncles

Is inwardly kind, for the betterment of the sons and nephews;
Outwardly, sharper than a thorn, the husk of the grain in a
    good year
Is inwardly blunted and filled with grain.
I, faultless Joru, banished from this place,
Do not deserve the reprimand of my uncle,
Yet I have no choice but to accept this burden that is my
    previous karma.
First I will accept the punishment of having broken the law,
But whether my actions have been right or wrong will come
    out in the end.
The uncles and fathers have been hard on me,
So now I can no longer stay, I must go.

Yet, white snow lion cousins and nephews of White Ling—
When your mighty turquoise mane, Joru, is gone
I wonder if the six provinces of Ling can find true happiness;
If they are to be happy, then the six provinces must live
    contentedly.
Wild striped tiger fathers and uncles
When your six smiles, Joru, are gone
I wonder if White Ling can keep its true splendor.
If they are to be splendid, then the six provinces must remain
    with glory.
Undulating fish mothers and aunts
When your golden eyes, Joru, are gone
I wonder if you'll be able to glide with ease.
To be at ease, the six provinces must live in peace.

This boy Joru is like the crystal snow mountain;
May the Ling warriors and the snow lioness naturally
    surround me.
I, Joru, am as boundless as the sky;[68]
May the southern clouds of the six provinces of Ling
    naturally surround me.
Mother Gogmo is the treasury of wealth;
May the prosperity of White Ling naturally surround her.

If you have understood this song, it is sweet to your ears.
If not, there is no way to explain it.

Having sung this, he mounted his staff and departed for Upper Ciphu. All the lamas blew conches to expel him, but Joru and his mother heard the horns sounding clear and lovely ahead of them as if they were a welcoming party. The youthful tigers shot arrows at him, but no matter how strongly they pulled their bows, the arrows all fell into Joru's hands as if they were offerings. In order to keep a fortunate connection with the warriors, he kept them all. No matter where they ceremonially tossed the barley flour, it descended directly on mother and son like falling snow. Mother Gogmo waved the longevity arrow and sang this song:

> Ho! Heed me!
> All the divine guardians who befriend and grant protection
>   and refuge to mother and son such as:
> Guru Uḍḍiyāṇa Padma,
> Yidam Hayagrīva,
> Ḍākinī Yeshe Tsogyal,
> Auntie Nammen Karmo,
> Drubpa'i Gyalmo who sustains life,
> Sister Gödcham Karmo,
> Elder brother Dungkhyung Karpo,
> The drala Nyentag Marpo,
> Nāga king Tsugna Rinchen,
> Zodor Gedzo Nyenpo,
> Yulkyong Chi-gyal Tagri [Guardian of the Place King Tiger
>   Stripe] and others—
> All the guardian deities who are the principal companions
>   and refuge for us, mother and son,
> And especially the wealth energy of these three—
> The people, possessions, and livestock of White Ling.
> Just as rivers and tributaries flow into the sea,
> Foals follow the mares, and children follow their mothers,
> So may everything follow after mother and son, rushing and
>   overflowing.

Thus she called out to them three times as she twirled the longevity arrow. Once she did so, all the springs of the thirteen valleys on both the sunny and shady sides of the Ci Valley began to flow together in the direction of Joru and his mother, and the face of the mountain Ci-gyal Tag-ri also turned toward them. To this day they still face that way. Then Mother Gogmo and son passed through Upper Ciphu, and at the upper encampment of Kyalo they arrived at the home of Tönpa Gyaltsen of Kyalo. Joru magnetized the three doors of body, speech, and mind of Sengcham Drugmo and the auspicious coincidence of upāya and prajñā was then complete. Although Kyalo Tönpa Gyaltsen tried to offer them whatever they needed, they would accept nothing from him but a hoe to dig the earth. Although he asked them to stay a long time, they stayed only about a month and twenty days. At the time of the waxing December moon, they, both mother and son, set out again for Ma Valley.

As they were traveling, Joru's little sorrel colt was carrying a light load on its back, when suddenly without thinking he struck the pony with his staff, and the colt ran away behind a hill. Then Joru mounted his White Willow Staff and rode after the colt, speeding away to the other side of the hill. Gogmo pursued them as fast as she could but, as the proverb says:

> Could see nary a trace of a bird in the sky nor the track of a mouse on the ground.

She went everywhere chasing them, and finally it fell dark and she found herself lost in a remote place. She thought, "I don't know where to go. It seems better if I just stay here tonight."

As she dismounted her horse and prepared to rest, she saw a ball of still-warm tsampa and, knowing that Joru had put it there, she partook of it and had a pleasant sleep. Then she was awakened by a voice that said, "Mother, have some tea," and she found that she was at Yulung Gadar* of Lower Ma.

There in that place, right on the heart of the black demon, their little tent was pitched and the stove, fire, firewood, and all of it was perfectly arranged, as though they had been living there for several years already. Then Joru offered her some tea, and she felt very healthy and clear-minded. She sat there relaxing, with a mind free from elation and lethargy, and delighted in the feeling of joyful happiness. Then Mother Gogmo invoked the gods, and picked up the hoe and dug a little bit in each of the four directions. As an indication of being welcomed by

---

* Another name for Yulung Sumdo [Turquoise Valley Three Crossroads].

the earth lords, from the east she unearthed a sweet yam the size of a horse's head; from the south, one the size of a yak's head; from the west, one the size of a dri's head; and from the north, a yam the size of a sheep's head. This was taken as a supreme auspicious indication of the way that the earth lords granted siddhi to Joru and his mother. It was then, on the fifteenth day of December at the end of the Water Sheep year and at the beginning of the year of the Wood Monkey, that Mother Gogmo and her son took over, first the Ma Valley, and then in Lower Ma, a place called Khenlung Ridrug [Six-Peaked Sage Valley]. Here the pika demons controlled the lands, the black earth of the mountain peaks had been turned over, the long grasses of the mountain slopes had been gnawed down, and all the herbs of the great plains had been devoured down to their roots. The people who had gone there were enveloped by dust storms; their livestock had died of famine. Joru realized that the time had come to liberate the pika demons, and he put three ewe-kidney-shaped god-demon life stones into his slingshot called Wazi Bi-tra [Brighter than Zi]. Preparing to empty their mountain hideouts, he sang this song called Swirling Melody of the North:

> It's Ala Ala Ala.
> Thala leads the melody of the song.
> The buddha, dharma, and sangha and
> The guru, yidam, and ḍākinī,
> Deities who lead, protect, and guard,
> Today come and befriend me.
> Please help guide these pika demons to liberation.
>
> Now, you who are embodied as demon pikas
> Have completely turned over the earth of the great grassy
>   plains,
> Scattered the flowers and leaves of the marshlands,
> Filled the air with the dust of the black earth of the mountain
>   peaks,
> And mowed down all the fragrant grasses and trees that grow.
> As it is said in the proverbs of the ancient people of Tibet:

It's a pika that turns the earth to black and
It's a thief that turns the district black,
And a deceitful woman who blackens the reputation of a man.

These are the three harms.

> Without them, then this land will be filled with goodness;
> With them, the land will be known as an evil nest.
> You have been embodied as pika demons.
> Look, this is because, in times gone by, your negative karma
>   produced this rebirth
> And now, once again your intentions are evil!
> First you delight in eliminating this great province,
> Ravaging the grass and foliage that sustain the inhabitants
> And destroying the herbs and flowers that are offered to the
>   Three Jewels.
> You've stolen the happiness of these people and their green
>   grassy meadows.
> In order to cut the flow of ripening of karma such as this,
> This very day, I, Joru, with my slingshot
> Will empty this realm of pika demons.
> May the divine Three Jewels lead them and show them the way;
> May the flow of their negative karma be severed;
> May the truth of the words of this boy Joru be accomplished.
> If my song causes confusion, I am at fault.
> If my speech has been in vain, I beg your forgiveness.

Then, having made his prayers, he loosed his slingshot with the roaring sound of a thousand dragons, and the stone struck and killed all three: the pika king Big Mouth, Many-Eyed Pika, and the pika minister Green Ears. By the power of his prayers and compassion, all the other pikas' eardrums burst with the piercing thunderous sound of the slingshot, and they died instantly, were sent to the higher realms, and their minds were placed in the state of liberation.

Meanwhile, there were merchants from Ladakh of upper Tibet enroute to China with a team of some two thousand mules. The mules were carrying assorted loads of gold, silver, and precious silks. The leaders were Palden Jigme [Fearless Glory], Namchag Norzang [Excellent Wealth Meteorite], and Lhadag Chöga [Dharma Joy from Lhadag], with their seventy porters. On the flat colorful meadows of Achen Nawa Tralep [Flat Colorful Meadows of Achen], they were overcome by seven bandits, and Joru knew that the three divisions of Shenpa Meru [Blazing Fire Butcher], Langpo Trabar [Blazing Colorful Elephant], and Chonglha [Lunging God] must be bringing up the rear. Instantly through his magical powers Joru arrived nearby the merchants. All the servants had been beaten and bound and were sitting there sobbing. Joru told them, "Here, in this mind mandala of the divine valley of Ma, once you connect with Magyal Pomra and me, you should realize that I am the earth lord Joru. I wonder why so many of you have crowded here without a reason, making such a disturbance in Ma Valley. If you must cry, then go home and cry! Forget about crying, you're not even supposed to laugh here. You must apologize to me, Chief Joru, and make offerings to the mountain Ma Pomra! If you don't do this, right now, today, I will smash your bloody brains with my short slingshot." Saying this, he loaded a stone the size of a sheep's stomach [rumen] into his short, colorful slingshot.

The three merchant leaders began offering him prostrations, saying, "O Joru, divine child Precious One, we are merchants from Ladakh." And they told him in detail how robbers from Yellow Hor had overcome them and so forth. "Could you just help us to get back a few of the provisions we need to return to our homeland and we will do whatever you command of us?"

Then Joru said, "Oh, what a pity! Since this land is my land, even the Lord of Death will not be allowed to come and pillage here. What's the point in being so afraid of a few butchers from Hor? It's possible to get back all of your possessions and wealth without exception. But from now on, whenever any merchant from Ladakh comes here, they must bring presents and offering scarves to me, Joru. Along with that, whatever I say that I need, they must promise to get. And if you do that, I myself will pursue them and get your things back from the bad men of Yellow Hor." Even though they answered, 'Yes, sir!' the merchants still sat there thinking, "How could he ever get our things back?"

Meanwhile those seven robbers had already arrived at Achen Thangpa Drushi [Square Plain of Achen] and had begun to divide up the booty of mules, boxes, and goods. Joru mounted his staff and, arriving there instantly, told them, "Hey, you seven thieves from Hor, I am Joru, and you had no call to raid my merchants. If I don't get even with you for what you've done, I will be as good as dead." As soon as they heard the sound of his haughty voice, the Butcher [Shenpa] said, "Oh, this is not good. We're in real trouble now. Let's go, it's every man for himself!" As they ran off, cast out by three strikes from Joru's slingshot, King Togtog Relchen [King Great Sword] was on the slope of the Nine-Pointed Vajra Mountain of Hor, where he was out for a jaunt with ninety-nine of his men, making a full one hundred in all. The three stones from the slingshot struck a crag above them, creating a rockslide that tumbled down and killed all two hundred, the men and their horses, leading their consciousnesses to the pure realm.

Then summoning the dralas and wermas to help him, Joru snatched up the thunderbolt sword called Barwa Tsegu [Nine Blazing Points] and the thunderbolt copper vessel called Barwa Kholyong [Blazing Boiler] as well as most of their helmets, armor, swords, and other accoutrements.* He gathered up all of the Ladakhi golden boxes and mules without losing any and then, taking these as two separate loads, riding his staff, made a horse path through Tsara Padma Tongden [One-Thousand-Lotus Pasture]. Joru returned all the merchants' possessions, horses, mules, wealth, and the lot and loaded his own newly claimed armor, helmets, weapons, and thunderbolt copper vessel on the backs of the mules; together with the merchants he went to Madro Lu-gu'i Khelkhung [Warm Ma Valley Lamb's Belly] of Ma. The merchants were joyful beyond measure, and although they tried to give almost all their wealth back to him, he refused to take it. Some of the merchants said he must be Ma Pomra. Then Joru said, "Now all of you can take your time coming to Mamed Yulung Sumdo [Conjunction of Turquoise Valley at Lower Ma], for up to that place you need have no fear of enemies or robbers. I have something small that I would like you to accomplish for me when you arrive there. Then I will escort you through the territory of the marauding Yellow Hor bandits, until we reach the end of the Makhog Valley. Until then you are responsible for my armor and so forth; don't lose anything!" and saying this he instantly departed for Lower Ma.

By that time Nyima Legchen [Sun of Excellence], Dawa Zangpo [Excellent Moon], and Keltri Döndrub [Accomplishes Aims for Ten Thousand Ages], three merchant chiefs from Omi Shen [Omi Mountain] in China, were traveling with four hundred thousand bricks of tea and a thousand attendants on their way to the upper plateaus toward the west. As they passed through that empty land of Ma Valley, they were terrified of the Yellow Hor bandits. When they arrived at Yulung Gapa Tramo [Colorful Canyon of the Turquoise Valley], they dismounted and set up their camps. Joru transformed his little sorrel colt into his supreme steed Noble Mount, so magnificent that if it ran, it ran like a bird in flight, and it possessed the great confirmation of a steed, with vulture-down tufts on the tips of its ears and four hooves with wheels of wind. All the merchants stared distractedly at the horse as Joru led it right on into the encampment. Joru said, "It's just me, King Joru, with only this horse, the excellent steed, Noble Mount. If I keep it, the bandits of Yellow Hor will surely steal it, but yet there are no buyers in this vacant land. Because of the good fortune of you merchants, this valuable wealth has come to you without you even pursuing it. From the good fortune of you merchants, something of value

---

* Items that had belonged to King Togtog Ralchen and followers.

that you have not pursued has come to you of its own accord. If you want to buy this supreme steed, I am ready to sell it."

Some of the merchants thought, "This can't be true! It's probably a magical apparition. Besides, even the Emperor of China doesn't have an animal like this to ride." Among them there was a skilled magician who was asked to examine the steed. After checking he said, "The characteristics of magic are not present here." The chief merchant Dawa Zangpo spoke, "If it's true that you are willing to sell this horse, I will give you whatever you want for it."

Then Joru replied, "This horse of mine is one of two brother supreme steed flying horses. Honestly speaking, its head is so fine, it is worth a hundred boxes of gold; its ears are so fine, they're worth a hundred boxes of silver; the four hooves are so excellent, they are worth a hundred boxes of silk; the tips of the hairs on its coat are so fine, they're worth a hundred mules; and the shaft of those hairs is so fine, it is worth a hundred dzomo; and the roots of those hairs are so fine, they're worth a hundred ewes. On top of that, there must be a tip for the mother, as we must reckon up with the mare that bore this steed. And I will insist upon a fee for removing the halter, and the celebration we must have in my honor!"

The merchant chief Nyima Legchen said, "This horse is a only little bit better than my horse, Yuja [Flying Turquoise], which I sold to the Tag-rong clan of Ling for a mere hundred pouches of gold and a hundred ingots of silver the size of a horse's hoof. I didn't ask for an arrangement of so many boxes of gold and silver. Not only that, even if each one of us completely gave all of our wealth to him, it wouldn't even equal the worth of a hundred boxes of gold. This man is not only dishonorable, but he doesn't seem to understand the value of horses, gold, and silver. Whatever the case, we can at least be sure he is not from Yellow Hor."

Then all the merchants held a secret meeting and unanimously plotted to kill Joru and steal his horse, and agreed that it would be better to send the magician and the horse back to China.

The chief merchant, Keltri Döndrub, then said, "If we merchants were to give you the value you have placed on every part of the horse, from the most valuable item we have down to the lowest, we would still not have enough; this is an incredible insult to the merchants from China in the east. Now we are going to take this horse from you. This will be your way of confessing and purifying before [the Chinese Emperor] Dungkün Trülgyi Gyalpo [Magical King of Dungkün]. Joru replied, "Isn't the horse on my land? Just leave it there. You vagrants get out of here to wherever you belong! I, King Joru, demand an apology for all the articles of wealth of the encampment."

This made all the merchants furious, and they began to stone Joru. They killed

275

one Joru, and two emerged. They killed two, and then there were four. They killed four, and then there were eight. Finally, the whole place was filled with an army of Jorus. Some of them started packing up the encampment. Others started leading the mules away, while others started tying up the merchants and beating them. He left all the merchants there, hog-tied. Without leaving even a needle's worth of wealth or provisions behind, the Jorus went off to Mamed Lhalung Sumdor [Divine Place of Three Junctions] in Lower Ma. Meanwhile, all the merchants were terrified and had decided that this was how they were all going to die. Still, one diminutive Joru remained there, and all the merchants begged him to spare their lives.

He replied, "We Jorus have anger but don't hold a grudge. If you promise to do what we command of you, then we won't steal your possessions."

The merchants became overjoyed and said to each other, "This is only a magical emanation. We merchants must apologize for our ignorance and do whatever he says.

Then the miniature Joru untied them and led them up to Lhalung Sumdo. Once there, they set up camp just as it was before, and each merchant regained his place.

"All of you killed many Jorus. If I took all of your possessions as blood money, it would not be enough. I won't take your goods, but you must sign a written contract that, from this day on, every Chinese merchant will greet Joru with a silken scarf and the best bricks of your tea. All of you must offer the best tea you have. The penalty is that you must build me a palace in the place called Ma Drodro Lu-gu'i Khelkhung. After that, I will return to you every bit of your wealth, but until then, I will just give you what you need to eat and drink. From today onward, wherever you go, up or down, I will protect you from fear of the Yellow Hor thieves.

"Yesterday, some merchants from Ladakh were robbed by the seven Hor bandits of Ayen. I, Joru, pursued them, took the blood money, and returned it to the merchants. Sometime today, they will arrive here where they must build a palace for me," he said.

The other merchants sat there in amazement. Later that day the Ladakhi merchants and their mules arrived and made their encampment all in one area. Through his magic, Joru manifested a feast with many varieties of food. Then all the merchants offered three tan mules laden with boxes of gold, five white mules laden with boxes of silver, and seven sorrel mules laden with boxes of silk. All fifteen mules, their loads, and silk offering scarves were offered in a single presentation to Joru. Then all the merchants from China offered a thousand bricks of tea with offering scarves and their oath to obey him. Joru created another feast for them.

The very next day, all the merchants from Ladakh and China went to Ma Drodro Lu-gu'i Khelkhung to build a four-storied palace with four pagoda-like fortresses in the four directions and to make a foundation to just begin a fifth story. Joru told them, "If the provisions I have given you are exhausted before the building is completed, you can come back for more." Each hundred men were given a bag of tsampa, and loads of butter, tea, and meat. Then, two Jorus arrived to be supervisors. The tea merchants from China were given the task to build the east, west, and north pagoda fortresses. The merchants of Ladakh were asked to build only the southern fortress. The southern fortress was thereafter known as the Ladakh Palace of Gu-dril [Nine Unifications]. Since the fortresses of the eastern and other directions were built by the Chinese tea merchants, they were given the names High Tea Fortress [Jakar Ringmo], Prosperity Tea Fortress [Jakar Chugmo], and Dark Tea Fortress [Jakar Mukpo]. These were the three names given to the three directional fortresses of the main palace. Likewise, the first story of the main palace was named Tongshong Karmo [White Assembly Hall of the One Thousand], the second Mukgu Gu-dril [Dark Assembly Hall of the Nine Unifications], and the third, Samdrub Tagdzong [Tiger Fortress FulfillingAll Wishes]. The fourth story became known as Gödtsang Kha-yel [Skylight Vulture Nest] as it was built with the assistance of Gödcham Karmo and others as well as that of the nāgas. The walls of the upper opening skylight were built so that they would just reach the fifth story. During the entire time of construction, the food provided for the merchants not only was not exhausted but didn't decrease in the slightest. Upon completion of the palace, Joru threw a large celebration and presented all the merchants with gifts, after which he sent each of them happily back to their respective countries. It became well known that through Joru's blessings, these merchants never before had had such a success in their business as this.

Later the fifth story was built by the nyen Gedzo and Ma Pomra. Since the stones for the walls were carried by many snow lion cubs, the roof laid by the gods, Nyentag, and others, and the wood carried from the Siblung Nag-gyal Chugmo [Shady Valley Rich Royal Forest] by tigresses, it thereafter became known as Sengdrug Tagtse [Lion Dragon Tiger Peak]. Perfectly accomplished both from without and from within, for a while the palace was maintained by the gods, nāgas, and nyen, these three, who resided there. This is how it became known that the upper, highest story was built by the gods; the second, middle story was built by the nyen; and that the third, lower story, was built by the nāgas.

CHAPTER SIX

When the land of Ling is covered by snow,
The land of Ma blossoms with the noble glory of spring.
When the people of Ling request to borrow the land,
Joru proclaims how the land will be divided.

NOW IT HAPPENED THAT [in the year of the Wood Bird] when the queen of garuḍas played in the wish-fulfilling tree, Joru was eight years old, and he knew that the time had come for White Ling to be established in the land of Ma. He went to the nāga king Tsugna Rinchen, asking him to make it rain, and this was when, with the help of the spirits of the eight classes, the rain turned into a snowstorm that descended on the land of Ling. From the first day of the first month of winter, the snow fell so hard in the land of Ling that if a spear were set in the ground of the mountain passes, only the banner at its peak could be seen. If an arrow were stuck in the ground of the lower valleys, only the notched tip could be seen. The snow fell so hard that the entire region of eastern Kham was buried. In particular the snows were so deep all over the upper, middle, and lower regions of Ling that a meeting was held. It was determined that no one could survive unless they left this land to go in search of a place without snow. Four warriors were dispatched all around the upper and lower regions to look for land. For many days, the warriors traveled even to farmlands,[69] but, in general, because it was winter and, in particular, because the spirits of the eight classes were changing the way things appeared, they didn't see a single place that they thought had less snowfall than the land of Ling. But the warriors who went toward Ma Valley, after looking around very carefully, found that where it bordered Dza, Dri, and Tra, these three, all the way to Om, Ga, and Nyi, these three, including the upper Ma Valley known as Sengchen Khogpa [Great Lion Belly]; the Middle Ma Valley, Lu-gu'i Tsera [Frolicking Lamb's Corral]; and the Lower Ma Valley, Lhalung Sumdo all the way to Yulung Gadar Tramo, had hills that were grassy and green. All the plains were rich with burgundy. The plateaus' grasses, herbs, and foliage, all three, were so abundant as to seem inexhaustible, even though the livestock of the six districts of Ling were grazing there.

During the same time, all the traveling merchants from China and Tibet gave gifts to Joru and paid the taxes for their goods. As a result they had no problems with the robbers and thieves, and a number of different groups of traders passed this way.

The four warriors of Ling who had been dispatched asked these merchants, "At the present time, who is the owner of this land? If we want to be loaned some land, who should we ask?"

The merchants replied, "Previously, this land was a vacant place, possessed by no one, and it was difficult for visiting merchants to pass through. Even apart from the thievery of the Yellow Hor bandits, we were never able to pass through here. Then the one known as King Joru came to Lhalung Sumdo—he who is the lord of the nonhuman godly demons, whose magical manifestations can move heaven and earth, and who has the complete power of the three realms of existence. Because we all presented to him greeting scarves and the best and first portions of our tea and other goods as an offering, we were able to travel here in safety. If you want to be loaned some land, you must request it of him," they said and then departed.

The warriors of Ling were afraid to approach Joru, so they returned home. At the moment that all the search parties arrived back, all the people of the six provinces of upper and lower White Ling had assembled to make inquiries. Those who had searched three of the regions explained that there was no land without snow, but the search party that had gone to the land of Ma explained in detail how there was no snow there at all, and that Joru was the owner of the land but that they had been too afraid to meet him. All the people of Ling conferred; the wise ones such as Chipön, Denma, Gyatsha, and so forth knew that according to the prophecy the time had come to occupy the land of Ma, but they pretended not to know. Then Gyatsha said, "Now, the place without snow is the land of Ma, and furthermore the owner of that land is Joru. From the beginning I have been the general representative of the people of the six provinces, so I, Bumpa, will go there, even though Joru's actions are not in accord with the country's customs, his thoughts are not in accord with humans, his crops are not in accord with the rhythm of the seasons, and he makes his own decisions according to only his own mind. I should not go alone, but with a few warriors, so that I can then have the upper hand," he said. Then,

Tshazhang Denma Jangtra, Tag-rong Pöntro* Trothung, Gyapön Sergyi Argham Kyalo Tönpa Gyaltsen, and Druga-de Chökyong Bernag [Joyful Black-Cloaked Dharma Protector of Dru], these five, volunteered to go. All six brothers in arms then departed for the land of Ma.

When they arrived in Lhalung Sumdo, Lower Ma, Joru omnisciently knew of it. Then, in order to subdue the pride of these mighty warriors, as the brethren in arms approached Yulung Gadar Tramo, their colors shimmering with brightness, Joru suddenly appeared standing before them. He placed in his slingshot, Wazi Bi-tra, a black nyen stone the size of a sheep's stomach and, standing about the distance of an arrow's flight away, without uttering any words, he sang this song of the Soaring Flight of the Great Garuḍa:

> The song begins with Ala Ala Ala.
> Thala leads the melody of the song.
> May this song be sustained by the Three Jewels,
> May this song be lead by the motherly ḍākinīs,
> And be befriended by the dralas and wermas.
> If you don't recognize this land,
> This place is called Yulung Sumdo.
> If you don't recognize me,
> In the great clan of the lineage of Mukpo Dong,
> I hold the great title that has been conferred by the higher
>   gods;
> My name is Little Chieftain King Joru.
> Now listen here, you six bandits.
> Among the earth lord keepers of these lands,
> For the gods there is Machen Pomra
> And for the humans there is King Joru.
> For us, the gods and humans, there are the animals;
> In the highlands are the grazing wild ass and the wild yak,
> In the midlands are the foraging deer, and
> In the lowlands are the stalking tigers and leopards.
> In particular, in Lhalung Sumdo,
> Since I, King Joru, have arrived,
> Not only is impossible for bandits to pass through in daylight,

---

* Wrathful Chieftain.

Even after nightfall, the godly demons don't dare to move.
The gold, silver, and mules of the merchants of Ladakh in
    upper Tibet
Were stolen by the five scorpion brothers of Hor.
I, Joru, pursued them, and
Even though the seven mounted thieves escaped without
    being caught,
I killed Hor Thog-gyal [Meteorite King of Hor] with my
    slingshot.
I took the nine-pointed blazing meteorite sword
As well as the meteoric copper vessel that boils naturally,
And I returned to the merchants of Ladakh their wealth,
Including their boxes of gold, silver, and silk, and their mules.
I followed the Ladakhi merchantmen going down to the
    lower regions
And that two-year-old colt was my, Joru's, first bounty.
A thousand Chinese merchants with their porters came
And tried to steal my little colt.
I captured and imprisoned a thousand of those merchants,
And they presented to me as offerings a thousand bricks of
    tea with silk offering scarves.
Their penalty was to build the Tea Fortress Palace—
And that was Joru's second bounty.
When displaying the strength of a great army
If a true warrior's power is not fully matured,
Then no matter how many warriors[70] there are, it is merely
    like dry grass on the hills—
Fuel for the fire that is Joru's to burn.
Today, you six bandits
Have run right into me
And have disrespectfully intruded upon me.

This slingshot that I hold in my hand
Is the first palace of the dralas.
It is the best of all things that are quick and swift.
First, the hair of a thousand motherly ḍākinīs,
Second, the turquoise mane of the white snow lion,
Third, the whiskers of the red tiger,

Fourth, the long shoulder hair of the brown wild yak,
Fifth, the chest hair of the white-shouldered grizzly:
These five are what make up the slingshot.
Its upper part is braided during three waxing moons.[71]
The waxing moon corresponds with the time of the dragon;
When the stone is thrown, the roar of the dragon resounds.
The lower part is braided during the three waning moons,
Braided only in the waning moon time of the bird;
When [the stone is] thrown, it takes flight on the path of the
     birds.
At the dawn of three full moons is the time of the tiger.
When the slingshot's pouch is prepared,
The auspicious connection for the tiger Nyèntag to surround
     this is made.
The whip tail is sewn at daybreak of the twenty-ninth day of
     these three months;
It then can strike wherever it is aimed.
This black stone that looks like a sheep's belly
Is the life-force stone of a thousand godly demons.
Look as I aim toward the cliff in front of you six men—
It will be split as if by a thunderbolt.
Watch this show while you're still alive.
The next stone that I will throw
Will be the stone thatis the support of the Nyentag drala,
And it will demolish the bodies of you six men.
The six horses will be my third bounty.
In this pleasing mandala of the divine valley of Ma,
There is no reason for demon samaya corrupters to wander.
If you understood this, it is sweet to your ears.
If not, there is no way to explain it.

Having sung, he swirled the slingshot with waves of many meteoric sparks and flames, and the white crag was crushed to dust. The booming sound filled the entire valley, causing several mighty warriors to faint. It was then that Gyatsha Zhalkar took his white silken offering scarf Nyinmo Delek from his inner coat and said, "O Joru! Precious one! O Joru, have mercy on us! In this unknown land, the empty valley of Ma, I am the stranger Gyatsha Zhalkar, with five important wise men." Saying this, he then broke into the song of the Six White Melodies:

The song begins with Ala Ala Ala.
Thala leads the melody of the song.
Gurus, yidams, ḍākinīs, these three
Abide inseparably as my crown ornament.
If you do not recognize me,
I am Gyatsha Zhalkar of Bumpa
With five mighty warriors as my companions.
Well then, honorable Joru, divine son,
Listen, and I'll tell you how things are.

The horns of the brown wild yak,
It seems, will destroy the bodies of whoever comes,
Yet it is unheard of that they would brandish their horns to their young.
The great fangs of the red tigress,
It seems, can devour whoever they meet,
Yet it is unheard of that they would threaten their own offspring.

Your elder brother has put himself out to come to visit you
Along with these wise and mighty warriors of White Ling;
Is it customary to welcome us with just these rocks?
Now listen, divine son.
The peace of the sandalwood forest has been destroyed by
	fire.
The colorful leopards are unable to roam their homeland.
Since you the youthful wild wolf are of the same clan as we
	carnivores of the plains,
We thought we could ask to make the rich grassy meadow
	our home.
The land of White Ling has been buried under snow.
Due to famine, none of the animals and beasts can survive.
Boy Joru of the lineage of the Bumpa clan,
We thought to ask you to loan us the land of the Ma Valley.
I, Gyatsha, came here as the one with the upper hand,
Thinking that the land of Ma was a place where the animals
	could freely roam:

The cuckoo bird is an eater of grapes,
And although it seems to be attached to the joyful land of Mön,

It has no choice but to carry them to the shelter of the juniper trees,
Hoping to return to its own country before long.

In the colorful land of Ling,
First, in the highlands are the meadows where the nomads
    live,
Second, in the midlands is the palace fortress of the Bumpas,
Third, in the lowlands are the patterned farmlands.
It's not that we have no want or wish for those.
First, in the highlands are the finest breeds of the farmers'
    horses.
Second, in the midlands are the nomads' dri and dzo.
Third, in the lowlands are the pleasant towns where flocks of
    sheep graze.
Until [the snow melts], we thought that we could all come to
    the Ma Valley.
The best would be if we could borrow the land for three years.
At least, we would like to borrow this land for six months.
So please, honorable Joru, do not send me, elder brother
    Gyatsha Zhalkar,
And this group of the best and mighty warriors of White
    Ling
Back empty-handed!
If you've understood this song, it is sweet to your ears.
If not, there is no way to explain it.

Thus he sang, and instantly Joru ran to receive them. Taking Gyatsha's horse by the bridle, he said, "Alas, brother Zhalkar and many warriors of White Ling, I failed to recognize you. Now, please, come here so that we can confer, but not only that, please don't be disgusted with me. Since my mother and I have been living here at the crossroads of the paths traveled by robbers and thieves and inhabited by demons and tsen, people like you are always passing through here." Saying that, he invited the chieftain and ministers to his tent, which looked small from the outside but was large and spacious within. Inside, there were chests of tea, gold, silver, and more, which gave a feeling of prosperous charm and warmth. All the mighty warriors were mesmerized. Then all of the guests were offered tea and a banquet of food and drink and, like the cakes of the divine, celestial delicacies possessing a hundred flavors. They repeated the stories of everything that had happened in great detail, after which Joru offered Gyatsha and each one of the principal warriors the best of white silk scarves, called Nyinmo Delek, and a gold coin, while he sang this song of auspicious connection called the Long Haunting Melody That Invokes the Divine:

> The song begins with Ala Ala Ala.
> Thala leads the melody of the song.
> Today may the divine, the nyen, the spirit-lords of existence,
> And the great nāga Tsugna Rinchen
> Lead and inspire Joru's song.
> May my intentions turn toward the dharma.
> Now then, listen, mighty warriors of White Ling.
> Especially you, Zhalkar of Bumpa!
> It is as the ancient proverb says:

For the merchant who ventures afar—
Unless he takes his own means into account,
The enticements of the marketplace will be never-ending.
The inhabitants of this island [marketplace] can weigh their own
*   gold dust,*
But this has no bearing on the merchant's purchases.

For the wild asses that take pleasure in grazing in the plains of the
*   deserted valley—*
Unless they sense when they are full,
The enticement of the grasses of the plains and mountains will never
*   be exhausted.*
The grass on the rocky crags may grow straighter than an arrow,
But this has no bearing on the wild asses' grazing.

> Although the chieftains of White Ling are bent on
>   scrutinizing everything,
> Unless they see the truth with their own minds,
> Then there will be no end to the confused dream-like appearances.

A starving beggar may dream of finding food,
But when examined, that dream will bring him greater despair.

> Not only that, there are even more examples:

A lama explaining the dharma with attachment and aversion
Is the first sign that the purpose of beings will not be fulfilled.
A chieftain freeing a prisoner with good connections
Is the first sign of falling short of integrity.
The tigers in their prime choosing the smaller army of enemies
Is the first sign that victory will not be won.

A bride who separates brothers
Is the first sign of a lack of good judgment.
When the humble are forced from their land by the mighty,
It is the first sign of losing one's own government.

Last year it was Joru who was the demonic force;
This year it is the snow that is the evil spirit—
The demon forces of White Ling are never exhausted.
Don't just leave the snow, get rid of it—
Just like you did me.
The six tribes of Ling should stay behind.
Oops, I shouldn't have said that, just kidding!

In the great lion's belly, the land of Ma,
The heads of the grasses are blooming with flowers,
The sheathes of the blades are laden with dew,
And the roots are rich with sap.
Forget about animals; it even satisfies humans.
It is the path of the heroes' reward,
The place where all beautiful women promenade,
And the place where racehorses run at leisure.
The land of Ling is a golden white parasol,
The valley of Ma is the silken fringe encircling.
The country of Ling is a silver mandala,
And the Ma Valley is the surrounding circle of iron mountains.
Don't stay in White Ling; prepare to come.
If you stay in Ma for a lifetime, that will be okay.
You can stay for three years; it is up to you.
There is no need to pay for the use of the land and its grass.
I do this to honor the elder and younger brothers of White
    Ling in general,

And especially out of respect for Chief Gyatsha.
Not only that, at the lower treasure gate of Sheldrag,
There is a treasure trove of sevenfold jewels,
As well as the palace built by the travelers of China called
    Sengtrug Tagtse—
All of which will be presented as a welcoming celebration for
    White Ling.
I, Joru, have no need for any of this.
The one you entrust as your leader should be
Endowed with uplifted windhorse and authentic presence.
Don't stay in Ling any longer.
Inhabitants of the six provinces, prepare now to come here.
If you understood this, it is like a songbird.
If you didn't understand, there is no melody for these words.
Brothers, bear this in mind.

Thus he sang, and they all replied, "Yes, sir! So be it!" Then the warriors came hastily to Ling. The people of the six provinces of Ling gathered to discuss the possibility of the exodus to the Ma Valley; Chipön made the final decision to go. Now, at this time each of the warriors had a fort in the upper and lower regions, and each day someone was delegated to oversee the farm fields and the fortresses. The nomadic tribes associated with each of the Thirty Warriors began their journey and chose the most convenient route to the Ma Valley, with plans to meet at Ma Dil-yag Tagthang Tramo [Colorful Tiger Plains and Hills of Ma] exactly on the tenth day of December. Like rain clouds in the summertime, all the people of Ling began their exodus through the lands that were both near and far from the Ma Valley, such as Ga, Tra-khog, Omgo, Nyi, and others. Then, on the tenth day of December, all the fathers, uncles, brothers, cousins, and others met precisely as planned at Ma Dil-yag Tagthang Tramo. They began to wonder, "Just how will Joru would divvy up this land?" All those who were in accord with Joru felt joyful; those who were his enemies sat there feeling depressed. Trothung thought about how it was said that some time ago Joru had killed the hunters of Tag-rong and was then exiled to the Ma Valley, but that finally, some fifteen days later, the hunters had returned to their own homes, and it became apparent that not only had Joru had not eaten them, but he was innocent. Even though he was a bit apprehensive and ashamed, Trothung thought it would be best to flatter Joru. He invited Joru to his place and gave him the third summer's milk of a dri, a platter of deliciously sweet cakes, and the fatty meat of the white prosperity sheep.

Then Trothung said, "Dearest nephew, may all your wishes be fulfilled, and please, do whatever you can to give me the most excellent portion of land."

Joru replied, "It is no problem for me to give you just what you want—a piece of land that is unlike any other. There is no need to worry."

Then in the midst of the great gathering of all the people of Upper, Middle and Lower Ling, King Joru donned his hat Gopo Chogzhu [Antelope Hat] as the gateway to the auspicious connection, while he sang the song of the division of the lands of Ma, called Quelling the Great Gathering through Splendor:

> The song begins with Ala Ala Ala.
> Thala leads the melody of the song.
> Guru Padma Uḍḍiyāṇa,
> Auntie Nammen Karmo
> Surrounded by one hundred thousand motherly ḍākinīs,
> Today come here to befriend me.
> I am the one known as King Joru.
> Outwardly, I am a beggar boy lonely vagrant.
> Inwardly, I am the pillar that supports the dralas.
> Secretly, I am the embodiment of all the victorious ones.
> Residents of the six provinces, listen to my song.
>
> In this valley of Ma, the great snow lion's belly,
> The west reaches to the land of India,
> The east reaches to the land of China,
> The north directly connects to Achen Hor,
> While in the south the land connects to Ati Rong.
> Here, the Ma River winds in three loops.
> The first loop is the portion of land called Ling.
> The remaining two are called the inhospitable plains of the
>   land of Hor.
>
> In the highlands of Ma, Tselha-ser Khamdo [Conjunction of
>   the Divine Golden Peak],
> The sky looks like the eight spokes of a wheel
> And the land is beautifully arranged like an eight-petaled
>   lotus.
> In between, the great mountains appear like the eight
>   auspicious symbols.

Of all lands, it is by far the finest.
It is a land for the most revered leader.
This portion of the land is to be given to Nyibum Daryag
    [Excellent Banner of One Hundred Thousand Suns]
Of the Elder Lineage of the eight Serpa brothers
Together with the Go'jo and Achag tribes.
From Upper Ma to the thirteen mountains of Tselha[72]
Take your seat, like the sun embracing the golden mountains.

The sunny side of the valley of Ma is like a lotus naturally
    blooming;
A land where great bucks frolic in play
And where the brown wild yaks butt their horns.
Because the grass is so abundant, the baby yaks get lost in it.
Because the trees are so dense, the deer hide there.
This is the land where the great ones should reside.
This portion of the land is to be given to Anu Paseng
    [Courageous Youthful Lion]
Of the Middle Lineage of the six provinces of Ombu
Together with the three tribes, Ga, Dru, and Den.
From Middle Ma to the place where the nine high mountains
    unite,
Take your seat, like beautiful flowers in a meadow.

The land of Madro Lu-gu'i Khelkhung
Is a place where the winds pay taxes by scattering the grass
And the river pays its tax by carrying logs downstream.
The background of mountains is like a drawn curtain
And the Ma River resembles a water offering.
This is the land where a chieftain of great power should
    reside.
This portion of land is to be given to Uncle Chipön Gyalpo
And his son Yutag.
On the great shady side of Ma, in the wealth valley of Drag-
    do [Lower Crag],
There is a fence of one hundred and eight stupas
And a thousand and two shrines with a hundred thousand
    tsatsas.

This is the land where the subterranean nāginīs constantly
bow down.
It is also the land where the animals of the humans and nāgas
mingle,
And a land where a sovereign leader should reside.
This portion of land should go to the great father King Senglön
And to Zhal-lu of Bumpa.

In the six upper regions of Ma called Darlung Chugmo
[Wealthy Silk Valley]
The plains resemble a perfectly arranged mandala,
The herbs and flowers resemble the mounds arranged upon it,
And the streams and rivers look like knotted silk scarves.
This is the land where a leader of great family lineage should
reside.
This portion of land goes to Rinchen Darlu [Precious Silk
Scarf]
Of the Lesser Lineage of the four districts of Muchang
Together with the tribes of Kyalo and Tshazhang.
From Lower Ma up to Lu-gu,
Take your seat, like arrows placed perfectly in aquiver.

In Sidpa Khölmo Rogdzong [Black Bellow Fortress of
Existence],
The snow falls throughout the summer just as in winter,
And the autumn and spring are but a driving blizzard.
If a human cries out, a demoness will answer.
If a dog cries out, then the wail of the fox is the answer.
Until a mare reaches nine years of age,
In this land, it cannot give birth to its foal.
Until a young dri meets a stud for nine seasons,
In this land, her calf will not be born.
Until the white prosperity sheep reaches three years of age,
In this land, her lamb cannot be born.
The narrow passageways are roads as thin as throats,
While the plains are expansive like lotus flowers in bloom.
This is a land where a mighty man should abide.
This portion of land will be given to Uncle Trothung.

In great Upper Ma, on the highest striated peak*
Stallion caribou reign over the three highest mountains.
Musk deer take the middle white crags to be their fortress.
The lower region of the king of rivers is teeming with
    undulating fish.
Even if there is no booty in the morning, it will be there by
    night.
During the three months of summer, the mountain peaks are
    cool and refreshing;
In the three months of winter, the hearts of the valleys still
    hold this warmth.
This is the land where a warrior should reside.
This will be the portion of land of Nya-tsha Aten [Stable
    Nephew Fish].

Alpine willows thrive on the great black crests of Ma's
    mountain ridges,
The land where the tigers show their six smiles,
And the summer and winter residence of the great tribes.
This is the land where the unruly warriors should reside.
This portion of land is given to Tag-rong Zigphen.

In the valley of Jang in Ma where nine turquoise manes are
    braided,
Each mountain has eighteen secluded valleys;
Each plain is an eighteen-day journey.
The men gaze over and over at this very sight.
This is the land where the mighty warriors should reside.
This portion is given to Sengtag Adom [Lion Tiger Youthful
    Bear].

In Nyima Lebchen Phorog [Crow Great Sun Flats],
The three months of spring come early
And the three months of winter are not so very cold.
In the early morning the sun envelops the homes;

---

* Mountain peaks streaked with snow.

At sunset the day turns instantly into night.
The only minor drawback is the presence of enemies;
If a man is lacks a brave heart, this is not the place for him.
This portion of land is for Chölu Darphen.

In Ma, on Churi Lhathang Tramo [Rippling Divine Colorful
    Plain],
The white husks of grain are like flocks of driven sheep;
There the sorrel mules scatter like herds of wild yaks.
It is a playful land where the flowers seem to dance.
This place, where the bees sing their little songs,
Is a land where a wise man should reside.
This portion of land is for Tshazhang Denma Jangtra.

Between the lower mountains of Ma at Padma Khyung
    Dzong [Padma Garuḍa Fortress]
And a mountain that looks like a poisonous snake slithering
    downward,
Is the rocky crag resembling the mouth of a red Yama.
This is the passageway of the eight classes of māras and tsen.
This is a place for black magicians who are unwanted by the
    enemies.
It is a land where a powerful man should reside.
This portion of land is for Gadei Bernag.

At the uppermost red hill in Ma, Tashi Tsel [Auspicious
    Vermillion Hill],
Is the center of this land endowed with prosperity.
It is a land where the white-ridged dri who calve each year
    roam,
A land where the supreme horse births twin foals,
A land where, even if the white prosperity sheep are
    slaughtered, they continue to multiply.
It is a land where a wealthy person should reside.
This portion of land is for Kyalo Tönpa.

At the vista of Dzachen Khujug in Ma
Where the Golden Yak Pass in Hor meets the summit,

Even though this is the winding path where the Hor bandits
  roam,
In this land you can see them clearly from afar.
This land is only for a swift-footed man.
This portion of land is for Dongtsen Nang-ngu Apel [Mighty
  Youthful Glory of the Tribe].

In the valley of Dzatri Ga'u-ser [Crag Throne Golden
  Amulet] in Ma,
The high mountains are snow-covered and rocky.
Below is the fortress of the forest, the tether of the earth.
This is the land where a high-ranking man should reside.
This portion of land will go to Michen Gyalwa'i Lhundrub.

In Ma on the sunny side of Dragkar Gudril [United White
  Crag],
This is a great plain spread out like a carpet
And a great mountain that seems as though it is summoning
  guests.
This is a place where a man of great decisiveness should abide.
This is portion of land is for Gyapön Sergham [Chief Sergyi
  Argham].

In the upper valley of Ma called Darthang Chugmo [Wealthy
  Silken Plain],
At the highest point are some three great valleys,
And in the foothills, three great plains unite.
Here is the land where the myriarchies barter, summer and
  winter.
This is a land where a man with a great following should
  reside.
This portion of land is for Tongpön Treltsei.

At Datra Lungpa'i Sumdo [Colorful Silk Conjunction of
  Three Valleys] in Ma
The high mountains are covered with great forests and musk
  deer reign,
And the resounding call of the cuckoo can first be heard.

The lower region is covered with lakes and plains.
It is here that the first blooms of summer flowers can be seen.
This portion of land is for the one who enjoys luxury.
This portion of land is for Yuyag Gönpo [Protector of
    Excellent Turquoise].

In Ma Dru-gu Gu-lung Tramo [Colorful Valleys of Ma],
If one goes to the nomadic lands, the valleys and pathways are
    spacious.
If one makes this their home, it is warm and close to the farmers.
If one wants to build a house, the earth and stones are already
    there.
This portion of land goes to Lingchen Tharpa.

In Ma, at Nachen Damgyi Gongwa [Collar of Marshes and Bogs]
Is the origin of the dense earth.
This is the headwaters of the Ma River
And the land where the fathers and uncles should abide.
This portion of land goes to Namkha Serzhal[73] [Golden Face
    of Space].

In Ma, at Nyikhog Padma Lung [Sunny Lotus Valley],
Is the route travelers take when they are upward bound, and
When they return, it is the gathering place of wealth.
It is a marketplace where judgments and reputations are
    made.
This is the place where a handsome cavalier should abide.
This portion of land goes to Tsangpa'i [Brahmā] Ngo-lug of
    Agê for one,
Second, to Dar-'jam [Gentle Scarf] Ngo-lug of Mupa,
And third, to Sintsha [Rākṣa Maternal Nephew] Ngo-lug of
    Tag-rong.
This portion of land goes to all three Ngo-lugs.

One, the junction of Tradong Sinpo [Falcon Face Rākṣa],
Two, Dza-zelmo Gang [Spotted Crag Hill Spur] of Ma,
And three, the shaded valley Lung-do[Royal Dark Lower
    Valley]—

These three are sacred grounds in Ma Valley.
Unless a man has great merit, he cannot reside here.
This portion of land should go to those endowed with karmic
    power,
Who are praised as three of the men named Victory Banner:
Guru Gyaltsen of Denma, Nyima Gyaltsen of Kar-ru, and
    Tharpa Gyaltsen of Nag-ru.

Buyi Phentag of Abar [Drawn Tiger Boy of Abar],
And Ca-nag Pönpo Singsing [Chieftain Black Metal];
Please take your seat on the land and join with the tribes of
    the Greater Lineage.

Changtri Ngamchen [Great Awesome Myriad Jackles] of Ombu
And the hero Nyima Lhundrub [Spontaneous Sun];
Please take your seat on the land and join with the tribes of
    the Middle Lineage.

Gung-gi Marleb [Upper Red Plain] of Rongtsha
And Shelkar Gyangdrag [White Crystal Far Famed] of
    Bumpa;
Please take your seat on the land and join with the tribes of
    the Lesser Lineage.

Bu-yag Drug-gyei [Handsome Royal Son Dragon]
    of Kyalo
And Tshazhang Kyalo Trikor [Myriarchy of Nephews and
    Sons] of Kyalo
Can have whatever portion of land makes them happiest.

In the colorful valleys of Lower Ma, which are arranged like
    astrological charts,
Are the naturally originating playing[74] stones of the godly
    demons.[75]
This is a land where a great magician should abide.
This portion of land goes to Khache Migmar [Kashmir
    Red Eye].

In the rich valley of Ja-shingnag Markhu Yölwa [Rich
  Rainbow Forest],
Which is the central land of Upper and Lower Ma,
If you look up, you can see all the way to the source of the Ma
  River, and
If you look down you can see all the way down to the
  Turquoise Valley.
This is a land where a man of great decisiveness should abide.
This portion of land goes to the great arbiter Zuchen Werma.

In the upper part of Ma at Di-yag Tagthang [Tiger Plain
  Knolls]
Is the place where the people of the great provinces convene.
Where the travelers from China and Tibet stop over to rest
Is the one who is the guardian of the general wealth of the
  merchants
As well as the one who makes arrangements for the meetings
  of the cousins and brethren.
This is a land where one of great power should abide.
This portion of land goes to Wangpo Darphen [Powerful
  Unfurled Silk].

In Middle Ma at Lu-gu'i Tsera,
Whatever plants grow here are medicinal flowers
And the animals are permeated with the scent of medicinal
  herbs.
This is a place where a doctor should reside.
This portion of land goes to Künga Nyima [All-Joyful Sun].

Upon the colorful ridged mountains of Ma,
At the convergence of three great valleys and
The confluence of the fords of three great rivers,
Is the land where a diviner should reside.
This portion of land goes to Künshei Thigpo.

That mountain over there is Ab Mountain [Mole Mountain]
And this mountain here is Ur Mountain [Bird Mountain].

Where Ab and Ur merge
The scurrying groundhogs come close enough to be prey
And the neighboring grouse come close enough to be game.
This is a place where a poor man should reside.
This portion of land goes to Khyishi Gu-ru [Hunchback
     Dead Dog].

At the lower valley of Ma, where three Turquoise Valleys
     merge,
Is a land where there are more moles than lice
And a place where the wild yams are more delicious than any
     other.
The Chinese tea merchants go up the staircase, and
The Ladakhi merchants come back down.
If one is begging, this is where provisions for a journey will be
     acquired.
If one waits, then the marks of success will come.
This is a place where a beggar should reside.
This portion of land goes to me and my mother Gogmo.

Even though previously I was kicked out of Ling,
Once again, I will stay in Lower Ma:

Rather than having a belly full of undigested food,
Don't eat at all, keep an empty stomach.
Rather than accepting wages to carry a backbreaking load,
Wander the kingdom begging and enjoy inexhaustible food.
Rather than fathers and uncles lacking in affection,
Take delight in travelers who are free from love and hate.

In the divine ranks of the great tribes of White Ling,
I, the beggar boy, had no hope of staying.
However, I am part of the paternal lineage,
So my mind must turn with my clan.

Those who are penniless but still obsessed with business
Seem to have sold themselves out to debt.

The beggar who is starving but still attached to his relatives
Has sold out to their frank ridicule.

Even though I know this, I can't let the situation go.
Joru's welcoming gift for the six provinces
Is not lacking wealth, for it is a fortress and a treasure trove.
But saying it is great still does not mean that there is any way
    to divide it up individually.
Why, there's nothing to do but to let this be the general
    wealth of all.
Well then, brothers of White Ling,
For the Wishing Land of Ling with its prime dzo
    tea-bearers,
There is the land of Ma abounding in the six grains.
For the ancestral castle of Chöphen Nagpo
There is a fortress for the nine tiger cubs of the Greater
    Lineage
Called Kukhar Tazhi Zilnön [Fort that Quells the Four
    Borders with Its Splendor].
For the eight warriors of the Middle Lineage
There is Tsendzong Nyima Khyilwa [Shining Sun Secure Fortress].
For the seven brothers of the Lesser Lineage of Bumpa,
There is Kukhar Khyugtrug Tagtse [Garuḍa Chick Tiger
    Peak Fort].

Inwardly, erect the three supports,[*]
Outwardly, maintain the integrity of protection, and
Place the golden spirals at the peak.
All of this must be upheld just as sons must follow in the
    footsteps of their fathers.
Concerning Ngulchu-tro Dzong [Ormolu Fortress] of the
    Bumpas,
Trakhar Namdzong of Chipön,
Uncle's Be'u-tag Dzong [Tiger Gem Fortress] and others,

---

[*] The three supports are statues, scriptures, and stupas.

You must not squander the outer or inner wealth of these
   three.
From among the twelve myriarchies of the districts of Ling,
Here we will have fifty neighborhoods of a thousand families
   each.
The leaders will be the Thirty Brethren.
The Super Warriors, who are the seven holy men,
And the Ultimate Warriors, who are Falcon, Eagle, and
   Wolf, must take their seats.
In their own districts, fortresses, and political affairs, and so
   on,
They must have total sovereignty, as vast as the sky.
They must be as great and steadfast as the support of the
   earth.
When the bandits of Yellow Hor pass through here,
The people of the six provinces of Ling have no reason to
   confront them
Because, first, the owner of the land is Joru.
The origins of the dispute are connected to me;
I, Joru, will stand up and face them.
If you understood this story, it's sweet to your ears.
If not, there is no way to explain it.
White Ling, bear this in mind.

Thus he sang. All the people of Upper, Middle, and Lower Ling who were
sitting there declared, "Well, then, it's like that! Joru is of the ancestral lineage of
the Mukpo Dong!" Trothung of Tag-rong did not take much pleasure in this. But
Aten, Dongtsen [his sons], and others had been given very special portions of land.
Though Trothung himself let a vulgar expression flit across his face, in fact his portion of land had a lower narrow defile[76] and an upper open range, so that the nine
hundred tent dwellers of Tag-rong would be able to relocate in the summer and
winter, and it was known that everyone was very contented. From that day onward,
the worldly zodors of the land of Ma protected the Lingites, and the poor became
wealthy, while the meek became mighty.

   Then, on the fifteenth day, below the treasure portals of Magyal, Joru said he
was going to open the gates to the treasure fortress. All the people of the six districts
gathered. Flowers rained down from the sky; the sky became a dome of rainbow
clouds. On the earth a delicious fragrance permeated everywhere, accompanied by

countless wondrous signs. The treasure keeper came and offered him the key to open the lower treasure portal of Sheldrag. Opening the lower treasure portals, he revealed a golden Śākyamuni, a conch Avalokiteśvara, a self-originating Yuyi Drölma [Turquoise Tārā], Trim-dung Karmo Gyangdrag [White Conch of the Law Resounding Afar], Trim-nga Selwa'i Ödden [Drum of the Law Radiating Light], Silnyen Nyima Drugdrag [Hand Cymbals Sun Dragon Thunder], Trimdar Drala Tendung [Banner of the Law Drala-Gathering Lance], and the key to open the upper treasure portal of Sheldrag along with the treasure code. These seven precious treasure objects were escorted to Sengtrug Tagtse [Lion Cub Tiger Peak]* Castle, primarily by the Tag-rongs of the Greater Lineage and all the mighty warriors. He specifically asked the Tag-rongs of the Greater Lineage to escort the seven precious treasure objects to Sengtrug Tagtse Castle as the inner supports. These were the general gifts for the six tribes.

Then Joru mounted his staff and instantly arrived in Lower Ma, where the three Turquoise Valleys merge. All the Lingites were in a state of inconceivable delight, and they selected one man from each circuit of the great districts to become a servant of the fortresses. Two knowing, mighty warriors were chosen to head each group of twenty men, and they stayed there, diligently making prostrations, offerings, and circumambulations. Not only that, concerning the general wealth of Ling, the nāga vase and the twelve-volume *Prajñāpāramitā Scripture* of the nāgas written in gold, the blue nāga tent with nine partitions, a bronze statue of black Mahākāla, a black scarf with a self-originating protector, and other objects had been placed as general supports.

From the start, Father Senglön and Kyalo Tönpa Gyaltsen were entrusted as the first two leaders in charge. This set up the auspicious connection for the future, when the Lesser Lineage would be the principle guardian of Drugmo and the owner of Kyalo's wealth.

This has been the episode called *The Settling of Ma*, like *The Knotted White Scarf*.

At this time, most of the warriors built fortresses in Ma Valley using the examples and names of those from their respective clans. Readers should

---

* Same as Sengdrug Tagtse.

not get confused thinking that these castles are the same as the originals. It is evident that even though Chipön and the other elders may have built as many as six castles, most of them carry the same name, such as Trakhar Namdzong.

Among the accounts of the Great One Gesar Norbu Dradül, the episode of *The Settling of Ma* called *The Knotted White Scarf* is now complete.

AFTERWORD

The lord of the world Gesar Norbu Dradül
Is known as the Enlightened Divine One who brought peace
    and well-being to the land of Tibet.
May this praise, like the melodious strumming of a guitar,
Be laden with the express purpose that brings benefit and
    happiness.

Sengchen Norbu Dradül is the embodiment of the
    enlightened activity of the victorious ones
Whose smiling youthful moon of compassion
Beams exceptional loving-kindness upon the people of Tibet,
Causing the night-blooming flowers to blossom
With the stainless dharma of scriptural learning and
    realization;
Whose kindness even gives the fortunate bees cause to delight
    freely in the nectar of the siddhis.

The life stories of this Sublime One are as vast and deep as the
    ocean.
Although it is impossible for this rabbit of low intelligence to
    cross such an ocean,
This excellent account, which is like the moon, has arisen
    from the churning of my devotion to the ancestral lineage
To vividly appear in my mind, like the crown ornament of
    Shiva.

The corpus of this flowing biography
Is like the stainless body of the Sita River,*
Carrying silt as it bends and turns.
Whatever faults may have occurred through twisting the
    meaning, like the activities of the king of Lanka,†
Are released through the blessings of the Lord of the Family,
    Hanumanta,‡
And through the threefold scrutiny,§ the intelligence of King
    Ramana.¶

This accumulation of virtue is like the radiant moon that
    holds the rabbit,**
Shining on the minds of beings, which are like the great
    treasury of water [the ocean].
May this bring pure white waves of benefit and well-being
    that are ever-increasing,
And may this world be beautified by the doctrine of scriptural
    understanding and realization.

The dense darkness of the suffering of all beings
Is completely dispelled by the buddha activity of the jewel of
    the sky [sun].
May the youthful lotus of the glorious age of perfection
Be free to smile.

---

* This is one of the four great rivers of Jambudvīpa.

† This refers to the chief hero in the epic known as the *Ramayana*, King Lanka, who was dishonest.

‡ Hanuman is the monkey warrior in the epic of *Ramayana*, the devoted general and messenger of Rama.

§ Threefold scrutiny means three forms of logic, which are inferential understanding, confidence in inferential understanding, and direct understanding.

¶ This refers to the Vedic epic about King Ramana. For those who are familiar with the epic, the author of this afterword is applying the subject of his praise to the examples that are similar in this famous Indo-Vedic epic.

** "Holder of the rabbit" is a poetic epithet for the moon. The imagery of Vedic poetry includes a rabbit within the moon, much as in the West there is the image of the man in the moon.

In this and all my future lifetimes
May the lotus feet of the Great Lion of Men,
Be placed on my crown like a flower diadem
And may I become a guide for limitless sentient beings.

Author's note:

Even though it may be that there are many different traditional biographical accounts of the great Lord Gesar, this account represents the unbroken ancestral lineage of Bumpa Zhalkar from the kingdom of Dokham Ling. What is clearly expressed here has arisen from the authentic ancient manuscripts of the ancestors of earlier generations. Based on that, in this version all illogical information as well as any scribal spelling errors have been eliminated. Then, by comparing this version with the Trung Ling documented by Bu-lha Norbu, I was able to complete this text. In particular, according to this text, the recognition of [King Gesar's] birthplace is Kyidsö, which is in harmony with the uncommon wisdom intent of the Great Tertön Chog-gyur Lingpa, the Venerable Guru Mipham Jampel Gyepei Dorje, the vidyādhara Drodül Pawo Dorje, the Great Tertön Lerab Lingpa, and others. Even though this recognition can be proven through scriptural authority, and confidence is thereby established, now is not the time to elaborate upon this; it will be discussed elsewhere. Not only that, I was also able to personally take in the following sites, like nectar for my eyes, such as Gyaza's tent site, Joru's footprint, the spring of his life lake, Amnye Gompa Raja's cave at the lower valley of Drag-nag [Black Crag], Kyigyal Tagri, and the thirteen streams and valleys of Kyi [Kyidsö].*

This authentic biography, documented by logic, words, and meaning, was written at the request of the lord of men, the earth guardian king of White Ling, who was honored with the name Wangchen Tendzin Chögyi Gyalpo Chimed Drubpei Dei by the Terchen Lama Rinpoche [Great Treasure Finder Precious Guru] Jamyang Kyentse Wangpo, like placing a diadem of flowers on the crown of his head. This king bestowed the gift of these ancient texts, writing materials, a scarf, a flower of the second precious substance [silver], and others upon me. With these gifts the king then conferred upon the crown of my head the command to write this, and I accepted that command with faith and devotion.

Through the power of receiving in my heart a small portion of the compassionate blessings of the supreme deity himself, I felt that the doubts concerning this

---

* An error in the original Tibetan text shows this as *lci* (heavy), but it should be *skyid* (happiness).

text had been primarily severed. I have read four of five different accounts of *The Birth in Ling*; however, doing so has only served to further increase my trust in this one. Placing the dust from the feet of the great sublime teachers as the ornament upon my crown, including the powerful scholar of Tibet the Venerable Guru Mipham Jampel Gyepei Dorje, the Terchen Lerab Lingpa, the Vidyādhara Drodül Pawo Dorje, and many others, and with the fortunate mind to partake of the ambrosia of their enlightened speech, I, this ordinary person, a vagrant monk known as Gyurmed Thubten Jamyang Dragpa, wrote this with the prayer that the precious doctrine of the victorious ones may be exalted to the peak of existence.

SARVA MAṄGALAM.

May it be virtuous!

VOLUME THREE

*Gesar Wins the Horse Race
and Becomes the King of Ling*

PART THREE CONTENTS

The Narrative Content of the Seven Chapters

I. A magical prophecy causes Trothung to be misled by false appearances. He discusses having a horse race to compete for the sevenfold wager. The people of White Ling gather and agree with his plan. This gives rise to the Saga of the Precious Wheel.

II. Zhalu Karpo sends Drugmo to invite Joru. They meet at Lower Ma valley. Obstacles are cleared, and auspicious connections set. This gives rise to the Saga of the Precious Queen.

III. On Joru's command, Sengcham Drugmo is sent to catch the divine horse. She accomplishes her mission. Wild Sorrel is offered to his owner and the horse's attributes are praised. This gives rise to the Saga of the Precious Supreme Steed.

IV. Joru is invited to upper White Ling. Drugmo offers him the golden saddle and other requisite accoutrements and supplicates by the truth of the eight great prayers.[1] This gives rise to the Saga of the Precious Minister.

V. The contest of the horse race between the fathers and uncles of White Ling gets under way. Joru, in disguise, goes to the end of the line. Drugmo introduces the men and their horses. This gives rise to the Saga of the Precious Elephant.

VI. During the competition of the horse race Joru subdues demons and devils and foils Trothung's fooling. Diviners, doctors, and others are put to the test. This gives rise to the Saga of the Precious General.

VII. Joru obtains victory in the contest of the horse race. He is enthroned on a golden throne; gods and humans offer him auspicious prayers. The name Gesar Norbu Dradül is conferred upon him. This gives rise to the Saga of the Precious Jewel.

VIII. Colophon

PROLOGUE

The Account of the Horse Race of the Great Lion Being of Jambudvīpa, called *The Sevenfold Jeweled Mirror:*[2]

> NAMO GURU MAHĀ SENGHA MAṆIRAJAYE
> The essence of the three secrets[3] of all the victorious ones, the
>   kāya with the major and minor marks,
> Blossoming atop[4] a thousand petals in the milky lake of the
>   southwest,
> In this pure land, I bow down to the guru who reveals
> The path of the essential definitive secret through his
>   wondrous and magical deeds.
> In the lake of the view free from the elaborations of the eight
>   extremes,[5]
> Where Takshaka* always abides in a state of meditation.
> You who have mastered the treasure jewel of the three
>   trainings,
> Spiritual guide known as Śāntarakṣita, please protect us.
>
> In this dark land of Tibet, a land of Masang demons,
> All beings are tormented by the three sufferings.[6]
> Lord Trisong Deutsen, you brought forth the white law of
>   the ten virtues, the moonlight of benefit and well-being,
> Through the chariot of your buddha activity.
> By virtue of your knowledge you are Mañjuśrī who dispels
>   ignorance;

---

* There are eight classes of nāgas, and Takshaka is a king of one of the eight.

311

By your loving-kindness you are the Lord of the World
    [Avalokiteśvara] who accomplishes the welfare of others;
By your power you are the Lord of Secrets [Vajrapāṇi] who
    conquers the hordes of māras;
To the embodiment of these three protectors, to you Great
    Lion King, I pay homage.
You, an expert when it comes to this life story,
Have opened the eight inexhaustible treasures of courageous
    eloquence;[7]
Jampel Gyepei Dorje [Mipham Rinpoche], may you always
    grant protection,
May your wisdom eyes guard the doctrine and sentient
    beings.
The meaning of the vajra words, your secret speech
Will be clearly presented here in this Jeweled Mirror
The Account of the Horse Race of White Ling,
Explicating these wondrous deeds in the sevenfold
    categories.[8]

THE NARRATIVE CONTEXT*

The renown of the name Gesar Norbu Dradül resounds like a drum roll throughout the four corners of Jambudvīpa. Even though his life stories are inconceivable, the principle sagas are: *The Birth in Ling, The Horse Race,* and *the Four Sagas of Subjugation: Düd, Hor, Mön, and Jang.* The *Account of the Horse Race of White Ling* is based on the faultless meaning of the vajra verses composed by Lord Guru Mipham Jampel Gyepei Dorje in a prayer he wrote called *The Wondrous Biography: The Symbolic Secret Jeweled Mirror.* This account is not only an authoritative source, it is also a manifestation of Mipham's vast enlightened mind coupled with the Great Lion Being himself. Not only that, he [Mipham] promised in all his lives to manifest as king [Gesar] as well as his ministers. Therefore, the points expressed in these verses come from remembrance of previous lives or mind terma, which are teachings drawn from the Sky Treasury Division of the Dharma.[9] Due to the kindness of flawlessly receiving these unbroken transmissions from the Aural Lineage [Great

---

* What follows is an introductory commentary added by the original editors, any clarifications that we, the current translators, have added appears in brackets.

Treasure Revealer of Ling] and the compassionate enlightened activity of the Great Lion Being himself, I intend to openly explain the profound meaning of the vajra words by explicating this in the form of a commentary that describes the meaning in a way easy to comprehend.*

First the homage:

> OM SVASTI
> Within the play that accomplishes welfare and well-being in
>   Jambudvīpa,
> Through the blazing glory of the garland of light rays of the
>   wisdom jewel,
> The great and powerful sorcerer has subjugated the enemy
>   demons of the dark side.
> Supreme Being Great Lion King, grant auspiciousness.

This single śloka explicitly reveals the homage, while implicitly presenting the entire meaning of *The Birth in Ling* and *The Settling of Ma*. In this passage [the first line of the śloka] the continent Jambudvīpa refers generally to the field of disciples and specifically to the land that is recognized as the birthplace [of Gesar]. Although generally there is no limit to the faculties and realms of beings, Jambudvīpa is recognized specifically as the field where he will tame his disciples through the four enlightened activities [pacifying, enriching, magnetizing, and destroying]. The region of White Ling in Dokham will be tamed through the three: pacifying, enriching, and magnetizing. Düd, Hor, Mön, and Jang, these four, will be tamed through wrathful activity, along with the lands of Persia, and others. Regardless of the manner of taming, reference [in the śloka] to accomplishing **benefit** and **well-being** refers to the purpose of the appearance of the rūpakāya. Although in every country there are opportunities to tame through the four enlightened activities, from the perspective of the principal activity this was directed toward the impure perceptions of those who dwell in the land of White Ling, namely their bias and competitive nature, which was suppressed through splendor, intimidating, and overcoming. Through all of these three enlightened deeds, he [Gesar] brought benefit by pacifying the pitfalls of turmoil through reversing temporary confused perceptions.

---

* "I" here refers to one of the original editors of the epic, Gyurmed Thubten Jamyang Dragpa, who composed this section entitled "The Narrative Context."

Ultimately, having satisfied them with the amṛta of the dharma that accords with an individual's fortune, he [Gesar] brought them the relief of the **accomplishment** of the spontaneous state of untainted bliss.

The demon lords and ministers who took rebirth due to their perverted prayers and wrong views had led the beings dwelling in the lands of Düd, Hor, Mön, Jang, Persia, and so forth, on an irrevocable path of killing, warfare, and conflict. When Gesar defeated them, the instigators of the wars of the age were actually tamed, the continuity of their armed conflict was cut off, and in that way he brought temporary benefit to them. Ultimately, having fully embraced great compassion, and not contradicting the inner meaning of the three ways to satisfy,[10] he simultaneously slayed and guided them [to higher states of rebirth and liberation]. It was thus that he spontaneously established these beings in a state of immaculate bliss. This is how Gesar revealed the reasons for the manifestation of the rūpakāya.

Hence the spontaneously present rūpakāya of benefit and well-being manifests through root causes and contributing circumstances, so it is referred to as having manifested. The cause of the **play** of joyful pleasure is both Senglön, the father of the clan, and Gedzo, the lord of the Nyen. The condition is the mother nāgī, who united with them in coemergent union. This brought about the condition for Gesar to enter his mother's womb, although the fact that he was unsullied by the obscurations of the womb is what is referred to by the words mentioned in the second line of the verse, a **blazing wisdom jewel**. Just as when a wish-fulfilling jewel is underground, its nature is always free from the fault of increase or decline, likewise [Gesar] was always free from any stain of faults. Not only had he perfected all the noble qualities of the rūpakāya, he had inherently perfected the powers of wisdom. This is comparable to a blazing jewel. Reference to the **garland of light rays** refers to the deeds performed from the time of his birth all the way up to the horse race.

When a wish-fulfilling jewel is still underground, it does not radiate light. As soon as it is taken from the earth, the light rays will arise unimpeded. Likewise, this reveals that at the moment of his birth his qualities arose unceasingly. Although the essential quality of a wish-fulfilling jewel is that it fulfills whatever wishes mind desires, nevertheless in this context that is not the main point. Here the radiance of light rays is reference to the display of his manifest qualities, such as his birth, the settling of the land of Ma, and all the events up to the horse race, which he performed in disguise through his yogic conduct as deeds that accomplished the benefit of beings. All of these unceasing enlightened activities performed [by Gesar] in the aspect of Joru are represented by the metaphor of the garland of light rays. His true bodily form and, similarly, the extent of his noble qualities were not revealed, but rather, until the moment he settled the land of Ma, he disguised his natural qualities and accomplished the benefit of beings by engaging in many feats based on magic.

The words the **dark side** refer to the māras of nonvirtue. As a result they are karmically destined to be reborn in the lower realms. That, combined with the circumstances of their perverted prayers, causes these creatures of the class of nonhumans to possess the power to be able to lead sentient beings along the wrong path. All such beings are generally considered to be of the dark side. He tamed those specifically considered to be members of the class of **demons**: Black Bird; Amnye Gompa; Vulture Demon; Colt Demon; Khase Rulu; the cannibal demoness Child Eater; Trothung, who was both overtly and covertly the hateful **enemy**; and the māras, Hor, and so forth. Reference to the **Great Powerful Sorcerer** means that, not only did he just slay and expel these warriors, he also intimidated, suppressed, and overcame them. In doing so his ability to benefit others through astonishing power and strength became unrivaled. This is a summary of the majority of his deeds while he was still known as Joru.

Furthermore, the passage that **Supreme Being** implicitly shows how the main emphasis of his supreme life story is the enlightened deeds that he performed from the time of his birth until the land of Ma was settled. Among his many names, reference to the name Great Lion King shows the fact that, although his ability and power to quell others through splendor was primordially complete, still, according to the ordinary perception of beings, his powers appeared to gradually mature, like the qualities that are innate within a lion cub. When a lion cub reaches maturity, its strength is complete and it naturally follows that it becomes the king of all wild animals of the jungle. Likewise, when the time was right, he [Gesar] became the king of White Ling; how this came about will be told in the course of the *Account of the Horse Race of White Ling*. Saying Supreme Being Great Lion King, **grant auspiciousness**, refers to the content of his life story during the period when, through his enlightened deeds, he actually becomes the king of Jambudvīpa.[11] This passage also indicates the prayer that uninterrupted peace and virtue be granted to the minds of those to come in future generations who will read and sustain this epic.

The extensive meaning of this homage was already explained in the contents of *The Birth in Ling: The Flower Garden,* and *The Settling of Ma: The Knotted White Scarf.*

When Gesar abandons his yogic conduct of poor attire and ugly body, the manner in which he reveals the actual rūpakāya just as it is will be explained in the verses:

At the moment the lotus appears from the mud,
The garland of lightning dawns in the center of the red
　　mirror.

Thus, these verses present the meaning of the horse race.

Recounting *The Horse Race: The Sevenfold Jeweled Mirror* begins with a prophecy and a playful game, as reflected in the Saga of the Precious Wheel. The way Drugmo goes to invite him [Joru, back to Ling for the horse race] is reflected in the Saga of the Precious Queen. The story of how the horse is captured is reflected in the Saga of the Precious Supreme Steed. The story of acquiring and taking possession of the horse's gear is reflected in the Saga of the Precious Minister. The account of how a disguised Joru entered the race of White Ling at the back of the line, displayed magical emanations to tame whoever needed taming, and instantly traversed the paths and stages[12] is reflected in the Saga of the Precious Elephant. The way he sought out his opponents and challenges, quelling humans and nonhumans with his splendor, is reflected in the Saga of the Precious General. Achieving the sovereignty of the golden throne, the way in which he accomplishes the deeds of gaining the admiration of gods and humans is reflected in the Saga of the Precious Rūpakāya Wish-Fulfilling Jewel. These are the seven [chapters].

CHAPTER ONE

A magical prophecy causes Trothung to be misled by false
    appearances;
He discusses having a horse race to compete for the sevenfold
    wager.
The people of White Ling gather and agree with his plan.
This gives rise to the Saga of the Precious Wheel.

FIRST OF ALL, to invoke the wisdom intent of the one to subdue the evil Düd,
the yoke upon the Yellow Hor, the destined savior of the black-haired Tibetans, the
supreme being of Jambudvīpa, Gesar Norbu Dradül himself, was called forth from
the higher gods, supplicated by the humans of the middle realm and assisted by the
nāgas of the lower realm. He was born as the son of the union of the three: nāga,
nyen, and humans in Eastern Upper Sparkling Ling in Kyidsö Yag-gi Khado.

While still a child, until he was five years old, in the Dri and Dza valleys, he
bound by oath all the formless beings of the dark side. Then when he reached six
years of age, his uncontrived yogic conduct caused the people of White Ling to lose
faith in him. At the age of eight, he settled the land of Ma, overcame White Ling,
captured the Chinese and Tibetan merchants, and emptied the place of the pikas.
Given that the predetermined time had not yet arrived, the dralas and wermas of
Ling influenced the minds of the people of Ling. Because of that, the devotion they
once had toward the joyful awakened sublime being Joru as their guru was now
scarce; their respect for him as a lineage chieftain had waned, and they hardly re-
tained any love for him even as a relative. So he [was banished] to Yulung Sumdo
in Lower Ma, the place where demons twirl their batons of fate, and tsen throw

their dice and stones; the place where menmo* perform the dramas of their dances. It is there that he remained with his mind dwelling in unchanging luminosity. He would reveal myriad nirmāṇakāya emanations at once, emanation bodies that could be seen by the disciples according to what was necessary for them to see. During the day he joked around with humans; in the evening he shot craps with the tsen; and at night he challenged the demons to games of dice. He [Joru] ran races with the gods and conversed with the demons. When he reached the age of twelve, in the year of the Earth Horse, toward dawn on the eighth day of the Iron Tiger month, Auntie Nammen Karmo appeared to him, riding upon a white lioness, accompanied by a hundred thousand clairvoyant ḍākinīs. And she sang this prophecy to Joru:

> The song is Ala Ala Ala
> And Thala Thala Thala.
> Ala is the source of the lyrics
> And Thala is the melody of the song.
> Now then, Joru, divine child,
> Listen to your auntie's song.
>
> In this vast plain of patterned fields
> Blue-green stalks of grain have shot up;
> Unless they are adorned with a good harvest
> The shoots are nothing but forage,
> Their burgeoning growth of no avail.
> In the high azure tent of the sky
> The constellations glitter;
> Unless they are beautified by the full moon,
> The stars are merely guides in the darkness,
> Their many clusters of no use.
>
> In the land of Colorful Sparkling Ling,
> Those myriad magical emanations of Joru,
> Unless you take your place as a chief of White Ling,
> Will merely add further scandal [to your name].
> It is as if your signs of accomplishment were merely to one-up
> your paternal uncle.

---

* Menmo (Tib. *sman mo*) are female demons.

The supreme horse of the land of Uḍḍiyāṇa
Is in the northern wilderness of the *kyangs;*
It is the same age as you, young Joru.
If you do not take possession of it this year,
The horse may vanish in a rainbow body.

Your wife, ordained by the gods,
Is to be Kyalo's Sengcham Drugmo.
Unless she becomes your bride this year,
There is the risk that she will marry Tag-rong's son.
If she weds him, the gate to your enlightened deeds will be
    disturbed.

Tomorrow in the predawn light,
Bring down to Mazhi Chieftain Trothung
A false prophecy from Hayagrīva,
Which says to Tag-rong that he must host a festive gathering
    of the brethren,
And that, if he wagers that the rider of the fastest steed
Will gain the position of chief and win Drugmo and a
    treasure trove,
It is then certain that Turquoise Bird will break the silken
    ribbon first
And Trothung will become the master of the bride Drugmo.

You must capture the steed with the lasso of great emptiness[13]
And acquire the fairest of maidens through myriad
    emanations.
It's best to tan a mighty tiger's skin;
Do not damage it for it will be useful as an ornament for the
    six smiles.[14]
If you understand this, it's sweet to the ears.
If not, there is no way to explain it.

Thus she sang, and Joru thought, "The only time my true form appeared to
anyone was when my mother saw me at birth, for otherwise I am concealed like a
lotus encased in mud, sitting here with this poor attire and this ugly body. Indeed,
this alone will not bring benefit to others. Although the time may have arrived for

my true form to appear, I still need to perform many unconventional yogic activities in order to gain the kingship with my horse [Noble Steed]."

Joru knew that before he could manifest the rūpakāya, he must join the festive horse race. Trothung was staying in solitary retreat[15] in the Ancient Black Fortress,[16] and as he was diligently engaged in the approach and accomplishment practices,[17] visualizing Red Hayagrīva in the single-pointed mirror of his mind, at about midnight on the ninth day, Joru manifested to Trothung as a crow. He proclaimed this false prophecy like a garland of lightning. In a state of altered awareness, this is what Trothung heard intermingled with dreaming, meditating, and wakefulness:

> It's Ala Ala Ala.
> Thala is the melody of the song.
> This land is called Be'u-tag Dzong [Tiger Gem Fortress].
> If you want to know who I am,
> I am the Red Hayagrīva.
> Don't sleep! Do you understand, Chief Tag-rong?
> According to an ancient Tibetan proverb:

> *That which waits for the southern clouds verging on seasonal rains*
> *Are the patterned fields.*
> *Until the blue grain has covered the earth,*
> *The seasonal rains must be delayed.*
> *It does not matter whether the winter snow falls or not.*

> The one who is pursuing the blessings of Red Hayagrīva
> Is King Trothung of Tag-rong.
> Until the great goal is in the palm of your hand,
> The prophecy must be delayed.
> It does not matter whether you listen to a false prophecy or not.

> Beginning tomorrow morning,
> The brethren of White Ling will gather
> In a festival, without regard to high or low station
> And the Tag-rong family must prepare for the occasion.
> Kyalo's Sengcham Drugmo,
> The treasure trove of the sevenfold jewels,
> And the throne of colorful Ling;
> These you must wager on the rider of the fastest steed.

The bridegroom of Sengcham Drugmo,
And the one who will attain the honorable golden throne,
Can be none other than Tag-rong.
Among the thirty karmically destined horses of the brethren
    of Ling
The fastest steed will open the great pathway.
That can be none other than Turquoise Bird.
Waste no doubt on this prophecy.

The best among men who place trust in their gods
Will turn out as certain as the rising of the sun in the azure
    firmament.
The middling among men who place trust in their chieftain
Will turn out free to stay in whatever land makes them happy.
The inferior among men who place trust in a wicked woman
Will only be brought down, since a wicked woman and a river never
    move upward.

If you understood these words, hold them in your mind,
If not, there is no way to further explain this prediction.

Thus he sang, and Trothung made abundant offerings of gold, silver, the select offering of food, and various grains. Considering that each of Hayagrīva's previous predictions hadn't been completely accurate, he still had a little doubt about this one. Just then, as he glanced at the raven, the raven dissolved into his statue of Hayagrīva on the altar. He gained confidence in the prophecy and suddenly stood up and sang this song to [his wife] Denza in the short and impetuous melody of Hara Hurthung:[*]

It's Ala Ala Ala.
It's Thala Thala Thala.
May the Gekhong[†] secret assembly of deities

---

[*] There is no way to literally translate "Hara Hurthung," which means singing a song in a rough and frantic manner.

[†] Bön deities are addressed because Trothung practiced a mixture of Buddhist and indigenous traditions.

Lead this song of Tag-rong.
In case you don't recognize this place,
It is Raven Heart Fortress.
I am the chieftain Trogyal of Tag-rong,
And this song is in the tune of Harmin Hur.
I would not sing this song, if it were not an important
    occasion.
Don't sleep! Do you understand, Lady of the Golden Lake?

There is no benefit for one who sleeps.
How could there be? Just look at a stone.
A piece of solid rock just lies there and becomes encrusted with dirt,
A tree trunk just lies there and its roots rot.
If the fatherly guru lies there, the dharma activities will be idle.
If the honorable dear chieftain lies there, the lawful decisions will be
    idle.
If the tigers in their prime lie there, the enemy will rear its head.
If a maiden lies there, she will be expelled from the household.

This morning during my early meditation session
The Northern God [Hayagrīva] gave me a prophetic
    pronouncement
To gather the brethren of the six provinces
And the people of White Ling to a festival.
He said that I, Tag-rong, must be the host.
And that if the golden throne, the treasure trove, and
    Drugmo as well
Are the stakes wagered on the rider of the fastest steed,
The winner will be the bridegroom of Kyalo's Sengcham,
And will take his seat upon the golden throne.
This will be none other than I, Tag-rong.

Personal power and precious gold—
The more you have them, the higher you go;
Both belong above to ornament your head.
Shameless friends and dirty boots—
The more you have them, the lower you go;
Leave them behind when you reach the gate.

I have even more analogies if you want them:

If you reach for something, don't let your hand be clumsy;
If you run somewhere, don't let your knees tremble.
The great flag of divine accomplishment
Must not be stained by corruption.
The stainless white copper pot of auspicious connection
Must be not be tarnished by the verdigris of samaya violation.

Don't sleep, quickly prepare for the festivities.
Get numbers of yak loads of sweet cakes
And prepare a hundred lamb carcasses.
There must be an inexhaustible supply of potent drink,
And the three types of teas called flower tea, milk tea, and
    highland tea.
Present them in the copper pot Tashi Kyilwa
And flavor them with white salt from the north.
Make them rich with the essence of the third summer's milk.

When the treasure wealth of a great chieftain
Is kept, it doesn't increase; but when given away, it does.
The food and clothes of one without merit
Need not be worn to wear out or eaten to run out.

[In the same way],

If you meet up with your true love,
There is no way to still be concerned about the cherished wealth.

If you understand this, it is sweet to your ears.
If you don't, there's no way to explain it.

Thus he sang, and Denza thought carefully, "It's well known that Gogmo's
Joru was ordained by the gods to be the destined bridegroom of Drugmo, the master of Kyalo's wealth, and the chief of White Ling; Tag-rong will not seize all of this.
This prophetic vision of Trothung's seems to be the magical deception of Joru. Even
though he probably won't give ear to my honest speech, I must try to speak out so
that I will have no future regrets." With this in mind, she sang this song:

It's Ala Ala Ala
And Thala Thala Thala.
If you don't know this place,
This place is the castle of Tag-rong.
If you don't recognize me,
I am the daughter of the king of Den
And the housewife of Chief Tag-rong.
Although I don't know the prophecy of the Northern God,
If I guessed, I'll bet I could get it right.
Here in the Ancient Black Fortress
That hoarse caw of the midnight raven[18]
Seems to be either a magical illusion of the māras
Or the neurotic upheavals of godly demons;
That cannot be called a prophetic vision.
When samādhi is lacking during sleeping,
How can there be a true prophecy in the dream state?
When just arising from bed with no daily practice,
How can the face of the meditation deity appear?
This seems not to be a prophetic vision but
A false demonic prophecy set up by Joru.
Ill omens are misfortune's guide,
So I choose not to prepare for such an occasion.
According to the well-known ancient saying:

Going to bed commends us to the fall of darkness,
The period of darkness commends sentient beings to slumber,
Getting out of bed commends us to the white sun,
And daytime commends us to our daily chores.

These are called the fourfold commends of humankind.
When Chieftain King Trothung
Is chased from behind by desire,
He can't wait for the darkness of nightfall to enter his bed;
When you are led around by your obstacles,
You can't even wait for sunrise to get up.
Don't let it be like this; tonight just rest;
When the sun rises, early tomorrow morning,
You can discuss matters and decide what must be done.

First, Anu Zigphen of Tag-rong,
Second, Dongtsen Nang-ngu Apel [Mighty Youthful Glory
    of the Tribe][19]
And third, young son Nya-tsha Aten.
Headed by these three brothers,
The ministers of Tag-rong, like a colorful tiger's lair,
Should gather to see if their minds are in accord;
If the minds of men and divine prophecy concur,
Then I will consider planning for the festival.
But still, here are a few analogies to consider:

The white garuḍa dzo, appointed to carry
A burden of six loads of tea,
Had better know exactly how to bear the load.
The noble stallion appointed to run,
Saddle and bridle inseparable from its body,
Had better know exactly how to proceed.

Since you, King Trothung, have been appointed to receive the
    Northern God's messages,
By now you have received many a prophecy;
You'd better know exactly what siddhis you get from this.
If my song has brought confusion, I confess the fault.
If my speech has been meaningless, I beg your forgiveness.

When the song was finished, she sat herself down. Although Denza's words bore some weight with Trothung, his desire for Drugmo surpassed that, for Drugmo's countenance was so mesmerizing that he was constantly losing his eyes to her face and his mind to her body. Even though he did not intentionally try to think of her, her form appeared vividly in his mind. Not only that, Hayagrīva's prophecy seemed to promise that he would also gain great siddhis, which was just what Trothung was hoping for, and above all, the dralas and wermas brought down great blessings of desire for Drugmo in the minds of not only Trothung but all other brethren as well. When they went to bed they were unable to sleep, and when they got up they were so distracted that they all suffered indigestion. He began to wonder if everyone would wager on this race or not. If so, then from among the thirty karmically destined horses of the brethren of White Ling, the one who will be the winner of the race is none other than Turquoise Bird, who is the fastest steed and the mount to open up the great pathway. Trothung thought these words must surely be true. Therefore there is no doubt that Turquoise Bird will be the first to break the silken ribbon. He thought that, once Drugmo was brought into his home, it would no longer be possible for him to stay there with Denza, so he felt he should sever their relationship immediately by blaming her for trying to ruin the auspicious connection of the prophecy. "Besides," he thought, "if I were to cast Denza out after Drugmo had already arrived in my home, people would say that I, Trothung, had no conscience and that Drugmo was a brainless [that is, careless and thoughtless] girl. An enormous scandal would ensue."

Having thought about it, Trothung spoke to Denza, "Now, you quarrelsome bitch, you've struck the golden stupa of this prophecy with your ax of evil words, and you've tossed the ashes of your false omens in the face of the dralas of auspicious connection. This chief of Tag-rong cares for you no longer," he said, and sang this song:

> It's Ala Ala Ala,
> And Thala is the melody of the song.
> God of the North, Red Hayagrīva, know me.
> Assist Tag-rong in his song
> And see that I get whatever I want.
> Denza, your poisonous tongue is always flapping.
> Listen, here are some analogies for you to consider.
> Your mind is so deluded you think that the compassion of the
>   imperial gods is unclear
> And that you, Denza, know more.
> You say that the prophecy of the emanation of Hayagrīva
> Is a bad omen, misfortune's guide.
> [Your doubts] have disordered the gateway of good fortune.
> The only reason I don't cut off your mouth and nose for this
> Is that we've lived together and had nine sons.
> The moment Sengcham arrives
> At the inner castle of Tiger Fortress,
> You should place in her hands
> The keys to the treasury, the jewel case, and the bedroom,
>   these three.
> The handle of the spoon, the ladle, and the cup,[20]
> You can keep in your own hands.[21]
> Or if not, if you want to go far away, then you should go.

In the three months of spring, wrathful wrinkles in the ice
Can't help but thaw for they are chased away[22] by the warmth.
In the three months of autumn, the frenzy to harvest the lentils and
  grain
Can't be helped, for the harvest is chased by the frost.

Denza, who resents the gods,
Will now have no choice but to wander off alone.
When the sun of Sengcham arises
It will then be time for this homely owl to fly away.
The divine flower of Sengcham
Ornaments the lake of the great province of Tag-rong;
Nectar for the eyes of those who behold her,
To be partaken of and enjoyed by the bee, Trogyal.
You, Denza, but a meadow flower
Blooming on the plains, think you are beautiful,
But the hoarfrost of age chases after you.
You are but a path for people to tread on.
Although this may be sad, there is no need to feel regret, for
    this is the decree of karma.
Concerning the treasure trove of Tag-rong's food,
If your hands are too clumsy for the work,
There is no need for you, Denza, to be there, just go your way.

My daughter Tromo-tso [Wrathful Lake],
Playmate of Sengcham Drugmo,
Must now quickly prepare for the festival.
You, the messenger Akhöd Tharpa Zorna,
Don't linger but go without delay
To upper Dil-yak Tiger Plain [Good Hill Tiger Plain]
And strike the great gong of the law
And quickly sound the loud conch of the law.
Take particular care to inform Gyatsha and
Formally invite Chief Zigphen.
Tell them that before the hailstorm of the other districts
Steals away the radiant lotus of Sengcham's smile,
I think that Kyalo's daughter as well as his wealth should be
    wagered along with

> The sevenfold jewels of the treasure trove
> As the prize for the fastest horse.
> This great festival to celebrate a noble goal
> Will be arranged by the Tag-rong clan.
> Let us invite all the brethren to join in.
> We will deliberate on the tenth day of the waxing moon;
> The horse race will be held on the fifteenth.
> These are my plans; please discuss them among yourselves.
> If you have understood this, it is sweet to your ears.
> If not, there is no way to explain it.

Denza thought, "A proverb tells us:

> *Just as karma from past lifetimes cannot be sidestepped,*
> *Wrinkles on one's forehead cannot be erased.*

That's just what this is like: I can't separate from my previous karmic connection with Trothung. Day or night I've always spoken to him with an open heart, yet not only does he not listen, he keeps on getting angry. Perhaps it is useless to try to explain myself." Hence she just gave up and began making preparations for the festival.

Akhöd Tharpa Zorna rushed off to sound the gong and the conch of the law. Besides Gyatsha Zhalkar, he invited all of Upper Ling with *ki!* and all of lower Ling with *so!* He made sure that Gyatsha was told, and he extended a personal invitation to Zigphen. So, when the highest mountains donned their golden hats, the Thirty Mighty Warriors, the Seven Super Warriors, and the Three Ultimate Warriors—Falcon, Eagle, and Wolf—all came together, just as the fine red tiger rises from his lair. They came thronging with drala flags on their threefold panoply, pennants flapping on their helmets, longevity knots billowing behind from their cloaks, the swift-gaited horses dazzling in formation. Once they had all arrived, Akhöd Tharpa Zorna began to relate the details of the planned festival in Tag-rong and recounted how Trothung had received the prophecy. He sang this song in the melody of A Gently Flowing River:

> The song is Ala Ala Ala.
> Thala is the melody.
> May the Three Refuges of guru, yidam, and ḍākinī
> Remain inseparable as my crown ornament.
> Dwelling there, may blessings be bestowed.

If you don't recognize this place
It is the gathering place of upper Tiger Plain,
Tshogs-sa A-lung Rawa [Assembly Ground Circle
    Enclosure].
If you don't recognize me,
I am known as Akhöd Tharpa Zorna.
I am the personal minister of Chieftain Tag-rong.
I have been sent here on an important mission
That concerns the political affairs of White Ling.

The night before last, in the predawn hour,
The chieftain of Tag-rong, Trothung, received
This prophecy from the God of the North:
In the rich field of Father Kyalo,
Grows the sprout of well-born Drugmo;
Now her youth has reached maturity like the six grains.
If the brethren don't know how to hold and cherish her,
It is said she will be carried away by the hail of foreign
    districts.
The golden throne, the status of king, along with
    Drugmo—
These precious jewels of the ocean of White Ling,
Will be received in reliance upon the ship of the noble steed.
If the karmic windhorse[23] of whoever is the fastest is placed
    atop the victory banner,
It is said that they will be honored by reaping all that is
    desired.
Now hear the command of mighty Tag-rong:
Today, on the excellent occasion of the tenth day,
Let us gather to celebrate and discuss the festivities;
On the fifteenth day the noble steeds should line up for the
    race.
What does everyone think?

In order to make a plan, invite the brethren to be seated in
    their ranks for the celebration.
Not idling I have come as the assiduous servant.
There is a well-known proverb of the ancient ones:

A beautiful maiden as a life companion
Many desire, but few receive.
The harvest of saṃsāric happiness
Many think feasible, but few reap.

With arrow, horse, or dice,
Of course you go all-out, hoping to win;
Whether you win or lose is your previous karma.
There's not a single chief in White Ling
Who doesn't fancy Sengcham Lotus Garland.
If only each one of you could win her!
It's such a shame that there can be only a single winner.
Even if you three great chiefs [Senglön, Trothung, and
      Chipön] and the mighty warriors
Were to beseech Kyalo Tönpa Gyaltsen at once,
There would be no way for him to bestow her.
In China, India, and Yellow Hor,
Sengcham appears like food to the hungry.
Therefore the youthful warriors should agree that,
No matter who wins this prize, they will have no regret.
I think this would align with the prophecy of the gods and
      accord with the wishes of humans.
I mean no disrespect; this is just how it is.
If you heard this song, it is an offering ornament to your ears.
If not, there's no way to explain it.

Thus he sang, and although Gyatsha, Darphen, Sengtag, and most of the war-riors saw no problem with the wager itself, nevertheless, given that Trothung had said that the reward would go to the winner of the horse race, they realized that Tag-rong's son Dongtsen's horse, Turquoise Bird, was the fastest horse of all. This made them feel that Tag-rong's idea was a bit self-serving. As a result, they didn't take to the idea, but still they said nothing while everyone sat there wondering what Uncle Chipön would say. Uncle Chipön already knew that it was predicted that "when Joru reached the age of twelve he would catch the noble steed and based on the wager, the sun [Joru] would rise [Gesar] from the eastern peaks, and that until then the blue swords would remain sheathed." Although he now knew that the time had arrived for what had been set down in the prophecy, Chipön thought it would be good to delay [the horse race], otherwise it would be meaningless, since it was predicted that Joru would capture a magical horse.

Then his [Chipön's] face broke out into a smile, and his chest shook with laughter as he said, "Ya, well then, Tharpa Zorna, you're right. Sengcham is renowned, and Kyalo is rich. This is going to pose a major calamity for the land of Ling. Now, according to the prophecy, there is no problem with wagering this prize on the horse race, but if the race is held in this particular place in the third month of winter, the mountain pass will be solid ice and there will be dust storms on the plains. If a horse gallops on frozen ground, even a robust rider will fall off, plus there is the danger that even a wild horse could be injured. Therefore, it is necessary to delay this for awhile. On the fifteenth day, all the people of Upper and Lower Ling without exception should assemble for the festival, and we can then discuss all of this in more detail." When the mighty warrior brethren heard this, they all agreed and went back to their homes.

Then Akhöd Tharpa Zorna went back to Trothung and recounted every detail of what had transpired. Trothung was overjoyed and was further convinced that this prediction of Hayagrīva had not been mistaken. At the same time, all the warriors of upper White Ling, from the highest elders of fathers and uncles to the youngest babies, from the highest Tag-rong to the lowest Gu-ru, yearned to win the lovely Drugmo even more than they all hoped to gain the golden throne and the treasure trove. Each one of them supplicated his own gods, each asked his own lama to pray, and each asked their ceremonial masters to do rituals just for him. Each made smoke offerings to his own local deity and raised windhorse as his own drala castle. Among them all, only the man of great vision, King Chipön, and the man of great wisdom, Denma Jangtra, knew from previous signs that Joru would take his seat on the throne.

Although Gyatsha Zhalkar of Bumpa knew that there was no other possible master than Joru, he still thought, "I'm afraid he might lose to Dongtsen," and sat there in a state of doubt.

Then, at the pinnacle of the Earth Ox year, on the fifteenth day of the twelfth month, in the community tent of Tag-rong, gurus like the sun and the moon in the firmament, fathers and uncles like royal Mount Meru, mothers and aunts like silken ice on a lake, young braves, the tigers in their prime swift as new-feathered bamboo arrows, and all the maidens fresh as blossoming flowers in the summertime, all arrived for the festival. They were like snow descending on a mountain pass and fog banks drifting into the valley. Then the great arbiter Werma Lhadar sang this song to arrange the seating of the ranks:

It's Ala Ala Ala,
And Thala is the melody of the song.
Machen, the cosmic Zodor,
Lha, nyen, lu, wermas, and so on,
All the dralas who keep the ancestral tradition of Mukpo
    clan,
Come here today and befriend this arbiter.
This place is near the Tag-rong castle.
Within this assembly ground of the Joyful Enclosure
Is the community tent that is in line with the law.
In case you don't recognize me,
I am the great arbiter Werma Lhadar.

Today on this auspicious occasion,
First is the gathering of the brethren for the festival
    celebration.
Second is the announcement of the prophecy that will lead us
    to happiness.
Third, the discussion of how the finish-line ribbon will be
    broken,
And fourth is the arrangement of the ranks for Tag-rong's
    festival.
Since the proper arrangement of the four stations[24] creates an
    auspicious connection,
This arbiter will begin with the arrangement of the ranks.

In the front are silver thrones on either side.
On stacks of cushions covered with silk brocade:
Gyatsha Zhalkar of Bumpa,
Nyibum Daryag of Serpa,
Anu Paseng of Ombu,
And Rinchen Darlu of Muchang
Will be seated as the Four Divine Heirs.

Next, in the middle rank upon rows of cushions,
Upon silken seats covered with silk brocade:
First, King Chipön will be seated,
Second, King Trothung of Tag-rong,

Third, King Senglön,
Fourth will be Namkha Sengzhal [Sky Lion Face],
Fifth will sit Guru Gyaltsen [Guru Victory Banner],
Sixth, Tönpa Gyaltsen [Teacher Victory Banner],
Seventh, Nyima Gyaltsen [Sun Victory Banner] of Kar-ru,
And eighth, Tharpa Gyaltsen [Liberation Victory Banner]
    of Nag-ru.
These last four are the men who hold the name Gyaltsen.

Then the row for the brethren
Seated in rank on the right upon stacked cushions,
And round seats covered with leopard skin:
Chieftain Zigphen of Tag-rong,
Second will be Chökyong Bernag of Gadei,
Third, Chölu Buyi Darphen of Mukpo Dong,
Fourth, incomparable Sengtag Adom,
Fifth, the royal maternal nephew Denma Jangtra,
Sixth, the fierce warrior Nya-tsha Aten,
Seventh, Dongtsen Nang-ngu Apel,
And eighth, fierce Nyima Lhundrub.

Next the row for the warriors
Seated in rank on the left upon stacked cushions
Colorful seats covered with tiger skins:
Michen Gyalwei [Great Man Spontaneously Accomplished
    Victor],
Second, the chiliarch Treltsei,
Third, the centurion Sergham,
Fourth sits Yuyag Gönpo,
Fifth, Buchung Daryag, [Young Lad Excellent Banner] of Serpa,
Sixth, Tsangpa'i Ngo-lug of Agê,
Seventh, Dar-'jam[25] Ngo-lug of Mupa
And eighth, Sintsha Ngo-lug of Tag-rong.
The last three are the Ngo-lug [Sheep-a-Peep] brothers.

Furthermore, at the row for the swift-horsed ones entitled
    Chieftains,
Seated in lateral ranks on stacked cushions

And seats covered with the spotted lynx fur
Is first, Norbu Lhadar, maternal nephew of Rong,
Second, sweet youth Yuyi Metog* [Turquoise Flower],
Third, handsome Drug-gyal [Victorious Dragon] of Kyalo,
Fourth, the young warrior Cho-nga Paser Dawa [Young
    Warrior of the Full Moon],
Fifth, Lynx Cub Kyatra,
Sixth is Chief Singsing of Ca-nag,
Seventh is Changtri Ngamchen of Ombu.
Eighth is Zhalkar Gyangdrag of Mupa.

Following them, in the row for the dear lads,
Seated in a lateral rank on the left
On neatly arranged cushions covered with white-breasted
    bear skin
Will be Lingchen Tharpa Sönam
And Abar Puyi Paljor [Prosperity of Abar's Son],
The judge Wangpo Darphen
And the great arbiter Werma Lhadar, myself,
The doctor Künga Nyima,
And diviner Künshei Thigpo,
The astrologer Lhabu Yangkar [Prince White Prosperity],
And eighth, the magician Khache Migmar.

Following them at the row for the relatives and friends,
Seated on the back rank at the right on cushions covered with silk,
Is first Sengcham Drugmo of Kyalo,
Second, Kyidkyi Nichung [Joyful Little Parrot] of Ngolo,
Third, Chipön's daughter Yudrön,
Fourth, Pekar Lhadzei of Drolo [White Lotus Divine
    Beauty],
Fifth, Denma's daughter Dzeidrön [Lovely Lamp],
Sixth, Yatha's daughter Ser-tso [Golden Lake],
Seventh, Tag-rong's daughter Tromo-tso.
These are the Seven Fair Maidens of White Ling.

---

* Also called Nangchung Yuyi Metog and Nangchung Metag.

Following them another beauteous line of fair maidens are
Seated on the back rank on the left on cushions covered with
    silk:
First is Tashi Lhatso [Auspicious Divine Lake] from central
    Tibet,
Second, Lhakar Drönma [Divine White Torch] of China,
Third, Kharagdza of Ser-tso [Golden Lake],
Fourth, the great father's daughter Ragza of Ge-tso [Lake of
    Virtue].
These in turn were the swift-horsed mothers and aunts.

Seated on the remaining long kyang-hide cushions
Are the Tibetan youth Michung Khadei [Young Clever
    Mouth],
The handy servant Pagyal Akhöd Tharpa Zorna,
The son of Khyishi Gu-ru,
And the rest, who will take their seats according to age.

In the white dharma tent on the highest seats of all,
I need not say that the gurus will be seated according to their
    ordination rank.
Each man, please sing of your pleasure;
Each fair maiden, step out a lovely dance;
Brethren, cheerfully meet and discuss your plans.
Today on the occasion of this festival,
May the blue sky show that there are no divine grudges.
May the dense earth show no enviousness among us.
May all disaster be gone in greater Tibet.
If my song has brought confusion, I confess it.
If my words were frivolous, I beg your forgiveness.

Thus he sang as each of them took their respective seats. The three whites and
the various victuals were like a swirling ocean; the three sweets and the fruits seemed
to fall like a pleasant rain. Like an avalanche from a crag there were meats, cheese,
and other victuals and drink; tea, liquor, and other beverages flowed like a river.
Each person sang a song of good cheer. The fair maidens gaily performed their playful dances. When everybody was enjoying themselves, the chieftain of Tag-rong,
Trothung, in order to tell how the festival had come about, how he had received

the prophecy, and why it would be best to have a horse race, raised this song in the melody of the Roaring Tigress:

Ala is the way to begin the song
And Thala is the way of making the melody.
The guru is inseparable from my mind;
The yidam arises as the display of the mind's nature;
The ḍākinī is the innate nature of the luminous and empty
    mind.
I supplicate you three to remain inseparable with me.

Here within this white community tent,
From the Four Divine Heirs
Down to Gu-ru, the son of Khyishi,
Listen to this song by Trogyal of Tag-rong.
If you want to know who I am, I am Chief Tag-rong.
The outer world is the pure land of Hayagrīva's Lotus Power;
The inner inhabitants are the kāya of the Supreme Horse
    [Hayagrīva].

Concerning the correct cognition of this generation stage
And the completion stage, which is all-pervading and
    nonconceptual:
First, not wandering from this during the day;
Second, not being confused by them at night;
Third, not solidifying by grasping and fixation.
Since I've been familiar with these three all my life,
On the face of the mirror of my luminous empty mind
Blazed the splendor of supreme direct knowledge.
Like a garland of lightning bolts, the prophecy arose
And I received the ornament of this excellent meaning.

Concerning Sengcham Drugmo, the daughter of the divine:
The prophecy says that if nothing is done, we will all meet
    with bad luck.
So she must be wagered as the prize for the horse race,
Not only her, but the golden throne, the treasure trove,
The achievement of the title of General Leader—

All these as well must be laid on the wager.
If these things go unclaimed, it will be an inauspicious
    connection.
These similes will show you how it is:

The Mighty Warriors are like tigers and leopards,
The Super Warriors are like wild animals in their prime;
Only a lion can be placed at the head of such a group.

The beautiful moon-faced Sengcham,
The fairest maiden of all, is given as the ornament source of bliss.
Besides that, those thirty who hold the title of leader
Although they have skill, accomplishment, and bulging-eyed
    fury in battle,
If they do not have the rank of minister,
Will be like Rāhu, with no head or body.[26]
Furthermore, the revered rank of thirty ministers,
If they don't have one leader,
Although they have the field of power to attain the booty,
Will be like shoulders moving without a head.
This lovely girl Sengcham,
If she is not drawn to a friend full of authentic presence,
Her beauty will be the likeness of a rainbow
That can't be caught and vanishes into the distance.
Rather than that, let's make her the prize for the horse race.
These karmically destined horses of the thirty warriors,
Although everyone agrees they are the fastest,
Their speed has never been tried in a race.
Why don't we test their swiftness in this year?

To call a horse fast or slow
Amounts to saying its supper's grass and water were good or bad.
To say that a man is fierce or weak
Amounts to saying his windhorse was up or down that day.

To speak of winning or losing the prize
Amounts to outlining where one's power field will be
    displayed.

In the paternal lineage of Chöphen Nagpo
All brothers and cousins belong to a single flock.
Whoever wins, whoever loses, there will be no regret.
For the golden stupa of our governance
This is offered as a cheerful song of joyful celebration.
I, your uncle, have made the arrangements;
First, concerning the distance of the horse race,
Second, the best day for it to occur.
All brethren must meet and concur.
If you've understood this song, it is an offering to your ears.
If not, there is no way to explain it.
Cousins and brothers keep this in your mind.

Thus he sang, but in truth:

> *His heart strove for his own selfish vested interest,*
> *Even though his sweet-talk pretended to be for the commonwealth.*

Yet on that day, the mighty warriors and all the brethren failed to harbor a single negative thought about Trothung's song, so they began their discussions.

The clan leader, the imperial king Chipön, said, "Well, now then, in this year according to the alignment of the constellations in the sky above, the timing of the seasons on the earth below, and the words of the prophecy in between, in whatever way we choose to construe this, there is nothing problematic about a horse race with this as a wager; I, Chipön, have decided that the race should go on. However, we must make certain that all of you who belong to the paternal lineage of Mukpo Dong, irrespective of whether you are from Upper or Lower Ling, have been told about this so no one can claim that they did not know. We must take care in advance to avoid any possible ground for disputes. Furthermore, if we don't postpone the horse race for another five or six months, then:

> *A foolish girl churning frozen milk[27] in winter*
> *Will not get butter, but just freeze her hands.*
> *A foolish boy racing his horse on frozen ground in winter,*
> *Aside from falling, will not remain on his mount.*

Not only that, but since this is the first horse race of White Ling, it won't be enjoyable for the spectators [if the track is icy]. We'll have to postpone this race for a spell, and meanwhile, let all the brethren in council make the best decision about the distance of the horse race."

What he really meant to imply was that they should summon Joru.

Then Bumpa Gyatsha Zhalkar proclaimed, "So be it for this horse race of White Ling, which was instigated by Uncle Trothung and decided on by Chipön:

> *You can consult the fathers and uncles when there's a marriage,*
> *But when you have an enemy, you are on your own.*

So this is as the proverb says. The divine child Joru of Mother Gogmo is from the royal lineage of Mukpo Dong. He is my, Zhalkar's, younger brother, and the older brother of Rongtsha. This is what the proverb speaks of when it says:

> *Although it's just a small piece of flesh, it's still a shank of the white*
> *prosperity lamb.*

Although he's just a little guy, he's our maternal uncle's nephew. Although his horse is small, its lineage is that of a noble steed. As for his mother Gogmo, she is the heart jewel of the first wager given to White Ling. She is the tent-wife of King Senglön and the daughter of Tsugna Rinchen. Both mother and son were first exiled, even though they were innocent. Unless he is called to the starting line of the horse race, then we of the Cadet Lineage will not compete in the race nor will we vie for the valuable prize. To be exact, Joru has his own inherent disposition. He turned his back on his father's house and went looking for a cave to sleep in, cast aside his own affairs and fought with dogs for a bone, and with birds for crumbs. Although I am not really expecting that Joru will actually win this horse race, if we don't summon him to join the end of the ranks of the brethren, then the race will be pointless," and saying this he advised all of them to keep this in mind.

Then Mazhi Trothung of Tag-rong thought, "That nephew of Gog, Joru, with his bitch mother Gogza, is [like the proverb]:

> *Ignoble, having never seen what is higher;*
> *Bringing ruin to the ranks, having never seen nobility.*

Even though he is of no use to this land of Ling, Chipön had brought him up and Gyatsha also followed his lead in saying that he must join us here. However, Joru is so gullible that even if he gets the booty in his hand, he'll probably just give it away to some stranger, just like:

Even though a windfall lands right in his mouth, he's someone
whose tongue will just spit it out.

My wife Denza and the whole Lesser Lineage are just like the proverb says:

Cats think their litter is as precious as gold.

Aside from that [even if he wins the kingdom], he's incapable of handling such affairs." Trothung said, "Zhalkar of Bumpa, you are right. Your uncle can't help but feel great regret that this worthy son of Senglön, the divine child of Gogmo, has yet to come join the ranks of this festival. But it's up to the Lesser Lineage to actually summon him here. We must determine the length of the race and when it will take place."

Then Dongtsen Nang-ngu Apel, proud of his swift horse, Turquoise Bird, joined in, "Concerning this horse race of the brethren of White Ling, if the distance is too short, everyone will jeer at us. If the arrangements are uncivilized, other countries will mock us. We must make this horse race famous throughout the world. What if we set the starting line in China and the finish line in India? Let's make this a great spectacle for the black-haired Tibetans." His remarks were not well-received by the chieftains and ministers of the Cadet Lineage, as they fell silent.

It was then that Sengtag of the Middle Lineage, knowing that the lad Dongtsen's words were not being well received by the brethren of Ling, thought, "If there's going to be a discussion, there's no point in bringing up things we won't agree on. So there must be a way to work this out." Then he said, "Okay then, if you want a horse race that will be renowned throughout the world: Take the azure firmament as the finish line and look to the dense earth for the start. Place the karmically destined prize next to the sun and moon and watch the spectacle from the middle space of heaven. Either follow Dongtsen's proposal or else follow these words of Sengtag. Otherwise just follow the words of the chief of White Ling." These were his words.

Then dear wise Bumpa Zhalkar said, "Let's make the finish line the Crag Mountain of Gu-ra and the starting line the Downs of Ayu. Make a smoke offering at the hill of the divine, and let the spectacle be viewed from the hill of the nāgas.

All brethren without regard for age were in total agreement [with Zhalkar's suggestion].

Then Uncle King Chipön answered, saying: "If we should send the destined prize, so hard-won, to India and send the gallant lad and his horse to China, then the black-haired Tibetans would have great difficulty coming to this spectacle. Between sky and earth there is no way to race; between China and Tibet the distance is too far. Rather, let's just do what Gyatsha has said. Concerning this matter of awesome import I'm afraid there may be some turmoil in the hearts of the brethren. So let the arbiter sing a song of mediation, and let the judge sing a song determining the judgment."

Then the great judge Wangpo Darphen thought he must be speaking to him, since the great arbiter had already sung the song that arranged the rows. He then offered the song known as One Decision Settles a Hundred in the melody called Swirling Melody of a Happy Song:

> The song is Ala Ala Ala.
> Thala is the melody.
> To the great god Brahmā,
> Nyen Lord Gedzo, god of power and authority,
> And the nāga king Tsugna Rinchen,
> Today please come and befriend White Ling.
> I am the magisterial Wangpo Darphen;
> First, I have great authority from my previous karma,
> Second, my mind is a ruler straight and true,
> Third, I am karmically ordained as the successor of my father.
> Fourth, I am the unity of these three.
>
> Concerning the horse race this year in White Ling—
> If you think about the situation, isn't it like this?
> First, the rays of the royal umbrella of the sun,
> Second, the abundance of warmth and moisture on the earth,
> Third, the fall of the droplets of sweet rain,
> Fourth, the roar of the turquoise dragon—
> All join to adorn the grassy meadow with flowers.
> Through their union the excellent season of summer dawns.
>
> First the Bön god of Zhang gave the prophecy,
> Second, the horse race was instigated by Tag-rong,
> Third, Chipön made the decision to hold the race,
> And fourth, Zhal-lu decided the distance.
> They join as ornaments of the horse race of White Ling.
> Through their union happiness will dawn in White Ling.
> Therefore, I, Wangpo Darphen,
> For the golden stupa of this horse race,
> Offer my advice as an array of silken ceremonial scarves.

Holding the horse race between China and Tibet
With a wager that's close to the sun and the moon,
May be fine, but it's just not workable.
Make the finish line Gu-ra Crag Mountain and the starting
    line the Downs of Ayu,
Make a smoke offering at the summit of the divine hill,
And let the spectacle be viewed from the summit of the Nāga
    Downs.
Between Ayu and Gu-ra
Is a journey of almost four days;
That should be a sufficient distance for a race.

Beautify the horses, deck them with beautiful ornaments.
The golden Elder Lineage, sons of the nyen,
Will wear coats of golden silk brocade,
Each with his Ling hat* topped with coral;
The Middle Lineage, descendants of the white lha,
Will wear uniforms of lovely white silk,
Each donning a Ling hat topped with a ruby;
The Lesser Lineage, descended from the blue nāgas,
Will likewise wear uniforms of blue silk,
Each donning a Ling hat topped with lapis.
The remaining mighty warrior brethren
Will be distinguished by the sparkling glitter of their jeweled
    ornaments.
If they were to come bearing arms
That would truly transgress the imperial law.
When stringing a garland of turquoise,
Among all grades the Chinese milk drop turquoise is
    supreme.
It should not be set aside, but strung with the rest.[28]

If we of White Ling are to wager for the prize,
Joru must be placed in the ranks of the brethren;
The Lesser Lineage must invite and take responsibility for him.

---

* The traditional hat of each district.

Whether the prize is won or not is up to previous deeds.
As for this spectacle of the horse race of White Ling,
The word is out that it is a wonder of the world,
And they say it must be so famous that it is renowned
    throughout Jambudvīpa.
If you think about it, doesn't it seem to be like this?
The profound dharma is in the land of India
And the field of suitable disciples is the snow land of Tibet.
If the lineage were not orally transmitted from the divine
    guru,
Then the snow land of Tibet and the field of disciples would
    have nothing.

The good rain comes from the nāgas of Lake Manasarovar;
The five types of grain are spread to the ends of the earth;
If the rain were not carried there by the white clouds,
Then hoping for barley grain and beans would be in vain.

Ling needs the fame of the horse race.
The entire world hopes to catch sight of it.
If we don't abide by this decision to race,
Then calling it a great wonder is just Ling praising itself.
The time of the waxing fourth moon
Is the holy gathering of the gods of the white side.
That is the best time of all, the first month of summer.*
So let's hold off four months until that date.
Then, on the thirteenth day of the waxing moon of the first
    summer month,
Near the left slope of Gu-ra Crag in Ma
On the fine land of Mönlam La,
Pitch the white community tent that holds a thousand people.
On the golden throne that quells the three realms,
Place silken parasols and heaps of jewels to adorn it.
First, the drum of the law, Selwa'i Ödden [Brilliantly
    Shining],

---

* The first month of summer (Tib. *dbyar zla ra ba*) is April or May.

Second, the white conch of the law, Karmo Gyangdrag
    [White Lady Furlong],
And third, the cymbals Nyima Drug-drag [Sun Dragon
    Voice]
Should be placed as ornaments of the jeweled throne.
That support spear of the great god Brahmā
Is in the hands of Senglön of the Lesser Lineage;
That symbolic spear of the drala Nyentag
Is in the hands of Trogyal of Tag-rong;
That silk-bedecked spear of the wealth god Yakṣa
Is in the hands of Tönpa Gyaltsen.
Including these three ceremonial spears in the principal
    position,
Place the thirteen banner spears to the right
And consider this a castle fortress shrine that the wermas will
    surround.
The longevity arrow of Drubpa'i Gyalmo
Is the prosperity support of Chipön,
The divine arrow of Bernag Gönpo [Mahākāla]
Lies in the heart of the armory of Gadei,
The golden notched arrow of the Power Lord, the drala
    Shug-gön [Juniper Lord]
Is the ornament of Tshazhang Denma Jangtra's quiver.
With these three principal divine arrows,
Set up the thirteen long-life arrows to the left
And consider them the ritual supports that gather the dralas
And the life-essence stones where the ḍākinīs land.
After the winner has the prize,
Then each one may take in hand their respective arrows or
    spears.

On the peak of the mountain place thirteen drala castles,
With thirteen smoke-offering urns before them.
First, the golden throne that quells the three realms,
Second, Sengcham Drugmo of Kyalo,
Third, the Sevenfold Jewel of the Ancestral Treasury,
Fourth, the twelve volumes of the *One Hundred Thousand*
    Verses of the nāgas,

Fifth, the little nine-portioned blue tent of the nāgas,
Sixth, the fortress Sengtrug Tagtse,
Seventh, the districts of Ling, the twelve myriarchies.
These seven will be wagered on the horse race.
From the highest, Chipön,
Down to the most humble, Gu-ru,
No matter who wins, all must accept this without feuding,
For the brethren have reached their agreement.

Led by the one venerated by all, Guru Künga [All-Joyful],
Rabten of Ga who increases virtue, and
Guru Darbum [Silk Myriads] of Yatha,
May the thirteen gurus of Ling
Perform a smoke offering and a mighty praise of the dralas
So that the brethren are not cast down
And the horses beneath them are not injured.
Implore the imperial gods for refuge and protection.
These are my main points in this song.

Now listen to the way things are:

The general interests of everyone are like the moon on the third day;
Although slender, they will grow in purpose and result.
Personal desires are like the moon on the sixteenth day;
Although sizeable, they will grow smaller and smaller.

Given that the sole ornament of Jambudvīpa, this field of
    power, is the prize;
I think to settle this through a horse race is a bit too much.
When the competition begins, concerning the question of
    the horse's speed,
I think that the determination of the winner can occur
    whether they run or not.
However the karmic patterns of the power field may be drawn,
What makes you think they can be uncovered by a mere
    animal?
If the power of your karma does not mandate leadership,
Do you really think just a horse could get the prize?

If you analyze it, it's strange to give that such importance.
Oops, not supposed to say that—just joking!

When the horses are running neck and neck
There's no way for there not to be one ahead and the others
    left behind;
There's no way for two to be the fastest.
One wins, all the others lose when you're competing for a prize.

Water can be free-flowing or held in a pot,
But when it turns to ice, the water is less yielding than the pot.
A beggar both has a head and [carries] a stick,
But until his dying day, the beggar's head is harder than the stick.
A man and a stallion each have their own pace,
But if the pathway is narrow, the man will be faster than the horse.

Whoever wins will depend on their previous karma.
Thinking you're the winner is fooling yourself.
This year, the horse race in White Ling
Is the dream of the humans that is revealed by the gods.
The divine prophecy has taken shape in your minds.
May whatever you wish for be placed in our hands.
May the gurus grant their blessings,
May the meditation deities dispel obstacles,
May the dharmapālas assist us in accomplishing miraculous
    activities,
And may the local deities befriend us.
May there be the auspiciousness of abundant well-being and
    happiness.
People of White Ling please keep this in mind.

Thus he offered this song.

Everyone thought that his words were true, because when honest speech is heard its nature is such that the listeners can gain confidence in their understanding. Feeling joy and gratitude, they each returned to their castles.

The decision of a goatskin-clad arbiter
Can't be defaced even by a tigerskin-clad ruler.

So the proverb says and so it was. However, there were three men who, overcome by selfish desires, intended to oppose the arbiter's decision.

Bumpa Gyatsha Zhalkar thought, "If the prize is lost to Dongtsen, it would mean that I had lost the horse race. I am not willing to give away this wager, and furthermore I will receive it through my own bravery. There is no way that I will leave my arms behind!"

Trothung of Tag-rong, not knowing what would come of it if Joru were in Ling, wondered what could be done to stop Joru from joining the ranks of the other brethren in the race.

Lowly Gu-ru, because he had none of the fine brocade and jeweled ornaments that were said to be necessary, sat there in a state of all-too-familiar anxiety.

———————

This concludes the first chapter, which begins with the prophecy and leads to the celebration, known as the Saga of the Precious Wheel.

Thus the meaning of the phrase,

At the moment the lotus appears from the mud
The garland of lightning dawns in the center of the red mirror,[*]

has been explained. However, to recap, "garland of lightning" refers to the fact that during this time Joru created the false prophecy that was hard to believe in. Trothung boastfully professed to be a practitioner of Lotus Power Hayagrīva, and he actually convinced himself that the deity of his generation stage practice had appeared in the clear "red mirror" of his mind.

———————

[*] At the end of every chapter there is a verse from the prayer written by Mipham Rinpoche, called the *Supplication for the Horse Race*. A short commentary by the author follows.

CHAPTER TWO

Zhal-lu Karpo issues an invitation to Joru
By sending Drugmo to lower Ma Valley.
They meet, obstacles are cleared, and auspicious connections
   set.
This gives rise to the Saga of the Precious Queen.

THE SECOND [CHAPTER] describing how Drugmo came to invite [Joru] is as follows:

Uncle King Chipön, elder of the clan, knew that there was no other way to invite Joru other than to send Drugmo. Therefore, Chipön spoke to the warrior Gyatsha and the minister Denma about inviting the divine child Joru from Lower Ma. He told them, "Of course, it would be fine for me, Chipön, Father Senglön, or somebody else to go to invite him, but in order to fulfill the divine prediction so that Joru can open the auspicious connection gateway to his enlightened activity, we have no choice but to send Sengcham Drugmo. The two of you must go to the upper encampment of Kyalo and tell Drugmo that she has to go and get Joru, since it is she who is the reason for his banishment to Lower Ma and the source of this dispute. Force her to go with threats and hostile speech."

Then the chieftain Bumpa Zhal-lu Karpo and the minister went up together and arrived at the tents of the upper encampment of Kyalo Tönpa Gyaltsen of Ga, where they engaged in extensive discussions. Finally, Bumpa Zhal-lu Karpo sang this song explaining the reason why Drugmo must go to invite Joru. It was sung in the melody White with Six Modulations:

The song is sung with Ala Ala Ala.
Thala is the melody of the song.
I supplicate the divine Rare and Precious Three Jewels.
Grant your blessings so that my speech may accomplish the
    words of truth.
In this place, the encampment of Kyalo,
I am Bumpa Gyatsha Zhalkar;
I am called the son of the Mu clan of the Lesser Lineage of
    Ling.
And I am Gyatsha, the nephew of the Chinese [emperor].
From the time I was born until today, like a father and
    mother
I have always taken care of my weaker cherished ones.
I have acted as the hammer that strikes the evil enemy.
Now at this time in this year [it has been said that]
The golden boulder of the governance of Ling
And Aunt Drugmo, the lake-born flower,
Are being placed as the trophy of the horse race.
If you really heard what I said, then the metaphors are like
    this:

The governance of Ling is the ocean of milk
Which, in this time of change, we must churn in a skin bag
Hoping to garner its essence of rich butter.[29]
If we don't get it, I think I'll just split the bag with my sword.
I won't have any regrets, even if my thirst is unquenched.
Maiden Drugmo is the divine cuckoo bird,
She must alight to adorn our juniper tree of the Mu clan.
If she doesn't, I think I'll just scatter her feathers everywhere.
I won't have any regrets, even if her song is no longer heard.

Just when my younger brother of Bumpa, Joru,
Thought to stay in his own happy land,
You, Drugmo, said you saw him kill the seven hunters;
That's the root of the scandal that expelled him from White
    Ling.
With that, the apple of warrior Gyatsha's eye was banished to
    the borderlands;

Joru paid the blood price of murdering no one.
In the end even though the falsity of these accusations has
    become clear,
The right hand of truth was never extended.

The brethren of Greater and Middle Ling are united,
But I, the chieftain of Bumpa, am without my younger
    brother.
Like a nose-less bride going to her in-laws
Seeing no happiness, my mind is pierced with pain
That cannot be cured even by the six good medicines.
So, to atone for your misdeeds, you must
Bring the boy Joru and his mother Gogmo
To the door of this warrior Gyatsha's home.
If not, from this day onward,
The maiden Drugmo will atone with her very body;
With her eyes, nose, and right arm, these three,
She will recompense the families of the Lesser Lineage.
Then I can give Drugmo, less these three body parts,
As the prize to the horse Turquoise Bird.
As the ancient Tibetan proverb states:

Rather than give a valuable jewel to an enemy,
We'd happily throw it in the harmless river.

If you manage to invite the boy Joru back,
That will expiate all your crimes, maiden Drugmo,
And spare Father Kyalo mental anguish,
For who wins the prize is the result of their previous karma.
If someone is a true warrior, the trophy is already in his hands.
If you understood this song, it is sweet to your ears.
If not, there is no way to explain it.
Maiden Drugmo, bear this in mind.

Thus he spoke, proposing that Kyalo Tönpa Gyaltsen and Drugmo deliver an invitation [to Joru]. Zhalkar and his minister then departed.

Sengcham Drugmo of Kyalo, an emanation of White Tārā, was an undeceiving child of noble family, with a keen mind and clear insight, and she was a trustworthy friend on whom one could infallibly rely with complete confidence. She kept her promises and had great courage. She had both great passions as well as morality. Her body was supple like bamboo; her face as white as the rising moon, with cheeks so red it was as if they were smeared with vermillion. The proportions of her body were perfect and lovely to behold. Her black shiny hair flowed down her back. She had almond eyes with clear pupils. Her white teeth were perfectly even, and her soft skin was not too warm and not too cool. Her lips had the beautiful lines of a lotus and her tongue was ornamented with the white syllable ĀH. Her voice was melodious, and she was a skillful speaker. She got along with everyone, was easily adaptable, and utterly beautified without exception with all the excellent qualities of a youthful maiden. She was also skilled in the art of love. From every angle she was faultless, and charming from every point of view. The hair on her right was combed to the right. The hair on her left was combed to the left. Her plaited hair resembled the spread wings of a garuḍa. The hair falling down was tied so that it would not fly in the wind. It was studded with precious amber that outweighed the weight of the world. So that the fine hair at her temples would not flutter, it was held down by loops of turquoise and coral. She wore a long colorful necklace of *zi* beads interspersed with red coral, and she held a blue turquoise mala and a ruby amulet. She had a sapphire bracelet and a golden ring like the rising sun. Her beaver-lined *chuba* was spotted with the nine layers of color similar to astrological trigrams,[30] and her silken boots were banded with the three colors of the rainbow. She was adorned with silk brocade encrusted with jewel ornaments. Even the sun and moon would lose their luster in comparison with her, even a divine celibate *rishi* would feel desire for her, even the radiance of the dazzling lotus would be stolen away by her, and even an enemy as murderous as Yama the Lord of Death would do whatever she asked.

Then Drugmo mounted her sorrel steed Garuḍa Wing and, carrying her provisions, set out for Lower Ma.

Meanwhile the divine child Joru told his mother Gogmo the following, "Mother, today Sengchen Drugmo of Kyalo is coming here. I must go to receive her," and he left. When Drugmo arrived at the neighboring valley of the land of the Beri tribe at the edge of the Ma Valley, she came to a deserted place in the foothills. Given that she was a young woman wearing many ornaments, without a companion, the thought suddenly occurred to her that there could be bandits and thieves in the vicinity. She continued on but was overcome by fear. It was then that Joru intentionally manifested himself as a man in black riding a black horse. Brandishing in space a spear with a black banner that reached into the sky, he sang this song to Drugmo:

It's Ala Ala Ala
And Thala Thala Thala.
In the palace of the Red Copper Castle
All classes of red tsen know me.
If you don't recognize this place,
It is said to be the solitary alcove of Jachen Yölmo [Great
    Rainbow Alcove].
If you don't recognize me,
The iron mountain beyond and the copper mountain
Merge as this fort of copper and iron
Where I reside and am known as Nyima Gyaltsen of Beri.
I'm a man who eats the raw flesh of the enemy;
I'm a man who quenches thirst with the enemy's blood;
I'm a man who takes as booty the enemy's possessions.
I've never let anyone get the best of me.
For the powerless, I know no pity.

Now then, you flashy young girl,
Listen, I have a few questions for you.[31]
A person carrying valuables on their back
Must have some plan in mind,
For if not, why carry all that baggage?

Merchants from Ladakh and central Tibet have mules laden
    with boxes of gold.
Their aim is to get the silk from the Chinese girls' looms.[32]
They hope to bring lots of silk back to central Tibet;
Thinking they will hawk it before a great man,
They aim to profit from the precious goods.

Merchants from China have dzo laden with boxes of tea.
Their aim is to get the white silver.
They hope to bring the shining silver back to China;
Wishing to make public their profit in the bazaar,
They hope to fill their treasury with white silver.

The maiden girl carries her gold as ornaments on her body.
Her aim is to attract a gigolo.

She hopes to hook a true love;
Planning to make her cunt and its coverings common
    property,
Her wish is to make the gigolo's penis her very own.

To rely on what your mind actually desires is difficult.
All your goods, the profit of good business, will be taken by
    this robber.
Young piece of ass desiring a gigolo, you will now just go
    naked.
Let's see if this is true, flashy young girl.

The mind of a girl and that of a pig are the same,
One will wiggle their ass in front of a boy and the other in
    front of food.
A raven and a girl are the same,
They will chatter while perched on a tree of paradise,
And will be cheerful when looking down upon the dunghill
    of misery.
The mind of a girl and that of a fish are the same,
If you pick them up with a gentle hand, they will quiver and
    thrash,
But if you pierce them with a cruel iron hook, they will ease
    off.

Your jewel ornaments seem to be the ancestral wealth of the
    nāgas;
Your body with its countenance makes you seem a daughter
    of the gods,
But without refuge, it seems that misfortune is your guide.
Now I will tell it like it is:

First, your bracelet of pure gold,
Second, your self-originating zi stone ornament,
And third, your earrings of excellent white turquoise—
If these jewels are in the hands of a rich person, it is the
    abundant wealth of a lifetime
Gathered here on a lovely woman's body for just one day.

Tell me honestly how you have collected this and
What father's name you have left behind
And to what family are you heading.
Don't keep it secret, quickly tell me the truth.

First, there is a wolf hoping for vittles,
And second, a white prosperity sheep roams the mountain;
This is how they come to meet up in the high mountains.

First the wild lad turns robber,
And second, a tender maiden brings her wealth as ornaments;
That is how they come to meet in the lower valley, an
    uninhabited deserted land.
It seems their way of meeting is the result of previous karma.
They say previous karma is like a dog and a deer;
They say karmic debts are like a body and its shadow.
The best choice is for you and I to be companions for a
    lifetime
Because a precious human birth is the heart jewel of the
    booty;
The wealth of having horses and cattle will gradually follow.
If that's not possible, then let's make love just once
And I will take your golden ornaments, horse, and jewels as
    my booty,
But I'll give you back your underwear as a sign of gratitude
    for your ass.
Or your third option is to return to your homeland stark
    naked
While this robber gets the wealth of all your jewelry.
You're so feeble, I'll just set you free.
Think about it, girl, what is your fancy?

Thus he spoke, and Drugmo, utterly terrified, began babbling, her mouth
quivering like a leaf in the wind as she sang this song in reply:

It's Ala Ala Ala.
Thala is the melody of the song.
From the pure land of Turquoise Leaf Array

Jetsün Ārya Tārā,
Surrounded by a hundred thousand ḍākinīs of the mother lineage,
Watching over the welfare of beings.
Come today to befriend Drugmo.
First, the way I am terrified and disheartened,
Second, the way the displeasing howl of the wind grates in my
    ears,
And third, the way this man in black appears like a robber;
Like an uninvited guest this all came together here today.

First the greatness of my parents' loving-kindness,
Second the brave-hearted gathering of brethren,
And third, the dwelling place in my happy homeland.
Although I had no wish to abandon them, I have left them
    behind.
What grief for this young girl
From this robber demon dressed in black!

First, at best I could escape from him,
Second would be that, if I fight him, I would be able to defeat
    him,
Third would be that, if I appeal to him, he will
    compassionately protect me.
If these three don't work, then the suffering will be
    overwhelming.

First, to strike a tiny flea with an ax,
Second, to shoot a poison arrow at a honey bee,
Third, for a warrior to overcome a girl;
Crowing about these will make you a laughingstock among the people.

Although I should hardly dare address you this way, that is
    how it is:
First, because Drugmo has great worth,
Second, because Gyatsha's prowess is great,
Third, because the tiger ranks of the young brethren are
    unified.

There's no way I'll ever be your life's companion.
Although you mentioned that we should make love at least
    once, that will never happen.
For first, the thought of ravishment makes me sick,
Second, there is no feeling of love toward you in my mind,
And third, you will just become a warrior who took ass as
    booty.
People will jeer, and misery will be brought upon us.

First, the jeweled ornaments fastened on my head,
Second, the garland of zi adorning my neck,
Those, and third, the gold jewelry on my body—
Take these treasures of mine, you robber.
First, a small turquoise knob adorning my hairline,
Second, clothing that protects my modesty,
And third, my chestnut horse to get me back to Ling.
At least allow Drugmo this as her rightful portion.

First, aging is the decline of the beloved four elements,
Second, the time when death arrives,
And third, the karmic ripening of one's own deeds.
No one has ever heard of a detour to avoid these three.

First, Trothung instigated this calamity,
Second, Gyatsha drives me with his ominous heavy words,
    and
Third, because Joru is the leader of the demonic force,
They hoped that Drugmo would be delivered into the hands
    of the enemy.
All patron gods who protect this maiden,
First, if you have compassion the time has come to watch over
    me,
Second, if you have power the time has come to reverse this,
And third, if you possess enlightened activity the time has
    come to enact it.
Not only has the time come, it's almost too late.

Thus she sang, and sat there weeping. Beri Nyima Gyaltsen addressed her, "Ya, well now, girl, maybe you're right. I won't take advantage of or ravish you, and I am not going to rob you, but you must be sure to return here in seven days with all the wealth you're going to give me and, if so, I'll let you go for today. As a token of this commitment, hand over your gold ring now. Oh, by the way, who is this Joru you're talking about? Is he a yak or a wild beast? Tell me who he is."

Then Drugmo replied, "He's not a wild animal, he's a human. All the people of White Ling say that Joru is a pika killing, sniveling, demon-necked, notch-nosed laughingstock. If, when offering to him, you ranked him among the gods, he is someone who would choose to pose as a demon. If you categorized him among the ranks of the demons, he would cause feuds with the gods. He seems to be one who delights to see the rich dying of famine. He appears to be the kind of person who would be shocked by a dog biting a warrior. He is one who appears to be happier in the body of a beggar than in the lineage of a chieftain. He turns his back on the affairs of his own state and squabbles over land and water with the pikas. He has no other vittles than the wild Himalayan yams. In actual fact, he is from the royal lineage of Mukpo and is the rightful son of Senglön and the nephew of Gyatsha. However, it's as though he was not born of these men, for he's just a vagrant who wanders the ends of the earth. Actually I'm on my way to summon him now," she said, placing in his hand her gold ring, which was set with a vajra. Agreeing to meet in seven days, she then left.

Since he knew that it would be the presentation gift marking the auspicious connection of the Great Lion's first meeting with Drugmo, for this reason, he felt he must take the golden ring. All of the words that Drugmo uttered turned out to be the words that symbolically invoked the miraculous activity of his enlightened intentions.

From there, Drugmo journeyed farther until she arrived at Gangkar Tsesum [Three-Peaked White Snow Mountain]. Beyond the mountain pass of the Seven Dunes, there was Joru, manifesting as a charming young man relaxing with seven white-clad men on white horses. Drugmo approached them to have a look. The main man there was outstandingly attractive. His complexion was creamy like a conch, his cheek color was redder than rouge, the ornaments on his clothes were like shimmering rainbow light, and his radiant complexion was like a lotus. He was a nonhuman miraculous child of the gods, cheerful, smiling, and extremely good-natured! She fell in love with him upon sight. She sat there wide-awake; her mind blank, her body frozen, and her eyes wide open, without blinking. After a while the magical man sang this song to Drugmo in the melody of Six Modulations:

It's Ala Ala Ala.
With Thala the song is sung.
Gurus, yidams, and the Three Jewels
Remain inseparable as my crown ornament.
Through your presence grant your blessings.
If you don't recognize me,
I'm not from around here; I come from far away,
From as far away as the land of India.
I am the Indian minister Berkar [White Cloak].
Honorable girl whom I meet today,
Listen, I have a few questions for you.[33]

Within the country of Colorful Upper Ling,
Who is the sovereign chieftain?
Who is the blessed guru that lives there?
How many warriors of great might are in residence?
How far away from here is this place?
The famous woman, Sengcham Drugmo,
If I beg for her hand, is there any chance to receive her?
If I were to look for her, is there any chance to catch a glimpse?
What about the way she looks? Is she as beautiful as they say?
Don't hide anything, speak out frankly.

A superior maiden has the looks of a goddess,
Longevity, merit, and splendor surround her.
Her mind and thoughts are like a crystal vase
That seems to be filled with the amṛta of everlasting
    companionship.
She can keep her speech secret, like a door that's been shut,
And her words are so sweet, they can steal the minds of the
    kingdom.

A middling maiden has a lovely moon face
With a waxing and waning karmic field of power.
Her mind is unstable, like a fish in the ocean,
And her companions come, bad after good, like patterns on
    the waves.
Her mouth is busy like a crossroads,

And her words are both true and false like a hundred travelers
    going and a thousand returning.

An inferior maiden is like a razor that severs the life of her
    companions.
Her impermanent mind is like a flag on a mountain peak.[34]
Any companion who stays with her is like the wind on the
    ridge.
Her speech is untrue, like a false treasure trove,
And her slanderous tongue stirs up trouble.

The superior maiden benefits everyone like medicine.
She would be a good consort for the divine guru's path of
    skillful means,
Or the queenly ornament of the imperial chieftain's
    government,
Or she could serve well as the quintessence of prosperity for a
    tiger in his prime.

The middling maiden is like crystal,
She can be beneficial or harmful, depending on
    circumstances.
Depending on the quality of the divine guru's experience and
    realization,
If he and she unite, it could be either virtuous or sinful.
Depending on whether the young tiger's windhorse rises or
    declines,
If they come together, the outcome could be good or bad.

The inferior maiden is like a poisonous flower.
Even if her exterior looks nice to the gaze,
As their bodies unite, she is the razor that severs her
    companion's life.

There are three ways of meeting with maiden girls.
The superior maiden, like the waxing moon,
Should join with the guru who has achieved siddhi,

Or the tigers in their prime when their windhorse is increasing.
She is their companion who increases their ocean of longevity
    and merit.
The middling maiden is like the divine cuckoo.
First, when the monks lose their vows in spring,
Second, in the time of renewal, when people work hard to
    support their worldly lives,
Third, when young tigers travel from their homes, such
    women are taken as lovers.
If it works out, it's neither good nor bad.
If it doesn't work out, it leads to contention.
The inferior maiden is like a poison pill.
She meets the divine guru just before he goes to hell;
She meets the young tiger just before he brings his own end.
Before her is unhappiness; she brings suffering to her new
    family.
Behind her is discontent; she brings the torture of scandal to
    the father's home.
The whole country is discontent, as she lays the ground for
    discord.
If you examine these words, I think you'll find them true.
Thinking in this way, this minister has come without delay.
I traveled this long road like rolling up a scroll,
Like the wind journeying through unfamiliar lands,
I came here, and today I met you, girl, on the path.
If you really examine this, here is how it is:

The parrot forages for food,[35] *but finds beer instead;*
After drinking his fill, unable to fly he will fall into the hands of
    another.
When young tigers go hunting, but find a bandit's stash,
Although not making a kill, what was acquired is an invitation for
    scandal.

I, the minister, was on my way to Ling and I met you, girl.
This seems to be the first sign that I won't meet the maiden
    Drugmo now.

361

There are more maidens here than grass on the mountains,
But an eligible life-mate is rarer than gold.
If you're searching for yellow gold, you will find it in the
    mountains.
I've wandered the borderlands but have not found the
    maiden girl.
If you understood these words, they are sweetness to your
    ears,
If not, there is no way to explain it.

Thus he sang, and then by the power of Joru's compassion, Kyalo Sengcham Drugmo's body, speech, and mind were overcome and she became vulnerable, like paper carried by the wind, while her mind was so filled with lust that her body could hardly bear it. It was like this:

Although her words maintain that she feels no affection,
The expression of lust is betrayed by her smile.
Although her heart wants to keep this secret,
The secret words escape from her mouth.
Although she tries to conceal her modesty,
Her inner feelings are obvious to all.
Although the outer body of flesh is covered by clothes,
The inner mind is nakedly revealed.

Not knowing what to do, she sang this song about the good fortune of this occasion in the melody of Unchanging Longevity:

Ala is the way the song is sung,
Thala gives the melody.
If you don't recognize this place,
This is the Seven Sandy Passes of Ma
If you don't recognize me,
Like the jewel amid the rocky white peaks,
Famed as the one called White Vulture,
I alone can boast six broad wings on my body.
Like the jewel in the snow-covered peaks,
Famed as the one called the White Snow Lioness,
I alone can boast a broad turquoise mane.

Like the prosperity jewel of White Ling,
Famed as the one called Maid Drugmo,
I alone can boast a brilliant radiant body.
The golden swan takes to Lake Manasarovar;
It would be senseless to veer from the lake and go elsewhere.
You, the minister, fancy Sengchen Drugmo;
It would be senseless to veer from the maiden Drugmo.
Don't you think so, O minister from India?

To the east in the colorful land of Ling,
There are four divine brothers, heirs of the sovereign leader.
The throne of gold is the general reward for the winner;
Whoever wins the horse race will be seated there.
There are Thirty Brethren of great skill;
Whoever has the fastest horse will become the most
    renowned among them.
I, Sengcham Drugmo of Ga Kyalo
Have been made the reward for the fastest horse.
If one's horse captures the path of the birds, then the wager
    will be in their hands.
If you want to see this spectacle, then that is how it is.
Suppose you thought to purchase me,
Even if the land of Ma were filled with gold dust, my worth
    would still be beyond your reach.
And though you may beg, there's no way I'd be given away.

The flow of the blue water's rosary of bubbles
Doesn't expect to acquire the undulating fish;
When the sparkling blue water fills the valley,
The Golden-Eyed Ones will karmically arrive there.
The spreading branches of the juniper tree
Did not expect the cuckoo bird to come;
Still, the way that the cool wind moves the branches
Seems to invite the melodious divine bird as its guest.
I, Sengcham Drugmo of White Ling,
Did not expect to meet a minister from a distant land;
I was lost on my way to inviting the boy Joru,
And so the minister Berkar appeared as though to escort me.

363

First, the warmth and moisture rising from the earth below,
And second, the sun and rain that descend from the azure
     firmament above
Do not plan a rendezvous, but the way they meet
Is the happy union of the pitched tent of rainbow colors.

First, the peacock bird aspires upward,[36]
And second, the southern turquoise dragon's thundering
     voice descends.
They didn't plan to rendezvous, but the way that they
     coincide
Is as though they thought to perform an extraordinary dance.
Not only that, but here are a few more examples:

First, bamboo from the southern province [of Gyalrong],
Second, the breast feathers of the white vulture:
If they are to last, it depends on how well they are joined in
     the making.
If these two are harmonious, they will be the ornament of the
     quiver.
Pure water from the crags of the snow land of Tibet
And the saffron flowers of India to the south:
If there is to be pigment, it depends on the temperature of the
     water.
If the two are harmonious, it will be the essence of the vase.
You, Berkar, the minister from India,
And this Sengcham Drugmo of Ga Kyalo:
Whether you capture her to become your companion or not
     depends on previous karma.
If we two are harmonious, we will become the ornament of
     the world.
If you understand this, it's sweet to the ears.
If not, there is no way to explain it.
O minister, keep this in your heart.

Thus she sang.
The minister said, "It's hard to trust the words of a person you have just met.
Are you really Drugmo?" "I am indeed Drugmo," she swore. She thought, "I suppose

I should offer the Long-Life Queen of Siddhi Liquor to Joru, but since he's a master of illusion, I think it's acceptable to offer it with my mind." Touching her ring finger to the nectar, she offered the first select portion, and a drop fell right at the foot of the minister. She thought that was curious, and then she offered the minister the rest of the drink, while the two of them shared a lengthy and very romantic conversation. They enjoyed the playful song and dance of empty bliss, and this generated the delight and authentic splendor of all the dralas of their body, speech, and mind. All haughty worldly spirits were magnetized to action. The auspicious connection for the defeat of the four māras of the four directions occurred. They sealed[37] their love for one another by placing a great boulder as a sign that their love was as enduring as the earth. They pledged their vows to one another by swearing an oath. To seal their decision, Drugmo gave the minister from India a white offering scarf with nine knots. The minister in turn gave Drugmo a crystal bracelet. Scarcely able to part, they planned to be reunited in Shady Valley Rich Royal Forest and each went their separate ways.

Then Drugmo went over the mountain pass and arrived in Khenlung Ridrug. Whether in the shade or in the sun, wherever there was a pika hole, there at the entrance she saw a Joru. Frightened by Joru's magical display, she dared not go any farther. She hid herself next to a boulder that was naturally shaped like a horse. After a short while, Joru condensed all his emanations into one, and that one Joru killed a large pika and just sat there. Drugmo stood up and called out "Joru!" three times. At the moment Joru saw her, he pretended that he mistook Drugmo for a demoness and, pulling out his slingshot Chumig Gudril [Spring Nine Turns], he loaded it with the pika's waste, intestines, and liver, and, standing up by the gateway, he sang this short song, Invocation to the Slingshot:

> The song is Ala Ala Ala.
> Thala is the melody of the song.
> I supplicate the Three Jewels of Refuge.
> May the boy Joru tame the māras and cannibal rākṣasas.
> This land of Lower Ma is a place of demons and pikas;
> The boy Joru is the one who subdues demons and māras.
> Since I, Joru, first arrived here,
> Forget about demons, even the humans can't pass through;
> Forget about humans, even the icy wind can't pass here
>   without my permission.
> This is the place where the gods on high bring down rainfall;
> This is the archery range of the nyen.

Here, in the seat of the wealth of the nāga Tsugna
Today a demoness has been running around.
Not only have you come, but you've been screaming and yelling.
If you're a tsen, get you to the peak of three mountains;
If you're a demon, get you down to three valleys;
If you're a demoness, get you between two towns;
If you're a the'u rang, go into a rocky cave;
If you're a gyalgong, go to the crossroads of the three paths.
If there's a success-preventing demon,[38] let it dissolve your
    teeth;
Those thirty teeth will be the ransom for the demon.
If there is a demon following behind you, then force it into
    your hair,
And I'll present your braids to the demon following you as
    material for an effigy.
More than the joyful laugher that was there before traversing
    these three mountain passes,
I delight in this tantrum of the negative demons of the
    mountain pass.

Happiness follows sadness just as day follows night;
The glow of dawn guides us out of the dark of night.

This unprovoked demon's splendor
Is threatening an unqualified exorcist.
When the exorcist targets the demons,
That suffering will lead them to bliss.
This colorful short slingshot is the drala's castle;
This waste and intestines are the mamos' power substance.
If you are a demon, then your consciousness will be led to
    Sukhāvatī.
If you're a human, you will be released from the obstacles of māra.
If you understand this, it's sweet to the ears.
If not, it cannot be explained.

Thus he sang, and loosed his slingshot, hitting Drugmo's hair and teeth. Becoming as hairless as a copper ladle, and with her mouth as toothless as an empty bag, she sat there, suffering unbearably as she wept.

Joru then went back home and told his mother Gogmo, "Today Drugmo came, but she was preceded and pursued by many demons and māras, and I tamed them all. Drugmo herself sat there, close to the horse-shaped boulder, screaming and wailing. In reality, I did this in order to tame the various bride demons and in order to increase the majestic splendor of Drugmo's body."

Immediately, Gogmo ran to Drugmo's side and asked her what happened. As Drugmo sat there in a helpless state, Gogmo said, "Girl, don't be miserable. Let's go up and ask Joru to come and make your appearance even more beautiful than before. Every act he performs is solely a feat of magical illusion, so there's no problem," and she led her [Drugmo] back up to Joru.

Joru asked, "Hey, are you Drugmo? Oh, I mistook you for a demoness. Looks like I've made a big mistake! Why didn't you just come in rather than screaming from over there? If you didn't wish to meet me, why did you come to Lower Ma? Besides, if you had just said, 'Hey, I'm Drugmo,' this wouldn't have happened. However, what's the point of regretting past deeds?" Then Kyalo Sengchen Drugmo sang this song about seeing suffering and the reason why she came to invite him to White Ling in the melody of Unchanging Longevity:

> The song is Ala Ala Ala.
> Thala is the melody of the song.
> Compassionate mother, White Tārā, goddess of longevity,
> Look upon this girl who possesses devotion with kindness.
> If you don't recognize this place,
> It is Yulung Sumdo of Lower Ma.
> If you don't recognize me,
> I am called Sengcham Drugmo from Kyalo, of the Ga clan.
> I wasn't born in the summer; I was born in the winter.
> That winter, between the months of the Tiger and the Hare,
> Is the time that I, this damsel, was born.
> At that time the lion's roar reverberated from the white snow
>   mountains,
> On the marshy fields a wild kyang neighed,
> In the midst of the azure firmament the dragon thundered;
> That's why I was named Sengcham Drugmo.
> Ever since I was born in my dearest mother's lap,
> My beauty has stood out from the crowd.
> Well then, good sir, divine son Joru,
> Listen here to some examples of how it is:

On the majestic mountains above the verdant grasslands,
Broad-racked bucks roam free.
The hunter who carries arrows thinks this place is their
     pathway.
He hopes to get the superb white horn,
He hopes to get the nutritious prime meat for food.
The innocent deer so content to wander,
How sad to think that this is the way of karma.
Rocked peacefully in the calming waves of the churning
     ocean,
The white-bellied fish frolic in the water.
The thought to pierce their cheeks with a curved iron hook,[39]
The thought to snare them in sturdy nets,
Thinking this delicious meat is food fit for a guest.
The innocent fish just drinking pure water,
How sad to think that this is the way of karma.

In the wealthy district of Father Kyalo
I, the maiden Drugmo, was content in my own home.
The hordes of mighty warriors of Ling think I am just a
     plaything,[40]
You think this is just a place where you can dance around on
     your horses,
And you, boy Joru, think I'm just somebody to disdain.[41]
This innocent maiden staying in her home,
How sad to think this is the way of karma.

The prayer flags hoisted on the high mountains peaks are
     lovely from a distance,
They are powerless to leave, their poles anchored in the
     mountains.
Unable to remain still, they are constantly flapping in the
     wind.
The high mountains don't suffer, they just happen to be there,
The icy winds don't suffer, they just happen to be moving
     through,
But the innocent prayer flags are the ones that are punished.
I, Sengcham Drugmo of wealthy Kyalo,

Am powerless to go because I belong to the brethren,
And powerless to stay because Joru scoffs at me.[42]
The brethren of Ling don't suffer, because they just happen to
    be competing,
Boy Joru, you don't suffer, because you just happen to be
    playing,[43]
All suffering and punishment falls on poor Drugmo's
    shoulders.
They say the boy Joru is a mandate from heaven.
If dissension has been spread among the gods, Drugmo
    confesses it.
If the nāgas have been troubled, Drugmo confesses it.
Well, then, good sir, divine son Joru,
When you came to the land of men, divine child,
It fell to me, Drugmo, to serve you.
You, Joru, are a lord of magical illusion.
Since that is the case, then make Drugmo's body a vessel of
    splendor and blessing,
Ageless, youthfully radiant,
Free from illness, and gloriously endowed with well-being.
Among the eighteen kingdoms,[44]
The eighteen fair maidens are equally gorgeous.
Bring forth a wealth of beauty to make Drugmo unlike them all.
If you do that, I'll accomplish your every command.
If you listen to this song, it is an ornament offered to your ears.
If you don't listen, there's no way to explain it.

Thus she sang, and Joru replied, "Yes, well then, the horse that has been karmically destined to be mine throughout the succession of all my lives resides in the
midst of the herds of wild kyang. It is neither a horse, nor a kyang; it is the knowing steed, which can only be captured by the two of you: Mother Gogmo and you,
Drugmo. Now you must go there. The horse understands human language and has
unobstructed clairvoyance. It has the power to show any sign of accomplishment
that needs to be shown. If you are afraid that you won't catch it or that once you
do it will be lost, then call out with intense yearning to both my elder and younger
brothers. They will come and help you catch him with their lasso Nyida Trüldzin
[Miraculously Catches the Sun and Moon]. If you catch him but lose him, it's
Mother Gogmo's fault; if you can't recognize the horse, it's your own fault, Drugmo.

369

If you fail to beckon him, then it's both your faults. If they don't help you, then it's my brothers' faults. Promise me that you'll catch the steed, and I'll bring forth the blessings of a splendidly youthful body and speech that possesses the power of truth." Drugmo then promised to accomplish his command.

Joru, the divine child of Gogmo, according to worldly customs of summoning prosperity along with the bride, sat in nonconceptual meditation and sang this song to bestow the body blessings to Drugmo with the melody called White Divine Invocation:

> It's Ala Ala Ala.
> Thala leads the melody of the song.
> All deities of the Three Roots and dharmapālas
> Come to befriend Joru.
> Elder brother White-Conch Garuḍa,
> The white man with the head of a garuḍa,
> Who always delights with laughter,
> And deities of the Three Roots, arise from your places;
> Gather the splendor and blessings of all the goddesses
> And confer it upon the body of Sengcham Drugmo.
> Younger brother, Ludrül Ödchung,[45]
> A dark man with the head of a snake,
> Always beaming with a radiant smile,
> Rise up from the land of subterranean nāgas.
> Bestow all the glamorous prosperity energy of the nāginīs
> On Drugmo's speech today.
> My only sister, Thalei Ötro,
> A maiden clothed in a coat of fine vulture feathers
> Coyly glancing with a seductive stare,
> Arise from the middle space of the nyen.
> Grant the prosperity energy of well-being and happiness of
>   the human lands of China and Tibet
> On Drugmo's mind today.
>
> Welcome guests, windhorse, wermas, and the like,
> All of the patron gods of my being,
> Today come and befriend this noble person.

The countenance of the youthful moon,
The radiant color of a blooming lotus,
The lustrous black like the bumblebee's hair;
Confer all of this on Sengcham Drugmo's body.
Sweet as the sound of a gandharva's lute,
Delightful as the sound of the divine cuckoo,
Melodious as a *kalavinka* bird;
Confer all of this on Sengcham Drugmo's speech.
Magnetizing the three worlds,
Splendidly quelling the three realms,
Seducing the life essence and minds of the elite;
Confer all of this on Sengcham Drugmo's mind.
Make her body more beautiful than before.
May she be famed among the people for her lovely form.
She, the supernal maiden of the tribe of Ling,
May she be the ornament of all maidens of the world.
May whatever this song has sung become the dharma.
May whatever tune I sang be filled with purpose.

When he finished singing he touched her with his hand, and Drugmo's beauty was more resplendent than ever, and everything about her changed for the better. As Drugmo felt unwilling to enter the tent of Joru and his mother when she saw how dirty and patched it was, she hesitated for a moment. Joru gazed into the sky, summoning the eight classes of deities: there was lightning, thunder, and hail as if the earth and sky were being stirred together. Drugmo, not having the slightest place of refuge outside the little tent, was forced to enter. It was then that Joru served her a meal of pika flesh and sweet potatoes. The food had been blessed with the hundred flavors of the gods, and Drugmo was seized with a measureless thirst and hunger. She consumed every bit of it, leaving not a bite. As soon as she finished eating, she immediately began to retch and filled the home with her vomit. This action sent forth auspicious connections of siddhis throughout the entire land. Kyalo Sengcham Drugmo was so confused by her experiences that she became afraid that she would forget the point of her mission. Sometimes she felt scared, sometimes sad, sometimes hungry, sometimes thirsty, and so on. So she sang this song in order to focus on the aim of her mission, singing in the tune White Melody with Six Modulations:

It's Ala Ala Ala.
Thala leads the melody of the song.
I, the maiden Drugmo of Kyalo,
Came to Lower Ma to invite the divine child.
Sometimes the sun of happiness dawns,
Sometimes the terrifying black winds of fear swirl.
My mind's thoughts, like a flag on the highest peak,
Are blown by the wind of fleeting experience
So that I have forgotten the crucial point of my mission.

The rich endowments of Father Kyalo
Are like the adornments of the six-smiled tigress.
If the tiger looks after his own body, there is freedom;
Once the hunter shoots an arrow, the freedom belongs to
    another.

I, this Sengcham Drugmo of Kyalo,
If my kind parents look after me, I belong to them;
Once the brethren look after me, I'm just their common
    possession.
Truthfully speaking, this is the way it is.

On the broad alpine meadow,
The white prosperity sheep, the shepherd, and the wolf in its
    prime, these three:
The white prosperity sheep think single-mindedly of the
    grass;[46]
The youthful shepherd's thoughts are to get the pelt of the
    wolf;
The wolf in its prime is focused on meat.
The sheep in their stupidity graze on the mountain,
    distracted by the grass.
The wolf in its prime stalks the delicious meat.
The cruel shepherd with his arrows spies from a distance.
Truthfully speaking, the whole thing seems ridiculous.
But following the advice of Chieftain Trothung's Northern
    God,
Father Kyalo has wagered me on a horse race.

Whoever is the fastest will take Drugmo as his bride.
That hero Bumpa Zhal-lu Karpo
Told me I must go and invite the boy Joru.
Not daring to stay at home, I, Drugmo, came here.
Child Joru, please don't stay here; come to Ling.
Mother Gogmo, don't stay behind; come along to Ling.
I, Drugmo, will be able to capture the noble steed.
If you know tricks, you can magically speed the running of
    your horse.
If you can magically disguise yourself, you can take your seat
    on the golden throne.
The people of White Ling, happy as a fish in water,
Will be all the happier if you show signs of the power of
    siddhi.
If you understand this discourse, it is sweetness to your ears.
If you don't, then there's no way to explain it.

Thus she sang. Then he [Joru] said, "Oh you and Mother must both capture this karmic steed, and then we will go to Ling. It will be easy to be the bridegroom of Drugmo, the lord of Kyalo's wealth, and the holder of the golden throne of White Ling. Not only that, but I will set my yoke upon the neck of Gurkar of Hor, pierce the forehead of the māra Lutsen with my arrow, and so forth. All this will come to pass. But if you don't get the horse, then I'm a beggar who can't win the kingdom anymore than riding this stick could get me first prize in the race. Do you understand this: without the horse I will have no choice but to remain in my present state?"

This ends the second chapter, the Saga of the Precious Queen, which explains how Drugmo extended the invitation.

    All of the above relates to the lines in the prayer [by Mipham Rinpoche] that state:

> By the roar of the dragon, the heroine rides the swift mount of the wind.
> I pray to the one who can bring everyone under his control.

The "roar of the dragon" refers to Drugmo [Dragoness], who was placed as the wager of the race, in order to invoke the gathering of the heroic brethren of White

Ling to "ride the swift mount of the wind." "Everyone" became excited, and their minds' attachments and desires became like "riding the swift mount of the wind." In that way "everyone" agreed to hold the horse race, which was what became the way that the blessings of Joru "brought everyone under his control." Saying "even" means that this refers not only to the brethren, but that "even" Drugmo's body, speech, and mind are included.

This completes the account of how he [Joru] overcame them all.

CHAPTER THREE

Following Joru's instructions, Sengcham Drugmo sets out
To capture the divine steed and accomplish the goal.
Offering Wild Kyang to his owner, she expounds upon the
  horse.
This gives rise to the Saga of the Precious Supreme Steed.

THE THIRD [CHAPTER], describing the capturing of the steed is as follows:

Then Kyalo Sengcham Drugmo thought, "I have no choice but to catch the horse. However since this Joru is a lord of magical illusion, I wonder if he isn't just playing a trick on me?

If one doesn't already have herds and wealth, how can they be sought after in the mountains?[47] If there is indeed a horse to be found, it must be a horse unlike any other. I'd better ask again what it looks like, because if I don't, how will I know how to find it?" Then she began to sing this song of inquiry as to where the divine horse resides, in the melody of Unchanging Longevity:

> The song is Ala Ala Ala,
> And Thala gives the melody.
> Well then, sir, divine son Joru,
> The duty to catch your divine mount has fallen to me.
> But if the horse is already in someone else's possession, I dare
>   not take it from the mountain.
> Drugmo doesn't plan to be a lasso-wielding horse thief.

Gogmo doesn't have the guts to be a horse rustler.

There has never been a horse that was captured in the
mountains that was without an owner.[48]

Even if captured there are no accounts of that ever bringing
any benefit.

There is no way to mount a stripe-muzzled kyang;

And there is no one who would consider that a dark-muzzled
drong could be domesticated.

This wandering steed is not really from the species of wild
kyang,

It only looks as though it were a light-colored kyang.

This fine steed is not the kind to belong in a herd of horses,

It is not really a horse; it only looks like the horses that roam
the mountains.

To tell the truth, the whole thing seems completely
ridiculous.

If the horse is a siddhi from the gods above,

What is preventing it from just falling into Joru's hands?

If it's a treasure trove of the nāgas below,

What is preventing it from just appearing at Mother Gogmo's
door?

If you're looking for a man, you need to know his full
name.

When you lose your cattle, you have to search for[49] their
markings and characteristics.

To identify a mountain in a vast deserted place,

The coloring of a certain animal in the wilderness,

And not mistake the characteristics of the noble steed,

Boy Joru, please give me precise instructions,

And whatever you say I will accept as sweetness to my ears.

If you heard this song, I offer it as an ornament to your
hearing.

If you didn't, there's no way to explain it.

Thus she sang, and Gogmo's divine child Joru said, "That's right, Drugmo. If
the characteristics of this horse are not explained, you will never recognize him."
Then he sang this song giving advice about the steed and the place where he could
be found in the melody of Unchanging Longevity:

It's Ala Ala Ala.
With Thala the song is sung.
My dear mother, who was the abode of my whole body,
And Kyalo Sengcham of Ga, you two,
If you want to hear me, then listen with your gentle silken
    ears.
If you know how to analyze, then think with your white snow
    mountain minds.

The vast field, seeds, and moisture,
Together these three ripen into the nutritious grains and legumes.
The arrow, bow, and the archer's potent thumb,
Together these three can utterly cut off the life of the enemies.

Joru, Mother, and Drugmo,
Together these three can bring the divine horse to the starting
    gate.

Whether there were skillful means or not, it is irrelevant,
But the interdependency of nonexistent phenomena seems to
    be undeceiving.
Even though karmic cause and result are inevitable,
It is difficult to find someone who deeply believes this.

It's obvious that the kindness of parents is great,
Yet few are the descendants who fully repay them.
It's obvious that relatives and neighbors are friendly,
Yet it's hard to find ones who are truly sincere.
Discursive thoughts are convoluted like a sheep's second stomach,
Sometimes cheerful and sometimes grim.
Sometimes conversations are just like an artist's drawing,
Looking good from the front but nothing there from behind.

Sengcham Drugmo's determination to catch the horse
Comes from her mouth but not her heart.
Mother's capture of the horse in the mountain
Is easy to imagine but difficult to bring about.
Therefore you must supplicate the gods,

And then give ear to me;
For within the wide world of Jambudvīpa,
The birthplace of the great steed is the mountains Ma and
    Dza.
At the good mountain Penne Ritra [Colorful Tamarisk
    Mountain]
This horse, karmically destined for all lifetimes to be mine,
And I, came simultaneously to this middle land of humans.

His father was White Sky Horse,
Even so, he is not called White Sky Horse
As he was born into the line of steeds who come from Magyal
    Pomra in the east.
His mother was Sorrel Earth Horse,
Even so, he is not called Sorrel Earth Horse
As he enters the womb of the Female Earth Mare.
He is not a kyang, but a noble steed.
He's not an ordinary horse, because he is of the species of
    wild animals that wander the mountain passes.
There will be no mistaking him; you will know him by the
    markings of his coat.
The horse is not light-colored but sorrel,
His coat is the color of ruby red.
The tips of his ears have fine hairs like the finest vulture
    feathers,
His four hooves have wheels of wind.
The poll of the horse's head is square like a shapely mountain;
His muzzle seems as though secured to its sides.
His throat is in the shape of a beautiful bell,
Supported by the muscles of his neck.
His belly looks like a budding water-borne lotus,
Supported by his four legs.
His legs are straight like the trunk of a tree,
With his four hooves attached.

Unlike other steeds, this great steed has nine special features.
His forehead resembles that of the bird-demon falcon.
His neck is like that of a pika-demon weasel.

His face looks like that of a goat,
With fine hairs like a naive little rabbit's chin.
His eye sockets resemble those of an older toad;
His pupils look like that of an angry snake.
On his musk doe's muzzle
His nostrils look like empty silken sacks.
The tips of his spy-demon ears
Have fine hairs like vulture feathers.
The abundance of his features totals more than nine.

There is no way to mistake him, you will recognize him!
Not only that,
His head and ears resemble that of seven animals,
He has eighteen special muscles,
As well as twenty heroic bones,
And thirty-two hidden marks.
All of these great qualities of a stallion
Are complete in the body of this supreme steed.

First, when he flies, he holds to the pathway of the birds.
Second, if you speak, he can understand human language.
Third, when he's spoken to, he can respond in the human
    language.
These are the characteristics by which you cannot mistake the
    horse.
As if that were not enough,
In the flowering meadows of the mountaintops,
He can be found frolicking with a hundred stallions
And sporting with a hundred mares.
His forelock calls forth the gods;
His tail calls forth the nāgas.
His front legs will seem to say that he must go;
His back legs will seem to say that he must run.
The stallion of karmic connection
And Joru who gathers authentic presence—
These two are helpless but to join together.
Whether I go to Ling or not depends on this stallion.
Don't just sit there, gods and protectors,

Come today and befriend my mother.
Gods, gurus, and protectors,
Don't forget to be mindful of Drugmo.

Thus he sang, and Mother Gogmo and daughter Drugmo, with the help of the gods, nāgas, and nyens, went off to catch the horse.

Looking across from the top of the mountain pass, the excellent land of Mön-lam La, they saw all of the kyangs on the face of the mountain Penne Ritra. Some were scattered throughout the valley, while others grazed the high grasslands. When they watched carefully they saw a horse unlike the rest; a lord of all horses, 'Dorje Kyang Göd with his turquoise mane and tail and his ruby coat, glimmering rainbows swirling at the tips of his hairs, his four hooves prancing.[50] From the front he looked like burnished metal. From behind he looked like a white vulture swooping for food on the meadow. His lower body was low to the ground like that of a stalking vixen. He was turning and twisting like an undulating fish, his hocks full-fleshed like those of a doe's calf. He had the delicate breast of a female crane. His four joints were well-proportioned. His four tendons moved in perfect synchrony. When Drugmo saw him, he seemed to be a steed unlike any other, since he possessed the thirteen penetrating qualities and was surrounded by a flock of many-colored falcons.[51] Then she sang this song to Mother Gogmo:

Ala Ala Ala the song is sung.
Thala is the way the melody goes.
Guru, devas, and dharmapālas
Accompany me as I sing this song.
If you don't recognize this place,
It is the excellent land of Mönlam La.
Look right over there at that spectacle;
There's a mountain that looks like a king on his throne.
The Chinese call it Dongchen Nya [Great Fish Mountain];
Tibetans call it Penne Ritra.
There are clouds of rainbows massing about its peak,
And on its slope, grass tips in full bloom.
At the foot of the mountain are brilliant flowers.
There, among a hundred mares and a hundred colts of white-
     mouthed kyangs,
Is the Lord of Steeds, Wild Kyang.
He mingles with a hundred mares

And dances with a hundred colts.
His tail and mane play with the wind.[52]
The tips of his hair ripple with the colors of the rainbow.
Is he real or unreal? I can't be certain.
Sometimes when I perceive him as an illusory appearance,
Above him a magical garuḍa soars,
Behind him a white snow lion assumes a haughty pose, and
In front a tigress is leaping.
On his eyes, heart, spleen, and each leg,
And on his shoulders, mane, and splayed-out ribs,
Perch many multicolored falcons,
And horse gods gather like massing clouds.
What would be the point of that being an illusion?
That must certainly be the true Wild Kyang over there.
If you address him, surely he will understand human
    language.
If he flies, surely he will hold to the path of the birds.
There are oh so many supreme horses, countless ones,
But this steed is indeed best;
Drugmo knows she has made no mistake.
If he can be caught, it will be the will of the gods and
    protectors.
Gogmo, you must know what to do now.
If you understand this song, it is sweetness to your ears.
If not, then there's no way to explain it.

Thus she sang. When Gogmo saw Wild Kyang she was filled with joy. She thought, "If I am to catch Wild Kyang, it will be due to my previous karma with the gods and the Triple Gem. Without their help this would be impossible. Son Joru said that this horse speaks human language, so, while I get a posse of the gods and Three Jewels together, I will sing a song to him explaining the past and the reason we are here. I'm sure he will understand me." And so, she offered this song in the melody called the Free-Flowing River:

Ala Ala Ala the song is sung.
Thala is the way the melody goes.
You who dwell in the crown chakra of great bliss,
Guru Padmasambhava and

My offspring Little White Conch, Dungchung Karpo,* know me.
Help me to lasso Wild Kyang
And give me, Gogmo, your assistance.
You who dwell in the throat chakra of abundance,
Great Power Hayagrīva and your assembly of deities,
By the truth of the words of the Great Being's predictions,
Help me to lasso Wild Kyang
And give me, Gogmo, your assistance.
You who dwell in the heart chakra of truth,
Assembly of yidams and
My offspring Little Luminous Nāga Serpent, Ludrül
    Ödchung,
Help me to lasso Wild Kyang
And give me, Gogmo, your assistance.
You who dwell in the naval chakra of emanation,
Intangible ḍākinī and
My offspring Completely Luminous [Thalei Ödkar] and
    others,
Help me to lasso Wild Kyang
And give me, Gogmo, your assistance.
You who dwell in the secret chakra that sustains bliss,
Oath-bound dharma protectors and
My offspring magical son Joru, all of you together
Help me to lasso Wild Kyang
And give me, Gogmo, your assistance.
Don't be idle, imperial gods and protectors;
Help me to lasso Wild Kyang
And please give Mother one end of the lasso.
Well then, Supreme Steed,
Listen, I have a few things to tell you:

The sharp arrow notched with gold,
Left inside the quiver
Only embellishes the warrior's panoply.
Unless it serves to tame the enemy,

---

* A variation of the name Dungkhyung Karpo.

Its razor sharpness matters not.
A cherished son, who is a hero with a brave heart,
Although he may be the family's core,
If he doesn't protect his kin by taming the enemy,
His status as a son matters not.
The sprouts of the six grains are the ornament of the field.
Although they are the ornament of the vast field,
If they are not brought into the family's storehouse,
The flowering blossoms matter not.
The Supreme Steed is the ornament of supreme horses.
Although he is the ornament of the king of mountains,
If he does not come under the golden saddle,
Then his Mongolian gait matters not.

Father, mother, son, these three
Have not been deliberately placed together.
Even if we tried this could not turn out as planned.
No one can mandate the karma of previous lives.
A girl's good or bad looks,
A boy's courageousness, great or small,
Have not been deliberately created by parents.
Even if they tried, this could not turn out as planned.
For this is the ripening of good and bad karma.

Joru, Wild Kyang, Gogmo, we three—
Even if we had planned to come together,
It wouldn't have come about;
It's the mandate of the gods above.
Therefore, Wild Kyang, Joru's horse,
Come here and make friends with Gogmo.

First this cake made of five types of grain,
Second this drink, the finest of teas,[53]
Third, this square wool horse blanket—
These are the presentation gifts for the arrival of the Lord of
    Steeds.
And not only that,
This year there will be a special event:

White Ling's golden throne, a treasure trove,
And the bridegroom of Sengcham Drugmo—
All will be waged as a bet on you.
First you, the divine horse, will be called Lord of Steeds;
Second, Joru will be able to attain the golden throne;
And third, it will accomplish the mandate and purposes of
    the gods above.
According to Joru's design all this will certainly come to be;
The Wild Kyang who is wise
Together with Joru who possesses authentic presence,
Even from here I can see over there that you have this
    potential.
He said if I call you, you would understand human language.
Therefore, Wild Kyang, please come here.
To just stay there and feed yourself
Would merely be surviving like a desperate animal.
But if you come and accomplish the benefit of others,
Then consider the uncommon benefit of illusory beings.
Help magnetize White Ling
And help bind the four māras by oath.
Help establish the world in bliss.
Wild Kyang, hold this in your heart.

Having offered this song, she moved toward him, and all the other kyangs ran away. But the divine steed showed Gogmo that he was slightly interested and felt some affection for her. Then he raised this song to Gogmo, in the melody of a Modulating Long Neigh:

The song is Ala Ala Ala.
Thala is the melody of the song.
If you don't recognize this place
It is Penne Ritra of Tibet.
This is the pasture land of thousands of white-mouthed
    kyangs.
If you don't recognize me,
I am the messenger of the gods above.
I am the karmic treasure trove of the nyen of the middle
    space.

I am the karmically destined god of the horses.
My full name is Lord of Steeds Ever-Increasing Wild Kyang.
Now then, Gogmo, listen to me:

It's hard to domesticate an animal you've neglected.
It's hard to get what you really want without trying.
It's hard to have prosperity without merit.
It's hard to have children without karmic fruition.

I am the Supreme Steed, Lord of Horses, Wild Kyang.
I've stayed in Red Wetland Pastures[54] for three years,
I was on the Crag Mountain of Gu-ra for three years,
I stayed on the slopes of Yutse three years more,
And now I've been in Penne Ritra for three more years.
In the three months of summer, I roamed and grazed
With no shelter to protect me from the rains;
In the three months of winter I was tormented by the icy
     winds
With no blanket to cover my flanks.
In the three months of spring, when my stomach was
     growling,
There was no one to feed me even three bites of grass.
I am a stallion twelve years old;
It's too late for me to be saddle-broken.
All through these twelve long years:
First, a great horse like me had no owner;
Second, I had no saddle or bridle to show off to others;
Third, no warm stall for sleeping and no horse blanket,
And no food to fill my stomach.
How I wished and wished for these things, but this stallion
     wished in vain.
What I wished for never came.

So, first, I've never heard of anyone called Joru,
And since I've never seen the one called Gogmo,
Now that this Great Steed has grown old,
I would not even think of accepting the bridle.
I just won't accept the mandate of the gods above.

Even if I tried there would not be enough time left in my life
    to do this.
The bit will never fit this square mouth.
The saddle blanket will never cover my broad back.
Sister Drugmo means nothing to this horse.

If you don't sow seeds in the three months of spring,
It's hard to get the six grains in the three months of fall.
If cows are not fed in the three months of winter,
It's hard to get milk in the three months of spring.

If the steed is not regularly fed,
When an enemy raids, it is too late to capture him.

I will not stay here now for I am going off to the pure land.
I will not serve the purposes of beings in the intermediate
    human realm.
Since the boy Joru doesn't care about this horse,
Rather than surviving on my own as a horse, a mere animal,
I had better wander in the ranks of the gods above.
If you understand this song, it is sweetness to your ears.
If not, there's no way to explain it.

Thus he sang and then began to fan his vulture wings as if preparing to take to flight.[55] Meanwhile Gogmo sat there and prayed to the gods with one-pointed devotion. Then in the sky, from within the white clouds, appeared elder brother White-Conch Garuḍa, younger brother Little Light Nāga Serpent, and sister Completely Luminous, surrounded by a great company of gods, nāgas, and nyen sparkling like motes in the rays of the sun. They threw the ring of the lasso around the divine horse's neck and gave the other end of the rope into Gogmo's hand. The assembly of gods showered them with auspicious flowers; rainbow light tents were pitched. Many wondrous signs showed forth as she captured the horse. She led him down a little bit, thinking, "The real ones who captured this horse are the gods, nāgas, and nyens, and the lasso itself is a magical lasso. This supreme horse knows how to speak and understand. He has six broad wings to fly across the sky and other features unique even among the karmically destined horses of White Ling. So I must praise him and expound his sublime qualities."

Turning toward them she said, "Ya, Sengcham Drugmo of Kyalo, among the

herds of wealthy Kyalo and even the thirty karmically destined horses of White
Ling, there is no horse that could possibly compare with this one." She was on the
verge of singing a song, but since the time had not yet arrived for Drugmo to open
his great secret and explain the qualities of the horse, the horse bolted and took to
flight like a vulture soaring into the sky.[56] As he flew, Gogmo was in tow, grasping
her end of the lasso like a protection cord. As they flew higher up in space, they
could clearly see the countries of China, India, Persia, Mongolia, Jang, Mongolia,
and the land of the māras. It was then that the supreme horse broke into song, singing to Gogmo in the melody of a Modulating Long Neigh.

> The song is Ala Ala Ala.
> Thala is the melody of the song.
> The assembly of deities of Cakrasaṃvara in my body,
> And all the ḍākas and ḍākinīs who abide in my channels,
> The absolute deities of the three kāyas are my awareness.
> Lovingly look upon this supreme horse.
> Grant your blessings that I may accomplish the purpose of beings.
> If you don't recognize this place,
> It is the middle path of the birds in upper space.
>
> Look down and there's a spectacle to be seen:
> That mountain, which looks like a vulture is perched upon it,
> Is Vulture Peak Mountain in India.
> That mountain, which looks like a great sleeping elephant,
> Is Posing Elephant Mountain in China.
> That one great mountain with five peaks,
> Which looks like a ḍākinī wearing the crown of the five
>   families,
> Is Five-Peaked Mountain in China.
> The mountain that resembles a pure crystal vase
> Is the supreme site for meditation practice, Mount Kailash.
> These are the four supreme sacred mountains in the south of
>   Jambudvīpa.
>
> That mountain over there that resembles a guru wearing his
>   initiation hat
> Is Yarlha Shampo [Flowing Silk of the Upper Gods] in
>   central Tibet.

That mountain, which looks like a curtain of white silk,
Is Nyenchen Thanglha in Dam [in central Tibet].
That mountain, which looks like a crouching white lion cub,
Is Kulha Rigyal in the south.
That mountain like a colorful tigress cuddling her cub
Is called Öddei Gung-gyal [Radiant Heavenly King] in the east.
Those are the four great mountains of Tibet.

Look down there, there's more to see:
The square earth is covered with clouds and mist.
Where it seems that the happy day is flooded by darkness
Is the mountain pass in the darkness of the north called
    Chu-drug [Turbulent Waters].
The mountain that resembles a man's dark fell of hair
Is Jowo Namri [Lord Sky Mountain] of the far north.
That which resembles a black iron stake driven in the ground
Is the castle of the māras, Sharu Namdzong [Stag Horn Sky
    Fortress],
Also known as the nine-storied castle Bangkhar Naro [Castle
    of Muck].
This is the land to be tamed by the boy Joru;
This is the place where this horse will accomplish the benefit
    of beings.
This is the meditation place where an inexhaustible
    accumulation of the merit of samādhi will be accomplished.
If you want to remember this, Gogmo, hold it in mind.

The mountain that looks like a white torma offering for the gods
Is Gurkar of Hor's Palo Tsegyei [Wide-Peaked Mountain].
That castle that resembles a crimson Chinese knot
Is Yazi of Hor's Karmo Tsegtong [Thousand-Storied White
    Castle].
That is the place where boy Joru and I must go.
This is the place where Sister Drugmo's marriage will first go
    awry.
This is the place where all sorts of wise and skillful
    emanations will be produced.
If you want to remember this, Gogmo, hold it in mind.

Look down there, there's more to see:
The black mountain that looks like a woman dressed in black
Is Khasha Nyug-ri [Deer Bamboo Mountain] of Mön in the
    south.
The land that resembles an iron vajra thrust in the ground
Is Zhuyi Zhoro Trabtsen [Mighty White Armor of Zhu].
That red crag mountain resembling an angry cannibal demon
Is Sogkya Relpa [Braided White Grass Canyon].
That castle that looks like a mass of molten rock
Is the kāya castle of King Shingtri in the south.
Some call it Pang-ra Yu-dzong [Fenced Meadow Turquoise
    Fortress],
Some call it Samdrub Lingdzong [Fortress That Fulfills All
    Wishes],
And others call it Tong-ri Namdzong [Thousand Mountains
    Sky Fortress].
It is the place where the black demon casts down his Mu cord.
This is a field the boy Joru will tame.
This is the place where this horse will travel through the skies.
If there is an arrow with white feathers, it will be useful in this
    place.
If you want to remember this, Gogmo, hold it in mind.

Look down there, there's more to see:
That black lake, which resembles boiling poisonous waters,
Is the poison lake of Beri.
The black castle that looks like a pillar between heaven and
    earth
Is the ancestral castle of King Sadam of the land Jang.
It is also called the ancestral kāya castle of Zimtri.
The mountain that looks like an old man sneaking out to spy
Is Mi-gen Jatri [Old Man Leading a Bird] in Ding-ri.*
That mountain, which resembles a cuckoo perched on a rock,
Is Colorful Tiger Nose Soul Mountain [La-ri Tagna Trawo].
This is a field the boy Joru will tame;

---

* This is a district in Tibet.

This is the place where this horse will bring the benefit of
   beings.
That is a valley of sin where the dharma does not flourish.
That is the place where the wishes of the White Fish Belly[57]
   will be accomplished.
If you want to remember this, Gogmo, hold it in mind.

Beyond these, we are unable to even count the mountains.
If the qualities of this horse were to be expounded,
Then it must be the people of White Ling who sing my
   praises,
If not them, then not you, Mother Gogmo, for that would
   embarrass me.
Nobody really knows all the good qualities this horse
   possesses
Except for Sister Drugmo,
So Mother Gogmo, don't stay here, return to Ling,
And I, the horse Kyang-bu, will not stay here but go to the
   land of the gods.
If you understand this song, it is sweetness to your ears.
If not, there is no way to explain it.

Thus he sang, and within an instant, like magic, he landed at the Five-Peaked
Mountain of China. It turned out that Joru was already there. He whipped the horse
three times, and it flew across the sky like a meteor, landing back at Mount Penne.

Gogmo was delighted. She led the horse down to Sengcham Drugmo, who
said to her, "Since we've caught the horse, it's time to leave. Once we've given the
horse to Joru, we will have accomplished our mutual goal." Accordingly, they hur-
ried to lead the horse to Joru. The horse started trying to break away from them. Just
when they couldn't hold him any longer, they called out, "Joru! Joru! We're losing
the horse!" Joru replied, "Just let him go, Mother. Today we two, the karmically
destined horse and Joru, chosen by the gods, have finally met."

After all of the ups and downs Gogmo had been through, she came to this
conclusion, "The only kind of person who could handle this horse would be a sorcerer endowed with the magical strength of the power of karma. Surely I cannot be
the one to pull this horse back." She threw her end of the rope back to the horse and
let him loose. Like an affectionate son going up to his mother, the horse pranced up
to Joru and stood close to him. Joru lovingly stroked him for a long time, and then,

taking the rope, he said "Ah, Sister Sengcham Drugmo, I, Joru, have finally acquired Wild Kyang as a gift from the gods. Now it's okay to go to Ling. We, mother and son, have no wealth that is greater than this horse. You, girl from Kyalo, are the owner of many herds of horses, and you have experienced the quality of the brethren's thirty karmically destined horses. So tell me if my horse is superior, inferior, or equal and whether he belongs in the ranks of the brethren's karmic horses. What are the qualities of horses in general, and, in particular, what are the good and bad points of this Wild Kyang? Please expound on the subject of horses." Then Drugmo sang this song, giving the history of horses and explaining the good qualities of the divine horse in the melody called Six Modulations in Nine Pitches:

> The song is Ala Ala Ala.
> Thala is the melody of the song.
> I supplicate the Supreme and Rare Three Jewels.
> Please remain inseparable as my crown ornament
> And befriend me today.
> No matter how many songs I sing, may they be imbued with
>   the dharma.
> Now then, Gogmo's divine son,
> Listen, I have some things to tell you.
> According to the worldly Tibetan proverbs:

> *If you don't know the good qualities of the divine gurus,*
> *Rendering them reverence is like rubbing oil into a stone.*
> *If the teachings of the Buddha, whether sutra or tantra, are not*
> *   mixed with the mind,*
> *Then reading dharma scriptures is like the chanting of a parrot.*

> *If humans do not know their ancestral lineage,*
> *They are like wandering monkeys in the endless jungle.*
> *If you do not know the value of something*
> *You are like a stranger who has lost his way.*

> If you don't understand what distinguishes a noble steed,
> You can't just go around calling every horse a thoroughbred.
> In the classes of noble horses there are four types:
> The Dowa [Noble Steed] itself, the Begto, and the Mu-
>   kheng, these three,

And the Gyiling steed, make up the four types.
Of the Dowa breed the long-torsoed ones are the best.
Of the Begto breed, the white ones are the best.
Of the Mu-kheng breed, the bulky ones are the best.
Of the Gyiling breed, the light ones are the best.
The larger noble steed is like the sun shining in the sky.
In all four directions it has perfect proportions.
The cross-breed resembles a taut silken thread,
Supple on the outside, firm on the inside.
The smaller noble steed is like an iron flute,
Its coat is fine and its body long.
There are three kinds of frontlets [the face] for a horse.
The superior horse must have a garuḍa frontlet,
The middling horse must have a goat frontlet,
And the horse with the frontlet of a deer is inferior.
There are also three varieties of hocks,[58]
The bull hock, deer hock, and goat hock,
Which correspond to the superior, mediocre, and inferior horses.

There are seven types of horse teeth:
The kyang type is big and concave,
The bull type is like pennycress,[*]
The sheep type is small and pearly white.
These three are the best teeth of all.
First, the teeth are mighty like a tiger's;
Second, the teeth jut out like a camel's;
Third, the teeth are snaggle-toothed like a pig's.
These are the three worst types of teeth.
The kyang teeth with their small concavity are of
    intermediate quality.

There are five different types of coats.
First, the long coarse fur, like that of a deer;
Second, the short coarse hair of a tiger;
These two are the superior coats.

---

* A medicinal herb with small leaves.

First, the long and smooth fur, like that of a fox, and
Second, short and smooth like that of a grizzly bear, are the
    two worst coats.
The donkey coat, which is neither smooth nor coarse,
Belongs to horses of middling breed.

There are seven kinds of hooves.
A hoof that is high and attractive like a fine cup made from
    rhino horn,
A hoof that is worn down with a rim like ridged copper
    petals,
A hoof that is short and straight down like iron fangs.
These are the three superior types of hooves.
Hooves drawn in with no cleft in the sole, that's one;
Second, rounded with no edge;
The third is flat and leaves no clear print behind.
These three are the worst types of hooves.
The quality of the four hooves is intermediate if they appear
    to be well proportioned.

In general a horse must have sturdy bones.
The sturdy upper neck bones [are like] those of a tiger,
One likes them to be nicely rounded.
The solid backbone is in the middle.
If the three main joints of the back are curved, it is best.
The lower sturdy bones are the hooves;
The large hooves should be thick and short.
What's more, there is the back of the head behind the ears.
It's best if it is low rather than high.
Behind the tail are the haunches,
It is better if this is high, rather than low.

The muscles of the thigh[59] should not be bulging
Like a pregnant woman's belly, but are better flat.
The forelocks on top of the head should be thick.
It is better if this is high, rather than low.
The mane that flows like smooth silk
Is better long, rather than short.

The forelock, like a pillar to the sky,
Should be lofty rather than low.
The neck, like a stretched-out scarf,
Is better long than short.

The rib cage,[60] where lungs reside,
It is better small than large.
The back of the torso where the kidneys rest
Is better to be pulsating than to be weak.
And as it pulsates, it's best if the ribs move in rhythm.

The lungs are the vessel for the breath; it's advantageous if
    they're buoyant.
The liver is the vessel of the blood; it's advantageous if it's small.
The intestines are the vessel for the grass; it's advantageous for
    them to be large.
The spleen is the vessel of the blood; it is best to be clean.
Those are the four vessels of the great steed.[61]

An important person's head must have a hat;
If the horse's head and ears are excellent then this is like
    having a hat.
Even an unimportant person must have shoes on their feet;
For a horse the four joints and hooves are best if they are large.
Above the tail at the rump
Must be large enough to just about place a liter of grain.
Between the eyes and ears there should be a clear cavity,
And a narrowing[62] between the two nostrils.
Between the front of the forehead and shoulders there must
    be definition.
And the four limbs must be solidly built,
The four cannon bones [lower legs] are best if spread apart.[63]

Now, there are five [kinds of] horses skilled in racing:
Falcon Breast, Yak Shoulder, and Crouching Lion,
With one such mount [Falcon Breast], the legs of the wild
    northern kyang can be whipped.

[Yak Shoulder] like an autumn yak, with its thick high mane
    and a head like a mattock,
Can catch a baby wild yak on the run in the hills with a lasso.
[Crouching Lion] with its stout loins and hunched back
Can get close enough to a shade-dappled doe to snap it with
    a whip.
[Fourth] the horse with a head like a spool of thread, flaring
    nostrils, and pika eyes
Can run so fast, you can catch a rabbit on the run.
[Fifth] the vicious horse that fights his friends looks like a rat,
    a tiger, or a red deer;
His speed is equal to that of the scudding clouds in the sky.
These are the five types of superior racehorses.

The Ūgpa Belpo [Abundance of Owls], which can beat a
    hundred of the finest horses in a race;
The Dru-gu Bershel [Turkish Lapis Crystal], which can beat
    a thousand;
And then Garwa Kang-ring [Long-Legged Dancer], which
    beats ten thousand mules;
And Dza Tshangpa Bumding [Rocky Brahmā One Hundred
    Thousand Leaps], which beats a hundred thousand:
Those four are called the Four Competition Brothers.

As if that weren't enough,
On the head of each of these excellent horses
One finds the seven features named after seven animals:
The forehead[64] of the brown drong [wild yak],
The protuberant eye socket like that of a tortoise,
The pupils of an angry snake,
The nostrils of a white snow lion,
The lips of the red tigress,
Fine vulture-down ears, and
A muzzle like the chin of a deer.[65]
These are the finest features that resemble seven
    animals;
This horse is endowed with them all.

As though that wasn't enough,
On the body of each of these excellent horses
One can find rippling muscles named after the young of
    eighteen [animals]:
The temporalis muscle shaped like the crossed neck of a crow
Can be found on the temple.
The muscle attached to the skull just behind the ear,
Looks like two tigress' necks crossed.
The masseter muscles on the cheek look like the stomach of a
    sheep full of water.
The muscle on the side of the horse's neck looks like the form
    of a fish.
The cervical trapezius muscle on the base of the neck looks
    like a saw.
The dorsal trapezius muscle around the collar that connects
    with the whole body resembles a split shoulder of a yak.
The muscle between the front leg and the chest resemble the
    form of a frog.
The muscle on the shoulder resembles the rising moon.
The muscles of the lower leg are like a taunt golden chord.
The muscles of the spine resemble a slithering black snake.
The latissimus muscle where the saddle is placed is like the
    pitched spokes of a golden wheel.
The intercostal muscles where the saddle sides touch are like a
    turquoise dragon entering its cave.
The croup muscles are like a heap of wool.
The gastroc muscles are like piglets asleep in their sty.[66]
The muscles of the loins are like a sack of barley,
The inner thigh muscle like a tightly wound ball of yarn.
The muscles under the intestines are like the tributaries of a
    great deep river.
Muscles that look like fingers are located at the base of the tail.
These are called the eighteen kinds of rippling muscles;
This horse is endowed with them all.

As though that wasn't enough:
The domed cranium should be thick,
The cheekbone should be prominent,

The cranial cavity[67] should be elevated three finger widths.
The poll should be like palms pressed together.
The head and the neck should be elegantly joined,
The withers should be thick.
The scapula should be fine and wide,
The humerus should be short and relaxed,
The fore cannon bones should be straight and supple,
Where the saddle is placed, the horse should be slightly broad.
The three intervertebral joints should be flexible.
The ribs should splay out like feathers.
The shape of the pelvis should be long,
The femur should be short, and the head of the femur should
    be wide.
The hind cannon bones should be straight, and the femur
    should be curved.
The four pastern bones just above the hooves should be long.
The four fetlocks are better to be short.
The root of the coccyx should be short and thick.
These are the twenty bones of a hero.
It is said that each superior horse has them;
All of these are complete within this horse.
This is a general explanation about horses.

Now as to this divine horse:
He is elegant and shimmers with the colors of a rainbow.
He is eager to run, and is dazzling as he goes.
He is an emanation of Hayagrīva.
He is not the usual piebald sorrel but is altogether red,
The color of a ruby.
The hair on his body is entirely red,
Indicating that he magnetizes the assembly of Hayagrīva deities.
He tosses his dark tail and mane,
Indicating that he magnetizes an assembly of wrathful
    annihilating deities.
His teeth and muzzle are exceptionally white, like the rays of
    the radiant moon,
Indicating that he magnetizes an assembly of deities who
    pacify illness and demonic forces.

His underbelly is a rich golden color,
Indicating that he magnetizes an assembly of enriching deities
    who increase longevity and merit.
The downy vulture feathers on the tips of his ears
Indicate that he magnetizes guardians who illuminate like a
    torch.
His shoulders are wheels of wind,
Indicating that he magnetizes the dralas who have mastery of
    long life.
The iron petals of his four hooves
Indicate that he magnetizes the dralas who tame the four
    māras.

This ever-increasing steed Lord of Horses
Has all the marks of a sovereign of saṃsāra and nirvāṇa:
The height and beauty of his head
Is a sign that he venerates the Three Jewels.
That the size of his body is comparable to that of all other
    horses
Indicates that he has mastered bodhicitta in his being.
His tail and mane being thick and long
Indicates his emanations are unceasing.
That his eyeballs are clear and sparkling
Indicates that he has the direct realization of the nature of
    phenomena,
And that there is a pair [of eyes]
Indicates that the scope of his knowledge encompasses both
    saṃsāra and nirvāṇa.
That they see congruently
Indicates the ultimate inseparability of the two [saṃsāra and
    nirvāṇa].
That both ears are extremely beautiful
Indicates that he is in harmony with the path of the two truths.
That these sense organs are complete on a single head
Indicates that everything is subsumed as a single nature.
That he is adorned with six sense faculties
Indicates that he maintains the conduct of the six perfections.
That he dances and prances with his four hooves

Indicates that he nourishes beings through the four
   gatherings.[68]
The white of his pale underbelly
Indicates that he is unstained by the faults of existence.
That he occasionally speaks human language
Indicates that he can reveal that the sound of words has no
   true inherent existence.
That he flies in the sky from time to time
Indicates that all appearances are an illusory play.
His bond of affection toward humans
Indicates that he sees all beings with loving wisdom and
   compassion.
That he could be caught with a lasso
Indicates that his buddha activity is ever-increasing.
If he is ridden, that he can carry a great being
Indicates that he can lead all beings on the path to liberation.
That his gait that is comfortable and swift
Indicates that he will accomplish the benefit of beings
   through skillful means.
For any other ordinary stallion
An explanation like this would be pointless.
But to praise this divine horse, the white-muzzled one,
Matches the truth of what he really is.
Just look at how pleasing this horse is!
That's not all; what a wonderful marvel this horse is!
For among the thirty winged horses of White Ling,
Once Dongtsen's colt Turquoise Bird
Was said to have the strength of a garuḍa in flight.
He may, but that's no great wonder;
Any animal that can fly has that quality.
Denma's Ngültrug Denpa
And Tag-rong's Gu-gu Rogdzong
Are both said to be horses with the gift of speech;
Even though everyone says this is amazing,
It's no great wonder.
There are other animals that know how to speak;
Sengtag's Tong-ri Darjam [Smooth Silk Thousand
   Mountains],

Gyatsha's Gyaja Sogkar [Pheasant White Shoulder],
And Chipön's Sha-kyang Drelgo [Ochre Mule Head], and
    others,
Have all the qualities of great steeds, yet
I think that's not such a great marvel.
For their outer bodies and inner thoughts
Are none other than those of animals.

But this horse outwardly appears as a beast of burden, a horse,
While inwardly possessing the wisdom mind of a buddha.
He is an emanation of the mighty Hayagrīva.
Just meeting him is enough to close the door to the lower
    realms.
Just riding him is to be carried to the citadel of peace.
Such a supreme horse as this,
It's amazing that we have encountered him today.

As if that's not enough:
When we saw this horse on the mountain
He was captured by the gods, nāgas, and nyen, these three.
The rope was a magical lasso.
He has wings that soar in the sky.
He has hooves to land on the earth.
When he lives outdoors, he is free and easy.
If one were to have a horse such as this,
If he flew, he would find the path of the birds.
Unrivaled even by a garuḍa,
If he raced, the swiftness of his speed
Would be difficult for the horses of Ling to equal.
The finish line is in the palm of your hand.
Now, don't stay, Joru, come to Ling,
Let the fame of this steed become public,[69]
And let it be that the boy Joru holds the throne.
If you heard this, let it be a melodious offering to your ears.
If you didn't, there is no way to explain it.
Boy Joru, take this into your heart.

Thus she sang, and Drugmo's previous karma awakened, and she realized the qualities of the horse just as they are. Although she knew that Joru possessed magical powers, she didn't understand that his poor appearance and ugly body were also his magical manifestation. She was hoping Dongtsen would win, but at the same time she fully understood that the winner of the wager would be Joru and this horse.

———

This completes the account of how the horse was caught, called the Saga of the Precious Steed, and concludes the third chapter.

> It is Hayagrīva who appears as the Sorrel Steed.
> The magical legged one is captured by the magical lasso.

Thus the meaning of this is that Great Power Lotus Hayagrīva emanates as the Sorrel Steed to be captured on the mountain by gods, nāgas, nyens, along with humans, showing how they mastered the power of the magical legged one. The account is now complete.

CHAPTER FOUR

Joru is invited to come to upper White Ling, and
Drugmo presents him with the golden saddle and other
    necessary appurtenances
Signifying the words of truth of the eight great aspirations.
This gives rise to the Saga of the Precious Minister.

THE FOURTH [CHAPTER] on the way Joru returns to Ling is as follows:

Joru says to Drugmo and his mother, "I can go to upper White Ling, but since this horse of mine isn't the least bit broken in, I won't be able to ride him. Furthermore, I don't yet have any gear such as a saddle, saddle blanket, or bridle. If I try to mount him without these, I could have a fatal accident and, if that happens, the blame will fall on Drugmo's head. Instead, it's better if Mother can lead my horse, and we go on ahead. But Drugmo, you have your own horse and I am holding a stick, so it might be hard to keep up with you."

Drugmo replied, "Joru, you ride Dromug [Roan], and I can walk. I can keep up with you on foot." Saying that, she came down a bit. Joru was gazing at a musk deer on the far side of the mountain, and he said to Drugmo, "Over there, hidden in the shady side of that mountain, is a deer called Chung-la Rogchung [Black Demonic Deer]. If he's not immediately bound by oath there will be trouble. You sing a song, and, and while he's distracted by listening to it, I'll rope him with the lasso." He started off, and Drugmo sang this song:

It is Ala Ala Ala.
Thala is the melody of the song.

Through the mountain pass ridge of Sa-nag of the shady side
   of Ma[70]
Joru and Drugmo are journeying to Ling.
Although we are trying to proceed, it seems like we are not
   moving,
Yet we are on our way.
Joru said that he would bind the demon musk by oath,
Not because he's a demon, but because of his musk.
He is thinking only of getting the buck's musk
And intending to eat the doe's meat.
Generally phenomena are not truly existent;
It seems that today nothing is true.
There's no reason this musk deer lives in shady Ma;
Why would he have left behind one untamed demon?
Joru himself is not real, he is just magical;
The musk deer is not real, he is an illusion.
Drugmo is not real; her song is merely false.
If all of this actually turns out to be true,
Keep in mind that Joru means to kill
And that Drugmo is planning to deceive you with this little
   song.
The musk deer are distracted by eating grass.
The way confusion occurs in our minds is similar.
Either the musk deer's life is over,
And Joru and I are on the same team,
Or Drugmo has been deceived,
And Joru and you and the musk deer are in cahoots.
I can't tell the difference!

Thus she sang this lovely song, and Joru threw the lasso such that the loop caught the musk deer by the neck. Then Joru pulled the deer in front of Drugmo, and as they struggled, Drugmo began stoning the deer to death. Suddenly Joru stood up and said, "Shocking! Sister Drugmo, I'm supposed to be the one who tamed the deer, but you jumped the gun and killed him. This deer's death was in vain, and Joru's opportunity to tame him was lost.[71] Now the mind of this deer has been cast down into the lower realms, and you have dishonored your father Kyalo's tribe. You even said something as crass as, 'if it is a buck, I want the musk; if it is a doe, I want the meat,' like the saying, *ruining one's wealth over a single meal.*

When it comes to the horse race of White Ling, since you are the heart jewel
for which the Noble Steed is competing, now I'm compelled to broadcast this story
using your name and reputation. Not only that, if I really think about the way you
spoke, pretending to see that appearances were not really as they seemed, I would
have thought you would never kill this deer. You seem to care about evil deeds ver-
sus virtue, but look at how viciously you killed him. Now listen to this song," and he
began to sing in the melody of Unchanging Longevity:

> It is Ala Ala Ala.
> Thala is the melody of the song.
> May the Three Jewels of Refuge
> Dwell inseparably as my crown ornaments.
> This place is Nyag-ma'i Dong [Notch Ridge]⁷² in the shade of
>   Ma,
> I am called Gogmo's Joru.
> Listen and I'll tell you how it is:

> *Meditation that is without learning*
> *Is like an arrow without a bow, and*
> *Learning without any practice*
> *Is like a bow without an arrow.*
> *It is hard to unite these two,*
> *But if it is done, that makes an authentic guru.*

> *Bravery without armor and weapons*
> *Is like a sword without a handle, and*
> *Armor and weapons without bravery*
> *Are like a handle with no sword.*
> *It is hard to unite these two,*
> *But if it is done, that makes a hero.*

> *A good-looking woman with no wisdom*
> *Is like a slingshot without a stone;*
> *Although fashionable, is not practical.*
> *A wise woman without good looks*
> *Is like a stone with no slingshot;*
> *There when you want her, but not useful.*
> *It is hard to unite them,*
> *But if it is done, that makes the perfect woman.*

With inner intelligence as sharp as the point of a lance,
Speech as elegant as the colorful banner,
Deeds as valuable as the sandalwood handle—
If these three unite, that's called a wise person.
But to have brought them together is difficult.

Mistakes that are made through lack of understanding
Are like the suicide of a madman.
Having understanding but applying it mistakenly
Is like an animal that licks its own ass.[73]

Words without deeds
Are like a bird without its six wings.

Saying that Joru does not really exist, but is an illusion—
What's the point of bringing a mere phantom to Ling?
Saying that the musk deer does not really exist, but is an
    illusion—
What's the point of killing a magical emanation with a stone?

Your intentions, words, and deeds, these three,
Each one is more exaggerated than the next.
Your devious intent, your critical words,
And your deeds only sow the seeds of sin.
Your name Sengcham, Lion Sister, means nothing,
Calling yourself Drugmo is full of conceit.

A raven carrying meat ascends to the mountain peak,
A deer carrying an arrow descends to the valley floor.

I, Joru, will bring this story to the attention of the brethren,
Explaining the basis of this quarrel.
Joru was mandated by the gods above
To be the one to bind the demon musk deer by oath.
But you, Drugmo of the middle world of nyens,
Unskillfully jumped the gun.
This act has denigrated the merit of the black-haired race,
Brought disgrace upon the female gender, and

Defamed the brilliance of Ling.
Now Joru is hard-pressed not to take action.
If you think my decision unfair,
Then among Kyalo Tönpa's innermost wealth,
The golden bridle called Wishing Gem,
And the golden crupper called Wish-Fulfilling,
Are really the karmically destined possessions of the gods
    above.
When there is a horse race of White Ling
Don't place them among the prizes, but give them to me.
If you do, then Joru will shut his mouth.
You, Drugmo, keep this in mind.

Thus he sang, and Drugmo thought that, no matter what, there was no choice but to offer the golden bridle, so she promised she would present it to him.

After that, they departed for Ling. As soon as Joru mounted Drugmo's mule (or horse), he whipped it once or twice with the white willow staff, Jangkar Berka,[74] and, like an arrow shot by a skilled archer, he crossed the mountain pass Lha-lam Gongma [Upper Divine Path] of Ma Kali [White Ma]. Even though Drugmo ran as fast as she could, she couldn't keep up with him. When she reached the top of the mountain pass, looking down, she saw Joru's severed head. Terrified and utterly bereft, she started down the mountain, weeping, and overcome with misery. There she saw Joru's severed right arm with the sleeve still stuck to it and, a little farther down, was his right leg with the shoe still on. His inner organs and guts were strewn everywhere. The horse (previously called a mule) Dromug was standing there, steaming in its own sweat, with Joru's other severed foot and leg still in the stirrup. Drugmo gathered all the pieces of his scattered body. His two eyes were bulging from his head. Saying, "Turn back the dead eyes that look upon the living," she threw ashes on the face, hiding it from view.[75] So that no one would walk over his corpse, she pilled many white stones upon it, stating, "Now I'm definitely not going back to my homeland of Ling. I don't want to suffer, since no one with a body can avoid death, but I failed in my responsibility to bring Joru, the younger brother of the Bumpa, back alive. If I, Drugmo, am not there, then the Lesser Lineage will be happy, and it will be easier for my parents as well." Thinking that she should go jump into the poisonous lake Beri, she left riding Dromug.

When she reached the shore of the poisonous lake, she thought to herself, "Now, there's no reason to take my own life as though I were truly insane, but instead I should supplicate my personal deity and transfer my consciousness and that of Joru together to the pure lands. It's best to throw this illusory material body into the lake." So she covered her head with her nomadic hooded cape and called on all the deities for help, while she sang this song:

> It is Ala Ala Ala.
> Thala is the melody of the song.
> From the tip of the central energy *avadhūti*,[*]
> Dharmakāya Great Vajradhara, know me.
> From the tip of the *lalana* channel,[†]
> Sambhogakāya Avalokiteśvara, know me.
> From the tip of the *rasana* channel,[‡]
> Nirmanakāya Padmasambhava, know me.
> From the sun and moon seat on the crown of my head,
> Kind and gracious root guru, know me.
> From the tent of light in the space in front,
> Buddha Amitābha, know me.
> In the ocean of suffering of saṃsāra,
> If one can abandon confused appearances there will be bliss
>   and well-being.
> Well-being and suffering rely upon each other.
>
> By working to attain happiness and well-being,
> One will succeed in producing a harvest of suffering;
> It's hard to accomplish the purpose of one's goals.
> It is said that the essence of saṃsāra is suffering;
> If so, then they have reaped the essence.
> Happiness and suffering are like ripples on the water.
> This material body is like a narrow valley;
> If too many things come its way, something's going to give.
> It's hard to put up with this for too long.
> Well, then, since Joru has died,

---

[*] The central wisdom nāḍi, or channel (Tib. *dbu ma*), that runs up the middle of the human body.

[†] The left nāḍi (Tib. *rkyang ma*) of the human body.

[‡] The right nāḍi (Tib. *ro ma*) of the human body. The right and left channels start at the nostrils and run alongside the central channel, connecting with it four finger-widths below the navel chakra.

Why should I regret my death?
I'll go to join the assembly of pure deities.
They say that saṃsāra is impermanent.
Merely saying that does not make it true.
Delighting in the objects of desire
Brings pleasure to the five sense faculties.
It is said that death is suffering.
Merely saying that does not make it true.

A guru steeped in practice will take joy in death,
A prisoner of great crimes takes joy in death,
A person maddened by demons takes joy in death,
Parents with a burden of great suffering take joy in death.

If you have whatever makes you happy, you have well-being,
    and
If that sense of well-being pervades your mind,
Then unhappiness is just an acquired label.
That's why Drugmo now takes joy in death.
May the unobstructed emptiness and luminosity of my mind
Mingle inseparably with the mind of Joru.
Unsullied by the confusion of hope and fear,
May we mingle as one taste in the expanse of the dharmakāya.
This karmic illusory material body
Came about from the three poisons,
And now it will be thrown back into the middle of the lake of
    poison.

May all the buddhas and bodhisattvas
Come to lead Joru to the pure land,
And Drugmo's view will push from behind;
Through this may Joru achieve the immutable state.
Through this deed that discerns saṃsāra from nirvāṇa,
Into the mental bardo body of further confusion
This girl will definitely not go.
If this girl can accomplish these words of truth,
May Dromug go back to Ling, and
May my parents have no suffering.

Thus she sang, and kicked her horse with the stirrups to ride forward, but she felt as if somebody was restraining the horse, and when she looked back to see, there was Joru, pulling the tail of her horse, Dromug. When Drugmo saw that, she was overwhelmed with shame and burst into tears as well as uncontrollable laughter that cleared away the pain. She dismounted, and Gesar said to her, "Hey, Kyalo Seng-cham girl, the worldly proverb says:

Cloyed by happiness like a buck howling in the wilderness,
Cloyed by suffering like an owl laughing in the darkness,
Cloyed by a full stomach like a wolf still crying for meat.

You are too beautiful; your father, Kyalo, too rich; and the brethren cherish you too much. Is this the suffering that makes you want to throw yourself in the lake? That may be true, but I, Joru, didn't die when you crushed me under those rocks. Why do you need to do Transference of Consciousness [*phowa*] for the living? From your own lips you said, 'I am happy to die,' but you must be afraid of death because you closed your eyes. You're afraid of being wounded, because you covered your head. You're afraid of getting wet, so you came riding the horse. What were you really thinking? Although you said you're not going to the bardo, does closing your eyes and covering your head stop you from entering the bardo? I'm going to tell my brother Gyatsha and all of White Ling what you've done. The renown of your beauty and the sweetness of your sweet voice have covered the earth, but the greater notoriety of your mind has been unknown until now."

Then Drugmo said, "Dear divine child Joru, I thought you were dead and, filled with fear, I experienced immeasurable sorrow. I had no idea you were displaying your magical powers. Torture me no further, and please come with me to Ling. If you tell these stories to others, what will it matter? It is no more than what the proverb says:

A person with a busy mind who leaves home,
Will return with many kinds of stories.

If you use a diseased head as a prosperity support,
Then the contagion itself will be unceasing.[76]

So, please don't say those things," she said.

Then Joru responded to her by singing this playful song:

It is Ala Ala Ala.
Thala is the melody of the song.
I supplicate the Three Jewels of Refuge.
This place is the inlet of the poison lake in the Be[ri] valley.
And I am the one called Gogmo's Joru.
I'm the heart son of a thousand buddhas
And a manifestation of the three families of protectors.
I am of the lineage of the clan of Mukpo Dong.
Listen, for I have something to say.
In Lower Ma, the homeland of demons and rakśasas,
Is the place where Joru and his mother made their home.
Sometimes we stayed in a state of magical phenomena,
And other times we stayed there in a playful state.
Those are all Joru's nature.
At that time there was no lama to perform Phowa.
If you don't have the power to transfer your own mind,
To then think that you can transfer the mind of another is a
    sign of delusion.

Your father, mother, and the brethren, who are so doting;
Your good family, youthful beauty, and wealth, these three;
Your golden jewelry, your zi garland, and your silken
    garments, these three; and
The gods, protectors, and Joru who play with you—
The twelve great sufferings, as you call them—
Throwing your own life away in the waters
You say is the best of all happiness.
Girl, it seems that you are really full of wisdom.
The way you take even my playfulness as real
Shows clearly just how far your view goes.
Intending to end your life in the lake,
Indicates that your meditation has reached the immutable ground.
That you covered your head with your hood
Seems to indicate how you distinguish saṃsāra from nirvāṇa
    through your conduct.
Your prayer for Dromug to return to Ling
Seems to indicate that you have severed all attachment.

The way you crushed me under stones before I was dead
And threw ashes in my living eyes
Really shows your pure intentions for Ling.
Whatever you said were words of truth indeed;
So the whole truth will be told to upper White Ling.

First, the plants on the mountain peaks,
Second the gray-haired meadows of green grass,
Third, the flower patches of the steppes;
Don't try to stop the animals from eating, but watch and see which
    one they eat.

The uneaten leftovers are a bonus.
If all three are eaten, there's nothing to regret.

Whether you win or lose is according to previous karma.
The white rack is on the head of the buck,
The musk is in the body of the deer,
The fine fur is on the mountain dog fox;
Don't ponder which one the hunter will kill today, just watch and see.

If none of them are killed and they're left there, all will be happy.
If all three are killed, there's no regret.
Whether you win or lose, it's due to previous karma.

All these mishaps are in Drugmo's mind,
And all of the story will be in Joru's mouth.
Both incompatible stories are in our minds.
Without keeping it secret, the story will be told as it is to
    Ling.

If it brings neither benefit nor harm, we'll both be happy.
If we both lose, there's no cause for remorse.
If you win or lose, it is because of your previous karma.
Isn't that the way it is, dear Sengcham Drugmo?

If you don't want to argue with me, then
Among Kyalo's wealth of prosperity supports

There is a golden saddle with nine circular designs,
Which is a karmic treasure of the middle land of nyen,
Where the life-force talisman of the steed abides.
The saddle blanket marked with the nine astrological
    diagrams at the four corners
Is the karmic wealth of the cold-blooded nāgas of Lake
    Manasarovar,
And it's the place where the white prosperity sheep's life force
    abides.
Wild Kyang has not yet gained these appurtenances,
And I, Joru, have not yet gained them.
If there's to be a horse race, there's no way I can do without
    them.
If you give both of them to me,
Joru will relax and stop doing magic,
And Joru won't speak of this, he'll be quiet.
Sister Drugmo, keep this in mind.

Thus he sang, and Drugmo thought, "Since Joru didn't die, everything he does must be purely a magical display. All the mishaps I've committed must not be told to anyone. Even if I have to steal these things to give them to him, I have no choice but to do it. Everything depends on this gift." With that in mind, she promised Joru she would offer them to him.

From there, they both went up to Seven Sandy Passes, where Drugmo had met the Indian minister Berkar when she first arrived. Joru had sat down for a brief rest when they heard the sound of many pikas running to and fro. Suddenly there emerged a sizeable white pika wearing the very scarf Drugmo had given the minister. Then that pika offered this song to Joru:

It is Ala Ala Ala.
Thala is the melody of the song.
If you don't recognize this place,
It's the Seven Sandy Passes of the land of Ma.
In case you don't recognize me,
I am Abthung Gapa Limig [Youthful Clear-Eyed Pika].
Among pikas I am the dharma minister, and
A dharma practitioner who has abandoned nonvirtue.
I am a great meditator who sleeps in the rocky crags.

Today I came here to greet Joru.
Have you had many difficulties on your journey?

This white scarf with nine knots
Was in possession of the girl from Kyalo a few days back.[77]
She said her name is Sengcham, and
Since she shacked up on the sly
With the Indian minister Berkar,
This is their secret tryst [of shacking] scarf.
Since they promised to be true to each other, this is also their
    pledge scarf.
Since they took an oath three times, this is their oath scarf.
Since it is a token that he not forget her, it is a reminder fee.
Then the minister gave this scarf to me,
And now I give it to you, Joru, in greeting.
What I have to say is with pure intention.

If all of your resources go to a horse,
One day you'll find that you've become a beggar.
If all of your attention goes to a girl,
You'll end up losing everything you've worked for.

Even though you look after your horse and provide for your wife,
If you go too far, you may be thrown to the ground.
Even though you cherish your sons and daughters,
If you go too far, your descendants could become your enemies.
Even though you accumulate much food and wealth,
If you go too far, you'll lose your own life.

It's madness to think the Noble Steed is the finest of the lot;
Even though it's the best, it will only last for a year or two.
It's madness to think the young girl is the best
When it's only that she's had a good upbringing.

Now here is how this all fits in:
A few days back,[78] this Drugmo from White Ling
Said she's the dearest child of Father Kyalo

And the heart essence of White Ling.
In the foreign land of the Seven Sandy Passes,
To the unfamiliar minister from India,
She told several familiar stories.
That left me concerned about the way she trusted this
    stranger;
Without any regard for her body, she hooked up with him,
With no concern for her own belongings, she gave him her
    precious wealth,
Not minding her mouth, she pledged an oath.
Seeing that, this pika meditator had some thoughts:

I thought this maiden girl was brainless,
Like a horned goat.
I thought, if she has any power, she is one who would destroy
    her own father's house.
I thought this maiden girl was like a water sieve
Since she exposed the secrets of her heart to the enemy.
She is one who will bring slanderous rumors to her own
    father's doorstep,
Giving our best words away and keeping the rubbish for herself.
I thought that this maiden girl was like a cow,
And her white smile like milk.
But it will not benefit her calf, only the stomach of her clever-
    mouthed useless lover.
I thought this maiden girl was like butter,
Easily melted away by the sun of happiness.
But if the harshness of the icy winds prevails then, like butter,
    she will be hard.
I thought this maiden girl was like a flea
Biting the warm bodies of those who have shown great
    kindness.
If you stay with her too long, like a nest of fleas, she will be
    the source of an unsuccessful household.
I thought this maiden girl was like the springtime weather,
Cold and warm, up and down with each passing day.
Oh well, when you think about this, it may be too late.

An inferior woman and the spirit of the deceased—
As she sees her [earthly] companions, so the spirit sees the protector
deities [in the bardo], as demons;
Their minds are so attracted to the harmful demons.[79]

When I see that, this meditating pika is saddened.
I think the brethren of Ling have made a mistake concerning
their wager for the race.
Boy Joru, I think you are being led on the wrong path.
Boy Joru, keep this in your mind.

So saying, the pika returned to his cave, flinging the Nine-Knotted scarf in front of Joru. Drugmo was so utterly ashamed that she was at a loss as to what to even do. Joru said, "Wow, Drugmo! I had no idea you would have done all of this! Everything the pika just said is the whole truth, and nothing but the truth! Now I must certainly tell all of this to the brethren of White Ling."

As he prepared to depart he stuffed the scarf into his chuba and, although she couldn't utter a reply, Drugmo [followed Joru back] to the place where she had met Beri Nyima Gyaltsen. There the foothills abounded with flowers in full bloom, and Joru stopped for a moment to listen to the melodious droning of the bumblebees. Then Joru said, "Well, this is the very place where Beri Nyima Gyaltsen and you, Drugmo, plighted your troth; right here you gave him your golden ring. You told me you would give me the other treasures, even if you had to steal them, but just look, on your way to call for me you have gotten yourself into this much of a mess. It is imperative that the principals of White Ling, Chipön, Gyatsha, and Kyalo, be told of this. Not to do so would be even more dangerous. Is this gold ring really yours?"

Drugmo bowed down to him, saying, "Sweet Jo, precious one, may your wisdom always be exalted. Listen, for here is what I have to say," and she sang this song in the melody of Six Modulations in Nine Pitches:

It's Ala Ala Ala.
Thala leads the melody of the song.
If you don't recognize this place,
It is Jachen Yölmo,
The place where Joru produced a magical manifestation.
If you don't recognize me,
I am the dear child, descendant of Father Kyalo,

And the main wager of White Ling, known as Sengcham.
Well then, divine child Joru,
Listen, for I have something to tell you.

Those who are confused by ignorance are called sentient
     beings;
Knowing without confusion is called Buddha.
In the dharmatā of awareness and nonawareness
Liberation and confusion are just mere words.
Not understanding that until now, I was confused.
Joru of unimpeded magical powers,
Thinking you were a demon child was Drugmo's mistake.
Those travelers to the uninhabited regions of Ma,
Without recognizing them as the buddha activity of Joru,
In joy and sorrow Drugmo was confused.
The rainbow of Joru's magical transformations,
By solidifying those, Drugmo was confused.
In the narrow passage of Jachen Yölmo,
The black demon man with pennants on his helmet
And, at the Seven Sandy Passes of Ma,
The man in white sporting a topknot,
Not knowing that these were your magical emanations, Joru,
Through attachment and aversion, Drugmo was confused.
This untrustworthy stallion of my mind
Was brought under control by the magical bridle
Of Gogmo's divine child Joru.

Wherever these aggregates of the contaminated illusory body
Are tossed hinges upon the chariot of karma.
These sounds and words are like a sweet sounding sitar;
Whether good or bad turns on the weight of the fingers and concepts.

This consciousness is like a drunken elephant;
Lead it where you will with your hook of compassion.

First of all, I confess all my past evil deeds,
And vow from this day onward not to commit them again.
On this day Drugmo makes a promise to you.

As the horse race of White Ling takes place,
First, may Joru who is like red fire,
Be fanned by the pleasant wind of this prayer;
Second, may Wild Kyang who runs on the path of the birds
Be urged on by the whip which cuts through the highest
    reaches of space;
Third, may this horse that has yet to develop the racing gait
Be shown the legacy that reveals the great secret.[80]
These three I, Sengcham, will secure for you.
First, may your omniscient mind be free from obscuration,
Second, may your loving-kindness not abandon this girl,
Third, through your power may you seize the golden throne.
Joru, you must never forget this.
It is difficult for the wealth of Kyalo to be the causal
    condition;
Through the convergence of karma and authentic presence, it
    is made easy.
It is difficult to be the bridegroom of the maiden Sengcham;
If this is mandated by the imperial gods above, it is made
    easier.
It is difficult to be the leader of the brethren of Ling;
If the skill and signs of accomplishment unite, it is made easier.
If you understand this, it's a supreme ornament to the ears.
If not, there is no way to explain it.

Thus she sang, and then Joru said, "Well now, whether or not I really under-stood what you meant by your remarks, here is the real story," and he sang the song in the melody of A Gently Flowing River.

It is Ala Ala Ala.
Thala is the melody of the song.
I supplicate the Three Jewels of Refuge
To dwell inseparably on the crown of my head.
I am called Gogmo's Joru,
And I have a few things to explain to you:
The royal parasol in the imperial path of the gods
Comes to adorn the four continents without invitation,
Bringing happiness to all beings,

418

But the owl, ghost bird of the night, sees only in the darkness.

The warmth and moisture of summertime

Come to adorn the earth without invitation,

And the meadows and flowers unite as companions,

But the snow mountains' mandate is to become a glacier of
   deadly frozen ice.

I, Gogmo's child Joru,

Came to adorn Lower Ma without being invited.

Although I was delighted to hook up with Sengcham as my
   companion,

These stories have filled my hopeful guts with pain.

Joru's mind is empty of magical emanation;

Drugmo's mind is empty of confusion.

Within this magical display of the appearance of empty reality,

Confusion and emanation are merely dharma jargon.

Furthermore, these are mere designations of a mind with no
   reference point.

When you see the mind's nature as without self,

Confusion vanishes like a rainbow in the sky;

At that time emanation brings neither benefit nor harm.

Joru has no choice but to emanate.

If emanation does not occur to benefit beings,

Realization alone will not liberate another's mind.

The appearance of Joru is emanation.

The interdependency of phenomenal existence

Is merely the magical emanation of cause and condition.

It's possible to have fire between stone and metal,

But without tinder there's nothing to do.

It's possible to have crops between the soil and moisture,

But if heat and moisture don't unite, nothing will grow.

This wager among the brethren,

If the horse is not free to run its fastest, there is nothing to
   attain.

For the kyang colt that runs on the swift path of the birds,

A whip guarantees that he's not a lazy runner;

There's no way I can be without that.

In order to fulfill the wishes of the rider,

The prayers and auspicious connections must not be disturbed.
For the racehorse not to get stuck in the narrow passageway,
You ought to open the great secret of this steed.
This is not an order, just a proper request;
This proper request must accomplish the goal.
These things won't obtain victory in the race;
But these are the things we will need to get the prize.
If there is any obstruction, then there cannot be omniscience;
If there is any partiality, then there cannot be love;
If there is any interruption, then there cannot be power.
If this animal doesn't take the swift path,
Then the so-called purpose of others is just empty speech.
If you have understood this, it is sweet to your ears.
If not, there is no way to explain it.

When he said this, Drugmo's previous karmic tendencies suddenly awakened. She was able to sever all doubt and wrong view that she had toward Joru, and she found the certainty of faith and devotion. She decided that except for Joru there could be no other leader of White Ling, bridegroom of Drugmo, and lord of the wealth of Kyalo. She promised to do whatever he said, and both of them departed. She safely delivered Joru to the Lesser Lineage. So it was said that the messenger Drugmo fulfilled her mission; the Great Being who arrived will accomplish all goals, and the minds of the residing fathers and uncles were satisfied.

Drugmo said to Joru, "When it's time for the horse race, come to the tents of Kyalo. There will be a saddle for the horse, the rider's horsewhip, and positive aspirations for both man and horse." Having said this, she returned to her own father Kyalo's home. The Lesser Lineage sent someone to bring Gogmo, as she and Wild Kyang were both invited. Joru and Gogmo, mother and son, once again joined the ranks of the Lesser Lineage and resided there in equal status with the other brethren. Nonetheless:

> Whether wealth is great or small depends on the fruit of previous
>   generosity.

Then, when all the brethren asked Joru where he got Wild Kyang and who he belonged to, he told some of them that he had bought the horse, and others that he had found it, and still others that it was the colt of a wild mare called Drolo Thödkya [Gray Skull], and so on, sitting there giving nothing but inconsistent answers.

420

One day Joru, riding his white willow staff Jangkar Berka and leading Wild Kyang, his nine-edged prosperity bag thrust inside his chuba's breast, arrived at Tagrong's door. "Uncle, Uncle! It's Joru at your door. Please, throw me a party and give vittles for my horse!" he called out again and again. Trothung saw not only Joru but, accompanying him, a supreme steed rarely found in this world. Bewildered, he ran down to the door. "Well, Nephew, I am so delighted that you have come here today! You weren't here yesterday when we had the banquet for the horse race of Ling, but I will certainly throw another party for you now! Where did you get this horse? Whose is it?"[81] Joru replied, "This little colt of mine was born to Drolo-ma [Silken], the mare that belongs to my mother and me. It's just that he's not able to be mounted because he's never been broken. For eight years he's been running free in the mountains. Now, if he's to run in the staged horse race of White Ling, tell me what should be done, so he'll be able to be ridden."

Trothung said, "O Joru, this horse is of no use to you. If you are going to run in the race then you have to be able to take charge of the government of Ling.[82] One's horse must be capable of competing with the fastest horses of all, the horse needs to have the best constitution, and you need to be in complete control. This horse has none of these qualities. Nevertheless, in a herd of colorful horses, this one would stand out as the most beautiful, so how about if uncle and nephew make a trade. Uncle will trade you Ragkar Yumog [Roan Turquoise Mane], including whatever else you say you need."

Joru replied, "That would be okay. Ya, Uncle, we can trade horses. But first you said you would give a party for everybody, from the eldest fathers and uncles of White Ling to the youngest infant. It was unfortunate that my mother and I missed the banquet. Now, if you don't give us a proper party, I won't join the ranks of the fathers and uncles of Ling. I really mean it—I won't line up my helmet pennants with the others for the race. Give me, Joru, what I need to eat. Give me, Joru, something to eat, and as much as I can carry for my mother, and then we'll both be happy to trade horses. Who wins the wager is the result of previous karma. The horse race is the common wealth of the brethren. I could ride the horse, and you could take care of it; surely that would gratify us both. This particular horse is very precious to me, but if I don't sell it there will be no trained horse for me to ride. If I do sell it, I'll be brokenhearted. My mother and I need provisions to last through the summer and the winter, just as much as we need some food right now. Not only that, in addition to thirteen scarves with perfect fringe, as well as thirteen silver ingots stamped in the shape of a horse hoof, if you give us thirteen pouches of gold, maybe we will trade, but I'm still not sure."

Trothung said, "I can give that. I'd much rather give my wealth to my dear nephew than anybody else. So let's agree upon this, and I'll throw a party." Joru said, "Now, Uncle, you give the best party you can throw, and then we'll bargain about the horse trade. Surely we will be able to strike a deal."

Uncle thought, "It seems the prophecy of Hayagrīva was not deceptive. I've heard that a horse like this is spoken of in some foreign countries—a race of horses born from an egg of the soaring garuḍa. If it's not that, it's still definitely unrivaled. Now, I myself am delighted to have a party and, above all, to give him all the things he has asked for. If I don't get my hands on this horse, it will be a big mistake."

The party began with third summer's dri milk, Chinese Prosperity Blossom tea, plates of sweet delicacies, portions of marbled meat, nine rounds of sacred year-aged beer, and numerous plates of fruits and sweets abundantly arranged. The things that were added to get the horse—thirteen scarves with perfect fringes, thirteen silver ingots, and thirteen pouches of gold—were placed before Joru. Then Trothung said, "Dear nephew, may your wishes be fulfilled. I, your uncle, haven't seen you in so long. In one lifetime there is much happiness and sorrow. It's just like this," and he sang a song in the melody of Hara Hurthung:

> It is Ala Ala Ala.
> Thala is the melody of the song.
> From the meditation cave of the unborn view,
> The unobstructed self-arising ultimate deity
> Red Hayagrīva, god of Zhangzhung, know me.
> Lead Trogyal in his song.
> Now then, listen, honorable Joru,
> Children, youth, elders, these three
> Are the ornaments of a long human life.
> If the kind parents are good, that's even better;
> Better yet is if there is happiness from beginning to end.
> Guru, student, patron, these three
> Are useful to the accomplishment of the divine dharma.
> If you cultivate the dharma, that's even better;
> Better yet is to reach perfect enlightenment.
> Leader, minister, subjects, these three
> Are the mandate for the prosperity of existence.
> If the leader is kind to the ministers, that's even better;
> Better yet is if they govern the people with kindness.
> Fathers and uncles, brothers and cousins, and family
>   descendants, these three

Are the pillars for the dignity of the country.
If they can tame the enemy through skillful means, that's even
    better;
Better yet is to look after the relatives with love.
Mothers, wives, and daughters, these three
Are the necessary foundation of the vibrant villages.
If they are of one mind, that's even better;
Better yet is if they get along for a long time.
Business, games, and weddings, these three
Are used as the stakes for pooling wealth and property.
If trade is without profit and loss, that's even better;
Better yet is if all minds are in harmony.
Uncle, Joru, and Gogmo, these three;
It's better if Uncle, who has many horses, has some that are
    wild,
Better if Joru, who has one horse, has the one that is tame,
Better yet if Gogmo, who is hungry, has plenty of food to eat.
Nephews and uncles making deals with each other is good;
Even better if their superior wares go to the family;
Better yet if their minds and aspirations are harmonious;
Best of all if their deals are without profit or loss.
Relatives, friends, and bosom buddies, these three
Are vital parts of a happy existence;
If they bring happiness and benefit to each other, it's even
    better;
Still better if they hold one another in great esteem.
The sun, the moon, the stars, these three
Are the ornament of the azure firmament.
The warmth and radiance of their light illuminates
    Jambudvīpa.
They remain together inseparably in the sky.
The southern clouds, the turquoise dragon, and gentle
    pleasant rains, these three
Are the ornament of the empty middle sky.
As they befriend and assist one another,
They are universally praised and coexist inseparably.
Grasses, crops, and fruit, these three
Are the ornament of the dense earth,

Guaranteeing all beings happiness and well-being;
Bringing both beauty and sustenance as they coexist
    inseparably.
Fathers, uncles, nephews, these three
Gather as ornaments of the world of Jambudvīpa.
Through skill and wisdom they tame the four enemies,
Bringing joy and well-being as they coexist inseparably.
Tea, meat, and beer, these three
Are for your banquet, Joru.
This Prosperity Blossom tea from China,
The more you drink it, the clearer your mind becomes;
Eating the marbled meat gives you great fortitude;
Drinking the potent beer lifts your spirits.
Silk and gold and silver, these three
Are the bonus given in trade for the steed.
According to the ancient sayings of Tibet:

Disciples who violate samaya will not gain buddhahood,
It doesn't matter whether you're wise and learned or not.
Without merit, wealth will not come your way,
It doesn't matter whether you work hard or not.
An unwise daughter will never know happiness,
It doesn't matter whether she's good-looking or not.

A weak Joru cannot rule the people,
It doesn't matter if you win the golden throne or not.
This untamed wild horse,
If nephew rides it, will place his life in peril.
Therefore, let uncle and nephew trade horses.
If you understand this, it's sweet to the ears.
If not, there is no way to explain it.

Thus he sang, and Joru partook of all the food, the tea, and the beer at the banquet. Their aroma and flavor suffused his body, and his spirits soared higher than the sky. His speech was imbued with charismatic eloquence such that his words reached farther than a river. Once the meal was digested, his mind was struck with the power of omniscience; his knowledge and his loving-kindness became more radiant than the sun and the moon. Behaving as though he were slightly intoxicated, he gazed up at his uncle and down at Wild Kyang, laughing and smiling as he broke into this song in the melody of A Slowly Rolling River:

It is Ala Ala Ala.
Thala is the melody of the song.
Guru, yidam, ḍākinī, these three,
Please remain inseparable as my crown ornament.
Dwelling there, please grant your blessings.
If you don't recognize me,
I am the divine child Nangwa Ödden,
And the human child King Joru,
And the nāga child Sampa'i Döndrub [Accomplisher of All
    Wishes].
Listen here, for I have something to say.
First, innocent as a child,
Second, without a guide as a youth,
And third, shameless as the elderly;
It's hard for there to be happiness from beginning to end.
The guru, overpowered by craving,
The view of the student opposed to dharma,
The mind of the patron tied by the knot of avarice;
It's hard for them to keep the vow of samaya.
A chieftain's mind and sights are set on wealth,
The minister turns the law on its head,
They bring punishment to innocent subjects;
It's hard to say they are kind-hearted.
Uncles with deception and conflict greater than a mountain,
Brethren with hearts more rotten than a corpse,
A helpless nephew exiled to the borderlands;
It's hard to both conquer the enemy and look after relatives.
Mother's face darker than a stormy sky,
Conniving sisters-in-law, wilder than goats,
Daughters' minds driven by desire;
It's difficult for them to stay together for long.
As business partners,[83] uncles are spiteful to the core,
As a business partner,[84] Joru is naturally smart,
The favored Wild Kyang is a high-priced horse;
It's hard to just get your own way.

Ultimately, relatives are burdened by animosity;
In the end, friends take sides in disputes;
Bosom buddies are finally divided by slander;
It's hard to say that they really value one another.

The sun flees behind the western mountains,
The moon is lost in the blackness of dark clouds,
The stars are driven away by dawn;
It's hard to say they are the ornaments of the azure firmament.
The southern clouds are scattered by the icy winds,
The turquoise dragon's tail is hidden in the earth,[85]
The pleasant rains vanish into empty space;
It's hard to say that they are inseparable companions.
Grasses are eaten by the hoofed wild ones,
The crops become the harvest that fills the silos,
Ripened fruit rots on the ground;
These are merely fleeting ornaments of the dense earth.
Father Senglön is rotten to the core,
Uncle Trothung has many schemes,
Nephew Joru is full of commotion;
It's hard for our minds to combine upāya and prajñā.
First, Joru, mandated by the gods,
Second, Wild Kyang, given by the nyen,
Third, the golden saddle, received from the nāgas;
If they come together, the race will be easy.
Then this beggar boy will make a fortune.
When a beggar boy gains wealth,
The mind of a rich man will bring him down.
When the prosperity sheep get plump,
The mouths of coyotes and wolves start to tremble.
When the buck's rack is full grown,
The hunter's spirit trembles to no avail.
I think all of this indicates meaningless confusion.
Not only that, I also think it's full of sin.
You who tend your sheep and your yaks;
When the time is right, the owner takes their fleece and hair.
You work your fields and acreage;

When the crops are mature the owner will just harvest the
　　grains and beans.
Fathers and uncles stockpile their food and wealth;
When sons and nephews arrive, they spread it before us.
That is the great joy gained from those with expectations.
Not only that, I think this is their way of accumulating virtue
　　and benefit.
The fuller my stomach, the more I count on my horse;
The more I drink, the more I miss Drugmo.
Now, I'm not going to trade my horse; I'm leaving instead.
I really could care less if I am able to unite the people of Ling
　　or not—
It's enough for me to just have Drugmo.
If you understand this, it's sweet to the ears.
If not, there is no way to explain it.
Uncle, keep this in your mind.

Thus he sang, and putting all the scarves, gold, and silver into his little bag, he prepared to leave. Uncle said, "If we don't trade horses, then don't take the extras. Of course you can take the banquet food since it was my gift to you, Nephew." Joru said to his uncle, "I told you to give me the best party you could and afterward we would talk about the horse trade. But if you ask me to return the whole party you've given me, it is for sure we'll have a falling out. Uncle, you must remember our agreement about the nine-edged prosperity bag." And leading his horse, he left.

Uncle was left without anything to do, even though his mind was full of regret. Chipön, Gyatsha, and Denma all realized that this horse of Joru's was acquired as a sign of the collective merit of many beings. They each offered an Auspicious-by-Day scarf. Then on the excellent day called Happy Good Fortune, Joru and his horse arrived at Kyalo's door. He said, "Ya, Sengcham Drugmo, you said that you would have the saddle for the horse, the whip for the man, and the prayer for the whip. Now, the time has come when they are needed." Then Kyalo Tönpa Gyaltsen erected a precious golden throne and placed a silken brocade cushion upon it. Arranging sweet delicacies for the party and offering the auspicious greeting scarf, he sang this song about the state of affairs:

It is Ala Ala Ala.
Thala is the melody of the song.

In the palace of the cannibal demons of Cāmara,
Outwardly he is the king of the rākṣasas,
Inwardly he is the Mahāsiddha Lotus Born,
Secretly he is the actual Great Vajradhara.
Vidyādhara Lotus Born, know me!
If you don't recognize me,
I am Kyalo Tönpa Gyaltsen.
I am a reincarnation of Jambhala,*
I am the patron of Uḍḍiyāna Padmasambhava,
And Sengcham Drugmo's father.
Kyalo, Ngolo, and Drolo, these three,
Are brothers whose wealth is equal.
One day we three brothers went to the mountain;
One guru, who came from who knows where,
Brought forth faith just by his mere presence.
Just meeting him inspired devotion.
Simply hearing his speech brought liberation.
He was driving some animals ahead of him
Loaded with his provisions.
When we met him, this is what the guru said:
"The saddle, halter, and the saddle blanket, these three,
Including the whip, these four,
Are the inner wealth of Migön Karpo from the nāgas.
Kyalo, I ask you to keep it safe and sound.
Someday, as mandated for the world,
A sublime being with unimpeded magical powers will come.
Once he comes into Kyalo's family home,
You must place this wealth into the hands of its owner."
My son Drug-gyal[86] came, but he has no magic powers.
Sengcham came, but she was born as a woman,
And not only that but as [your mother]
Nāginī Yelga Dzeiden.
When Ling acquired her as booty,
I had a mixture of dreams and visions so profound
That even the wide sky could not cover them,

---

* Jambhala is the wisdom deity representing wealth.

The dense earth could not hold them,
And all of these signs point to you, Joru.

The towering white crag peaks reach higher and higher.
Although not intentionally created for the white vulture,
It is the natural circling place of this king of birds.
The juniper treetop reaches higher and higher.
Although not intentionally planned for the cuckoo bird,
It is this happy divine bird's own merit.
Beneath the surface are the churning depths of the ocean.
Although this churning is not intentionally made for the sake
    of white-bellied fish,
That the undulating female fish swims here is her own karmic
    ripening.
The abundant wealth of Kyalo Tönpa,
Although not intentionally accumulated just for Joru,
Seems to be the result of Joru's own merit.
The ring of an abundance of endowments
Is ready to be invoked by the hook of merit.
Yet to win the golden throne and the mother's womb,
It is unheard of that this could be done with just a fast-running horse.

When life is over, even an artist can't reconstruct it,
Negative character can't be pounded into shape by a blacksmith.

Previous karma can't be wagered by the stallion in the horse race.
The power of karma can't be blocked by a hand.
If the mind of the great knower is accurate,
For Joru [to become the holder of] the imperial golden
    throne, the leader of Ling,
And Sengcham Drugmo's bridegroom, all three,
Is how things were ordained by the gods.
If you understand this, it's sweet to the ears.
If not, there is no way to explain it.

Thus he spoke. Then Kyalo Sengcham Drugmo offered the tack for the horse,
the whip for the man, and she sang this song in order to open the great secret of the
steed, in the Six Melodies of the Divine Drum.

It is Ala Ala Ala.
Thala is the melody of the song.
From the pure realm of Turquoise Leaves,
Jetsün Ārya Tārā, know me.
Look upon me with your omniscience, and lead Drugmo in
    her song.
This is the day of the auspicious sun;
The constellations in the sky are excellently aligned,
The signs of good fortune in the middle are excellent,
On earth the time for humankind is excellent.
Therefore, on this divine horse Kyang-bu,
In the finest vulture down at the tip of his ears
Dwells the great secret of unimpeded sound.
This whip that fulfills all wishes
I will wave three times over the tips of the ears,
But not too hard, for I'm afraid it might disturb his finely
    feathered hair,
And not too weakly, or the great secret will not open.
If there is a great secret, may it open it today.

In the pupils of this horse, like those of a hostile snake,
Exists the great secret of unimpeded form.
I will wave this whip three times over his eye sockets,
But not too hard, so as to disturb his hair,
And not too weakly, or the great secret will not open.
If there is a great secret, may it open it today.

In the nostrils of this horse, like those of a white snow lion,
Is the great secret of unimpeded smell.
I will wave this whip three times over the sinus cavity,
But not too hard, so as to disturb his hair,
And not too weakly, or the great secret will not open.
If there is a great secret, may it open it today.

In the mouth and tongue of this horse, like those of a red tiger,
Is the unimpeded great secret taste.
I will wave this whip three times over the muzzle.[87]
But not too hard, so as to disturb his hair,

And not too weakly, or the great secret will not open.
If there is a great secret, may it open it today.

The horse's body is like a red flag blowing in the wind.
This body has the great secret of unimpeded feeling.
I will wave this whip three times over the horse's body,
But not too hard, so as to disturb his hair,
And not too weakly, or the great secret will not open.
If there is a great secret, may it open it today.

In the tent of the precious heart of this horse
Dwells the great secret of all-pervasive awareness.
I will wave this whip three times over the heart,
But not too hard, so as to disturb his hair,
And not too weakly, or the great secret will not open.
If there is a great secret, then may it open it today.

The great secret, which is the crucial point of the Secret
    Path,
I will symbolically open today through skillful means.

I will open the great secret that brings benefit to others
Through the divine horse, the white-muzzled kyang colt.
The body of this horse is composed of the four elements
Obstructed by this narrow passageway based on material
    substance.
Unimpeded travel is the outer secret;
Today may this open with Sengcham's words of truth.

The supreme horse possesses an enlightened mind,
Yet the temporary five poisons represent the narrow
    passageway of fixating upon true existence.
Freedom from accepting and rejecting is the inner secret;
Today may it open with Sengcham's words of truth.

The wisdom of omniscience, loving-kindness, and power,
Is obscured by the secret narrow passageway of the dualistic
    mind.

Freedom from conceptualization is the secret of the great
    secret;
Today may this open with Sengcham's words of truth.

Just like beating a drum with a stick,
Opens the great secret of sound,
For this divine horse today
May the great secret of enlightened activity be opened
    through this wish-fulfilling whip.
In addition to that,
The wool saddle blanket Meiwa Druzhi, marked with the
    nine astrological diagrams at the four corners,
The special treasure of Tsugna Rinchen,
Is the place where the white prosperity sheep's life force
    abides;
Today may this be placed upon the back of Wild Kyang.
Joyful wish-fulfilling jewel, Joru,
May you become the ruler of Jambudvīpa
And take your seat on the imperial golden throne.
This is my first aspiration prayer.

On the golden saddle patterned with nine circles, called
    Rimo Gu-kor [Nine Circular Designs],
With a yellow pommel made of gold in front, and
In back, a pale cantle made of silver,
Is the place where the great steed's life force abides.
This is the karmic treasure of the middle nyen;
Today may this be placed upon the back of Wild Kyang.
May this divine son of Gogmo
Be able to place yokes upon the māras with perverted
    views, and
May you be able to sponsor and serve
All beings who uphold the scriptures and realization.
This is my second prayer.

The wish-fulfilling golden bridle and
This golden girth that accomplishes all desires

Are the karmic treasure of the gods above,
And the place where the prosperity life force abides.
Today, may Wild Kyang be adorned with them.
May you, Joru, the divine son of Gogmo,
Keep all beings confused by bad karma
Away from the path of the lower realms,
And may you be able to turn their minds to the dharma.
This is my third prayer.

These white stirrups with a conch ring
Suspended by silken fenders,
And the front girth called Drug-gi Shagyur [Dragon's
    Blood],
And the cinch called Lhadrei Chingthag [Rope that Binds
    Gods and Demons];
All these are the inner wealth of the local deities.
Today, they will adorn the golden saddle.
May you, Joru, the divine son of Gogmo,
Fully perfect the four buddha activities and
Accomplish uninterrupted benefit of beings.
This is my fourth prayer.

These reins called Drülnag Shagpa [Black Snake Lasso],
The leather seat with the eight auspicious symbols, and
The saddle pads[88] made of nine layers of fine silk
Are the special treasures from the humans of the middle realm.
Today they are placed on Wild Kyang.
May you, Joru, the divine son of Gogmo,
Be the protector and refuge of humankind
And the chieftain of the land of White Ling.
This is my fifth prayer.

This hard bamboo that fulfills all aspirations
Is the wish-fulfilling jeweled handle of the whip.
The whip cord itself is woven from the silk of ḍākinīs;
And is an inner treasure of my father Kyalo Tönpa.
Today this is offered to Joru's hands.

May you, the divine child of Gogmo, Joru,
Become the king who enforces the renouncement of
    nonvirtue
And the dharma king who establishes the ten virtues.
This is my sixth prayer.

This stainless white scarf
Is the longevity scarf that ensures immortality.
It is the power scarf of authentic presence
And the merit scarf of great accumulations.
It is the action scarf that increases windhorse.
Today this scarf is offered to Joru's neck
As the single white scarf of life expectancy,[89]
Unsullied by the stains of obstacles.
Through the power of your enlightened deeds,
May the field to be tamed be entirely gentle and virtuous.
This is my seventh prayer.

This white-mouthed great steed Kyang-bu,
Mandated by the command of the imperial gods,
Birthed at the birthplace of the king of mountains,
When captured was captured by your mother and Drugmo,
Whose master is you, Lord Joru.
Today I offer [this horse] adorned with jewels
To you, Joru, Gogmo's divine child.
May you inherit the wealth of Kyalo Tönpa
And become the bridegroom of Sengcham.
That is my eighth prayer.

This great steed with magic wheels of wind,
Don't let any swift ones go before you;
Kyang-bu, don't fall behind.
May these well-intended prayers be realized.
Excellent prayers made by gurus, parents, and
Life-long companions,
Hold the words of truth to accomplish whatever is wished for.
Therefore my song is not meaningless.
Joru, keep this in your mind.

Thus she prayed, and the tack for the horse, the whip for the man, the prayer for the whip, and other especially noble indications of good fortune arose. It was that day that Joru took his place in the ranks of competitors for the race, and Chipön, Gyatsha, and others offered advice and prayers while placing the scarf of auspicious connection around his neck.

This completes the fourth chapter, the Saga of the Precious Minister, recounting the story of how Joru came to possess all the necessary articles.

> **From the illusory treasury, articles of the three worlds were amassed.**
> **I supplicate you who are respected by all the Great Ones.**

Thus through many apparitional emanations you realized the lack of true inherent existence, and from the treasury of magical deceptions like an illusion, you gained control of the treasure articles of the gods, nāgas, and nyens.

This completes the explanation of how Joru gained the respect of everyone.

CHAPTER FIVE

The contest of the horse race between the fathers and uncles
    of White Ling gets under way.
Joru, in disguise, goes to the end of the line.
Drugmo introduces the men and their horses.
This gives rise to the Saga of the Precious Elephant.

FOR THE FIFTH [CHAPTER], the way Joru, cunningly disguised, goes to the
back of the line of the brethren is as follows:

Then it happened that they all gathered at the mind mandala of the land of
Ma, upon the seat of the solid earth, the gathering place Tagthang Tramo, the jeweled seat of the dragon's piercing roar, where the vivid melody of the cuckoo is heard
and where the mind-captivating clear sound of the lark reverberates.

Those who came to line up for the horse race were the eight brothers of the
Serpa clan of Upper Ling, headed by the nine sons, tigers of the Elder Lineage, along
with their brethren and distant brethren. In the cloth of glistening gold that they
wore, they appeared like the sun embracing a golden mountain.

As for the six tribes of Ombu of Middle Ling, they were headed by the eight
heroes of the Middle Lineage and were accompanied by their brethren and distant
brethren wearing white cloth as beautifully radiant as the moon, such that they appeared like snowfall blanketing a mountain.

Next came the four tribes of Lower Ling, headed by the seven brothers from
Bumpa of the Lesser Lineage and accompanied by their brethren and distant brethren wearing blue clothes the color of lapis lazuli. They appeared like massing storm
clouds in the sky.

Furthermore, to the right were the tribes of Ga clan; to the left the tribes of Dru, and the eighteen tribes of Tag-rong, the ruddy people of Ta'u, the district of wealthy Kyalo, the clan of Denma on both the sunny and shady banks of the river, the nine hundred families of Tshazhang, and so forth. In addition to the brethren, all the rest of heroes and mighty warriors of White Ling gathered in full costume, their bodies completely bedecked, their minds full of courage, and their hearts full of joyful happiness.

Among all of them, the one with great fervor for the race, a human who had received the prophecy of the gods, and whose mind was changed by the gods, was Chieftain Trogyal of Tag-rong. Along with him came Dongtsen Nang-ngu Apel, Tag-rong Pönpo Zigphen, Aten Dug-gi Metog, and so forth. They all thought that no horse but Turquoise Bird could win the race. They came with pride greater than that of a tiger; their sixfold panoply resplendent as the tiger's six smiles. That mighty tribe of Tag-rong was as boastful as a snarling tigress rousing from her lair.

Those of the Greater Lineage, Nyibum Daryag of Serpa, Michen Gyalwa'i Lhundrub, Chölu Buyi Darphen of Dong, Abar Buyi Phentag, and so forth, the illustrious ranks of the Greater Lineage, stood more firm than a mountain. Their bravery rivaled that of a lion; their garments were like its flourishing turquoise mane. Haughtily poised like snow lions on a mountain, that's how they came.

Anu Paseng of the Middle Lineage of Ombu, Chökyong Bernag of Gadei, unrivaled Sengtag Adom, dauntless Nyima Lhundrub, and so forth, the illustrious ranks of the Middle Lineage, stood as one. Appearing like a turquoise dragon in the sky; draped with clouds, they were ready to all but rival the fame and glory of the dragon.

From the Lesser Lineage came Rinchen of Muchang, Gyatsha Zhalkar of Bumpa, Chipön Rongtsha Tragen, Denma Jangtra of Tshazhang, and others. The dauntless sense of divinity of the Lesser Lineage was completely intact. Their minds were endowed with complete bravery and able to quell the four enemies through their splendor.

Even though the brethren of Ling did not give them authority, the karmic winds would be enough to carry them to the state of leadership. Outwardly their constitutions were the same. Inwardly, the strength of their courage and bravery was unlike that of any other. Whether or not they agreed that they would prevail in the horse race, one thing was certain: the entire Lesser Lineage was determined not to lose the throne of White Ling to the others. They readied themselves, just like a garuḍa inside its egg with all six wings fully developed.[90]

Furthermore, Lhabu Namkha Sengzhal, Kyalo Tönpa Gyaltsen, Kar-ru Nyima Gyaltsen, the arbiter Werma Lhadar, the judge Wangpo Darphen, and the four gurus of Ling, as well as the entire assembly of mighty warriors and their fledglings were full of the arrogance of their personal power, strength, and abilities. They arrived confident enough to contend with a herd of intoxicated elephants.

Gogmo's divine son Joru wore an unsightly antelope buck hat, and his body was unsightly in his untanned calfskin coat. His legs were unsightly in their cruddy horsehide boots, and so forth, all of which were pale with no sheen at all.[91] The white-muzzled divine kyang colt had been equipped with a jeweled saddle and tack, but he had transformed into an ugly horse with a shoddy constitution. Joru, alternately wielding his white willow staff and sticking it under his belt, was ill-mannered, like someone pathetic with no class, or someone completely lacking monastic discipline.

> *Ready to freeze in a blast of cold air,*
> *Ready to melt in the midday sun,*
> *Ready to be blown away by a breeze.*

Up until that day, Joru had done what he could with his outrageous yogic conduct to tame the minds of beings. Although no one there understood this, it seemed that all the signs indicated that now was the proper time for him to give up this behavior, since his ugly body and ugly demeanor only served to conceal the treasure.

All the spectators for the horse race were like massing clouds, and as many as there were atoms on the earth; it seemed that every country under the sun had converged there. Then the Lingites lined up in rows, turned their mounts toward Ayu Downs,* and rode off in a line. By that time, Sengcham Drugmo of Kyalo, Kyidkyi Nichung of Ngolo, Pekar Lhadzei of Drolo, Chipön's daughter Yudrön, Tshazhang [Denma's] daughter Dzeidrön, Yatha's daughter Ser-tso, and Trothung's daughter Tromo-tso, all seven, had dressed in silken garments, with headdresses of jeweled ornaments and zi and other jewels around their necks. They were so bedecked that it seemed as if their clothing had come from the gods and their jewels had come from the nāgas. So beautiful and charming, they arrived at Lha Downs, making a smoke offering, and joined the other spectators to watch the race from the top of the Nāga Downs.

The riders lined up at Ayu Downs in a perfectly even line, so that not even one bridle was in front or in back of the others. Then the race began.

Riders from the Greater, Middle, and Lesser Lineages, Tag-rong, other

---

* This is the place where the race will commence.

individual villages, these five just mentioned, started to run[92] together, led by the great god Brahmā, the lord of the nyen Gedzo, and the nāga Tsugna Rinchen. The spectacle was a treasure for the eyes.

> Seeing this, bitter enemies would be shaken to the core;
> Close relatives would have genuine delight.

While the race continued, all the spectators said to one another, "Who do you think is going to win the prize of this horse race here today?" Some said that there could be no other winner than Dongtsen, and others had various different opinions.

At the Crag Mountain of Gu-ra the ritual masters of Ling gathered to fill the sky with lhasang smoke from the thirteen smoke-offering chambers. They embellished the drala castles,[93] hoisted flags, and, sounding the white conch, invoked the activity of all the guardian deities. They remained there, praising the countenances of the dralas.

Then the Seven Maidens of Ling, gazing coyly out of the corner of their eyes and swaying as they walked, were like goddesses moving through pleasure gardens, graceful and youthfully radiant were they as they offered juniper and prayers on the Divine Downs. Then as they watched the spectacle from the Nāga Downs, Ne'uchung Lu-gu Tshar-yag [Marvelous Little Lamb],* suddenly remembered several astonishing dreams that she had had, and Manenei influenced her mind to want to speak about them. So she sang this song to all the maidens in the Six Melodies of the Lark:

> The song begins with Ala Ala Ala.
> Thala is the melody of the song.
> May the guru, yidam, ḍākinī, these three
> Remain inseparable as my crown ornament.
> This place is Middle Nāga Downs
> And I am called Nichung of Ngolo but my full name is
>   Nichung Lu-gu Tshar-yag
> Kyalo, Ngolo, and Drolo, these three—
> If there is wealth, they are three brothers;[94]
> If there is no wealth, then they have the status of master and
>   servant.

---

* Also known as Kyidkyi Nichung [Joyful Little Parrot] of Ngolo.

Drugmo, Nichung, and Lhadzei, these three,
If we have a bond, then we are three sister maidens;
If not, we are like mistress and attendants.
Dear sister Sengcham Drugmo,
Today in this horse race of White Ling,
The public can't decide who is the most handsome man.
The finish line won't be won by racing;
The youthful warriors who wish to race
Can't win the race just by distance.
But Joru, who holds the power of karma,
Seems to already possess the throne without even needing to race.
Last night in my dream,
Within the mind mandala of the valley of Ma
I dreamed that a garuḍa and a dragon were frolicking in
     space.[95]
Even though they had the ability to soar to the limits of space
In my dream they returned.
I dreamed that a tiger and a lion roamed the earth,
And that an elephant trod mightily.
Although they were able to tread to the ends of the earth
In my dream they stayed behind.
I dreamed that a colorful rainbow tent was pitched.

I dreamed that from Chugmo Namtsho [Wealthy Lady Sky
     Lake] on Gu Mountain,
Clouds and sun moved across the sky.
I dreamed that all the clouds vanished into middle space
While the royal parasol of the sun arose;
Its light reached to the ends of space
And its light rays encompassed Jambudvīpa.
I dreamed that everyone who was there was proclaiming,
"O joyful sun, your warmth is great kindness."

This dream was not negative, but positive.
The garuḍa indicates the life-force symbol of the Lesser
     Lineage,
The dragon indicates the life-force symbol of the Middle
     Lineage,

The lion indicates the life-force symbol of the Greater Lineage,
The tiger indicates the Tag-rong tribe,
The elephant indicates the brethren.
The skill to soar across the sky and
The might to tread on the earth
Are the signs of unrivaled strength and power.
Failing to reach the limits of the sky and earth,
The pitched rainbow tent,
Plus not gaining the throne by racing
Are all signs that the prize will dissolve into a rainbow.

That the sun and clouds rose into the sky
From Chugmo Namtsho of Gu Mountain
Indicates that Joru's origin is from the nāgas.
That the clouds dissolved in space
Indicates that he will discard his ugliness and bad manners.
The rising of the radiant golden sun
Indicates that Joru will hold the golden throne.
That its light rays encompass Jambudvīpa
Indicates that his buddha activity will increase to benefit all
    beings.
The people singing the praise that the sun's warmth is great
    kindness,
Indicates that all beings will be established in happiness.
Such are the marvelous dreams I had.

Actually, this Gogmo's Joru
With his ugly looks is just a magical display.
His shortness is just for looks,
His spit and snot are amṛta,
His fleas and lice are siddhis.
If you look at him from the outside he is a wandering beggar
    child, while
Inwardly he is the prince of the victorious ones;
Secretly he is the embodiment of the Three Roots.
By the evening of this very day,
The difference between good and bad will be revealed.
When this is revealed there will be no argument.

The sun of happiness will dawn.
The darkness of suffering will be cleared.
If you understand this, it's sweet to the ears.
If not, there is no way to explain it.
Drugmo, keep this in your mind.

Then Kyalo Sengcham Drugmo thought, "Considering the swiftness of Wild Kyang, Joru's magical displays, Nichung's dreams, and all the astonishing signs that appeared when we captured the horse, how could there be any other winner than Joru?"

But Trothung's daughter Tromo-tso was rather offended [by this song]. Her body showed her displeasure, twisting like a black snake. Her disapproving head rocked back and forth like a ḍamaru; her hair swung with annoyance like a cow's tail. Displeasure flashed in her eyes like bolts of red lightning, her nose like an elephant's trunk scrunched up in annoyance, and her face swirled with black clouds of anger, her mouth raw with its quivering flesh. And she spoke, "Oh Ngolo's daughter, listen here. You, the daughter whose father wanders the path of a mendicant, your arrogance seems to be higher than the azure firmament.

> *A girl whose mother died of famine*
> *Still tossing her braid high up in the air.*

As it is, I don't need your prophecies because my father Trothung has a prophecy from the Northern God," she said, as she sang her own praises in a song with the melody of the Mind like a Whirlwind:

It is Ala Ala Ala.
Thala is the melody of the song.
Northern God Red Hayagrīva, know me.
May Father Trothung be raised to the sky.
Please deliver the scarf of victory to Brother Dongtsen's
    hands,
Sustain the speed of the noble steed Turquoise Bird.
Don't be idle, don't be idle, imperial gods!
If you don't recognize me,
I am the daughter of the exalted father of Tag-rong,
And the daughter of the wise mother Denza.
Then listen here, Nichung,
To this worldly proverb of Tibet:

The worst land blows away like dust in the sky;
Neither grass nor flowers can survive.
The worst monk's mind is driven by passion;
He has neither dharma nor vows.
The worst leader's mind is full of deceit;
He has neither karmic cause nor result.
The worst mother with a headstrong daughter
Has neither knowledge nor intuitive wisdom.

Before knowing what the guru will chant,
The monk jumps the gun and chants just nonsense.
Before understanding what is required of a leader,
The minister barks sharp reprimands.
Before knowing what her master wants to eat,
The servant girl is already yapping orders about the food.
Even before she sees the four walls that will be her home,
The servant is already consumed with avarice.
Even without getting three square meals a day,
The scrawny dogs still pretend to be the guards of their families.

How could anything compare with the truth of these
examples?

Unworthy Mother Gogmo's Joru
Is short, but that is the final display of his manifestation;
As this is his last such display, you should wait for him.
You said his fleas and lice were siddhis;
If so, then you should receive them.
You said his spit and snot were amṛta;
If so, then you should drink them.
From Sidpa Kholmo Rogdzong,[96]
The prophecy of Red Hayagrīva
Says the scarf of victory will belong to Turquoise Bird
And that he will come to be Sengcham's bridegroom.
It says that he will come to possess the wealth of the wager.
The prophecy couldn't possibly be mistaken.
Look up and see the spectacle for the eyes.
On the lower path of the divine white plain of Ling,

This blue flag that seems to be carried by the wind
Is the blue colt, swift Turquoise Bird;
It looks like the horse is not running but flying.
The man in white garments with a face like the moon
Is Dongtsen Nang-ngu Apel;
It looks like the man is not approaching, but rising
Like the moon appearing in the sky.

A man, a steed, a male dzo, these three—
If there is nothing on the outside, there is nothing on the inside.

Food as empty of nutrition as lungs that have exhaled their air—
If it's not good in your mouth, it won't be good for you later.

From the outside, he's a wandering beggar boy;
On the inside, his stomach meditates on emptiness.
With the snap of a finger, someone will lose.
Then your mind will be washed of happiness and your
    suffering will intensify.
His little horse is not like a bird but more like a chick.
He doesn't look like he is racing; he seems to be swerving
Like a scrawny dog that sniffs around.
Gogmo's little boy Joru,
Seems to be snatching up the leftover crumbs of the brethren.
If there is a scarf for the loser who comes in last,
Whatever that is, Joru will get it.
Only Dongtsen will get the victory scarf,
Sister, there is no other winner!
If you have understood this, it is sweet to your ears.
If not, there is no way to explain it.

Thus she sang this song, and Nichung thought, "If I give this girl an answer now, nothing will be resolved, but we'll just drag down the clan of all the maidens. By tonight, the rightful one will be known." With this in mind she sat there pretending not to have heard.

At that point Sengcham Drugmo realized that Nichung was right; therefore she felt that it would be pointless to argue. She said, "Long life to you, sisters! Until this matter is finished, there's no use in us arguing with each other. Listen to this discourse to determine what abundance the eyes can behold," she said and sang this song in the melody of Six Modulations in Nine Pitches.

> It is Ala Ala Ala.
> Thala is the melody of the song.
> May the guru, yidam, ḍākinī, these three,
> Remain inseparable as my crown ornament,
> And may they grant their blessings.
> Hail to my playmates;
> When we were little we shared the job of taking care of the
>   little lambs.
> When we were even younger, we were flower-picking
>   companions,
> Friends who dressed up in soft lambskin chubas, and
> We were eating companions who shared delicious food.
> Listen to Sengcham's song:
>
> You can't predict which horse will be the fastest;
> But we will know it when the winning rider assumes the
>   throne.
> You can't say which boy is best;
> But it will be obvious when one of them assumes the
>   kingdom of White Ling.
> As for knowing who will conquer the southern continent
>   Jambudvīpa,
> There's no need to bicker, we'll know soon enough.
> For today,[97] we view this spectacle,
> This horse race of colorful Ling.
> For those up to and including the highest lineage of
>   chieftains,
> Down to and including the lowliest Gu-ru,
> The main booty is Drugmo, they say.
> I'm not so sure if Drugmo is the main draw here but,
> Their is the value of Kyalo's great wealth [and]
> There are the precious valuable treasures.
> Among the Thirty Brethren who are all hoping to win this
>   wager:

Nyibum Daryag of Serpa,
Anu Paseng of Ombu,
Rinchen Darlu of Muchang, those three
Are the Three Ultimate Warriors.
To the enemies they are the ones called Falcon, Eagle and
     Wolf, those three, and
They are the heart, eyes, and life force of White Ling.

First, Gyatsha Zhalkar of Bumpa,
Second, unrivalled Sengtag Adom,
Third, Tshagyal* Denma Jangtra,
Fourth, Chieftain Zigphen of Tag-rong,
Fifth, Chökyong Bernag of Gadei,
Sixth, Chölu Buyi Darphen,
Seventh, Nya-tsha Aten of Tag-rong;
These are the Seven Super Warriors.
They are the hammers that strike the head of the enemy;
They are like parents who watch over vulnerable relatives.
They are the very ground for the existence of Ling.
They are the leaders of the seven ten-thousandfold armies.

First is Uncle King Chipön,
Second is Senglön Gama-ri Kyei,
Third is Mazhi Chieftain Trothung
Fourth is the divine Namkha Sengzhal;
These are the four paternal uncle brothers of Ling.
The extent of their minds is vaster than space,
The depth of their minds is deeper than the ocean.
They are the men who hold the patriarchal castle of the
     diplomatic counsels.
Among brethren they are the eldest statesman.

---

* This is a variation in the way the name is provided in the text (Tib. *tsha rgyal*); elsewhere it is
given as Tshazhang (Tib. *tsha zhang*).

Nangchung Yuyi Metog,
Gung-gi Marleb of Rongtsha,
Shelkar Gyangdrag of Mupa,
Changtri Ngamchen of Ombu,
Cho-nga Paser Dawa,
Gungpa Buyi Kyatra,
Chief Sengseng of Ca-nag,*
Yuyag Gönpo Tongthub,
Dongtsen Nang-ngu Apel,
Gödpo Nyima Lhundrub,
Bu-yag Drug-gyei of Kyalo,
Buchung Daryag of Serpa, and
Abar Buyi Phentag
Are the Thirteen Cherished Sons of Ling,
The newest ones to join the ranks of the warriors.
They resemble lions with the three skills perfected,
And are like garuḍa chicks with fully developed
    wings.
Outwardly, they are like jagged poison thorns,
Both sharp and painful.
Inwardly, they are soft and gentle as a lambskin chuba,
Both soft and comfortable.
Among the brethren they form the lower rank,
Among the valued they form the highest rank.

Michen Gyalwa'i Lhundrub and
Lingchen Tharpa Sönam
Are the two men of karmic power.
Gyapön Sergyi Argham and
Tongpön Treltsei Shemchog
Are the two unrelenting warriors.
Those are the four miscellaneous tribes.
When they stay in one place they are like Sumeru.
When they advance they are like the royal parasol of the sun.
They resemble the four stays that hoist the white tents.

---

* Also known as Chief Singsing.

They are like the fourfold pillars from which the square home
 is built.
They are the generals of the four tribes, and
They are the highest-ranking chieftains among the fathers and
 uncles.

Tönpa Gyaltsen of Kyalo, and
Next, Guru Gyaltsen of Denma,
Nyima Gyaltsen of Kar-ru, and
Tharpa Gyaltsen of Nag-ru
Are the four who carry the name Gyaltsen.
Among those endowed with merit they excel.
In the hierarchy they are in the middle, and
When it comes to their victory record, they rank lower.

First, Tsangpa'i Ngo-lug of Agê,
Second, Dar-'jam Ngo-lug of Mupa,
Third, Sintsha Ngo-lug of Tag-rong
Are the three men who are called Sheep-a-Peep Ngo-lug.
Their good looks are renowned among the masses.
To glimpse their faces will cost a whole sheep;
That's exactly the reason they are called Sheep-a-Peep.

First, the arbiter Werma Lhadar,
Second, the judge Wangpo Darphen
Are the two arbiters of Ling;
They are the two men whose broad-mindedness is renowned.[98]
They are the men who call together hundreds of meetings.
No one can overrule their authority;
No one can reverse their decisions.

Those were the Thirty Brethren.[*]
They are the reincarnations of the thirty mahāsiddhas from
 previous lifetimes;

---

[*] Actually she has listed thirty-seven warriors, which include the Thirty Brethren plus the Seven Super Warriors.

Now they have the honor of being the ThirtyBrethren.
They are the men who stroke the whiskers of tigers,[99]
They are the men who seize the horns of the wild yak,
They are the men who grab the turquoise mane of the snow
    lion.[100]

First, the doctor Künga Nyima,
Second, the astrologer Lhabu Yangkar,
Third, the diviner Künshei Thigpo, and,
Fourth, the magician Khache Migmar—
These men are the four minor warrior mentors.
Here is the man who cuts the lasso of the Lord of Death.[101]
Here is the man who dispels the invisible spells of enemies
    and spirits.
Here is the man who directly reveals the future.
Here is the man who as a last resort can confuse the minds of
    the enemy.
You'd never make it without these four men.

First, the Tibetan child Michung Khadei [Young Clever
    Mouth],
Second, Gochöd [Handyman] Pagyal Tagyu [Victorious
    Warrior Tiger Horn], and
Third, Akhöd Tharpa Zorna
Are the Three Servants of Ling.

First, Gu-ru son of Khyishi, and
Second, the divine son Joru of Gogmo,
Are the two beggars of Ling.
By birth they are in the ancestral lineage of the mighty
    warriors.

Furthermore here are some more examples:
The wager among the brethren,
If it goes well, will lay the groundwork for well-being in
    Jambudvīpa.
If it goes poorly, I fear there will be war.
Therefore, this girl has ordered things like this:

Those Three Ultimate Warriors, Falcon, Eagle, and Wolf,
Are as exalted as the sun, the moon, and the stars.
If one of them wins the wager, the treasure should go to all
    three.
Set like jewels in the azure firmament,
May their sovereignty be as all-encompassing as the sky.

Those seven sublime Super Warriors,
Resembling the seven golden mountains,
Should unite to become the ornaments of the earth.
May their fervor be as staunch as the earth.
Those thirteen little Cherished Sons,
Like the thirteen ancient arrows of existence,
May they equally share and grace the tiger-skin quiver.
Until the time comes to tame the enemies,
May they continue to grace the ground of White Ling.
If the buddha activity of the auspicious connection isn't
    bungled,
They will come to be the weapons that tame the four māras.
I pray that the ancient arrows are not scattered.

Those four very wise brethren
Are like the four great rivers that flow from the mouths of
    four animals.[102]
May they merge together as the ornament of the great ocean.
They will come to suppress Jambudvīpa with their power.
I pray they may flow on without interruption.

Those four wise men from the miscellaneous tribes,
Are like the four pillars that support a square house.
Let them unite to adorn the noble ancestral castle.
I pray that they will be immovable.

Those four men who have earned the name Gyaltsen,
Are like the four claws of the haughty white lion.
May they unite to adorn the white snow mountains.[103]
They will come to splendidly suppress the bestial enemies.
I pray that they will never age or decline.

Those three men who have earned the name Sheep-a-peep
   Ngo-lug
Are like the sheath that perfects the beauty of the threefold
   panoply;
May they unite and become the ornaments of the tigers in
   their prime.
They must come in order to show they are the finest of all.
I pray that their youth will never decline.

Those two arbiters of White Ling
Are like the two eyes that distinguish good and bad karma;
May they unite to become a repository of upāya and prajñā.
Whatever they utter is exactly right, like the speech of the
   gods.
I pray that their karma may be untainted.

Joru's perky, ever so perky;
Gu-ru's crooked, ever so crooked;
Although it's hard for them to unite,
Today, I, Drugmo, will force them to be together.

The straight arrow prefers to go,
The curved bow is happy to stay.
Even though their actions and form are dissimilar,
When they collaborate, the enemy's life is cut off at the root.

Therefore, both the clean and the filthy should be
   complementary.
Even though shit and piss are not part of the food,
They are the best companions for the growth of beans and
   grains.
The irrigated paddies are the ornament of China,
Yet the stalks of the excellent crops will bring benefit to
   Tibet.
Therefore, both the best and worst [horse and donkey]
   should be complementary.
Even though a donkey is not part of a horse,
It must be the father of the little bronze mule.

And a great man's wealth is enhanced by a mule;
The great steed mule is the ornament of the herd of horses.
Therefore Joru and Gu-ru should have a pact to join together.
May the difference between good and bad be discerned.

Let the four minor warriors have equal benefit,
Let the three beggars be in accord.
Then for the brethren of Ling,
No matter who wins the wager, may it become the general
    wealth of their tribe.
I pray it will not become grounds for dispute.

Well, then, this is such a spectacle for the eyes.
From the Ma Kali middle path of the gods:
The man dressed in white with a face as white as a conch
Who seems to be led by an army of celestial gods
Is Dongtsen Nang-ngu Apel.
That swift steed that he's riding,
Is the steed Blue Colt Turquoise Bird.
The horse doesn't seem to be running, but flying.
Flying, it seems to have captured the path of the birds.
In the lap of mother Ahza a special boy was born;
If a boy such as that is born, then that is all anyone needs.
In the mare Yoma's lap a special colt was born;
If a colt such as that is born, then that is all anyone needs.
After that, the next one to come is
The supreme being Tharpa Gyaltsen.
That swift steed that he is riding
Is the steed called Tshal-lu Tshamshei [Sorrel Dancer].[104]
After him, the next one to appear is Chief Zigphen of
    Tag-rong;
His steed is called Phorog Thongcham [Black Crow One-
    Thousand Dances].
After him the next one to come is
Nya-tsha Aten of Trothung;
His steed is Gang-ri Dingshei [Snow Mountain Jumper].
After him the next one to come is
Trogyal the son of Gungwa;

His steed is Nag-tra Phurshei [Black-Spotted Flyer].
After him the next one to come is
Sintsha Ngo-lug of Tag-rong;
His steed is Kyung-nag Phurshei [Black Garuḍa Flyer].
After him is Chief Sengseng of Chagnag;[105]
His steed is called Lunggi Trülkhor [Magic Wheel of Wind].
After him the next one to come is
Mazhi Chief Trothung;
His steed is Pharwa Nga-nag [Jackal Black Tail].
Those are the eight men and horses of Tag-rong.
They are like a lineage of great and majestic tigresses.
With the fearlessness of tigers,
They run through the sandalwood forest,
Snapping the trees into bundles of twigs.

Well then, this is such a spectacle for the eyes.
On the peak of the existence of the Greater Lineage,
That swarthy man with conch-white teeth
Is Nyibum Daryag of Serpa.
He is of the royal lineage of the Mukpo clan,
He is the chief Serpa of Upper Ling,
He is the head of the Three Ultimate Warriors,
He is the elder brother of the four lineages of the chieftains.
That swift mount that he rides
Is called Serdang Nyima Trülkhor [Magic Wheel of the
    Golden Sun].
After him the next one to come is
Chölu Buyi Darphen of Dong;
His steed is Mug-gu Dingshei [Maroon Flyer].
After him the next one to come is
Michen Gyalwa'i Lhundrub;
His steed is Gapa Trijam [Blaze Gentle Seat].
After him the next one to come is
The great Ling Tharpa Sönam;
His steed is Khyung-nag Dingshei [Soaring Black Garuḍa].*

---

* This name sometimes appears in the Tibetan text as Khyung-nag Phurshei [Flying Black Garuḍa].

After him the next one to come is
Phentag son of Abar;
His steed is Meri Tsubshei [Turbulent Volcano].
After him the next one to come is
Gyapön, Leader of a Hundred, Sergyi Argham;
His steed is Gya-gyug Serja [Racing Golden Bird].
After him the next one to come is
Chief of a Thousand, Tongpön Sotra Yami [Unrivaled
    Sparkling Teeth];
His steed is Tong-gyug Phenpo [Swift Racer].
After him the next one to come is
Tsangpa'i Ngo-lug of Agê;
His steed is Gang-ri Ödden [Radiant Snow Mountain].
These are the eight men and horses of the Greater Lineage.
The Greater Lineage is like a glacier,
The eight men are like great posing lions, and
The eight horses are like [the lions'] lavish turquoise manes.
Therefore the Greater Lineage should go to roam in the
    snow-capped mountains;
You can see their trial on the glaciers right now.

Well then, this is such a spectacle for the eyes.
That ceiling beam that established the Middle Lineage
Is a boy as vigorous as a turquoise-maned lion.
He is Anu Paseng of Ombu.
He is the middle of the Three Ultimate Warriors,
And the middle of the Four Divine Heirs.
That swift mount he is riding is
The winged horse called Marpo Lung-shog [Red Wings of
    Wind].
After him the next one to come is
The warrior Sengtag Adom;
His steed is Tong-ri Rag-kar [Thousand-Mountain
    Palomino].
After him the next one to come is
Chökyong Bernag of Gadei;
His steed is called Lung-nag Jeichöd [Captures the Black
    Wind].

After him the next one to come is
Dzongpön Lha-lu [Divine Nāga] of Ma Nyin [the sunny side
   of Ma];
His steed is Maja Tshal-lu [Vermillion Peacock].
After him the next one to come is
Nyima Lhundrub of Gödpo;
His steed is Mug-gu Tongcham [Sorrel Dancer].
After him the next one to come is
Gönpo Tongthub of Yuyag;
His steed is the turquoise horse called Norbu Lungdzin
   [Jewel Catches the Wind].
After him the next one to come is
The only son Drug-gyei of Kyalo;
His great steed is Gugya Rachig [Select Unicorn].
After him the next one to come is
Mikar Lhabu Samdrub of Dru;
His steed is Ngangkar Dro-kyid [White Swan Happy Gait].
They are the eight men and the eight horses of the Middle
   Lineage.
These eight men are like turquoise dragons rising from their lair.
The eight horses are like massing southerly clouds.
The Middle Lineage is racing in the colorful crag mountains.
Look and you can see that the rocks are notched with their
   trails.

Well then, this is such a spectacle for the eyes.
The first man who is coming there is
Chipön Rongtsha Tragen;
His steed is Sha-kyang Drelgo [Ochre Mule Head].
After him the next one to come is
Senglön Gala Rigshei [Knowing Awareness];
His great steed is called Gangkar Gyengchen [Great Haughty
   Mountain].
After him the next one to come is
Lama Gyaltsen of Gojo;
His steed is Tringyi Shugchen [Great Strength of the
   Clouds].
They are the three brethren of the Lesser Lineage.

Well then, the next spectacle for the eyes is
Like a black eagle swooping down for prey,
That son who is like a garuḍa chick with fully developed
　　wings;
He is Rinchen Darlu of Muchang.
He is the lesser of the Three Ultimate Warriors.
He is the youngest of the four brothers.
He is the rope ladder that leads to the sky.
That swift mount that he rides is
The steed Turquoise Bird Increasing Myriad [Yuja Triphel].
Then that man that is coming over there is
The unrivaled Gyatsha Zhalkar.
He is an emanation of the divine king of the swans,
He is the middle one of the four princes of Ling,
He is the nephew of the king of China to the east.
He is preferable to seven hundred thousand warriors in battle.
Among the mighty warriors of Ling he is a super warrior;
He is the leader of the Seven Super Warriors.
That swift steed that he mounts is
The noble steed Gyaja Sogkar [Pheasant White Shoulder].
After him the next one to come is
Denma Jangtra of Tshazhang;
His steed is called Ngültrug Dempa.
Then, the man who is coming over there is
Rongtsha Norbu Lhadar;
His steed is Maja Trikar [White Throne Peacock].
Then, the man who approaches over there is
Dar-'jam Ngo-lug of Mupa;
His steed his called Dzamling Rabkar [Glittering White
　　World].
Then the man who is coming next is
Darphen Nagpo of Mupa;
His steed is called Serdang Ya-med [Incomparable Golden
　　Radiance].
Then the next man coming is
Chipön's son Nangchung Yutag.
He is the support of the life essence of the Thirty Brethren of
　　Ling,

He is the one that uplifts the abundance for every human
    being;
His steed is Maja Trichen [Great Peacock Throne].
Then the next man approaching is
Cho-nga Paser Dawa;
His steed is Dungja Yu-ngog [Conch Bird Turquoise Mane].
Those are the eight men and their horses of the Lesser
    Lineage.
The eight men are like great soaring garuḍas, and
The eight horses are like fully extended wings.
The Lesser Lineage is racing in the hilltops;
Look, you can see that the grassy hills are already beaten
    down along their path.

Well then, the next spectacle for the eyes is
That fair man with golden ornaments.
He is Tönpa Gyaltsen of Kyalo;
His steed is Gugya Rachig [Select Unicorn].
Then the man coming next is
Lhabu Namkha Sengzhal;
His steed is Norbu Chamshei [Jewel Dancer].
Then the man coming next is
Nyima Gyaltsen of Kar-ru;
His steed is Log-mar Khyugshei [Red Lightening Bolt].
Then the man coming next is
The great arbiter Werma Lhadar;
His steed is Ngangpa Tselden [Agile Swan].
The man coming next is
The judge Wangpo Darphen;
His steed is Serden Phurshei [Golden Flyer]
Then the next man to come is
The doctor Künga Nyima;
His steed is Sernya Rag-kar [Golden Fish Palomino].
Then the next man to come is
The diviner Künshei Thigpo;
His steed is Tshal-lu Tingkar [Vermillion Fetlocks]
The next man to follow is
The astrologer Lhabu Yangkar;

His steed is Dung-dog Chamshei [Conch-Colored Dancer].
The next man to come is
The skillful magician Khache Migmar;
His steed is Gapa Dröden [Blaze Prancer].
The next man to come is
The Tibetan youth Michung Khadei;
His steed is Khamkya Chukar [Palomino White Muzzle].
The next man to come is
The handyman Gochöd Yogpo Pagyal;
His steed is Nag-tra Yak-gying [Spotted Haughty Yak].
The next man to come is
Akhöd Tharpa Zorna;
His steed is Gawa Geiring [Old Long Life].
Those are the general public servants of Ling.
The three knowledgeable mighty warriors and
The four mentors who are minor warriors,
Down to the servants, beggars, and dogs,
Not even counting the fact that they all think they have the
    fastest horse,
Not a one of them thinks himself to be the loser.
Joru and Gur have fallen behind,
And Dongtsen has taken off in front.
Moreover, the other brethren of Ling
Are somewhere in between.
We have no way of knowing how things will turn out tonight.
Which steed is taking the deepest breaths,
And whose windhorse is highest;
Those are not things this sister can know.

The next man to come along is
One who looks like he is carrying a great heavy load, yet
Has never dropped his load to the ground;
He really has nothing but pretends to have it all.
He wears an unusual lead pouch hanging off his side.
His name is Khyishi Buyi Gu-ru;
His horse is Gapa Trikyid [Blaze Happy to Be Led].
The next man to follow him is
Gogmo's cherished son Joru;

His steed is Kyang-bu Khakar [White Muzzle Kyang Colt].
It doesn't look as if he is going; it looks as if he is staying.
Staying, and still preparing to get the wager?
That man over there seems to be just a likeness of Joru;
That horse over there seems to be just the emanation of Kyang-bu.
Where the child Joru really is, no one knows;
Where the horse Kyang-bu rides, no one can tell.
Those two beggars of White Ling,
Whether they are rich or poor this sister doesn't know.
All the noble steeds of colorful Ling
Are running up the mountain pass like banking fog,
Running straight out like falcons flying, and
Running downhill like a tumbling avalanche.

No one can gain merit through theft;
No one can block previous karma with their hand.

If you have understood this, it is sweet to your ears.
If not, there is no way to explain it.

Thus she sang, and at that time Dongtsen was ahead, while Joru and Gu-ru fell behind. As for the rest of the mighty warriors, some were on the mountain, some were at the crags, and some were by the meadow. Not a single one was ahead or behind. In fact, it was rumored that they were running neck and neck.

Racing like tigers, lions, dragons, garudas, and herds of elephants
Looking as if they were all madly intoxicated with the most potent liquor,
They seemed so splendid as they competed with each other, but
The one coming last hidden in disguise, it is to You that I supplicate.

The meaning of this has for the most part been explained already. By hidden is meant that even though he is racing in last place in the race of White Ling, nevertheless, [Joru] will reveal the way of traversing the bhumis and paths simultaneously, like the stride of the precious elephant. This concludes the fifth chapter, the Saga of the Precious Elephant. Even though this chapter is now complete, one must understand that the horse race continues and Joru continues along with the stride of an elephant.

CHAPTER SIX

During the competition of the horse race
Joru subdues demons and demons and foils Trothung's ruse.
Diviners, doctors, and others are put to the test.
This gives rise to the Saga of the Precious General.

THE SIXTH [CHAPTER], the way all his rivals were splendidly suppressed, is as follows:

During the spectacle of the horse race of White Ling, which was a feast for the eyes, while Joru was racing along, back at Ayu Downs the spirits of the land appeared as the great hills of Tiger Head, Leopard Head, and Black Bear[106] Head. They thought to themselves, "Today at this horse race of White Ling, all we three sisters can see are the crooked hocks, the bulging buttocks, the tails whipping our heads, while the horses fling their manure in our direction. Furthermore, they are wearing down the mountain pathways of the land of Ma, knocking rocks down as they make a trail, and tram'pling the meadows into dry earth. The zodors of the land of Ma are distracted and don't notice, but we three will bring disease to the humans, and death and injury to the horses. If we couldn't do that, we would not be the sisters of Ayu Downs. Not only that, when the tea merchants of China as well as the merchants of Ladakh, from the highest lamas and chieftains down to the youngest herdsman, see us, they each take off their hats and arrange stones in offerings. This is an uninterrupted tradition. Today White Ling and especially the Lesser Lineage have offended us greatly. Now we must give an overt sign that shows our displeasure."[107]

The three of them gathered with their retinue army of the dark side. First a black cloud about the size of a sheep suddenly appeared, growing larger until it seemed to join heaven and earth with thunder and lightning. And just as hail and thunderbolts were about to be sent down, Gogmo's divine son Joru thought, "Today whether I win the wager or not, if I don't bind by oath these great hills, these three evil demon sisters and their assembly from the dark side, it will be hard for the doctrine of the Buddha to spread, and it will be hard for sentient beings to have happiness and well-being. Particularly since they will insult the brethren in the horse race of White Ling, and certainly cause mishaps for the racehorses, I must return to take care of this."

Instantly he came to the base of the great hills and, in the prison pit of the three doors of liberation,* through the four immeasurables,† he shackled, bound, and crazed the demons, and as he tamed them through the four buddha activities, he sang this vajra dohā called Never Straying from the Enclosure of Compassion, in the melody of the Swirling Ocean:

> The song is Ala Ala Ala.
> Thala is the melody of the song.
> Buddha, dharma, and sangha, these three,
> Please guide impure sentient beings.
> If you don't recognize me,
> When I'm not angry, I'm the Great Compassionate One,
>   Avalokiteśvara.
> When I am angry, I am the wrathful Hayagrīva,
> The yoke upon both the māras and rākṣasas.
> Well, then, listen here, three sisters of the great hills.
> Evil karma, which is your own doing—
> See how this negative karma[108] ripens within yourselves.
> You, the ones with human bodies and heads of animals,
> The nonhuman rākṣasīs,
> Like to kill and eat flesh.
> You create obstacles for the dharma of the side of virtue, and
> Befriend the sinners of the evil forces.
> In the prison of your own karmic consequences,

---

* Three doors of liberation: emptiness, freedom from aspirations, and characteristics.

† The four immeasurables: evenness, love, compassion, and joy.

Caught by the compassionate hook of no escape,
I will liberate you with the weapon of unborn realization
And suppress you under the vajra mountain of no release.
Until you give rise to bodhicitta
I'll never set you free, great ladies of the hills.

Thus he sang, and while performing the vajra dance of Hayagrīva, they offered the essence of their life force to him. They promised to be his servants, to befriend dharma practitioners, and uphold the teachings of the Buddha. They took refuge in the Three Jewels. At that he transformed them into the bodies of women.[109] He took their tiger, leopard, and black bear[110] heads as a sign of his own bravery. At that moment, the hail and clouds vanished of their own accord, and the sun came out shining brighter than ever.

Also at that time, the Treasure Lady[111] of Lower Ma appeared holding a crystal vase full of amṛta and a key to open the door the treasury of Gu-ra Crag as well as a treasure offering scarf. He took these and then went off to reenter the race.

He immediately caught up with Gu-ru, Khyishi's son, and he sang this song to test Gu-ru, in the melody of A Conch with Nine Spiral Turns:

The song is Ala Ala Ala.
Thala is the melody of the song.
If you don't recognize this place
It is Nathang Dzomo Tadra [Pasture of Dzo Mares].
If you don't recognize me,
I'm Gogmo's divine Joru.
I'm the heart son of White Brahmā,
I'm the nephew of the nāga king Tsugna,
I'm Jo, alert to the hostile enemy;
When the enemy tries to escape, I will easily capture him;
When the enemy tries to hide, I will easily suppress him.

Ru means the clan of my loving relatives.
I am the chief of the five tribes.
As the head of the brethren of White Ling,
I am the one born as the rowdy Joru.
Now Gu-ru, listen here!
Tell me about yourself, Gu-ru!
Today the gathered brethren of Ling

Are racing some of their swift horses.
All their valuables are worn on their backs.
The horses make great strides as they traverse the high
	mountain passes;
The horses make short strides as they traverse the low passes.
What have they wagered as the trophy of the race?
What is to be gained by running this race?
What is to be lost by losing this race?
Jo and Gur will equally share.

Suppose you, Gu-ru, are the wealthy one, then also
So am I, Joru, the nephew of Tsugna;
Together, both acclaimed as rich men.
Suppose you, Gu-ru, are the mighty one, then also
So am I, Joru, the descendant of the nyen;
Together we are the mighty tigers and lions.
Suppose you, Gu-ru, are a beggar,
And I, Joru, am the penniless child of Gogmo;
Then we naked beggars must join back to back.

The light rays of the royal parasol of the sun
Equally befriend all the mountain peaks.
It's not that the sun has chosen them to be so high,
It is the way that the earth and the valleys have come to exist.

The white conch moon of the fifteenth day,
Moves in a star-studded sky;
It's not that it is unable to travel alone,
It is the astrological arrangement of the cosmos.

In this horse race, the divine son Joru
Will run along with you, Gu-ru.
Even though I can get along without you, Gu-ru,
This is the plan of the girl Sengcham.
If you have understood this, it is sweet to your ears.
If not, there is no way to explain it.

Thus he sang, and Gu-ru became irritated, thinking, "This Joru, like black ink, has evil intentions toward whomever he meets in upper White Ling. He was already been expelled once, as his wickedness had shown itself like tongues of fire. Now today, he must surely know the significance of this horse race, but, since he can't catch up with the other brethren, all his negativity is directed toward me. He has told me only desperate lies, saying that not only couldn't he find a horse, but he had to run around from valley to valley just to get a saddle. From the start he has fallen way behind all the mighty warriors, so now he says that we'll both be left behind. If we join together, then it's just like the saying:

> On top of not having enough to eat,
> A debt is owed.

If that were not the case then maybe we could unite, but he says his father is great, his mother is precious, and he boasts about himself telling nothing but lies. But unless I answer him right now, we surely won't join forces. As the proverb states:

> You can't lean back with a yoke pressing your neck,
> The yoke on your neck will never break.
> You can't bend over bound by a black rope at the calves
> The black rope at the calves will never break.

That's how it seems to me."

[He spoke aloud:] "Hey Joru, the reason these horses are racing is to become the owner of Kyalo's wealth, the owner of the treasury of wealth of the Mukpo clan, the bridegroom of Drugmo, the leader of all districts of White Ling; don't you understand these are the reasons for the race? These are the only reasons that I'm here to race. If you don't know about any of this, why are you racing at all? Therefore there's no hope for either of us to win the wager. Even if it were possible, were I to win, I wouldn't share it with you; and if you were to win, I wouldn't want to share that with you. If I don't win the wager, I still don't want to have to give anything away. If you have a debt that needs to be repaid, there's no way that I'm going to do it for you." Saying, "We should not even share our fleas and lice," Gu-ru sang this song:

> The song is Ala Ala Ala.
> Thala is the melody of the song.
> I bow down at the feet of the ocean of the victorious objects
>   of Refuge.

If you don't recognize me,
I am the divine hunchback [Lha Gur] of all of Upper Ling;[112]
They say that without a Gu-ru, the state of the gods will
    decline.
I'm the wealthy hunchback [Chug Gur] of Middle Ling;
They say that without Gu-ru, the riches will decline.
I'm the prosperity hunchback [Yang Gur] of Lower Ling;
They say that without Gu-ru, prosperity will decline.
This hunchback Gu-ru is not bad, he is good;
It is good if the waxing moon is curved,
For it is the ornament of the azure firmament.
It is good if the sprout of a good crop is curved,
For it becomes the food of all living beings.
It is good if a rainbow in the sky is curved,
For it is the pillar between heaven and earth.
I've got even more examples than that.
All curved males are mighty, wild warriors.
All curved females are deep and wise.
All curved swords are powerfully sharp.

I'm the owner of nine female dzo;
I have yogurt in summer and yogurt in winter that never runs
    out,
I am the owner of nine irrigated fields;
I have wine in summer and wine in winter that never runs out.
Compared to the wealthy fathers,
I'm not a wealthy man,
But compared to the beggar Joru, I'm rich.
The rich and the poor are like butter and ashes.
We aren't compatible and should go our separate ways.
I am the master of nine daughters;
I am the master of nine brothers.
There are many who love me, and I have no enemies.
I don't claim to be an unrivaled mighty warrior,
But compared to you, Joru, I am mighty.
Mighty and cowardly, like fleas and fingernails,
We don't share, just go our separate ways.
You tattered, worn-out tent,

When the royal parasol rises,[113]
You will remain together in its hundred shafts of sunlight;
When the soft white snow falls,
You will remain together in its hundred piles of snow.

Inwardly, a hungry stomach and Joru, these two
Share the lap of Mother Gogmo.
Outwardly, the icy wind and the cold, these two[114]
Are the ornaments of the child Joru.
I, Gu-ru, who stays among the ranks of the warriors of Ling
Don't have time to stay here; I must go farther to adorn them.
If you have understood this, it is sweet to your ears.
If not, there is no way to explain it.

Thus he sang, and Joru said, "Well then, Gu-ru, as for how I feel, I am miserable, since I can't think of anything besides Drugmo and the golden throne. But Drugmo, the object of my desire, is too beautiful, and the warriors are too formidable, so that I can hardly think about it. This morning, Drugmo said that whoever gets the prize should share and that we, Joru and Gu-ru, must divide it among us. That's what I understood her to say, and that's exactly what I had said to you. But if you don't need it, it's not because I was unwilling to give it to you. You didn't want it, so don't be disappointed later.

The owner of Kyalo's wealth, the bridegroom of Drugmo, the head of White Ling; whether there's a horse race or not, don't you understand that there is no one but me, Joru, who can be the lord of all that?

At any rate, now that the auspicious connection between Joru and Gu-ru has been somewhat spoiled, as you said, we should go our separate ways. Don't ride right behind my horse Kyang-bu, for he is a divine horse and you will be punished, so you must be careful. Not only that, there are still more examples, so hold this in your mind." With that, he sang this song in the melody Playful Song of the Nightingale:[115]

The song is Ala Ala Ala.
Thala is the melody of the song.
Well then, Gu-ru, listen here,
For I have a few examples to give you.
If the outer illusory body is bent over, it's grounds for illness;
If the illness erupts into disease,[116] it will consume your life.

If the inner mind is crooked, then that is confusion;
When confusion erupts, you will go mad.
If your speech is crooked, then your words are lies.
If lies erupt, you'll be dragged into court.

They say that a curved sword can take one's own life,
They say that a curved horn of an animal can poke its own eye out,
They say if your hands are curved, your fists will beat your own chest.
They say if you are really bent over your mouth will meet your
*   buttocks.*

Where could you find proverbs more truthful than these?

Water cannot be held in a bent bucket.
Words can't be understood by someone whose mind is bent on
*   foolishness.*
Fine clothes don't fit well on a bent-over body.

If a hundred men all line up at attention,
The crooked one will look like he has a burden on his back;
Once there it seems to be fixed.
If a hundred men walk up a mountain pass,
A bent-over man looks like he's going downhill.
If a hundred men are getting up,
A bent-over man looks like he's lying down to sleep.
You, Gu-ru, aren't like anyone else.
When the brethren race, they go uphill;
When Gu-ru races, he goes downhill.
This divine horse white-muzzled Kyang-bu
Is different today than he used to be;
Sometimes he's ready to fly,
Sometimes to jump.
Whatever is in front, he bites and scratches;
Whatever is behind, he will give a square kick.
Therefore, Gu-ru, you must get out of his way.
I don't have time to hang around; I must go to capture the
    throne.
Gu-ru, keep this in your mind.

Thus he sang, and Gu-ru thought that neither one of them were likely to win the golden throne. Whatever the case, he determined to never let this wicked Joru get there ahead of him. Then he cracked his whip once or twice and raced ahead of Joru. The horse Kyang-bu reared up alongside of him, and as though dancing gave [Gu-ru's horse] Gapa Trikyid a side kick. With that, the horse [Gapa Trikyid] was flung almost one mile away. Gu-ru was then eaten by Joru's horse, consumed in one swallow. Gu-ru found himself in Kyang-bu's stomach, which appeared to him as a temple. Then he was shat out and landed in a great pile of horse manure. Man and horse were left unscathed, but Gu-ru was left with no hope of racing, and he then returned home.

But Joru caught up with Sheep-a-peep Tsangpa'i Ngo-lug and sang this song to put Ngo-lug to the test:

> The song is Ala Ala Ala.
> Thala is the melody of the song.
> I supplicate the Three Rare and Precious Jewels.
> Remain inseparable as the ornament of my mind.
> If you don't recognize this place,
> It's a pasture of dzo mares.
> If you don't recognize me,
> I am Gogmo's cherished son Joru.
> I am of the royal lineage of the Mukpo clan;
> I am one of the heirs of the lineage of King Senglön;
> I and only I have received the name of Joru.
> Joru has no choice but to be jo [alert].
>
> Of all the descendants of the Mukpo clan,
> Only I, Joru, was expelled without my share;
> I had no choice but to stand up for my own ru [dignity].
> Deprived of my wealth and possessions, I alone was expelled.
> Deprived of my fair share of good looks, I alone was expelled.
> Deprived of my castle and treasury, I alone was expelled.
> Deprived of my maiden Drugmo, I alone was expelled.
> I had no choice but to stand up for my own dignity.
> Thinking of my wealth and endowments, I stood up for my
>   dignity.
> Thinking of my castle and golden throne, I stood up for my
>   dignity.

Thinking of my lifetime companion, I stood up for my
    dignity.
Thinking of my good looks, I stood up for my dignity.

Well then, Tsangpa'i Ngo-lug,
Among handsome men you are the most handsome.
Poor Mother Gogmo's Joru,
Among ugly men I am the ugliest.
Among sons who come from the same paternal lineage,[117]
Why is it that are some handsome and some are so ugly?
Among the ancient arrows of a single quiver,
Why is it that some are short and some are long?
Therefore, we should divvy up the handsomeness and
    ugliness;
Our bodies must appear as neither handsome nor ugly,
    neither good nor bad.
Our height must be neither tall nor short.
Our wealth should be neither great nor small.

According to previous karma, Joru is the best.
Over many previous births,
Joru never committed any nonvirtue.[118]
In the mind of Joru there are no evil thoughts.
Joru who is free from sin,
Why is it that I am cursed with this ugly body?
Joru who has perfected the pāramitās
Is a bodhisattva who has attained the tenth bhumi.
Why haven't I obtained an excellent support [body]?
Therefore we two, you and I,
Outwardly, we must dress the same,
Inwardly, we must make our appearances equal.
If you don't do what I say, then don't call me Joru.
If you have understood this, it is sweet to your ears.
If not, there is no way to explain it.

Thus he spoke, and Tsangpa'i Ngo-lug thought, "Joru must be an unimpeded
magical emanation. He must be a fully enlightened bodhisattva manifesting for the
benefit of others. Therefore, since the merit of White Ling is sufficient, it's certain

that he can become the lord not only of the tangible humans but of the intangible godly demons. The way he appears with an ugly face and an ugly body is nothing but a magical emanation. Even now he's just testing me, since the meaning of the song for the most part seems true. So as not to defile the auspicious connection, I must offer him a song." Furthermore, the hat called Jeweled Meditation Hat of Uḍḍiyāna, which is the ritual support of the Greater Lineage, was tied around his body for protection. He thought he should untie it and offer it, and so he said, "Oh dear divine Joru, on this great occasion of auspicious connection, other than my protection Uḍḍiyāna Padma Meditation Hat, I have no possessions worthy of you, Joru. Please be so kind as to grant me the opportunity to receive your blessings and protection. Furthermore, everything that you find contemptible about your appearance, give to me, and if I have anything worthy, take it for yourself. Your power, your siddhis, your signs of accomplishment, your merit, your authentic presence; if I would have the good fortune to receive these, please grant them to me. There's no question that these qualities are hard to expect, because that would be a result that does not merit a cause. Nevertheless, here is a song that explains the history of the hat and the meaning of my request." He then offered this song in the melody of Fluctuating Pitches:

> The song is Ala Ala Ala.
> Thala is the melody of the song.
> Suppressor of rākṣasas in Cāmara,
> Guru Rākṣa Skull Garland Power,
> Your compassionate blessings are swifter than lightning.
> Bless this devoted child.
> If you don't recognize this place,
> It's the pasture of the dzo mares,
> The highest of four great plains.
> If you don't recognize me,
> I am called Tsangpa'i Ngo-lug of Agê.
> I am famous among the masses as the one with the best looks.
> But that which is called looks is just flesh and skin;
> Saying "handsome" and "ugly" is just a conceptual label.
> The characteristic of the body is that it is impermanent;
> Ultimately it is food for the birds and dogs.
> Saying a statue looks good is due to the paint;
> Without any blessing, it is just earth and stone.
> If a guru looks good, it's because of the robes he wears;

Without experience and realization, he is just a stuffed shirt.
If a tiger in his prime looks good, it's because of his weaponry;
Without courage, he is just a coward.
If a girl has beauty, it is just a matter of clothes and
    ornaments;
Without being ingratiating, she is just known as a vagrant.
If you are just handsome, that will not keep you warm.
If you have good looks, that will not fill your stomach.
Beauty and ugliness are in the eye of the beholder.
Good and evil are just the way the mind fathoms things.
Even so, if it pleases you, I shall offer this to you,
This Jeweled Meditation Hat of the nature of emptiness.
It is the inner wealth of Kyalo Tönpa,
It is the inheritance of the ritual support of the Greater
    Lineage,
It is the abhiṣeka hat of Uḍḍiyāna Padma.
Today I offer it to you, the divine child.

The hat symbolizes both saṃsāra and nirvāṇa.
For saṃsāra, this includes the six classes and the three realms.
Its top is adorned with four feathers;
This symbolizes the four realms of infinite perception
    [formless realms].[119]
Then it is adorned with seventeen silken scarves;
This includes the seventeen abodes of the form realm.
The hat is adorned with six lotus petals;
This symbolizes the six classes of the gods of the desire realm.
The four sides represent the four great continents.
Each side also has two corners
Making eight corners, which stand for the eight
    subcontinents.[120]

That the end of the hat's chin strap has three tassels
Symbolizes the places of the three lower realms.
That the hat has six edges
Symbolizes the six classes of beings.
The immense empty cavity within the hat
Signifies that saṃsāra has no essence.

The brilliance of the white color of the hat
Symbolizes the unchanging ālaya.
The trim of cloth around the hat
Is a sign of being bound by the fetters of adventitious stains.
The progressive order of saṃsāra is complete in the hat;
The reverse order accords with the path of nirvāṇa.
The incisive empty cavity of the hat
Symbolizes the empty essence of the ground.
As for the material of the hat[121] being naturally white,
This symbolizes the intrinsic nature of luminosity.
That it appears in the form of a hat
Means that it can be used in any way,
Indicating that compassion pervades everywhere.
If you lay it flat, it becomes two-sided,
Symbolizing that all phenomena are subsumed in the two
     truths.*
If you open it out, there will be four sides,
Which indicate the four truths respectively.†
That the hat has six edges
Symbolizes the conduct of the six pāramitās.
The four faces, which are white, pure, and smooth
Symbolize that it possess the four immeasurables.
The eight corners are the noble eightfold path,‡
Symbolizing familiarity with the conduct of the bodhisattvas.
That it is ornamented with the six-petaled lotus
Symbolizes having purified the habitual patterns of the six classes.
The height of the ear flaps on the right and left
Symbolizes the union of upāya and prajñā.
The fact that the hat has three points
Symbolizes the attainment of the fruition of the three kāyas.
That it is adorned by a variety of silk ribbons

---

* The two truths are relative truth and genuine truth.

† The Four Noble Truths: suffering, the cause of suffering, the cessation of suffering, and the path that leads to the cessation of suffering.

‡ The noble eightfold path: correct view, correct thought, correct speech, correct conduct, correct livelihood, correct action, correct intentions, and correct samādhi.

Symbolizes expansive wisdom beyond partiality.
That it is adorned with the great garuḍa feather
Symbolizes always abiding as the dharmadhātu realm.
That it is adorned with the feather of a white vulture
Symbolizes the insight that dispels ignorance.
That it is adorned with feather of a parrot
Symbolizes transmitting instructions to others with loving-
    kindness.
That it is adorned with the feather of an eagle
Symbolizes subjugating the hordes of māras through power.
That there are a pair of chin straps hanging from the hat[122]
Symbolizes the certainty of the two paths to liberation and
    confusion.
That three tassels hang from the hat[123]
Symbolizes abandoning the obscurations of the three poisons.
That the sides of the hat are open
Symbolizes that the ground of saṃsāra and nirvāṇa is the same,
While the path is what makes the difference.
Concerning the dharmas of saṃsāra and nirvāṇa
There is not a single one that does not accord with the hat.
Wear this hat as the great auspicious connection.
You who are the divine child Joru of Mu,
May your buddha activity be limitless.
Moreover, concerning your buddha activity and authentic
    presence,
If there is a way for me to share this, I would only be happy.
If you heard this, it is an ornament for your ears,
If not, there is no way to explain it.

Along with the song, he [Tsangpa'i Ngo-lug] offered his hat. Joru removed his own antelope hat and put it in his chuba, and then placed the colorful meditation hat on his head. Then, as a support for his faith and to bless him, Joru gave Tsangpa'i Ngo-lug the crystal vase filled with ambrosia, which had been given to him by the female treasure holder of Ma, and the Auspicious-by-Day scarf. Then he rode on and arrived before many of the brethren. As he looked back, he saw the diviner approaching. He went to the diviner's side saying, "Oh, dear diviner Künshei Thigpo, today I, Gogmo's Joru, need to have a divination performed," and he sang this song in the melody of the Northern Swirling Song:

The song is Ala Ala Ala.
Thala is the melody of the song.
Great god Brahmā with Four Faces know me.
Lead this song of Joru.
If you don't know this place,
It is the path of the shady side of Ma Silken Plains.
If you don't recognize me,
I am Gogmo's Joru of Lower Ma.
Well then, precious diviner,
Listen, for I have a few things to request.
Now, whether our happiness and well-being are great or small
Is said to be cast up by the karma of our previous lives.
They say that karma is inescapable.
Whatever my karmic results are, I don't know.
What will come of the rest of this life, I don't know.
Therefore, I need a divination from the diviner.

At this time of the horse race of White Ling
If it's merely a game, it's wonderful.
If it's about winning or losing the wager, I think that's just as
    important.

First, the great value of the treasure trove,
Second, the wealth and endowments of Kyalo,
Third, the vast extent of all the districts of Ling,
Fourth, the great worth of Drugmo;
It is said that these four great treasures
Will be the booty that falls to the hands [of the winner].
For that this is what Joru has to say.

The dharma king of India
Does not win the throne by racing a horse,
The secular king of China
Does not win the throne by racing a horse.
In the eighteen principalities where the valleys converge[124]
There are many kingdoms like these.
They didn't win their kingdoms by racing a horse.
The king of White Ling will be established by a horse.

Even the two beggars Joru and Gur are riding horses;
If their horses win, they'll be the kings of Ling.
All the great royal ancestral lineages of the Mukpo clan,
If their horses aren't fast, will be the servants of Ling.

Isn't it quite strange, my dear diviner?
First, the males are both wild and brave and weak and
    cowardly,
Second, the inner qualities of females can be either good or
    bad,
Third, the power of karma is both high and low,
Fourth, the father's lineage and the mother's background
Divide the leaders from their subjects.
It seems that Ling has no need of all this;
Whoever is fastest is the custom for becoming king.
Therefore, concerning Gogmo's son Joru,
He has a horse that if he flies, can cross over the sky,
That if he runs, will win the ribbon.
He is the noble steed, a breed of the wild kyang.
I can't imagine that Turquoise Bird will break away ahead of me,
I can't imagine that I won't get the victory scarf;
The thing that is difficult is attaining the golden throne.

The unskilled rider racing downhill
Is just asking for a broken head.
The foolish man who sits at the head of the line
Is just asking for some embarrassment.

Thinking about that, Joru has returned.
That this beggar Joru is riding this swift horse
Is either leading me to disaster
Or it is the life-force mountain of good fortune.
Whatever will be, Joru doesn't know.
So please cast a divination for me.
I'm not asking for a mo [divination] to determine who is
    faster or slower but rather
Whether the golden throne will be held and,
If so, whether I will be able to be the chieftain,

And become the life companion of Drugmo, these three.
Please make the knots in the divination cord.
Please give a deep explanation of what it means,
Please analyze whether it is good or bad through your
    wisdom knowledge.
Since a divination that lacks an offering cannot be accurate,
I offer you a precious golden coin
Wrapped in an auspicious offering scarf.
If you have understood this, it is sweet to your ears.
If not, there is no way to explain it.

Thus he sang, and he offered a single golden coin with an offering scarf, requesting the divination to be cast. The diviner thought, "Today at this horse race, we
can measure who's ahead and who's behind by the length of the reins, and estimate
the height of the horse by the length of the ears. Usually I would lay out the divination board, clear out the confounding demons, and supplicate to the gods of the mo,
but today I don't have time for all that. In order to satisfy Joru's hopes I better do this
mo quickly, or else there is no choice." He took the divination cord out from inside
his chuba's pocket and sang this song of requesting the divination and the outcome
in the melody of Galloping as a Soaring White Vulture:

The song is Ala Ala Ala.
Thala is the melody of the song.
The Three Jewels of Refuge,
And the swiftest of dralas, and
The most powerful of the wermas,
Come here today to befriend this diviner.
Great god White Brahmā;
A man in white with a conch topknot,
On a white horse surrounded by banking clouds; how
    amazing!
Holding the divination cord of the gods,
Assist with this cosmic divination.

Lord of the nyen, Machen Pomra;
A man in yellow with a golden turban,
On a golden horse in shimmering rainbow light.
Holding the divination cord of the cosmos,

Today come and assist at this divination.
Divination god and the three Phuwer brothers,[125] and
Four gods of knowing, eight gods of seeing, I supplicate all
    of you.
To clear it, polish it with the silk of the queen,
To bathe it, wash it with pure water,
To purify it, purify it with a blade of poison grass.
May it be clearly cast and honestly revealed.
For this young child of Gogmo's, Joru,
First, if he races will he win the victory scarf?
Second, if he wins will he be a good leader?
Third, will he become the bridegroom of Drugmo?
Please show directly what this divination predicts.
With the six strands of the divination cord
May this swift and honest result be cast.
Atsi! The divination looks great.

First, the knot of the life force of the sky is cast,
Which shows you can cover and suppress like the vast
    covering of the sky.
If you take the throne, it shows you can hold it.

Second, the knot of the life force of the earth is cast,
To show that the earth is immutable and thus stands firm.
The mo says if you take the throne you'll be a good leader
And that you'll place all beings in happiness.

Third, the knot of the life force of the ocean is cast.
In the great fathomless ocean, the edge of the earth
Where all tributaries gather into one,
Even though the waves may seem to go elsewhere,
They will always return to the ocean.[126]

The mo says you will become the bridegroom of Drugmo.
However, it shows that there will be marriage and separation,
But the mo says that finally she will come back to you.
Also, this mo can be analyzed as follows:

At the spiritual level, the knot of the life force of the sky,
The mo says that the strength of your spiritual activity is
     higher than the sky.
Just as the sky befriends the sun and the moon,
It shows that the guardian deities will inseparably befriend
     you.
The knot of the life force of your own earth
Shows the pattern of the field of authentic presence
Ripening as the six grains of wealth and endowments.
The mo here shows the future, for it reveals in this cast a great
     king of all rivers.
The river doesn't stay; it is commanded to go.
If you go in the four directions, you'll accomplish the four
     aims.
The mo says that from the beginning, you will subjugate the
     four enemies.[127]
It shows the goings and comings of men and their horses.
And that there is freedom from the narrow passageway of the
     three evils,[128]
And freedom from any faults of making mistakes through the
     three mediocrities;[129]
The way this divination is cast shows three excellences,[130]
Making it a suitable divination for White Ling.

Child Joru, it follows that this divination is good for you.
Either this is a sign that the diviner should prepare to die,
Or else it seems the mo is inaccurate.
No matter what, if you run your race, good fortune will
     follow you.
There's no way to cast a divination that could be any better
     than this.
If you have understood this, it is sweet to your ears.
If not, there is no way to explain it.

As soon as he had sung, Joru felt deeply that this man was worthy of both
the name "diviner" and its meaning. Without this diviner guiding the religion and
politics of White Ling, it could not survive. Placing a stainless white scarf around

the neck of the diviner, he rode off on his horse, the lord of all steeds, speeding away as though it had wheels of magic. Catching up with the doctor Künga Nyima, he pretended to be extremely ill and sang this song to test the doctor in the melody of Playful Modulations:

The song is Ala Ala Ala.
Thala is the melody of the song.
Guru, yidam, ḍākinī, these three,
Please remain inseparable as the ornament of my crown
And dwelling there, grant me your blessings.
If you don't recognize me,
I am Gogmo's Joru of Lower Ma.
Well then, precious doctor,
Listen, I have a few things to tell you.
I, Joru of Lower Ma,
Unclothed, have been tormented by the icy winds.
First, the physical vitality of my body is exhausted,[131]
Suffering from lack of food and hunger, so that
Second, my inner strength has declined.
Without a family I am always the target of everyone's
    aggression, so that
Third, my frame of mind is one of utter depression.
Those three are inseparable as this life's illness.
Not only that, but today I've got a new illness;
It came upon me suddenly, and I don't know what it is.
I wonder if it's heat in my upper abdomen.
The pain feels like tongues of blazing fire,
My waist feels both hot and cold at the same time.
This illness seems like something stirred up by a black wind.
I wonder if it's coldness in my lower abdomen.
The pain feels like boiling hot water,
If I move it's uncomfortable, and heavier than a mountain.
If I stay still it's uncomfortable and lighter than the wind.
This illness along with Joru is
Like a mixture of water and milk.
Alas! What a grave illness.
I fear this is going to damage my body,
I fear that this will cut off the flow of my channels.

My inner mind is just about worn to shreds.
I wonder if it's a sign that Joru is meant to die?
If I die, this death will bring suffering, for the dying child Joru
    is lacking the dharma.
The mother I would leave behind has neither food nor
    clothing.
Please give me some medicine to cure this illness,
And check my pulses to see if I would live or die.
Please identify whether the illness comes from heat or cold,
And if it's a harmful dön, expel it.
If you have understood this, it is sweet to your ears.
If not, there is no way to explain it.

Thus he sang, and sat there acting utterly helpless. The doctor thought, "I don't have my medicine kit with me, but I can certainly check his pulses, and I do have one medicine called White Panacea, and also several general medicines that I always keep with me as a token of a doctor's commitment. If it's just a temporary illness, I can cure it," he thought as he carefully checked Joru's pulses. He determined that there was no obvious illness, and he knew that Joru's corporeal body was untainted. Internally, the impure blood and lymph had ceased to circulate since his channels, winds (nāḍī and prāṇa), and his body, all three, were stainless. Realizing that all of this had arisen based on pure interdependent origination, with a slight smile on his face, he offered this song in the melody of Six Undulating White Scarves of a Physician:

The song is Ala Ala Ala.
Thala is the melody of the song.
From the pure realm of beautiful-to-behold*
Medicine Buddha, and Lord Brahmā Atreya,†
The Youthful Physicians, and others,
Hold us with your compassion and grant your blessings.
If you don't recognize me,
I'm called the Doctor Künga Nyima,

---

* This is the pure land of the Medicine Buddha.

† Tib. *rgyun shes gyi bu*, Child of Your Stream of Knowledge.

The one who has never lost a child to death.
Now, Gogmo's Joru, sir,
Listen, for I have a few things to tell you.

Illness comes from wind, bile, and phlegm, these three,
Born from the root causes of passion, aggression, and
    delusion;
These three come together, and through the way that they
    mingle
The four hundred and four illnesses emerge.
In the human realm, where sentient beings abide,
Since the cause of disease, the three poisons, is not abandoned
It's impossible to find a pulse that is not free from illness.
Therefore this pulse of Joru's is definitely not
A pulse that comes from a disease of the elements.
Forget the fact that the coarse four elements don't even seem
    to exist;
When I examine the pure interdependent elements of the
    channels,
According to my diagnosis, the meaning of these signs seems
    to be that
Not even the slightest illness has been found in your pulses,
Indicating that you are free from the cause of illness, the three
    poisons.
The beat of your pulse is clear and calm,
Meaning that your knowledge and compassion are without
    obscuration.
Except for what arises in the mind of the doctor,
It seems that your pulses don't really give a clear reading,
Indicating that you are a magical manifestation for the
    welfare of others.
If illness or demonic forces are not apparent in the pulses,
The doctor won't know the treatment.
Your body and channels are not synchronized;
Joru and his channels are not the same.
Either these channels are an illusion,
Or else Joru is magical manifestation.

If what these pulses tell me is true,
It shows that whatever he wants will be spontaneously
    accomplished.
It shows that the purpose of his actions will be brought to
    perfection.
If you have understood this, it is sweet to your ears.
If not, there is no way to explain it.

Thus he sang, and Joru thought, "The name of this doctor matches his qualities." Placing the stainless scarf around the doctor's neck, he rode off on the Lord of Steeds, the swift magical horse. When he caught up to Chipön, his uncle Chipön said, "Joru, where have you been all this time? You'd better hurry up, Dongtsen is about to seize the throne."

Joru replied "Uncle, I was appointed by the imperial gods, so what's the point in losing this race to a mere animal? The gods and gurus are in control here. Earlier, on my way here, I accomplished both the benefit of self and others and witnessed several amazing spectacles. Even now I'm not concerned about speeding up or slowing down. If it's a question of speed, then, Uncle, ride faster, for there's no difference between uncle and nephew in terms of who holds the throne. Did you understand me?" Saying that, he rode on ahead.

Trothung's greatest fear was that Joru would get ahead of Dongtsen, and just then he saw Joru run off in the opposite direction from the race. Then Tro-thung thought, "Well, then, now there can be no other winner than Dongtsen. Hayagrīva's prophecy was truly undeceiving." He had more joy and elation than his guts could hold. He was so excited that he didn't know what to do with himself, and he swiveled in his saddle, riding at ease. It was then that he met up with Joru.

When Trothung saw Joru, his chest filled up with air. His nerves flared, and his anxiety heightened such that he didn't know what to say. He let out a big sigh and suddenly blurted, "Hey, Joru, what are you doing racing back and forth like this? How far has my son Dongtsen gone? Who do you think will win today's horse race?"

And Joru replied, "Uncle, I've already been near the golden throne twice, but I didn't dare to sit on the brocade cushion. There's no one ahead of Dongtsen, however:

> *Even though a man shouldn't sweat, his forehead is sweating.*
> *A horse shouldn't quiver, but his calves are quivering.*[132]

I don't know what he'll be like by the time he gets to the golden throne. His calves will be shaking while he receives the spiritual attainment.[133] Not only that, another proverb says:

> When good fortune comes to the mouth, the tongue accidentally
> pushes it out.

It doesn't seem like he will be equipped to hold the throne.

I've examined those famous steeds of the Thirty Brethren, looking them all up and down twice, and I have seen nothing over there but nostrils panting like bellows and bodies steaming with sweat. Not even one horse turned out to be an exception. Still, your horse, Trothung, Pharwa Nga-nag, and Denma's, Ngültrug Denpa, are supposed to be exceptional because they know the human language. Well, perhaps that will be to your favor, but otherwise they certainly won't be able to accomplish the goal.

No matter how high your position in the lineage of White Ling, that's not going to help you win the wager today. There is absolutely no horse that is faster than my Kyang-bu. My horse has not even broken a sweat yet and is but lightly breathed. I don't know how useful this prize would be for me, so, although I arrived at the throne, I did not sit on it. I'm not sure whether I will even continue [to race]. If I don't, then I think perhaps Dongtsen will be the one to win," he said.

Trothung thought, "If I don't trick this nephew Joru, who knows what that demon in a human skin will do?" Then he said, "Nephew, you're right. The booty of this horse race of White Ling is a farce, luring the reckless youth and leading them astray. Actually, it's laying the foundation for a den of corruption. It will only add to our hardships. Nephew, what you've figured out is absolutely right. Still I will clarify this further; there are many stories that the youngsters need to know. Therefore listen to this advice from your old uncle." Then he sang this song of deception in the melody Long Slow Gentle Tune:[134]

> The song is Ala Ala Ala.
> Thala is the melody of the song.
> From the palace of mighty Padma,
> Yidam Red Hayagrīva, know me
> And guide me, the wrathful King Tro.
> Grant me the ultimate support of your prophecy.
> If you don't recognize this place,
> It is the upper valley of Darthang [Silken Plain].
> If you don't recognize me,

I am known as the Uncle of Dong, Trogyal.
Well then, nephew, listen here.
That which is called the wager of the horse race,
If you think about it, here is what it's like.

It is well known among the guru's teachings that
They teach not to be bound by hope and fear,
And not to maintain attachment and aggression that create
    saṃsāra.
They teach that effort-based practice brings more confusion;
If you're confused, they say this is the source of suffering.
I think that these teachings are true.
If you're confused, you'll do all sorts of things,
You might laugh out loud while you're fast asleep at night.
If you're a glutton, you'll think all sorts of things,
And will even think the taste of pure white yogurt is bitter.
If you're hungry, you'll eat all sorts of things,
You'll say the starving flesh of cattle in spring tastes terrific.
The clans of Ling say all sorts of things;
They say the booty of the horse race is fantastic.
All of that is confusion.
Let me explain the root of this confusion,
The drum of the law, Selwa'i Ödden,
Is just a dry piece of wood covered with leather.
The white conch of the law, Karmo Gyangdrag,
Upon inspection, is just the empty shell of a bug.
Those cymbals called Nyima Drug-drag
Are actually cymbals made from a piece of metal.

Killing them won't supply meat or fat,
Milking them won't bring down any milk,
Wearing them can't take the place of clothes,
Trying to eat them won't be good for your stomach.

That Kyalo Sengcham Drugmo,
Getting to know her will just lead you into sin.
To become the chieftain, winner of the golden throne of the
    many districts of Ling,

Is a position of leadership that just adds to your misery.
Not only that, I have a few more points to make.

The flower that grows in a pile of manure,[135]
Although the color is brilliant,
If offered to the gods, it will pollute them.

The good looks of that reckless maiden
May be pleasant to look at,
But if you get together with her, it will be a den of corruption.

The sweetness of poison fruit,
May be sweet to eat,
But you risk your life when it hits your stomach.

Becoming the leader of the people of these many
    districts,
Sounds good to the ears but
Actually carries with it more suffering than anything.

This is the advice of your uncle.
Don't race, let uncle and nephew ride on slowly,
If we tell stories as we go, the path won't seem as long.
First of all, the way the eon of this world was created,
And afterward, the way in which this kalpa endures, and
Finally, the way that it will be destroyed and emptied.
Except for me, Trothung, it's rare to find another who
    understands all of this.
The way of taking a precious human rebirth,[136] and
After birth, the way of maintaining life in the world, and
At death, the way of passing through the bardo.
Except for me, Trothung, it's rare to find another who
    understands all three.
Those are the things I have to tell you;
There's an important reason for my telling you this.
From among the ancestral six clans of Tibet
How the great people of Mukpo became an offshoot, and
How the Thirty Brethren all branched off.

Except for me, Trothung, it's rare to find another who
    understands all of this.
Those are the things I have to tell you.
The four kingdoms that border White Ling,
Yellow Hor, Multicolored Mön, Black Düd, and Maroon
    Jang;
The way the diverse clans originated in these countries, and
All about the ranks of the ministers and the rest of the
    population.
Except for me, Trothung, it's rare to find another who
    understands all of this.
I'll tell you everything as we ride along.
I will share with you many meaningful and helpful things.
Besides, we could have some lighter fascinating discussions.
We'll loosen our muscles with melodious songs and
Decipher the difficult words.
As we ride along, we'll talk and talk about all sorts of things.
If you have understood this, it is sweet to your ears.
If not, there is no way to explain it.

Thus he spoke, and Joru replied, "Yes, Uncle, your words are true, but right now I'd like to tell you some of my own thoughts," and he sang this song in the melody Reverberating Playful Song:[137]

The song is Ala Ala Ala.
Thala is the melody of the song.
Buddha, dharma, and sangha, these three,
Please remain inseparably as my crown ornament.
This land is the upper valley, Darthang,
And I am the one called Gogmo's Joru.
Now then, Uncle, listen here.
The finish line of the horse race of White Ling,
I don't think it's such a big deal that I am intimidated.
Nor do I think it's so insignificant that it offends me.
For this, each person has their own karmic portion;
That is the mandate of the imperial gods.
First, telling stories about all the great cultures, and
Second, the exciting stories that break one's jaw to recount,

And third, the chronicles of the history of Ling called the
    Precious Lamp
Are gifts that I, Joru, inherited when I was born in this world.
That is why I don't have any need for your advice, Uncle.
As for this hat of the unsightly heads of all these antelopes,
The fathers and uncles are getting more and more irritated by
    the sight of it;
I just wish that one day I could be the person to wear a white
    pennon helmet.
My back is being bitten over and over by the lice in my
    calfskin chuba;
I just wish that one day I could be the person to wear a long-
    sleeved cloak.
Everybody insults me again and again by putting me down;
I just wish that one day I could be a powerful and mighty
    chieftain.
The frigid icy cold winds whip me again and again;
How I wish I'd be the one to get a turquoise tent.
I'm tormented time and again by the desire for a companion;
I wonder when the day will come that I will get Drugmo for
    my bride.
In fact, I don't even have time to keep singing this song.
I shouldn't be too early; they'll just make fun of me.
Now I'm not staying here any longer, for I must go on to
    fulfill my dreams.
Now, Uncle, keep this in your mind.

Thus he sang, and the Lord of Steeds instantly departed. All this set Tro-thung's nerves on edge, but there was nothing he could do.

Elder brother Gyatsha Zhalkar was wearing his armor Karmo Lhazang [Pure Benevolent God] underneath his chuba on his bare skin, and he was putting his sword Yazi Kartren [Invincible Sword Little Star] into the pouch of his chuba. Joru was rac-ing along and thought to himself, "Older brother Gyatsha was the kind of man who would hold his sword above his fellow brethren and flex his biceps. Now he should see what [Gyatsha] would do if he suddenly encountered an outside enemy." He then emanated himself as a man in black on a black horse and like a storm cloud filling the sky, its dark shadow extending across the lake. He held a black iron spear that seemed to reach into the heavens, shouting *ki! so! ho!* With a shout that shattered the earth and the sky, he bore down on Gyatsha. Then the warrior Gyatsha Zhalkar of Bumpa saw him and thought, "It is impossible for this to be happening on this happy occasion of the horse race of White Ling. This has to be a māra or a rākṣasa. What an unbelievable insult to White Ling and particularly to me personally. I will stand firm even at the cost of my life, for I will have no regrets." He stroked the pommel of his sword and waited. Instantly the man in black drew his sword and sang this song to Gyatsha in the melody of Six Modulations of the Māras:

> The song is Ala Ala Ala.
> Thala is the melody of the song.
> From the inner chambers of the Red Copper Crag,
> Red tsen and your retinue, know me.
> If you don't recognize me,
> My father is a māra, and my mother a tsen.
> This son of the union of a māra and a tsen
> Is Beri Nyima Gyaltsen.
> Half my retinue is from Hor and half from Düd, and
> I'm the general of the troops of both Düd and Hor.
> Well then, man in white with a pale white horse,
> Listen, for I have some stories to tell you.
>
> Last year in the wintertime,
> In the alcove of Jachen Yölmo,
> Sengcham Drugmo of Kyalo
> Was traveling alone across the valley when I found her.
> The maiden Sengcham said,
> "I'll give you all the wealth and possessions of Kyalo;
> Because it is all mine to give,
> I'll surrender it all to you."

Once making a verbal commitment,
The chop that seals the deal is still fresh.

Once the six grains are cut down with a sickle,
The bundles of ten remain perfectly intact.[138]

> The personal property of Kyalo,
> Just hand over to this man.

If you don't, but want to talk instead,
First I'll fill the hills with corpses, and
Then I'll fill the valleys with blood;
I'll conquer all of White Ling.
If I can't do that, then I'm not the warrior of Düd and Hor.
If you have understood this, it is sweet to your ears.
If not, there is no way to explain it.

Thus he sang, and then Gyatsha Zhalkar of Bumpa said, "All this, the wealth
possessions of Kyalo, I wouldn't even think of placing in the hands of the Thirty
Brethren. If I handed it over to you, the Demon-Hor, this warrior Gyatsha would be
nothing but a dead corpse. So, I have a few things to tell you," and he sang this song
in the melody Short Song of the Warrior:

The song is Ala Ala Ala.
Thala is the melody of the song.
Inseparable Three Jewels of Refuge, know me,
Imperial gods lead me in this song.
If you don't recognize me,
From the immutable castle Ngülchu Tro-dzong,
I am the steady warrior Gyatsha Zhalkar.
Among the daughters of the Emperor of China in the east
The eldest is Lhakar Drönma.
She is the wife of King Senglön,
And she is my own mother.
The middle daughter, Gazi Lhamo [Worthy Zi Divine Lady],
Is the queen of the chieftain Gurkar of Hor,
Who bore their son, Lhabu Legpo [Excellent Prince].
The youngest sister is Jangza Metog Drön [Lady of Jang
    Blazing Lotus],[139]
She is King Sadam's queen and
The mother who gave birth to Nyitri.
Gyatsha, Nyitri, and Lhabu, these three
Are the three nephews of the Emperor of China;
Pheasant, Duck, and Peacock, these three horses
Are the Gyiling supreme steeds of China.
Pheasant is the horse beneath dear Zhal-lu,
Duck is the mount of the son of Jang,

Peacock belongs to the Yellow Hor, and
Is the mount of Lhabu Legpo.
Their weapons Yazi, Guzi, and Azi; these three
Were gifts from China.
This poison blazing sword Azi
Just now is in Yellow Hor,
In the hands of Shenpa-bu [Butcher]*
Guzi, the pale white one,[140]
Is now in dark Jang,
In the hands of Yulha-bu [Divine Turquoise Son]†
The sharp-cutting invincible sword Yazi Kartren
Was not entrusted to another; I have kept it.
If you hold it, it protects your life.
If you wield it, it subdues the hordes of enemies.
It was fashioned by the blacksmith of the the'u rang,
Forged in the darkness of the three waning moons,
Forged in daylight of the waxing moons.

The blunt edge is well-made,
Resembling a flowing braid of hair.
The sharp edge is well-made,
Resembling the lengthening shadows that reach across the lake.
The scabbard is a model of beauty,
Long and straight resembling two elegant chopsticks in their
     sheath.
The coarse father iron is a model of beauty,
Resembling the fur of deer on snow.
The mother iron is a model of beauty,
Resembling fire tongues touching crystal.
When the sword is raised, it is more like a flame than a sword,
As though it were ablaze with its own dralas.
When you strike with the sword, it's not like striking; it's as
     though it can consume.

---

* The Butcher is one of Gurkar's five poison ministers.

† Sadam's son.

It seems to be consuming the breath and life of the vindictive
    enemy.
For the blade of a sword of such action
To encounter a warrior like you would be wonderful.
Now that you and I are together,
Apart from the wind, nothing could come between us.
Apart from the solid earth, nothing else could drink our
    blood.
Apart from the blue sky, nothing can be such a spectacle.
The daughter of Kyalo and all of his wealth
Should not be handed over to a vengeful enemy and
Are not to be handed over to the brethren of Ling.
If you have understood this, it is sweet to your ears.
If not, there is no way to explain it.

Thus he sang, and as he struck once with his sword Yazi, except for an empty sky there was nothing to penetrate. Then a pale-colored Joru appeared standing upright.

Joru said, "Brother Zhalkar, why are you so upset with this emanation of me appearing in front of you? If you were not so against me, I was hoping that you could run off and seize the golden throne, while I pretend to be fighting with the brethren of White Ling. Now, brother, if you're not interested in this throne and its status, then this beggar Joru has no need for the throne or the power. Do you understand?" As he spoke, he dismounted and lay down naked on his calfskin chuba, relaxing.

Then Gyatsha Zhalkar of Bumpa responded, "O Joru, Joru you precious one, may your wisdom be exalted! There's no point in my being put to the test since the divine prophecies of all the gods and gurus repeat again and again that it is you, Joru, who will quell the four māras through your splendor. You are the one who will become the vast covering of the sky and the great support of the dense earth. I was only thinking to serve the general purpose of the doctrine and all beings—that's the reason I was going to fight you. I have no hope to get the golden throne or Drugmo. Even if I did, I was thinking to offer it to you. As they say: 'The Buddha will never tire of working for sentient beings.' So, increase your magical powers, for if you procrastinate any longer I'm afraid there will obstacles to the welfare of the doctrine and the happiness of sentient beings. Keep in mind that if right in front of all these people Dongtsen wins the throne, even though you have magical powers, it will then be difficult." Thinking that Gyatsha was right, he [Joru] put his clothes back on, mounted his horse, and rode off.

Just as an image reflects from a clear crystal
In front of so many [people] your myriad songs of experience
Have clarified the minds and desires of individuals.
I supplicate this magical display of instrumentation.

Thus, the meaning of this verse is explained through this chapter. This recalls how Joru sought out all those human and nonhuman rivals, annihilating and intimidating and quelling them with his splendor. This completes the sixth chapter, which is the Saga of the Precious General.

CHAPTER SEVEN

Joru obtains victory in the contest of the horse race.
He is instated on a golden throne; gods and men offer him
    auspicious prayers.
The name Gesar Norbu Dradül is conferred upon him.
This gives rise to the Saga of the Precious Jewel.

THE SEVENTH [CHAPTER] depicts the way he obtained the golden throne:

After meeting with Zhalkar, Joru continued to ride on his magically swift steed. Then, in the space in front, in a floating[141] bank of white clouds there appeared in the midst of multicolored rainbow light the five Tsering [Long-Life] sisters holding long-life arrows and trays loaded with jewels. Nenei [Auntie] Nammen Karmo held an arrow and a mirror; Sumo [Sister] Gödcham Karmo held a treasure vase. Surrounding them were a retinue of many countless ḍākinīs who clearly appeared there.

Auntie Nammen Karmo spoke, "Boy Joru, don't just tarry, hurry up and run! Dongtsen has slipped ahead of you! Being overconfident, lazy, and distracted, these three, are the three faults that prevent the benefit of others. Even though the dralas might catch the horse Turquoise Bird, I'm afraid they won't be able to catch the boy Dongtsen." Thus she spoke.[142]

Meanwhile, downhill in the ravine on the left of Gu-ra Crag was the golden throne, and Dongtsen was almost there when the drala Nyentag Marpo unleashed lameness* on Turquoise Bird. Turquoise Bird wheezed and gasped for air until he collapsed; Dongtsen tugged on his bridle but as [the horse] had gone lame, he could not get up. Not knowing what to do, but realizing he was very close to the golden throne, [Dongtsen] abandoned his horse and ran on foot toward the throne. It was then that all the dralas and wermas made the throne more distant. Dongtsen ran, but as before, the more Dongtsen ran, the farther away the throne moved, so that he was unable to reach it.

Then Joru, riding on the magically swift Lord of Steeds, arrived there and transformed into many Jorus who started talking to each other and said, "If we slay Turquoise Bird, his flesh will be fat and delicious." They pulled out their knives as if they were about to start butchering him. Then some of the Jorus starting removing his saddle and bridle and such, causing Dongtsen to feel overwhelmed at the thought of losing his precious horse. He turned back and began running and started prostrating to all the Jorus saying, "Please don't slaughter the horse! Please bring my horse back to life, and I promise to serve you and do whatever you say."

Joru replied, "Well, then, when I conquer the Tea Treasury of China, promise that you'll loan me this horse just once. If you do, I have the know-how to heal him."

When Dongtsen said, "Not only will I loan him to you once, I'll loan him to you three times," that created the auspicious connection by which it would take more than one miraculous manifestation to conquer the Tea Fortress.[143]

With his mouth at Turquoise Bird's ear, Joru screamed the sound of *ki!* three times, and just like the moon escaping from Rāhu, Turquoise Bird was revived and was just as he'd been before. By then most of the other brethren had arrived there as Joru, with his magical swift Lord of Steeds, was already next to the golden throne. At that moment the force of the karmic connection and windhorse of Dongtsen and the Tag-rong tribe reached full maturity, like the full moon. All the members of the Greater Lineage shone as clear and bright as the sun. Joru himself became like Rāhu, and the Lesser Lineage, Middle Lineage, and individual warriors became like garlands of constellations.

The way of appearing in the firmament is the same, yet Rāhu robs the power of the sun and moon while not harming the constellations. For these three reasons, by analogy Rāhu symbolizes Joru, yet his strength like that of a karmic river and his energy of the magical powers of all the dralas and wermas did not just come from the speed of the horse. It was through the culmination of these karmic forces that

---

* "Lameness" has been used to translate the Tibetan word *lhad*, which is the name of a disease that affects horses in their tendons and muscles.

Joru captured the golden throne. Thus it is that by decisively winning the wager of the horse race, the banner of this renowned account of his ascent to the throne would be hoisted to fly at the peak of existence.

It was at that moment that the major and minor marks of his body blazed forth, and his true nature appeared. Everyone's hearts were filled with joy and delight expansive as the rising sun. All their hopes were fulfilled, and they were established in happiness and well-being, like the cooling and refreshing moonlight. An astonishing celebration ensued.

Through his energy, power, and skill in debate, he raised anew the great victory banner of enlightened activity to become fully victorious over the hordes of form and formless obstructing spirits in all directions. At that time the gods and humans gathered to celebrate, and the people cheered the awesome deeds by which Gesar won the wager of the horse race. It was like a dragon roaring in the sky amid massing cloud formations, and even the earth shook so that most beings everywhere, below, upon, and above, could hear and witness this to some degree. Hence Joru laid claim to the great throne of the divine kingdom of White Ling.

The way that Joru had hidden his true innate form was just like the sun when it is hidden in dark clouds or the brilliance of a lotus hidden in mud. But from this time onward he cast off his ugly appearance and unsightly clothing and assumed the rūpakāya with the manifold astonishing major and minor marks. His true appearance was like nectar to the eyes of all gods and humans. Even the great earth itself trembled in the face of his authentic presence, as though unable to contain it. From the rainbow tent of the sky, the many gods and guardians sang songs of auspiciousness and sent down showers of flowers.

At that moment, the emanation of Lotus Power, the supreme Hayagrīva, Lord of Horses, neighed three times in the melody of Eight Laughters. This caused the earth to shake, the rocks to split, and the door to the treasury of Crystal Crag naturally opened. Ma Pomra, the nyen Gedzo, and the nāga Tsugna Rinchen, these three came to welcome him and offer him tea. During that time Gesar revealed the treasures from within the Crystal Crag: the lord of helmets Gyalwa Thödkar [Victorious White Skull], the lord of armor Tro-nag Zilpa [Resplendent Bronze], the shield Ba-mar Lingzab [Red Cane Deep Backing], the amulet Mamo Lado [Life-Essence Stone of the Mamos], the tiger-skin quiver Drala Dzongchen [Great Fortress of the Dralas], the leopard-skin bow case Werma Lanei [Werma's Source of Life Essence], the longevity clothing Tongden Jigme [Indestructible Myriarchy], the belt Drala Tsedüd [Longevity Knot of the Dralas], and the Mongolian boots [Quelling the Eight Classes of Demons]. He adorned his body with all of these treasures.

Brahmā offered prayers and thirteen talking arrows emanated by the werma s plus eighty-six more to make up ninety-nine divine arrows. Rāhu, the great upāsaka, offered the bow Ragöd Khyilpa [Curving Wild Horn], Ma Pomra offered the sword Tabpa Lenmei [Strikes without Riposte], Gedzo offered the lance Khamsum Dradül [Quells the Enemies of the Three Realms], the nāga Tsugna offered the lasso Beltrül Domgu [Nine-Fathomed Frog Emanation], and Vajrasadhu offered the slingshot Phawong Tongkhor [Slings a Thousand Boulders], which is a support for the oath-bound guardians. The drala Nyentag Marpo gave the thunderbolt Shelgi Pudri [Crystal Razor], and the great king Lijin Harleg gave a great ax Drag-ri Harshag [Crag Mountain Rock Splitter].

Each one, according to their activity, presented an offering scarf. Younger brother Dungchung Karpo, older brother Ludrül Ödchung, younger sister Thalei Ödkar, and auntie Gödcham Karmo all magically emanated as many little children beating the drum of the law, blowing the conch of the law, sounding the cymbals, offering the scarves of the law, and so forth, making a great raucous sound as an actual offering presented to him by the formless gods.

As for the offerings directly presented by the human beings, right at the moment when everyone was completely distracted by the spectacle of the various magical manifestations of the gods and nonhumans, all the crowds gathered there began to doubt what they were actually witnessing. "Could this be a dream? An illusion, rather than the simple truth? This is beyond what is possible," they thought, and for the moment they were at a loss as to what to do. Then the Great Vajra Lion [Gesar] sang the dohā called Unceasing Natural Vajra Sound in the melody Quelling the Great Crowds through Splendor:

> Ala is the way the song is sung.
> Thala is the way the words are recited.
> Guru Uḍḍiyāṇa Padma, and
> Yidam Padma Wangchen, and
> Ḍākinī Vajravārāhī
> Remain inseparably as my crown ornament.
> If you don't recognize this place
> Upon the left shoulder of Gu-ra [Crag],
> This is the excellent land called Aspiration Pass.
> If you don't recognize me,
> I was sent here by the imperial gods.
> I'm of the ancestral lineage of the middle nyen,
> And I am the maternal nephew of cold-blooded nāgas.

I was given my name among the middle humans
By my brother Gyatsha Zhalkar,
Who named me Joru.
I was given my name among the imperial gods,
By the guru Uḍḍiyāna Padma, who named me
The supreme personage of Jambudvīpa as well as
Gesar Norbu Dradül.
My personal name is Sengchen Kyebu [Great Lion Being];
I am the suppressor of the demons of the dark side,
I am the yoke upon the Yellow Hor,
I am the wealth lord of both China and Tibet,
I am the sovereign of Jambudvīpa.
I'm not here to wander in impure saṃsāra,
I'm not attached to the pure state of nirvāṇa,
I work for the welfare of all sentient beings.
Now then, you brethren of White Ling,
Listen, for here are some points I have to make:

The Thirty Brethren, mighty warriors,
The seven true men, the Super Warriors,
The Three Ultimate Warriors, Falcon, Eagle, and Wolf,
And, in addition, some from the bordering kingdoms,
Including some fortunate dharma ministers,
Are emanations of the eighty great mahāsiddhas
From India, the land of the āryas.
Their fate will be to join with me.
I am the king of the law of abandoning nonvirtue,
I am the dharma king who establishes the ten virtues.
All the mighty warriors of White Ling
Seem to be pure beings;
Still they are thick with obscurations from the womb.
Some of them have total recall in their dreams,
Some of them see in their visions;
Ultimately they are only pure,
Their courage is unrivaled.
In the morning they are the butchers who slaughter,
In the evening they are the gurus who guide the ones they've
    butchered.

In this golden kingdom of White Ling
I, Sengchen Norbu Dradül,
Have been mandated by the imperial gods,
Sent to engage in the two activities of forming an army and
    subjugating the enemies.
Ultimately this spreads forth the happiness and well-being of
    all beings.
My function will be to establish the Buddha's doctrine,
My law will be to practice the holy dharma of the ten virtues.
In all those regions of the demons of the dark side,
If you try to explain the holy dharma, it won't be understood;
If you try to teach cause and fruition, it won't be respected.
If they are not tamed through powerful mighty means,
They lack the fortune to be tamed by peaceful compassion.
In order to directly tame all of them,
I am the king of the wrathful army.
The general who guards the eastern gate is Bumpa Gyatsha
    Zhalkar;
It is he who will quell Sadam of Jang.
The general who guards the southern gate is Sengtag Mi-
    chang Karpo;
He is the yoke upon Shingtri of the southern māras.
The general who protects the western gate is
Tshazhang Denma Jangtra;
He is the shadow demon who breathes down the necks of the
    Yellow Hor.
The general who guards the northern gate,
Is Trothung Nya-tsha Aten;
He will quell both [countries] of Rong and Düd.
The chief of the elders of the Greater Lineage will be
Serpa Nyima [Daryag] Bum-thub;
His personal minister will be Zigphen of Tag-rong.
The chief of the elders of the Middle Lineage
Will be Ombu Anu Paseng;
His personal minister will be Chölu Darphen.
The chief of the elders of the Lesser Lineage
Will be Muchang Rinchen Darlu;

His body guard is Gadei Bernag.
The man to be the stable council leader
Will be Uncle Chipön Gyalpo.
And as for all the other mighty warrior brethren,
They must guard their own tribes and clans.
Other than the general enemies of the Buddha's teachings,
I, Gesar, have no personal enemies.
Other than the general welfare of all beings,
I, Gesar, have no other personal aims.
It has fallen to me to accomplish the general welfare;
This is the reason for the command of the imperial gods.
If we spread the doctrine of the Buddha
And place all sentient beings in bliss,
The welfare of Ling will be accomplished as a matter of course.
From this day onward,
The chieftain will be called Sengchen Norbu,
The ministers will be called the Thirty Brethren.
The country will be known as the Highlands of White Ling.
We will implement the practice of the ten virtues,
And the abandonment of nonvirtue will be the law of the
    land.
When destroying the māras of the dark side,
Be brave in knowing that it is virtue;
That is the swift path for perfecting the two accumulations.
If your mind can't discern virtue from nonvirtue,
Saṃsāra and nirvāṇa will not depend upon the body and
    speech.
All beings who are māras of the dark side,
Even if they are temporarily slain and tortured,
If they are not placed in ultimate bliss,
This great being's aim for others is in vain.
Today for my insignia of rank,
The gods scatter flowers from above,
The nyen pitch rainbow tents in between,
And the nāgas play music from below.
The eight classes of nonhumans become subservient.
Country of Ling, did you see? Did you hear?

Society of humans in the middle realm,
Will you submit and become my subjects in the Kingdom of
    Ling?
Brethren, will you accept me?
Warriors, do you have confidence in me?
Until now my name and form, Great Lion,
Was previously hidden and not revealed;
This was because the time to tame the māras had not yet
    arrived.
Today I show myself directly.
May the Black Düd and the Yellow Hor,
The Dark Jang and the Wrathful Mön,
All hear this with their ears.
Having heard, may it bring them pain.
May all sentient beings be liberated
And may their minds turn to the pure and sacred dharma.
If you have understood this, it is sweet to your ears.
If not, there is no way to explain it.

Thus he sang, and everyone heard his song, the vajra dohā. No one had the power to transgress it; everybody embraced it and placed it on the crown of their heads. All beings, gods and humans alike, threw flowers of celebration for the occasion, and Chipön Rongtsha Tragen brought out the Mother Chronicles* of Mukpo and offered them with the five kinds of scarves as he sang in the melody Long Slow Gentle Tune:

The song is Ala Ala Ala.
Thala is the melody of the song.
Guru, yidam, and the Three Jewels,
Please remain inseparably upon the crown of my head.
If you don't recognize this land,
It is the left side of Gu-ru Crag.
This patrimony accumulated by White Ling,
Is arranged here as the prize for the horse race.
If you don't recognize me,

---

* These are the original ancient chronicles of the Mukpo clan, also known as the Mother Text.

I am King Chipön of Mukpo Dong.*
Upon the throne of yellow gold,
The bronze-skinned man with teeth as white as a conch
Is King Sengchen Norbu Dradül.

Clouds of dralas mass denser and denser,
A sweet rain of wermas falls pattering and pattering,
Renowned like a dragon's roar the sound blazes up.
Above among the wondrous gods,
The sky is filled with everlasting banners of victory.
In the middle, the virtuous mark of the humans
Is the sound of the victorious gods as *ki! ki! so! so!*
Below, among the offerings of the nāgas,
Is the wish-fulfilling rain, *si li li.*
All the gods are celebrating with delight.
And all the humans are joyfully dancing;
The merriment of the nāgas sets the clouds in motion.
The race of demons wails at their loss.
All brethren, do you understand the source of this joy?
Country of Ling, do you understand this happiness?

I offer this single white scarf to you, Gesar,[144]
So that all the dralas and wermas above
May be like the sun and its light rays,
Inseparably accompanying you, Gesar;
This is the scarf that exalts the imperial gods.
This single golden scarf[145]
Is the greeting scarf for the body guard Nyen Gedzo.
This single blue scarf[146]
Is the greeting for the nāga Tsugna.
This single red scarf[147]
Is the greeting scarf for the Red Nyentag drala.
This single green scarf[148]
Is the greeting scarf for Maneni.
I offer all of these scarves to you, Sengchen.

---

* He was the ruler until Gesar took the throne.

These are the signs of the inseparable companionship
    between
Gods and humans, like a body and its shadow.[149]

Given that you possess stainless wisdom knowledge,
It is not appropriate to offer you this prophetic book;
Nevertheless, I will place these ancient original chronicles* in
    your hands.
May I, the sovereign of the clan of Rong, Chipön Gyalpo,
Be inseparable with you as my lord and I as your minister.
By offering you this single white scarf for our entire
    lifetime,[150]
Together may our buddha activity turn everything into
    dharma.
Never separating from you, Great Being,
May the purpose of beings be perfectly fulfilled.

If the gods as well as the eight classes,
Place their topknots at your jeweled feet,
Then why wouldn't the brethren of the Wishing Land of Ling
Respect you as well?

From this day onward,
The wishes of White Ling will be fulfilled.
Prepare to sing the songs of delight,
Prepare to dance the dance of happiness.
Keep all of this in your heart.

Thus he sang, and similarly the chieftain of the Greater Lineage, Nyibum Daryag of Serpa, starting with the beautiful golden scarf of auspiciousness, offered the golden treasure vase that fulfills all desires, and all sorts of tiger and leopard skins. The leader of the Middle Lineage of Ling, Ombu Anu of Paseng, starting with the long scarf whose color and splendor rival that of the lotus, offered the auspicious conch that swirls to the right, and all sorts of silk and brocades. The jewel of the ocean of the Lesser Lineage, Rinchen Darlu of Muchang, starting with the blue

---

* That is, the Mother Text or Mother Chronicles.

scarf the color of lapis, offered the wish-fulfilling cup made of zi filled to the brim with white pearls, and all kinds of precious gems such as gold, silver, turquoise, and coral.[151]

Prostrating respectfully as they made these offerings, they placed the crowns of their heads at his lotus feet. They prayed that throughout all lifetimes the king and ministers would be inseparable and that, as the ministers, all their buddha activity would steer toward the dharma.

Likewise Bumpa Zhalkar, starting with a white scarf the color of a snow mountain, offered a wish-fulfilling jewel with a coil of joy on it, pieces of silk brocade, and many skins of wild leopards and lynx. Tshazhang Denma Jangtra, starting with the blue silk scarf, offered the nine-eyed zi of the wealth of the nāgas. The warrior Sengtag Adom offered the eight auspicious symbols in red pearl stone. Yamed Darphen of the Chölu clan offered a purple agate archer's bow, and Gadei offered a black cloak and Mahākāla's personal arrow. Nya-tsha offered the coral helmet of the tsen, Zigphen offered a gleaming gilded copper jewel, along with silk brocades and varieties of jewels. Each of them offered vast numbers of the finest furs and skins. With the auspicious scarves out in front, they made these offerings and placed their heads at his feet and prayed never to be separate as the ministers of this great lord for all their lifetimes.

Furthermore, since all the mighty warrior brethren had the good fortune to become members of his retinue, they cultivated irreversible faith and devotion. The three venerable gurus, the four individual chieftains, the Thirteen Favorite Sons, the four men called Gyaltsen, the three men called *Ngo-lug* (the Sheep-a-Peeps), the two final authorities, the judge and the arbiter, and others including all the other mighty warriors and the minor warriors, bowed down respectfully, and with their scarves of good fortune out in front, each offered many special gifts with prayers to never be separate from him in all their lifetimes and supplicated to be cared for by the king and his ministers. From the firmament, music resounded while a shower of white flowers descended. At that time and for the next thirteen days, everyone sang and danced in celebration.

The festivities were launched by the seven sister maidens of Ling, the most beautiful of all the maidens, accompanied by others all bedecked in their most expensive garments and jewels and looking like goddesses strolling in their pleasure gardens. As they began to dance, Kyalo Sengcham Drugmo asked Ne'uchung Lugu Tshar-yag [Drugmo's paternal cousin] to bring her the golden vase filled with Drubpa'i Gyalmo longevity wine and the refined year-old beer. Then Drugmo herself offered nectar three times from the prosperity support of the wealth of Kyalo, Yakṣa Jambhala's own cup, Tashi Yuring [Auspicious Long Stem]. This cup was filled with nectar, and she held it up as an offering along with a long white offering scarf. Then she offered prayers to consecrate the success of the weapons and armor as she sang this song in the melody of Six Modulations in Nine Pitches:

> The song is Ala Ala Ala.
> Thala is the melody of the song.
> In the pure land of Turquoise Leaf Array,
> White Ārya Tārā know me
> And be this maiden's friend and companion.
> If you don't recognize this place,
> It is the excellent land of Aspiration Mountain Pass.
> If you don't recognize me,
> I am Kyalo Sengcham Drugmo.
> They call me the fairest maiden in Jambudvīpa;
> They call me the heart essence of the country of White Ling.
> I am the daughter of Kyalo Tönpa.
> Now then, precious Sengchen,
> Today I, Sengcham Drugmo,
> Chose you as my destined deity by tossing the flower.
> I greet you now with thirteen offering scarves.
> As well as the auspicious cup with the long stem filled with
> Drubpa'i Gyalmo longevity wine.
> The grape wine of the land of India,
> Rice liquor from the land of China, and
> Fresh barley beer of Tibet
> Are the drinks that please the dralas,
> The select offerings that please the wermas,
> And the longevity nectars that lengthen life expectancy.
> Please partake of these drinks that will uplift your spirits.
> The Queen of Siddhi longevity scarf and
> The three activity scarves of lha, lu, and nyen,
> The treasure scarf of the Queen of China,
> The divine cloth of the land of India,
> A pearly scarf from the mouth of an oyster,
> A water scarf from the cold-blooded nāgas, and so forth;
> These are the thirteen offering scarves.
> Today they are offered to greet the Lord Great Lion.
> They are the khatas to greet your actual kāya.

This golden throne that quells the three realms with its
    splendor,
I thought it was the highest ornament of White Ling.
Although it doesn't even touch the ground,
Today it's still not high enough as the white lions hoist it up
    with their paws.[152]
The silk umbrella Rinchen Pungpa [Heap of Jewels],
I thought it was the highest ornament adorning the golden
    throne,
Yet today the pole-bearers aren't even holding it up
As it reaches into the sky on its own, turning and spinning.
The drum of the law, Selwa'i Ödden, and
The conch of the law, Karmo Gyangdrag,
And the cymbal, Nyima Drug-drag,
Today don't need to be sounded or struck;
Their melodious sounds naturally resonate.
Isn't this delightful, Lord Great Lion?
Isn't this joyous, people of Ling?
And not only that,
The wealth of the treasury of Crystal Crag,
The self-existing weapons of the dralas,
Today have come together as the ornaments of this great
    being.

This lord of helmets, Gyalwa Thödkar,
Is offered to adorn your crown chakra of great bliss.
The silk pennon Nyima Rangshar [Self-Arising Sun] and
The victory banner Tashi Gu-tseg [Auspicious Many-Tiered]
    and
The garuḍa pennon Vulture Down,
The colorful studded gems in the front, like five-colored silks and
The helm ornament Lhayi Sopa [Divine Sentry];
All these unite as ornaments of the white helmet.
May this helmet be mightier than others,
And may its glory surpass the heavens.
Along with the king of armor, that finery of the dark bronze
    coat of mail,
The billowing of the longevity knots on the back flag, and

The shield called Red Cane Deep Backing,
Massing rainbow clouds of wermas
Unite as the ornaments of the Great Being's kāya.
May his life force be as solid as a rock.

From the longevity clothing called Fearless One Thousand
    Tribes,
The amulet life-essence stone of the mamos,
The sash, the karmic scarf of the ḍākinīs,
Blessings abound like scudding clouds of mist, so amazing,
A drumming rain of siddhis
Unite to adorn the three nāḍīs [avadhūti, rasana, and lalana].
May your lifespan be longer than a river,
Firm and stable, without aging or infirmity.

Mongolian boots, which quell the eight classes with their
    splendor,
Along with the knee covering that protects from all harm,
Unite to adorn the feet of the Great Being.
May he suppress and reverse the classes of demons.

The tiger quiver Great Fortress of the Dralas
And the leopard sheath Werma's Source of Life Essence
Naturally unite as the ornaments of his weapons.
May your wisdom and means be indivisible.

The sword Strikes without Riposte
Sparkles with local guardians;
The lance Subjugates Enemies of the Three Realms
Shoots the poison flames of the nyen;
The lasso Nine-Fathomed Frog Emanation
Makes the panting sound of nāga demons;
The bow Curving Wild Horn
Chokes the air with the poison vapor of Rāhu demons;
The divine arrow that knows human language
Is the thick glottal click of the dralas.[153]
The slingshot Braided Nine Eyes[154]
Blows the black winds of the mamos;

The life-essence stone that attracts the oath-bound guardians
Is a lightning-born meteorite,
That radiates the light of the the'u rang.
The ax Crag Mountain Rock Splitter
Sends out the sparks of king demons,
The razor knife Crystal Razor
Causes the Nyentag to descend like lightning.[155]
Unite today in the hands of the Great Being.

May you be the yoke upon the Hor and Düd,
And may you bind nāga and tsen to the oath.
May you annihilate Shingtri.
May you turn Sadam to the dharma.
May you bind the four māras by oath.
May you turn the four borderland countries to the dharma.

Just as when the moon arises from the mountain peak
To blossom the jasmine flowers in the gardens and swell the
     milky lakes,
Lord Great Lion, when your lotus feet place a yoke upon the
     haughty ones
The doctrine of goodness and decency will flourish.[156]

Lord Great Lion, the golden mountain of your presence
Is as though embraced by the youthful clouds of dawn;
The radiance of your armor and weapons, and
Your authentic presence, are unrivaled.
Lord Great Lion, your presence,
Like a blazing jewel,
Constantly emits a shower of benefit and well-being.
Please hold me inseparably.

At the tip of the creeper's pliant body
Is the wondrous beautiful face of the *utpala* [lotus] flower,
With coyly glancing eyes, like a hovering honeybee,
I offer myself to you, Lord Great Lion.
Beautiful to hear
Is the song of the kalavinka bird,

Revealing all inner desires;
This voice intoxicated by the amṛta of great bliss
I offer to you, Lord Great Lion.
The waves of wandering thoughts
When overcome by the desire of great bliss
Are an ocean of amṛta of blissful emptiness free from
    thought;
Partake of this with pleasurable delight, Lord Great Lion.
Floating on the ocean of desire and attachment,
The jeweled ship of the wealth of Kyalo,
Guided by the oarsman of compassion;
Make it your own, Lord Great Lion.
From now until the heart of enlightenment,
By accomplishing the great purpose of the doctrine and of all
    beings,
May I, like a body with its shadow,
Be held inseparable from you, Lord Great Lion.
Great Being, hold this in your heart.

Thus she sang, and the other warriors and maiden sisters also offered songs of auspicious connections and greeting scarves. Then the antelope-head hat, the fringed calfskins, and the red leather boots were buried underground as the *phywa** wealth and prosperity supports for the future generations.

Then it was Trothung's turn to offer prostrations and a scarf. As he promised to do, Gesar now returned to Trothung the ancient sacred supports of Tag-rong that he had used in the guise of Joru, such as all the articles for his yogic activity: the white willow staff, the nine-edged prosperity sack of Jambhala, and the like.

Joru [Gesar now] said, "Now, since these are my magical implements, you must lend them to me later on when the time comes to strike the forehead of the demon Lutsen with an arrow," and Trothung replied, "Yes, and not only for Lutsen, but whenever the time comes to yoke the necks of the Hor Gurkar and so forth, just ask to borrow it again!"

It became well-known that because of this connection, when the time came to tame the distant Hor, it would only be able to be done through magic.

---

* This is the word for divination, lot, luck, fortune, and so on.

Even at that time there were early signs that the minds of the māras of the four demon kingdoms of the four directions were turning to the dharma.

For instance, there were seven tiger brothers who were the life-force animals of the earlier king of Hor, Relchen; six of them were killed by lightning. Also, the life-force lake of Lutsen turned into milk, and [Lutsen's] life-force wolf was buried under a mountain avalanche. In addition, at the entrance to Jang Sadam's fortress, the sacred life-support castle of Namtel [Celestial Seal],* a conch stupa, naturally crumbled to the ground. The monstrous Mu cord of Lho Shingtri [in the south], a staircase of wind reaching up to the sky, snapped for the first time, and likewise many other calamities occurred in the lands of the māras.

The sound of the bellowing and crying of both the form and formless spirits foreshadowed the decline and fall of the great countries of the māras and their armies. Therefore, from the moment that he was enthroned as the head of the kingdom, all those inclined to virtue, whether of high or low station, just like a snake shedding its skin, immediately gave up any notion that they could equal or rival him.

From then onward, Machig Drubpa'i Gyalmo gave him long-life initiation and blessed his body to be as indestructible as the vajra.

In any case, since his body did not exist as the result of karmic ripening but rather as the essence of vajra wisdom, the pure appearance of his light body was such that this alone could effortlessly overcome the very core of saṃsāra and nirvāṇa. Until the time that all sentient beings are set free, these qualities will be spontaneously present with his kāya, like a wish-fulfilling jewel, and his actual kāya will remain firm, free from aging or decline and transition or change. Actually seeing his form is itself an unsurpassed astonishment, since this establishes the ground for the propagation of the Buddha's doctrine. Through his unceasing buddha activity he will continue to increase both temporarily and ultimately the happiness and well-being of all beings, in accordance with their own abilities to be tamed.

Their celebrating and feasting were unimaginable, and soon after Gesar went to reside in the great palace Sengtrug Tagtse.† The four enemies were suppressed through his splendor, and the four categories of endowment flourished.‡ The fame

---

* Sadam's main god of refuge, from the class of the'u rang.

† This is the same as Sengdrug Tagtse as in volume 2.

‡ The four categories of endowment: (1) the flourishing of the Buddha's doctrine, (2) the endowment of wealth and prosperity, (3) the ability to utilize the five sensory experiences, (4) the ability to achieve the state beyond sorrow and awakening by relying upon the sacred dharma.

of his name pervaded the three realms like the roar of a dragon; the extent of his sovereignty spread forth like the covering of the sky. All the inhabitants of Ling basked in the joy and happiness of the newly arisen sun.

Just then Denza said to Trothung, "Well then, Tag-rong Sidpa'i Trogyal! What happened to the wager of the horse race that was predicted by the God of the North?[157] What happened to the golden throne and Drugmo? Do you think the other warriors are disappointed?"

Trothung replied, "Oh, Lady Denza, the reason I arranged this celebration, predicted by the God of the North, is that I am the one to find and inaugurate the holder of Ling's golden throne—the one who is the support for the warriors and ministers, the heart son of the imperial gods, the all-encompassing guardian of Jambudvīpa, the warrior who will tame the classes of māras, the one who is Dzamling Sengchen Gyalpo, King Gesar of Ling. I have been so busy polishing the golden stupa of the general affairs of the kingdom that I, Tag-rong, have not had time to consider even one teacupful of my own personal interests."

Even though there were a few more songs exchanged between Trothung and Denza, I [the author] did not write them down since I did not see any great import contained there, but rather they seemed to be inherently ordinary confused perceptions.

In this way, having composed the account of the Horse Race, by the strength of the interdependency with the supplication, Padmasambhava, embodiment of the Three Protectors, magically emanated as the Great Lion King of the Dralas [Sengchen Drala Gyalpo]. The object of faith and devotion, the youthful utpala flower of the mind, for the time being abides in the indestructible *bindu* in the center of the heart as one taste with your own mind. All living beings without measure will enjoy the glory of adventitious happiness and well-being, and ultimately this results in the desire to attain the state of Great Enlightenment. Hence, the siddhis of accomplishment will be granted.

Hence, this brings the story to an end. The reason for this composition as well as the colophon will be clarified in the following supplication.

> In the presence of the hosts of beautiful youthful gods,
> Like the movements of the sun, moon, planets, and stars,
> The force of the mighty wind stirs
> The waving banner of fame to whom I supplicate.

Under the glare of the blazing appearance of the blissful and
    happy sun and moon,
Beneath the royal banner victorious in all directions,
As the fame of the dragon's roar shakes the great earth;
I supplicate the one who holds the great throne of the kingdom.

Just as the sun appears from the clouds, or
A youthful lotus emerges from its casing of mud,
Your stainless supreme body is favored by the gods and all
    who live;
I supplicate you who now appears in your true form.

No matter how pompous they may be in their power,
In your presence, as one they bend their topknots to the ground,
The great classes of māras bemoan their defeat;
I pray to the victor of the forces of good.

Then saṃsāra and nirvāṇa helplessly surrender their essence
To this wish-fulfilling kāya,
Who is permanent, stable, and naturally free from old age
    and decline;
I supplicate the one who propagates the well-being and
    benefit of the doctrine and all beings.

By the karmic power of this prayer
To the King of the Dralas, the manifestation of the Lotus
    Born and the three protectors,
May you dwell in the center of the youthful utpala flower of
    my mind,
And may you bestow the siddhi that accomplishes whatever
    mind desires.

Thus, this meaning has been explained in the body of the epic. Having captured
the throne, the way of accomplishing the goal of fulfilling all the mind's desires completes the seventh chapter, The Saga of the Precious Rūpakāya Wish-Fulfilling Jewel.

For the time being, this concludes our understanding concerning the epic account of the horse race.[158]

Hence, this conscientiously composed commentary
Based upon the meaning
Of the epic account of the horse race,
The supplication called *The Symbolic Secret Jeweled Mirror*,[159]
Has come to mind through the blessings of the unsullied oral
    instructions
That flow like nectar from the Lion of Speech, Jamgön
    Mipham.*
Having had the great fortune to receive the force of these
    blessings upon the crown of my head,
I was inspired to write this down.

All facets of the habitual patterns of previous lifetimes
Arise as the form of conceptual phenomena.
Although nonexistent in the nature of self-liberated
    awareness,
These interdependent illusory appearances continue to arise
    without ceasing.
Although there are some so-called scholars who object
To the accounts of the biography of Gesar Norbu Dradül
Claiming they are a string of lies;
In that case, if asked to write the true account, they will have
    no clear source or answer,
Like one who, beholding the face of a friend,
Arrogantly denies that he recognizes him.

Those who do not see the true nature of what is being shown
Are nihilists who only believe in material relative
    phenomena.
This life story is based on the speech of the sublime ones
And the names and sadhanas
That are clearly revealed in the profound scriptures of the termas.
To just write this off as idle gossip is to fault the activities of
    the victorious ones.

---

* Mipham Jampel Gyepei Dorje.

Moreover there are those who claim that this subject [the
    biography] gives rise to attachment and aversion
And thus this epic contradicts the dharma.
If so, wouldn't one also have to claim that the philosophical
    texts, Buddhist and non-Buddhist histories alike,
Are also not the dharma?

The eighty-four thousand categories of dharma
Are teachings that serve as antidotes for the rejection of
    attachment and aversion.
If some practitioners are born into the lower realms through
    their own mistaken views of hope and fear,
Would you then say this is the fault of the dharma?

There are many who exaggerate and try to denigrate these
    epic accounts.
If one were to ask what then the true story is,
They would only sit there scratching their heads,
Knowing nothing at all about it or when it actually took place.

Seeing this situation,
I wrote this in accordance with the profound mind treasure
    lineage and the authentic oral transmissions of the realized
    ones.
That this small degree of confidence dawned in my mind like
    the sunrise
Is due to the kindness of the root guru.

Hence may this excellent accumulation of merit like a
    stainless sky,
Adorned by the illuminating sun and moon of scriptural
    understanding and realization,
Fully blossom as this lotus garden of benefit
For the doctrine and for the happiness of sentient beings.
Throughout the continuity of all of my lifetimes,
May I never be separated from the cool shade of the Great
    Lion Being's compassion.

And may you place your ever-extended stainless smooth hand
> upon the crown of my head
So I may always have the opportunity to hear your sacred
> speech.
May the hazards of temporary illness, weapons, famine, and
> decline
And the turmoil of war be completely pacified.
By the three secrets of the Sakyong Great Treasure Revealer
> Guru,[160]
May this be the cause for this enlightened activity to remain
> forever firm!

This wondrous avadāna was written by the incarnation of the Lord Lion of Speech, Mipham Jampel Gyepei Dorje. I have compiled this biography in a way that is complementary to the crucial points of *The Symbolic Secret Jeweled Mirror,* with the primary aim that it would be easy for ordinary people to understand.

I received the reading transmission of the supplication to the horse race and the guru yoga of Subjugating Hor from the tertön Sakyong of White Ling. He [the king of Derge Lingtsang] assured me that this is faithful to the words of the oral instructions [*tri*] bestowed by Lord Mipham Rinpoche. As he conferred upon me the extraordinary written biography and the thangkas that accompany it, along with a concise oral commentary, he told me to compose *The Sevenfold Jeweled Mirror,* and thus I received the diadem of his command on the crown of my head.

And from the lord guru Padma Ödzer [Lotus Ray of Light], the ocean-like vidyādhara who realized the nature of the definitive secret Great Perfection, I received the reading transmission for Gesar's guru yoga. He told me, "If you internalize this through practice, then the dharma epic will well forth from your mind." Based on this encouragement and his speech that could clearly predict the future, I gained confidence. Later on, due to his insistent command that I must record this, gradually, as I began to write, it came easily to me, like a freely flowing river. I recognized that this potential was due to the kindness of the guru and the Great Lion Being, whom I hold within my heart.

This was written by the tattered monk, the sadhu Akaśara Muniśa [Gyurmed Thubten Jamyang Dragpa], who has on the crown of his head the dust from the feet of Lord Guru Mipham Jampel Gyepei Dorje, Vidyādhara Drodül Pawo Dorje [Vajra Warrior Tamer of Beings], the great tertön Lerab Lingpa, and many holy gurus who are both learned and realized. Through this, may the lotus feet of the glorious guru remain firm for a hundred kalpas, and may the glory of the victorious ones be raised to the peak of existence!

SARVA MAṄGALAM.

POSTSCRIPT

THE STORY OF THE HORSE RACE from the biography of Gesar Norbu Dradül was previously renowned as the edition written by a warrior from the land of Hor. It did not contain many details about the horse race itself, but it did include other information. The bard Ragu [Grandfather] Amnye revealed a horse race from the epic that is very similar to this edition. There are various other editions that are dissimilar, such as the five versions of the horse race that came from central Tibet. As I read those accounts, I [Gyurmed Thubten Jamyang Dragpa] memorized the content, and that inspired me to practice the above-mentioned guru yoga with heartfelt enthusiasm.

I continued to supplicate Gesar as the sole precious embodiment of the Three Roots, and a long time passed. Then one day the great tertön Sakyong Lama Rinpoche shared with me some teachings that he had received from Mipham Rinpoche about the Supplication to the Horse Race and the narrative thangka. He gave me oral instructions on *The Symbolic Secret Jeweled Mirror*, after which he asked me to write a saga called *Gesar Wins the Horse Race and Becomes the King of Ling*. I thought I would be able to write it, so I answered that I would do so. Even though I was determined and pushed myself repeatedly, I began to wonder if I knew anything to write down. Even going over and over the accounts of the previous epics, I had no idea about how to write a table of contents for *Gesar Wins the Horse Race and Becomes the King of Ling*. Not only that, I was unable to understand some of the crucial points of the Symbolic Secret, so I was left at a loss.

Then, while I was tirelessly supplicating, I had a dream in which a man was pointing at a horse that he said was Gesar's divine horse Kyang-bu. He wore a jeweled saddle, and the man said I was to take the horse to the city of the northern country of Shambhala. Leading the horse by the reins, I found myself in a place I had never seen before, the mountains and dwelling places of Shambhala. I didn't know what happened to the horse, but one man gave me a small volume of the horse race. Although it seemed to me that I had read the book, I did not know the meaning of the content. Nevertheless it seemed that the man had said that the subject of this book was the horse race.

From that time onward, the content of the Symbolic Secret arose within my mind. Hence I understood how to place the account of the horse race into seven chapters corresponding to the seven royal signs. As I wrote them down, one by one, I was able to clarify any misconceptions concerning the meaning and accuracy of the existing epics.

By the time I was beginning the sixth chapter, again I was at a loss as to what to write and was stuck there for about a year. I was extremely frustrated and did not know how to reconcile this.

Previously I had received from Guru Padma Ödzer some practices from Khentsei Yeshe Dorje's Gesar dharma cycle. At that point Guru Padma Ödzer said, "If you are able to practice this guru yoga, the dharma epic will come to you!" I responded by saying that I had completed the epic up to this point, and then he strongly insisted that I write the rest down as quickly as possible. Even the Great Dharma King of Ling told me to write it down quickly and promised several times that he would carve it into woodblocks.

Then once again when I was single-pointedly supplicating to the Great Lion Being, I dreamed that I had found the epic, met the brethren, and that Sengtag, Zhalkar, and Denma, these three, were lining up their troops, and so forth. From this dream state, many visionary experiences arose that I wrote down as well.

Concerning this subject it cannot be definitively determined that the life stories of buddhas and bodhisattvas occur in only one way; however, that this appeared to me in this way accomplishes the command of the guru and recalls the kindness of Great Lion, while hoping in some small way to remedy the disease, famine, and war of the world. For these reasons I have written this down.

I have no experience, realization, or noble qualities, and in addition have spent my entire life overpowered by confused perception, so in no way am I claiming that this epic falls in the category of authorized prophetic command or revelational pure vision. Nevertheless this epic is not other than the appearance of the dynamic strength of buddha nature, the *tathāgatagarbha*.

Any small virtue accumulated through this work, I dedicate to the welfare of sentient beings. Whatever mistakes have been made due to confused appearances, I confess before the assembly of deities. Since I alone know that my motivation has never become sullied by poisonous passions, may this be the cause that, throughout all my lifetimes, I am never separated from the Great Lion Being.

KARMA YAMARADZA MAHĀDEVA TIŚTHRA.

This epic is based on the original woodblock of the Ling family of Derge. Comrade Thubten Nyima [Alak Zenkar Rinpoche] and others used several handwritten versions of the horse race to add a few passages to the text of the original woodblock of Ling province. They also edited the text and wrote a table of contents.

NOTES

1. For clarity we have chosen to create titles in English for the volumes. The original title in the Tibetan text for volume 1 is "The Divine Land of Ling: The Nine-Squared Divination Board" (Tib. *lha gling: gab rtse dgu skor*), so-called because it forms the basis of the epic, or is the source from which the rest of the epic emerges and the life and enlightened deeds of Gesar can gradually come to be known. In this way, the saga is similar to the divination board that is used in Tibetan astrology, whereby drawings and numbers are prepared in order to calculate a prognosis and allow one to discern the resultant situation. The number nine in Tibetan is a generic plural implying multiple numbers: this tells us that there will be many accounts concerning the Great Being's enlightened deeds as his life story unfolds through the epic.

2. This is a piece of formal poetry written in the compact style of Sanskrit kāvya, or court poetry. Since this kind of language is distinctly unbardic, it is probably an introductory contribution by the person who compiled this edition, expressing an interpretive agenda and bringing out, in this edition, the Buddhist message seen in the epic.

3. *Dharmatā* means "the ultimate nature of phenomena or reality itself" and is a word for the absolute level of reality, beyond the illusion of mere appearance. Gesar has his true or ultimate existence at the absolute level of reality as the enlightened mind of a buddha. The idea is that King Gesar, before he incarnated as a human being, dwelled, like all enlightened beings, in a state of mind where he directly saw the ultimate nature of things, the dharmatā, or the very nature of phenomena. All his actions may have expressed themselves on the relative plane, but are seen by Gesar from an ultimate, nondual point of view.

4. "Awakened mind" (Tib. *byang chub kyi sems*; Skt. *bodhicitta*): The Tibetan literally means the "mind of enlightenment" or the "thought of enlightenment." Here the thought of enlightenment is the experience of compassion that intends the benefit of all sentient beings. Since this compassion is based on the dharmatā, or the absolute, it is not clouded by false perceptions and does not play favorites. It is impartially directed toward all sentient beings equally.

5. The one who can perform the magical rituals known as the four karmas possesses ultimate skillful means (Tib. *thabs;* Skt. *upāya*). These are symbolized by the vajra, the adamantine lamaic scepter. "Hundred points" is a classical epithet for the vajra. The one-hundred-pointed vajra is a hand implement, the undefeatable weapon of the great god Indra. Well

known among the Vedic parables, the one-hundred-point vajra scepter is a metaphor for the four enlightened activities that have the same potential.

6. "Fourfold buddha activity" refers to the four enlightened activities of pacifying, enriching, magnetizing, and destroying. *See* glossary: buddha activities, fourfold.

7. "The teaching of cause and effect"(Tib. *rgyu 'bras*; Skt. *hetu phala*) refers to the Buddhist teachings about the nature of karma that impinge on the moral life. Much of Buddhist moral philosophy is based not on absolute principle but rather on a rational understanding of the causal or karmic consequences of one's actions. The epic will illustrate moral causality at many levels, teaching the kind of relative understanding necessary to lead an ethical life in the Buddhist religion.

8. Each chapter of this edition includes a descriptive stanza that is not in the original Tibetan woodblock print. This style is reminiscent of the humorous verses at the beginning of each chapter of a Ming or Ch'ing dynasty Chinese novel and also reminiscent of the *argumento* at the beginning of Renaissance heroic literature (such as *The Fairie Queen*), as well. The argumento describes the coming chapter, but in a riddling way. Heroes are referred to not by their names but by their epithets.

9. The five degeneracies of the dark age are those of lifespan, the passions, sentient beings, time, and view.

10. The causal vehicle of characteristics (Tib. *rgyu mtshan nyid*; Skt. *mahāyāna*), the so-called Greater Vehicle of Buddhism, is divided by the Tibetans into two sub-*yānas*, or vehicles: the *sūtrayāna* and the *mantrayāna*. Sūtrayāna is the exoteric vehicle of bodhisattvas that relies on the Buddhist scriptures known as sutras. Mantrayāna is the division of mahāyāna that uses the esoteric techniques of the tantras. One of its many names is the secret mantra vehicle, because its teachings cannot be received without first receiving an empowerment. If empowerment has not been received, then the teachings must be kept "secret."

11. "Naturally pacify": English does not have an exact equivalent for the Tibetan, *rang sar zhi*. The word *naturally* here actually means "in its own place." There is a sense of leaving something as it is while nevertheless changing it; *rang sar* does not evoke the existence of an absolute essence, the way the term "nature" does. The native deities were "pacified in their own place."

12. "Glorious gateway" (Tib. *rten 'brel dpal kha*), also expressed as "glorious gate of good fortune" (see glossary). This term represents the idea that a particular astrological conjunction, probably understood according to the five elements, twelve roots, and ten branches of Chinese astrology, made this the perfect moment to establish a connection between heaven and earth and create an enlightened kingdom. The "glorious gate" is a gateway to energy and good fortune. The Tibetan *rten 'brel* (pronounced *tendrel*) literally means "causal linkage," a technical Buddhist concept. But here it is often used to indicate a positive string of causally linked events, in which case it is translated as "good fortune" or "auspicious coincidence."

Had Lotus Skull Garland succeeded in binding the anti-Buddhist demons of Tibet three times, the flourishing of dharma in Tibet would have begun. There would have been no effective opposition and the negative events upon which the epic is based would not have occurred.

13. Sukhāvatī, the realm of great bliss, is the pure land or heaven of Amitābha, who is the buddha of compassion, just as Avalokiteśvara is the bodhisattva of compassion. It should

be observed at this point that all of the deities thus far mentioned belong to one particular "family" among the five buddha families.

The tantric mandala is a structure containing five buddhas facing in five directions; center, north, south, east, and west. All of the characters in this chapter of the Gesar epic are members of the Lotus (Padma) family, which presides over the western direction of this mandala. Chief among them is the Buddha Amitābha, then the bodhisattva Avalokiteśvara, the guru Lotus Born (Lotus Skull Garland), and then later the yidam and protector of the Lotus family, Hayagrīva, the horse-headed one, and of course the warrior protector of the Lotus family, Gesar himself. All are manifestations and emanations of the same general principle of compassion and discerning wisdom (the wisdom that allows one to be precise), that are the characteristic of the Lotus family.

14. This brief supplication and its response are phrased in the conventional terms of Sanskrit court poetry, but the underlying metaphysical situation is odd. Avalokiteśvara, the bodhisattva of compassion, is considered an emanation of Amitābha, the buddha of compassion. On Amitābha's command, Avalokiteśvara will go to another emanation of the same principle, the enlightened tantric yogin Padmasambhava, and request him to cause the birth of Gesar. Most of the conversations in this chapter will occur between individuals who are in essence the same person.

15. Usually Amitābha's name in Tibetan is *'od dpag med,* Limitless Light. Here it is *'od mi 'gyur,* Unchanging Light.

16. By asking the buddha of compassion to "reveal skillful means," Avalokiteśvara is requesting that he create and cause Gesar to incarnate. Gesar's specialty is to use magic mischievously to benefit beings.

17. This is a traditional figure of Buddhist kāvya. The would-be disciples are drowning in a whirlpool of delusion. The lords, who look down on them from above, the bodhisattvas such as Avalokiteśvara, offer to the disciples a stick with a hook on the end, symbolizing their compassion. If the disciples have an iron ring of faith in the buddhas, the hook will snag that ring and pull them from the ocean.

18. The heaven of the thirty-three is the abode of gods who are practicing and studying the dharma. Divine deities abide in this realm.

19. *Evam* is Sanskrit for "thus," the first word of any Buddhist sutra—for example, "Thus have I heard." But in tantric buddhism, Evam is a code symbol for the unification of male and female principles; of wisdom and skillful means, wisdom and compassion, and so forth.

20. "Unfabricated compassion." The Gantok edition has the Tibetan as *mi skyod,* whereas other editions have *mi spyod* rather than *mi skyod.* This would translate as "through the light rays of Akṣobhya's compassion," which would seem to be the wrong buddha for the occasion, since we already have Amitābha presiding as the dharmakāya principle behind events leading to the Gesar's birth. Therefore we have chosen *mi spyod,* reading "unfabricated compassion."

21. The phrase "emanation of their blessings" refers to the style of reproduction of gods. There are five kinds of birth. For example, mammals are born from a womb, whereas snakes and birds are born from eggs, and certain kinds of bugs are thought to be born from heat and moisture. Unlike these, the method of birth for the gods is *rdzus skyes,* or "miraculous birth." Thus this child is not an ordinary descendant, but a *sprul,* an emanation, considered to be magical.

22. This appears in various places in the epic as Jampei Künkyab [All-Pervading Mercy], Jampei Lingchen [Great Garden of Mercy], and as Jampei Künkyab Lingchen [Great Garden of All-Pervading Mercy]. We have chosen to use the latter for uniformity.

23. Tibetan epic ballads begin with a half-line of alliterative nonsense syllables that give the tune of the song. A literal rendering of these lines would be "Ala, this is the head of the song. / Thala, the melody goes this way." These musical sounds are like "tra-la" in English and begin every epic song.

24. The demon is speaking in the epic manner, like a nomad making an eloquent argument, proving his point by citing well-known proverbs. The proverbs in this case all contain a pun on the homonyms of the word pronounced *dön*, which when spelled *don* means affair, wealth, court case, meaning, and benefit. But when spelled *gdon*, it refers to an invisible evil spirit and the resulting evil, misfortune, madness, and disease.

    The demon minister, through these proverbs, argues that the child must have an extraordinary reason (*don*) for doing something so foolhardy as to visit an island of demons. His reason must be unusual, like the case of a man suddenly possessed by a dön (*gdon*), which would force a traveler to jump off a cliff, or force a rich man unnecessarily into court.

25. The word *sin* in the name Blood Lake of Sin is a translation of the Tibetan *sdig* (Skt. *ppa*), which is often paired with *sgrib*, meaning "obscurations." "Sin" does not quite have the right connotation in English and often, in order to dispense with Judeo-Christian notions of guilt and stain and innate evil, we translate *sdig* simply as "evil deeds." These are simply activities that plant seeds of negative karma. The Sanskrit for obscuration is *āvaraña*, which literally means "veil," since it represents the two veils that darken conventional mind and keep it from seeing reality.

26. This proverb refers to the caravan path followed by Tibetan merchants conducting trade with China.

27. The demon minister has asked his questions implicitly in proverbs. He has asked whether the magical child's case is important enough to merit the danger of approaching Padmasambhava's demon-ridden domain. Since the question was subtly implied (*rang bzhin zhugs*) in the proverbs rather than asked directly, he asks the demon boy if he has understood.

28. This is the first of a series of cosmological and climactic extended similes that fill the epic. In spring the frozen earth warms, ice melts, and the earth becomes tillable. Rain falls and the thunder is like a dragon's roar. If there were no spring, the dragon would be like a snake, silent as a frozen mouth.

29. "Spinning head" (Tib. *mgo 'khor*) is an expression that refers to people who are confused and distracted by a con artist. The point of this proverbial argument is that fancy words that don't tell you something important are just a trick to confuse naive minds.

    The extended metaphor is taken from a mixture of Indian and Far Eastern cosmology found in the worldview of the Kālacakra tantra. Mount Meru is the mythical mountain at the center of the world. The heavenly bodies all rotate around it, creating the seasons and all cycles of nature. Thus rain and sun are brought to the fields and crops can grow as the cycling of the heavens brings the seasons. This is the practical meaning to humankind of the spinning of the heavens. If this benefit did not occur, there would be no point in the ceaseless, ever-repeated rotation of heavenly bodies, which would serve no purpose but to confuse people by their senseless spinning.

It is the same with words that hide a point in symbols and figures of speech; if the meaning is not understood, then the speeches serve no purpose but are mere distractions for brainless dupes.

This is a telling point in the oral culture of the Tibetan highlands, where the ability to give long, florid speeches loaded with proverbial instances and using fancy rhetorical figures is considered a powerful personal weapon and an instrument of power.

If the continents were people, then they would be grateful for the circulation of the sun and moon, showing them due respect. The sun and the moon are the leaders and the four continents are the subjects. When the leaders increase, the subjects increase. But if the leaders were unable to bring benefit to the four continents, their subjects would not respect them.

Although a person may try in his or her lifetime to have wealth and spiritual accomplishments, if people fail, it is probably because they have not planted the karmic seeds that would ripen into a successful life. For example, if one wants to be wealthy, the best way is to practice the Buddhist religion and to be generous. This will make wealth in the next lifetime occur naturally. When a businessman with such a karmic store creates an enterprise, it tends to be successful. But planning an enterprise without such a basis is pointless, and a person exerting him or herself that way would be merely a brainless dupe.

30. Here Avalokiteśvara begins to argue that his case is important enough to merit being brought before Lotus Skull Garland. This line is missing from later editions of the Tibetan.

31. Literally, the Tibetan here (*tshugs la zad*) translates as "no more stations," but the real meaning is that the continents come to an edge.

32. A common village expression, as if to say, "If this is so important to you, go to China and come back in a day."

33. "The transcendent dharma" (Tib. *chos pha rol phyin*) is the dharma of pāramitas, or in other words, the mahāyāna—the path of the six perfections: generosity, patience, discipline, exertion, concentration, and wisdom. This supplication introduces a verse sermon on the mahāyāna path of compassion, sung by the patron saint of mahāyāna himself.

34. The magical child continues to play on the same untranslatable pun. The word for benefit is *don* (pronounced *dön*), a translation for the Sanskrit term *artha*, which means "wealth" and "meaning" and "ultimate," as well as "benefit." It also means a reason for undertaking an action, and it means a cause such as in a litigation or court case. Therefore the speech in which the demon minister asked the magical boy what was his cause for coming to the island of the demons was full of different uses of the word *don*. Now the boy uses it to mean "benefit" as in the classical Buddhist formula, "the benefit of others."

35. In other words, this means "the wealthy, those who bear the burden of material possessions." A wealthy person may be so attached to his possessions that he is separated from others and finds himself alone.

36. Literally the Tibetan translated as "is just asking to bind himself up with his lucky mouth." This refers to a poor person who out of pride and boasting may turn away from help.

37. "Thus he requested and the demon minister answered, 'Hey, you!'" The cosmic encounter between an ironic Avalokiteśvara and a blustering demon functionary continues with the demon's grotesque speech on the terrors of the court of Padmasambhava. The minister's speech is thick with colloquialism and clever folksy puzzles. He is minister to a cannibal

demon king who rules over a continent of these man-eating monsters. But somewhere along the line Master Lotus, Padmasambhava, has secretly replaced the demon king, assuming his form. That is why he is called Lotus Skull Garland because he is secretly Lotus, but wears a garland of skulls and other accoutrements of a cannibal demon. The demon minister's language would be absurd and incongruous in any other situation. But we must remember that this man-eating demon does not realize that a buddha in wrathful aspect has taken over the government of his country. He still believes that the ancient lineage of demon kings rules, for Padmasambhava appears in his Lotus Skull Garland form, which is indeed the shape of a rākṣasa or cannibal demon.

38. Rāhu (Tib. *gza' rgod*) is a planet with a body like a thread. It is nearly invisible, but periodically it eats the sun, causing an eclipse. It also has an influence on the earth. There is an expression, *gza' rgod kha rlang dug gi spu gri*, that means "the razor-sharpness of the poisonous breath of Rāhu." When it passes overhead, sometimes its breath strikes an individual who suddenly falls under its terrestrial influence. The person cut down by Rāhu's breath falls to earth in an epileptic fit. It is considered quite dangerous. Even on auspicious days, such as Padmasambhava's feast day, you might see a person suddenly have an epileptic attack. Tibetans would say that "Rāhu struck him down." Or they would say that "he was cut down by the razor-sharp poisonous breath of Rāhu."

   As a metaphor it means that the force of these demon kings' charisma is so powerful that one responds to their commands in a split second, as if struck down by the poisonous breath of Rāhu. This is one of numerous metaphors used for the personal power of a king. Sometimes his command is likened to the sting of a scorpion: "If he gives the command, you will surely obey, even as the sting of a scorpion will surely bring death."

39. The truth is that some time ago the great Buddhist tantric yogin Padmasambhava took over this island of demons masquerading as its rākṣa chieftain. The interior minister does not realize that his king has become more open-minded because he is no longer a flesh-eating monster.

40. The Tibetan *rtswa bsre zhing bsre* means "to mix roots and sticks," signifying that the rules of the government and the code of ethics of the monastic institutions must not be mingled or confused.

41. Presentation offerings (Tib. *phyag rten*) are offerings given to an important personage at the moment of greeting. There is an art to greeting an official or high lama; the language of greeting should be elaborate, high-flown, and poetic. Scarves and bundles of smoking incense sticks are presented along with ornamental foods and precious objects. In this case, Avalokiteśvara's offerings amount to the thirty symbolic gifts as a list of the main practices of the mahāyāna and vajrayāna paths. Repeating the six-syllable mantra OM MAṆI PADME HŪṂ again and again is the most widespread religious practice in Tibetan popular religion, especially among the laity who not only repeats it, but spins wheels upon which it is engraved. It literally means "OM the Jewel in the Lotus HŪṂ." Books are devoted to explaining multiple levels of meaning to this cryptic expression. The six perfections are the heart of mahāyāna practice. They are virtues such as generosity and discipline, which promote the deep and profoundly contemplative life of the bodhisattva, whose life is devoted to the vow of compassion. The Maṇi mantra is not taught or learned but rather is culturally ingrained into Tibetans even as children. Avalokiteśvara is the chosen deity of Tibet, and Tibet is his field to tame.

The last eighteen offerings are nothing more than the sense perceptions and their objects, the ordinary world of form and the ordinary consciousnesses that connect the sense organs with their objects of color, sound, and so forth. In tantra these ordinary things, which are the basis of the saṃsāric confused mind, are transmuted into sacred manifestations of wisdom energy. The idea is that this is a daring offering, as if the bodhisattva were saying to Padmasambhava, "What more precious thing could I offer you than the ordinary phenomenal world, which is a heavenly buddha field when seen by an enlightened mind?"

42. A dzomo is the female of a cross between a yak and a domestic cow. Raising such fancy hybrid milk cows is not the bandit's way, but a professional bandit would not hesitate to steal one. Although the dzomo may be valued for its milk, a bandit, apt always to be fleeing from the authorities, would not stay put long enough to care about such luxuries and would simply roast up the dzomo for a meal.

43. When pilgrims visited Tsari, they would cut a piece of the abundant bamboo to use as a walking stick or to fashion as a frame for a homemade backpack.

44. "Free and well-favored" (Tib. *dal 'byor*) is a fixed expression from a standard Tibetan contemplation on the advantages of being born as a human being. It means we should practice the dharma strenuously right now, because it is difficult to be reborn as a human being, possessing the qualities of being free to practice Buddhism and well-favored in the physical circumstances that makes this possible. Thus the human body, which is free and well-favored, is a precious possession. The magical boy is making, as his offering, his own body with its sense organs, good karma, and consciousnesses. From his point of view it is a precious offering, because it is free and well-favored and capable of gaining enlightenment.

45. "If you do not possess an analytical mind" refers to a distinction made in the scholastic tradition between two kinds of people, those who have developed the critical mind of prajñā, or analytical intelligence, and those who have not. These terms usually occur in philosophical texts, but sometimes, as above, in the simple expression, "If you possess analysis." The idea here is that it is difficult to obtain rebirth in a human body. If you possess critical intelligence, that body can be used to gain worldly success and transworldly enlightenment. But if you do not possess analytical intelligence, then the body becomes involved in grasping and fixation, and you sink into the whirlpool of cyclic existence.

46. The Tibetan original of this passage—*skyid sdug gnyis kyi yo ge red*—is questionable: It could mean "the boundary between happiness and unhappiness."

47. "There on top of a wrathful seat of corpses": In tantric iconography, tutelary deities (yidams) appear standing or sitting on special platforms that reflect the "mood" of the figure, mood here being a question of metaphysical posture toward the practitioner's path to enlightenment. Moods are wrathful, peaceful, semiwrathful, and so on. A wrathful deity symbolizes the destruction of ego through decisive actions such as suddenly cutting thoughts. Such a deity stands on a "wrathful seat" formed by the corpses of evildoers. Contemplation of wrathful deities is supposed to cut through conditioned psychological patterns and deluded thoughts. The corpses represent the thoughts and conditioned patterns that contemplation on this meditational deity in a wrathful aspect has subdued.

48. In Tibet, clouds coming from the south always bring rain, while clouds from the north bring snow, if anything. "Southern clouds" are therefore auspicious.

49. Like tantric Buddhist mandalas, the city of Padmasambhava on Cāmara on the Copper-Colored Mountain is surrounded by an iron mountain wall. Actually, there are two encircling walls, and this is the inner one. So this is the second gate, the eastern gate in the inner encircling wall.

50. In tantric visualization practices, the central deity sits on a special symbolic throne that represents that buddha's mastery of the phenomenal world. The throne involves "seats" or cushions stacked one on top of another, with each seat representing a different metaphysical principle. Some thrones have at their base as a seat a huge lotus with hundreds or thousands of petals. This represents compassion and is a "peaceful" throne. The corpse seat placed on top of the lotus represents, among other things, the fact that the deity sitting on top of it has conquered ego fixation and is a wrathful seat.

51. "When the golden rays of the royal parasol / Struck the peak of [Glorious Copper-Colored Mountain]" is a conventional poetic figure for the dawn. "Royal parasol" is a figure from classical Sanskrit poetry for the sun. In Tibet the sun's light strikes the mountain peaks in the west before the globe of the rising sun is itself seen above the eastern horizon.

52. Usually when a petitioner approaches a king, he gives a presentation scarf to the minister or servant, who then carries that scarf to the king as token of the request to enjoy his presence.

53. The real point of the song here seems to be that the minister wants to help the magical boy, but cannot figure out how to, because he does not entirely understand the subtle points and poetic figures in his speech; the boy's message is too subtle for the demon to interpret or transmit. He therefore thinks the best thing to do is to simply deliver the boy into Padmasambhava's presence.

54. These proverbs are a good example of one of the ways the epic teaches the Buddhist doctrine of "cause and effect." An example of such a connection (*rten 'brel*; pronounced *tendrel*) would be a connection with a guru. For example, if you have devotion and so experience a genuine sense of connection (tendrel) with a guru, that is ultimately more valuable than material goods, not only because it will bring spiritual happiness, but because it will contribute to one's long-term success and good luck, for tendrels are luck-bringing connections.

55. This, of course, is a version of the mantra of Avalokiteśvara. It ends with ĀḤ, the seed syllable of emptiness or of speech. It seems that each time in the epic the bodhisattva of compassion's mantra appears, it has another seed syllable tacked on to the end. Of course, Padmasambhava and Avalokiteśvara are omniscient and know everything that is going on in their reciprocal masquerade. The demon minister—demons being as dense as they are wise—fails to recognize the mantra of compassion, which is a quintessential form of the bodhisattva himself. This is just the kind of mistake a demon, by nature unacquainted with virtuous dharmas, would make.

56. The Tibetan appears as *bsam blo skor brdzogs bcu gnyis / blo rtse nyi zhu rtsa lnga btang*. A *blo skor*, a "mind circle," is apparently an attempt to figure something out. A *blo rtse*, a "mind point," seems to be a stratagem. The two lines together, however, mean to think a lot and try to figure something out.

57. One interpretation of this line is that the demon is trying to build his own confidence by saying, "Why should I worry, since the mind is by nature empty. Perhaps I should just relax."

58. "Like relic pills from the grave of a pig": When an enlightened or highly realized being dies, after their cremation, in their ashes, can sometimes be found small, circular or oblong pearl-shaped pills. These *ring bsrel,* or "relic pills," are considered to be a sign that the person has reached the ground of liberation and has left behind this sign for the faithful to honor and hold as a support for their prayers and devotion.

    Of course, the grave of a pig would not produce spontaneous relic material. But if it were to, there would still be no point in collecting the relic pills of a pig, for no blessings could come from such an unenlightened creature. So, "relic pills of a pig" suggests a pointless inefficacious substance.

59. Classical analogy for a person who has not had a certain meditation experience trying to understand the words of one with that experience.

60. "Auspicious connection" (translating once again the Tibetan term *rten 'brel*) here refers to the visionary experiences and experiences of sudden insight that a meditation practitioner has when his or her practice is successful. "Accumulating merit" in this case means doing religious practices. Every disciple waits, in theory, for the marks of advancement toward enlightenment that occur from time to time. If such signs do not occur, it may be an indication that the practice instructions are not being carried out correctly, and one might seek fresh instruction or counsel.

61. A magician's basis for transformation" (Tib. *sprul gzhi*) refers to a certain kind of traditional Asian illusionist who uses mantras to fool people into believing that an ordinary object is something extraordinary. The mantras exercise their power over the eyes of the spectators. There is a story that once, for example, a *rdzu 'phrul,* an illusionist (or literally, "a wonderworker"), used the power of his mantras to make an entire audience think that a shoe was the Potala Palace. The shoe was the basis (*gzhi*) for the illusion or transformation (the *sprul pa*). He attached a rope to it and made people think he was pulling the Potala into a lake. One man, however, arrived late and, since the mantra had not been pronounced when he was there, his eyes were unclouded. He saw the *sprul gzhi,* the basis for transformation, as it truly was. He saw, in other words, an illusionist pulling a shoe into the lake with a rope.

62. This proverb in Tibetan is *gangs dkar sems la 'thud lugs / khra chung mig la mdzes lugs.* In other words, "it's a matter of taste" or "it's a matter of previous karma." For example, if a boy and girl fall in love despite the wishes of their parents, the parents may think that this is a bad match. But another relative might correct them with this proverb, as if to say, "No matter what you think, no matter how unsuitable the match seems to you, they are beautiful to each other. It's a matter of how the mind sees things."

63. Like many oral epics, much of the story is known through folktales and village lore but is not literally part of the text of any given volume of the epic. Here Avalokiteśvara gives us more of the background of the epic, a summary of the background story not actually told in this edition. In theory, other versions of the epic or folktales about Gesar would describe how certain tantric Buddhist disciples turned against their gurus when they were criticized in the course of their training. In frustration at their gurus' disciplining of them, they turned against the dharma itself and swore to use their power to defeat the religion. Although they had turned to evil, because of their previously accumulated good merit and their special tantric powers, in the next lifetime they were reborn as powerful and wealthy demon kings, the sworn enemies of Ling and the buddhadharma.

64. The song that follows is an invocation designed to call forth a deity who will become Gesar of Ling. The deity is an emanation of Avalokiteśvara, who himself is an emanation of the Buddha of the Lotus Family, Amitābha. When the mind-stream is evoked from the breast of Padmasambhava, it will arise as the mind of Thöpa Gawa, the deity who will later be born in the human realm as Gesar. Strictly speaking, this continuity is simply one transformation after another of Avalokiteśvara, each dissolving into the next in the characteristic style of tantric visualization practices.

   The calling forth (Tib. *bskul ba*) is an important aspect of the technology of tantric ritual. The idea is that by singing this song Avalokiteśvara can provoke, excite, stimulate, and arouse Lotus Skull Garland to action, arousing him to generate Thöpa Gawa/Gesar. Thus we have a complex series of emanations. First Amitābha confers authorization on his bodhisattva emanation, Avalokiteśvara. Avalokiteśvara transforms himself into a magical demon-child. The demon-child becomes a lotus, the symbol of compassion and the mahāyāna. The lotus becomes rays of light, which dissolve into the heart center of Padmasambhava. Now, Avalokiteśvara, even though he has evolved into rays of light, still exists in an absolute sense outside of this series of transformations. Thus his voice can sing the following invocation, which comes from the absolute wisdom mind (Tib. *dgongs rgyud*) beyond time and space and asks Padmasambhava to call forth from the absolute mind stream of Thöpa Gawa. *See* glossary: mind stream.

65. "Oath-breaking demons" (Tib. *dam sri*; pronounced *damsi*): *Damsi* are a particular type of demon that has violated tantric vows. They figure extensively in the Tibetan Buddhist oral literature. And they seem to function roughly in the same way demons do in Christian heroic narratives. That is to say, damsi are not simply another style of demon in the cosmology. They are the demons who play the role of villain in Tibetan Buddhist narratives. As far as their role in plot construction is concerned, the damsi remind one of the fallen angels in *Paradise Lost*. They are the nine greater enemies of the four cardinal points and the other demons of the intermediate points; some are ministers, rather than kings. *See* glossary: *damsi*.

66. Southern Throne [Lhotri] Tiger Eye (Tib. *lho khri stag mig*) is actually a place name, as if this were "Tiger Eye from Lhotri." Sadam [Sa Dam] is also a place name. White Tent [Gurkar] The'u rang Cub (Tib. *gur dkar the'u rang bu*) is called "the child of the *the'u rang*." This implies that he is a gambler because the one-legged the'u rang demons are the patron deities of gamblers, who supplicate them in order to win at cards or dice. This is actually how new the'u rang are made. If the gamblers depend on them too much, in their next lifetimes they become "servants of the the'u rang" and have the form of these creatures themselves—a terrible price to pay for good luck in gambling. Since they have but one leg, they travel riding tornados as their mounts. Children are sometimes told to avoid cyclones when they see them in the distance, because these are the mounts of the'u rang, who are coming to steal the children.

67. Here begin the demons of the intermediate directions. Turquoise Peak (Tib. *g.yu rtse*) is actually the name of a mountain near the Kokonor region, which is considered in the north, insofar as epic geography is concerned. This region figures in the history of the Gologs. In principle it is a region that borders the tribal lands of the Kingdom of Ling, a land where many of the Gologs settled.

68. Each of the major demons is subject of a complete volume of the epic. Beyond the main

demons, one for each of the eight cardinal points, there are minor demons who receive sagas and chapters in the larger versions of the epic, depending upon their particular powers.

69. Notice that at this point Avalokiteśvara directly addresses Thöpa Gawa, who still exists as a potentiality in the breast of Padmasambhava. This is the "calling forth" of Gesar from the wisdom mind of Padmasambhava. The universality of the principle that becomes Gesar is stressed here. He is called primordially pure (Tib. *kun bzang*), as in *kun tu bzang po*, that is, Samantabhadra [Always Excellent], the primordial buddha of the dharma body (dharmakāya) level in the Nyingma tradition. The three protectors (Tib. *rigs gsum mgon po*) are the three main bodhisattvas in mahāyāna and tantric iconography: Mañjuśrī, Vajrapāṇi, and Avalokiteśvara.

70. "It falls upon you to invoke your samaya" means "the time has come to fulfill your sacred vow." This is a standard expression in any Buddhist supplication, but within the context of the epic narrative it has a specific reference. In effect, Padmasambhava has already taken a sacred vow, a samaya, to produce a manifestation on the earthly plane, a transformation body (nirmāṇakāya), who will complete the taming of the demons threatening Tibet. This promise is implied in Padma's original failure to complete the taming of the demons when he first arrived in Tibet. Since he did not bind them three times, he still is bound by his vow to see to their permanent enslavement. Thus there is a preexisting samaya within Padmasambhava, which Avalokiteśvara can "call forth" when he calls forth Gesar from within Padmasambhava.

71. "In the limitless sky of your enlightened mind of bodhicitta": This stanza shows one of the most frequently used extended figures in epic language. In the sky are stars, constellations, the sun, and the moon; each of these different kinds of lights, according to its nature, is a metaphor for a particular religious principle. When it speaks of the moon surrounded by the moving stars, the idea is that the moon is brighter when it is surrounded by all these other lights.

72. The perfection of aspiration (Tib. *smon lam pha rol phin*; Skt. *praṇidhānapāramitā*) is the perfection practiced at the eighth level, or *bhumi*, of the bodhisattva path. It is a measure of Avalokiteśvara's degree of enlightenment, for complete buddhahood is attained just after the bodhisattva passes beyond the tenth level.

73. Here begins the section in which Padmasambhava initiates the process by which Thöpa Gawa is miraculously born (Tib. *rdzus skyes*) as a deity in heaven. *Miraculous birth* is a term for the way gods come into being. Just as humans and animals are born from wombs, eggs, and so forth, so gods are "miraculously born." The entire process of emanating and gathering lights, sounds, and tantric symbols and hand implements that are depicted in this passage could be regarded as a technical description of the birth of a deity.

The passage is quite remarkable for its detail. In this case, however, it is a very special deity—a deity who is not just a long-lived intelligent creature living in an immaterial realm, but a being who is a manifestation of ultimate truth and will become in his next incarnation an avatar of such. It is this evolution or devolution, if you will, from reality to appearance that is represented by the birth of Thöpa Gawa, the Buddhist equivalent of the "word becoming flesh."

74. This passage could actually be interpreted as saying that White Supreme Bliss Good Nature not only imagined himself as the horse-headed Buddha but that his appearance changed into that of Hayagrīva.

75. "Passionless union" means that the union was not based on ordinary sexual desire. According to the tantric tradition, this is a union that symbolizes the indivisibility of the method of compassion and the wisdom of emptiness.

76. "Space" is a coded way of referring to a woman's genitalia. She and her consort are in *yab yum*, sexual union.

77. In other words, that wisdom prajñā became the nirmāṇakāya of a buddha, the magical or emanation body, which is an interesting point. Usually it is said that the ultimate body of the Buddha is the dharma body, and his or her visionary body, which appears like a god wearing ornaments, is the enjoyment body (sambhogakāya), whereas the human body of a buddha, the physical form he assumed to walk the earth is the nirmāṇakāya. Here, however, the nirmāṇakāya is actually a godling (Tib. *lha sras*; Skt. *devaputra*).

78. The passage just concluded follows the logic of many Buddhist tantric ceremonies. It shows how a buddha manifests as a nirmāṇakāya, a historical buddha, when prayers are made to draw forth from the formless void his incarnation.

    First the Great Compassionate One and Padmasambhava sing songs to "invoke and call forth the mind stream." This means that although the buddha abides on a level of absolute enlightenment, beyond time and space, an invocation to his pure mind can draw him down into the realm of manifestation.

    All the thus-gone ones, all the buddhas who abide in the ten directions, when they were bodhisattvas had made vows help beings out of compassion. The two songs remind them of those vows and call them down through the power of those vows.

    Later at a tantric ritual feast, Padmasambhava sends out rays of light, which get the process of incarnation going. A green ray of light, symbolizing action, radiates from his head and strikes the ultimate buddha Samantabhadra. This evokes a blue vajra from that buddha, which flies to the Heaven of the Thirty-three and lands on the head of a local deity. It transforms him into the special demon-slaying tantric buddha, Hayagrīva, the horse-headed one.

    At the same time, presumably also in response to Padmasambhava's catalyst, the female buddha of the element of space sends out a red lotus that enters the head of a female local goddess in Heaven. Just as a blue vajra turns a god into a male buddha, the red lotus turns a goddess into a female buddha, the Vajra Sow.

    Thus a buddha and his consort have used their power to bless two local deities and transform them into absolute principles. Those two manifest buddhas enter into union, not out of lust or desire but rather in order to bring together the absolute male and female principles. This act of divine coupling sets off a chain reaction throughout the universe. Innumerable male and female buddhas send out rays of light throughout the universe. These rays of light benefit countless beings invisibly and then gather into a double vajra, the symbol of all accomplishing activity. That double vajra enters the horse-headed buddha, then passes through his body and out his vajra into the lotus of the Vajra Sow. There it transforms into a nirmāṇakāya buddha, Thöpa Gawa. He is a godling, but later he will incarnate as Gesar.

79. The song that follows, by Thöpa Gawa [Gesar], presents divine Ling's first complete picture of the political theory of Mipham Rinpoche. Like many thinkers of the ecumenical school of Tibetan Buddhism, Mipham was fascinated by political theories that were, in effect, fresh ideas for Tibetan culture in the nineteenth century. Although fresh, they

hearken back to theories of a golden age when the Tibetan Empire was founded in the time of Padmasambhava, and they evoke Indian notions of a hierarchical society.

In this song we see the details of his theory of monarchy as the ideal political system. Society is constructed of classes or orders of humans. Sometimes Mipham presents five orders: *rgyal po,* or kings; *blon po,* or ministers; *btsan po,* or "mighty ones"; *phyug po,* the rich; and *sde,* the commoners, the people. Technically the *blon* are advisors to the king, but actually they are often powerful heads of clans, provincial leaders in their own right whose accord the king must attain for his major decisions to become actions. The *dbang po* are people who have power because of the possession of lands, wealth, and (principally) arms. According to Tendzin Samphel, one of the Tibetans who Robin Kornman worked with at the Sorbonne, they are considered to be people whose power rests on their use of force as much as on their political connections. The words *btsan po* and *dbang po* can in certain contexts be considered as equivalent, in which case "the mighty ones" are in effect the aristocracy. Their wishes also must be taken into account when the king makes important decisions. The *phyug po* are rich people. They are considered to have a special nature because of their wealth; their wealth is a sign that they possess an extraordinary accumulation of good karma from actions in previous lifetimes. Chapter 2 of the epic describes this ideal hierarchical order as it presents in detail the social strata of Ling.

The song begins with a traditional sermon on the "Four Thoughts Which Turn the Mind." This contemplation ordinarily is used to motivate the disciple to practice meditation with greater diligence. However, in this case, it is given a special twist and becomes the basis for a political message. The Four Thoughts aim to develop general motivation to tread the path to enlightenment.

Here, on the other hand, the motivational force is directed toward the classes of society. If a king understands the force of karma, the certainty of death, and the difficulty of finding a precious human rebirth, then, understanding cause and effect, he will rule virtuously and wisely. The same pertains to the other classes of society; they will fulfill their duties properly if they have a correct perspective on karmic causality.

The horrors of sickness, old age, and death, the last stages of the twelve niḍānas or causal links, are graphically described. Realizing the impermanence of ordinary human life and the certainty of suffering should motivate the proper detachment in the high, the middle, and the low orders of society. Detached from materialistic goals in that way, they will perform the duties of their station properly and will thus create an enlightened society.

80. The usual three kāyas are the body, speech, and mind of the Buddha. The five-body (kāya) system includes qualities and action, along with body, speech, and mind. The five kāyas are the kāya of nature as it is, the kāya of truth, the kāya of complete abundance, the kāya of emanation, and the vajra kāya. The five wisdoms are the wisdom of the basic space of phenomena, mirrorlike wisdom, equanimity, discerning wisdom, and all-accomplishing wisdom.

81. Continuing the traditional sermon on motivation, Gesar speaks of the obstacles to practice, which are twofold: neither being free (Tib. *dal ba*) nor well-favored (Tib. *'byor pa*). The "eight states of being" mentioned here are the opposite of the eight freedoms or leisures (Tib. *dal ba*), which are the eight conditions of life in which one has an opportunity to hear and practice the Buddha's teachings.

82. "And when you are born in the central land, with faculties whole, with faith, / Without reversed karma, inclined to virtue": This is a list of five of the ten endowments with which one is well-favored. The ten endowments (Tib. *'byor ba bcu*), are the ten positive qualities or prerequisites that one must possess in order to be able to seek enlightenment. And so, altogether there are eighteen elements—"the precious eight leisures and ten endowments"—with which one is "free and well-favored."

83. There are two kinds of fatal illnesses. The first is *chi ba'i nad*, a sickness unto death. In that case, you get sick and die quickly. But then there is *gcong chen nad*, a great fatal illness—that is, a long fatal illness. This occurs because a person has evil karma from a previous lifetime and cannot die until it is brought to fruition in suffering before dying. The long illnesses produce bedsores, one becomes hypersensitive, the body is weak, and the mind depressed. Tibetans often pray to avoid this kind of illness: "In this life to avoid the suffering of a long fatal illness and after death to avoid the suffering of the lower realms."

84. Tibetans believe that it is unhealthy to sleep during the day if you are ill. Sleeping in the day is believed to cause fever. And so people take turns sitting by the sick person keeping him awake. The "sleep guardian" may even fashion little devices to keep the sick person awake by prodding him or her.

85. The Tibetan here, meaning "auspicious connections are reversed in your spells and divinations," is *mo dang phywa la rten 'brel log*. Mo are divinations using dice and the like, and *phywa* are usually ceremonies to deflect magical attacks or to call back loved ones who are dying. In this case, because of the nearness of death, you have run out of auspicious connections, tendrel, or good fortune. Tendrel is the driving force behind *mo* and *phywa*; therefore, in this state of exhaustion of the energy of good luck, the divinations are misleads and the spells do not work. The theory is that a person has a certain amount of karma for life. When that karma is exhausted, the person will die, no matter what magical interventions are employed. Furthermore, the signs are no longer reliable when you have no more karma to live.

86. It seems that the negation that appears in the Tibetan text as *min (chos rnam dag min cing dge rtsa phyi)* should read *yin*. Then the reading would be, "But even though you have pure dharmas, it's too late to plant virtuous roots." The idea is that any meritorious actions you perform now, such as making great offerings, will ripen in your next life and not come to fruition now, preventing your death. The karmic seeds for your death were planted long ago.

87. The Tibetan phrase translated as "help in the forty-nine days" (Tib. *zhe dgu'i re ba*) literally means "hope for the forty-nine." "Forty-nine" refers to the length of time an individual spends in the intermediate state (bardo) between death and rebirth. Tibetan Buddhists believe that if relatives and loved ones pray and make offerings to the Three Jewels during the forty-nine days of the bardo, then the departed one's rebirth will be higher or more fortunate.

88. The Tibetan *bsod nams* [sönam] ordinarily means "merit," as a translation of the Sanskrit word *punya*. But in Tibetan it can also refer to a field of power around a person, a kind of karmic aura. When it is strong, a person is in good health. But your aura of merit may leak and degrade, particularly in the hour of death.

89. The Tibetan has a misspelling in the text: *mthur bud* (reins fall off) should be *thur bud* (fall down, upside down).

90. Dralas are, among other things, tiny energetic beings who perch on the body of the warrior and help to give him energy. Drala castles or temples are tiny shrines to these drala (Tib. *dgra bla* or *lha*). There are visualization practices in which places on the body that the dralas are to bless are pictured as little castles inhabited by the dralas. The expression "the castle of the dralas is turned away" (Tib. *dgra lha'i bse mkhar phyir log*) thus means that your dralas have deserted your body/mind complex and left you unblessed, vulnerable. This happens at the time of death, when all the positive energies organized around the body depart, including the protecting dralas. *See* glossary: drala.

    For the warrior, there are practices that serve to increase one's windhorse (see glossary), raise one's field of power, and attract the dralas. A person fully invested with these elements would be completely healthy, but at death they scatter and the energy drains away.

91. "Inner stores" (Tib. *phug zas*) means "long-term provisions." In Khampa dialect, the most inward room where long-term storage of foodstuff (Tib. *zas*) is kept is the *phug ma*, the innermost room. When food is stored for the winter, there is always an emergency store in the furthest room. It is held for a last resort, the last stores to be eaten. By extension, *phug zas* are anything stored away and the object of the greatest attachment, such as gold and precious gems—things with which the stingy would never part.

92. "A wooden stake of attachment driven into the ground": Attachment to the things of this life interrupts the process of rebirth and, like a stake driven into the ground, the deceased person, instead of journeying on to the next rebirth, remains as a ghost.

93. "Now even regret is merely cause for more suffering": Buddhist teachings emphasize "the force of regret" as a mental influence that can lead to personal moral reformation. When a person regrets their negative actions, this leads to confession of sins. This act of confession leads to actions that favor religion and so to the eventual lessening of suffering as one becomes free of negative karma. Thus, for ordinary people, regret ordinarily leads to a lessening of suffering.

    But when the gods die, their regret does not improve their karma. By regret they simply increase their own suffering. They have led a dissolute life of self-indulgence in heaven and failed all that time to practice religion. Now it is too late to regret their laziness.

94. "Determine to resolve the nature of mind": This is a step on the way to enlightenment. "To resolve" (Tib. *kho thag chod*) here means arriving at a sense of intellectual certainty through reasoning and reference to scriptural authority. Once a lama has resolved for him or herself that the nature of the mind is buddhahood, then it is possible to meditate with determination directly on the nature of mind. This leads to direct realization and thus to enlightenment.

95. "Think through their actual meaning" (Tib. *don 'bras dpyod*): The homonym *spyod* would make this "put their meaning into practice."

96. The Tibetan text here says *ma go glu la 'brel ba med*; literally this means, "If you did not understand [this discourse], there is no connection." We have chosen to translate the final phrase as "there is no way to explain it."

97. What follows will be a detailed description of a tantric empowerment ceremony, with which the chapter ends. Many tantric practices require taking part in such a ceremony before one has the right to do the practices. Usually there is a mandala that represents the deities, the buddhas, and retinue, and that is involved in the practice. The mandala is represented as a palace with four gates and a center. On each of these five points sits or

stands a particular buddha. Each of these buddhas grants empowerment to the disciple in the ceremony. In theory, these five actions repeat the ancient ceremony of coronation in which a prince is turned into a king.

Generally the details of these ceremonies and the buddhas within them are quite secret. But here the compilers of the epic have obviously decided to teach the people the general principles of the empowerment ceremony, using the nonsecret buddhas of the five families. Thus, this is a sort of generic or, you could say, training abhiṣeka. Several verses that are found in the praise are taken from the *Mañjuśrīnāmasaṃgīti*, a text used to teach the poetic language used in tantric practices.

98. "Additives" (Tib. *kha tshar*) are additional ingredients that perfect a medicine by changing its flavor or quality.

99. Since the enemy is ignorance, it cannot be slain unless the warrior has compassion.

100. In an ordinary empowerment the guru-preceptor blesses a scepter that represents the Buddha Vairocana and the enlightened principle of body. Then he or she touches the disciple with this scepter while uttering verses of empowerment. Here the scepter itself performs the empowerment, and the words are uttered magically without a speaker being present. The scepter of Vairocana is an eight-spoked wheel.

101. He is like a child who throws a stone in the air not realizing where it will fall, and sometimes it falls on his own head. In other words, since he does not think of cause and effect, he does not pay attention to the inevitable result of mistreating his subjects. He enforces the law too strenuously, and they either revolt or the country suffers harm.

102. "Disciple with no samaya" refers to a disciple who does not keep his vows and commitments to his guru—in other words, a disciple without proper devotion. The phrase "whose open mind shows him to be learned" is based on the Tibetan wording *mtong rgya*, which is literally "seeing widely." It generally means having great vision or open-mindedness, but here it probably means being merely scholarly.

103. "Great source of jewel wisdom, Ratnasambhava" (Tib. *rin chen 'bhyung gnas*): This, like many lines written into this empowerment ceremony, was taken from the *Mañjuśrīnāmasaṃgīti*.

104. The order of these five empowerments is somewhat strange. Usually one begins with the body empowerment, and the order continues with speech, mind, quality, and finally action. Here he is empowered with the speech of the buddhas last, instead of second.

105. "Support of the samaya of all the tathāgatas" (Tib. *de bzhin gshegs pa thams cad kyi dam tshig gi rten*): *rten* refers to "support," an instrument used in a ritual to contain or receive spiritual energy. It becomes both the symbol and the embodiment of that energy, and thus we call them "symbolic supports." So this vajra has become the support of the vows of devotion of all the buddhas. Presumably in holding it one holds all the power and virtue of each guru's devotion to beings, their samayas, their intensity, and commitments.

106. Here we have a classical list of the three levels of local spirits, corresponding to heaven, earth, and subterranean; also corresponding to sky, mountains, and streams. The triad is mentioned constantly. It is pronounced *lha, nyen, lu,* the *lu* being the nāgas or serpent spirits. *See* glossary: *nyen* and *nāga*.

107. Yellow Hor: In the epic there are three brothers of the Hor clan to be subjugated by Gesar. They are Gurkar (White Tent), Gurnag (Black Tent), and Gurser (Yellow Tent).

108. "Conquered by the logic of the learned" (Tib. *mkhas pa'i grub mthas ma bcom na*): Literally, "if he is not converted by a philosophical system put forward by a paṇḍit."

109. If he does not recognize his mistakes by immediately suffering personally the karmic result of his misdeeds, he will continue to torture and oppress the people.

110. The skandhas, or five aggregates, are form, feeling, recognition, reaction, and consciousness. These are the five psycho-physical constituents of ego. Each of the five empowerments purifies one of the five aggregates, transforming it into one of the five wisdoms. Therefore this verse is a summary of the effects of the empowerment, for by destroying the five aggregates one destroys ego-clinging, and the five wisdoms emerge. *See* glossary: skandha.

111. A complete abhiṣeka or empowerment is divided into four empowerments: outer, inner, secret, and the nature as it is. The first of these, the outer empowerment, sometimes called the vase empowerment, is divided into five sub-empowerments corresponding to the five buddha families of the five directions of the mandala. This first of the four was presented in complete detail. The rest are only mentioned in this sentence.

112. The land of Ling has many epithets: White Ling, Divine Ling, Brilliant Ling, and Multicolored Ling, to name a few. There is no Black Ling and, although white is good in this system, black is not its opposite and is not evil. "White" when used refers not to the color, but to qualities of fighting the forces of evil.

113. "Middle land of humans" (Tib. *bar mi yi yul*) refers to the three levels of native Tibetan cosmology: the heaven realm of the gods, above; the human realm, in the middle; and the realm of the water spirits, below. The water spirits are called *klu* (pronounced *lu*) in Tibetan or *nāgas* in Sanskrit, the familiar dragon spirits of East Asian culture. Sometimes the three levels are given as *lha* (upper gods), *mi* (humans), and *lu* (serpents), and sometimes just as three gods. In that case the human realm is replaced by the realm of the mountain gods, who are, after all, the original proprietors of most of the human inhabited land in this epic. Mountain gods are called *nyen*. Thus the famous triad would be *lha*, *nyen*, and *lu*, an expression that occurs constantly in epic discourse about the structure of the world. This triad matches in some ways the Confucian triad, which also describes the universe in three levels: Heaven, Earth, and Man.

114. "Breathtaking to behold" (Tib. *mthong ba kun smon*): literally, "whose sight everyone aspires." It is a term of Sanskrit court poetry indicating that the place is so beautiful, and possesses all positive qualities, so that everyone who came upon it would find it breathtaking, and would aspire to be in such a place.

115. The Thirty Mighty Warriors are the main heroes of the epic. Later on, when Gesar together with these thirty conquers other kingdoms, there come to be eighty warriors. Those eighty are considered to be emanations of the eighty great mahāsiddhas of India.

116. "In the sleep of luminosity" (Tib. *'od gsal gzim gyi srang lam na*): that is, during a phase in his sleep of lucid dreaming. Great yogins are supposed to practice a kind of meditation that is done while they are asleep. This special sleep, in which one is aware of the state of sleeping, is called "sleep of luminosity" and is the dreaming that occurs in the early morning hours of sleep.

117. Heavily ornamented ceremonial parasols are a symbol of kingship. A servant holds the parasol over the head of an official, high monk, or king and then turns the handle slowly in his hand, causing the parasol to slowly rotate.

118. This describes the great yogin who founded Tibetan Buddhism, Padmasambhava. He is escorted in this case by the wrathful female buddha Vajrayoginī, who appears wearing the bone ornaments of a wild inhabitant of the charnel grounds.

119. The three seed syllables or seed mantras, OṂ ĀḤ HŪṂ, represent the body, speech, and mind of the Buddha. The song has OṂ as an auspicious beginning, ĀḤ is in the middle as the speech of the Buddha, and it is sealed with the syllable HŪṂ, a sign that the commitment of the singer is unchanging. The eight meanings refer not to eight individual meanings, but to general auspiciousness.

120. There are four orders, or lineages (Tib. *rgyud*), in the society of Ling. They express a matrilineal point that is difficult for Westerners to understand. Although they are called the Elder, Middle, and Cadet Lineages, they are not really a matter of age at all, but of families related to the founding mothers of the Mukpo clan, who were of three ages. For details see the Historical Introduction.

 The tribal group descended from the elder matriarch is known as the Elder Lineage and is also called the Order of the Garuḍa. The Middle Lineage is the Order of the Dragon. The Cadet Lineage is the Order of the Snow Lion. The people or masses (Tib. *sde mangs*) are the Order of the Tiger.

121. " Smile-striped" refers to tigers in classical poetry and the fact that their stripes resemble six smiles.

122. "Windhorse flag" (Tib. *las dar*; literally "action scarf") refers to the special flag that is raised in this ceremony to invoke the dralas. It has the figures of a tiger, snow lion, garuḍa, and dragon in the four corners around a central figure of a horse carrying on its back a wish-fulfilling wheel.

123. "Practice groups" (Tib. *sgrub khag*) refers to the custom of breaking up an assemblage into distinct groups, each of which practices a different deity invocation simultaneously, for increased effectiveness. So here the inhabitants of Ling are being ordered to divide into thirteen groups to simultaneously supplicate thirteen different wealth gods.

124. "Summon prosperity" (Tib. *gyang 'bod*) originates with the shamanist culture of ancient Tibet. Later this practice was incorporated into the Buddhist path by using different deities and mantras. This practice can invoke not only wealth but also prosperity and basically whatever enriching qualities may be desired.

125. "What's the point?" This is a traditional close to an epic song; the singer formulaically challenges the audience's understanding of the song.

126. "Slowly like the sun in springtime" because the days are long and the sun therefore moves slowly across the sky. For example there is the Tibetan proverb *dpyid ka'i nyi ma lo red*, meaning "one day in spring is like a whole year."

127. "Cursing": The Tibetan words in the original, *pha sha*—literally "father's flesh"—are the first words of a Tibetan's famous curse, *pha sha zo*, "eat your father's flesh."

128. Since he had neglected to put on his belt, his robe hung loose and he had to hold it together with his hands. He had to gather the front of his robe like the protective cloth that hangs in front of a thangka is gathered up by a ribbon in order to reveal the painting.

129. The Jowo image of the Buddha in Lhasa is a universal object of devotion in Tibet.

130. Image of the perfect Tibetan king: every morning he practices meditation and says a tremendous number of prayers before even rising from his bed. Actually, the custom among many Tibetan meditation practitioners is to make their meditation seat directly on their bed, instead of moving to another place to begin practice. The servant is thus surprised to see him out of his bed, not meditating at this hour of the morning. For ordinarily he does not open his cross-legged posture until he has finished meditating.

131. The chieftain debates with himself whether or not it is necessary to perform the rituals designed to make the events in the dream come to happen, since they seem to be happening of their own accord.

132. "Milk of the third summer" (Tib. *sum yar 'o ma*): In *sgrong yig*, village dialect, this is the very best milk. The first year that the female yak, the *dri*, suckles her calf, the calf is called a *be-u* and the cow a *trid-ma*. The second year the calf becomes a *yar-ri* and the cow a *yar-ma*. If the calf is weak and undernourished by the third summer, the cow may still provide milk even to this large a calf. That milk of the summer months of the third year is the richest and most potently flavorful milk, making the best butter available among the nomads.

133. The lines of this proverb in Tibetan are as follows: *sgo mo bde skyid ngag grol glu yi sgo mo de/ bkra shis byin chags rten 'brel mgo ma red.* The two "go(s)," *sgo mo* and *mgo ma,* are pronounced alike and could mean, respectively "gateway" and "head" or "start." They can be taken to mean practically the same thing in village dialect, with the *ma* ending being more usual.

    On the other hand, there is an interesting metaphorical message if their meaning is different. When song is a gateway to expression of an inner reality, it may be the beginning of good fortune: "There may be many people in a room, but they all have to leave by one door." In the same way, there are many thoughts in the mind, but they all have to be expressed in this song via the one gate of speech (Tib. *ngag*). Thus, if one were not using speech, if one's speech were not set free, then it would be as if the doors were closed; the gate would be closed and there would be no song.

    For example, inside the body there may be happiness and bliss. This *sde skyid* within is liberated through speech when we express it. As a result, it is through this gate of song that auspicious blessings or splendor (Tib. *byin chags*) are released, because this is the result, the auspicious connection or good fortune (Tib. *rten 'brel*).

134. The "Auspicious-by-Day" scarf (Tib. *dar nyin mo bde legs*) is a special offering scarf inscribed with the eight auspicious symbols and a four-line poem that begins *nyin mo bde legs*, "auspicious by day." The entire text on the scarf goes like this:

    > *nyin mo bde legs mtshan bde legs*
    > *nyin mo'i gung yang bde legs shes (or shi)*
    > *nyin mtshan rtag rgyu bde legs pa'i*
    > *rkyabs gnas dkon mchogs gsum kyi bkra shi shog*

    > All is well by day and well by night
    > All is well even before the dawn;
    > Bringing continuous well-being both day and night
    > May the auspiciousness of the Rare and Precious Three Jewels be present
    > and everywhere.

135. The cuckoo bird is considered the most melodious of all birds when he first appears at the onset of summer. Although the cuckoo's song is the most haunting in the beginning of summer, as the season goes on it loses its appeal. Tibetans believe the cuckoo's song is very special.

136. "Sublime prosperity animals" (Tib. *phugs gyang*; literally, "wealth-prosperity") is a term

referring to domesticated animals that are outstanding in fortitude, beauty, and character, so that they are spared from the ordinary drudgeries imposed upon other beasts of burden. For example, a yak that displays the signs of being a sublime animal will be referred to as a *lha* yak (Tib. *g.yag*), a yak of the gods. Some yaks have beautiful horns; some have beautiful fur. The broad chest and sturdy frame and long locks will be ornamented with bells and bangles and the beast; so ornamented, will be left to wander in freedom and its fur will not be shorn.

This is similar to the expression *g.yang mdzas* (wealth substance), a material used in wealth ceremonies that is sometimes made from the skin of a baby yak that has good countenance. Sometime the wealth substance is made from beautiful silk brocade, etc.

137. As the servants sing this song they make offerings to a shrine. This line of verse is chanted at the moment when they hold up butter lamps as an offering of light.

138. The literal meaning of Ser (Tib. *gser*) is "gold." This is the clan name attached to members of the Elder Lineage, based on the name given to the founding mother of this lineage, Serza, who established the homeland of this clan group in the highlands of the Machen Pomra region. She was given the name Ser because she found a golden yoke in Upper Ling as a sort of totemic magical object.

139. *Ombu* means "son of Om." Om (meaning "tamarisk") is the name given to the founder mother of the Middle Lineage, Omza, who quested and later settled in the lands of middle altitude around Machen Pomra Mountain and found there a tamarisk tree as her totemic object.

140. The Lesser, or Cadet, Lineage was founded by a woman who was given the name Chang ("wolf") and told to settle in the lowlands of the same region as her fellow wives. Her totemic quest object was a wolf's tail. The Mu (Tib. *dmu*) family is traditionally a group of priests of the native religion, people involved with the original descent of the Mu chord, linking heaven and earth. Members of that family are thus associated with shamanistic priestly matters. They are also involved through intermarriage with the Chang descent line of the Lesser Lineage of the Mukpos. Stein (1959) explains that Gesar is a member of the Mu within the Mukpo clan and therefore a member of the Cadet Lineage. Both clans are descended from the gods, who are considered in this tradition to have the divine color of dark brown (*smug po*).

141. The metaphors here are based on an epic vision of the traditional provinces of Ling, which are grouped into districts with their respective tribes. They are the Eight Golden Brothers (Tib. *gser pa mched brgyad*) of Upper Ling, the Six Tribes (Tib. *tsho drug*) of Middle Ling, and the Four Districts (Tib. *sde bzhi*) of Lower Ling. The epic's Thirty Mighty Warriors come from these provinces. The leaders of these three tribal regions were Nyibum Daryag of Serpa, Anu Paseng of Ombu, and Rinchen Darlu of Muchang. The first, Serpa was said to be like an eagle, perhaps referring to the arc of gold that his ancestress found. Ombu was like an offering wood, a reference to tamarisk. Muchang, in keeping with the matrilineal name, was said to be like a wolf.

142. The six medicinal herbs are perfected or augmented by the six minor ingredients (Tib. *bzang drug sman gyis kha tshar btab*) The *bzang drug*, six precious ingredients, is either a list of substances such as myrobalan and musk, or a list of six culinary ingredients such as nutmeg, marigold, cardamom, and saffron. The *kha tshar*, minor ingredients, is yet another classical list of substances used to improve the flavor and appearance

of medicines, and may be poetic license to claim this was all added to the tea. The six medicines (Tib. *sman*) are *ka ko la* (cardamom), *cu gang* (bamboo manna), *sug smel* (Himalayan cardamom), *dza ti* (nutmeg), *li shi* (caryophyllus, or wild carnation), *gur gum* (saffron).

143. "Unarranged . . . arranged itself": The distinction here cannot be directly translated into English. In the Tibetan *ma bsgrigs rten 'brel rang 'grigs,* there are two forms of the verb: *bsgrigs* is a form that describes an action, which is *byed pa po med pa,* without an agent, and *'grigs* is the form of the verb that describes an action that has an agent. Thus the most literal translation would be "the fortunate connection that nobody arranged has arranged itself." It is as if to say, "The connection that just happened to occur and had nobody arranging it or intending to arrange it has arranged itself." Our translation of these two verbs into active and passive is thus slightly misleading, for the real point here is that there is no third party that brought together the various elements which, when conjoined, amounted to good fortune. Rather, they themselves, the various elements that formed the fortunate conjunction, were responsible for their own coming together, or they came together *rang bzhin gis,* "naturally or by their own nature."

144. "Self-proclaimed" (Tib. *ma bsgrags*): The Tibetan does not really say "self-voiced," but rather "*un*voiced," which is as much as to say "voiced by no one and yet voiced." This line ends a paragraph that reflects upon the auspicious events that are arising of their own accord. The full Tibetan is *ma bsgrags gyi 'brug sngon mo'i gsung red,* which means "this is the unproclaimed roar of the blue dragon."

145. Letters to people of rank should not begin by naming them directly; rather such a letter should refer to them indirectly with honorifics and titles, or by mentioning their qualities.

146. In this letter Chipön is asking Michen Gyalwa'i Lhundrub to join him in performing specific ceremonies that will induce the birth of Gesar. The ceremonial acts are represented by the rays of the sun. The idea is that unless the sun shines at the right time, the time when the lotus is ready to bloom, the lotus will not bloom at all. Chipön's symbolic dream enjoins him to gather with the leaders of his kingdom to perform ceremonies that will take advantage of the mystical conjunction of events represented by the opening of the "glorious gate," the cosmic conjunction of elements, mystical energies, and buddha intentionality that lead to Gesar's incarnation.

147. The "treasury" (Tib. *mdzod*) refers to the special place in the home where the priceless, precious possessions were stored. It was from such a treasure chest that the bolt of brocade offered here with the letter was drawn.

148. The word *timely* in this passage points to a view of how prayers and psychic phenomena work in a world of beings and buddhas. The enlightened Padmasambhava knows, and doesn't even have to wait for Chipön to finish his wish; already he is in action to finish it. There is an implied synchronicity of actions of sentient beings in saṃsāra and actions of buddhas to help them. This is reflected in the instantaneous "timely" appearance of Padmasambhava in Thangtong's dream telling him to go to Falcon Castle Sky Fortress.

149. "Divine dharma" (Tib. *lha chos*) is a technical term to distinguish it from more worldly magical practices. The distinction is between *lha chos,* which we translate as "divine dharma," and *mi chos,* the dharma of men. Buddhism is divine dharma and the dharma of men refers to ordinary life as a human being.

150. "Mighty one" (Tib. *btsan po*) could be translated as "nobleman," but the emphasis here is

on the military power of the man. This is sort of a positive term for a warlord—a person of great military power who rules well by virtue of that. In the epic such "mighty ones" are almost a class of society, alongside the lamas, the rich patrons, and the common people.

151. A reference to a story found in the aphorisms of Śākya Paṇḍita. As the story goes, a farmer was unable to sustain his hungry donkey in his own field, so he found the fertile field of another that was near to the forest. He turned his donkey loose there to graze, but before doing so he covered the beast with the skin of a leopard. The donkey grazed to its heart's content until one day someone noticed that indeed this was a donkey and killed him.

152. "View" (Tib. *lta ba*) can refer to any kind of theory that the ordinary mind holds. Here this refers to gaining certainty about a philosophical position about the nature of reality. For example, the view of the *yogacārya* sect is that the phenomenal world is simply a projection of mind. One who merely accepts this idea intellectually would not be said by virtue of that to "have the view." Possession of the view means that one has deeply contemplated it and understands it on an instinctual level so that it can subtly guide one's meditation practice and way of seeing ordinary reality.

153. An accomplished siddha is a yogic master who can control the subtle energies in the body and, for example, by practicing mystic heat can stay in the cold without being affected by the elements.

154. The *gaṇacakra* offering is often referred to as a "feast." Actually this means a gathering of necessary components that come together to present offerings in the context of inner vajrayāna practice. The gathering includes the mandala of deities of the Three Roots, the male and female practitioners, and the offering substances which represent that which is not to be discarded or rejected due to concepts and the gathering of both ordinary and wisdom merit. According to inner tantra practice, this is the supreme method for offering and thus the supreme method through which merit is accumulated. A pure dedication occurs when the merit gained by performing the ritual practice is entirely given over to others without concern for the benefit of one's own vows.

155. Here the yogin is challenging the chieftain in return, pretending that he is just another self-centered political leader who "consumes the people." The chieftain's song had challenged the yogin by saying he might be a false lama.

156. The *ālaya* means the basis of all, which is the ground of both saṃsāra and nirvāṇa. The characteristic of this basis is neutral, which means that any karmic seeds can be sown here and anything can arise from this.

157. "Advice" (Tib. *kha brda*): The Tibetan is a colloquial expression from Golog that here means "advice" but can also mean just "chitchat."

158. An error in the text gives the word *se ru* (yellow) here; it should be *bser* (wind).

159. "Dralas faring forth from their nests" (Tib. *dgra lha tsang nas*) means the thought of the dralas is such that one feels the energy of their presence as they fill up an environment. So magnificent was the departure of the great Michen Gyalwa'i Lhundrub from his palace that it resembled what it would be like if all the war gods were to rise up from their nests or dwelling places and travel as an army to another destination. This gives the sense of how great was Michen's field of power.

160. The term used here, *skor khyi*, refers to the large mastiffs that must be chained or harnessed to a pole. They guard the tents of the Golog nomads, yet they must not be allowed

to run loose due to their ferocious power and inclination to kill and tear apart not only intruders, but any stranger they meet.

161. A makara (Tib. *chu srin*) is a mythological sea monster. Ancient Tibetans believed that when a dragon aged, it became a sea monster. When the sea monster aged, it became a paisley-shaped design known as *patra*. The makara is thus depicted with the head of a sea monster and the design of a patra.

162. "Leaders of the auspicious connection": In the Buddhist and shamanistic world, magic political strategies are based on natural karmic relations that are a kind of naturally occurring power. Kyalo is a man who has collected great merit in his previous lifetimes and so is now rich. Michen is powerful for the same reason. Both of them, therefore, have flourishing windhorse, a broad and impressive field of power and natural good fortune. Thus they are the masters and leaders of the auspicious connections for this province. The energy of fortunate connections of tendrel focuses on them and by inviting them to the great assembly, Chipön gains additional control over the fortunate connection, which will bring about Gesar's rebirth in Ling.

163. These proverbs refer to daily events in a *sde,* a division or province. The chieftain or leader operates like a judge, deciding the constant disputes that occur between tribesmen in a seminomadic region. If he fails to exercise leadership, the number of disputations and formal cases increases. The province sends spies to watch its ever-shifting boundaries. If they become excitable, they begin to imagine enemies attacking, and the resulting alarms and posses run the horses off their legs. If a yogin in his or her cave loses perspective, he or she begins to hallucinate demonic attacks, and the cave is thronged with armies of phantasms.

164. "Incarnation" (Tib. *sprul tshul*): literally, about the "manner of manifestation" of Gesar. Note that here Thangtong Gyalpo is using the same word (*sprul*) used for the reincarnation of a great lama, *sprul sku* (pronounced *tülku*). *Tulku* is the typical word for an enlightened being who reincarnates on purpose or a divine principle that chooses to take the flesh. In Tibet many of the famous lamas are considered to be tulkus, reincarnations of great lamas from the past.

165. Gesar's elder uncle Trothung, his most persistent related enemy in the epic, is actually an incarnation or emanation of the wrathful yidam Hayagrīva. Although he seemingly strives to hurt Gesar, his interference serves to help him succeed.

166. It is interesting to note that this point-by-point commentary is on the dream itself, rather than on Chipön's song describing it. His song is not complete in its details. Thangtong Gyalpo, being an omniscient yogin, knows the dream directly instead of through hearsay.

167. This section is like the "catalog of ships" in *The Iliad*. It is the first mention of the principle heroes who will figure in the rest of the epic. Actually there will be several such catalogs in the first three volumes of the Gesar epic in order to establish the powers, possessions, and family relations of each warrior.

168. "Innermost mind" is an attempt to render the Tibetan word *phug*, which refers to an inner treasure, stored within the house in its deepest recesses.

169. "Remain on the crown of my head" is one of several standard requests that the teacher and the student be inseparable.

170. "Cosmic song" translates the Tibetan, *srid pa glu yi. srid pa* (pronounced *see-pa*) is the word for all of conditioned existence, all possibilities, the world sphere. In that case,

the worldly element would be that it is a song (Tib. *glu*) dealing with political matters and the practical realization of the dream prophecy.

171. This phrase is odd, since it does not occur in the original narration of the dream. The Masang are a kind of local deity associated with Vajrasādhu. *See* glossary: *Masang* and *Vajrasādhu*.

172. The four rivers of Kham: Dri Chu (Tib. *'bri chu*) [Yangtze River], Ma Chu (Tib. *rma chu*) [Yellow River], Gyalmo Ngül Chu (Tib. *rgyal mo ngul chu*) [Salween River], and Da Chu (Tib. *zla chu*) [Mekong River].

173. The six ridges of Kham are: Zelmo Gang (Tib. *zal mo sgang*), Tshawa Gang (Tib. *tsha ba sgang*), Markham Gang (Tib. *dmar khams sgang*), Pombor Gang (Tib. *spo 'bor sgang*), Mardza Gang (Tib. *dmar rdza sgang*), and Minyak Rabgang (Tib. *mi nyag rab sgang*).

174. Around Mount Meru sublime in body are the four continents (Tib. *gling bzhi*): Pūrvavideha [Noble Body] in the east, Jambudvīpa [Rose Apple] in the south, Aparagodānīya [Enjoyer of Cattle] in the west, and Uttarakuru [Unpleasant Sound] in the north.

175. This is the conclusion of an argument Michen has given to support the agenda he is about to unfold. His point is that because of natural karmic connections between the different classes and groups in the audience, they all effortlessly understand the symbols in the dream in the same way. Just as the sun and moon naturally illuminate the entire world ("the four continents") and Buddhism has spread naturally in Tibet, likewise the people of Ling naturally have the same understanding of what they are to do in terms of ritual activities to receive the incarnation of Gesar. Or to look at it another way, just as the sun, which is clear and bright, illuminates the earth, so the Tibetans' intelligence is clear and bright, so that it naturally accepts Buddhism. And since their intelligence is clear, they have no need for coercing to agree about the functional meaning of the prophecy.

176. Animals saved from the slaughter are animals caught and then released with an injunction that they not be killed for food. This transforms them into an offering to increase one's good merit.

177. The two laws refer to the religious law and the secular law that rule respectively in monasteries and in homes. This may mean that if the people participating in the ceremonies do not obey Michen's injunctions, they will have to report either to a monastic court or a civil court, depending on their vocation. The celebrants are enjoined to not simply perform the ceremonies together but to spread news of the ceremony that has occurred throughout the surrounding countryside.

178. Though Hor and Düd are both mentioned, they are not separate; the Hor are Düd—but there are also other Düd (Tib. *bdud*), which can be translated as "demon" or simply as the Sanskrit, *māra* (the type of obstacle demon that tried to prevent the Buddha from gaining enlightenment). But here Düd refers to the famous Demon of the North, an evil king who will be one of Gesar's greatest enemies. The long and complex saga in which King Gesar fights the Demon of the North is one of the two central battle sagas of the epic and thus is called the *bdud gling* [Düd Ling], the fighting between this Demon and Ling.

179. "Great space dome": The Tibetan, *rlung gi go la,* literally means "the globe of wind," meaning the firmament—the globe of the heavens, in which are fixed the stars and planets and which spin around each day with the sun, moon, and the stars.

180. "Sunny and shady slopes" (Tib. *nyin srib*): The highlands of Tibet are full of lateral valleys and rocky canyons. The western side receives the sun's rays and is called *nyin* (sun), the sunny side. The eastern slopes or sides of valleys are called *srib*, the shady side. So

these light-based terms are actually names of geographical features that name east and west. Of course, all words for east and west in Tibetan are descriptors. For example, the basic word for east is *shar*, which means "rising," and west is *nub*, which means "setting."

181. The song that follows is rather complicated, since Thöpa Gawa cites distinct sets of proverbs for each of his conclusions. First he decides that he must obey Padma, for he is the guru and one is bound by the samaya oaths to follow a guru's instructions. Second, there is no question that obeying Padma's instructions will be beneficial ("the benefit the guru brings," "When a boy is born, he benefits himself"). Then with "When a guru speaks to disciples" he begins to relate a series of proverbs to prove he must be obedient.

    Having accepted the command, he begins to think of assistance he will need. Padma has already ordered Gesar to reincarnate in the area of Ling, ("The time has come to perform enlightened activity for the benefit of others.") and he has commanded various spirits to help Gesar invisibly ("Werma keep company with his body"). Now Thöpa Gawa asks for divine companions to be reborn alongside of him. They will be the "basis" of his spiritual action, and he will depend on them like a deer does on a mountainside or a fish on the lake. Furthermore, he demands magical weapons and devices, just the way a young tough who is independent nevertheless must rely on his sword.

182. "Fancy trappings": This could also be rendered as "earthly entanglements." The Tibetan, *sa chus,* is a very colloquial expression that literally means "earth mixed with water."

183. Thöpa Gawa continues to give himself arguments for obeying the guru's commands and continues to cite proverbs that support this; his resolution gradually increases, and his mind gets gradually stronger in its commitments.

184. Cattle in nomadic herds slowly starve over the winter, so that when spring comes they are terribly thin. "Nephews" (Tib. *bu tsha*) actually refers to cousins and sons or nephews and sons. The idea is that since a nomadic tribe travels together, even after the longer winter, relatives with an excess load will transfer weight from their overburdened oxen and yaks to those of their kin. It is an irritating practice, particularly when one's own cattle are just skin and bones; but one cannot deny a relative.

185. Gesar is requesting here that Padmasambhava have various kinds of assistants incarnate with him as humans or commit themselves to him as gods and spirits, so that he has a team to work with him on his great project of protecting Ling from spiritual enemies. These friends and helpers are to assist him with the *mi chos,* or way of humans, and the *lha chos*, the way of the gods. This could mean that some incarnated assistants will help him materially and others magically. Alternately these two terms could be translated as if they referred to different aspects of religious practice. Then they would be translated as the dharma of humans and the dharma of the gods. Usually the dharma of humans is the local shamanistic and animistic religion, and the dharma of the gods is really the buddhadharma, which talks about transworldly matters. In this case, *lha chos* and *mi chos* would mean that some would help him in his spiritual goals and others would help him in his material goals.

    According to some teachings of the Nyingma lineage, there is the *lha mi theg pa*, the vehicle of gods and the vehicle of men. This refers to religious practices that are helpful but do not transcend the world. In this case the word *mi*, man or human, would refer to worldly ethical practices, and *lha* would refer to practices that deal with worldly gods. Neither of them would deal with the higher teachings that concern the ultimate nature of reality and how to realize it.

186. "Dancing eyes" (Tib. *gar mig*) refers to the different expressive glances and poses of expression used in classical dance. The eyes of fish are being compared to the expressive eyes of a dancer.

187. Gesar continues to argue that Padma must send him to Tibet accompanied by all sorts of assistants. Otherwise he goes with empty hands. A "tough guy" still needs his sword. Even excellent cattle need grass. Empty words don't bring joy, and empty hands won't kill the enemy.

188. In other words, it is no shame to have assistants.

189. "Pacified in its own place" is a very literal translation for the Tibetan *rang sar zhi*—which could also be translated as "naturally pacified."

190. In the section that begins here, Padmasambhava contemplates the map of all Tibetan-speaking regions, trying to decide the place most suitable for Thöpa Gawa's manifestation as Gesar. He reviews the geography of Tibet following traditional categories that can be found in annals of Tibetan royal dynasties and early histories of Tibet. There is a great deal of room here for interpretation in the translation, because the reception of this passage differs widely among Tibetan informants.

191. This is a confusing line in the Tibetan: *tsha rong rma zla chu bzhi'i gling.* But traditionally the four great rivers are those of Kham: the Dri Chu (Tib. *'bri chu,* the Yangtze River), the Ma Chu (Tib. *rma chu,* the Yellow River), the Gyalmo Ngül Chu (Tib. *rgyal mo ngul chu,* the Salween River), and the Da Chu (Tib. *zla chu,* the Mekong River). The Salween or Gyalmo Ngül Chu is sometimes referred to as the Tsharong because of the metallics salts (*tsha* is "salt") that it contains.

192. "Four farms" translates the Tibetan *rong bzhi* which could literally be the "four cultivated valleys."

193. The problem here is that although the passage then says there are thirteen myriarchies (Tib. *khri skor*), they do not add up so. This could be another bardic misenumeration; the bard simply losing track of the numbers as he chants them.

194. Serpa, Ombu, and Muchang are the names of three branches of the Mukpo tribe who settled the area in which the epic takes place. In this version of the epic they form, respectively, the three orders of Elder, Middle, and Lesser Lineages of the tribe.

195. Prosperous Wealth Enclosure of the River Ma (Tib. *rma gyang nor gyi ra ba*): The river Ma, or Yellow River as it is known today, has always been referred to as a river of wealth, a treasure of prosperity.

196. Modern-day historians of the Gesar epic have made two assertions concerning the term Kyidsö (*skyid sos*), "happiness and leisure" (taking *sos* as short for *sos dal,* "leisure"). One is that this is the name of an area in eastern Tibet that is close to the Shechen Monastery. Tsab Tsa Kuchen Pakya Rinpoche built a temple to Gesar and his warriors on the site that is said to be the birthplace of Gesar. However, though the name of the place is logical, according to geography and the locale of the Ma River, it is not possible that this could be the correct location. Another assertion is that the term *skyid sos* simply refers to Gesar's birthplace in terms of the qualities of the land rather than the geographical location. His Holiness Jigme Phuntsog recognized the palace of Gesar to be close to the Ma River. *See* glossary: Kyidsö Yag-gi Khado.

197. "Paternal and maternal families" (Tib. *rus* and *rigs*): Tibetan nobility can name two sorts of family lineages. One, the *rus,* or bone lineage, relates to the line of paternal descent. The

other, the *rigs,* is a more inclusive term for family but is often used to refer to the tribe, clan, or family of the mother.

198. "Changmoza" (Tib. *spyang mo bza'*): Ordinarily *za* would mean that this wife's natal family was Chang, literally "the family of the wolf." Here, however, the word "wolf" (Tib. *spyang*) probably does not refer to the father's family but instead to the fact that she is descended from the Lesser Lineage of Ling. The founder of the Lesser Lineage married a grandson of the founder of the Mukpo family. In some versions she married Lama Phen (Tib. *bla ma 'phen*), the son of founder Ratra (Tib. *ra kra*). In other versions she married Chöphen Nagpo, another grandson. In any case, she was given her name based on the fact that she found a wolf's tail as a totemic object when she was sent on a quest to Lower Ling by her grandfather. Thus she came to be known as Changza (Tib. *spyang bza'*), "the wolf wife." Apparently the mother of Chipön, Trogyal, and Senglön is a descendant of Changza and belongs to the Mu family of the Lesser lineage. And according to this version of the epic, she is a daughter of a mountain god named Dzagyal Dorje Phenchug (Tib. *rdza rgyal rdo rje phen phyug*). This is confusing, because there is a myth in which the three lineages of the Mukpo clan are based on three granddaughters of Ratra, who are descended from Mount Magyal Pomra. This is three generations too early to be Muza, the mother of Senglön, the paternal grandmother of Gesar. The confusion may come from a lacuna in the oldest version of this text.

199. In some versions of the epic these three brothers are sons of three different wives, all married to Chöla Bum (Tib. *'chos la bum*). The three wives come respectively from the Rong, Ga, and Mu families. Thus Senglön's mother is Muza, the wife from Mu.

200. Usually the nāgas are represented as having four castes, which are the same as the Indian castes: the baronial or royal caste (Tib. *rgyal rigs*), the brahmans (Tib. *'bram ze*), the merchants (Tib. *rje'u*), and the low caste (Tib. *gdol ba*), the untouchables.

201. "Tibet" (Tib. *bod*) here refers to central Tibet—that is, Ü and Tsang—perhaps as if to say that the Yarlung River valley, the home of the ancient kings of Tibet, is quintessential Tibet.

202. Padmasambhava is engaging in word play in order to "create a *rten 'brel*"; that is, in order to create an auspicious connection through a kind of pun-magic. First the words *happiness* and *leisure* are used as descriptions, and then they become part of the proper name for the region, Kyidsö, happiness and leisure or ease. The name of this valley is Kyidsö Yag-gi Khado. *Kyidsö* (Tib. *skyid sos*), "happiness and leisure," Yag-gi a nominalizing term, and *Khado* (Tib. *kha mdo*) is a geographical term that refers to a place where two valleys meet or where the upper and lower parts of a valley or canyon come together. *Kha* can also mean the open end of a valley, and *do* (Tib. *mdo*) the closed end of the valley. The upper open end of the valley, the *kha*, is a place called *skyid*, happiness. The lower end, the closed end of the valley, the *mdo,* is a place called *sos*, leisure or relaxation. The place where these two geographical features meet is the *khado*, the conjunction of the two parts of the valley or the conjunction of two valleys.

203. The Tibetan, *mdun ru smon lam brag dkar yod,* would give, "In front is Aspiration White Boulder." However, here *ru* ("in") is a misspelling and should be *ri* ("mountain"), giving us *ri smon lam*, Aspiration Prayer Mountain.

204. "Six powers" (Tib. *rtsal drug*): literally, "the six skills"; things such as fangs, claws, courage, the lion's ability to leap, and so forth.

205. Tibetan iconic dragons are shown holding a jewel in their claws. This is the wish-granting gem, which gives the dragon his magical powers, such as the power to fly. When the dragon grows old, he cannot hold his jewel anymore and it drops from his claws, forcing him to become a mere sea monster such as a *chu srin*, a makara.

206. "Does not burn terribly" (Tib. *kha ru tsha*; literally, "hot to the mouth"): Often in Indic literature, poison burns. In theory, the peacock eats poison without harm. The poison gives the colorful "eyes" in the tails of peacocks their unique luster.

207. "Tarbu berry"(Tib. *star bu*): The sea-buckthorn (*Hippophae rhamnoides*); an edible orange-colored berry that grows in the highlands of Golog and is used to polish tarnished silver.

208. "Enemy" in this context does not simply mean a person who preaches against Buddhism, but a demon who seeks to eradicate the religion by killing its adherents and enslaving their tribes.

209. The brilliance of this stratagem lies in the fact that this kind of pollution (Tib. *mnol*) is the classical irritant that excites the wrath of the dragons or nāgas. As spirits of water, they represent the prehuman purity of the environment. They react against the stains typical of human habitation such as fetid smoke, the smell of rotten meat, human excreta in streams, or the occult pollution created by acts of violence and bloodshed. Padma's use of black magic to pollute their realm is the perfect attack on the nāgas' peace of mind.

210. Literally, the Tibetan *'og ma klu* refers to "subterranean nāgas": The nāgas live in water, which is considered to be the lower realm, beneath the earth. Tibetans believe, as a matter of fact, that beneath the earth is water throughout, and therefore the nāgas can live throughout the world beneath the earth, not just where there are visible bodies of water.

211. The Tibetan, *mgo bo par la zhog,* literally means, "the beginning of this song is sent far away." Usually a song begins with an auspicious or happy beginning, but today they are sad and worried and skip the evocation of happy sentiment.

212. Without a boundary or some other excrescence, there is nothing on which a bird could land in this treeless land. The argument of the proverb seems to be simply that the nāgas must have done something wrong, otherwise they would not be suffering now.

213. A strange three-line proverb that means "there must be a reason for our suffering."

214. The dawn is the nāga child, and it is led by the sun, the nāga king, Tsugna Rinchen. The nāga child is helpless not to obey his command, just as light, lead by the sun, must suffuse the world.

215. The original text has an error: *seng* ("lion") should be *sang*, then *kar sang* is "yesterday."

216. "Blood relatives": The Tibetan, *sha phu nu,* literally means "flesh relatives"; *phu nu* means something like "elder and younger brother" or "brother and cousin." But it is used to indicate a general relationship of being sworn kinsmen. Sometimes there is a *phu nu* relationship between two people not related by marriage or blood, the phrase simply indicating that they are as loyal to each other as blood relatives would be. Here the dragon child is saying that the race or species known as *nyen*, the mountain gods, may dwell in the middle world between heaven and earth, while the *lu*, the dragons, live in the earth below—nevertheless, they are kin, as we would say, "blood brothers."

217. The Tibetan, *ma mthun dgu mthun,* literally means "nothing accords many (nine) accord." It means that they are naturally in accord without any external cause.

218. Another strange expression of the same form as "nothing accords many (nine) accord": The Tibetan is *rtsa rtsi thog mi skye dgu skye.*

219. The term *grib* in Tibetan that appears here in the original can be understood in many different ways. Here we are translating it according to the result that has occurred, that of deadly disease. The term literally means to render something impure or obscured so that it is no longer clean or clear. This comes about due to root causes and contributing circumstances that are based upon concepts and superstition.

220. An error in the original text here gives the Tibetan as *stong,* "one thousand," when it should be *sdong,* meaning "grooved."

221. This passage, like most of the nāga chapter, has a tone of authorial sarcasm. The divination, of course, is completely fake in these circumstances. Padmasambhava has already secretly ordered the diviner to give a specific divination, no matter what the signs and augury might actually suggest. The bard is probably making fun of the way Tibetans superstitiously ask for a mo, a divination, whenever they must make a serious decision. In fact, this is a characteristic of Buddhist practitioners throughout North Asia.

222. Pronounced "so," this exclamation is actually spelled *bswo.* It is a native Tibetan mantric sound, a sign of Bön or non-Buddhist religion. It may originate from a sort of yodel or victory cry that Tibetans give when they have reached the summit of a mountain: *ki! ki! so! so!* The fact that the Tibetan *bswo* contains so many silent letters is a sign of its antiquity and native origins. This is particularly so in the case of the "w," which is almost never sounded in modern speech. This song is a showcase of Bön and native Tibetan religion, with its many bizarre and anachronistic words: *chwa,* spelled *phywa, or yel,* spelled *dbal.* It strikes the ear much the way references to Celtic literature and culture would in a Walter Scott novel and gives a sort of gothic sense to the passage.

223. "Yel, Thor, and Dar"(Tib. *dbal, 'thor,* and *bdar*): In the Bön religion these are three clans (*ru*) of gods who incarnate to fight demons out of compassion for sentient beings.

224. *Ibid.,* endnote 215.

225. Although the nāgas are high and magical creatures, paradoxically they still belong technically to the animal realm. They are the highest of the animals, but still animals.

226. Padmasambhava is pretending that the bodhisattva of compassion is his guru and has sent him into retreat. There in his cave he is virtuously practicing and can't attend to worldly affairs.

227. An error in the original text here gives the Tibetan as *dad* ("faith"); it should be *'ded,* or *ded,* meaning "pursue."

228. "The wealth god" (Tib. *dkor bdag*): An epithet of Kubera, the Indic god of wealth. The central term in this section of the song is *dkor,* which means wealth and riches in general but is also used to refer to monks and religious people who consume religious offerings for their own wealth. This section describes people who use religious terms to appropriate personal riches. They give sermons on compassion but only work for their own good. They invoke deities such as Kubera and the dharma protectors, but just for their own minor benefit.

229. "Oath-bound protectors" (Tib. *bka' srung*), perhaps also could be translated "the guardians of the word." These are the deities called dharma protectors, wrathful deities who have been deputized by enlightened beings to protect practitioners in their dharma practice. Padma sarcastically describes false gurus calling on these protectors

for worldly things instead of the essentially mental or spiritual protection these deities truly offer.

230. "Philosophical dialectics" (Tib. *grub mtha'*), literally, "philosophical tenet systems." This is a translation of the Sanskrit term *siddhānta*. Half the study of Buddhist metaphysics is devoted to learning classical and systematic descriptions of philosophical systems that developed in India and were elaborated in Tibetan schools of philosophical dialectics. In this verse we see a learned lama who upholds one siddhānta and harshly criticizes others, with the result that when he or she meditates they contemplate mere points of philosophical debate and develop emotionality over issues of doctrine, a detour from the path of enlightenment that aims for equanimity.

231. "When training in the completion stage, to have a focal point" (Tib. *sbyangs na rdzogs rim dmigs gtad can*): In the developing stage of meditation one focuses the mind on religious visualizations. But in the completion stage one is supposed to meditate resting in openness without having a visualized focal object. This raises a problem sometimes, for there are yogic practices in the completion state that involve control of psychic energies and channels inside the body. Sometimes meditators fail to work directly with these channels and instead simply visualize or imagine them. Padma could be saying that concentrating too much on such visualizations in this case is a mistake.

232. Remorse is one of the stages in the Buddhist act of confession, which if properly done, sincerely and in a timely manner, may bring a remedy to evil deeds. But at the moment of death it is too late for remorse to operate as one of the powers of confession, for the power of remorse is itself karmic and has a greater effect on the future than the present. Meanwhile, when you are dying, Yama, the god of death, is appearing: conditions far in the past are already in the act of ripening.

233. Here Padma's song takes a turn the nāgas must have been dreading. It is comforting to hear a lama denigrate material possessions. It makes him sound unworldly and harmless. On the other hand, as wealth-hoarding magical beings, what the nāgas fear most is the typical rapacious lama whose spirituality is a mere pose. Such a man will charge them dearly for his services as an exorcist. In this song Padmasambhava seems to perfectly fulfill that stereotype.

234. The word translated as "golden river" here is *gser ldan*, literally, "the gold-bearing." This refers poetically to the Tibetan notion that broad rivers have bits of golden sand in them.

235. "Go wherever he wants" (Tib. *brgya 'gro stong 'gro*): Literally, "go a hundred paces or a thousand paces."

236. The following section is meant to be humorous and probably seems as ridiculous to a Tibetan as it does to the Western reader. Padma has come to cure the kingdom of a plague he secretly started. The nāga king, like all dragons, is attached to wealth. Padma plays the part of a typical corrupt lama who gives pious sermons about self-denial and then expects extravagant fees to pay for the rituals he performs. He is pompous and prolix until the moment comes to bargain for his stipend. Then his language becomes earthy, almost vulgar. The best joke is the sense of irony the reader shares with the bard, for we know that Padma is actually beyond greed, but must play to the nāga's expectations in order to achieve his goals.

237. "Are you exhausted from your journey?" (Tib. *byon si phebs si 'o re rgyal*) is a very formal idiomatic expression. Tsugna Rinchen's short speech here is very flowery and stylized. It

contrasts nicely with the informal, village style of speech that has humorously accompanied most meetings so far in this epic.

238. Actually, the following verses read more like formal Indic court poetry rather than Tibetan songs. They are full of extended metaphors that can be read at several levels and use classical imagery. And like everything the nāgas say, there are constant references to a nāga sense of reality: the elemental world of water, mountains, and cycles of nature.

239. As a guardian deity, a zodor is the local proprietor of the region, an "earth lord." If the zodor becomes angered by pollution or mistreatment of his locality, he may punish the people who live there with hailstorms that destroy their barley crops and harm their livestock.

240. Zodors can become touchy and irritable if the environment is polluted or mistreated. In this stanza the dharmapālas are regarded as being similarly reactive. Tsugna imagines the anger of such local deities could be the cause of the epidemic. It is interesting, because, if such an epidemic were to happen to humans, they might very well attribute it to the irritability of nāgas.

241. This probably refers to ransoming (Tib. *bslu*) ceremonies, in which a shaman or Buddhist priest cures a person's illness by offering the spirits a ransom for the return of the person's stolen life essence.

242. Obviously one should cook an animal's head first and only then remove the tongue to eat it. Furthermore, Tibetan dinners usually include a noodle soup. One should evidently eat the noodles before finishing the broth. "*Ki! ki!*" is a Tibetan shout equivalent to "hurray." Apparently there is a proper way to do that, too.

243. "All this I need for my preparations." Padma has given a list of the offering substances that must be collected to perform this part of the ceremony: offering water filled with medicines (that is, herbs), the kind of precious stones a nāga could acquire, five kinds of milk, a rare conch that swirls in the opposite direction from most, an offering cake made in the shape of a lotus, and two objects used for divination: a divination board and a ritual divination arrow. Some of these offerings are reminiscent of the special offerings made in ceremonies to pacify attacks by nāgas who have been infuriated by human pollution.

244. This ceremony has the form of a lhasang (Tib. *lha bsang*), a smoke purification practice. A white column of smoke is produced and used to purify objects that have been polluted with "obscurations." The aim of the ceremony is to cure the nāgas of the poison that has polluted their realm. But in the ritual liturgy Padma chants, he allegorizes the impurity, the poisoning of their waters, so that the real poisons are the so-called poisons of the emotions, the kleśas.

245. When a disciple enters into a tantric practice often there is an empowerment, and as part of that ceremony one receives a tutelary deity, a form of the buddha with whom the disciple identifies. This deity is chosen seemingly by chance: The disciple throws a flower into a mandala of deities, and his or her tutelary deity will be the buddha on whom the flower falls.

246. Although the reference in the original is to the black-haired Tibetans (Tib. *bod dbu nag*), we have interpreted it to be a reference to the nāgas, since that is the context. Perhaps the bard made a mistaken reference to the Tibetans at the juncture.

247. They are laughing because the low-caste nāga was so bold. People always make fun of the low caste—this is the nāga equivalent of ethnic slur jokes.

248. "Slightly darker" (Tib. *sha tsa sno shad*): Literally, "tinged with blue," but actually the phrase means almost "olive-complexioned."

249. A Tibetan maiden wears her entire dowry on her body in the form of gold, silver, and precious stones. She dresses this way for special occasions and when she goes traveling to her new family by marriage. We see an example of this in volume 3, when Drugmo wears her wealth as she goes looking for Gesar, her fiancé.

250. Now Tsugna Rinchen is speaking prophetically with apparently full knowledge of the cosmic situation. The drala nyen who will be born among humans is Gesar, whose father is regarded as a nyen, a mountain god.

251. In some versions of Tibetan cosmology, the original kings of Tibet and the leaders of the Tibetan people descended from the Mu (Tib. *dmu*), primordial Tibetan sky gods. The first king was actually a god who was lowered to earth via a cord attached to the crown of his head, the *mu* cord. Since then the column of smoke that rises during a juniper smoke cleansing offering is called "the Mu cord." Thus, "holding the celestial (Mu) cord" means that Gesar will be a divinely appointed king.

252. This refers to a symbolic field of protection that will surround her, and she will remain unscathed as though having donned armor.

VOLUME TWO. GESAR'S BIRTH AND CHILDHOOD

1. The Tibetan, *'jig tshogs lta ba*, literally means "view of the transitory collection as real." The transitory collection is the five skandhas, the components of self, which are, of course, impermanent and empty of self-nature.

2. In Buddhist mythology, the Sindhu River flows from Lake Anavatapta, or Manasarovar as it is also called. There Padmasambhava first tamed the nāgas. It is associated historically with the now-lost Saraswati River, which was an important part of the ancient Indus civilization in India.

3. These four lines signify that Gesar is an emanation of Guru Rinpoche [Padmākara], Trisong Deutsen [the king referred to as "the flower of the god Brahmā of the snow land of Tibet"], and the current king of the northern pure land Shambhala [Rigden Raudracakrin].

4. This is a story about a person who developed wrong view based on misunderstanding about authentic spiritual teachers and so took rebirth as a suffering nāga.

5. The rūpakāya is the enlightened body of form, which refers to the sambhogakāya and nirmanakāya, as these two kāyas appear according to the phenomena of beings. *See* glossary: bodies of the Buddha, three.

6. "Authentic historical accounts": This could be an important claim for the oral sources of the epic. Here is the precise Tibetan: *rtogs par brjod pa sngon gyi lo rgyus khungs can rnams la ji ltar grags pa bzhin*—literally, "as I have proclaimed this avadāna just like the previous stories, which are original sources."

7. In Tibetan there are actually four volumes or accounts of the epic that are being put together here in one book. Those four are the *lha gling* [Divine Land of Ling]. Combined together are the *'khrungs gling* [Birth in Ling] and the *rma sa bzung* [Settling of Ma], which are really two separate volumes, and finally the *rta rgyug* [Horse Race].

8. "Intelligence and knowledge" (Tib. *blo shes*): This refers specifically to practical intelligence, what we call in our urban culture being "streetwise."

9. "His was the final word" translates a colorful Tibetan expression, *blo phug*—literally, intellect's (Tib. *blo*) cave or recess (Tib. *phug*); what we call "innermost mind."

10. "General of all bandits" (Tib. *jag gi dmag dpon*): In the culture of the Golog region of northeastern Tibet, banditry is an honorable profession.

11. "Like a falcon" (Tib. *rgya khra hor pa*): Literally, it seems to say "like a Mongolian bird of prey," taking *rgya khra* as "bird of prey" and *hor pa* as "Mongolian."

12. An error in the original text here gives the Tibetan as *sbom*; it should be *spom*, to make the proper name Magyal Pomra.

13. An error in the original text here gives the Tibetan as *'phan* (ribbon); it should be *phan* (benefit).

14. "White turquoise" (Tib. *drug dkar*): The highest quality turquoise. If you put a drop of milk on it, it turns the milk pink, which is a sign of its high quality. We don't know what the other five orders of turquoise are.

15. The fish Trawa Kha comes up at different times during the epic and other ancient stories. It is uncertain how one can understand how this relates to the scarf, but it may be an item that is made from some parts of the fish guts. *See* next endnote.

16. According to the story, in the land of Hor there was a famous river called Khampa Zhungdrug [Murky River of the Six Districts]. There was a bridge across this river guarded by a fish named *nya dpral ba kha che*, which would give Trelwa Khache. The name of the fish is spelled both ways but the common one is *nya dpral ba kha che* [Huge Forehead and Gaping Mouth]. Here in the text we have *spra ba kha*, which is another, less common, spelling of the name of that fish and gives Trawa Kha.

17. We have added a few words to a cryptic passage. Chipön is explaining why the Mukpo clan is divided into three clans, which they call "lineages" (Tib. *rgyud*). The three lineages descend from the three wives of a single ancestor. They are distinguished as Lesser, Middle, or Greater based on their respective ages or it may be the order in which they were acquired in marriage.

18. "Harrying from behind": The Tibetan *ltag bdud* is a colorful expression that literally means "nape demon": a māra or demon who attacks from behind the nape of the enemy's neck. It fits neatly with the previous epithet regarding a "yoke" (Tib. *gnya' non*, "yoke that presses down").

19. These three terms, masculine metal, feminine metal, and the metal of their offspring, are literal translations of the Tibetan (*pho lcags, mo lcags, bu lcags*), but also likely refer to different grades of iron used in fashioning sword blades. The masculine would be coarser less refined steel, the feminine finer and more ductile steel, and the offspring a combination of both the male and the female. A sword blade generally has a softer iron core, and a harder steel (iron forged with varying amounts of carbon) edge and point which, combined, give it flexibility as well as strength.

20. Tibetan has *rlung khri* "wind sword." It could be a misspelling of *klung khri* which would mean "river blade."

21. "Spoken of by the rest of the world": The Tibetan, *brgya sdes bshad*, means literally "told by the hundred districts."

22. Zhalkar is embarrassed by the beggar woman because his relatives could not bear to give him bad news. This is not unusual behavior among the nomads of northeastern Tibet, who live by word of mouth. The song with which Zhalkar attacks his uncle, Chipön,

criticizes the tendency of political leaders to keep things secret, which he sees as a sign of corruption. On the other hand, the ability to keep a secret is a prime virtue in a culture whose principal religion is esoteric Buddhism.

23. Zhalkar refers here to events that preceded this chapter of the epic. Lenpa Chögyal is actually Zhalkar's cousin, but he calls him his elder brother. Apparently he married a woman from one of the tribes of the Yellow Hor, Zima-tso, the daughter of one Künga. Zhalkar claims that this outlander brought bad luck into his family. He calls her a prostitute and demands that she be returned to Hor. Although marriages in the epic are nearly always exogamous, numerous rituals surround the importation of a wife from another clan. She may bring with her alien clan spirits, which function as demons in her new family.

24. "Ninefold revenge" (Tib. *sha lan dgu skor len*): The Tibetan *sha lan* literally means "flesh price." It is the blood price extracted for personal injuries. A blood price is usually an amount of money or cattle given as restitution for an injury or injustice. Here it seems to be a matter of life for life. Zhalkar is demanding, metaphorically, that nine people die for the single death of his cousin. Actually, however, he is asking for more. The army of Ling has already killed most of the male population of Gog. Zhalkar is demanding that the rest of the people be killed. As Chipön is about to argue, it is an immoderate demand, but not totally outside the scope of punishment in nomadic law. Whatever injury or violation of treaty inspired the first Ling raid on Gog—that crime has been paid for with the death of the Gog warriors. In the process a Ling prince was killed. This, Zhalkar argues, is an additional injury and must be paid for with an additional *sha lan*.

25. Chipön's speech to Zhalkar, which follows, is a classic example of a chief diplomatically moderating the hot blood of a young brave. He would rather not conduct another raid on Gog, a raid whose only aim would be to wipe out Ralo Tönpa's village and the women and children of the eighteen tribes. But Zhalkar's grievance is legitimate; he lost face because Chipön withheld vital information from him. Chipön's compromise is to propose that the whole clan accompany Zhalkar on a second mission to Gog, but this time with no immoderate killing. Instead, he proposes that they kill no one, but rather that they rob Ralo Tönpa of his new wife and her magical dowry. He politically proposes that the theft be celebrated as Zhalkar's maiden-raiding expedition. He backs up his argument with quotes from the Mukpo book of prophecies called the Mother Text, arguing that this less violent undertaking is fated and part of Zhalkar's special destiny.

26. Chipön believes this cryptic couplet from the Mother Text is a coded prophecy about their upcoming raid on Gog. The "jewel" mentioned in the verse is the nāga princess. Nāgas possess a jewel in their forehead. "Victory banner" refers to Ralo Tönpa Gyaltsen's full name; Gyaltsen means "victory banner." The "pinnacle" refers to the fact that the nāga princess took with her the best of the nāga kingdom's treasures. "Mouse" refers to the year of the Mouse—the year that Gyatsha will actually go and fight Gog and win the princess. "White" here refers to White Ling, whose wishes will be fulfilled by the raiding expedition, because on a raid on Gog they will gain the nāga princess, and she will give birth to the new king of Ling, Gesar.

27. The action here becomes somewhat complex, despite the compactness of the narrative. The young warriors find that Ralo Tönpa has hastily struck his tents and fled, leaving only cushions for seats and beds on the ground. Finding no loot, they think to return to Ling, but Chipön stops them, saying that Ling never returns empty-handed from a raid.

He then asks Senglön, Gesar's future father, to do an arrow divination in order to determine their next step. Senglön's reading is somewhat cryptic, but it seems to say that they should stay, for thus they will gain great wealth without even fighting. Trothung, as usual, misunderstands the prophecy and thinks it means that there will be no booty today, but in the long run the wealth of Ralo, including the nāga princess, will all fall to his clan of Tag-rong. He therefore proposes that Senglön be given whatever they find that day as his fee for the divination (thinking this will be nothing).

Chipön, who is of the Lesser Lineage of Mukpo just like Senglön, quickly accepts Trothung's proposal, realizing that in this way the prophecies will be fulfilled, and his family will get Gesar and his mother's wealth.

He therefore proposes that they continue to search for booty in Gog. He then orders Sengtag Adom, who serves as a priest for practices of the local religion, to perform a smoke offering and purification while they serve tea.

28. A support (*rten*) is an object that has a symbolic value and is the ritual basis for magical ceremonies. It is often a scepter or religious icon to which a spirit may be invited or in which a spirit may reside. Sengtag Adom is a *rten mkhar*, a castle (that is, a temple) which is a support for the dralas of White Ling. *See* glossary: support.

29. One of the functions of the dralas is to land on the head, shoulders, and heart of a warrior, strengthening his or her body and defending the body's energy field. When the juniper smoke forms a white column rising into the sky, it acts to invite dralas, who descend down the column and take their positions as protectors on the bodies of the officiates. Thus all the soldiers of Ling will now perform together this lhasang, this smoke purification ceremony, in order to reinvest their persons with the blessings of the dralas.

30. Here the hearth is a metaphor for the female buddha of the element of earth (Buddhalocana). Having created a hearth with the goddess of earth and a liquid to be offered with the goddess of water (Māmakī), we place substances in the liquid and melt them down into further liquid with the goddess of fire (Pāṇḍaravāsinī). Samayatārā is the goddess of wind. The wind blows across the flames and kindles them to blaze higher.

31. This is a speculative translation: Literally the Tibetan seems to say that White Ling and the lha have *mnyam chas*, that is, equal appurtenances.

32. Here already she is given the name she will keep for the rest of the epic, Gogza, the wife from Gog. Even though they simply adopted her into their tribe, she is regarded as a family member now, meaning that when she marries Senglön, this will draw Gog, Ralo Tönpa's homeland, politically closer to Ling again.

33. The idea here is that since she originates in the nāga country, this human realm is not her native home and the loyalties of humans for each other are not exactly her loyalties. So she might as well tell the truth, even if it betrays the Gog people.

34. "Went out for a stroll" (Tib. *skyo sangs*): an interesting expression that literally means a "sadness cleansing." But here *sangs* stands for a break or a brief holiday. Sometimes in the winter, when Tibetans are feeling bored and claustrophobic, they will go out on a "sadness cleansing" walkabout or solitary hike. It may simply be leaving the house and walking around for a while or it may be a more extensive holiday walk.

35. Even though exogamous marriage is the custom, and wives tend to be from other tribes, there seems to be a culturally instilled distrust among nomads of these women—who come from other families and must switch their loyalties. In a country where neighboring

pastoralist groups are constantly raiding each other, questioning whether a recent arrival from another family is good or bad is a conventional and sensible precaution.

36. The tent is named *sbris tshe bse ru ltag kha ma*. The term *sbris tshe* means 'little tent' and the term *bse ru* is based on the tent's color which is dark brown like the horn of a rhinoceros. The term *ltag kha ma* means that the tent is pitched behind that of Gyaza, it is the tent that is to the back side. This name also evokes the jealousy that Gyaza feels for the new woman (the nāginī) who has arrived. The fact that the little tent was pitched to the back is meant to indicate that Gyaza is still the woman in charge of the household.

37. All along the Tibetan editor of the early woodblock edition that gave rise to this particular version has had before him several different editions of this volume of the epic, his job being to choose among them the version he found most correct. At this point he has had to change the text so much that he feels at odds with the previous editions before him and feels compelled to correct them. But rather than starting new controversies by discussing the weaknesses of the other editions and his specific reasons for changing the edition, he will just present his corrected version and move on—for the epic is a dharma text, and he does not wish to create doubts in it that would put stumbling blocks in the way of the faithful.

38. "Their own karmic mandate" (Tib. *rang gi bskos thang red*): a karmically appointed naturally process, the same as *las skal*, the karmic portion that falls to an individual. It functions like the term "fate" or "destiny" in Western languages, but has a different material explanation, since one's las *skal* is a certain way not because of the will of a higher being, and not as the result of natural physical processes, but as a result of previous karma.

39. "Another spin of his hapless brain" (Tib. *klad gcig 'khor*): A "spinning head" means a moment when a person does a foolish thing because they are distracted and duped. It is difficult to say why the nāga king suddenly makes these two finely honed critiques. Perhaps his point is that Gogmo should not seek to avoid her karmically mandated fate, the way a lama might sacrifice his comfortable situation in order to chase women or a warrior ignore the wealth he has inherited in order to steal a goat.

40. The garuḍa is a giant magical bird who figures in the first volume of the Indian epic the *Mahābhārata*. His egg takes ages to hatch, but when it does, the garuḍa arises completely mature, possessed of all his powers. He is a symbol for enlightenment that arises not gradually but full-blown in the consciousness of a confused practitioner.

In the *Mahābhārata*, the garuḍa's mother has two children, both egg-born. She broods over both eggs, impatient that they may hatch so that she will have children to support her in a power struggle with her co-wife. She impatiently cracks open one of the eggs. It contains a powerful god, who would have been her protector if she had waited for him to mature in the egg. Instead, he is half-formed and departs for heaven. Having learned her lesson, she therefore waits for the other egg to hatch in its own time. It produces the garuḍa, a being powerful enough to fight all the gods at once.

41. This line says that Gesar will not need the traditional ritual protections that mothers ordinarily undertake to ensure the well-being of their newborns. Literally it says that the three thoughts of "protection (Tib. *srung*), demons (Tib. *sri*), and modesty (Tib. *'dzem bag*)" are a mother's apprehensions.

The word *sri*, pronounced *si*, in this context refers to a certain type of demon. Ordinarily si demons are murderous invisible spirits of various kinds, which visit their destruction cyclically. One kind of si acts as a family curse, visiting the same destruction generation after generation on descendants. *See* glossary: si demons.

Tibetan mothers are sedulous to protect their children from such evil forces. The term *'dzem*, refraining, and *'dzem bag*, modesty, may refer particularly here to the activity of avoiding curses and pollution that might be spread by objects or by attracting to the child the wrong kind of attention from the spirit world. For example, articles of clothing that have been worn by an unfortunate person may be charged with negative energy of some kind, and so a mother would be careful not to allow her children in contact with such infected articles.

42. In other words, forgo the usual birthday parties and special observances that would focus attention on the child.

43. When a child or a foal is first born, it is given a morsel of warm butter to soften its palate.

44. Because the guru has blessed her, she has no need of ordinary comforts and necessities, but wears instead, as they say, "the food and clothing of samādhi."

45. "Masang Norbu Dradül" (Tib. *sku masang rdo rje dgra 'dul*) is a name for Gesar. It literally means something like "the honorable Masang Jewel Tamer of Enemies." (*See* glossary: Norbu Dradül.) In other words, while sleeping with her husband, Senglön, Drugmo dreamed that she spent the evening making love to a high status mountain deity named Gedzo, who thus became the spiritual father of Gesar in his human incarnation. Then Gesar "blessed her womb"—that is, resided there in her womb until he was born as a human child.

46. It's clear from the context that this means that Gesar had entered her womb and was now dwelling there. Therefore, Gesar has two parents in this situation: Senglön, his earthly father, and Gedzo, the father who made love to Gogmo in her dream. An "immeasurable palace" is the exalted dwelling of a deity in a Buddhist mandala.

47. In other words, Gesar experienced in the womb the exact opposite of ordinary human experience, which, according to Buddhist texts, is excruciatingly painful. The Tibetan word we translate as "delighting" literally means that he "played" (Tib. *rol pa*) there, indicating the spontaneity buddhas experience and by which they live, in contrast to the conditioned state of suffering ordinary beings experience.

48. Each of these ḍākinīs intentionally took rebirth in the different lands surrounding Ling. In that way they could assist the godling to accomplish his enlightened deeds once he became Gesar of Ling. His companions are Küntar, Chödrön from Hor, and Bumkyid from Düd. These are the lands that Gesar will conquer in future epics.

49. This foreshadows an event in later volume of the epic that recounts the battles of Hor and Ling; after he returns from Düd and has defeated the evil king Gurkar, Gesar and his warriors place the golden saddle on Gurkar's neck in order to humiliate this former king.

50. This poison is a toxic alkaloid produced in the tuberous root of the wolfsbane (*Aconitum vulparia*) plant. It has cardiac and neurologic toxicity, causing cardiovascular depression, paresthesias, vomiting, and ultimately respiratory arrest.

51. This refers to a proverb: When a lamb dies, it goes to the door of the wolves' den. When a person dies, he or she will go to the door of the rākṣasas.

52. The splendor of the torma is its power, which comes from the deities who guide the torma and go along with it when it is flung. Fire and wind refer to the natural power, which is instilled into the torma as the power of the elements—a result of the meditator's practice focused on the torma.

53. Since Trothung believes Joru's disguise as Amnye, and then thinks that Amnye killed Joru, he wonders if the power (that is, the black magic) of the vengeful gods of Ling is affecting Amnye, and that's why he seems different. If this were true, then soon this black magic power would cause Amnye's death.

54. The term "three skills" here does not refer to three specific skills but rather to the idea of fully developed maturation and power.

55. "Ram grass" (Tib. *ram pa*), also called conch grass, is a short grass with a small fuzzy white seed-head that matures to red and then is filled with many tiny round seeds, resembling mustard seeds.

56. At other times Atag Lumo is called Atag Lhumo. This is just a difference in spelling her name as *a stag klu mo* (nāginī) or *a stag lha mo* (goddess). She was a great archer and the foremost female warrior of Ling. She started out as an inhabitant of Düd but then became a warrior of Ling. She was a great hunter and a bodhisattva who could slay and liberate simultaneously. There are prophecies about her in the sutra of Lord Buddha concerning the Eighty Mighty Warriors. Atag Lhamo never broke samaya with Gesar even for a second; she was also a consort of Gesar.

57. Mongolian: An error in the original text here gives the Tibetan as *sogs* (and so forth); it should be *sog* (Mongolian).

58. Forest: An error in the original text here gives the Tibetan as Tib. *nag* (black); it should be *nags* (forest).

59. This is the valley that Khenpo Jigme Phuntsog (1933–2004) recognized as the original site of Gesar's palace, Sengtrug Tagtse, and now a Gesar shrine and Rigden temple have been built on this site which is nearby the Ma River (Yellow River).

    Khenpo Jigme Phuntsog was a Nyingma master with great realization and incomparable knowledge of dharma. Due to his efforts during his life the monastic traditions were revived and reestablished, particularly that of the Nyingma Order.

60. *Ibid.,* endnote 58.

61. The ḍākinī is giving indications of what will transpire. The idea is that they will exile Joru to the Ma Valley as a form of punishment. In the three years that he will remain there, a great snowstorm will come to Ling forcing the inhabitants to move or else all people and animals will die. Because of these events all the inhabitants of Kham, where Joru was born, will be forced to move to the Ma Valley, where he has been exiled. Mention of the white conch stupa refers to Gesar and the adornment of the five-colored scarf refers to the warriors who will finally come there to join him. The term *rong* means "farmer" and this indicates that the inhabitants of his birth land were of the class of farmers who must then come to the land of nomads which is Ma.

62. Saying "Gogmo's Joru" is a way of insulting Joru, calling him a "mommy's boy." It is not that Chipön himself is insulting Joru, but he is taking on the tone of the villagers in referring to Joru.

63. The names Yongdzom (Tib. *yong 'dzoms,* "gathering place") and Yangdzom (Tib. *yang 'dzoms,* "meet again") have similar meanings as a place where people gather, but Yongdzom refers to a place where people gather to see someone off and say farewell, whereas Yangdzom is more auspicious and implies a place where "we'll meet again soon."

64. "Rising patterns within a skullcup" refer to the river-like imprints that through the course of a lifetime are carved on the inside of the skull by blood vessels that traverse the dura mater, the outermost layer of the meningeal covering of the brain.

65. In Tibet, a bride's family does not give a dowry, instead the husband's family gives gifts. After the marriage, the bride assumes control of her new household, and her life and its outcome are bound to that of her husband and his family.

66. "Min-drug Dawa" (Tib. *smin drug zla ba*): Literally, *smin drug* is the "ripened six" and refers to the Pleiades, and *zla ba* is the moon. The moon of the Pleiades is the four weeks between the full moon of the ninth month and that of the tenth month—that is, the second half of the ninth month and the first half of the tenth month. In the lunar calendar, this is approximately late November–early December.

67. In the practice called *chöd* or "cutting through," the identification with the ego and body is meant to be severed as the view of emptiness is sustained and the consciousness ejected out of the crown aperture to become a wisdom kāya in the space in front. Then the corporeal body is blessed and offered, to become whatever is desired by those who will partake of it.

68. An error in the original text here gives the Tibetan as *kha,* "mouth"; it should be *mkha',* "sky."

69. In general, farmlands are less likely to be snow-covered.

70. An error in the original text here gives the Tibetan as *pho nga,* meaning "weak"; it should be *phong,* meaning "no matter how many."

71. The slingshot is an important tool and weapon for the nomads of Golog. Here we see the significance in terms of how the original slingshots were made and kept sacred.

72. We have adjusted the locations given in this and the following paragraph, as the geography is inaccurate in the Tibetan text.

73. An error in the original text here gives the Tibetan as *sen*; it should be *ser,* meaning "golden."

74. An error in the original text here gives the Tibetan as *brtse,* "love, kindness"; it should be *rtse,* meaning "play."

75. The unusual agates that are to found here and there in the terrain are considered to be the playing stones of the godly-demons. If these stones are gathered up for one's own purpose without asking permission from the local spirits then there could be dire consequences. Many nomadic parents will warn their children not to unearth or destroy the natural formation of the rocks as they play.

76. An error in the original text here gives the Tibetan as *dogs,* "uncertainty"; it should be *dog,* "narrow."

VOLUME THREE. GESAR BECOMES KING

1. In this chapter Drumo offers several aspiration prayers that represent the context of the horse's gear: The first aspiration prayer is made when Drugmo offers the saddle blanket to Joru. She prays, "May you, Joru, be able to take your seat on the golden throne and become a sovereign of this earth." The second prayer occurs when she offers him the golden saddle: "May you, Joru, be able to suppress the yoke of the perverted demons and become the patron for those sublime upholders of Buddha's doctrine of scripture and realization." The third prayer is made when she offers the golden bridal and girth and prays that "You, Joru, may be able to turn the minds of all those who are confused by the ignorance of their negative karmic accumulations so they never fall to the lower realms again." For the fourth prayer she offers the fenders along with the front girth and

prays, "May you, Joru, be able to perfect the four enlightened activities to work unceasingly for the benefit of beings." For the fifth prayer she offers the reins and prays, "May you, Joru, become the protector of sentient beings and the leader of the White Ling." For the sixth prayer she offers the whip and prays, "May you, Joru, become the dharma king who eliminates non-virtue and sets into motion the practice of virtue." For the seventh prayer she offers a white scarf and prays, "May there be no obstacles to your life and through the power of your enlightened deeds may all beings' minds be brought to the path of virtue." For the eighth prayer when she captures the horse and then offers the horse to Joru she prays, "May you become the Lord of the Wealth of Kyalo Tönpa and the husband of Sengcham Drugmo."

2. "The Sevenfold": (1) the Golden Throne called Subjugates the Three Realms [Ser-tri Khamsum Zilnön], (2) Sengcham Drugmo of Kyalo, (3) the Sevenfold Jewel of the Ancestral Treasury, (4) the twelve volumes of the *One Hundred Thousand Verses* of the nāgas, (5) Tingshog Gung-gu [Azure Nine-Panels] the little nine-partitioned blue tent of the nāgas, (6) the fortress Sengdrug Tagtse [Lion Garuḍa Tiger Peak], and (7) the twelve myriarchy districts of Ling.

3. The three secrets are enlightened body, speech, and mind.

4. An error in the original text here gives the Tibetan as *brtser,* "kindness"; it should be *rtser* "atop."

5. The eight extremes refer to origination, cessation, permanence, negation, going, coming, single identity, and separateness.

6. The three sufferings are: the suffering of suffering, the suffering of change, and compounded suffering.

7. These are the eight treasures of confidence: (1) The treasure of memory that does not forget; (2) The treasure of intelligence that discerns without mistake; (3) The treasure of realization that internalizes all meanings; (4) The treasure of total recall or retention that holds everything that has been heard; (5) The treasure of fearlessness due to the ability to satisfy all beings; (6) The treasure of holding the profound dharma that annihilates heretics; (7) The treasure of bodhicitta that holds the lineage of the Three Jewels; (8) The treasure of profound accomplishment that realizes the unborn nature of truth.

8. The words in boldface indicate the title of this volume as *The Account of the Horse Race of White Ling called The Sevenfold Jewel,* and correspond to words marked in the Tibetan text as the words of Mipham Rinpoche whose Supplication to Gesar was received as mind terma. *See* Translator's Introduction.

9. This refers to the inexhaustible source of mind termas and does not necessarily refer to a category of mind terma that belongs only to Mipham Rinpoche. Mipham was not renowned for terma revelations, yet here it is clearly stated that his recollections of the Gesar epic originate from that source.

10. (1) Partaking of the enemy's longevity and merit satisfies the one who is liberating them; (2) partaking of the enemy's flesh and blood that is transformed into wisdom nectar satisfies the wrathful deities; and (3) severing the continuity of the enemy's negative state of mind and liberating them satisfies the object being liberated. These are the three.

11. Gesar does not actually become the king of the entire world, but this implies that he has conquered so many kingdoms that his sovereignty is likened to a ruler of the world.

12. This does not directly refer to the five paths and the ten grounds of the bodhisattva's ascent to fully enlightened buddhahood, but it is metaphorically implied by the fact that the young Joru was able to jump to the finish line of the horse race instantaneously through his enlightened powers.

13. The reference to capturing the steed with the lasso "of emptiness" implicitly suggests the fact that the horse can be captured only by the lady Drugmo, who represents the feminine principle of emptiness.

14. Six smiles is an epithet for the tiger, which actually refers to Gesar and the fact that he will need to rely upon the mighty warriors to assist him once he becomes king.

15. An error in the original text here gives the Tibetan as *'tshams,* "necessity"; should be *mtshams,* "retreat."

16. In the original text this place name appears as *srib pa 'khor mo'i rong rdzong;* however, it should read *srid pa 'khor mo'i rog rdzong,* which means "ancient black fortress."

17. These are the two phases of mantra recitation that occur during a deity sadhana practice.

18. An error in the original text here gives the Tibetan as *rogs,* "friend"; but it should be *rog,* "black"—here, "raven."

19. An error in the original text here gives the Tibetan *gdong btsan snang du a pan* as "*du a pan,*" which has no clear meaning; it should be *gdong btsan snang ngu a dpal* giving "Mighty Youthful Glory of the Tribe" (his correct proper name).

20. An error in the original text here gives the Tibetan as *pho ru;* it should be *phor yu,* "cup."

21. This means that Denza can still stay there, but she will be reduced to the position of a cook in the kitchen.

22. An error in the original text here gives the Tibetan as *red,* "is"; it should be *ded,* "chased by."

23. An error in the original text here gives the Tibetan as *klung,* "river valley"; it should be *rlung,* "wind."

24. The four stations are the propagation of the Buddha's dharma, being endowed with wealth and prosperity, utilizing the five desirables, and achieving the state of quiescence in dependence upon the dharma.

25. An error in the original text here gives the Tibetan as *dar 'dzom;* it should be *dar 'jam* (his correct proper name).

26. This is reference to the wisdom protector of the *dzogpa chenpo* (Tib. *rdzogs pa chen po;* the Great Perfection, or Dzogchen). He has no body, as his appearance is that of faces and eyes, and his lower torso is a serpent. *See* glossary: Rāhu.

27. An error in the original text here gives the Tibetan as *zho,* "curd"; it should be *'o ma,* "milk."

28. This is a reference to Joru, who is likened to the best grade of Chinese turquoise called the "milk drop." A drop of milk is placed upon a piece of turquoise to indicate its grade. If the milk turns a pink color, this denotes the best turquoise.

29. The Tibetan term that appears here, *rkyal ba,* refers to the material used for making butter in the nomadic culture. There are two ways to do this. One is to pour the milk into a large wooden container and churn the milk. The other way is to pour the milk into an animal skin bag and then to tie it and shake the milk until it turns to butter.

30. These nine relate to layers of different colors, which are white, black, indigo, green, yellow, white (again), red, cream, and maroon.

31. "A few questions for you": An error in the original text here gives the Tibetan as *dri,* "odor"; it should be *'dri,* "to ask."

32. An error in the original text at this line gives the Tibetan as *rgyal mo,* "queen"; it should be *rgya mo,* "Chinese woman or girl."

33. *Ibid.,* endnote 31.

34. "On a mountain peak": An error in the original text here gives the Tibetan as *dgong,* "night"; it should be *gong,* "high" i.e., "on a mountain peak."

35. An error in the original text here gives the Tibetan as *gzan,* "shawl"; it should be *zan,* "food."

36. According to the Vedic scriptures, when the peacock is in heat and hears the sound of thunder, the dragon's roar, she becomes pregnant. The peacock is aspiring upward toward the sky in order to meet the dragon's roar.

37. An error in the original text here gives the Tibetan as *'tshams,* "necessity"; it should be *mtshams,* "boundary, retreat" and is the notion that one is "sealed" or "bounded."

38. "A success-preventing demon": This kind of demon, called a *sna dre,* is one who gets between a boy and girl who are hoping to marry. This demon or spirit will attempt to make obstacles for their union together and their life in general.

39. An error in the original text here gives the Tibetan as *'gug,* "invoke, summon"; it should be *gug,* "curved."

40. An error in the original text here gives the Tibetan as *brtse,* "love"; it should be *rtse,* "play."

41. An error in the original text here gives the Tibetan as *brngan,* "to reward"; it should be *rngan,* "to disdain." *See* note 42, "to disdain" or "scoff at."

42. *Ibid.,* endnote 41.

43. *Ibid.,* endnote 40.

44. This refers to the kingdoms that existed around Ling at this time. The epic makes reference to four borderlands and eighteen minor kingdoms. The eighteen maidens are the fairest women in each kingdom of the earth.

45. "Light": An error in the original text here gives the Tibetan as *'ong,* "pleasing, will become"; it should be *'od,* "light," giving "Little Light Nāga Serpent" (Ludrül Ödchung).

46. An error in the original text here gives the Tibetan as *rtsa,* "channel, nāḍī"; it should be *rtswa,* "grass."

47. An error in the original text here gives the Tibetan as *nyug,* "stroke, extend"; it should be *nyul,* "search for."

48. Generally in Tibet there are two varieties of horses. One is a sorrel-colored wild horse or mustang, which is actually smaller in size than a regular horse. The other is a spotted domestic-type horse that comes in different sizes and shapes. Reference to the horse that has never been captured suggests that she is thinking of the domesticated horse, which belongs to the second category. Joru's horse belongs to the first category and has always been wild up until the capture.

49. *Ibid.,* endnote 47.

50. "His four hooves prancing": An error in the original text here gives the Tibetan as *brtse,* "love"; it should be *rtse,* "peak"—hence, *rtse gar,* "prancing (on tips of his hooves)."

51. The number thirteen indicates the thirteen wermas, and the falcons indicate the dralas and wermas naturally surrounding him.

52. *Ibid.,* endnote 41.

53. In Golog the horses love to drink strong tea and eat barley for feed. This is the most common diet in the winter months and is also good for their health.

54. An error in the original text here gives the Tibetan as *gzhung,* "government"; it should be *gsher,* "wet."

55. An error in the original text here gives the Tibetan as *bya'u* (one of the constellations); it should be *bya'i,* "of the bird" which we took as "to take flight."

56. This reference to a "great secret" refers to the sacredness of the horse. This also means the horse's hidden qualities were supposed to be revealed by Drugmo, not Gogmo. Since Gogmo almost told the secret, the horse then bolted away to show that the timing was off.

57. This is a prediction about how Gesar will emanate in the future disguised as a great fish, and in that body he will be able to accomplish his goal. This account relates to another story in the epic.

58. An error in the original text here gives the Tibetan as *skyid pa,* "happiness"; it should be *sgyid pa,* "knee joint or hock."

59. An error in the original text here gives the Tibetan as *gla,* "wages"; it should be *brla,* "thigh."

60. An error in the original text here gives the Tibetan as *nam tshong*; it should be *nam tshong,* "upper chest bones, ribs."

61. This may disagree with traditional Tibetan terminology, but we assume the bard is knowledgeable in stating the five visceral organs (Tib. *don lnga*) as the heart, lungs, liver, spleen, and kidneys. The six hollow organs (Tib. *snod drug*) are the stomach, greater and lesser intestines, bladder, ovaries or testicles, and gall bladder.

62. An error in the original text here gives the Tibetan as *dogs,* "doubts"; it should be *dog,* "narrow."

63. An error in the original text here gives the Tibetan as *da ra,* "buttermilk"; it should be *ngar,* "forepart" which we interpreted as the most distal bone, the cannon bone.

64. An error in the original text here gives the Tibetan as *ci,* "what, whatever"; it should be *spyi,* "top of head."

65. An error in the original text here gives the Tibetan as *sha bo,* "enemy"; it should be *sha ba,* "deer."

66. An error in the original text here gives the Tibetan as *tshong,* "marketplace"; it should be *tshang,* "nest, den."

67. An error in the original text here gives the Tibetan as *khyims*; it should be *khyim,* "home"; here we have taken this as meaning "cranial cavity."

68. "The four gatherings" (Tib. *bsdu ba'i dngos po bzhi*) are the four means of magnetizing: being generous, speaking kind words, giving appropriate teachings, and keeping consistency between words and actions. These four can be summed up as generosity, pleasing speech, appropriate teachings, and consistency in behavior.

69. An error in the original text here gives the Tibetan as *khram,* "false word"; it should be *khrom,* "public."

70. This place was identified by Khen Rinpoche Jigme Phuntsog as the original site of Gesar's palace, called Sengtrug Tagtse. The actual location is close to the present-day town of Darlag and the Traling Monastery in Golog.

71. The Tibetan in this passage, *go ma chod,* means that the opportunity was wasted in the sense that nothing was satisfied by the girl killing the deer. Nothing was paid off. For instance, if a man is killed, the family may demand that the killer's family pay life for life or put the

murderer in jail, but instead they send a poor person with no background and have that person killed. It still does not satisfy the vendetta. And *go ma chod* literally means "does not satisfy" in the sense of being "unproductive." Hence this death was unproductive.

72. Nyag-ma'i Dong [Notch Ridge] (Tib. *nyag ma'i gdon*) is a small mountain in a ridge, sometimes called Dong Nyag. It is also a nickname for people with no bridge to their nose who are called *sna nyag,* meaning "notch nose."

73. This means that one could apply understanding incorrectly.

74. An error in the original text here gives the Tibetan as *rkyang dkar,* "white mule"; it should be *lcang dkar,* "white willow."

75. When someone dies in the Tibetan culture, it is considered very bad to have the dead eyes still staring at a living person. That could mean the dead person is still attached to something based on mental passions and poisons. Although Drugmo respects and loves Joru, because of this bad sign she tries to reverse his gaze with the ashes.

76. The Tibetan term *god mgo* in this passage refers to a ritual object that is used when an animal dies of a disease. This object should not be used in a wealth prosperity ceremony, for it will spread the disease—which is the exact opposite of what is wanted as the outcome of a prosperity ceremony.

77. An error in the original text here gives the Tibetan as *khar seng*; it should be *khar sang,* "yesterday."

78. *Ibid.,* endnote 78.

79. This explains a woman as inferior who is incapable of upholding tradition and who is always disrespectful. The spirit of the deceased is similar since it has entered the bardo and due to negative karmic accumulations sees the wisdom deities only as demons. He is comparing these two and linking them together in his sarcasm directed towards Drugmo.

80. In other words, she prays that the inner qualities of the horse will become functional to reveal its enlightened qualities and then accomplish his enlightened deeds.

81. An error in the original text here gives the Tibetan as *'dug nas lon*; it should be *ga nas lon,* "Where did you get it?"

82. The Tibetan in this passage uses an alternate spelling of Ling; usually it is *gling,* but here it is given as *brling*.

83. An error in the original text here gives the Tibetan as *tshang,* "nest"; it should be *tshong,* "business."

84. *Ibid.,* endnote 84.

85. This is a reference to the ancient Tibetan story about hibernating dragons. In the highest mountains there are empty cave-like holes that are hidden by grass, and it is said that in these vast empty holes the dragons hibernate through the winter months.

86. An error in the original text here gives the Tibetan as *rgyas,* "bloom"; it should be *rgyal,* "victorious."

87. An error in the original text here gives the Tibetan as *mtshur,* "color"; it should be *mtshul,* "muzzle."

88. An error in the original text here gives the Tibetan as *ha 'jog*; it should be *a 'jog,* "seat on a horse saddle."

89. An error in the original text here gives the Tibetan as *sku che,* "greatness"; it should be *sku tshe,* "lifetime, longevity."

90. An error in the original text here gives the Tibetan as *sgang nga*; it should be *sgo nga,* "egg."

91. An error in the original text here gives the Tibetan as *mi mdza,'* "enemy"; it should be *mi mdzes,* "ugly," here written as "unsightly."
92. An error in the original text here gives the Tibetan as *rgyag pas,* "putting"; it should be *rgyug pas,* "running."
93. Drala castles are roadside shrines that are adorned with colorful silk flags and large arrows still in the quiver.
94. These three are blood brothers; however, because of his wealth, Kyalo is the only one known in the land of Ling. If all of them were of equal wealth, then they would all be well known, and in a sense, more equal.
95. An error in the original text here gives the Tibetan as *brtse,* "love"; it should be *rtse,* "play."
96. An error in the original text here gives the Tibetan is *kho mo*; it should be *khol mo,* that is, Sidpa Khölmo Rogdzong [Black Bellow Fortress of Existence], the place Trothung was given to live.
97. An error in the original text here gives the Tibetan as *de rim*; it should be *de ring,* "today."
98. An error in the original text here gives the Tibetan as *blo brgya*; it should be *blo rgya,* "mental capacity."
99. An error in the original text here gives the Tibetan as *kha spor*; it should be *kha spur* (that is, *kha spu*), "whiskers."
100. An error in the original text here gives the Tibetan as *lan,* "reply": it should be *zin,* "capture, seize."
101. The order of this line and next three lines have been changed from the Tibetan text to "match up" with the four names above.
102. The source of the rivers are as follows: the river from the east, the Ganga, flows forth from the mouth of the great elephant. The river from the south, the Sindu, emerges from the mouth of a peacock. The river from the west, the Pakyu, flows from the mouth of a horse. The river from the north, the Sidha, flows from the mouth of a lion.
103. An error in the original text here gives the Tibetan as *gra sdeb mjod*; it should be *gra sdebs mdzod,* "unite in proper order."
104. An error in the original text here gives the Tibetan as *'tsham,* "suitable"; it should be *'cham,* "dancer."
105. The Tibetan text here has another variation in this name. It was previously given as Sengseng and Singsing (Tib. *sing sing*); here it appears as *sring sing*.
106. An error in the original text here gives the Tibetan as *dam,* "holy"; it should be, *dom,* "bear."
107. These environmental justifications for their evil activities are just an excuse. All the demons will try to make a case for their evil obstructions as though they were really virtuous, when in fact they are evil.
108. An error in the original text here gives the Tibetan as *lus ngan,* "ugly body"; it should be *las ngan,* "negative karma."
109. When the demon sisters of the great hills first show themselves, they appear as frightening and as terrifying as a tiger, a leopard, and a bear. Once Joru tames them, he then transforms them into the bodies of human females.
110. *Ibid.,* endnote 107.
111. The sudden appearance of this treasure keeper of the land of the Ma Valley, and her bestowal of gifts upon Joru, indicate that he will reveal the treasures hidden at Gu-ra Crag during another episode of the epic.

112. This means that he sees himself as the most divine among the hunchbacks, as the wealthiest and the one with the most prosperity.

113. An error in the original text here gives the Tibetan as *gdug*, "evil, harmful"; it should be *gdugs*, "parasol, umbrella."

114. An error in the original text here gives the Tibetan as *ser bu*, "breeze"; it should be *ser ba*, "hail" or "sleet," here written as "icy wind."

115. *Ibid.,* endnote 41.

116. An error in the original text here gives the Tibetan as *lhangs*; it should be *lhang*, "become active," written here as "erupt."

117. An error in the original text here gives the Tibetan as *pha ru*; it should be *pha rus*, "paternal clan."

118. "Joru never committed any nonvirtue." An error in the original text here gives the Tibetan as *jo ru sa*; it should be *jo rus*, "by Joru." Literally the sentence would read "Nonvirtue was never committed by Joru."

119. In saṃsāra there are three realms and six classes of beings. The three realms are the formless Ārūpyadhātu, form Rūpādhātu, and desire Kāmadhātu realms. The four formless realms are also referred to as the fourfold spheres of perception. These are four unenlightened meditative states of dwelling on the thoughts called Infinite Space Ākāśānantyāyatana, Infinite Consciousness Vijñānānantyāyatana, Nothing Whatsoever Ākiṃcanyāyatana, and Neither Presence nor Absence of Conception Naivasaṃjñānāsaṃjñāyatana.

   The seventeen form realms are heavenly abodes consisting of the threefold four dhyāna realms or realms of concentration and the five pure abodes (Tib. *gnas gtsang ma lnga*; Skt. Śuddhāvāsa) or the five highest heavens in Buddhist cosmology, where realized beings who will never return to samsara abide.

   Another way of delineating them is that the fourth dhyāna realm is said to have eight inner realms or stages. The beings there have bodies of light, long lives, and no painful sensations.

   The desire realm is where the beings of the six classes reside. It is said that there are six levels of the gods of desire: They are the four classes of the great kings Cāturmahārā or Lokapāla, the thirty-three levels of gods, the Limitless Gods, the gods of Tuṣita, the gods who Enjoy Emanation Nimmanarati, and the gods who Enjoy the Abundance of Others Paranimmitavasavattin.

120. There are four great continents: In the east is Pūrvavideha, in the south, Jambudvīpa, in the west, Aparagodānīya, and in the north, Uttarakuru. Along with these are the eight subcontinents: Deha and Videha, Cāmara and Aparacāmara, Śātha and Uttaramantriṇa, and Kurava and Kaurava.

121. An error in the original text here gives the Tibetan as *zha*, "face"; it should be *zhwa*, "hat."

122. *Ibid.,* endnote 122.

123. *Ibid.,* endnote 122.

124. This refers to many small kingdoms scattered about. It is a classical list that we are calling the eighteen principalities. For instance, in volume one this is variously called the eighteen great wings of Tag-rong or the valley of the eighteen falcon caves, which is also referring to these eighteen small kingdoms or principalities.

125. The Phuwer brothers are indigenous spirits of the land. Here the diviner is performing an

extremely abbreviated version of the norm, and so in some ways he is synthesizing to make the song sound melodious.

126. The ocean refers to Gesar; the tributaries refer to Drugmo, telling that she will come to belong to Gesar. The reference to the waves that seem to go elsewhere refers to Drugmo being captured by Gurkar and then one day returning back to her king.

127. "The four enemies" are the adversaries in the four directions, which are the subject of future battles in volumes of the epic to come.

128. These three are the spiritual side, the personal side, and the future, and the divination says that there will be only positive circumstances concerning these three situations.

129. This means that this mo divination is the best among the three possible types of mos, which are: excellent, mediocre, or bad.

130. These "three excellences" means that the outcome of his questions is excellent in all three cases.

131. An error in the original text here gives the Tibetan as *lung,* "shastra, scripture, valley"; it should be *rlung,* "prana, vital energy."

132. The worst place for a man to sweat is from the forehead; that means he's working too hard. And if a horse's calves are quivering, that means he is barely able to run.

133. At the conclusion of an important ceremony the spiritual attainment is received in the form of ambrosia nectar. Here Joru is saying that Dongsten will be so exhausted and shaky that his hand will quiver as he extends it out to receive the nectar.

134. Usually Trothung's songs are in the melody of Hara Hurthung, which is sudden and abrupt, but now he's trying to hide his nature, so he sings in this slow, gentle style.

135. An error in the original text here gives the Tibetan as *lung phug*; it should be *lud phung,* "dung hill, manure."

136. An error in the original text here gives the Tibetan as *mi 'u*; it should be *mi yi,* "as a human."

137. *Ibid.,* endnote 40

138. In Tibet, when grain is harvested, the cutting of a single bundle of grain stalks usually involves about ten strokes with the sickle. Then those stalks are bound up in a bundle and placed upright in the field where the grain was cut, and the bundle stays there until it has dried. The number ten is a generalization, as there would be more or less than ten strokes per bundle with the sickle.

139. She married into the Jang clan, so she is called Jangza. However, according to the Tibetan culture even when a girl marries she maintains her maiden family name. Since she and her sister Gazi Lhamo married into different cultures and countries outside of Tibet, they assumed the names of their husbands.

140. An error in the original text here gives the Tibetan as *ring*; it should be *rings.* Then the Tibetan *skya rings* in this line would mean "pale."

141. An error in the original text here gives the Tibetan as *long lang*; it should be *lang long* "languid, slowly moving," here translated as "floating."

142. She is saying that Dongtsen is very close to the throne, and even if his horse were to have an accident brought on by the dralas who favor Joru, she is afraid that Dongtsen could then run by foot to capture the throne.

143. In a future time, Gesar is destined to conquer this kingdom in China; at that time the

horse Turquoise Bird will be a crucial part of the epic. But because of the overstated answer from Dongtsen at this moment, the destined process of conquering this kingdom is further complicated and will thereby take three attempts in order to achieve success.

144. An error in the original text here gives the Tibetan as *yugs gcig*; it should be *yug gcig*, "in one piece, single."

145. *Ibid.,* endnote 145.

146. *Ibid.,* endnote 145.

147. *Ibid.,* endnote 145.

148. *Ibid.,* endnote 145.

149. The point is that King Gesar and the imperial gods above are now inseparable, so that all the subjects can have the confidence of knowing that Gesar embodies all the gods. That means once the king gives a command, the inhabitants are receiving a mandate from all of the gods simultaneously.

150. *Ibid.,* endnote 145.

151. An error in the original text here gives the Tibetan as *byur,* "mishap"; it should be *byu ru,* "coral."

152. This indicates that the authentic presence of Gesar surpasses even the splendor of the throne. Until this time no one had ever sat upon the throne, which seemed to be so lofty and exalted, but now in Gesar's presence even the throne seems to be dwarfed.

153. This is a palatal click, quite loud, that Gologs make to indicate determination. It is made after a good meal, or when you bravely determine to do something, or when you are angry and about to fight. Lama Chönam explains that this secular sound was outlawed in his monastery, and monetary penalties were assessed if the young monks made this sound, as if it were a curse word.

154. The nomadic people of Golog would keep such a slingshot close to them for protection, as it safeguards against demons, even while a person is sleeping. It is made from a braided rope with a diagonal pattern that changes direction every eight or so lines and forms the shape of an eye every two lines.

155. All of these couplets are really saying that each item "possesses the energy" of such and such a deity.

156. This translation is not literal, because of the cryptic nature of the poetry in Tibetan, but the basic meaning is as translated.

157. An error in the original text here gives the Tibetan as *bya,* "do, make, bird"; it should be *byang,* "north."

158. The reason it says "temporarily" is so as not to make a bad omen about the future of the text. It is hoped that these stories of the activities of buddhas and bodhisattvas will continue to be brought into the world.

159. An error in the original text here gives the Tibetan as *gsar,* "new"; it should be *gsang,* "secret."

160. This must be a reference to the clan of Derge Lingtsang's leader, who was a treasure revealer prior to the Cultural Revolution.

GLOSSARY OF TERMS

The Wylie transliteration of the Tibetan term is shown in parentheses.

abundance dralas, the three kindred (Tib. *rgyas byed dgra lha spun gsum*). A society of dralas that increase and expand one's energy and accomplishments, increasing windhorse, eloquence, and possessions.

Achen (Tib. *a chen*). A tribe and a region in the Kingdom of Hor, in the area of the upper Yellow River.

Akaniṣṭha (Skt.; Tib. *'og min*). The highest of the god realms, but normally this term is used to mean the highest Buddhist pure land of all.

Ākāśadhātvīśvarī (Skt.; Tib. *dbyings phyug ma*). *See* buddha families, five.

Akṣobhya (Skt.; Tib. *mi skyod pa*). Literally, "immovable." This is the buddha of the Vajra family in the eastern direction of the mandala. However, according to some other traditions, this buddha is in the center and represents the Buddha family. *See also* buddha families, five.

Amitābha [Limitless Light], Lord of Sukhāvatī (Skt.; Tib. *'od dpag med*). Buddha of Sukhāvatī, which is also known as the land of bliss, the pure land, or the western buddha field.

Amoghasiddhi. *See* buddha families, five.

amṛta (Skt.; Tib. *bdud rtsi*). Nectar or ambrosia; literally, "antidote for demonic forces." Amṛta can refer to a sacred substance made from particular medicinal herbs and blessed in a great ceremony that is carried out for ten days under strict conditions. More generally, it simply refers to any nectar-like substance that has special spiritual properties to grant blessings and increase health and vitality.

ancestral lineage (Tib. *gdung brgyud* or *rus brgyud*). The paternal lineage of a clan (Tib. *rus*).

antelope demon (Tib. *rgo 'dre*). One of the wild animal demons in the Snake Head Valley in Kham (eastern Tibet).

appeasement and fulfillment offerings (Tib. *rngan gsol*). Ceremonies of sacrifice in order to reverse the opposition of gods, which is caused by violation of taboos or other transgressions.

approach and accomplishment practice (Tib. *bsnyen sgrub*). Two stages of mantra recitation in deity yoga practice, corresponding to the root mantra accumulation, followed by the accomplishment mantra accumulation.

ārya (Skt.; Tib. *'phags pa*). A noble being who has entered the ten grounds of realization. See also *bhūmi.*

Aspiration Mountain Pass. *See* Mönlam La.

Auspicious-by-Day scarf (Tib. *dar nyin mo bde legs*). The name of a silk presentation scarf inscribed with a famous prayer of aspiration.

auspicious coincidence (Tib. *rten 'brel;* Skt. *pratitya-samutpāda*). Good fortune, fortunate connection. The Sanskrit term means "codependent origination." The term refers to causality mediated by karma, but here it is used to mean a magical or karmically destined fortunate situation.

Auspicious Intertwined Dragons scarf (Tib. *bkra shis 'brug gor kha sprod*). The name of a presentation offering scarf, described by its dragon motif.

authentic presence (Tib. *dbang thang*). An invisible field of power that extends around the shoulders of a warrior or a great being, like the Byzantine notion of a saint's charisma. An important part of the cosmology of Tibetan village and nomadic culture, the *wông tông*, as it is pronounced, though it is often written as *wang tang*, is actually an aura that surrounds the body and can be gathered, collected, and built up into a powerful force that makes a person's actions penetrating and effective. This expression is translated as "authentic presence" because it is regarded in a subtle way as a kind of field of wealth and fortunate power investing one with natural charisma. *See also* life force.

avadāna (Skt.; Tib. *rtogs pa rjod pa*). *See* biographical account.

Avalokiteśvara: A bodhisattva, the embodiment of compassion, and one of the three principle protectors of this world, the other two being Mañjuśrī and Vajrapāṇi.

averting ceremonies (Tib. *bzlog pa*). Special ceremonies and recitations that are performed by qualified vajrayāna adepts in order to reverse obstacles and turn back calamities.

awareness (Tib. *rig pa;* Skt. *vidyā*). Also translated as "wisdom awareness." In the context of the tantras of the Great Perfection, this refers to the highest direct and unfabricated awareness of the true nature of mind and phenomena.

Ayu, Downs of (Tib. *a yu dis*). A sequence of hills in Ling. This is the site where the horse race began.

azure firmament (Tib. *gung sngon*). An epithet for the sky.

bardo (Tib. *bar do*). The intermediate state between death and rebirth, or simply the period of time that comes between two other determinations of time. In the bardo between death and rebirth, one's karmic accumulations dictate the length and quality of the experience, which is usually no longer than forty-nine days. There are many books that specialize in the subject, such as *The Tibetan Book of the Dead: The Great Liberation through Hearing in the Bardo,* trans. Chögyam Trungpa and Francesca Fremantle (Boston: Shambhala, 2003).

baton of fate (Tib. *khram shing*). A magical stick carried particularly by local Tibetan deities such as the *tsen.*

Beri tribe or clan (Tib. *ldong be ri*). A tribe inhabiting a land near Ma.

Bernagchen (Tib. *ber nag can*). Also known as Pernagchen. The two-armed Mahākāla, one of the major tantric dharma protectors. In the world of the epic, he is associated with the region of Gadei (Tib. *dga' bde*) and the tribe of Dru (Tib. *'dru*). His name refers to the fact that he wears a black *ber,* or cloak. He is famous for his power of mantra.

Bhagavat (Skt.; Tib. *bcom ldan 'das*). The Blessed One; an epithet for the Buddha.

bhūmi (Skt.; Tib. *sa*). The grounds or stages of realization that are accomplished by those who have directly realized the true nature of reality. Such practitioners are also referred to as bodhisattvas who have entered the grounds of realization. Once the first ground or *bhūmi* has been achieved, the individual no longer needs to be subject to ordinary rebirth in saṃsāra; that is, to rebirth in cyclic existence. He or she will continue to ascend through the grounds and paths to the tenth bhūmi, and from there achieve fully enlightened buddhahood.

biographical account (Tib. *rtogs pa rjod pa;* Skt. *avadāna*). One of the twelve divisions of Buddhist literature.

Black Bird (Tib. *bya nag*). This could be short for *bya nag gshog ring* [Black Bird Long Wing], a messenger of the demon king Lutsen.

Black Month (Tib. *nag zla*). The third month of the lunar calendar.

Blossom Wealth Holder (Tib. *me tog g.yang 'dzin*). In the world of the epic, a name for one of many varieties of jasmine tea.

Blue Turquoise Plain of Ne'u Seng (Tib. *ne'u seng g.yu thang sngon mo*). A plain where the nāgas gather.

bodhicitta (Skt.; Tib. *byang chub kyi sems*). Mind that is directed toward clarity and compassion.

bodhisattva (Skt.; Tib. *byang chub sems pa*). One who aspires to attain the state of fully enlightened buddhahood in order to lead all beings to that state. A bodhisattva will consider the needs of others before himself or herself, and dedicates his or her life to benefiting beings until samsara is emptied of suffering. A bodhisattva has entered the bhumis and is no longer an ordinary individual subject to karma and passions. See also *bhūmi*.

bodies of the Buddha, three (Tib. *sku gsum;* Skt. *trikāya*). Three enlightened bodies of the state of enlightenment. The three are also presented as a twofold division: the dharmakāya (Skt.; Tib. *chos sku*), or truth body; and the rūpakāya (Skt.; Tib. *gzugs kyi sku*), or form body. The dharmakāya is enlightenment itself; it is wisdom beyond any reference point, self-occurring primordial mind that is devoid of characteristics. The form bodies, or rūpakāya, refer to the other two kāyas: the Body of Abundance (Skt. *sambhogakāya*), and the Manifestation Body (Skt. *nirmāṇakāya;* Tib. *tülku* or *trulku; sprul sku*). The nirmāṇakāya is the actual form that a buddha manifests through, in order to reach disciples according to their ordinary and diverse perceptions.

body god (Tib. *sku lha*). A deity who protects the body of a specific warrior, much like the kind of dralas called patron gods, which perch on the head, shoulders, and chest of warriors.

borderland kingdoms, twelve (Tib. *mtha' yi rgyal khag bcu gnyis*). Twelve countries that bordered Ling.

Brahmā (Skt.; Tib. *tshangs pa*). The Hindu god of creation; in Buddhist cosmology, the ruler of the gods of the Realm of Form. Literally, *tshangs pa* means "pure one." Also called White Brahmā (Tib. *tshangs pa dkar po*).

Brethren of Ling, Thirty (Tib. *phu nu sum cu*). Literally means "fraternal cousins" or "elder and younger brothers." Generally it is used to suggest kinsmen, but in the context of the list of thirty, it means a group of warriors who are linked to each other by relations of equality and loyalty, as if they were brothers. The Thirty Brethren are the same as the Thirty Mighty Warriors.

bride demon (Tib. *sna 'dre*). Literally, a "leading demon." The arrival of a bride at her new family's dwelling is taken very seriously, and is considered a moment when the alien and perhaps malevolent spirits of the bride's old family could enter and harm the balance of the home. There are complex ritual actions involved in ensuring that the bride does not arrive in an inauspicious manner. For example, when the bride dismounts her horse, she must face her new home, not the direction of her native clan's home. If such a ritual is not followed, it is believed that the marriage could be plagued by mishap. Although this term can apply to other situations, it usually refers to marriage.

Bright Blaze (Tib. *gwa pa*). Gyalwa'i Lhundrub's horse, also sometimes called Bright Blaze Gentle Throne (Tib. *gwa pa khri 'jam*).

brothers and cousins (Tib. *phu nu*). This is a collective noun for the younger generation of braves, which describes the sons of the fathers and uncles, who are related either as brothers or cousins. All of these groups are referred to in the translation as "brethren" or "kinsmen." *See also* Brethren of Ling, Thirty.

brothers of Serpa, eight (Tib. *gser pa mched brgyad*). The principal warriors of Upper Ling (Tib. *stod gling*).

buddha activities, fourfold (Tib. *phrin las bzhi*). Four enlightened activities that buddhas engage in for the benefit of beings. They are described as ritual or magical practices: pacifying, enriching, magnetizing, and destroying: (Tib. *zhi ba, rgyas pa, dbang,* and *drag po 'phrin las*). These four can also be considered as a set of instructions for enlightened conduct within the world.

Buddha ḍākinī (Tib. *sangs rgya mkha' 'gro;* Skt. *buddha ḍākinī*). The ḍākinī, or female enlightened one, from the central direction or Buddha family of the mandala. *See also* buddha families, five.

buddha families, five (Tib. *sangs rgyas rigs lnga;* Skt. *Dhyani Buddha*). The five points of the mandala. The five buddha families abide in the east, south, west, north, and central directions of a mandala, representing specific qualities of enlightenment that correspond to the particular direction, as well as color, passion, dynamic strength, and wisdom. These five families are often known as the five *tathāgatas* (Skt.), "thus-gone ones," and by their Sanskrit appellations from Indian tantra: Vairocana Buddha in the center, Akṣobhya in the east, Ratnasambhava in the south, Amitābha in the west, and Amoghasiddhi in the north.

These five primordial Buddhas and their consorts participate in most empowerments in the epic. Each buddha family is identified by its hand emblem: Vairocana by the wheel; Akṣobhya by the vajra; Amitābha by the lotus; Amoghasiddhi by the double vajra; and Ratnasambhava by the jewel. Numerous personas in Tibetan tantra are taken to be emanations of one of these families. For example, the bodhisattva Avalokiteśvara; the yidam (tutelary deity) Hayagrīva; the guru Padmasambhava; and the king, Gesar of Ling are all emanations of the Lotus family of Amitābha. Matching the five male buddhas of the five buddha families are five female buddhas who represent the five elements. They are the consorts of the five tathāgatas. In the east and south are Māmakī and Buddhalocanā, water and earth elements respectively. In some texts, these two reverse the positions, consorts, and elements that they represent. In the center is Ākāśadhātvīśvarī, goddess of space. In the west is Pāṇḍaravāsinī, goddess of fire. In the north is Samayatārā or Tārā, the goddess of wind.

Other fivefold homologies are correlated with the five buddha families, such as the five poisons and the five skandhas. Just as the five passions or poisons are by nature the five wisdoms, they are represented by the five Buddhas.

buddha realm (Tib. *zhing khams*). An environment in which the wisdom-mind transmission occurs, and there is no distinction between teacher and listener. Also referred to as a pure land.

Buddhalocanā (Skt.; Tib. *sangs rgyas spyan ma*). Literally "Buddha eye" in both Sanskrit and Tibetan. She represents the element of earth. *See also* buddha families, five.

Bumgyel Tongthub [One Hundred Thousand Victories and a Thousand Defeats] (Tib. *'bum bsgyel stong thub*). The turquoise armor given to Nyitri by the Chinese emperor.

cakra (Skt.; Tib. *'khor lo*). Literally meaning "wheel," the word *cakra* (anglicized as *chakra*) can refer to a magical weapon, such as a sharpened wheel, which is thrown at an enemy. However, it usually refers to the network of channels that are formed into energy centers at key locations in the body. Each wheel, or chakra, is the nexus of a system of channels, or nāḍīs, which regulates physical and mental activities in the body. In most systems, there are five chakras, which are located at the crown, throat, heart, navel, and the genitals.

cakravartin (Tib. *'khor lo sgyur ba'i rgyal po*). Universal monarch. Also written as chakravartin.

Cāmara (Tib. *rnga yab*). Literally, "tail-fan island." The island southwest of the continent of Jambudvīpa where the cannibal demons live. Padmasambhava lives there as Lotus Skull Garland.

cannibal demons (Tib. *srin po;* Skt. *rākṣasa*). Fearsome demons with long tongues, claws, and fangs, who are enemies to humankind; similar to the notion of a vampire.

chakra. See *cakra*.

Cherished Sons, Thirteen (Tib. *gces phrug*). A way of referring to the most beloved youngsters among the youthful Ling warriors.

chieftain (Tib. *dpon*). Sometimes *dpon* is translated as "leader," but when referring to the head of a tribal group, it is translated as "chieftain," with the term "chief" reserved specifically for Chipön Rongtsha Tragen.

Chiliarch [Leader of a Thousand] (Tib. *stong dpon*). A Tibetan military honorific.

chuba (Tib.). A long, wrapped woolen or sheepskin garment; the traditional dress of Tibetan nomads.

clairvoyance (Tib. *mngon shes;* Skt. *abhijñā*). Sometimes translated as "superior knowledge." A collection of paranormal powers of insight gained through inner realization.

clear light (Tib. *'od gsal*). A code term for the special yogic accomplishment of seeing the clear-light nature of appearances.

Cloud Valley of Wealth (Tib. *sprin lung phyug mo*). The name of a treasure chest of scarves (Tib. *dar mdzod*) in Chipön's home.

coemergent connate wisdom (Tib. *lhan cig skyes pa'i ye shes;* Skt. *sahaja jñāna*). From the point of view of the unsurpassed tantras, moments of ignorance do not arise totally divorced from wisdom. Even in a confused person's stream of consciousness, wisdom and ignorance always arise simultaneously. Thus wisdom can be found even in moments of confusion. This is the wisdom that coemerges with ignorance.

completion stage (Tib. *rdzogs rim*). See generation and completion stages.

confidence (Tib. *spobs pa* or *gdengs*). *See* splendor.

constellation (Tib. *rgyu skar*). Literally, the "moving stars." Refers to classical Indian astrology's list of "lunar mansions" (Skt. *nakṣatra*), which are constellations of stars identified by the position of the moon in the sky. Altogether, there are twenty-eight of these constellations.

Cosmic Turquoise Lake [Sidpa Yutso] (Tib. *srid pa g.yu mtsho*). The lake that is the domain of the nāgas.

country god (Tib. *yul lha*). Literally, "god of the place." A term for a native Tibetan deity, who is usually attached to a specific place. Sometimes this refers to a god of the hunt.

Country of Demons (Tib. *bdud yul*). A country to the north of Ling that is ruled by a monster king named Lutsen. Gesar fights this country in the second-longest saga of the epic, the Düd Ling. *See also* demon.

Crag Mountain Meteorite-Proof (Tib. *khrab rdza ri thog thub*). The name of the armor given by the Younger Lineage to Zhalkar on his birth celebration.

crown chakra of great bliss (Tib. *spyi gtsug bde chen khor lo*). One of the chakras, usually having thirty-two channels, located in the crown. See also *cakra*.

Crystal Light One Eye (Tib. *shel 'od mig gcig*). The name of a jewel originally owned by the dragons.

ḍāka (Skt.; Tib. *dpa' bo*). Literally means "warrior" or "hero," but in this context it refers to the male equivalent of a ḍākinī, usually wrathful or semi-wrathful yidams of masculine gender.

ḍākinī (Skt.; Tib. *mkha' 'gro ma*) Literally, "sky-goer." A female deity who signifies the absolute as a messenger principle. Ḍākinīs can be tricky, playful, seductive, motherly, or punishing as they serve the tantric practitioner and bring messages of enlightenment and guidance. They represent the basic space out of which they manifest in order to meet the needs of beings in the world. Lower goddesses who are essentially fairies or demonesses deputized by Buddhism are sometimes called ḍākinīs in Tibetan texts; however, they represent the worldy aspect of the term. The wisdom ḍākinīs manifest as female yidams in the context of the five families of Buddhas, and they are named according to those families, such as Buddhaḍakinī, Vajraḍakinī, and so forth.

Dalung (Tib. *zla lung*). The lower plain of Ling's Moon Valley, located in Kham, eastern Tibet, where the inhabitants would gather for communal events. Sometimes this is rendered *brda lung,* and hence it would be called Indication Valley.

damsi [oath-breaking demons] (Tib. *dam sri*). These are terribly powerful demons who began as tantric practitioners and then turned against the dharma. As enemies of the dharma, they have some degree of power because of the virtue they accumulated through previous dharma practice when they were Buddhists. Now they use this power to literally serve the dark side (Tib. *nag po'i 'phyogs*).

dark side (Tib. *nag po'i phyogs*). Literally, the "side or direction of the black or darkness." The opposite of the "white side," which is represented in expressions such as "White Ling." These are gods and humans who are opposed to the buddhadharma, either by nature or because they have perverted the intention of their vows.

Deep Blue Blazing Rays of Splendor Jewel (Tib. *nor bu mthing 'od gzi 'bar*). A magic jewel in the possession of the nāgas.

demons (Tib. *'dre*). Malevolent spirits who cause harm and are usually connected with specific kinds of disasters. In general, they are death spirits who bring disease and loss of wealth. For example, the Tibetologist Giuseppe Tucci, using a Bön source, names five classes of 'dre: food demons (Tib. *za 'dre*); demons causing loss (Tib. *god 'dre*); executioners (Tib. *gsed 'dre*); water sickness demons (Tib. *chu 'dre*); and material loss demons (Tib. *gson 'dre*). *See also* māra.

Den (Tib. *'dan*). A region in Kham (eastern Tibet) ruled by the Den family. On Chinese maps, this appears as Teng k'o (Tib. *'dan khog*). The home of the famous minister Denma is located in this region, probably along the trade route from Tatsienlou to Jyekundo. It was also the family home of Trothung's wife, and for this reason she became known as Denza (Tib. *'dan bza'*), the lady from Den. Den was often allied with Dru (Tib. *bru* or *'dru*) and Ga.

Derge (Tib. *sde dge*). The largest city in eastern Tibet and the center of the ancient kingdom of the same name, ruled for 1,300 years by a lineage of kings. It is the home of the great publishing house that still exists to this day.

dharma (Tib. *chos*). The term *dharma* can be understood in two ways: spiritually and worldly. Spiritually, the dharma refers to the teachings of the Buddha and his disciples which lead to enlightenment. Worldly dharma or phenomena refers to the way of life of sentient beings who are still in the realms of existence. Worldly dharma is in harmony with the goodness of the world and brings temporary well-being and happiness that will gradually lead beings to the path of liberation from *saṃsāra*. Another definition of *dharma* is "truth" or "law," which refers both to natural laws as well as to the body of teachings on the nature of mind. *Dharma* also means "phenomena." *Buddhist dharma* refers to the Buddha's speech, which is thereby known as the law or order of truth.

dharma robe (Tib. *chos gos*). The outer robe, patched and of certain specific dimensions, which a monk or nun receives upon ordination and wears as the principle mark of the monastic vow.

dharmadhātu (Skt.; Tib. *chos kyi dbying*). This means the nature of phenomena, or the basic space of phenomena. Phenomena is *chos* in Tibetan, referring to all appearances, and *dbying* is space, referring to emptiness as the nature of phenomena.

dharmakāya (Tib. *chos sku*). *See* bodies of the Buddha, three.

dharmapāla (Skt.; Tib. *chos skyong*). Those who guard and protect the spiritual aspect of dharma, and also guard those who are practitioners. The dharmapālas were bound to oath by Padmasambhava to assist in ensuring the pure presence of the vajrayāna Buddhist doctrine in the world. Since this is dependent upon practitioners, the dharmapalas guard and protect the lineage holders and authentic practitioners from obstacles and conflicting circumstances.

Dhātviśvarī. *See* Vajra Dhātviśvarī.

dignity. *See* splendor.

disaster (Tib. *kha 'dre*). Literally, "mouth demons," which is a village expression for problems that coincidentally arise when a person is praised too much. For example, if a child's qualities are overly praised or exaggerated, it might attract disaster, and the demons drawn to inflict the disaster are called mouth demons, because they are drawn by the words of praise.

districts, six (Tib. *sde* or *tsho*). In the epic, this term refers to the six districts into which Middle Ling is divided, under the heading of the tribally based province of Ombu; these were probably originally tribal districts. For consistency, *sde* has been translated as "district," and *tsho* as "province."

divination arrows (Tib. *lha mda'*). Often used by Gesar for divination. They are decorated with ribbons and used in formal settings to indicate an official message. The term also refers to the arrows used by Gesar's warriors.

divination stones (Tib. *mo rdil*). Pebbles that are used to make a divination.

divination threads (Tib. *ju zhags*). Threads that are braided and used in divination; also called *ju thig*.

Divine Heirs, Four (Tib. *lha sras mched bzhi* or *lha sras spun bzhi*). Four princely warriors from four tribes of Ling: Gyatsha Zhalkar of Bumpa, Nyibum Daryag of Serpa, Anu Paseng of Ombu, and Rinchen Darlu of Muchang. Nyibum is the divine heir (Tib. *lha sras*) for the

Greater Lineage; Anu Paseng for the Middle Lineage; and Rinchen Darlu for the Lesser Lineage.

Divisions of Muchang, Four (Tib. *mu spyang sde bzhi*). Four districts in Lower Ling (Tib. *smad gling*).

dohā (Skt.; Tib. *mgur*). A spiritual hymn or yogic song of experience. A spontaneous song sung by a tantric practitioner to express his or her experience in meditation practice. The Bengali *mahāsiddhas* were famous for these songs, but the form saw its greatest development in the collected songs of the Tibetan yogi Milarepa and his successors.

Dokham (Tib. *mdo kham*). Another name for Kham, or eastern Tibet.

Dorje Luphen (Tib. *rdo rje glu 'phen*). A name for Vajrasadhu. Also known as the *genyen* Dorje Legpa.

downs (Tib. *dil*). Colloquial term for a little hill or series of hills.

drala (Tib. *dgra lha*). Deities that represent the strength and physical integrity of a warrior. Iconographically, they are usually shown as armed figures on horseback. Some, dralas are more like nature spirits, and these are represented as animals or as part animal and part human. These are also referred to as *werma,* and in fact the two terms are interchangeable. The term *drala* is so popular in Tibetan stories and native Tibetan religion that its reference has expanded beyond the range of its original definition as a defensive spirit of war, and is used instead to mean any sort of local deity.

There are two spellings for this word with similar pronunciations but slightly different meanings: *dgra lha* and *dgra bla.* The first literally means, "enemy god," the idea being that this deity protects warriors against enemies; *lha* is the Tibetan term for "deity" when it is translating the Indic word *deva,* which is the generic term for god. The second literally means "above the enemy" and implies a sort of life force that resides on the body of the warrior and protects him or her from psychic and physical attacks. For more on the notion of *bla, see also* life stone.

drala castles (Tib. *bse mkhar*). Shrines to local spirits where juniper smoke offerings are performed. These shrines often appear in the form of piles of stone that look somewhat like castles and, along with prayer flags and other shrines that hold long arrows and flags, are considered to be the dwelling places of the dralas.

Drala Ceremonial Spear (Tib. *dgra lha rten mdung*). One of the Sevenfold Treasures; the name of a banner. For the meaning of *rten, see* supports.

dralas, praise of (Tib. *dgra lha'i ngo so bstod*). A ceremony usually performed after a *lhasang* (smoke offering) as a thanksgiving offering to the dralas. This will uplift, encourage, and invoke the dralas to action.

Dri Valley (Tib. *'bri lung*). A valley or region where the Dri Chu, also known as the Yangtze River, runs. The Yangtze River flows south into China and northwest of Jyekundo.

Drigung (Tib. *'bri gung*). Place name in middle Tibet.

Dromug [Roan] (Tib. *gro smug*). Drugmo's mare.

Drong (Tib. *'brong*). A wild yak that runs in herds on the high planes and is never domesticated.

Dru (Tib. *'dru*). One of the tribes of Ling living near the Ga, and therefore, like the Ga, it is labeled "rich."

Düd (Tib. *bdud*). Usually this refers to *bdud yul,* the country of māras or demons. Its king is the Demon of the North, and the greatest battle saga of the epic, the Düd Ling, is devoted to the bitter and violent war between this demon king and Gesar. *See also* māras and demons.

dzo (Tib. *mdzo*). A male beast of burden, the result of crossing a yak bull with a cow. This is considered to be the hardiest beast for merchants' travel and for caravans.

dzomo (Tib. *mdzo mo*). A female dairy beast; a hybrid of a yak and a cow. This animal is prized for the richness of its milk and butter.

E ma ho. A Tibetan expression of wonder and jubilation.

Earth Mare [Sata Dromo] (Tib. *sa rta gro mo*). The mother of Gesar's horse.

earth lord (Tib. *sa bdag*). A spirit who is the proprietor of a certain region, usually an impressive local deity complete with a palace, personal army of spirits, consort, and retinue.

East Mountain Dragon Fortress [Shar-ri Drugdzong] (Tib. *shar ri'i 'brug rdzong*). The palace of Chief Rongtsha Tragen.

eight classes of gods (Tib. *lha sde brgyad*). A classical list of eight kinds or races of local, non-Buddhist deities who inhabit Tibet. In the Yamantaka tantra, they are listed as follows: *gshin rje* (lords of death); *ma mo* (wrathful ḍākinīs); *srin po* (cannibals); *gnod sbyin* (wealth deities); *mi'am ci* (nonhuman entities); *sa bdag* (earth lords); *btsan* (local haughty spirits of the land); and *bdud* (demons). In other texts, they are listed as *lha* (gods); *klu* (nāgas); *gnod sbyin* (wealth deities); *dri za* (gandharvas); *lha ma yin* (demigods); *nam lding* (space dwellers); *mi'am ci* (nonhumans); and *lto 'phye chen po* (big-bellied spirits of the earth).

ego-clinging (Tib. *bdag tu 'dzin pa* or *bdag 'dzin*). Literally, "grasping to a self." The mental condition produced by ignorance that prevents enlightenment.

empowerment (Tib. *dbang;* Skt. *abhiṣeka*). A tantric ceremony of initiation that confers the power and authorization to begin vajrayāna practices.

enemies in the four directions (Tib. *phyogs bzhi'i dgra bzhi*) Also known as the demons of the four directions (Tib. *phyogs bzhi' bdud bzhi*). The four principal kingdoms that are opposed to the direction of virtue; Gesar must oppose and tame their rulers. The four kingdoms are the Düd, Hor, Mön, and Jang.

evil deeds (Tib. *sdig pa*). The Tibetan word is sometimes translated as "negativity," and sometimes as "sin"; this translation generally uses "evil deeds" in order to avoid Judeo-Christian terminology.

Fair Maiden (Tib. *dwangs sman*). Literally, "stainless maiden." An expression in the epic indicating a respected female.

Falcon Castle Sky Fortress [Trakhar Namdzong] (Tib. *khra mkhar gnam rdzong*). Rongtsha's palace. Also called Wealthy Sky Fortress [Namdzong Chugmo] (Tib. *gnam rdzong phyug mo*), and Upper Falcon Sky Fortress [Tratöd Namdzong] (Tib. *khra stod gnam rdzong*).

Falcon Cave [Traphug] (Tib. *khra phug*). The seat of Chipön Rongtsha Tragen, the chief of Ling. Also called Upper Falcon, or Tratöd (Tib. *khra stod*).

Ferocious Roaring Dragon (Tib. *rngam pa 'brug grag*). Kyalo Tönpa's guard dog.

field (Tib. *zhing;* Skt. *kṣetra*). A term from Buddhist cosmology that refers roughly to what Westerners would call a "world" or a "domain." Sometimes these are called "lands," as in *dag pa'i zhing*, which means "pure land." A pure land is the manifestation of pure appearances, which is the experience of those who are able to see the true nature of reality. On the other hand, if appearances are misinterpreted and based upon ignorance, then the ordinary realms of the world come into play.

Field of Lotus Power (Tib. *pad ma dbang gi zhing*). The assembly hall located to the west in Padmasambhava's Palace of Lotus Light on the continent of Cāmara; this is the room where the most secret tantras of Hayagrīva were taught. "Lotus Power" is a synonym for the yidam Hayagrīva.

Fills with Admiration (Tib. *mthong ba kun smon*). Literally, "inspired by seeing." Refers to the sight of the Ma Valley, or the land of Ling.

Five-Peaked Mountain. *See* Wu-t'ai Shan.

Five Topknots (Tib. *zur phud lnga pa;* Skt. Pañcaśika). This name refers to a way of tying up hair in a topknot, and may imply Mañjuśrī. In the Gesar epic, this refers to the king of the *nyen* gods or mountain gods, a figure associated with the great nyen Nyenchen Thanglha.

foreign kingdoms, eighteen (Tib. *rgyal khag bco brgyad*). Eighteen provinces or kingdoms surrounding Ling.

Form body of the Buddha (Tib. *gzugs kyi sku;* Skt. *rūpakāya*). The form body is the nirmāṇakāya, or transformation body—the visible, physical form of the Buddha. For example, Gautama Śākyamuni was a supreme nirmāṇakāya buddha who manifested in human form. The rūpakāya also includes the sambhogakāya; this is a wisdom form, which means it can be known by bodhisattvas who have true seeing. *See also* bodies of the Buddha, three.

Fortresses, Eight Minor (Tib. *rdzong phran brgyad*). The eight minor kingdoms.

fortunate connection (Tib. *rten 'brel*). An auspicious coincidence, good fortune.

Four-Gated Prosperity Corral (Tib. *g.yang ra ba sgo bzhi*). The area where Senglön first established the tent of Gogmo, Gesar's mother; so named because Gyaza, Senglön's primary wife, had given Gogmo four different animals as an auspicious connection in order to magnetize wealth for her. The animals were a yak, a horse, a goat, and a sheep.

Four Rivers of Dokham. Four rivers in the province of Kham, or eastern Tibet: the Dri Chu (Tib. *'bri chu,* the Yangtze River); the Ma Chu (Tib. *rma chu,* the Yellow River); the Gyalmo Ngül Chu (Tib. *rgyal mo rngul chu,* the Salween River); and the Dza Chu (Tib. *rdza chu,* the Mekong River).

free and well-favored (Tib. *dal 'byor*). Two conditions necessary to entering the Path. There are eight freedoms and ten conditions of being well-favored or endowed. For example, not being born in hell is one of the freedoms, because hell beings cannot practice meditation. An example of an endowment is being born in a country where the doctrine of the Buddha is taught.

Gadei (Tib. *dga' bde*). A place in Ling associated with the tribe Ga. The Tibetologist Rolf Alfred Stein identifies the locality with Jyekundo, which is around the first bend of the Yangtze River. The Ga tribe is associated with Tönpa Gyaltsen.

gaṇacakra (Skt.; Tib. *tshogs kyi 'khor lo*). A tantric or religious feast ceremony. In these practices, a group of vajrayāna practitioners who share a certain mandala or secret teaching will assemble and make offerings to the wisdom deities, according to the particular liturgy they are practicing. They share in the feast with the devas, sing songs expressing meditational experiences, and enjoy sensual pleasures that are transformed through ritual into dharma practice. Feasts are often given in order to purify a *tāntrika's* shortcomings or damaged commitments.

gandharva (Tib. *'dri za*). Literally, "smell eater." A spirit that feeds on fragrances as if they were food. These refined beings are celestial musicians.

Gangkar Tsesum [Three-Peaked White Snow Mountain] (Tib. *gangs dkar rtse gsum*). A mountain near the land of Ma.

garuḍa (Tib. *khyung*). A gigantic divine bird that was initially prominently mentioned in the first book of the great Indian epic, the *Mahabharata*. In Hinduism, he is the mount of Viṣṇu; in the Tibetan religion, he is the king of the birds and a divine principle of a mythical warrior's impeccability and vastness.

Ga'u Ser Dzong. *See* Golden Amulet Fortress.

Gekhöd (Tib. *ge khod*). A category of Bön deity.

generation and completion stages (Tib. *bskyed rim* and *rdzogs rim*). According to vajrayāna Buddhist practice, these are the two meditation stages: In the generation stage, one produces a mental image of a deity and his or her palace. In the completion or fulfillment stage, this visualization is resolved into emptiness, and one meditates formlessly without an objective focal point.

genyen (Tib. *dge bsnyen;* Skt. *upāsaka*). A class of wrathful, local Tibetan protector deities. The Tibetan word is a translation of Sanskrit *upāsaka*, a lay devotee who has taken certain vows. The name indicates the fact that these particular native Tibetan spirits are now committed to the buddhadharma as a result of oaths to Padmasambhava. Often they are depicted wearing a crystal *mala* or other explicitly Buddhist ornaments in order to indicate their status as genyens. Along with Nyenchen Thanglha and Machen Pomra, they are still called upon today during vajrayāna rituals in order to guard the doctrine of the Buddha, elevate the status of the practitioners, expand the community of the sangha, increase the life and splendor of the practitioners, raise the banner of fame, blow the conch of renown, and increase prosperity.

ghosts (Tib. *'byung po;* Skt. *bhūta*). A class of pathetic invisible spirits of the same order as *pretas* (Skt.), or hungry ghosts. They are sometimes called elementals, which follows the meaning and the fact that this class of deities includes deities of fire, earth, water, and the like.

Glorious Copper-Colored Mountain [Zangdog Pelri] (Tib. *zangs mdog dpal ri*). The mountain on the subcontinent of Cāmara. Padmasambhava resides here on its peak in the palace called Lotus Light.

glorious gate of good fortune (Tib. *rten 'brel dpal kha*). A moment in which astrological and karmic forces combine to offer the perfect conditions for the occurrence of a fortunate event, such as an event of some historical or political importance. At such moments, group rituals, sometimes carried out in unison by the entire political community, must be executed in order to take advantage of the "glorious gateway" and allow the supernatural energy to manifest. It might be better to say that the rituals performed during these perfect junctures stimulate these events to occur. The right conjunction is usually understood in terms of the four or five elements and the Chinese twelve roots and ten branches—a moment when heaven and earth may be united.

gods of the chase, thirteen (Tib. *mgul lha*). Literally, the "shoulder gods." The principal local gods in Tibet.

Gog (Tib. *'gog*). The country of Kyalo Tönpa Gyaltsen, which neighbors Ling. Since Gesar's mother lived in Gog, she is known as Gogmo, the woman from Gog; and as Senglön's younger wife, she is Gogza, the wife from Gog.

Golden Amulet Fortress (Tib. *ga'u gser rdzong*). The palace of Chief Michen Gyalwa'i Lhundrub. Later in volume 2, Gesar gives Michen an area of land near modern Derge called Golden Amulet Valley (Tib. *ga'u gser lung*).

Golden Provinces of Upper Ling, Eight (Tib. *stod gling gser pa ched brgyad*). Upper Ling is the highland area where Chöphen Nagpo's elder wife, the matriarchal founder of the Ser (or Golden) family of the Elder Lineage, found her totem, which was a golden yoke.

great encampment (Tib. *sgar chen po*). The great gatherings called *garchen,* which included semipermanent accommodations for a large number of people, were a particular feature of traditional Tibetan life. The encampment might serve as a monastery, or a village on the move, or a place for trade and business connections. *Gar* is also the name for a temporary encampment for disciples who are gathering around the guru for teachings and practice. It is also used in the context of military encampments.

Great Power (Tib. *dbang chen lha mchog*). One of the epithets of the yidam Hayagrīva. Another epithet is Lotus Great Power (Tib. *pad ma dbang chen*). *See also* Lotus Great Power.

Greater Lineage of Ling (Tib. *gling che rgyud kyi gdung rgyud*). The Elder Lineage of the three lineages of Ling, the Serpa clan. Their divine prince is Nyibum Daryag.

Grimacing One (Tib. *khro gnyer can ma*). Also known as Wrathfully Grimacing One. A wrathful form of Tārā.

Gu-ra, the Crag Mountain of (Tib. *gu ra rdza*). A mountain in Ling that was determined to be the finish line for the horse race.

gyalgong (Tib. *rgyal 'gong*). Literally, "king demon," this is a kind of spirit with a characteristic combination of tyrannous pride and sectarian aggression who some worship, but others regard as a pest. Those who worship gyalgongs may feel bliss at first, which is the gift of that spirit. But if they try to break off the relationship, the spirit becomes their enemy, chasing them in their dreams and inflicting diseases such as paralysis.

The gyalgong has a wrathful quality, and if there is a hotheaded schism or angry rebellion, some Tibetans will say it is the result of an infestation of gyalgongs or kingly demonic forces. Hence it has been said that the destructive behavior of the Red Guard during the Cultural Revolution had the appearance of an attack of gyalgongs.

habitual patterns (Tib. *bag chags;* Skt. *vāsanā*). Patterns of conditioning that exist in the subconscious mind, which are the cause of ego fixation.

Hara Hurthung [Short and Impetuous] (Tib. *ha ra hur thung*). A style of melody used by Trothung for his songs.

Haughty Turquoise Dragon Fortress (Tib. *g.yu 'brug 'gying rdzong*). Chipön's palace.

Hayagrīva (Tib. *rta mgrin*). A horse-headed tantric Buddhist yidam, or tutelary deity. Hayagrīva is a wrathful form of Amitābha, the Lotus family Buddha. He is especially revered as a deity that should be supplicated for the removal of obstacles and the liberation of demons. He is the personal deity of Trothung and the Tag-rong.

heart cakra of dharma (Tib. *snying kha chos kyi 'khor lo*). The network of wisdom channels located at the heart center. See also *cakra*.

heruka (Tib. *khrag 'thung*). A wrathful male yidam, or tutelary deity, in the sambhogakāya aspect of enlightenment. The Tibetan *khrag 'thung* translates as "blood-drinker," and in vajrayāna symbolism, the heruka drinks the blood of ego-clinging and dualistic thinking.

hidden lands, four (Tib. *sbas yul bzhi*). Theoretical secret lands that are similar to the notion of Shangri-la.

hocks (Tib. *sgyid pa*). The hamstring.

Hor (Tib. *hor*). A kingdom to the east of Ling, ruled by demons who are enemies of Ling as well as enemies of virtue. A later volume of the epic is devoted to the war between Ling and

Hor. The Hor are divided into three tribes, each governed by a king: King Gurkar [White Tent]; King Gurnag [Black Tent]; and King Gurser [Yellow Tent].

horse gods (Tib. *rta lha*). Horse spirits, or the forces that accompany a horse in order to assist it in various ways.

hundred-syllable mantra. The mantra of Vajrasattva. *See also* Vajrasattva.

hungry ghost (Tib. *yi dwags;* Skt. *preta*). The realm of the hungry ghosts is one of the three lower realms in the six realms of rebirth in saṃsāra. Hungry ghosts have huge stomachs and tiny mouths; they are always hungry and thirsty, but can never be satisfied. They are often depicted with fire spewing from their mouths, since whatever they try to ingest turns into molten fire.

interpretable meaning (Tib. *drang don;* Skt. *neyārtha*). Literally, "leading to the meaning." The teachings of the Buddha and the commentaries written based on these teachings will either directly introduce the definitive nature of reality, or implicate that nature. The scriptures that emphasize the latter are referred to as scriptures with "interpretable meaning," because they will implicate the truth but not point it out directly.

Jachen Yölmo Corners (Tib. *'ja' chen yol mo gru khug*). Literally, "great rainbow in the alcove of Yölmo." A solitary place known as Great Rainbow Alcove, near Ma.

Jambudvīpa (Tib. *dzam bu gling*). The southern continent in the cosmology of the Buddhist world-system. It is named after the *jambu* (rose-apple) tree. Jambudvīpa is the world populated by human beings, so it is roughly equivalent to planet Earth in the Western cosmological system.

Jang (Tib. *'jang*). A country south of Batang, ruled by King Sadam. Gesar conquers this country in later volumes of the epic.

Jowo Buddha (Tib. *jo bo*). A famous statue of Amitābha Buddha in Lhasa.

Jowo Namri [Lord Sky Mountain] (Tib. *jobo gnam ri*). A mountain in the kingdom of Düd, the Demon of the North.

Kailash, Mount (Tib. *gangs ti se*). Located in southwest Tibet, this mountain has been a pilgrimage point for Buddhists and Hindus for centuries. In Hindu mythology, it is said to be the home of Śiva.

kalavinka bird. A kind of Indian cuckoo known to Tibetans through their study of Indian poetry. Sometimes called a *kalapinka* bird, this is an allegorical, sweet-voiced bird of immortality.

Kaling Temple of Ma (Tib. *rma ka li lha khang*). A gathering place in Ling. Although it is not an actual temple, it is called one because of its divine beauty.

kalpa (Skt.; Tib. *kal pa* or *bskal pa*). An extremely long period of time; an aeon or an age.

Kar and Nag tribal wards (Tib. *dkar nag stong skor tsho pa*). A place in Ling. Although the expression makes Kar and Nag seem to be two separate places, they are always mentioned together as if they were a single unit.

karmically destined horses of White Ling, thirty (Tib. *gling dkar po'i las rta sum bcu*). Most of these horses can fly, and possess the power of speech. Each has a name and is specially destined to belong to its particular warrior.

kāya (Tib. *sku*). The Tibetan honorific term for "body" is *sku*. Throughout the text, the Sanskrit word *kāya* is used as the translation for "body" in order to indicate the word's esoteric meaning as the Enlightened Body of the Buddha. *See also* bodies of the Buddha, three.

kāyas, four (Skt.). This refers to the three bodies of the Buddha plus the *swavavivakāya,* which is the enlightened body of the nature as it is. *See also* bodies of the Buddha, three.

khaṭvāṅga (Tib. *khat wang ga*). A tantric scepter in the shape of an ornamented iron pole, which is adorned with three heads at the top and a three-pronged fork like a trident. This is one of the important hand emblems held by tantric yogis such as Padmasambhava. This emblem often indicates the consort.

Khenlung Ridrug [Six-Peaked Sage Valley] (Tib. *mkhan lung ri drug*). A valley in the curve of the upper Yellow River, near Ma. An unpopulated region inhabited mainly by *pikas,* the Yellow Hor robbed passing merchants here until the area was settled by Gesar's kingdom.

ki and so (Tib. *ki* and *bsvo*). Part of the warrior's cry. In full, the cry is: *ki! ki! so! so! lha gyal lo!* (*"ki! ki! so! so!"* means "Divine victory!"). This is also a mantric sound in native Tibetan religion. This sound originates with the Bön, a shamanistic sect of the indigenous people of Tibet. When invoking the gods and trying to incite their deeds, Bönpo utter this sound along with other syllables. This sound will uplift the windhorse for a situation, and once offerings are made, it ensures success. *See also* windhorse.

know me (Tib. *mkhyen* or *mkhyen no*). An expression that calls out to one's object of devotion, such as a god, guru, or buddha, in order to ask for blessings and support. This expression is used particularly in the practice of guru yoga, or devotion to the guru. This is one of the most common practices in vajrayana Buddhism. For example, in the practice of Calling the Gurus from Afar, one might invoke a guru by repeating the refrain "Guru, know me" several times over. (Tib. *bla ma mkhyen no*).

Knowing Steed [Changshei] (Tib. *cang shes*). An epithet for Gesar's horse, meaning "all-knowing." Refers to the fact that the horse possesses a human intelligence and complete knowledge of the future of the epic. The horse is also called Noble Steed (Tib. *rta mdo ba*), an elegant term for a special horse.

Kukurīpā. One of the eighty-four mahāsiddhas who taught Marpa Lotsawa the Mahāmāyā Tantra. He was famous for his eccentric association with dogs.

kumuda (Skt.). A kind of lotus flower that opens in moonlight.

Kyalo Wealthy Pasture Land (Tib. *skya lo phyug gi mtsher sa*). Homeland of Kyalo Tönpa. The word *wealthy* (Tib. *phyug*) in this context tends to mean "livestock," since the wealth of a family is often indicated by how many heads of yak, dru, and sheep they have in their family herds.

kyang (*Equus kiang*). The Tibetan wild ass. Unlike Westerners' negative notions about the ass, this is an exceptionally impressive and noble creature who wanders the high plains and mountains.

Kyang-bu (Tib. *kyang bu*). Gesar's horse; the name means "kyang colt." *See also* Wild Kyang.

Kyidsö Yag-gi Khado [Conjunction of the Excellent Joyful Spring] (Tib. *skyid sos yag gi kha mdo*). A region of Upper (western) Ling. This is now recognized as a place near Shechen Monastery, and close to the monastery built by Tshabsha Kuchen (Tib. *tshab tsha sku chen*). A temple in honor of Gesar and the Thirty Mighty Warriors has been erected on the site. Many scholars of Gesar also claim that the place known as Sengdrug Tagtse Palace (Tib. *seng 'brug stag rtse*) in Golog, where the Dar River merges with the Yellow River, is also the site of Kyidsö Yag-gi Khado. Both positions are openly accepted.

Kyigyal Tag-ri [Tiger Mountain King of Joy] (Tib. *skyid rgyal stag ri*). A place in Ling. This name has many variants, including *spyi rgyal* (general king); *skyi rgyal* (sparkling king); and *lci rgyal* (king of Ci).

Lesser Lineage of Ling (Tib. *gling chung rgyud kyi gdung rgyud*). One of the three lineages of Ling, the Muchang clan; the lineage that comes from the youngest of the heirs, also sometimes referred to as the Cadet Lineage, or the Younger Lineage. Their divine prince is Rinchen Darlu.

Lha Downs [Divine Downs] (Tib. *lha dis*). A group of hills in Ling where the spectators observed the horse race. Drugmo was positioned there, and this is the place from which she described the qualities of each of the warriors.

lhasang. *See* smoke offering.

life duration (Tib. *tshe*). A kind of force or energy that a person possesses at birth as the result of his or her previous karma. A person's longevity depends on the amount of life duration they possess, because short of extraordinary interventions, a person dies when their allotted life expectancy is exhausted. *See also* life force.

life essence (Tib. *srog*). The life energy that is possessed by every living being, which is responsible for health and a general sense of physical well-being. If a person has an illness associated with their life essence, they will become weak, depressed, and frequently ill. Often this term is presented as part of a triad: *tshe*, life duration or expectancy; *bla*, the life force; and *srog*, the life essence.

life force (Tib. *bla*). A kind of entity or nexus located in the human heart center that functions like a soul. It is responsible for the sense of identification with the body. If the life force should journey away from the body and not return, death will soon follow. The life force can exit the body if an individual is suddenly frightened, and this can lead to the shortening of life. *See also* life duration.

life stone (Tib. *bla rdo*). Literally, "soul stone," the life stone is a kind of soul that dwells in a person. When the life force leaves a person, they will die soon after. Some people believe they can keep part of their life force locked safely in a material object, such as a stone or a mirror, or in the famous Russian fairy tale of Koschei the Deathless, an egg. The Tibetans have ceremonies for locking a portion of the life force in a token stone, usually turquoise, which is then worn around the neck for security and protection.

Limitless Palace of Lotus Light (Tib. *pad ma 'od kyi gzhal yas*). Padma's palace on Cāmara on the Copper-Colored Mountain.

Lion Cub Tiger Fortress [Sengtrug Tagdzong] (Tib. *seng phrug stag rdzong*). A castle built for Gesar by Gedzo and Machen Pomra. It is one of the prizes given to the winner of the race. In modern times, this place was honored through the rebuilding of a temple at the original location, which was identified by the great twentieth-century lama Khenpo Jigmed Phuntsog Jungney. The site is in Golog, close to the place where the Yellow and Dar Rivers merge. Also known as Lion Dragon Tiger Peak [Sengtrug Tagtse] (Tib. *seng 'brug stag rtse*).

Ling, epithets for (Tib. *gling*). Ling is a country presumably in eastern Tibet or Amdo Province that has several epithets in the Gesar epic: it is called White Ling (meaning "Ling, the good"); Sparkling Ling; Multicolored Ling (meaning "Ling, the beautiful"); and Wishing Land Ling (meaning that Ling is such a wonderful place that everybody wishes they were there).

Lingtsang (Tib. *gling gtsang*). A tribe or a small kingdom in northeastern Tibet (or northwestern China), also known as Derge. This tribe is said to be associated with Ling.

Long-Life Queen of Siddhi Liquor (Tib. *grub pa'i rgyal mo'i tshe chang*). The name of a liquor, blessed by the goddess of longevity named Drubpa'i Gyalmo. This is the long-life liquor that Drugmo has with her in order to offer it to Joru when she meets him.

Lord of Secrets. *See* Vajrapāṇi.

Lord of Steeds ['Dorje Kyang Göd] (Tib. *'do rje kyang rgod*). Epithet for Wild Kyang, also referred to by his full name, 'Dorje Kyang Göd Phelpo [Lord of Steeds Ever-Increasing Wild Kyang] (Tib. *'do rje kyang rgod 'phel po*).

Lord of the World (Skt.; *Lokeśvara* Tib. *'jig rten dbang pyhugs*). An epithet of Avalokiteśvara, the bodhisattva of compassion.

Lotus Crystal Cave of Ma Dentig [**Ma Dentig Padma Shelphug**] (Tib. *rma dan thig pad ma shel phug*). A sacred cave in the Ma Valley where Padmasambhava revealed *termas,* and where Gesar, when he was just eight years old, revealed many earth treasures that were warriors' accoutrements. This set up the auspicious connection for his future taming of the māras in the four directions. Another epic is fully dedicated to how he revealed these treasures from this cave. See also *terma*.

Lotus Great Power [**Padma or Pema Wangchen**] (Tib. *pad ma dbang chen*). A name for Hayagrīva.

loving-kindness (Tib. *byams pa;* Skt. *maitrī*). The Tibetan and Sanskrit terms are translated variously as "loving-kindness," "mercy," or "friendliness."

lunar month (Tib. *bod rtsis*). Type of calendar that is based on the cycle of the moon, so that the first day of the month is the first day of the waxing moon, the fifteenth day is the full moon, and the thirtieth day is the new moon day.

Ma (Tib. *rma*). A region localized sometimes in eastern Tibet, sometimes in Amdo. Usually Ma refers to the region of the upper Yellow River (called Ma River in Tibetan), which is located near the mountain Magyal Pomra; Upper Ma is in the present-day Tibetan prefecture of Golog. In this version of the epic, Ma seems to be located somewhat to the south, because it neighbors the land of Den (Tib. *'dan*). At the beginning of the epic, Ma is a wild, unpeopled land full of gods and demons. Later on, after a famine, Gesar resettles all of Ling in Ma.

Ma, Lower (Tib. *rma smad*). In the land of the Gologs, the Ma River—that is, the Yellow River—turns from east to west at the thirty-fourth parallel, and forms a region enclosed on three sides by the river. This is *rma smad lha lung sum mdo* (Tib.), which means roughly the Divine Valley of Lower Ma at the Three Confluences.

Ma Dentig Padma Shelphug. *See* Lotus Crystal Cave of Ma Dentig.

magnetize (Tib. *dbang du bsdu*). Used here in the sense of "overcome." This is the ritual action by which a being or object is brought under one's influence. It is one of the Four Karmas (Tib. *phrin las bzhi*)—that is, four ritual acts of power that a buddha can perform.

mahāsattva (Skt.; Tib. *sems can chen po*). Among bodhisattvas, the mahāsattvas are the ones who have attained the level of the sixth bhūmi and beyond. This means they have accomplished the perfection of knowledge, or *prajñā,* and can directly see the empty nature of all things.

mahāsiddha (Skt.; Tib. *grub thob*). Literally, "great accomplished one." The Indian mahāsiddhas were unconventional yogic practitioners of tantra. They are famous for pursuing livelihoods not usually associated with the practice of buddhadharma, and thereby demonstrating the continuity of the dharmakāya through all things. They are traditionally represented wearing bone ornaments and the informal clothes of a tantric layman. There is a classical list of eighty-four mahāsiddhas, most of whom lived in Bengal. Their dohās, or "songs of experience," collected in the Caryāpadas, give esoteric instructions in symbolic form while often appearing to be popular genres of secular ballads.

makara (Skt.). An abstract design shaped like a mythical sea creature of Hindu mythology, reminiscent of a crocodile. It is displayed on ornaments and jewelry, as well as on temples.

Māmakī (Skt.). Māmakī is the female buddha who represents, and ultimately is, the element of water.

Mamed Yulung Sumdo. *See* Yulung Sumdo.

mamo (Tib. *ma mo*). Female demons; wrathful ḍākiṇīs that represent the aggressive enlightened activity that averts all negativity concerning upheavals with the elements. Mamos will actively turn back those who intend to bring harm to others, particularly through the elements and through imbalances with the humors of the body.

Manasarovar, Lake (Tib. *ma dros pa*). A mythical lake where Padmasambhava tamed the nāgas. From this lake flow the four great rivers, which are known by many names in various countries: the Sutlej, the Brahmaputra, the Indus, and a river called the Karnali in Nepal (Ghagāra in India). Manasarovar is also called Anavatapta, which is the name of a nāga who lives in the lake. The lake is just south of Mount Kailash, and like Kailash, it has been a pilgrimage spot for both Hindus and Buddhists.

Maṇi mantra. The six-syllable Sanskrit mantra particularly connected with Avalokiteśvara, the Lord of Compassion. Repeated as: OṂ MAṆI PADME HŪṂ. This mantra translates as "OṂ Jewel-Lotus HŪṂ," indicating the bodhisattva of compassion, as well as the indwelling Buddha nature that abides as the basic enlightened nature of all living beings. By repeating this mantra, compassionate awareness is stirred, and one realizes that all beings have this enlightened potential and so should be honored and cherished above oneself. Sometimes amended as OṂ MAṆI PADME HŪṂ HRĪḤ; the syllable HRĪḤ is Avalokiteśvara's heart essence or seed syllable.

Mantra Holder (Tib. *sngags 'chang*). A master of *mantrayāna* of the tantric path. Lotus Skull Garland [Padma Tötreng] is called the Mantra Holder.

Mapham Lake (Tib. *ma pham gyu mtsho*). Another name for Lake Manasarovar.

māra (Tib. *bdud;* Skt. *māra*). This is a term that can be translated as "demon." and refers to a class of native Tibetan malevolent deities that can cause obstacles or even death; one of the eight classes of gods (Tib. *lha*) of the native religion. The evil demon king of the north, whom Gesar must destroy in the central battle saga of the epic, is known as Düd, the Demon of the North.

When capitalized as Māra this refers to the tempter of Śākyamuni Buddha, who appeared just prior to his attainment of enlightenment. More generally, in the Indic tradition, māras are difficulties that the practitioner may encounter along their path, such as obstacles and interruptions to their meditation practice. *See also* demons.

Marshöd (Tib. *smar shod*). The dwelling place of the prognosticator, Dorje Ngangyag. The longer name "Marshöd Shelkar Lhadrag" has been translated here as Lower Valley of Mar Crystal Divine Crag.

Masang (Tib. *ma sang*). An ancestral tribe of Ling. Masang is also an epithet for Gesar, in the title Masang King of Magic (Tib. *ma sang 'phrul gyi rgyal po*). Another similar epithet is Masang One Who Accomplishes His Goal (Tib. *ma sang skye bu don 'grub*).

medicinal herbs, six (Tib. *bzang po drug*). This may refer to six culinary herbs: nutmeg, which is good for the heart; musk, which is good for the lungs; saffron, for the liver; cloves, for the aorta or central life vein; elettaria cardamom, for the kidney or *avadhūti;* and castor oil, for the spleen. Another listing includes: yellow myrobalan *(Terminalia chebula)*; beleric myrobalan *(Terminalia belerica)*; emblic myrobalan *(Emblica officinalis)*; bamboo manna; musk; and solidified elephant bile.

meditational deity (Tib. *yi dam*). The vajrayāna practitioner's personal deity, or tutelary deity, who embodies the practitioner's awakened nature. The word *yidam* is explained as a contraction of *yid kyi dam tshig* (Tib.), which means the *samaya,* or commitment of one's mind. Yidams are sambhogakāya buddhas who are visualized in accordance with the psychological makeup of the practitioner. They are male, female, peaceful, enriching, powerful, and wrathful, and carry symbolic ornaments that are an esoteric commentary on the nature and manifestation of the practitioner's mind. Examples of famous yidams are Vajrayoginī, Cakrasaṃvara, Vajrakīlaya, Yamantaka, and Hayagrīva, among others.

meditative equipoise (Tib. *mnyam par bzhag pa;* Skt. *samādhi*). "Evenness," a state in which meditative concentration or perfect stillness is attained; this term can also be used as a general expression for the practice of meditation.

meekness (Tib. *chog shes*). "Contentment" or "complaisance," as in *chung ngus chog shes pa* (Tib.), which means "to be content with little."

melodious speech, sixty aspects (Tib. *gsungs dbyangs yan lag drug cu*). Sixty aspects of melodious speech that are ascribed to the Buddha as the epitome of enlightened speech, including the gift of tongues and so forth. This list is found in both sutras and tantras.

Melody of a Modulating Long Neigh (Tib. *'tsher ring mo'i rta*). The tune to which Wild Kyang, Gesar's horse, sings his melodies.

Melody of the Roaring Tigress (Tib. *stag mo'i ngar glu'i rta*). Another name for Trothung's traditional melody. The word *tigress* relates to the name of his clan, Tag-rong [Tiger Valley].

menmo (Tib. *sman mo*). A female formless spirit that resides in the mountains and the rocks. Often the important great "sisterhoods" of goddesses—that is, classical lists of goddesses, such as the five Long-Life Goddesses—are called menmos. As native Tibetan feminine deities they can be wrathful, and hence they are similar in aspect to the Greek furies. In smoke purification chants, the menmo may be paired with dralas, as in "May all dralas and menmos come." They are also referred to as the twelve menmos, or the menmo of the four directions. Literally, *sman* means both "medicine" and "woman," thus *menmo* can also be a respectful term for a woman.

merit (Tib. *bsod nams*). In the context of the Gesar epic, merit is not an abstract possession of positive karma, but rather an actual energy or glow possessed by people with an abundance of virtue.

Middle Lineage of Ling (Tib. *gling 'bring rgyud kyi gdung rgyud*). Of the three lineages of Ling, in order of age the Middle Lineage is between the Elder and the Lesser Lineages, and represents the Ombu clan. Its divine prince is Anu Paseng.

Middle Ling (Tib. *'bring gling*). Comprising the six districts of Ombu. *See also* districts, six.

mighty and terrible ones, 360 (Tib. *kha drag sum brgya drug cu*). A list of local wrathful deities and guardians of the land. The number 360 is generic, and simply means that there are many of these deities.

Mighty Warriors, Thirty (Tib. *dpa' brtul sum cu*). The chief knights in Gesar's army. In addition to these thirty, there are seven warriors of a higher degree called the Seven Super Warriors (Tib. *yang thul;* literally, "even mightier") and Ultimate Warriors (Tib. *zhe thul*). Most of these warriors have their own sagas in the greater epic. In the beginning there are thirty warriors, but in future epics there are eventually eighty warriors, and they are all incarnations or aspects (Tib. *cha shas*) of the eighty mahāsiddhas.

mind stream (Tib. *thugs rgyud*). An honorific term for the mind of a meditation master who one respects. The Tibetan term *rgyud* refers to the continuity of mind of an ordinary individual. This term is indicative of the Buddhist view that the mind is a continuity or stream of movement and impressions, which permanently endure from one lifetime to another. In the case of the honorific term *thugs rgyud,* this would be the continuity of wisdom awareness as opposed to ordinary mind.

mind terma (Tib. *dgongs gter*). This aspect of the secret revelations concerns Padmasambhava's direct disciples during the Master's life and journey in Tibet. At that time, he gave many empowerments and teachings to his most qualified disciples, and they in turn went on to practice and accomplish these teachings and achieve higher states of realization. It was predicted that these disciples would reincarnate in future generations, and reveal different aspects of this spiritual teaching to destined disciples in those times. These revelations, which simply emerged from the recollection of that previous lifetime and were taught according to these prophecies, are known are mind terma. There are treasure revealers who continue to spread this tradition even in the present day. Based upon a moment of total recall, they will bring forth all the information they received during their life with Padmasambhava, and they share these teachings with the modern-day disciples according to the tradition. It is a remarkable lineage of direct transmission and blessing. See also *terma.*

Mind's Amusement (Tib. *sems rtsed*). The miraculous waterproof shoes in the possession of the nāgas.

Modulating Long Neigh (Tib. *'tsher 'gyur ring mo'i rta*). The tune that Wild Kyang, Gesar's horse, uses for a song he sings.

Mongolian gait (Tib. *rta 'gros ldan*). The unique style or gait of horses found in the highlands of Tibet and Mongolia, a gait that is fluid even at high speed. There is no need to post or postulate while a horse is running with this gait, because it is as smooth as if they were walking. Some horses are actually trained by having them run in thick sand, so they will lift their hooves up higher and gradually assume this gait.

Mönlam La [Aspiration Pass or Prayer Pass] (Tib. *smon lam la*). A sacred site in Ling near the castle of Chief Rongtsha Tragen. It is sometimes called Aspiration Mountain Pass, and is also known as Mönlam Dragkar [White Boulder Aspiration Prayer Mountain] (Tib. *smon lam brag dkar*), which is the place where Padmasambhava originally decided that Gesar would be born.

morning star (Tib. *skar rgyan*). Likely refers to Venus.

Mother of Basic Space. *See* Vajra Dhātvīśvarī.

Mother Text (Tib. *ma yig*) **of the Mukpo clan.** The original manuscript of this book, which contains prophecies about the future of Ling.

mountain dog (Tib. *ri khyi*). A metonymic term for wolf.

mountain ranges, six. Zelmo Mountain (Tib. *zal mo sgang*); Tsawa Mountain (Tib. *tsha ba sgang*); Markham Mountain (Tib. *smar khams sgang*); Pombor Mountain (Tib. *spo 'bor sgang*); Mardza Mountain (Tib. *dmar rdza sgang*); and the Minyag Rab Mountain (Tib. *mi nyag rab sgang*) or Minyag (Tib. *mi nyag*). Zelmo can be divided into two mountain ranges, Ma (Tib. *rma*) and Dza (Tib. *rdza*). These mountainous regions are closer in nature to provinces or states as they are really territories or political divisions whose borders have been defined by natural boundaries, such as mountain ranges.

Mu (Tib. *dmu*). A tribe in the Lesser Lineage of Ling. Gesar's human father is Senglön, whose mother was known as Muza, the "woman of the Mu tribe." Thus Gesar is closely related to the Mu of the Lesser or Younger Lineage, as is Chipön, the chieftain of the Lesser Lineage. There is another meaning of *dmu* which refers to Mu demons. This demonic force is the most detrimental of the eight classes of gods and spirits. Its power is based on deluded obstruction that obscures clarity, virtue, and goodness, such that the victim is completely unaware of the plague.

Mu cord (Tib. *dmu thag*). A magical rope that reaches from the heavens to the earth.

Muchang (Tib. *dmu spyang*). One of the clans of origin of the Lesser Lineage; the others were the Ombu and Serpa.

Mukpo Dong (Tib. *smug po gdong*). The name of the ancestral lineage of the Mukpo tribe or clan. *Dong* by itself means "tribe." The tribe may be called Dong, or Mukpo, or both together; all are proper names of Gesar's tribe. *Mukpo* means "dark-skinned," which refers to the maroon or dark reddish-brown color that is associated with many of the local deities.

Myriarch [Leader of Ten Thousand] (Tib. *khri dpon*). A Tibetan military honorific.

myriarchy (Tib. *khri skor*). A group numbering ten thousand. The term literally means "ten thousand householders," and when applied to the military it indicates an army with ten thousand soldiers.

myrobalan (Tib. *a ru*). Yellow myrobalan *(Terminalia chebula)*, the herb held in the hands of the Medicine Buddha in most traditional iconography. *See* medicinal herbs, six.

nāḍī, prāṇa, and bindu (Skt.). In Tibetan, these are *rtsa, rlung,* and *thig le.* According to the system of inner yogic discipline found in vajrayāna practice, the psychic channels called nāḍī run throughout the body. The major ones run down the middle of the body along the spine, and to the left and the right of the central channel. The essential fluid that passes through these channels is called bindu, which literally means "essential drops." The movement of energy through these channels is called prāṇa, or "wind." The goal of this level of practice is to gain mastery over these three constituents so that the karmic winds can enter the central energy channel, and therefore the flow of energy becomes that of wisdom rather than ordinary discursive movement.

nāga / nāgī (f.) (Skt.; Tib. *klu / klu mo*). Dragons, serpents. A class of deities associated with water in all its forms. The most prominent nāga in the epic is Tsugna Rinchen, the king of the nāgas who rules a realm at the bottom of the ocean. Iconographically they are usually represented with human torsos and blue-skinned, serpent-like lower bodies, and the women (nāgī, or nāginī) have turquoise hair. As an Indic deity, the nāgas also figure prominently in the Indian epic tradition, particularly the *Mahabharata,* which begins with a description of the war between the nāgas and garuḍa.

Nāga Downs (Tib. *klu dis*). A series of hills in Ling. This is the site where the smoke offerings were performed during the horse race.

Nāgārjunagarbha (Skt.; Tib. *klu sgrub snying po*). Another name for the great Indian Buddhist philosopher Nāgārjuna, the developer of the mahāyāna school known as Madhyamika or the Middle Way. According to Tibetan tradition, he became a tantric practitioner and lived for hundreds of years. Nāgārjuna means "friend of the nāgas," which refers to the story that Nāgārjuna fetched the Perfection of Wisdom Sutras from beneath the sea, where they were being held in trust by the nāgas for future generations.

Ngari (Tib. *mnga' ris*). The western section of the greater Tibetan Autonomous Region that borders India and Nepal, also called the Three Areas of Ngari (Tib. *mnga' ris skor gsum*).

nidānas, twelve (Skt.; Tib. *rten 'brel bcu gnyis*). Twelve links in a causal chain that describe the enslaved life cycle of beings that live in cyclic existence: ignorance, volitional factors, consciousness, name and form, six sense sources, contact, sensation, craving, grasping, becoming, birth, old-age-and-death.

nirmāṇakāya (Skt.; Tib. *sprul sku*). The physical emanation body of the Buddha. *See also* bodies of the Buddha, three.

Noble Excellent Great Compassionate One (Tib. *'phags pa thugs rje chen po*; Skt. *Avalokiteśvara*). Refers to Avalokiteśvara, the bodhisattva who embodies the compassion of all the buddhas.

Noble Steed. *See* Knowing Steed.

nonhuman (Tib. *mi ma yin*). A nonhuman spirit or entity. *See* eight classes of gods.

nonhuman, eight orders of (Tib. *mi min sde brgyad*). *See* eight classes of gods.

Northern God (Tib. *byang lha*). An epithet for Hayagrīva.

nyen (Tib. *gnyan*). Gods of mountain ranges. In the threefold hierarchy of native deities (*lha, nyen,* and *lu*), they occupy the middle realm between heaven and the underground, equivalent to the sides of mountains. Nyen are usually powerful gods who exercise a certain proprietorship over the lands where their mountain ranges lie, and hence are often referred to as *sadag* (Tib. *sa bdag*), or earth lords. Famous nyen are Machen Pomra and Nyenchen Thanglha, and Gesar's patron Gedzo.

Nyida Khatröd [Conjoined Sun and Moon] (Tib. *nyi zla kha phrod*). This complex name occurs with numerous variations in the text. The Tibetan, *nyi zla kha sprod* (literally "sun and moon face-to-face") is also written as *yag nyi kha sprod* (Tib.), Conjoined Excellence of the Sun, or *nyi zla kha* (Tib.), Sun and Moon Facing. It is a site at which two lateral valleys containing streams meet at the valleys' openings, and is the great gathering place of White Ling.

oath-breaking demons. *See* damsi.

Offering Treasures of the nāgas, nine (Tib. *dkor nor sna dgu*). Nine precious objects in the possession of the nāgas: the jewel Ting-öd Münsel [Blue Light That Dispels Darkness]; the seahorse Ziwang Phurshei [Splendid Stride Flying Knowledge]; the precious stole called Drojam Phagpa Rinchen [Soft Precious Skin]; the waterproof shoes called Chulam Samtsei [Freedom to Walk]; the little crystal vase Chuchüd Shel [Water Quintessence Crystal]; the turquoise branch Shing Chüd [Wood Quintessence]; the armor Yamed Bendrilya [Rustless Lapis]; the antidote to poison Dugkyöb Dugzil Zhuntig [Crystal Dew Poison Curing Potent Drop]; and the febrifuge Tsenden Trulgi Nyinpo [Cooling Sandalwood Serpent Essence].

One Hundred Thousand Verse Wisdom Sutra. A twelve-volume (or sometimes sixteen-volume) collection of Prajñāpāramitā texts, which was kept for centuries by the nāgas before being brought to the human realm by Nāgārjuna. In the epic, the nāgas give the texts to Gogmo, Gesar's mother, then they are appropriated by Tönpa Gyaltsen of Kyalo along with Gogmo, and as a result they passed into the common possession of the Ling tribe. These highly ornamented Perfection of Wisdom Sutras are one of the tribe's prize possessions, and they are so revered that people even swear by them. The same sutra is also known as the One Hundred Thousand Verse Prajñāpāramitā, the Greater Prajñāpāramitā Sutra, and the One Hundred Thousand Verses of the nāgas.

One-Thousand-Lotus-Fringed scarf (Tib. *pad ma lan tsar stong ldan*). The name of an offering scarf.

oral instructions (Tib. *gdams ngag;* Skt. *upadeśa*). In tantra, the guru personally communicates the essence of meditation practice to his students orally.

Padma Rāga Palace (Tib. *pad ma ra ga'i pho brang*). Ruby Palace, an abode of Buddha Amitābha.

Pāṇḍaravāsinī [Clothed in White Robes] (Skt.; Tib. *gos dkar lcang lo can* or *gas dkar mo*). The female buddha who resides in the west and is the pure aspect of the element of fire. *See also* buddha families, five.

panyacalika silk (Skt.; Tib. *pa nya tsa li ka*). A kind of special brocade silk.

pāramitās, six (Skt.; Tib. *pha rol tu phyin pa*). The six perfections, which are the six virtuous practices that constitute the discipline of the mahāyāna path: generosity (Tib. *sbyin pa;* Skt. *dāna*); discipline (Tib. *tsul khrims;* Skt. *śila*); patience (Tib. *bzod pa;* Skt. *kṣānti*); exertion (Tib. *btson 'grus;* Skt. *vīrya*); concentration (Tib. *bsam gtan;* Skt. *dhyāna*); and incisive knowledge (Tib. *shes rab;* Skt. *prajñā*). The perfections are six transcendent actions that serve as the transcendental tools for attaining the stages of awareness that lead to enlightenment.

passionless union (Tib. *ma chags thabs kyi sbyor ba*). To engage in the act of sexual union in a state of awareness that unites emptiness and exaltation, so that the state of awareness is no longer involved with grasping or self-gratification.

path of means (Tib. *thabs lam*). Synonym for the practices of karma yoga, also known as the practices of the third abhiṣeka.

patriarchal clans of Gog, eighteen (Tib. *'gog pha tsho bco brgyad*). Literally, the "eighteen paternal districts of Gog," which are areas of Gog apparently organized according to the clans' patriarchal origins. This is significant because matriarchal filiations are also noted in the epic's genealogies. Gog is probably in the region of Jyekundo.

patron gods (Tib. *'go ba'i lha*). Five deities who perch on the body of a warrior and protect him or her from attack. Here is one typical list of locations with their gods: on the crown of the head is the Tib.country god (Tib. *yul lha*) [sometimes Garuḍa]; on the right shoulder, the Tib.drala (Tib. *dgra lha*); on the right armpit, the male god (Tib. *pho lha*); on the left armpit, the female god (Tib. *mo lha*); and at the heart, the life-force god (Tib. *srog lha*).

Pehar (Tib. *pe har*). A Central Asian deity who was brought to Tibet when the Tibetan empire was founded, and who became a guardian of Samye, the first monastic center. He is easily identifiable by his peculiar circular hat.

Penne Ritra [Colorful Tamarisk Mountain] (Tib. *spen ne ri bkra*). A mountain in upper Golog in the Yig Valley.

phywa (Tib.). Pronounced "chwa," this is an ancient term from the time of the Bön that refers to a divination or prosperity ritual drawn from native Tibetan religion.

pika (Tib. *bra ba*). A prairie dog–like rodent that burrows and creates complicated tunnel systems. High-pasture nomads consider them a pest, because they believe that their burrowing activity destroys grasslands, and turns the ground into barren "black earth" (Tib. *sa nag po*).

pointing-out instructions (Tib. *sems kyi ngo sprod*). Oral teachings in which the guru directly indicates the nature of mind to a disciple. This is an individual instruction that some tantric lineages consider a necessary prelude studying deeper meditation practices.

Poison Curing Potent Drop (Tib. *dug zil zhun thig*). A magical medicine that cures poison, which in the possession of the nāgas.

poisons, five (Tib. *myon mongs lnga;* Skt. *kleśa*). The five passions are delusion, anger, pride, desire, and jealousy. Also called the five passions.

Potala Mountain (Tib. *po ta la*). The pure land of the bodhisattva of compassion, Avalokiteśvara. In our world, the physical location of this mountain is in northeast China.

prajñā (Skt.; Tib. *shes rab*). Incisive knowledge. The innate quality of the mind's true nature that is capable of discerning with wisdom awareness, and hence accurately knowing the nature of things as they are and as they appear.

prāṇa (Skt.; Tib. *rlung*). Sanskrit word for the psychic energy that flows through the body and sustains the life essence. *See also* nāḍī, prāṇa, and bindu.

precious jewels that fulfill all needs and desires, thirteen (Tib. *dgos 'dod nor bu bcu gsum*). A set of offerings that the nāgas made to Padmasambhava.

precious vase that destroys poison (Tib. *dug sel rin chen bum pa*). A precious vase in the possession of the nāgas.

preserver dralas, the three kindred (Tib. *skyob pa'i dgra lha spun gsum*). A society of dralas that protects the body of a warrior from attacks by weapons.

prosperity energy (Tib. *g.yang*). Also translated as "enriching presence," prosperity energy can simply refer to the fact that a person is wealthy, but it also means a kind of radiant and infectious power of wealth. Objects can also be infused with this energy. For example, a yak may be dedicated to the earth deities, so it will become the support for that particular family's prosperity. To indicate this, the family will adorn the yak by gilding its horns and weaving colorful ribbons into its shaggy coat in order to celebrate and augment the prosperity.

prosperity support (Tib. *g.yang rten*). A ritual object to increase one's Tib. enriching presence or prosperity energy.

protectors, three (Tib. *rigs gsum mgon po;* Skt. *dharmapāla*). The three families of protectors, who are the three bodhisattvas that respectively represent wisdom (prajñā), compassion, and power: Mañjuśrī, Avalokiteśvara, and Vajrapāṇi.

Purang (Tib. *spu rangs*). A region in Ngari in western Tibet.

pure land. *See* field.

quintessence of medicine (Tib. *sman bcud bdud rtsi;* Skt. *amṛta*). A tea offered by the nāgas to Padmasambhava.

Rāhu (Tib. *gza' rgod*). A malevolent heavenly body that causes eclipses by swallowing the moon. It has a threadlike body that is invisible, but the shadow of this body falling across a human being causes epileptic fits. The name in Sanskrit means "obstacle." This Rāhu, who is constantly mentioned in court poetry, is not to be confused with the yidam protector known as Rāhula, who is a guardian of secret mantra vajrayāna.

rainbow body (Tib. *'ja' lus*). The act of dissolving the corporeal body into light; a physical manifestation of enlightenment among Dzogchen (or Great Perfection) practitioners. When some fully realized practitioners of the Great Perfection die, their bodies do not decay, but rather slowly transform into rays of light. This is called the rainbow body accomplishment.

rākṣasa / rākṣa (Skt.; Tib. *srin po / srin mo*). Often translated as "cannibal demons," rākṣasas are man-eating, shape-shifting monsters with magical powers. They generally appear in Indian epics.

ransom (Tib. *glud*). An offering made in order to distract or deflect a demon (or other harmful deity) from an afflicted person. There are many kinds of ransoms in Tibet, and numerous varieties of ransom ceremonies. The ransom objects are cakes (Tib. *torma*), either in the shape of items to be offered (such as cattle and horses), or in the shape of the afflicted as a replacement object for the attack. Buddhism does not engage in the sacrificial offering of animals, so these sculptures are used to symbolize support for the visualizations. *See also* torma.

Rare and Supreme Ones, Three (Tib. *dkon mchog gsum*). The three Buddhist objects of refuge, namely the Buddha, Dharma, and Sangha. Also expressed as the Rare and Precious Three Jewels, or simply the Three Jewels.

Raven Heart Fortress (Tib. *pho rog snying rdzong*). Trothung's castle.

realms, six (Tib. *'gro ba rigs drug*). Six states of possible rebirth for beings trapped in saṃsāra: the deva (or god) realm, the *asura* (or jealous god) realm, the human realm, the animal realm, the hungry ghost realm, and the hell realm.

realms, three. *See* worlds, three.

Red Wetland Pastures (Tib. *na dmar gzhung*). The high-elevation plateau where Wild Kyang grew up. It is also a descriptive term for wetlands that appear red due to the presence of minerals in the soil.

renunciant (Tib. *bya bral*). A person who has renounced even the most elementary of domestic or daily activities, in order to devote themselves to the development of realization during that lifetime.

Rich Like Massing Clouds (Tib. *sprin lang phyug mo*). The name of silk flags given by the Lesser Lineage to Zhalkar on his birth celebration.

Rigden Raudrachakrin (Tib. *rigs ldan drag po lcags kyi 'khor lo can*). Sometimes spelled Rigden Raudracakrin, the Tibetan name means "One of Noble Family the Fierce Holder of the Iron Wheel." He is the twenty-fifth Rigden king of the mythical Kingdom of Shambhala, the last Rigden predicted by the *Kālacakra* tantra. During his reign, Shambhala will become visible to the human realm: its gates will open and an army will flow forth to conquer the enemies of the dharma, bringing in a new golden age on this earth.

River Slowly Flowing (Tib. *chu bo dal 'bab*). The melody used in the songs sung by Chipön Rongtsha Tragen.

rivers, four (Tib. *chu bzhi*). Four rivers in the province of Kham, or eastern Tibet: the Dri Chu (Tib. *'bri chu,* the Yangtze River); the Ma Chu (Tib. *rma chu,* the Yellow River); the Gyalmo Ngül Chu / Tsharong (Tib. *rgyal mo ngul chu / tsha rong,* the Salween River); and the Da Chu (Tib. *zla chu,* the Mekong River).

root causes and conditions (Tib. *rgyu* and *rkyen;* Skt. *hetu* and *pratyaya*). Close to the Western concept of primary and secondary causes.

sādhana (Skt.; Tib. *sgrub thabs*). A ritual text and liturgy for meditation practice and mantra recitation; used in order to accomplish the wisdom mandalas of the vajrayana deities.

samādhi (Skt.; Tib. *ting nge 'dzin*). A Sanskrit word that has entered into common Western usage, meaning a state of deep meditative absorption or evenness in meditation.

Samantabhadra (Skt.; Tib. *kun tu bzang po*). A Sanskrit name whose Tibetan translation is rendered as "Küntuzangpo," meaning "ever-excellent." He is the primordial dharmakāya buddha, and he is depicted naked, blue in color, and often with consort Samantabhadrī or Küntuzangmo, who is either blue or white in color. There is also a bodhisattva of the same name who is famous for making elaborate offerings in the chapter of the *Flower Garland Sutra* titled "The Vows and Practices of Samantabhadra."

samaya (Skt.; Tib. *dam tshig*). Literally, "sacred word" or "word of honor," samayas are tantric commitments that seal the practitioner to their vows, binding the disciple to a certain commitment that must be maintained under oath. Once one receives empowerment according to vajrayāna, the samaya of the tradition must be taken on as a requirement to engage in the practices. The refuge and bodhisattva vows are implicit within the samaya.

Samayatārā [Damsig Drölma] (Skt.; Tib. *dam tshig sgrol ma*). The goddess of wind.

sambhogakāya Buddha (Skt.). The visionary wisdom body of the buddha. *See also* bodies of the Buddha, three.

Samdrub Lingdzong [Fortress That Fulfills All Wishes] (Tib. *bsam 'grub gling rdzong*). King Shingtri's castle fortress. Also appears as Samdrub Dzong.

saṃsāra (Skt.; Tib. *'khor ba*). In contrast to nirvāṇa, saṃsāra is the vicious cycle of transmigratory existence that arises out of ignorance and is characterized by suffering. Also translated as "cyclic existence," because saṃsāra means "to circle round and round." One Tibetan etymology traces it to a longer expression that means "whirlpool." The idea is that if one behaves properly according to consensus reality or relative truth, one is like a drowning person slowly sinking in a whirlpool, circling round and round as one repeats domestic patterns, slipping ever lower with each circle, until one drowns.

Śāntarakṣita (Skt.). Abbot of Nālandā University, he is the eighth-century author of important works on mahāyāna philosophy such as the *Madhyamakālaṃkāra* (a work on Madhyamakan philosophy) and the *Tattvasaṃgraha* (a summary of all philosophical systems). He arrived in Tibet from India and taught advanced Buddhist teachings widely, developing the basis for the philosophical school that provided the metaphysical foundations for much of Nyingma practice, the Yogācāra-Madhyamaka-Svātantrika. He invited Padmasambhava to Tibet when he encountered obstacles to building Samye Monastery, the first great Tibetan monastery.

secrets, three (Tib. *gsang gsum*). The esoteric nature of body, speech, and mind.

select portion (Tib. *phud*). The select portion is the first offering of food or drink made during a ceremony that involves a series of offerings. It may symbolize making an offering first to the central deity before the retinue deities are served. In a *ja phud* (Tib.), or select offering of tea, it might mean making an offering of tea to the deities before the humans partake, usually to the Three Jewels of Refuge and the Three Roots [gurus, devas, and ḍākinīs].

Select Unicorn (Tib. *dgu brgya rwa gcig*). Kyalo's horse; *dgu brgya* means "nine-hundred" and implies that the animal is as rare as one in nine hundred, and *rwa gcig* means "single-horned."

self-luminosity (Tib. *rang gsal*). The state of natural radiance.

self-occurring (Tib. *rang 'byung*). To originate of itself, independent of root causes or contributing circumstances.

Seven Sandy Passes of Ma (Tib. *bye ma'i la bdun*). A series of hills near Ma.

Sevenfold Treasure. *See* Treasure, Sevenfold.

Shady Valley Rich Royal Forest [Siblung Nag-gyal Chugmo] (Tib. *srib lung nags rgyal phyug mo*). The "shady side of the valley" is a standard Tibetan topological expression. North-eastern Tibet is full of lateral valleys that oftentimes have one side in the shade (Tib. *srib*) and one side in sun (Tib. *nyin*). These valleys usually end in a box canyon.

Shapho Dumchöd [Dresses a Deer] (Tib. *sha pho sdum chod*). The name of a sword given to Zhalkar by the Lesser Lineage on his birthday celebration.

Sheep-a-Peep (Tib. *ngo lug*). The three Ngo-lug were three young men so handsome that people would travel great distances just to get a glimpse of their faces, and would pay an entire sheep to do so. Hence they came to be called the three Ngo-lug (Tib.), literally, "sheep faces." However, the term *ngo lug* actually implies something like "One glimpse, one sheep," and in the spirit of the original, *ngo lug* has been translated here as "Sheep-a-Peep." The three Sheep-a-Peep were Tsangpa'i Ngo-lug of Agê, Dar-'jam Ngo-lug of Mupa, and Sint-sha Ngo-lug of Tag-rong.

si demons (Tib. *sri*). Ancient invisible Tibetan demons that cause cyclical patterns of misfortune. For example, if the firstborn child dies for several generations, it would be regarded as a family curse of si demons.

siddhi (Skt.; Tib. *dngos grub*). Literally, "accomplishment." Siddhis are abilities that are developed through meditation practice, and they are either ordinary or supreme. The eight ordinary siddhis are physical powers; for example, there is the siddhi of the sword, whose touch grants whatever is wished. Supreme siddhi is enlightenment.

Sidpa Khölmo Rogdzong [Black Bellow Fortress of Existence] (Tib. *srid pa khol mo'i rog rd-zong*). The name of Trothung's castle. This site is in present-day Golog, close to the point where the Yellow and Ko rivers merge.

Sidpa Yutso. *See* Cosmic Turquoise Lake.

śila, samādhi, and prajñā (Skt.; Tib. *tsul khrims, ting nge 'dzin, shes rab*). The three disciplines (śila): discipline, concentration, and wisdom or incisive knowledge.

six attributes of a warrior (Tib. *dpa' bo'i chos drug*). Armor, helmet, shield, arrows, spear, and sword.

Six Modulations in Nine Pitches (Tib. *dgu seng 'brug 'gyur*). A melody that is sung by Drugmo.

six-syllable mantra. *See* Maṇi mantra.

skandhas, five (Skt.; Tib. *phung po*). The five skandhas are aggregates that make up the individual person. These five aggregates arise in coordination with each other in order to produce the complex of experiences known as ego-clinging. The five are: form (Tib. *gzugs;* Skt. *rūpa*); feeling (Tib. *tshor ba;* Skt. *vedanā*); recognition (Tib. *'du shes;* Skt. *samjnā*); reaction (Tib. *'di byed;* Skt. *saṃskāra*); and consciousness (Tib. *rnam par shes pa;* Skt. *vijnāna*).

sky meteorite (Tib. *gnam lcags thog*). A substance that is produced by lightning, and solidifies as it falls to earth. The indigenous people of Tibet believe that lightning and thunder relate to the magical activity of dragons.

sleep of luminosity (Tib. *'od gsal gyi ngang du nyal*). To sleep in a state of lucidity, and at the same time to be in the nature of the mind as clear-light awareness. Highly advanced meditators abide this way during sleep.

Slingshot Braided Nine Eyes, the (Tib. *'ur rdo chu mig dgu sgril*). Also called Wazi Bitra [Brighter than Zi]; Joru's slingshot. The slingshot is a standard weapon for a shepherd boy. In Tibetan culture, someone who possesses a braided slingshot with nine eyes will be protected from demonic evildoers.

śloka (Tib. *sho lo ka*). A song or verse written in Vedic meter with sixteen syllable couplets, with each sixteen-syllable line consisting of two eight-syllable submeters. Much of epic Indian verse is written this way, including the *Mahabharata* and *Ramayana*.

smoke offering [lhasang] (Tib. *lha bsangs*). Literally, "divine purification." A *lhasang* is a ceremony in which clouds of juniper smoke are offered along with tea, liquor, and various offerings from native Tibetan religion. The lha, or gods, are invited to descend down along the column of smoke and purify the physical space.

Snow Mountain Haughty Gait (Tib. *gangs ri 'gying shes*). The nyen Gyogchen Dongra's horse.

solidification (Tib. *a 'thas*). A term found in the Great Perfection texts and liturgies that indicates the deep-seated habitual patterns of conceptualization and perception. These patterns make the transparent phenomenal world seem solid; they make that which is not truly existent seem truly existent; and they make the unreal illusory manifestations of mind seem externally real. It is the same as habituation. The term also refers to the tendency to solidify the sense of existence of the self or the subject.

sons and nephews (Tib. *bu tsha*). The younger generation—as compared with *pha khu,* the fathers and uncles [brethren] of the older generation.

splendor (Tib. *ziji; gzi brjid*). A kind of energy of magnificence, magnanimity, and power that surrounds warriors and great people. Chögyam Trungpa Rinpoche translated the Tibetan as "dignity" and sometimes as "confidence." It implies majesty, a kind of radiance that one would expect to see and feel from a great and noble king.

spring of the nāgas (Tib. *klu yi chu mig*). A body of water (a lake or stream) where Gogmo met her father after she had entered Senglön's family.

stupa (Skt.; Tib. *chos rten*). An ornamental tower or obelisk-like monument containing the relics of enlightened beings. The Tibetan term *chöten* literally means "representation of the dharma." A stupa represents the nature of enlightened mind. There are eight traditional types of stupas, each one having a particular significance that relates to the deeds of Buddha Śākyamuni's life.

Sugata [Gone to Bliss] (Skt.; Tib. *bde bar gshegs pa*). An epithet for the Buddha.

Sukhāvati (Skt.). The pure land of exaltation; the name of Buddha Amitābha's pure land.

Super Warriors, Seven (Tib. *yang thul*). A group of superior warriors among the Thirty Mighty Warriors: Gyatsha Zhalkar (Tib. *rgya tsha zhal dkar*); Sengtag Adom (Tib. *seng stag a dom*); Tshazhang Denma Jangtra (Tib. *tsha zhang 'dan ma byang khra*); Anu Zigphen (Tib. *a nu gzig 'phen*); Druga-de Chökyong Bernag (Tib. *'bru dga' bde chos skyong ber nag*); Chölu Buyi Darphen (Tib. *chos lu bu yi dar 'phen*); and Nya-tsha Aten (Tib. *nya tsha a rten*).

supports (Tib. *rten*). In rituals, the supports refer to the basis, that is the iconic element or ritual object that represents the deity. So for example, a thangka or icon of Hayagrīva would be a *rten,* a support for Hayagrīva. Often deities are invoked and invited to invest or dwell in their supports on a shrine.

sweet potatoes [droma] (Tib. *gro ma*). Droma are a characteristic Tibetan sweet, a wild, yam-like root that grows wild in the lower valleys in places without grass. It ripens in both spring and fall; its green leaf that turns red when the root is ready to harvest. The fall troma are the sweetest and the most nutritious. . The bigger ones are the size of a thumb joint; the smaller ones are the size of a bean and are less tasty. For the northeastern Tibetan tribes it is a staple delicacy with melted butter and yogurt.

sweets, the three (Tib. *mngar gsum*). Sugar, honey, and molasses; three sweet substances that stem from the Vedic tradition and that represent all edible sweets. These are offerings that are used in peaceful ceremonies as well. *See* whites, three.

Swirling Auspiciousness (Tib. *bkra shis 'khyil ba*). Rongtsha Tragen's teakettle.

Tagtang Tramo [Colorful Tiger Plain] (Tib. *stag thang khra mo*). The same as Upper Tiger Plain Gathering Place.

tantric feast. *See gaṇacakra.*

Tārā (Skt.; Tib. *sgrol ma*). A female emanation of Avalokiteśvara, the bodhisattva of compassion. She is invoked as a remover of obstacles, but also as the patron female Buddha of women. There are several forms in which Tārā is visualized, the white and the green aspects being the most popular. The liturgies directed toward the different aspects focus on different services requested of the goddess.

Tashi Nyinmo Delek. *See* Auspicious-by-Day scarf.

tenma (Tib. *bstan ma*). Female protectors who were *zodors* converted by Padmasambhava to protect the land of Tibet and the Buddha's doctrine. There are twelve of these protectors who are sisters. *See also* zodors.

terma (Tib. *gter ma*). Sacred material objects and texts that were hidden during the lives of Padmasambhava and Yeshe Tsogyal, and were predicted to be revealed by their designated disciples in future centuries. Many terma are immaterial, in that the teachings simply well forth from the mind of the reincarnated disciples when they are predicted to remember them.

tertön (Tib. *gter ston*). One who discovers or reveals hidden terma teachings.

the'u rang (Tib.). One of the eight classes of gods, this is a class of local deities generally harmful to humankind. According to one description, the'u rang are invisible one-legged demons who ride mounted on tornados. They are harmful to children, and gamblers pray to them while playing dice. Whoever receives the blessings of the the'u rang will win when they gamble, but after death the person must become a servant of the the'u rang.

Thirty Skulls (Tib. *thod pa sum cu'i che 'go yin*). The eldest member in a tribe among thirty warriors. For example, this could refer to Chipön or Senglön.

three gates (Tib. *sgo gsum*). The gates of body, speech, and mind.

three sufferings (Tib. *sdug bsngal gsum*). Suffering of pain on top of pain (*duḥkha duḥkhatā*); suffering of change (*vipariṇāma*); and suffering of compounded phenomena or conditioned existence (*saṃskāra duḥkhatā*). The three sufferings permeate the experience of rebirth in any of the six classes of living beings that inhabit samsara or cyclic existence. The third is considered to be the most all-pervasive and difficult to purify in terms of releasing the mind from the bonds of ignorance.

three trainings (Tib. *bslab gsum;* Skt. *triśikśa*). Training in discipline (Skt. *śila*); concentration (Skt. *samādhi*); and incisive knowledge (Skt. *prajñā*).

thüd (Tib. *thud*). Hearty yam cakes (Tib. *skyid snum thud*); literally, "happy, oily cheese." A round cake made by mixing cheese, ghee, ground yam and sugar.

tigers in their prime (Tib. *stag shar*). Also "young tigers" and "youthful tigers"; a term in the epic for young warriors.

Ting-öd Münsel [Blue Light That Dispels Darkness] (Tib. *mthing 'od mun sel*). A jewel owned by the nāgas. Also called Ting-öd Zibar [Deep Blue Blazing Splendor].

Tingshog Gung-gu [Azure Nine-Panels] (Tib. *g.yu shra mthing shog gung dgu*). Also called the Turquoise Yak-Hair Tent in Nine Partitions. A magical possession of the nāgas given by King Tsugna Rinchen of the nāgas to his daughter prior to her departure for the human realm, where she is destined to become Gesar's mother. From her, it passed to Tönpa Gyaltsen of Ralo, and hence to the Ling tribe at large who took this as booty. Eventually it was possessed by Senglön, but it still accompanied Gesar's mother wherever she went.

torma (Tib. *gtor ma*). Offering cakes. Some tormas represent deities and buddhas who are worshipped on the shrine, and others represent offerings of food and other desirables. They are made from roasted barley flour, painted with food dyes, and ornamented with colored wheels of butter.

Trakhar Namdzong. *See* Falcon Castle Sky Fortress.

tramen / Wangchugma (Tib. *phra man / dbang phyug ma*). An animal-headed wrathful female ḍākiṇī who holds hand emblems and serves as a messenger and emissary, and protects the perimeter of the mandala of deities. Each tramen has a deeper significance pertaining to the transformation of the passions and poisons in the ordinary world into the wisdom nature through invoking the ḍākiṇī. These explanations are found in secret vajrayāna teachings that one must have empowerment for in order to study and practice.

Tratöd (Tib. *khra stod*). Another name for Upper Falcon (Valley). *See* Falcon Cave.

Trawa Kha [Sparkling Mouth] (Tib. *spra ba kha*). The name of a legendary fish in Hor.

Treasure, Sevenfold (Tib. *gter cha bdun*). Seven precious objects that were the common wealth of the tribe. They were a statue of Śākyamuni made of conch shell; a statue of Avalokiteśvara in conch; a turquoise statue of Tārā; the conch of the law called White Conch of the Law Resounding Afar; the drum of the law called Radiating Light; the hand cymbals called Sun Dragon Thunder; the banner called Drala Gathering Lance; and the key and code to open the treasure portal of Sheldrag [Crystal Rock].

tribes, nine (Tib. *tsho dgu*). Another list of ancient aristocratic families of Tibet: Ga (*sga*), Dru (*'bru*), and Dong (*ldong*); Sed (*sad*), Mu (*dmu*), and Dong; and Pel (*dpal*), Da (*zla*), and Tra (*'pra*).

tribes of Tibet, six (Tib. *mi'u gdung drug*). In Drigung, the Kyura tribe (Tib. *'bri gung kyu ra*); in Taglung, the Khazi tribe (Tib. *stag lung kha zi*); in Sakya, the Khön tribe (Tib. *sa skya 'khon*); in Chögyal, the Nam tribe (Tib. *chos rgyal gnam*); at Kyungpo, the Gya tribe (Tib. *khyung po gya*); and at Ne'u Dong, the tribe of the Lha (Tib. *sne'u gdong lha*).

Trisong Deutsen (714–797 c.e.) (Tib. *khri srong lde'u btsan*). Ruler of the Tibetan empire four generations after its founder, Songtsen Gampo (Tib. *srong btsan sgam po*). Trisong Deutsen was predicted by the Mañjuśrīmūla tantra. He brought the great founders of the Nyingma lineage and mahāyāna to Tibet; that is, the tantric guru Padmasambhava and the great abbot Śāntarakṣita. Therefore the three are sometimes known as a triad: the Guru, Abbot, and King (Tib. *mkhan slob chos gsum*). Trisong Deutsen is regarded as an emanation of Mañjuśrī, the bodhisattva of wisdom.

tsatsa (Tib. *tsa tsa*). A miniature clay image of a deity such as Avalokiteśvara, or an image of a stupa.

tsen (Tib. *btsan*). A type of earth lord, or local spirit of the land that inhabits the rocks and crags of mountainsides. In the threefold order of gods (lha, nyen, and lu [nāgas]), they stand with the nyen in the middle or intermediate space between heaven and earth. Often represented as red in color.

Tsharong (Tib. *tsha rong*). A kingdom that is a vast farmland, and the place where the treasure of barley is acquired in the Saga of Tsharong and Ling.

Turquoise Bird (Tib. *g.yu bya*). The horse belonging to Dongtsen, the son of Trothung.

Turquoise Leaf Array, pure land of (Tib. *gyu lo bkod pa'i zhing*). Tārā's pure land.

Two Excellent Ones, the Sun and the Moon Conjoined (Tib. *yag gnyis nyi zla kha sprod* or *kha 'dzom*). The word *conjoined* probably refers to a geographical feature where two or more canyon entrances meet.

Ü (Tib. *dbus*). One of three provinces of Tibet located in the central region, which is referred to today as the Tibetan Autonomous Region.

Uḍḍiyāna (Skt.; Tib. *o rgyan*). An epithet of Padmasambhava, and the name of the semi-mythical land northwest of India in which he was born. The many names of this land, Orgyan, Oḍḍiyāna, and Uḍḍiyāna, are all also epithets of Padmasambhava.

Ultimate Warriors, Three (Tib. *zhe thul gsum*). Falcon, Eagle, and Wolf, three supreme warriors who are even greater than the Thirty Mighty Warriors and the Seven Super Warriors.

uncontrived conduct. *See* yogic conduct.

upāya (Skt.; Tib. *thabs*). Literally "skillful means" or "method"; refers to the ability to teach in a way that is appropriate to a student's understanding, to a bodhisattva's display of compassion, or to a meditator's capacity to work with whatever situation arises.

upheavals (Tib. *lhongs tshad*). False visions that occur in the course of *chöd* practice. These involve apparitions that occur to the mind that has been focusing intensely upon the nature of emptiness and the lack of true inherent identity. Such experiences are encouraged as an integral part of the practice in order to induce realization in the mind of the practitioner.

Upper Dil-yag Tiger Plain in Ma (Tib. *rma dil yag stag thang gong ma*). The gathering place where the people of Ling assembled to discuss important affairs, and a plain used for encampments. It was one stage on the trade route between Tibet and China. Upper Tiger Plain is surrounded by beautiful mountains.

Upper Falcon Sky Fortress. *See* Falcon Castle Sky Fortress.

Ü-Tsang (Tib. *dbus gtsang*). Central Tibet is made up of four districts, or ruzhi (Tib. *ru bzhi*). They are Ü (Tib. *dbus*) within which are Üru (Tib. *dbu ru*) and Yoru (Tib. *gyo ru*), and Tsang (Tib. *gtsang*) within which are Weiru (Tib. *gwas ru*) and Rulag (Tib. *ru lag*). In the seventeenth century, they became known as Weiru (Tib. *gwas ru*), Wönru (Tib. *gwon ru*), Püru (Tib. *spus ru*), and Gung-ru (Tib. *gung ru*).

u-zi (Tib. *u zi*). A kind of Chinese tea.

Vaiśakha (Skt.; Tib. *sa ga zla ba*). One of the twenty-eight nakśatras (Tib. *rgyu skar nyi shu rtsa brgyad*), which are divisions or phases of the lunar zodiac. It is also the name for the fourth month of the Tibetan lunar calendar. *See also* constellation.

Vaiśravaṇa [Kubera] (Skt.; Tib. *rnam thos sras*). The deity of wealth. He has the form of a king and wears glorious, effulgent clothes.

vajra (Skt.; Tib. *dorje; rdo rje*). The ritual scepter used by tantric practitioners in their liturgical practice. The original vajra was the weapon of Indra, the king of the gods. It was made from an adamantine substance so hard that it could cut anything, but it could not be cut itself. This is why the word *vajra* is sometimes translated as "diamond" as a noun, and "indestructible" as an adjective. It is also translated as "thunderbolt." The shape of the vajra is a short rod with three, four, five, or nine points at both ends. The points are curled in and touch each other to make a flower-bud shape.

Vajra Dhātviśvarī [Dorje Yingchugma] (Skt.; Tib. *rdo rje dbyings phyug ma*). Vajra Mother of Basic Space; she is the ḍākinī of the central direction, who represents the basic space of phenomena or the nature of emptiness. She is also the consort of the central Buddha in the mandala of the five buddha families. *See also* buddha families, five.

Vajradhara [Dorje Chang] (Skt.; Tib. *rdo rje chang*). Literally, "holder of the vajra." The divine source of the tantric teachings and the compiler of the vajrayāna teachings. He is a dharmakāya buddha, or a deity who represents the absolute state of enlightenment.

Vajrapāṇi (Skt.; Tib. *gsang ba'i bdag*). A bodhisattva, the Lord of the Secret the embodiment of power, and one of the three principle protectors of this world, the other two being Avalokiteśvara and Mañjuśrī. He is called the Lord of the Secret because he is considered a primordial figure in esoteric Buddhism.

Vajrasādhu [Dorje Legpa] (Skt.; Tib. *rdo rje legs pa*). One of the most important protector deities in Tibet; a wrathful protector who rides a brown ram and holds the implements of a blacksmith. He is also known as the "genyen Vajrasādhu" and as the "samaya-bound Vajrasādhu" (Tib. *dam can rdo rje legs pa*).

Vajrasattva [Dorje Sempa] (Skt.; Tib. *rdo rje sems dpa'*). Among the five buddha families, he is the buddha of the East, white in color, holding a vajra in the right hand and a bell at the waist. In a sense Vajrasattva is the generic tantric god; his name means "vajra being." His hundred-syllable mantra is used to purify violations and corruptions of the samaya or tantric sacred vows, as well as all aspects of negative karma. He is the head of the pantheon of one hundred wisdom deities: the forty-two peaceful deities and the fifty-eight wrathful deities. *See* buddha families, five.

Vajravārāhī [Dorje Phagmo] (Skt.; Tib. *rdo rje phag mo*). A form of Vajrayoginī, the female, semiwrathful Buddha. She is often just called the Sow (Tib. *phags mo*), which is a more noble expression in Tibetan than in English. She is probably originally related to Varaha, the third incarnation of Viṣṇu, who became a gigantic boar and saved the earth from perishing in a flood by lifting it up on a tusk. This is the wrathful female red buddha who led Padmasambhava in a dream in volume 1. She is one of the greatest objects of devotion in Tibet, particularly for inner vajrayāna practitioners who see her as the representative of the nature of emptiness and the birthplace of all the Buddhas, as well as as phenomenal existence.

Valley of Eighteen Falcon Caves (Tib. *lung khra phug bco brgyad*). The region where Rongtsha Tragen's fortress is located.

valleys, four (Tib. *rong bzhi*). A geographical division of Lower, or eastern, Ling.

Vast as the Sky (Tib. *nam mkha' leb chen*). A helmet given by the Younger Lineage to Zhalkar on his birth celebration.

vidyādhara [awareness holder] (Skt.; Tib. *rig 'dzin*). There are four states of vidyādharahood, which are: the mature vidyādhara (Tib. *rnam smin rig 'dzin*); the immortal (Tib. *tshe dbang*); the *mahamudrā* (Tib. *phyag chen*); and the spontaneously present (Tib. *lhun grub*). These four represent the higher stages of accomplishment on the path of realization, which leads to the final state of buddhahood.

vināyakas (Skt.; Tib. *bgegs*). Literally, "obstructers." A kind of demon that obstructs a person's dharma practice. *Vināyaka* is also an epithet for Gaṇeśa, the elephant-headed deity with a baby's body who removes obstructions to practice. He appears in semiwrathful form in Tibetan tantra as a king of the dralas and as a local protector deity. In the case of Ganeśa, the name refers to a protecting rather than an obstructing spirit.

virtues, ten (Tib. *dge ba bcu*). Abandoning killing, stealing, sexual misconduct, lying, slander, harsh words, idle gossip, covetousness, ill will, and wrong views.

Vulture Peak (Tib. *bya rgod spungs ri*). The mountain in northern India where Śākyamuni Buddha turned the second wheel of the dharma.

Wazi Bitra. *See* Slingshot Braided Nine Eyes.

Wealthy Sky Fortress. *See* Falcon Castle Sky Fortress.

Wealthy Upper Valleys of Nelchag (Tib. *nel chag phu drug phyug mo*). There is no translation for the term *nel chag,* which simply indicates a place or area, as well as being the name for the home of Kyalo Tönpa.

werma (Tib. *wer ma*). One of the eight classes of gods; a species of warlike spirits such as the dralas. Some texts say that originally the werma were the spirits of the tips of arrows that guided the arrows' flight.

White Law and Order (Tib. *khrims shong dkar mo*). A tent used for gathering to make legal decisions or to have legal discussions, including events that are associated with law and order. Sometimes this is rendered as *khri shong dkar mo,* meaning "the white [tent] that could hold ten thousand," referring to the place where the nobles of Ling met in Tag-rong.

White Ling. *White* is a common adjective connoting the "good," as opposed to black, connoting the "bad." Those who pursue the positive side of moral virtue are considered to be "white," or correct. *See also* Ling, epithets for.

White Melody with Six Modulations (Tib. *dkar mo drug 'gyur*). The melody used by Gyatsha Zhalkar.

White Sky Horse [Namta Karpo] (Tib. *gnam rta dkar po*). The father of Wild Kyang, Gesar's horse.

whites, three (Tib. *dkar gsum*). Offerings of three kinds of dairy products: milk, yogurt, and sugar; used in ceremonies of native Tibetan religion and lhasangs (smoke offerings). *See also* sweets, three.

wife (Tib. *gza'*). Many of the heroes' genealogies are traced both from the standpoint of being patriarchal and matriarchal. So for example, all the wives of Chöla Bum, the ancestor of the Lesser Lineage of Ling, are identified by their maternal tribal origins—that is to say, they are identified as descending from one of his three wives: Rongza, the wife from the Rong tribe; Gaza, wife from Ga; and Muza, the wife from Mu. The sons of these wives are given names that indicate their maternal lineage; all the names use the word *tsha,* which means "maternal nephew." So for example, Zhalkar is the son of Senglön and Lhakar Drönma, who is also known as the Gyaza or the "Chinese wife." Thus he is known as Gyatsha, the "Chinese maternal nephew."

Wild Kyang [Kyang Göd] (Tib. *rkyang rgod*). One of the names of Gesar's wondrous horse. A kyang (Tib. *kiang*) is a wild ass, a large and impressive animal that roams the highlands of Tibet. Herds of them inhabit the vast plain of Changthang and northeastern Tibet. Gesar's horse is not literally a kyang, but it lived wild among them before it was captured by Drugmo and Gesar's mother, Gogmo.

wild yak. *See* Drong.

windhorse [lungta] (Tib. *rlung rta*). 1. An ancient Sino-Tibetan diagram that shows four beasts, sometimes the eight trigrams of the Chinese Classic of Changes [I Ching], and a flying horse with a flaming jewel on its saddle. It is often presented on a flag or pennant that flaps in the wind, and thereby propagates blessings and uplifts windhorse (see next meaning) to the place and its inhabitants. These lungta flags can be found by the hundreds in front of Tibetan residences or temples, decorating flagpoles and cords stretched between two high places.

2. Windhorse is also a kind of energy of dignity, confidence, and personal power that must be awakened by a warrior in order to have success in battle. People with perpetually opened windhorse have a field of power about themselves that gives them an air of success and invincibility. This field is called *dbang thang,* meaning "field of power" or "authentic presence."

wisdom (Tib. *ye shes;* Skt. *jñāna*). In this translation of the Gesar epic, the Sanskrit term *jñāna* (*yeshe* in Tibetan) is rendered simply as "wisdom" rather than "primordial wisdom," which would be a literal translation of the Tibetan term. Usually this term refers to the highest mystical wisdom, or nondual wisdom. In this text, the term "incisive knowledge" is used for *prajñā,* and *prajñāpāramitā* is translated as the "perfection of incisive knowledge" or "transcendent knowledge."

wisdom ḍākinī (Tib. *ye shes mkha' 'dro ma*). A goddess who represents an absolute wisdom principal and is therefore enlightened.

wish-fulfilling jewel (Tib. *yid bzhin nor bu*). Literally, "jewel that fulfills whatever mind desires." Usually a symbol for the dharma or the guru. According to ancient tales, there were jewels that when acquired would fulfill all needs and desires; in particular, if one were to pray to the jewel, one's prayers would come true.

words of truth (Tib. *bden tshig*). Vows and statements so true that they have their own power. For example, chants such as the Heart Sutra are said to be "words of truth" and have incantation powers. Vows made by great yogins and yoginīs are "words of truth" that come true through the undeniable strength of merit and positive virtue.

worlds, three (Tib. *khams gsum* or *srid gsum*). The three worlds of saṃsāra: the heaven of the gods (Tib. *lha*); the world of humans (Tib. *mi*); and the underworld of subterranean nāgas (Tib. *klu*). This term is often used to refer to the three realms: the desire, form, and formless realms.

Wrathful Grimacing One (Tib. *khro gnyer can*). A wrathful form of Tārā.

Wu-t'ai Shan (Tib. *rgya nag ri bo rtse lnga*). The famous Five-Peaked Mountain in China, traditional home of Mañjuśrī and the presence of the great rainbow transference kāya of Paṇḍit Vimalamitra located in northeast Shanxi Province in China. To this day, it is said that faithful pilgrims who visit this sacred site will have visions of Mañjuśrī as well as Vimalamitra.

Yakṣa Wealth God (Tib. *gnod sbyin nor lha*). A name for Kubera, the Indic god of wealth who is universally worshipped throughout Asia and across religions. He has the fleshy, luxurious body of a yakṣa, and is considered the king of a city of yakṣas who live on the peak of Mount Meru.

Yama (Skt.; Tib. *chi bdag*). The traditional lord of the underworld, a wrathful god with a bull's horns. He is an ancient, pre-Buddhist deity of the Hindu pantheon. Yama wears a mirror-like breastplate in which all of one's previous actions appear, and based on what he sees, Yama judges one's karma and determines whether birth will occur in the lower realms or above.

Yarlha Shampo (Tib. *yar lha sham po*). A sacred mountain in the Yarlung Valley in central Tibet; also the name of the province where the original kings lived in central Tibet, and the name of the patron mountain deity of the kings of Tibet.

Yellow Hor. *See* Hor.

Yeshe Tsogyal [Wisdom Lake Queen] (Tib. *ye shes mtsho rgyal*). A famous female tāntrika; the consort of Padmasambhava and one of the founders of tantrism in Tibet.

yidam. *See* meditational deity.

yogic conduct (Tib. *brtul zhugs kyi sbyod pa*). The uncontrived or fearless conduct of a completely accomplished and realized yogin. In yogic conduct, no rules or moral laws need to be obeyed. Rather, every action is performed based on direct perception of the nature of truth and spontaneous nondual compassion. Sometimes translated as "uncontrived conduct."

young tigers. *See* tigers in their prime.

youthful tigers. *See* tigers in their prime.

Yulung Sumdo in Lower Ma (Tib. *rma smad yul lung sum mdo*). The unpeopled land near Mount Magyal Pomra where Gesar and his mother spent his childhood. Also called Mamed Yulung Sumdo, Lhalung Sumdo (Tib. *lha lung sum mdo*), or Divine Valley Three Canyons. Note that here *sum* does not mean "three," but simply a confluence, such as a confluence of two rivers or two valleys called a *sum mdo*.

Yutse (Tib. *gyu rtse*). A holy mountain in Minyag that lies in the first curve of the Ma (Tib. *rma*) River, or as the Chinese know it, the Yellow River. Its long name is *mi nyag gyu ri rtse rgyal* (Tib.); literally, Turquoise Mountain King of Longevity of Minyag.

zi beads. An agate found in the highlands of Tibet, which are said to be fossilized worms that have petrified into stone. The value of this stone is based upon the patterns and the number of eyes that appear within it. Among the many different explanations of the power of the zi bead, it is said to prevent disease, demonic force possession, and obstacles, while inciting good health, luck, and prosperity.

zodor (Tib. *zo dor*). A class of worldly deities from the Bönpo pantheon and native Tibetan religion. Often they are the country gods (Tib. *yul lha*), the local naturally existing deities who are the true "proprietors" (Tib. *bdag po*) of the land. In the epic of Gesar, the term *zodor* in the singular usually means the god of Mount Magyal Pomra or Gedzo, a special epic mountain god who protects and advises Gesar.

GLOSSARY OF NAMES

This list is not meant to be comprehensive, but rather it is intended to include many of the major as well as some minor characters, and to clarify their relationships. The names are usually given in both the phonetic Tibetan and the English; the order varies to correspond with the language used most often for a particular name. In some cases, the English is not given because it is never used. In most cases, the Wylie transliteration is included.

Abar Buyi Paljor. *See* Abar Buyi Phentag.

Abar Buyi Phentag [Drawn Tiger Boy of Abar] (Tib. *a 'bar bu yi 'phen stag*). One of the Thirteen Cherished Sons of Ling and a member of the Elder or Greater Lineage; one of the Thirty Brethren [Mighty Warriors]. His father is Singsing and his mother is Abar. Also called Abar Buyi Paljor [Prosperity of Abar's Son] (Tib. *a 'bar bu yi dpal 'byor*).

Akhöd Tharpa Zorna [Hook-Nosed Tharpa] (Tib. *a khod thar pa'i zor sna*). The personal minister and messenger of Chieftain Trothung; one of the Three Servants of Ling.

Amnye Gompa Raja [Grandfather Meditation Prince] (Tib. *a mye sgom pa raja*). An evil Bönpo sorcerer or shaman called upon by Trothung to eliminate Joru as a rival; however, ultimately he is the one who is tamed by Gesar.

Anu Paseng [Courageous Youthful Lion] of Ombu (Tib. *'om bu'i a nu dpa' seng*). The chief elder of the Middle Lineage. He is one of the Four Divine Heirs (the heir of the Ombu clan), and one of the Three Ultimate Warriors (the one called Eagle).

Anu Zigphen. *See* Zigphen.

Aten Dug-gi Metog [Stable Poisonous Flower] (Tib. *a brtan dug gi me tog*). One of Trothung's sons, and a famous warrior with a central role in later volumes of the epic.

Berkar [White Cloak] (Tib. *ber dkar*). Indian ministers wear white cloaks, and this is the disguise adopted by Gesar when he meets Drugmo.

Berkar Tharpa Gyaltsen of Nag-ru (Tib. *ber dkar thar pa rgyal mtshan*). A chief in Ling, not to be confused with the Indian minister Berkar. One of the four Gyaltsens and one of the Thirty Brethren [Mighty Warriors]. Often called simply Tharpa Gyaltsen.

Bloody Single-Tress Demon Woman [Düdmo Trag-gi Relpa] (Tib. *dud mo khrag gi ral pa*). A demoness who, along with her brother Life-Essence Demon [Sog Düd] (Tib. *srog bdud*), was tamed by Joru, who appointed them terma guardians of Buddhist and Bönpo doctrines.

Buchung Daryag of Serpa [Young Lad Excellent Banner] (Tib. *bu chung dar yag*). One of the Thirteen Cherished Sons of Ling; one of the Thirty Brethren [Mighty Warriors].

Bu-yag Drug-gyei [Handsome Royal Son Dragon] of Kyalo (Tib. *bu yag 'brug rgyas*). One of the Thirteen Cherished Sons of Ling; one of the Thirty Brethren [Mighty Warriors].

Cannibal Demoness Child Eater [Sinmo Buzen] (Tib. *srin mo bu zan*). The cannibal demoness, or *rākṣasī*, destroyed by Gesar. He finds her in the act of eating several dead children and lures her to the middle of the Dza River, where she drowns.

Cham Thalei Ödtro. *See* Thalei Ödtro.

Changmoza (Tib. *spyang mo bza'*). An important woman from the Muwa clan; the matriarch of the Mukpo clan into which Chipön, Senglön, and Trothung were born. She was the third wife of Chöphen Nagpo and mother of Dragyal Bum-me. Sometimes called Changza.

Changtri Ngamchen [Great Awesome Myriad Jackals] of Ombu (Tib. *spyang khri rngam chen*). One of the Thirteen Cherished Sons of Ling; one of the Thirty Brethren [Mighty Warriors] and a member of the Middle Lineage.

Changza. *See* Changmoza.

Chatül, King. The father of Ratra Genpo, the first king of Dokham. He was the brother of the thirteenth king in the line descending from Yemön Namkhai Gyalpo.

Chipön Rongtsha Tragen (Tib. *spyi dpon rong tsha khra rgan*). Chief of the Lesser Lineage, brother of Trothung, brother of Senglön (and therefore Gesar's uncle); the first born of the Thirty Brethren [Mighty Warriors], the reincarnation of Mahāsiddha Nāgārjuna and Paṇḍita Sergyi Dogcan, the incarnation of Mahāsiddha Kukurīpā, and prophesied to be the dharma king of Shambhala, Dawa Zangpo. He was the son of Chöla Bum and his first wife, Rongza. Chipön married Metog Tashi-tso and they had four children: three sons (Yu-pen Tag-gyal, Lenpa Chögyal, and Nangchung Yutag), and one daughter (Lhamo Yudrön). Literally, *chipön* means "chief" or "leader," *rong tsha* is "nephew of Rong," and *tragen* means "colorful elder," which refers to his home in Upper Falcon.

Chökyong Bernag [Dharma Protector Black Cloak] of Gadei (Tib. *chos skyong ber nag*). One of the Seven Super Warriors, and bodyguard of Rinchen Darlu. Also called Gadei Bernag.

Chöla Bum [For the Dharma Hundred Thousand] (Tib. *chos la 'bum*). The eldest son of Thoglha Bum of the Lesser Lineage, and the father of Chipön Rongtsha Tragen, Yu-gyal, and King Senglön.

Chölu Buyi Darphen [Dharma Son Unfurled Silk] (Tib. *chos lu bu yi dar 'phen*). One of the Seven Super Warriors and personal minister of Anu Paseng. Later on in the epic, he figures prominently in the war with Hor. Also known simply as Chölu Darphen or Darphen.

Cho-nga Paser Dawa [Young Warrior of the Full Moon] (Tib. *bco lnga dpa' gsar zla ba*). One of the Thirteen Cherished Sons of Ling; one of the Thirty Brethren [Mighty Warriors].

Chöphen Nagpo [Dharma Benefit Black] (Tib. *chos phan nag po*). Ancestral leader of the Mukpo clan. He had three famous wives—Serza, Omza, and Changza (Changmoza)—who gave birth respectively to the three lineages of Ling: the so-called Elder, Middle, and Lesser (Younger or Cadet) Lineages. The suffix *za* attached to the tribal names means "wife" (Tib. *gza'*). By marrying into these leading families, he increased the power of the Mukpo clan. Ser (Tib. *gser*), Om (Tib. *'om*), and Chang (Tib. *spyangs*) are three tribes with important relationships with the Mukpos, probably through the politics of the tribal state of Ling.

Dardzom of Muchang (Tib. *dmu spyang dar 'dzom*). A judge, mediator, or arbiter (Tib. *gzu pa*) who appears in the epic.

Dar-'jam Gentle Scarf Ngo-lug of Mupa (Tib. *mu pa dar 'jam ngo lug*). One of the three

Sheep-a-Peep brothers; one of the Thirty Brethren [Mighty Warriors] and a member of the Mupa tribe.

Darphen. *See* Chölu Buyi Darphen.

Daryag. *See* Nyibum Daryag.

Demchog Karpo Ngangyag [White Supreme Bliss Good Nature] (Tib. *bde mchog dkar po ngang yag*). Gesar's divine father. This name combines the variations "Demchog Karpo" and "Demchog Ngangyag" that appear in the epic. Gesar refers to him as Jangsem Künkyab Gön [Compassionate Sovereign Lord] (Tib. *jang sems kun skyabs gon*).

Demkar Lhamo [Undulating White Goddess] (Tib. *ldem dkar lha mo*). A nāga princess.

Denma (Tib. *'dan*). Gesar's personal minister, also a great archer, and one of the Seven Super Warriors. His full name is Tshazhang [Maternal Uncle] Denma Jangtra (Tib. *tsha zhang 'dan ma byang khra*).

Denza (Tib. *'dan bza'*). Trothung's wife; a princess, the daughter of the king of Den (Tib. *'dan*). Also called Ser-tso [Golden Lake Lady] (Tib. *gser mtsho ma*) and Kharagza [Wife from Kharag] (Tib. *kha rag gza'*).

Divine Child Joru (Tib. *lha sras jo ru*). An epithet for Joru used by the Lingites. This could be translated as "child of the gods." The Tibetan also appears as *lha phrug,* literally "god cub" or "godling."

Döndrub. *See* Gesar.

Dongtsen Nang-ngu Apel [Mighty Youthful Glory of the Tribe] (Tib. *gdong btsan snang ngu a dpal*). One of Trothung's sons, leader of the Lesser Lineage, and rival of Gesar in the horse race, the contest for the throne of Ling. One of the Thirty Brethren [Mighty Warriors] and one of the Thirteen Cherished Sons of Ling.

Dorje Gyaltsen (Tib. *rdo rje rgyal mtshan*). Ralo Tönpa's guru.

Dorje Ngangkar [White Vajra] (Tib. *rdo rje ngang dkar*). A nyen, and the prognosticator or diviner of the nāgas. Also called Dorje Ngangyag [Vajra Domain] (Tib. *rdo rje ngang yag*).

Dorje Ngangyag. *See* Dorje Ngangkar.

Dradül Bum. *See* Dragyal Bum-me.

Dragyal Bum-me [Victorious over Enemies Hundred Thousand Flames] (Tib. *dgra rgyal 'bum me*). The founder of the Lesser or Younger Lineage of Ling, which were the four Mukpo tribes of Muchang. Son of Chöphen Nagpo and Changmoza, and father of Thoglha Bum. Also called Dradül Bum.

Drubpa'i Gyalmo [Queen of Siddhis] (Tib. *grub pa'i rgyal mo*). The goddess of long life, one of the protectors; also called Machig Drubpa'i Gyalmo (Tib. *ma chig grub pa'i rgyal mo*) [Sole Mother Queen of Siddhi] and Machig Sidpa'i Gyalmo (Tib. *ma chig srid pa'i rgyal mo*) [Sole Mother Queen of Existence].

Drug-gyal [Victorious Dragon] of Kyalo (Tib. *'brug rgyal*). Kyalo Tönpa's son.

Drugmo, Queen (Tib. *'brug mo*). Gesar's wife, who was born a princess as the daughter of Kyalo Tönpa Gyaltsen, and who was also an emanation of White Tārā, the goddess of longevity. One the Seven Fair Maidens of White Ling. Also called Sengcham Drugmo [Lion Sister Dragoness] (Tib. *seng cham 'brug mo*).

Dungkhyung Karpo [White-Conch Garuḍa] (Tib. *dung khyung dkar po*). A protector who was Gesar's older drala brother and his personal bodyguard.

Dzeidrön [Lovely Lamp] (Tib. *mdzes sgron*). Denma's daughter, one of the Seven Fair Maidens of Ling.

Excellent Rain Falls [Legpa Charbeb] (Tib. *legs pa char 'bebs*). A nāga prince.

Flower Divine Beauty. *See* Yelga Dzeiden.

Gadei Bernag. *See* Chökyong Bernag of Gadei.

Garza of Kyalo (Tib. *skya lo'i gar bza'*). A woman from the Gar tribe who married into the family of Kyalo.

Gaza (Tib. *ga bza'*). One of the wives of Chöla Bum, a woman (*bza'* means "lady" or "queen") from the Ga tribe, mother of Yu-gyal, who was lost to the Hor in battle.

Gazi Lhamo [Worthy Zi Divine Lady] (Tib. *dga'gzi lha mo*). The queen of Gurkar, wife of Achen the king of Hor; the middle daughter of the emperor of China.

Gedzo, Lord of the Nyen (Tib. *ge 'dzo*). The nyen of the mountain Gedzo Rimar Wangzhu (Tib. *ge 'dzo ri dmar dbang zhu*), which is probably located in the snow mountains of Lower Kham; the principal zodor, the protector mountain-spirit, of the Muwa clan from which Chipön and Senglön descended. He is also Gesar's spiritual or lineage father.

Gesar, King of Ling (Tib. *gling rje ge sar*). The epic hero of Tibet, known by various epithets at different points in the epic:

> **Döndrub [Accomplisher of Benefit]** (Tib. *don sgrub*). The divine child of Demchog Karpo Ngangyag and Gyuma Lhadzei. Döndrub will appear in Jambudvīpa through the sadhana performed by Padma Tötreng.
>
> **Künphen Nyinje [All-Benefiting Compassion]** (Tib. *kun phen snying rje*). Gesar's name for himself as he approaches Padmasambhava while still in the god realm.
>
> **Thöpa Gawa [Joyful to Hear]** (Tib. *thos pa dga' ba*). The name given to him by Padmasambhava during the Empowerment ceremony.
>
> **Joru** (Tib. *jo ru*). The name given to him by Gyatsa Zhalkar as the son of Senglön and Yelga Dzeiden. In his Joru aspect, Gesar was an ugly and misshapen juvenile delinquent who wore offensive clothes and caused havoc.
>
> **Sengchen Norbu Dradül [Great Lion Jewel Tamer of Enemies]** (Tib. *seng chen nor bu dgra 'dul*). His name as the King of Ling, which was conferred by Padmasambhava when Gesar won the horse race and attained the throne of Ling. Also said as Great Lion King (Tib. *seng chen rgyal po*). Of the many epithets of Gesar of Ling, Norbu Dradül is one of the most familiar and popular ; for instance, the Tibetan lama Chögyam Trungpa Rinpoche confided to translator Robin Kornman that as a small boy, when he was playing war games with his friends, he would call himself Norbu Dradül, just the way an American boy might call himself Superman or Batman.

Gesar is prophesied to become the foremost Rigden king of Shambhala, Chag-gi Khorlochen [Wielder of the Iron Wheel].

Gochöd [Handyman] Pagyal Tagyu [Victorious Warrior Tiger Horn] (Tib. *stag rgyal gyog spyod*). One of the Three Servants of Ling; Drugmo's personal attendant, who is also known as Gochöd Yogpo Pagyal [Practical Servant Victorious Warrior].

Gödcham Karmo. *See* Nammen Karmo.

Gödchung Karmo [Little White Vulture] (Tib. *rgod chung dkar mo*). The eldest daughter of Tsugna Rinchen, promised to the son of the Yakṣa queen.

Gogmo (Tib. *'gog mo*). Literally, the "woman from Gog." A sobriquet given to Yelga Dzeiden,

Gesar's *nāginī* mother, when she was first accepted by the people of Ling. It is short for Gogza Lhamo (Tib. *'gog bza' lha mo*), goddess wife from Gog, and she is also simply called Gogza. *See also* Yelga Dzeiden.

Gogza / Gogza Lhamo. *See* Gogmo *and* Yelga Dzeiden.

Golden Lake Lady [Ser-tso] (Tib. *gser mtsho ma*). *See* Denza.

Great Lion King (Tib. *seng chen rgyal po*). One of Gesar's names, used especially in volume 3, *Gesar Wins the Horse Race and Becomes the King of Ling*.

Great Sorcerer (Tib. *mthu bo che*). Epithet of Gesar of Ling.

Gung-gi Marleb of Rongtsha. *See* Rongtsha Marleb.

Gung-men Karmo. *See* Nammen Karmo.

Gungpa Buyi Kyatra [Middle Son Hawk] (Tib. *gung pa skya khra*). One of the Thirteen Cherished Sons of Ling and one of the Thirty Brethren [Mighty Warriors].

Gurkar Gyalpo (Tib. *gur dkar rgyal po*). The king of the northeastern land of Hor.

Gu-ru (Tib. *rgu ru*). A hunchback and lowly beggar, companion of Joru. Not to be confused with *guru* (Tib. *gu ru*) as in "teacher" or "lama." *See* Khyishi, Gu-ru son of.

Guru Gyaltsen [Guru Victory Banner] (Tib. *gu ru rgyal mtshan*) **of Denma**. One of the four Gyaltsens; a leader in Den and one of the Thirty Brethren [Mighty Warriors].

Gyalwa'i Lhundrub. *See* Michen Gyalwa'i Lhundrub.

Gyapön Sergyi Argham. *See* Sergyi Argham.

Gyatsha Zhalkar of Bumpa (Tib. *rgya tsha zhal dkar*). Gesar's elder half-brother, son of King Senglön and Gyaza Lhakar Drönma. One of the Four Divine Heirs, and the leader of the Seven Super Warriors; belongs to the Lesser Lineage. He qualified as the second in line after King Gesar. His family called him Zhal-lu Nyima Rangshar [Face of the Self-Arising Sun], or affectionately, Zhal-lu. Outside he was given the name Bumpa Gyatsha Zhalkar [Chinese Nephew White Face of the Bum Family].

Gyaza Lhakar Drönma [Chinese Divine White Torch] (Tib. *lha dkar sgron ma*). Often simply called Gyaza (Tib. *rgya bza'*); one of the principal mothers and aunts of Ling, the eldest daughter of the emperor of China, the primary wife of Senglön, and mother of Gyatsha Zhalkar.

Gyogchen Dongra [Great Cannon Face] (Tib. *sgyogs chen gdong ra*). A nyen, or mountain god, a deity-protector of Golog and other regions in northern Tibet who is often called the Spiritual Friend (Tib. *dge bsnyen*). He is a member of the nine deities of phenomenal existence (Tib. *srid pa chags pa'i lha dgu*), as well as a member of the orders of the great nyen.

Gyuma Lhadzei [Illusory Divine Beauty] (Tib. *rgyu ma lha mdzas*). Gesar's divine mother.

Illusory Divine Beauty. *See* Gyuma Lhadzei.

Jampel Gyepei Dorje. *See* Mipham Jampel Gyepei Dorje.

Jangsem Künkyab Gön. *See* Demchog Karpo Ngangyag.

Jangtra. *See* Denma.

Jangza Metog Drön [Lady of Jang Blazing Lotus] (Tib. *jang bza' me tog sgron*). Youngest daughter of the emperor of China, wife of Sadam, and mother of Nyitri.

Joru. *See* Gesar.

Kha-se Rulu [Gray Beard] (Tib. *kha se ru lu*). A demon spirit that haunts riverbanks or any narrow, dangerous pathway, and causes accidents and misfortune to befall certain unfortunate travelers. In volume 2 of the epic, he was tamed by Gesar along with other demon forms of wild animals.

Khache Migmar [Kashmir Red Eye] (Tib. *kha che mig dmar*). A magician.

Khatsar Lumo-tso [Joking Nāginī Lake] (Tib. *kha mtshar klu mo mtsho*). The middle daughter of Tsugna Rinchen, promised to the Chinese Hamipaṭa.

Khyishi, son of Gu-ru (Tib. *khyi shi bu yi rgu ru*). "Khyishi" is the name of a clan in Ling with the poorest, lowliest warriors. Gu-ru is one of the clan. The Tibetan, *khyi shi,* literally means "dead dog." *See also* Gu-ru.

Künga Nyima [All-Joyful Sun] (Tib. *kun dga' nyi ma*). A doctor in Ling. There are also two other men named Künga: one who is one of the Thirteen Lamas of Ling; the other is the father of Zima-tso.

Künphen Nyinje. *See* Gesar.

Künshei Thigpo [All-Knowing Accurate One] (Tib. *kun shes thig po*). A diviner.

Kyalo Tönpa Gyaltsen. *See* Tönpa Gyaltsen.

Kyidkyi Nichung. *See* Ne'uchung Lu-gu Tshar-yag.

Lamaphen. One of the three sons born to Mutritsen.

Langdarma, King (Tib. *glang dar ma*). The king of Tibet from approximately 838–841 C.E.; he suppressed Buddhism, and was ultimately assassinated.

Leader of a Hundred (Tib. *rgya dpon*). An epithet for Sergyi Argham. *See also* Sergyi Argham.

Legpa Charbeb (Tib. *legs pa char 'bebs*) **[Excellent Rainfall]**. A nāga prince.

Lenpa Chögyal [Simple-Minded Dharma King] (Tib. *glen pa chos rgyal*). The middle son of Chipön Rongtsha Tragen and Metog Tashi-tso. He was killed in a battle between Ling and Gog.

Lhabu Legpa [Excellent Prince] (Tib. *lha bu legs pa*) **of Hor**. Son of Gazi Lhamo and the Gurkar king, Achen of Hor; nephew of the emperor of China.

Lhabu Namkha Sengzhal. *See* Namkha Sengzhal.

Lhabu Yangkar [Prince White Prosperity] (Tib. *lha bu gyang dkar*). The astrologer.

Lhakar Drönma. *See* Gyaza Lhakar Drönma.

Lhamo Yudrön [Goddess Turquoise Torch] (Tib. *lha mo gyu sgron*). The daughter of Chipön Rongtsha Tragen and Metog Tashi-tso, and one of the Seven Fair Maidens of Ling.

Lhayag Darkar [Good Divine White Silk] (Tib. *lha yag dar dkar*). The son of Chöphen Nagpo and his first wife Serza; founder of the Elder or Greater Lineage, which was composed of the eight tribes of Serpa.

Life-Essence Demon [Sog Düd] (Tib. *srog bdud*). *See* Bloody Single-Tress Demon Woman.

Lingchen Tharpa Sönam [Great Ling Meritorious Liberation] (Tib. *gling chen thar pa'i bsod nams*). Leader of the Middle Lineage, an elder and chieftain of one of the six districts of Middle Ling, and one of the Thirty Brethren [Mighty Warriors].

Lotus Skull Garland. *See* Padmasambhava.

Ludrül Ödchung [Nāga Serpent Little Light] (Tib. *klu sbrul od chung*). Gesar's younger drala brother; a protector. Also called Ludrül Ödtrung [Born as Nāga Serpent Light] (Tib. *klu sbrul od 'khrung*).

Machen. *See* Magyal Pomra.

Machig Drubpa'i Gyalmo. *See* Drubpa'i Gyalmo.

Machig Sidpa'i Gyalmo. *See* Drubpa'i Gyalmo.

Magyal Pomra (Tib. *rma rgyal spom ra*). The local mountain spirit, a realized bodhisattva. Magyal Pomra, or Machen (Tib. *rma chen*), is the deity of the Machen Pomra mountain range, also known on Chinese maps as Amnye Machen. It is a series of peaks in the heart of the Golog district, in what is now Qinghai Province and close to the present-day town of Da'u.

Mandā Lhadzei [Celestial Flower Divine Beauty] (Tib. *manda lha mdzes*). A goddess, the mother of Demchog Karpo Ngangyag [Gesar's divine father], and hence Gesar's divine or celestial grandmother.

Manenei Nammen Karmo. *See* Nammen Karmo.

Mazhi Trothung. *See* Trothung.

Metog Lhadzei. *See* Yelga Dzeiden.

Metog Tashi-tso [Flower Auspicious Lake] (Tib. *me tog bkra shis mtsho*). A Chinese maiden, Chipön Rongtsa Tragen's wife; they had four children—the older son Yuphen Tag-gyal, the middle son Lenpa Chögyal, the younger son Nangchung Yutag, and a daughter, Lha-mo Yudrön.

Michen Gyalwei Lhundrub [Great Man Spontaneously Accomplished Victor] (Tib. *mi chen rgyal ba'i lhun grub*). Chieftain of one of the six districts of Middle Ling, a most respected leader among the aristocrats of the Elder Lineage of Ling, and one of the Thirty Brethren [Mighty Warriors]. Later on in further volumes of the epic, he fights with the Hor when Gesar's queen Drugmo is captured, and at that time he loses his life in battle.

Michung Khadei [Young Clever Mouth] (Tib. *mi chung kha bde*). A Tibetan youth; one of the Three Servants of Ling. Originally from the land of Gog, he lost his father and mother, and as an orphan he was brought into the family of Chipön.

Migön Karpo [Kind Protector of Humanity] (Tib. *mi mgon dkar po*). A nāga prince.

Mikyong Karpo. *See* Sengtag Adom.

Mipham Jampel Gyepei Dorje (Tib. *mi pham 'jam dpal dgyes pa'i rdo rje*). A Nyingma master (1846–1912), considered an emanation of the bodhisattva Mañjuśrī. Among his myriad collected works, many arose as mind terma associated with the Gesar epic. In particular, the Gesar Supplication found here is the basis upon which one of his students, Thubten Nyima, compiled this epic.

Mutritsen, King. The second king of Dokham, son of Ratra Genpo, and father of Chölipen, Lamapen, and Chöphen Nagpo.

Muza (Tib. *rmu bza'*). One of the wives of Chöla Bum, mother of Senglön.

Nāga Serpent Little Light. *See* Ludrül Ödchung.

Namkha Sengzhal [Sky Lion Face] (Tib. *nam mkha' seng zhal*). Head of the Greater or Elder Lineage of Ling, and one of the Thirty Brethren [Mighty Warriors]. Also called Lhabu [Prince] (Tib. *lha bu*) Namkha Sengzhal, or Namkhai Serzhal [Golden Face of Space] (Tib. *nam mkha'i gser zhal*).

Namkhai Serzhal. *See* Namkha Sengzhal.

Nammen Karmo [White Sky Goddess] (Tib. *nam sman dkar mo*). Gesar's aunt, and one of his principal guardians; sometimes called affectionately Manenei or Nenei [Auntie] (Tib. *ma ne ne*). Also known as Gödcham Karmo [White Vulture Lady] (Tib. *rgod lcam dkar mo*), Gung-men Gyalmo [Sky Goddess] (Tib. *gung sman dkar mo*), or as Gung-men Karmo [White Sky Woman] (Tib. *gung sman dkar mo*).

Nang-ngu Apel. *See* Dongtsen Nang-ngu Apel.

Nangchung Yutag [Sweet Youth Turquoise Tiger] (Tib. *snang chung gyu stag*). The youngest son of Chipön Rongtsha Tragen and Metog Tashi-tso; one of the Thirteen Cherished

Sons of Ling; and the youngest among the Thirty Brethren [Mighty Warriors]. Also called Yuyi Metog [Turquoise Flower] (Tib. *gyu yi me tog*), and Nangchung Yuyi Metog [Sweet Youth Turquoise Flower (Tib. *snang chung gyu yi me tog*).

Nangchung Yuyi Metog. *See* Nangchung Yutag.

Nangsid Zilnön. *See* Padmasambhava.

Nangwa Ödden. *See* Nangwa Ziden.

Nangwa Ziden [Majestic Appearance] (Tib. *sngang ba gzi ldan*). The young nāga child who offers to approach the prognosticator Dorje Ngangkar for a divination regarding the pestilence endangering the nāga kingdom. Also called also Nangwa Ödden [Appears Filled with Light] (Tib. *sngang ba 'od ldan*).

Nangsid Zilnön. *See* Padmasambhava.

Ne'uchung Lu-gu Tshar-yag [Marvelous Little Lamb] (Tib. *ne'u chung lu gu mtshar yag*). Drugmo's paternal cousin, and one of the Seven Fair Maidens of Ling. Also called Kyidki Nichung [Joyful Little Parrot] (Tib. *skyid kyi ni chung*), or simply Nichung.

Nenei Nammen Karmo. *See* Nammen Karmo.

Ngogüd [Wild Face] (Tib. *glen yu ngo rgod*). A nāga of the commoner's caste.

Nichung. *See* Ne'uchung Lu-gu Tshar-yag.

Norbu Dradül. *See* Gesar.

Norbu Lhadar. *See* Rongtsha Marleb.

Nya-tsha Aten [Stable Nephew Fish] (Tib. *nya tsha a brtan* or *a bstan*). One of Trothung's sons and one of the Seven Super Warriors.

Nyen Gedzo. *See* Gedzo.

Nyenchen Thanglha. *See* Thanglha.

Nyentag Marpo [Red Mountain Tiger] (Tib. *gnyan stag dmar po*). A mountain god and an important drala in the Gesar epic. Also known as Red Nyentag.

Nyibum Daryag [Excellent Banner of One Hundred Thousand Suns] of Serpa (Tib. *gser pa'i nyi 'bum dar yag*). The chief of the elders of the Greater Lineage, one of the Four Divine Heirs (to the Ser tribe), and one of the Three Ultimate Warriors (the one called Falcon). Also called Serpa Nyima [Daryag] Bum-thub [Capable of Hundred Thousand] (Tib. *'bum thub*), or Daryag of Nyibum.

Nyima Gyaltsen of Beri (Tib. *be ri nyi ma rgyal mtshan*; variation, *be ru*). An alias used by Gesar when he appears to Drugmo as a bandit.

Nyima Gyaltsen [Sun Victory Banner] of Ka-ru (Tib. *dkar ru nyi ma rgyal mtshan*). One of the four Gyaltsens and one of the Thirty Brethren [Mighty Warriors].

Nyima Lhundrub [Spontaneous Sun] (Tib. *nyi ma lhun grub*) **of Gödpo.** One of the Thirty Brethren [Mighty Warriors], and one of the Thirteen Cherished Sons of Ling. Also called Gödpo Nyima Lhundrub.

Nyitri (Tib. *nyi khri*). Son of Jangza Metog Drön and King Sadam of Jang; nephew of the emperor of China. Also called Jang Nyitri Karchen [Twenty Thousand Great Stars] (Tib. *nyi khri skar chen*).

Ödden Kar [White Luminosity] (Tib. *'od ldan dkar*). A god who is the father of Demchog Karpo Ngangyag [Gesar's divine father], and hence Gesar's celestial or divine grandfather.

Omza (Tib. *om bza'*). The second wife of Chöphen Nagpo, and mother of Trichang Pagyal.

Orgyen. *See* Padmasambhava.

Padma Thötreng. *See* Padmasambhava.

Padmasambhava [Lotus Born] (Tib. *pad ma 'byung*). A sage born in the eighth century in northwest India, the land of Uḍḍiyāṇa; his name means "born from a lotus," which is an indication of his magical origins. He was invited to Tibet by the Tibetan king, Trisong Deutsen, and while in Tibet he transmitted Vajrayāna Buddhism. He is known by many names, including Uḍḍiyāṇa Padma, or Orgyen Padma, the Lotus Born from the land of Uḍḍiyāṇa or Orgyen. In the epic, he is called Nangsid Zilnön [Who Quells Existence with Splendor] (Tib. *snang srid sil gnon*), and in his wrathful form living on the subcontinent of Cāmara, he is called Padma Thötreng [Lotus Skull Garland] (Tib. *pad ma thod phreng*), or Rākṣa Skull Garland.

Pekar Lhadzei [White Lotus Divine Beauty] (Tib. *pad dkar lha mdzes*). One of the Seven Fair Maidens of Ling.

Ralo Tönpa Gyaltsen of Gog (Tib. *ra lo ston pa rgyal mtshan*). King of Gog, and the man who raised the nāginī princess Yelga Dzeiden as his own daughter until she became Gesar's mother. Not to be confused with Kyalo Tönpa Gyaltsen, known as Tönpa Gyaltsen of Kyalo, one of the four Gyaltsens.

Ratra Genpo. The first king of Dokham, and the first king of the clan thereafter known as Mukpo. Father of Mutritsen and Ritritsen (Rutritsen).

Raudrachakrin. The last of the Shambhala kings prophesied in the Kalachakra tantra, who will appear in the year 2424 to defeat the degeneracy of the world. It is prophesied that Gesar will become this Shambhala king. Also known as Rigden Raudrachakrin or Rigden Dragpo Chag-gyi Khorlocan [Wielder of the Iron Wheel] (Tib. *rigs ldan drag po lcags kyi 'khor lo can*).

Rinchen Darlu [Precious Silk Scarf] of Muchang [Wolf Clan] (Tib. *smu spyang rin chen dar lu*). The chief of the elders of the Lesser Lineage, one of the Four Divine Heirs, and the lesser of the Three Ultimate Warriors (the one called Wolf).

Ritritsen, King. One of the sons of Ratra Genpo, and an ancient king of Dokham. Also spelled Rutritsen.

Rongtsha Marleb (Tib. *rong tsha dmar leb*). Gesar's younger half-brother, son of Senglön and Rongza. He is one of the Thirteen Cherished Sons of Ling and one of the Thirty Brethren [Mighty Warriors]. Also called Norbu Lhadar (Tib. *nor bu lha dar*), or Rongtsha Norbu Lhadar.

Rongtsha Tragen. *See* Chipön Rongtsha Tragen.

Rongza (Tib. *rong bza'*). One of the wives of Chöla Bum, and mother of Chipön Rongtsa Tragen. Her name simple means "Lady of Rong." Not to be confused with Rongza Sheldrön, who is also called Rongza.

Rongza Sheldrön [Crystal Torch, Wife from Rong] (Tib. *rong bza' shel sgron*). The first wife of King Senglön, and mother of Rongtsa Marleb, also called Norbu Lhadar, who is Gesar's younger half-brother. She is also simply called Rongza, but she is not to be confused with another woman of the same name, who is the wife of Chöla Bum and mother of Chipön Rongtsha Tragen. *See* Rongza.

Sadam, King (Tib. *sa dam*). King of the northern land of Jang.

Sengcham Drugmo. *See* Drugmo.

Sengchen Norbu Dradül. *See* Gesar.

Senglön [Lion Minister], King (Tib. *seng blon*). Gesar's human father, brother of Chipön and Trothung, and the leader of the Thirty Brethren [Mighty Warriors]. He is an incarnation of the Brahman Legjin Nyima, Sergyi Dogcan, also known as Anāthapi, and in the epic he was said to be an emanation of the Brahman Halikapa and prophesied to be the Shambhala dharma king Zijid Thaye. Senglön was born to King Chöla Bum and his third wife, Muza. Senglön had three wives: Gyaza Lhakar Drönma, who bore their eldest son, Gyatsha Zhalkar; the nāginī Yelga Dzeiden, who bore the boy Joru who was destined to become King Gesar; and Rongza, who bore the younger son, Rongtsa Marleb.

Sengtag Adom [Lion Tiger Youthful Bear] (Tib. *seng stag a dom*). A leader in the Middle Lineage of Ling, and one of the Seven Super Warriors. Also called Mikyong Karpo [Kind Guardian of Humanity] (Tib. *mi skyong dkar po*), sometimes spelled Michang Karpo [White Wolf among Humans] (Tib. *mi spyang dkar po*). Oftentimes he was actually referred to as a wolf among humans, so the second spelling could be more accurate.

Sergyi Argham (Tib. *gser gyi a rgham*). The head of the Middle Lineage and one of the Thirty Brethren [Mighty Warriors]. Also known as Gyapön [Leader of a Hundred] (Tib. *brgya dpon*) Sergyi Argham.

Ser-tso [Golden Lake] (*gser mtsho*). There are two women named Ser-tso: one is one of the Seven Fair Maidens and the daughter of Yatha (one of the Thirteen Lamas of Ling); the other is Trothung's wife. *See also* Denza.

Serpa Nyima. *See* Nyibum Daryag.

Serza (Tib. *gser bza'*). A woman from the Ser tribe, from whom the Greater or Elder Lineage descended; the first wife of Chöphen Nagpo, and mother of Lhayag Darkar.

Shelkar Gyangdrag [White Crystal Far Famed] (Tib. *shel dkar rgyang grags*) **of Mupa**. One of the Thirteen Cherished Sons of Ling; one of the Thirty Brethren [Mighty Warriors].

Shingtri, King (Tib. *shing khri*). The king of the southern lands of Mön.

Singsing [Sengseng] of Ca-nag, Chief (Tib. *sing sing lcags nag*). One of the Thirteen Cherished Sons of Ling and one of the Thirty Brethren [Mighty Warriors].

Sinmo Buzen. *See* Cannibal Demoness Child Eater.

Sintsha [Rākṣa Maternal Nephew] Ngo-lug of Tag-rong (Tib. *stag rong srin tsha ngo lug*). One of the three Sheep-a-Peep brothers and one of the Thirty Brethren [Mighty Warriors]; a member of the Tag-rong tribe in the Lesser Lineage of Ling.

Stupid Mute Stone Target. *See* Yelga Dzeiden.

Tag-rong. *See* Trothung.

Tagphen. *See* Zigphen.

Takshaka (Tib. *'jog po*). A nāga king, one of the Five Eminent Beings who received the *anu yoga* transmission of the higher tantras.

Thalei Ödkar. *See* Thalei Ödtro.

Thalei Ödtro [Completely Luminous] (Tib. *tha le 'od 'phro*). Gesar's drala sister, a protector. She is also called Sing Cham, or Cham [Sister] Thalei Ötro, or Thalei Ödkar [Completely White Light] (Tib. *tha le'od dkar*). *Tha* probably refers to *thale,* which is a kind of robe or coat.

Thanglha (Tib. *thang lha*). Also called Nyenchen Thanglha (Tib. *gnyan chen thang lha*); a powerful nyen, or mountain deity.

Thangtong Gyalpo [King of the Empty Plain] (Tib. *thang stong rgyal po*). A mahāsiddha, yogi, or wandering ascetic; the Buddhist lama who serves as the spiritual advisor to the Mukpo tribe and the Kingdom of Ling.

Tharpa Gyaltsen. *See* Berkar Tharpa Gyaltsen of Nag-ru.

Tharpa Sönam. *See* Lingchen Tharpa Sönam.

Tharpa Zorna of Akhöd. *See* Akhöd Tharpa Zorna.

Thoglha Bum [Lightning God Hundred Thousand] (Tib. *thog lha 'bum*). One of the sons of Dragyal Bum-me, and father of Chöla Bum, grandfather of King Senglön.

Thöpa Gawa. *See* Gesar.

Thubten Nyima. A Tibetan Rinpoche who is an incarnation of Do Khyentse Yeshe Dorje from Golog, and who is responsible for the discovery and preservation of thousands of Buddhist scriptures that would have otherwise been lost forever. Well-known as Zenkar Rinpoche, or simply Alak Zenkar, he was actively involved in the compiling and editing of the first three volumes of the Gesar of Ling Xylograph edition during the 1980s in Chengdu, China.

Tongnyid Chödrön [Emptiness Dharma Torch] (Tib. *stong nyid chos sgron*). Gesar's name for his divine mother. This is also the name of the daughter of a blacksmith in the kingdom of Gurkar when she emanates as [Tongnyid] Gardza Chödrön [Dharma Lamp of the Blacksmith Caste] (Tib. *mgar gza' chos sgron*). Later in the epic when Gesar invades the kingdom of Hor, she is his main helper and also becomes Gesar's lover as was prophesied.

Tongpön Treltsei Shemchog [Chiliarch Supreme Knowledge] (Tib. *stong dpon gral rtse shes mchog*). Leader of one thousand (chiliarch) of the clan of Dra, chieftain of one of the six districts of Middle Ling, and one of the Thirty Brethren [Mighty Warriors].

Tönpa Gyaltsen [Teacher Victory Banner] of Kyalo (Tib. *skya lo ston pa rgyal mtshan*). Drugmo's father, the king of Gog, one of the four Gyaltsens, one of the Thirty Brethren [Mighty Warriors], an emanation of Jambhala. Also called Kyalo Tönpa; not to be confused with Ralo Tönpa.

Tricham Dzeiden, Queen. The mother of Ratra Genpo, the first king of Dokham. She was from the Drong (also called Dri) clan, and married King Chatül.

Trichang Pagyal [Wolf Throne Victorious Warrior] (Tib. *khri spyang dpa'rgyal*). The son of Chöphen Nagpo and his second wife Omza. He founded the Middle Lineage, which consists of the six Mukpo tribes of Ombu.

Trogyal. *See* Trothung.

Tromo-tso [Wrathful Lake] (Tib. *khro mo mtsho*). Tag-rong's daughter, one of the Seven Fair Maidens of Ling.

Trothung of Tag-rong (Tib. *khro thung*). Gesar's uncle, brother of Chipön, king of Tag-rong, and one of the Thirty Brethren [Mighty Warriors]. He is sometimes called King Trowo, or simply Tag-rong. He is also called Trogyal (Tib. *khro rgyal*), which means "wrathful king" and is a reference to the wrathful yidam Hayagrīva, of whom he is an emanation. He is an incarnation of the Indian Mahāsiddha Naropa, and is prophesied to manifest as the dharma king of Shambhala, Lhayi Wangpo. He is often referred to by the epithet Mazhi Chieftain (Tib. *ma bzhi dpon po*). The Tibetan literally means "chief of four mothers." There are many explanations of this name, one being that four women nursed Trothung when he was a child, but it may simply be a tribal name.

He was a mighty warrior alongside Chipön and on the side of Ling, but out of jealousy he was always opposed to Gesar and repeatedly attempted to betray him. The reader is reminded however that while he was still in the celestial realm Gesar requested that he would have an adversary in the human realm, and to this end Hayagrīva incarnated as

Trothung's role as a foil is actually an indispensable part of Gesar's primal retinue of deities and dralas.

Trowo. *See* Trothung of Tag-rong.

Tsangpa'i [Brahmā] Ngo-lug of Agê [Ram Face of Purity] (Tib. *a ge tsang pa'i ngo lug*). One of the three Sheep-a-Peep brothers; a member of the Elder Lineage, and one of the Thirty Brethren [Mighty Warriors].

Tshazhang. *See* Denma.

Tsugna Rinchen [Precious Jewel at the Crown] (Tib. *gtsug na rin chen*). King of the nāgas. Literally, his name means "Jewel in the Crest," referring to a classical Asian belief that all serpents have a jewel in their heads just above and between the eyes. He has three daughters: the eldest Gödchung Karmo, the middle daughter Khatsar Lumo-tso, and the youngest Lenyu Khatam, who is also called Metog Lhadzei. This third and youngest daughter is brought to the human realm as Yelga Dzeiden, where she becomes Gesar's mother and is known by the name of Gogmo.

Vajra Lake-Born Lord of the Victorious Ones (Tib. *rgyal dbang mtsho skyes rdo rje*). An epithet for Padmasambhava.

Wangpo Darphen [Powerful Unfurled Silk] (Tib. *dbang po dar 'phen*, or *'phan*). A judge; one of the Thirty Brethren [Mighty Warriors].

Werma Lhadar [Werma Divine Banner] (Tib. *wer ma lha dar*). One of the great arbiters (Tib. *gzu chen*) of Ling; one of the Thirty Brethren [Mighty Warriors]. He is the one who establishes the order of the great council meeting in volume 3.

White-Conch Garuḍa. *See* Dungkhyung Karpo.

White Supreme Bliss. *See* Demchog Karpo Ngangyag.

Wrathful Lake. *See* Tromo-tso.

Yamshüd (Tib. *yam shud*). The king or leader of the tsen.

Yatha (Tib. *ya tha*). One of the Thirteen Lamas of Ling who assume a more prominent role in future volumes of the epic.

Yelga Dzeiden [Lovely Branch] (Tib. *yal ga mdzes ldan*). Gesar's mother, also known as Gogza or Gogmo, was born as Lenyu Khatam Do-to [Stupid Mute Stone Target] (Tib. *glen yus kha 'tham rdo tho*), the youngest daughter of the nāga king Tsugna Rinchen. Because she was not as beautiful or smart as her sisters, the nāgas gave her this name; however, she was also the ḍākinī Metog Lhadzei [Flower Divine Beauty] (Tib. *me tog lha mdzes*). She is the nāginī princess brought to the middle realm of humans by Padmasambhava. When she comes to the human realm, she is called Gogmo (Tib. *'gog mo*), literally the "woman from Gog," and she is raised by the king of Gog, Ralo Tönpa Gyaltsen, as her human father. She becomes the second wife of King Senglön, and is known as Gogza Lhamo (Tib. *'gog bza' lha mo*), goddess wife from Gog, or simply Gogza. Senglön is thereby Gesar's earthly father.

Yemön Namkhai Gyalpo. The first king of the ancient clan that was eventually called the Mukpo clan.

Yerpa'i Trin-ga [Cloud Lover of Yerpa] (Tib. *yer pa'i sprin dga'*). The nāga child of the untouchable caste who volunteered to invite Padmasambhava to the land of the nāgas.

Yu-gyal [Turquoise King] (Tib. *g.yu rgyal*). The son of Chöla Bum and Muza; later on in the epic, he is lost to the Hor in battle.

Yudrön. *See* Lhamo Yudrön.

Yuphen Tag-gyal [Turquoise Benefit Tiger King] (Tib. *gyu phan stag rgyal*). The eldest son of Chipön Rongtsha Tragen and Metog Tashi-tso. Also simply called Yutag.

Yutag. *See* Yuphen Tag-gyal.

Yuyag Gönpo [Protector of Excellent Turquoise] (Tib. *g.yu yag mgon po*). One of the Thirteen Cherished Sons of Ling; one of the Thirty Brethren/Mighty Warriors.

Yuyi Metog. *See* Nangchung Yutag.

Zhal-lu. *See* Gyatsa Zhalkar.

Zigphen (Tib. *gzig 'phen*). Trothung's eldest son, leader of the Elder Lineage, and one of the Seven Super Warriors; personal minister of Nyima Daryag. Also called Anu Zigphen [Youthful Leopard Leap] (Tib. *a nu gzig 'phen*), or Tagphen, a contraction of his full name "Tag-rong Zigphen."

Zima-tso [Ocean Froth] (Tib. *zi ma mtsho*). The lover or wife of Lenpa Chögyal, who was sent to Ling from Hor.

BIBLIOGRAPHY

Fremantle, Francesca, and Chögyam Trungpa, trans. *The Tibetan Book of the Dead: The Great Liberation through Hearing in the Bardo.* Boston: Shambhala, 2003.

Goldstein, Melvyn C., ed. *The New Tibetan-English Dictionary of Modern Tibetan Dictionary.* 2nd ed. Berkeley: University of California Press, 2001.

Karmay, Samten Gyalsten. *The Arrow and the Spindle: Studies in History, Myths, Rituals, and Beliefs in Tibet.* Kathmandu: Mandala Book Point, 1998.

———. "The Social Organization of Ling and the Term *Phu-nu* in the Gesar Epic." *Bulletin of the School of Oriental and African Studies* 58, no. 2 (1995): 303–13. doi: 10.1017/S0041977X00010788.

———"The Theoretical Basis of the Tibetan Epic, with Reference to a 'Chronological Order' of the Various Episodes in the Gesar Epic." *Bulletin of the School of Oriental and African Studies* 56, no. 2 (1993): 234–46. doi: 10.1017/S0041977X00005498.

Kongtrül, Jamgön. *The Torch of Certainty.* Translated by Judith Hanson. Boston: Shambhala, 2000.

Nālandā Translation Committee under the direction of Chögyam Trungpa, trans. *The Rain of Wisdom: The Essence of the Ocean of True Meaning.* Boston: Shambhala, 2010.

Rangjung Yeshe Tibetan-English Dharma Dictionary. CD-ROM. Erik Hein Schmidt. Rangjung Yeshe Publications (licensed to Nitartha International by Rangjung Yeshe Publications).

Roerich, George N. *The Blue Annals.* 2nd ed. Delhi: Motilal Banarsidass, 2007.

Sarat Chandra Das, Graham Sandberg, and Augustus William Heyde. *A Tibetan-English Dictionary, with Sanskrit Synonyms.* Delhi: Motilal Banarsidass, 2000.

Stein, Rolf Alfred. *L'épopée tibétaine de Gesar dans sa version lamaïque de Ling.* Paris: Presses Universitaires de France, 1956.

———. *Les tribus anciennes des marches sino-tibétaines; légendes, classifications et histoire.* Paris: Presses Universitaires de France, 1961.

———. *Tibetan Civilization.* Stanford, Calif.: Stanford University Press, 1972.

Wayman, Alex. *Chanting the Names of Mañjuśrī: The Mañjuśrī-Nāma-Saṃgīti.* Boston: Shambhala, 1985.

Yeshe Tsogyal. *The Life and Liberation of Padmasambhava.* Translated by Kenneth Douglas and Gwendolyn Bays. 2 vols. Berkeley, Calif.: Dharma Publishing, 1978.

———. *The Lotus-Born: The Life Story of Padmasambhava.* Edited by Marcia Binder Schmidt. Translated by Erik Pema Kunsang. Boudhanath: Rangjung Yeshe, 2004. First published 1993 by Shambhala.